A DICTIONARY OF
CHRISTIAN ETHICS

A DICTIONARY OF CHRISTIAN ETHICS

EDITED BY
JOHN MACQUARRIE

SCM PRESS LTD

1967. Edition.

334 00320 2

First published 1967
by SCM Press Ltd
56 Bloomsbury Street London
Second impression 1971

Printed in Great Britain by
Fletcher & Son Ltd Norwich

PREFACE

What does it mean to live as a Christian in the modern world? What moral obligations are imposed by membership in the Christian community? Are such concepts as 'sin' and 'grace' of any relevance to the contemporary problems of mankind? Are there distinctively 'Christian' virtues or policies or patterns of behaviour?

Questions such as these constitute the subject-matter of Christian ethics. This dictionary is meant to be a guide through this difficult territory. The extent and the complexities of the subject are so great that, although this is a big book and contains some fairly substantial articles, it remains a dictionary and aims at setting forth only the essentials of the subject. However, all the major articles have bibliographies, so that the reader can move on to more detailed study of the matters under discussion.

It cannot be stressed too strongly that this dictionary is not a manual of Christian morality – that is to say, the reader cannot look up 'Divorce' or 'Suicide', let us say, and find pat answers to his questions of what is right and what is wrong. In Christian ethics, as in Christian theology, there are many controversial matters where sincere and able men take different points of view. Many points of view are represented in this book. The book is a guide to Christian ethics not in the sense of laying down rigid norms, but in the sense of letting the reader see what the problems are, letting him know what leading Christian moralists are thinking about these problems, and so enabling him to come to his own intelligent and responsible decisions.

In saying that different points of view are represented in the dictionary, I am also disclaiming that it speaks for what is sometimes called the 'new morality'. (Incidentally, there was a 'new morality' when I was an undergraduate thirty years ago, and I hope there always will be new moralities, in the sense of fresh moral thinking in the face of new problems.) We have followed no party line, but have tried to bring together in this volume some of the most significant thinking that is currently going on about Christian ethics.

Let me now indicate briefly the subjects which the reader may expect to find treated in this dictionary.

First of all, since Christian ethics talks, like every other kind of ethics, of 'duty', 'goodness', 'values', 'conscience' and so on, there is a considerable number of articles dealing with *basic ethical concepts*. Most of these articles have been written by professional philosophers. We have also provided articles on some of the great philosophical systems of ethics, especially those that have been influential in Christian ethics, such as the thought of Plato, Aristotle and Kant; and further, since we are all living more closely in the shrinking world of the twentieth century, there have been included articles on Jewish, Buddhist and other non-Christian ethics, including the ethics of Marxist Communism.

Next, since Christian ethics, however contemporary its approach, stands in a definite tradition and has its roots in the revelation of God in Jesus Christ, there are important articles on what may be called the source material, that is to say, *biblical and theological ethics*. The ethical teaching of the Old and New Testaments (and of their backgrounds); the classic interpretations of such theologians as St Augustine, St Thomas, Luther, Calvin and many others; the approaches and methods of contemporary schools; topics such as sin and grace, the virtues and vices, the basic concepts of moral theology – these are all treated by theologians, biblical scholars and church historians, in the belief that only a thorough grasp of this foundational material can make possible any adequate formulation of a Christian ethic for today.

Finally, we come to 'where the action is', so to speak – to the *substantial ethical problems*: war and peace, international order, industrial relations, property, race relations, sex, marriage, the family, with all the attendant problems of birth control, divorce, prostitution and the like; alcohol and drugs; crime and punishment, and many other problems. Since so many of these questions carry us beyond purely ethical matters, a specialized knowledge of the facts obtaining in each particular field is necessary if a responsible judgment is to be reached. Clearly, a dictionary of this kind cannot provide information about economics, politics, physiology and all the other subjects that might be relevant to this or that ethical question. But it did seem that some of the modern behavioural sciences impinge so closely on ethics that some knowledge of them is required in considering moral problems, so to the articles on contemporary moral problems we have provided a background of articles on psychology (including psychoanalysis), sociology (including a survey of the characteristics of contemporary society) and anthropology.

An editor's lot is not always a happy one, but to edit a book of this kind is an exciting educational experience. A glance at our list of contributors will show that we have been fortunate in enlisting the help of many distinguished philosophers, theologians and other scholars. They also represent an unusually wide range of traditions – Protestant, Anglican, Roman Catholic, Orthodox and Jewish. It is an interesting but unplanned feature of the *Dictionary* that of its eighty contributors, exactly half belong to the Old World and half to the New. To all of them, let me express warm thanks for their co-operation. Special thanks are due to those contributors who also gave advice on the making of the dictionary, and to some other scholars who, though unable to contribute themselves, suggested possible contributors to the editor. These contributing and non-contributing advisers included J. Luther Adams, John C. Bennett, V. A. Demant, E. Clinton Gardner, Abraham J. Heschel, Robert S. Lee, Wilhelm Pauck, Ronald H. Preston, Cyril C. Richardson, John R. Sheets, s.j., James A. Whyte. The late H. Richard Niebuhr was keenly interested in the beginnings of this project, and would undoubtedly have participated in it, had he lived.

JOHN MACQUARRIE

CONTRIBUTORS

Rabbi Jacob B. Agus, *Beth El Congregation, Baltimore*
Professor Charles B. Ashanin, *Christian Theological Seminary, Indianapolis*
The Rev. Canon D. Sherwin Bailey, *Chancellor of Wells Cathedral*
The Rev. Professor William Barclay, *University of Glasgow*
Professor Emeritus M. Searle Bates, *Union Theological Seminary, New York*
The Rev. President John C. Bennett, *Union Theological Seminary, New York*
Professor Vernon J. Bourke, *St Louis University, Missouri*
The Rev. R. E. C. Browne, *Canon of Manchester*
The Rev. Professor Emeritus John Burnaby, *University of Cambridge*
The Rev. Professor Henry B. Clark, *Duke University, North Carolina*
The Rev. C. H. Cleal, *Christian Citizenship Department, The Baptist Union of Great Britain and Ireland*
The Rev. Professor Harvey G. Cox, *The Divinity School, Harvard University*
Professor Iris V. Cully, *The Divinity School, Yale University*
The Rev. Thomas E. Davitt, s.J., *Professor in Marquette University, Milwaukee*
The Rev. Professor V. A. Demant, *University of Oxford*
Professor M. J. Dresden, *University of Pennsylvania*
Professor Emerita Dorothy Emmet, *University of Manchester*
Professor A. C. Ewing, *University of Cambridge*
The Rev. Richard M. Fagley, *Commission of the Churches on International Affairs, New York*
The Rev. Professor Joseph Fletcher, *Episcopal Theological School, Cambridge, Massachusetts*
The Rev. Professor E. Clinton Gardner, *Emory University, Atlanta*
The Rev. Professor William B. Green, *Colorado Women's College, Denver*
The Rev. Graeme M. Griffin, *Ormond College, Melbourne*
The Rev. John S. Habgood, *Principal, The Queen's College, Birmingham*
The Rev. Professor Robert T. Handy, *Union Theological Seminary, New York*
The Rev. Professor E. R. Hardy, *Berkeley Divinity School, New Haven, Connecticut*
R. M. Hare, *Fellow of Balliol College, Oxford*
The Rev. Professor Joseph Haroutunian, *University of Chicago*
The Rev. J. B. Harrison, *The Church of England Council for Social Aid, London*
The Rev. Professor Roger Hazleton, *Andover-Newton Theological School, Massachusetts*
The Rev. Professor Martin J. Heinecken, *The Lutheran Theological Seminary, Philadelphia*
The Rev. Professor Ian Henderson, *University of Glasgow*

Contributors

The Rev. Professor Seward Hiltner, *Princeton Theological Seminary, New Jersey*
Major C. W. Hume, *The Universities' Federation for Animal Welfare, London*
Professor Emeritus T. E. Jessop, *University of Hull*
The Rev. Professor Charles W. Kegley, *Wagner College, New York*
The Rev. S. J. Knox, *Holburn Central Church, Aberdeen*
Professor James Kuhn, *Columbia University, New York*
The Rev. Professor James N. Lapsley, *Princeton Theological Seminary, New Jersey*
The Rev. Professor William H. Lazareth, *The Lutheran Theological Seminary, Philadelphia*
The Rev. Professor Robert S. Lee, *San Francisco Theological Seminary*
The Rev. Professor Paul L. Lehmann, *Union Theological Seminary, New York*
The Rev. Professor David Little, *The Divinity School, Yale University*
The Rev. Professor Harvey K. McArthur, *Hartford Seminary Foundation, Connecticut*
The Rev. William McKane, *Lecturer in the University of Glasgow*
Professor D. M. MacKinnon, *University of Cambridge*
The Rev. Arthur McNaughtan, *St Columba's Church, Brechin*
The Rev. Stewart Mechie, *Lecturer in the University of Glasgow*
The Rev. Professor Carl Michalson†, *formerly of Drew University, New Jersey*
The Rt Rev. R. C. Mortimer, *Lord Bishop of Exeter*
Johanna Mott, *Director of Windham House, New York*
The Rev. Professor Emeritus James Muilenberg, *Union Theological Seminary, New York*
The Rev. Professor C. Ellis Nelson, *Union Theological Seminary, New York*
The Rev. Professor R. A. Norris, Jr., *The Divinity School, Philadelphia*
The Rev. H. P. Owen, *Lecturer in the University of London*
The Rev. Ronald H. Preston, *Canon of Manchester*
Sheila Ralphs, *Lecturer in the University of Manchester*
The Rt Rev. Ian T. Ramsey, *Lord Bishop of Durham*
Brian Rodgers, *Senior Lecturer in the University of Manchester*
The Rev. Edward Rogers, *Department of Christian Citizenship, The Methodist Church in Great Britain*
The Rev. James P. Scull, S.J., *Professor in the Creighton University, Omaha, Nebraska*
The Rev. Professor Harvey J. Seifert, *School of Theology at Claremont, California*
The Rev. Professor Roger L. Shinn, *Union Theological Seminary, New York*
The Rev. Ulrich Simon, *Lecturer in the University of London*
John F. Sleeman, *Lecturer in the University of Glasgow*
William A. Smalley, *Translation Consultant to the Bible Societies in South East Asia*
Professor R. Ninian Smart, *University of Lancaster*
The Rev. Professor Ronald Gregor Smith, *University of Glasgow*
Professor John E. Smith, *Yale University*
The Rev. Professor E. J. Tinsley, *University of Leeds*
The Rev. J. Spencer Trimingham, *Reader in the University of Glasgow*
The Rev. Alec R. Vidler, *Fellow of King's College, Cambridge*
The Rev. Herbert Waddams, *Canon of Canterbury*
The Rev. Professor Charles C. West, *Princeton Theological Seminary, New Jersey*
Professor Alan White, *University of Hull*
The Rev. Professor James A. Whyte, *University of St Andrews*

The Rev. Professor Daniel D. Williams, *Union Theological Seminary, New York*
The Rev. Professor Thomas Wood, *St David's College, Lampeter, Wales*
The Rev. Professor G. F. Woods†, *formerly of the University of London*

ABBREVIATIONS

AER   H. Frankfort, *Ancient Egyptian Religion*, 1948
AV   Authorized Version (King James Version)
ANET   J. B. Pritchard, *Ancient Near Eastern Texts relating to the Old Testament*, 2nd edn., 1955
BCP   Book of Common Prayer
CQR   *Church Quarterly Review*
CTSR   *Chicago Theological Seminary Register*
DAB   *Dictionary of American Biography*
DNB   *Dictionary of National Biography*
ET   English translation
HERE   James Hastings, ed., *Encyclopaedia of Religion and Ethics*, 1921
IDB   *Interpreter's Dictionary of the Bible*
LAE   A. Erman, *The Literature of the Ancient Egyptians*, tr. by A. M. Blackman, 1927
LXX   Greek Translation of the Old Testament (Septuagint)
NEB   New English Bible
NT   New Testament
OT   Old Testament
PACPA   *Proceedings of the American Catholic Philosophical Association*, Washington, D.C.
RSV   American Revised Standard Version
TWNT   Gerhard Kittel, ed., *Theologisches Wörterbuch zum Neuen Testament*, ET: *Theological Dictionary of the New Testament*, tr. and ed. by Geoffrey W. Bromiley, Grand Rapids, Michigan: Wm. B. Eerdmans Publishing Co., 1964—
UN   United Nations
USA   United States of America
USQR   *Union Seminary Quarterly Review*
USSR   Union of Soviet Socialist Republics
WA   Martin Luther, *Weimar Ausgabe, Werke*

A DICTIONARY OF
CHRISTIAN ETHICS

Abandonment

The word is used in several senses that have ethical import. (1) Abandonment of children is, like abortion, a crude and primitive method of family limitation. Exposition of unwanted children was a practice opposed by the Church in its early days, and from then until now it has tried to make provision for children abandoned by their parents. The persistence of the practice points to the urgency of facing in a realistic way the question of making available information and facilities for contraception. *See* **Children; Infanticide; Population Policy; Procreation.** (2) The term is used by some existentialist writers to point to what they take to be a fundamental characteristic of human existence. Man is abandoned to himself, in the sense that his is an existence which he has not chosen and yet for which he is responsible. The consequence of such a view is that man must construct his own values. *See* **Existentialist Ethics.** (3) The term has been used in traditional Christian spirituality to mean the complete surrender of the will to God. Although such abandonment has often been supposed to have a quietist and other-worldly tendency, there are nowadays attempts to interpret the idea in a more active and socially concerned way. Something like a secular equivalent of abandonment is found in Heidegger's idea of *Gelassenheit*.

EDITOR

Abelard, Peter

Peter Abelard (1079–1142) was a moralist as well as a philosopher and theologian. His ethical thought is found in his *Ethics* or *Scito Teipsum*. As a moralist, Abelard, unlike his successors in the following century, was free from the dominating authority of Aristotle whose ethical writing was available to him in a few fragments only. It may be partly for this reason and partly because of his own speculative ability that Abelard showed considerable ethical originality. Over against the traditional objective view according to which morality is to be estimated by conformity or the reverse to a standard set by authority, Abelard developed a subjective view which placed the emphasis on intention. Actions can be characterized as good or bad not according to what is done but according to the underlying intention. The intention may be good in itself; the action which flows from it is only good through the good intention from which it proceeds. Thus the same action may be good or bad at different times.

Since the test of conduct is not dogmatic conformity but subjective intention, Abelard can bring pagan and Christian morality together. The philosopher of pre-Christian days, by aligning himself with the natural law, could act with the same kind of good intention as the Christian who bases his conduct on his trinitarian belief, the main difference being that for the Christian good conduct has been more clearly and attractively set forth in the incarnation. Moreover, Abelard's exemplarist doctrine of Christ's atonement is in harmony with his ethical standpoint, for it makes it possible to say that good men in ancient times could respond to divine wisdom and love, as they apprehended these, in the same way as the Christian who makes his loving response in conduct to the divine love manifest in the obedience and sufferings of Christ.

Abelard's Ethics, tr. by J. R. McCallum. 1935.

STEWART MECHIE

Abjuration

Abjuration is a solemn and formal act of renunciation. The term is chiefly used nowadays for the renunciation of a false opinion. For a discussion of the moral characteristics of such solemn declarations, *see* **Oaths; Vows.**

Abortion

Abortion is the expulsion from the womb of the mother of a living fetus which cannot survive outside it. Natural abortions occur not infrequently and are normally termed 'miscarriages'. Artificial abortion is abortion induced by artificial means of any kind, whether by external interference or by taking medicines or drugs internally.

From the earliest times Christian opinion was strongly opposed to abortion, which was a serious social evil in the first and second centuries of the Christian era. Nevertheless all abortions were not considered equally sinful until comparatively recent times. St Augustine made a distinction between abortion of an animate and an inanimate fetus. The fetus was presumed to be animated, that is, imbued with a soul, sixty or eighty days after conception. English law for a long period distinguished between abortion before and after quickening, that is, the first movement felt by the mother of the fetus in her womb. The pope decided against the lawfulness of direct abortion at the end of the nineteenth century.

Roman Catholic teaching holds that direct

intentional abortion can never be morally justified. If abortion is the unintended result of some other necessary moral action, then it may be accepted according to the law of double effect, as, for example, when a hysterectomy has to take place for the purpose of removing a cancerous growth. It is not permissible for a doctor to kill the fetus in order to save the mother in any other circumstances; it is regarded as on the same moral plane as to kill the mother directly in order to save the unborn child.

This view is not held by most other Christians, many of whom would think it morally right to procure an abortion in order to save the life of the mother. But there is uncertainty as to what other circumstances would justify an abortion morally. There is no doubt that large numbers of unskilled abortions take place in countries where its legal arrangement is difficult. In recent years there have been experiments in some countries, such as Japan and Hungary, permitting abortions to be performed freely at the simple request of the mother, but the results have led the authorities to try to diminish abortions where possible.

Among Christians the opinion is gaining ground that abortions are morally permissible in cases where there is a direct clash between the interests of the fetus and those of the mother. Where the mother's life is directly threatened, there is little dispute that its preservation should weigh morally more than the preservation of that of the fetus. The question of the mother's health and well-being may also be considered to be a moral value in coming to a decision. Although the fetus is certainly a potential person, its status before it is viable outside the womb is uncertain, and, if its existence threatens the well-being of the mother, this uncertainty may be taken into account. There are some Christians who think that abortion should be permitted in cases of rape and in cases where girls conceive under the legal age of consent, but these suggestions carry their own dangers and are difficult to justify on the basis of traditional Christian beliefs.

The more general ethical question which is raised by abortion (as well as by other medical and surgical advances) is that of the moral responsibility of man to use his increasing knowledge and skill to determine for himself, according to his best moral insights, the right course to take in each particular case. The growth in scientific knowledge and the possibilities which arise from this growth make it possible for man more and more to control life and death. In the case of abortion this knowledge is still limited, but it is likely to increase in the next decades. It is difficult for one to adopt any longer as a moral rule a general prohibition which implicitly seems to identify 'nature' with the will of God. If 'nature' already provides a natural form of abortion for those fetuses which for some reason or another are not viable, the ethical question arises whether, with his greater knowledge, man has not a moral obligation to use that knowledge to do more perfectly what 'nature' does in a hit or miss fashion. It may be assumed that natural abortion occurs so as to guard against harm for the mother and against imperfect births. If present-day knowledge and skill can do better what 'nature' does less well, that may well be considered to be an action more perfectly in accordance with the will of God who desires that the mothers should have their full health and well-being and that children should be born as perfect as possible.

There are clearly dangers, both social and moral, in making abortion easy, but practical questions should not prevent the fundamental moral issue from being frankly faced.

Abortion: An Ethical Discussion, Report of the Committee of the Church Assembly Board for Social Responsibility, 1965.

HERBERT WADDAMS

Absolutes, Ethical

By an 'absolute' value or good is meant one that maintains its validity under any and every circumstance, no matter what. Thus the ancient maxim of the Stoics, 'Let justice be done though the heavens fall' is a dramatic way of expressing the absolute validity of justice as a principle. For the moral theologians of the Middle Ages the general principle, 'Follow the good and avoid the evil' was regarded as a major or ultimate premiss carrying with it absolute validity. In modern philosophy the ethics of Immanuel Kant furnishes the best example of an ethical absolute. The good will which Kant defined as the will that acts out of respect for the moral law has absolute validity; it is good in any context and has a worth that cannot be calculated because it surpasses all values in exchange.

Ethical absolutes have come under attack from at least three distinct points of view. From the standpoint of some forms of subjectivism in ethics there can be no absolutes because moral judgments have neither objectivity nor universality and there is not sufficient constancy in human nature to guarantee for any good or value a place of absolute validity. It is important to notice that not all forms of subjectivism are thus relativistic but only those positions according to which human nature has no universal structure. The second and more powerful source of relativism in ethics stems from anthropological and cultural analyses that make paramount the great variety of customs and practices to be found in different cultures. From this vantage point ethical absolutes are ruled out because there cannot possibly be a universal agreement or consensus of opinion with regard to any standard or norm. Each set of values is 'relative' to a geographical time and place and we have no way of transcending this situation and of establishing any one set of norms as *the* final criterion.

Ethical absolutes have been attacked from a third source, this time in the name of a religious standpoint. Kierkegaard, for example, in his famous 'teleological suspension of the ethical' was calling attention to the problems that arise when the ethical standpoint is absolutized and becomes free of any critical vantage point beyond itself. If the ethical becomes absolute, then legalism and moralism result. The ethical must be limited by the mercy and forgiveness of the religious and if it is not the ethical will absolutize itself with evil consequences. A similar point about absolutizing the ethical is made from the standpoint of the dialectical theology so-called; the counsels of perfection stemming from the teaching of Jesus are not meant to apply absolutely and literally to the world of actual existence but rather are said to define the ideal standard in terms of which man and the world are judged. As absolute, the Christian ethic is said to be an 'impossible ideal' and yet it retains its relevance for historical life.

Reinhold Niebuhr, *An Interpretation of Christian Ethics*, 1935; H. J. Paton, *The Moral Law*; *Kant's Groundwork of the Metaphysic of Morals*, 1948; Edward Westermarck, *Ethical Relativity*, 1932.

JOHN E. SMITH

Absolution

Absolution is the act of freeing or loosing from sin and its penalties. When Jesus said to the paralytic, 'My son, your sins are forgiven', he was accused of blasphemy, and it was argued that God alone can forgive sins (Mark 2.5–6). However, the NT makes clear the belief of the early Church that the power to remit sins belonged not only to Jesus but had also been committed by him to the Church's officers. This is made explicit in such passages as Matt. 16.19 and John 20.23. In the NT, remission of sins is closely associated with healing and exorcism.

The conditions for receiving absolution are that the offender has repented of his sin, that he has made a full confession of it, and that he is willing to make reparation for it. Absolution may be given in various forms, and three of these may be distinguished in the BCP. (1) The *indicative* form, '. . . by his authority committed to me, I absolve thee from all thy sins', is used on hearing a private confession, as in the Order for the Visitation of the Sick. (2) In the context of the eucharist, the *precatory* form, 'Almighty God . . . have mercy upon you, pardon and deliver you from all your

sins', is used after the general confession. (3) In the orders for Mattins and Evensong, a *declaratory* form is used: 'Almighty God . . . hath given power and commandment to his ministers, to declare and pronounce to his people, being penitent, the absolution and remission of their sins.' *See* **Confession; Penance.**

EDITOR

Abstinence

Abstinence may be used in various senses, such as abstinence from sexual intercourse, temporary (cf. 1 Cor. 7.5) or permanent; or total abstinence from alcoholic beverages, the form which the temperance movement has taken among many Protestants since the 1820s. Its most technical use is for a lesser form of fasting (q.v.) which reduces the quality of food, though not necessarily the quantity. In the second century some Montanists and other rigorists added periods of abstinence (*xerophagiae*, 'dry meals') to the fasts commonly observed in the Church. Later abstinence from flesh meat, assumed on fast days, came to be the common observance of the less solemn fasts. The early Middle Ages discussed whether this should also exclude fish and meat products (*lacticinia*) such as cheese and eggs. The Eastern Orthodox Church still assumes that it should; in its calendar Lent is preceded by Carnival Sunday after which meat is given up and Cheese Sunday after which the strict fast begins. To this idea is due the custom of using up eggs in pancakes on Shrove Tuesday, the day before Lent, and returning to their use with Easter eggs (or the Russian Easter cake, called Paska). St Benedict directed his monks to abstain from the 'flesh of quadrupeds' except when sick (*Rule*, Chap. 39), perhaps in the interest of simplicity as much as that of asceticism. But the Middle Ages commonly assumed that strict monastic asceticism demanded perpetual abstinence from flesh; this is still practised by the stricter monks of the Eastern Church, as on Mount Athos, and by the Cistercians of Strict Observance (Trappists). The Protestant Reformers generally opposed compulsory abstinence as legalistic – the first formal act of protest at Zurich was a secret supper of sausages in Lent of 1522. But in England the custom not only continued on Fridays and in Lent, but was increased by civil days of abstinence (under Elizabeth I called 'Cecil's fasts') ordered to encourage fisheries for the benefit of the navy. A modern parallel to these occurred in the 'meatless days' encouraged in the USA as a form of rationing during the first and second World Wars.

Abstinence may be undertaken for various reasons. Many Orientals and some Westerners practise vegetarianism, either as an expression of reverence for life or out of conviction that meat is unhealthy and unnecessary. The dietary laws of the OT may be partly based on sanitary grounds, partly on the association of certain kinds of food with pagan sacrifices. For whatever reason adopted, abstinence often becomes a formal badge of religious profession – Hindus generally abstain from beef, Jews and Moslems from pork, Catholics traditionally from meat on Friday, many Protestants from alcohol and tobacco, some Mennonite sects from forms of dress associated with worldly display, Mormons from hot drinks of all kinds.

E. R. HARDY

Accidents

Accidents are events which normally cannot be foreseen, and the word is used especially for such events when they cause damage, injury and death. Accidents may be due to human error or to failure of equipment or to abnormal conditions, such as storm and flood. It is obvious that human life cannot be entirely protected from accidental happenings. Whatever policies we formulate, there is always the possibility that the execution of them will be frustrated by some chance happening. Provided that the accident was not due to negligence, one cannot be held guilty for the failure of the policy. On the other hand, there is a duty to take every reasonable precaution, and because accidents do happen, policies of action should be flexible enough so that they can be adapted to unexpected circumstances.

Many events that we call 'accidents' are undoubtedly preventible. They are traceable to lack of due care, or to unwillingness to spend time or money in producing safe equipment, or to lack of consideration for other persons, or to other causes that could be removed. The prevention of accidents is an important duty, especially in contemporary society where so much potentially dangerous equipment is in constant use. The appalling number of highway accidents is perhaps the most conspicuous example of the incidence of accidents in contemporary society, but accidents take a steady toll in industry, in the home, and elsewhere.

The duty to prevent accidents has both a personal and a social dimension. On the personal level, it means the avoidance of acts that could be dangerous to oneself or others (e.g., mixing drinking and driving, mountaineering in bad weather, etc.) or using unsafe equipment. Some activities that seem on the surface glamorous and adventurous are to be judged morally wrong if they increase the likelihood that other persons may be endangered, either directly or indirectly. Nowadays, however, the problem of accidents is so vast that it must be considered on the social level. It can be attacked only with the help of legislation, and there is a duty to support such legislation as will reduce the incidence of accidents in the various fields. Most countries already have a long history of legislation designed to promote safety in

industry. The various kinds of public transport, by land, sea and air, are governed by strict safety regulations. But much more could be done; for instance, automobiles could be made safer, even if this means higher prices or a cut in the manufacturers' profits. Tightening of legislation on toys and domestic equipment is also desirable in many countries. There is a duty for legislators to exercise constant vigilance in this whole matter of preventing accidents, especially as new gadgets are continually coming on the market.

No matter how much is done in the way of prevention, accidents will still happen. While our moral duty is primarily to prevent accidents, it does not end there. Allowing that some accidents must happen, we have a duty to minimize the evils arising from them. One of the most obvious ways in which to do this is through insurance. The law requires employers, drivers and others to carry insurance that will make it possible to compensate any persons accidentally injured by their operations; and, more generally, there is a personal duty to insure against unforeseen happenings, especially any that would be damaging to one's dependents. *See* **Negligence**.

EDITOR

Accidie

Accidie or *acedia* is a state of sad heaviness in which the mind is stagnant and the flesh a burden. It is said to be particularly bad at midday. In the past monks used the psalmist's words to describe it as 'the sickness that destroyeth in the noon-day'. *See* **Sloth**.

R. E. C. BROWNE

Act, Action, Agent

Act, action, agent are all words derived from the Latin verb *agere*, 'to do', and they are commonly used in ethics. The 'act' is the deed done; the 'action' is the doing of it; and the 'agent' is the doer. While some moral philosophers (e.g., Sir W. D. Ross) have distinguished rather carefully between 'act' and 'action', the distinction is difficult to maintain and is not observed by many other writers. An act, as what is done, need not be overt behaviour. An act of mental prayer, let us say, is certainly something done by an agent, but it is not an observable occurrence. If the distinction between 'act' and 'action' has value, then it would seem to be that it draws attention to two aspects of ethical behaviour, which may be considered as appropriate or inappropriate ('right' or 'wrong') in the context in which it is done, or which may be considered good or bad with reference to the end which the agent had in view in the doing of the deed.

A first step toward delimiting the meaning of 'act' or 'action' is to distinguish it from mere process or happening. A leaf falling to the ground is a mere happening or occurrence, not an act. What is distinctive in a human act is that there is both an outside and an inside to it, so to speak. Normally, there is an outside, that is to say, an observable occurrence in the world, though we have conceded that in exceptional cases, an act may be entirely internal to the agent. But what differentiates the observable occurrences of human conduct from the falling of a leaf is that in the former case there is a whole complex of mental events associated with the occurrence and, we believe, initiating it – events that we call by such names as 'decision', 'choice', 'responsibility', 'deliberation', 'intention', 'motivation' (qq.v.). These internal concomitants of overt human behaviour are, however, not always all of them present, or not always present to the same extent. Thus not all human behaviour can be reckoned as 'action' that would be of interest to ethics. What is done in abnormal states of mind, or again, 'reflex acts' over which we have no conscious control, are not reckoned 'acts' or 'actions' having moral significance. Whereas descriptive sciences such as psychology and sociology are interested in all human behaviour, ethics is concerned only with the kind of behaviour that is sufficiently differentiated from mere happening to show at least some of the characteristics mentioned above; and ethics is further concerned with the problem of how such behaviour can be thought capable of being evaluated, as right or wrong, or good or bad.

Obviously there are border-line cases, and our language for talking about action and its characteristics is far from precise. However, we may try to set down what seem to be the conditions that must obtain if we are to talk of 'acts' or 'action' in an ethical sense, and recognize these as the doings of an 'agent'. (1) To qualify as an 'act', what is done must be done freely, that is to say, not because of any compulsion, external or internal. Words like 'decision' and 'choice' point to this experience of freedom. Needless to say, the freedom is always a matter of degree, and choices are always limited, sometimes severely so. Yet it would seem that the notion of action presupposes some area of free choice. *See* **Free Will and Determinism.** (2) Closely connected with the idea of freedom is that of knowledge. The agent must be aware of what he is doing. Different kinds of knowledge are involved here. Some of this knowledge is factual – knowledge of the circumstances of the act, knowledge of the persons affected by it, and so on. There is also the question of knowing what is right in the particular situation, or knowing what are the ends at which one ought to aim. Both our knowledge of facts and of ethical values is bound to be more or less deficient in every situation, so that all ethical action would seem to imply an element of risk, inseparable from our human finitude. But some basic minimum of knowledge there must be before we can talk of 'action' or recognize anyone as the responsible 'agent' of a deed. *See* **Ignorance; Responsibility.** (3) An act is intentional, that is to say, it is directed upon some definite state of affairs (sometimes called the 'object' of the act) which the act seeks to realize. Because of the limitations of our knowledge, we often do things unintentionally. What we have done might still be an act with moral quality, if, for instance, we had acted with negligence (q.v.). The typical act, however, from an ethical point of view, is one that is done with definite intention. If we think of the intention as relating to some limited, well-defined situation, this enables us to distinguish it from (4) the end of the act. Action is purposive. My immediate intention may be to catch a train, but the end or purpose of this act is, let us say, to attend a meeting to forward some cause in which I am interested. Thus acts cohere together in policies of action, and the unifying factor is some long-range end or some overarching commitment. Here again we have to notice that it is impossible to draw hard and fast lines. In any particular case, it is likely that we act from 'mixed motives' (q.v.). Some motives may become dominant, and their dominance sets up patterns of action which, in turn, form a recognizable character (q.v.). Specially discussed in ethics and moral theology are the ulterior or ultimate ends of human action – self-love, love of mankind, love of God. *See* **Conscience; Ethical Language; Ethics; Motives and Motivation.**

EDITOR

Addiction

Addiction is the state of being given over to the habitual use of alcohol or other drugs. *See* **Alcoholism; Temperance and Temperance Movements.**

Adolescence. *see* Development.

Adoption

Adoption is the procedure whereby a child deprived of a home with its natural parents, because it is orphaned or illegitimate or for some other reason, is taken into the home of other persons who become legally the parents of the child. The practice is very ancient, and, from a Christian point of view, it is, under normal circumstances, entirely commendable and to be encouraged. It is a mistake to think that the child is the only or even the principal beneficiary of such an arrangement. The benefits are reciprocal, especially if the parents would otherwise have been childless. On the other hand, a couple should not be deterred from adopting a child because of the feeling that their motives are not sufficiently altruistic. In such cases, motives will always be mixed, and it is in the actual living relationship that adjustments will be made and a true parent-child relation established. One important moral implication of adoption has to do with the question of artificial insemination (q.v.) by a donor. It is sometimes argued on behalf of this morally dubious practice that it is justified as satisfying the natural desire for a parent-child relationship, but this argument can have little force so long as large numbers of homeless children are awaiting adoption. *See* **Orphans.**

EDITOR

Adultery

Adultery is sexual intercourse between a man or woman who is married and someone other than the marriage partner. Its prohibition as a moral offence among Christians derives from the OT in which it is specifically forbidden in the seventh Commandment (Ex. 20.14), though the Ten Commandments are concerned with more than the external act, as can be seen from the tenth Commandment: 'You shall not covet your neighbour's wife' (Ex. 20.17).

In his Sermon on the Mount Jesus does nothing to lessen this moral offence of adultery, but points the attention of his hearers to the springs from which a desire to commit adultery rises (Matt. 5.27–32. The Greek word *porneia* in this passage is probably a general term referring to the sins of the flesh). The teaching of Jesus in this, as in other matters, does not deal with the outward offence, which he assumes to be wrong, but concentrates attention on the inner thoughts and desires of man, implying that it is here that the moral offence has its origin, and that therefore this is the point where action needs to be taken.

Christians have allowed divorce (q.v.) for adultery, even when they have forbidden it for any other reason, on the basis of the passage from St Matthew's Gospel (5.31–32).

In the early days of the Christian Church the effect of Christian attitudes on the practices of the time was one of moderation. Severe penalties for adultery were in force in the ancient world, including the death sentence and mutilation. The discipline of the Church itself was more rigorous in the early days, when the end of the world was regarded as imminent, than in later times.

Roman Catholic teaching holds that adultery is a sin against the threefold good of marriage (q.v.), and that the consent of the other marriage partner in no way diminishes its evil. Adultery is held to be a more serious moral offence when committed by the wife on the grounds that the practical effects are usually more damaging to herself and to others concerned in the marriage.

In recent years it has been suggested that artificial insemination by donor (AID), that is, from the semen of an unknown man, may be considered as an act of adultery and that legislation should be framed accordingly. It would, however, seem clearer to discuss and legislate for AID without using terms derived from different concepts. *See also* **Artificial Insemination.**

Adultery from a moral point of view is damaging to the good of the family and is a direct betrayal of the most sacred human relationships. It has certainly increased during the last half century owing to greater facilities for divorce and to the availability of contraceptives. The atmosphere which is created by easy divorce facilities weakens the resistance of many men and women when temptation to be unfaithful to their marriage vows assails them, and this, together with the availability of contraceptives, has assisted the growth of adultery.

HERBERT WADDAMS

Advertising

Advertising has become an essential part of modern society, for business firms, having undertaken the investment necessary to produce a new product, must ensure that there is a market for it. In practice, there is no clear distinction between informing the public of a means of satisfying existing wants, and creating new wants. It is claimed that advertising by making possible larger markets, leads to greater economies of scale and hence to reduced costs and prices. This is true in part, but much advertising between large combines, e.g., for detergents and cigarettes, tends to be purely competitive, to protect the market against rival firms. It is also claimed that advertising enriches our lives, by making us aware of new forms of satisfaction. This also is true in part, but Christians cannot be happy about the types of satisfaction often encouraged, nor about the general encouragement of acquisitiveness and 'getting on' as the most important things in life, nor about the doubtful claims often made for certain goods. Christians must accept advertising, as being part and parcel of modern life, but they must be alert against its dangers and abuses. *See* **Business Ethics.**

JOHN F. SLEEMAN

Affection, Affectivity, Affects.
see Emotions.

Affinity

Affinity is the word used to denote those relationships arising from marriage, as distinct from those dependent on birth and parentage. Certain degrees of affinity constitute an impediment to marriage after the death of a spouse. Regulations vary somewhat from country to country and from one Christian communion to another. For the Church of England, *see* 'A Table of Kindred and Affinity' in BCP. *See* **Marriage.**

Affirmation

Affirmation is a solemn declaration of truth, made before a magistrate or other officer. It is equivalent to an oath, and may be made by those who have conscientious objections to oaths (cf. Matt. 5.34). The right to affirm was originally provided for Quakers, but has been extended to other groups, including atheists. *See* Oaths.

Affluence. see Contemporary Society.

Agape. see Love.

Aged, Care of the. see Old Age.

Aggression

Aggression is unprovoked self-assertive violence. The word is used of individual behaviour, but from an ethical point of view, a more important concept is that of aggressive behaviour on the part of nations. *See* International Order; Peace and War.

Akhnaton. see Egyptian Ethics, Ancient.

Alcoholism

Alcoholism is a disease in which the addictive cycle starts with a compulsion to drink in order to drown the effects of previous drinking. While excessive repetitive drinking causes physical complications, particularly vitamin B1 deficiency, the basic problem is the motive for repetition. Some 6% of social drinkers become addicted in a ratio of about five men to one woman; this gap appears to be narrowing. Patients of good pre-alcoholic personality show an 80% recovery rate, neurotic alcoholics about 30%, but psychopathic alcoholics cannot offer the co-operation essential to successful treatment. No physical heredity has been demonstrated.

Vulnerability is created by personal tensions arising from inadequacy and guilt. Excessive self-criticism demands perfectionism, creating a sense of inferiority and social diffidence which alcohol serves to allay. Over-sensitive to the gap between ambitions and achievements, the alcoholic cannot tolerate frustrations, yet has a high spiritual potential leaning to over-anxiety about ultimate religious questions. Alcohol first appears as a solution rather than a problem by diminishing his guilt feelings sufficiently for him to accept himself and feel accepted. He seeks pseudosatisfaction where only faith can fully satisfy. The 'Twelve Steps' of Alcoholics Anonymous presuppose capacity for a high spiritual response.

The disease involves body, mind and soul. Excessive alcohol intake depresses the self-critical centres giving an illusive sense of confidence eventually dissipated in a 'hangover', but dependence increases tensions while diminishing tension outlets. 'The excessive drinker lives to drink, but the alcoholic drinks to live'; while the former can control his drinking at a decisive crisis and may continue to enjoy it, the alcoholic cannot, and, from the time that alcohol has trapped him in the tension of helpless dependence on it and hopeless hatred of it, his moral and mental faculties degenerate to the extent that he will sacrifice everything for it. A single drink now becomes the inevitable prelude to an uncontrolled bout; ultimately he can neither conceal his excess nor remain concealed and isolates himself and his family from normal social relationships. Children who are victims of authoritarian moralism, rejection (spiritual or physical) and success-worship are particularly vulnerable.

It is impossible to help an alcoholic without his co-operation and it may be necessary to deprive him of his props to induce the 'rock-bottom' of acknowledged helplessness. Alcoholics Anonymous offers a non-judgmental fellowship to which he can bring his despair and in which he can accept himself as a sick man needing the group and the 'Higher Power'. This group-therapy might find greater effectiveness by a definition of the 'Higher Power' sufficient to assure absolution. Restoration demands a therapeutic programme engaging many skills, medical, psychiatric and social in the adjustment of the family as well as the patient. The Alcoholics Anonymous group and the spiritual counsellor offer the spiritual hope essential to the restoration of dignity and meaningfulness. Authoritarianism provokes resistance and religion must slip in through genuine personal identity. God is recognized as present in the relationship between helper and the helped rather than as someone to be dragged in on religious conditions. Councils on Alcoholism promote the team-work between these skills. Institutional treatment should be brief followed by supportive out-patient and group therapy within the family and social setting, as discharge may be followed by quick relapse if the patient remains alone with his load of indecisions. National Councils also establish Information Centres for spreading knowledge of the disease as a public health problem so that its early signs (preoccupation with drinking, sneaking drinks, secretiveness about the amount drunk or 'blackouts') may be made so well known that sufferers can come forward without shame for treatment before the devastating stages are reached. Thus incidence can be prevented and the 'rock-bottom' elevated to earlier domestic or social crises.

Persuasion to 'sign the pledge for life' increases the guilt already associated with failure of will-power so treatment programmes are built up on a day-by-day technique of evading the first fatal drink and eliminating loneliness and worry about past failures or future problems, while the patient is trained to help himself in helping others. 'Sufficient unto the day is the evil thereof' and 'Bear ye one another's burdens' are accepted therapeutic maxims. Spiritual 'conversion' can break the power of this addiction, but a swing to a spiritual pride in compulsive religion may provoke a relapse. Drugs like 'Antabus' guard against the depression which may follow spiritual exaltation by preventing a sudden drink from becoming a 'skid'; even such a relapse may be given therapeutic value as the prelude to a new stage of stability. The spiritual counsellor, while replacing shame with hope and isolation with fellow-feeling, should always seek co-operation with the physician, for, in this field of healing, doctors, clergy and social workers welcome each others' skill in the total effort of treating the personality as a whole. Alcoholism is of such complicated malignity that every therapeutic weapon must be sharpened by the research which is only beginning.

Marvin A. Block, *Alcoholism*, 1965; H. J. Clinebell, *Understanding and Counselling the Alcoholic*, 1956; J. C. Ford, *Man takes a Drink*, 1956; Marty Mann, *New Primer on Alcoholism*, 1958; Lincoln Williams, *Tomorrow will be Sober*, 1960.

J. B. HARRISON

Alienation

Alienation is a concept used both in existentialist philosophy and in depth psychology. It refers to the individual's condition of being cut off from some larger whole, to which he nevertheless feels that he ought to belong. This alienation can take place on several levels. An individual may be alienated from himself, in the sense that he has not been able to accept himself, or that he has not been able to fulfil himself and feels himself falling short of what he takes to be his 'true' self. An individual may also be alienated from his fellow human beings, and perhaps feels himself cut off from society as a whole. This kind of alienation is related to the phenomenon which sociologists call 'anomie' (q.v.). At a still deeper level, there is ontological alienation. In this case, the individual feels that he has no place in the scheme of things. Some existentialists have used the expression 'lostness'. Theologians have seen a connection between alienation and the biblical concept of sin, as a falling away or separation from God.

EDITOR

Almsgiving

Though giving to the poor has been a part of the Hebraic tradition, the word 'alms' does not appear in the OT. In this form the concept is Christian and is highly commended in the NT, where it is regarded as an act of virtue. Until modern times, almsgiving has been one of the most important of 'transfer payments'. This persisted while there was no established machinery for giving regular aid to the poor, and royal families and the great nobles would often appoint 'almoners' who would distribute largesse for them. In England the Queen's High Almoner is the Bishop of St Albans. The monasteries would also appoint almoners, but though it should have been possible for them to develop into something like social workers this did not happen. Almsgiving was an essential part of the social system, and many would have starved to death without the alms that were given to them. Almsgiving suffered from three defects: (1) it created in many a monetary calculus of virtue, (2) it created a relationship of subordination and superordination between people, (3) it resulted in the growth of professional begging. During the nineteenth century a considerable opposition developed to almsgiving on the part of those who wanted to suppress professional begging and in some measure on the part of some socialists who wanted aid to be given to the poor as a right, and not as an act of virtue on the part of others.

When the first social worker was introduced into the Royal Free Hospital in London in 1894, she was given the title of 'almoner'; since then the word almoner in England has come to mean a medical social worker.

With the growth of social services and the reduction of poverty, direct almsgiving has tended to decline and the very large numbers of those who give money away do so by subscribing to charities and voluntary social service organizations. Almsgiving has become a vicarious act.

David Owen, *English Philanthropy*, 1965; Cherry Morris, ed., *Social Case-work in Great Britain*, 1950.

BRIAN RODGERS

Alphonsus Liguori, St

St Alphonsus (1696–1797) was a leading Roman Catholic moral theologian. He founded in 1732 the society of missioners known as Redemptorists and devoted to pastoral work in rural areas of Italy. His preaching and pastoral concerns led him increasingly into the study of moral theology. Of his many writings, the most celebrated is his *Theologia Moralis* (I, 1753; II, 1755). He opposed the harshness of rigorism (q.v.) and developed equiprobabilism (q.v.). His authority on moral theology in the Roman Catholic Church was very great, and he continues to be influential. According to a leading contemporary Roman Catholic moral theologian, B. Häring, who names St Alphonsus with Augustine, Cyril of Jerusalem and Thomas Aquinas as the outstanding Christian moralists in the classic tradition, the work of Alphonsus has both the strength and the weakness of its time; but he points out that this work should be judged not only by the *Theologia Moralis*, but by the whole *corpus* of Alphonsus' writings on the Christian life, including his book *Pratica di amar Gesu Cristo*, which stresses the place of love in the Christian life, with reference to I Cor. 13 (cf. *Das Gesetz Christi*, p. 70). *See* **Moral Theology; Roman Catholic Moral Theology (Contemporary).**

EDITOR

Altruism

Altruism (Latin: *alter*, 'the other') is conduct aimed at the good of other persons. The Christian is commanded by the NT to love his neighbour as himself, and even to love his enemies. Other religions likewise teach an altruistic ethic. Some exponents of a naturalistic ethic (e.g., Sir Charles Sherrington) have argued that since co-operation has proved more successful than competition in the evolutionary process, altruistic conduct has its basis in the way things are. However, altruism usually runs so counter to man's self-regarding tendencies that it might seem almost unnatural. Many philosophers have argued that altruistic actions are at bottom self-regarding, and are done to win esteem or to enjoy the gratitude of the person benefited or to bask in the feeling of having done 'the right thing'. No doubt there is some truth in this, but it would surely be cynical to suppose that all altruistic conduct is a disguised egoism; and it is in fact possible to point to many deeds which have been done for the sake of others and which could not possibly have benefited the agent even in the most subtle ways. On the other hand, it must be acknowledged that purely altruistic acts are probably very rare, and that when we leave the sphere of individual ethics and think of social ethics or international order, pure altruism is presumably never found at all. Reinhold Niebuhr has remarked: 'The new life in Christ represents the perfection of complete and heedless self-giving which obscures the contrary impulse of self-regard. It is a moral ideal scarcely possible for the individual, and certainly not relevant to the morality of self-regarding nations' (*Man's Nature and his Communities*, 1965, p. 42).

EDITOR

Ambition. *see* Pride; Self-love.

Ambrose, St

St Ambrose (*c.* 340–397), one of the four 'Doctors' of the Latin Church, was born in a Christian family prominent in the public service of the western Roman Empire. Trained in law and administration, he was a provincial governor, and still a catechumen, when in 374 he was elected bishop of the metropolitan see of Milan, then the imperial capital in the west.

His episcopate was marked by a successful campaign to suppress open Arianism in the western empire, as well as by a continuing struggle with the forces of resurgent Roman paganism. As adviser to the emperors Gratian, Valentinian II and Theodosius I, Ambrose was led to shape in preliminary form that view of the relation of the Church to the Christian state which came by and large to prevail in the west.

Ambrose's work *On the Duties of Ministers*, modelled on Cicero's treatise *On Duty*, enunciates the principal themes of his ethic and, as the first handbook of Christian morals, exercised a formative influence on mediaeval western thought generally. Ambrose combines the best of the ancient Stoic ethic with Christian insight. Thus he adopts from Stoicism the scheme of the four cardinal virtues – prudence, justice, temperance and courage – but transforms their meaning by interpreting them in terms of Christian notions of faith, altruistic love, and dedication to the will of a personal God. God's will is made known in nature and in conscience, but above all in Scripture; and the goal of the moral life is not virtue for its own sake (the Stoic ideal), but the soul's enjoyment of God in a blessed immortality. This goal is attained through the control of passion by a reason enlightened and inspired by a grace-given love for God, which impels the soul to practise not only the imposed 'precepts' of the Gospel, but also its 'counsels' (e.g., celibacy or virginity).

The emphasis in Ambrose's ethic is on renunciation of the goods of this world in aspiration towards, and obedience to, God. Thus he regards the possession of worldly 'goods' as an affliction for which the only medicine is sacrificial almsgiving, and he is dubious about any absolute 'right' to private property, which, like slavery and the inequities of worldly political systems, he sees as products of man's sin.

Ambrose, however, accepts the State as a necessity for man in his fallen condition. He enjoins obedience to its laws except in cases where the State's transgression of divine law requires that the Christian practise passive disobedience. The Christian State, however, is the ally of the Church. It has a duty to protect the Church, though it may not interfere in her administration of spiritual affairs; and the head of a Christian State is subject as an individual believer to the doctrinal and disciplinary authority of the Church. Ambrose thus sees the Church and the (Christian) State as associated but independent authorities.

R. A. NORRIS, JR

Amos

Amos (*c.* 750 BC) was the earliest Hebrew prophet whose writings have come down to us, and he may be regarded also as one of the earliest protagonists of a 'secular' or 'lay' form of faith. He did not think of himself as a professional prophet or man of religion, but as an agricultural worker whom God had called to prophesy (7.14–15). This understanding of his mission is expressed in the context of an incident which shows Amos as a stern critic of the political and ecclesiastical establishment of his day. It was a time of relative affluence in Israel, but the wealth of the country was very unevenly distributed and there seems to have been much corruption, oppression and injustice. In the midst of all this, 'religion' flourished, tithes were paid, sacrifices made, and rites (sometimes licentious) observed. Against this empty cult Amos directed his polemic, and warned that the 'day of the Lord' would be one of punishment for the nation, rather than of vindication. Positively, he calls for righteousness and justice. His message is summarized in the famous verses: 'Take away from me the noise of your songs; to the melody of your harps I will not listen. But let justice roll down like waters, and righteousness like an everflowing stream' (5.23–24). Like many later advocates of 'religionless' faith, however, Amos does not fully appreciate the complexity of the relation between morality and religion. He demands righteousness rather than cult, but there is no suggestion as to how this righteousness is to be realized in the face of human weakness and sinfulness. It was left to later generations to wrestle with the problem of divine grace, and of the place of prayer and worship in the formation of the kind of life which God demands. *See* **Old Testament Ethics.**

EDITOR

Amusements

Amusements are activities which divert us from the everyday routine of life. They include games and sports, spectacles and entertainments, hobbies and leisure-time activities. From the earliest times, men have had some amusements. What is common to such activities is their non-serious character. They are play, and play has a legitimate place in human life (as perhaps also in animal life). Play serves as a relaxation from work, and indeed only if he has periods of relaxation can a man work effectively. There is nothing in the Christian religion that should be considered hostile to legitimate amusements, and only puritanical distortions of Christianity have frowned upon play-activities. Even if this puritanical prejudice against enjoyments is today much rarer than it has sometimes been, it lingers on in the superstition that somehow amusements ought to be edifying or educative if Christians are to give them wholehearted approval. Many amusements do in fact increase skills, and are therefore useful; but there is nothing whatever wrong with amusements which are entirely frivolous, and do not aim at being useful or edifying in some kind of oblique way. Moreover, Christian ethics should not allow itself to get involved in questions of taste, especially where these are usually dictated by middle-class and middle-aged preferences. Listening to Beethoven has no merit, from an ethical point of view, over listening to the Beatles. On the other hand, amusements are not exempt from the ethical standards that apply in our more serious activities. Cruel spectacles, dangerous sports, lewd shows – in short, any amusements that are detrimental to the well-being of participants or spectators, must be condemned by the Christian. There are many borderline cases. The question to be asked is whether an amusement excites states of mind that are either sinful in themselves or predispose to sinful acts. For the question of cruel sports, *see* **Animals**; for the question of a conflict between ethical and esthetic interests, *see* **Censorship.**

EDITOR

Anarchy

Anarchy is the absence of government. Such a state of affairs is indeed advocated by a few small extremist revolutionary groups. The Christian attitude to anarchy is perhaps best stated by Calvin. He acknowledges that in an ideal world (that is, where man had not fallen into sin) the restraints of civil government would be unnecessary; but in our actual world, he argues that even a bad government is better than none at all.

Anger

It is impossible to imagine a person incapable of anger and terrifying to picture one whose anger is ungovernable. A man's neural system and the sharpness of his five senses have a good deal to do with his proneness to anger. A man of deep love and loyalties is more likely to be angry than one who cares little for any person or institution.

Anger upsets one's mental and spiritual organization; the more delicate the organization is the more damage anger can do. This is noticeable in members of a community or in the case of others whose work demands close co-operation and provides occasions when it is difficult to control anger. Anger distorts a man's perspective so that he sees life out of proportion and does what he does not want to do and therefore, for the time, he is the sort of person he does not want to be. Habitual anger can keep a person in such a state that he continually contradicts himself in what he says and in what he does. It is sometimes held that a man is not responsible for what he does in the heat of anger but it cannot be denied that he is responsible for being angry.

The sources of anger are complex, among them are: (1) greed, whether for food, amusement, importance, security or sanctity, (2) pride, specially when it is on its guard against suspected attacks or is asserting its independence, (3) fear of losing freedom, security, power, importance, etc.

While anger cannot be banished or cured by acts of will it can be indirectly controlled by the maintenance of a right disposition towards God, the world, others and self. Christianity does not say that Christians are never to be angry. The Scripture says 'Be ye angry and sin not'. It would be subhuman for anyone not to be moved to anger by cruelty, deceit, treachery or readiness to defraud or destroy the weak. A Christian is expected to control, or rather to attempt to control, the expression of his anger.

It is a serious thing to incite others to be angry. On the other hand a Christian dare not advocate the avoidance of anger at all costs. The image of our Lord advancing on the tables of the money changers and traders with a scourge in his hand is not a picture of the suppression of anger but of its control.

R. E. C. BROWNE

Anglican Ethics, Anglican Moral Theology

There is no generally accepted body of moral teaching that would permit one to speak of 'Anglican moral theology' in the same way as one can speak of 'Roman Catholic moral theology'; and there is no single dominant figure in Anglicanism, like Luther or Calvin, so that one could not point to a coherent body of 'Anglican ethics' comparable to 'Lutheran ethics' or 'Calvinist ethics'. On the other hand, a great deal of important ethical thinking has been done in the Anglican communion, though according to Thomas Wood, 'in the present century it has been the most neglected of all aspects of Anglican theological studies'. No doubt some common attitudes run through all this thinking, but on the surface, the differences are more striking than the common characteristics. In the current situation are to be found all the views on the spectrum, from adherents of the traditional moral theology to advocates of a situational ethic without rules. Here we can only direct the interested reader to the separate articles on different topics in Anglican ethics. *See* **Butler, Joseph; Caroline Moral Theology; Christendom Group; Christian Social Movement; Hooker, Richard; Kingsley, Charles; Maurice, Frederick Denison; Moral Theology; Sanderson, Robert; Taylor, Jeremy; Temple, William.**

EDITOR

Animals

To formulate the Christian attitude towards animals in terms of texts from the Bible would be almost, though not quite, as difficult as to formulate objections to slavery in the same way. In the former as in the latter case our obligations arise from the humility and charity which should characterize a sincere Christian.

Nevertheless although St Paul, a townsman. had little thought for animals (except in Rom. 8.19–23), on the whole the biblical view is that man and beast form one community under the providence of God, who makes a covenant with 'every beast of the earth' (Gen. 9.10) as well as with men, spares Nineveh for the sake of not only the children but 'also much cattle' (Jonah 4.11), and commands a sabbath rest for domestic animals in the same way as for human beings (Ex. 20.10). All the beasts of the forest are his, and the cattle upon a thousand hills; he knows all the fowls upon the mountains, and the wild beasts of the field are in his sight (Ps. 50.10, 11). In the apocalyptic vision the worship in heaven is led by four representative animals (Rev. 4.6–9). Lambs were to the Jews what dogs are to the English. It is true that they were sacrificed, but killing must be distinguished from hurting, and the Jewish method of slaughter was the most humane that was known before the pistol was invented.

For a time our Lord lived 'with the wild beasts' in the wilderness (Mark 1.13), and he must often have referred to them afterwards (cf. Matt. 8.20, Mark 4.4, Luke 12.24). God cares for sparrows (Matt. 10.29); it is true that the Apostles were 'of more value than many sparrows', but death, not suffering, was here in question (cf. Matt. 10.17; 23.34). The premature death of the Apostles, unlike that of birds, would have had a disastrous effect on world history.

A heavy superstructure of exegesis has been imposed on a single text in the Genesis story of creation, of man being made in the image of God (Gen. 1.26, 27; cf. I Cor. 11.7). The essential difference between the minds of men and those of animals lies in men's capacity for abstract thought, which in animals is rudimentary at best (birds can only count up to five or six), and this endowment is felt to bear a certain resemblance to God's wisdom in creation. But animals are like men in having sensations (sight, hearing, pain), perception of objects and persons as such, emotions (fear, anger), sentiments (hatred, affection), instincts (mating, hunting, territorial dominance, peck order), curiosity, love of play, aesthetic sensibility of a primitive kind, self-consciousness ('a cat, though unable to use the pronoun "I", does not mistake itself for some one else', as Auguste Comte pointed out), and language, though the latter is not of a syntactical kind. They can learn by experience, and their psychosomatic response to stress is similar to that of man. Of moral and spiritual qualities animals must presumably lack those components which depend on abstract thought and syntactical language, but beyond that inference we can only speculate.

A Christian attitude towards animals derives from the basic Christian virtues of humility and charity; hence the innumerable legends of neighbourly relations between saints and animals of many kinds, such as the horse of St Columba, the hind of St Giles, the rats of St Gertrude of Nivelles and of St Martin of Porres, and the lion of even grumpy old St Jerome. St Francis also deserves mention. But since Aquinas the minds of most theologians, though with honourable exceptions like Bishop Butler and William Paley, have been hermetically sealed against the fact that animals exist and have rights. The Prayer Book, except inadvertently in excerpts from the Bible, nowhere shows the slightest awareness of the responsibility which dominion over the animals imposes on man, or even the faintest hint of compassion for them. Hymn books almost ignore their existence.

Aristotle taught that the only part of a man which is capable of surviving death is his intellect, and through Aquinas this led to the view, widely insisted on in Roman Catholic circles, that 'animals have no souls' and hence, by a palpable *non sequitur*, no rights; and this contemptuous attitude was strengthened by the humanism of the Renaissance, which influenced the casuists. The late Dr Joseph Rickaby, s.j., wrote that 'we have no duties of charity, nor duties of any kind, to the lower animals, as neither to sticks nor stones', for the reason that our nature is 'immeasurably above' theirs.

But the Christian doctrine is that the Son of God, whose nature is 'immeasurably above' ours, humbled himself for our advantage, and that Christians should take him for their exemplar. We are, therefore, under an obligation to have enough humility and charity, in imitation of his, to concern ourselves actively for the welfare of creatures which we regard as our inferiors. In sealing up the windows of her official mind against her animal neighbours, the Church has surely erred against their Maker. On the other hand where the influence of the Bible on character has generated humility and charity, neighbourliness towards animals has often ensued unofficially; this has occurred in many of the saints, including St Francis of Assisi. The modern animal-welfare movement originated in the matrix of Protestant Christianity, whereas pagan cults have generally entailed sadistic practices, the Arabs still treat animals as things, and in the Orient the place of compassion is taken by a superstitious reverence for life which often results in cruelty.

When, however, we ask how this responsibility is to be discharged in practice, we find a need for painstaking thought and much factual knowledge; for lack of these, many kind-hearted Christians have fallen in with an approach which is sentimental rather than humane. Sweeping generalizations are dangerous in such a complex field. If we say that the end can never justify the means we shall never

plough a field for fear of crushing a field-mouse. If, going to the other extreme, we take the greatest good of the greatest number as our rule we shall justify the lethal experiments carried out by Nazis on Jews. Some commonsense compromise has to be reached, and for this purpose the Golden Rule must be the Christian's guide. We must ask ourselves always 'How, *mutatis mutandis*, would you like it yourself?' (Matt. 7.12).

One basic principle is clear, however: the distinction between killing and hurting is fundamental. The oriental doctrine called 'reverence for life' has been responsible for an incalculable amount of cruelty. Hindus let old cows starve to death rather than put them out of their suffering. Buddhist scientists after an experiment entailing surgical interference, leave unanaesthetized animals to die in pain rather than take the responsibility of killing them. But Christianity values the quality, not the duration, of life (Mark 8.35), and our Lord teaches compassion (Luke 6.36) and neighbourliness which extends to the despised (Mark 2.16). It follows that a Christian's sympathy for animals must not be restricted to those species which happen to be popular or useful. A sensitive test of his sincerity is, for example, the care with which he chooses the least cruel poison when he has to destroy rats.

The sins which give rise to cruelty are chiefly avarice, pride (contemptuousness), and uncharitably selfish indifference. The profits to be made in the fur trade lead annually to the crucifixion of millions of musquash, beaver and other animals in gin traps. Of the whaling industry it has been said that if whales could scream audibly, nobody would be able to stay in it. The indiscriminate use of excessively cruel poisons for destroying rodents and other over-abundant wild animals has been generally dictated by considerations of convenience and contemptuousness towards any animal denominated 'vermin'. The enforcement of preliminary stunning in the slaughterhouse was for long resisted for commercial reasons by the British meat trade, and still is incomplete in most American states. Objectionable methods of raising calves are due to a contemporary fashion for white veal, but methods of producing other animal food may arise in part from the endeavour to stave off for a time the world starvation which must come from reckless overpopulation. But there is also a streak of sadism latent in human nature, becoming patent in, for instance, the beast-baitings, martyrdoms, etc., of the ancient Roman amphitheatres and in contemporary Spanish bullfights. As regards what is called 'vivisection', sincere and largely successful efforts to reach a reasonable ethical compromise have been made in Britain, and a few other nations have laws of a sort, but in most countries, including the whole American continent, there is no restriction on what may be done to an animal if it be called 'experimentation'. On the other hand field sports ('blood sports') have attracted disproportionate attention by their spectacular character. Although the pursuit and killing of animals for pleasure can hardly be called neighbourly, and although grievous cruelty is entailed in irresponsible and incompetent shooting and in otter-hunting, yet fox-hunting and deer-hunting entail an immeasurably smaller aggregate of suffering than, say, neglected foot-rot in sheep or the savaging of stock by dogs, which have been ignored by emotional propagandists.

These examples will show that, while the duty of neighbourliness towards animals is binding on Christians, its application in particular cases may demand accurate knowledge. Hence the most practical course for Christian leaders is, perhaps, to include in the regular language of public worship some clauses which express this neighbourliness in general terms.

Anon., *The Church and Kindness to Animals*, 1916; R. P. Jean Gautier, *Un Prêtre et son Chien*, ET, *A Priest and His Dog*, 1957; *Un Prêtre se Penche sur la Vie Animale*, 1959; C. W. Hume, *The Status of Animals in the Christian Religion*, 1957; *Man and Beast*, 1962. A. W. Moss, *Valiant Crusade*, 1961; Fr Aloysius Roche, *These Animals of Ours*, 1939; E. C. Rust, *Nature and Man in Biblical Thought*, 1953.
                                                    C. W. HUME

Anomie

From its Greek roots, anomie (or *anomy* or *anomia*) may be defined as 'broken limits'. The concept of anomie was initially developed by Emile Durkheim to refer to a condition of relative normlessness in a society or group. In his study of suicide (q.v.) Durkheim noted that anomic suicide is common among individuals who lack self-identity with a system of norms or values. Anomie refers to the absence of guiding or governing norms, the state of rulelessness, of deregulation, or of social anarchy. By extension, the term is now applied to individuals, as the theme of uprooted man in quest of self-identity and community has become prevalent in our time.

The anomic man is spiritually sterile and responsible to no one. Anomie conceived sociologically refers to the strain towards normlessness occurring when there is a disjunction or malintegration between cultural goals and the capacity of people to act in accord with these goals. Anomie is a useful concept for understanding deviant behaviour. Social chaos, moral confusion, and disintegration of value systems are marks of an anomic society. *See* **Alienation.**

Emile Durkheim, *Le Suicide*, 1930; Robert K. Merton, *Social Theory and Social Structure*, 1957; David Riesman, Nathan Glazer and Ruel Denney, *The Lonely Crowd*, 1950.
                                                    ROBERT LEE

Anthropology

What are the dynamics of human culture? What are the processes by which differences of custom arise? How are habitual ways of doing things transmitted within a society? How does change take place in deep-seated habits to give rise to the rapid social change of our generation? What is the effect of society on the individual and of individual on society? What are the value systems under which a people operate? What are the experiences and assumptions which give rise to ethical judgments or morality? Questions like these are some of the many contemporary concerns of cultural anthropology as practised in the USA. Cultural anthropology is the largest branch of general anthropology, which includes prehistoric archaeology, linguistics and physical anthropology as well. The most complex aspect of man is his culture, and cultural anthropology is the most extensive branch of the field.

Anthropology has not given all parts of human culture equal treatment. Language and kinship structures, for example, are treated with high sophistication and elaborately developed research and analytical techniques. Enormous amounts of information have been collected on religions of various peoples, and their interpenetration with other aspects of life studied. Ethics, however, has received little specific attention (*see* **Primitive Ethics**), although it is a most pertinent potential area of anthropological investigation.

Traditionally anthropology has made 'primitive' (pre-literate) peoples its principal subject matter, and anthropologists continue to give them a large share of attention, although anthropological techniques are more and more being applied to the study of non-primitive groups in present and industrial societies. In earlier workers the stress on the primitive was an attempt to find in them earlier stages of human cultural evolution. All peoples have an equally long history, however, and 'primitive' society has been undergoing innovations for millennia, which made that search somewhat illusory.

Modern research among 'primitives' may still often be historically motivated, but historical inferences are drawn from the study of the processes of culture change, from distributions of culture traits, from correlations with archaeology and with written records.

Modern cultural anthropology is seeking to understand the nature of culture, how it is rooted in personality, in history, in ecology. It seeks for the meaning of behaviour within a society, for the inter-relations between value systems, religion, mythology, social structure and the many other aspects and manifestations of culture. It sees culture holistically, and individual customs as parts of a fabric which has meaning primarily as the sum of its parts and in the inter-relations of its parts. The suicide of an elderly Eskimo compelled by his sense of the importance of preserving the meagre stock of food for the young and the fit, the self-immolation of the Buddhist priest on the streets of Saigon, the *hara-kiri* of the Japanese officer who has lost face, and the plunge of the neurotic young man who steps from the fortieth floor of a New York building have vastly different meanings because they stem from vastly different sets of assumptions and attitudes, as well as custom. Cultural anthropology today seeks to compare systems, compare structures, rather than simply to compare isolates.

The world-wide variety of cultures is the anthropologist's laboratory. Since he cannot place man in an artificially controlled laboratory system he searches out the different groups of men who have reacted to different ecological and social situations in different ways. By studying their variety and the dynamics behind it he learns more of the very nature of culture.

In the field of religion anthropology has provided the comparative religionist with most of his information about the religions of primitive peoples, and with such concepts as animism, animatism, mana, taboo. Anthropology makes no attempt to deal with concepts like life, mind, soul, etc., leaving them to theology and psychology. It seeks to study the manifestation of these in human behaviour, and to understand what people mean by these when they have them as parts of their religious system.

One of the fruits of anthropological study on a world-wide basis is a better understanding of the interplay of nature and nurture in the development of different group personalities, talents and aptitudes. African propensity to rhythm, Japanese rigidity, lack of competitive spirit in the Hopi Indian of the American south-west and many other variants of national or cultural temperament are the product of biological and cultural forces working together, and particularly appropriate for a discipline which relates the study of both biological and cultural man.

Because of their emphasis on the meaning of behaviour in relation to its cultural context, their comparative point of view, their attempt to see life through the eyes of other peoples, all anthropologists develop a somewhat relativistic point of view towards culture, including morals, ethics and other value judgments. Some insist that no moral judgments are possible outside of the meaning of a given cultural situation. Further research in the area of value judgments will certainly modify such extreme positions, but cannot diminish the importance of an understanding of the meaning of behaviour within its own cultural context for ethical judgment about that behaviour.

Melville J. Herskovits, *Cultural Anthropology*, 1955; John J. Honigman, *The World of Man*, 1959; Clyde Kluckhohm, *Mirror for Man*, 1948; A. L. Kroeber, *Anthropology*, 1948; Eugene Louis J. Luzbetak, *The Church and Cultures*, 1964; A. Nida, *Customs and Cultures*, 1954.

WILLIAM A. SMALLEY

Antinomianism

Antinomianism is the view that, for the Christian, faith has abolished the law so that he is no longer subject to it. The extreme antinomian point of view, which leads into licentious conduct, is condemned both in the NT and by the Reformers. Yet both the NT and the Reformers were clear that the gospel ruled out any legalistic ethic. The place of law in the Christian ethics is still being discussed. *See* **Law; Law and Gospel; Justification by Faith; Moral Theology; Natural Law.**

Anti-Semitism

Anti-Semitism, as popularly used, refers to the attitude and practice of prejudice against the Jewish people, ranging from acts of violent persecution to unexpressed dislike. Strictly speaking, the Semites include the peoples in several linguistic groups of South-west Asia and North Africa (Hebrews and Arabs among modern peoples; Assyrians, Phoenicians, and Babylonians among more ancient peoples). Thus it would be a contradiction to speak literally of Arab anti-Semitism. But the word has come to refer to anti-Jewish attitudes, whether among Semites or among other peoples.

Anti-Semitism is a problem of special concern to Christian ethics, because of the peculiar relations between Christians and Jews. 'Spiritually we are all Semites', said Pope Pius XI (1938). But from early times hostility has been common between Christians and Jews. The indications appear even in the NT. Jews sometimes regarded Christians as heretics, and Christians regarded Jews as recalcitrant unbelievers. As Christianity grew in numbers and power, Christians subjected Jews to many forms of discrimination, sometimes to outright persecution. Christian spokesmen attacked Jews as 'Christ-killers', guilty of the crime of deicide. In the Middle Ages the Jewish people were generally consigned to ghettoes and denied any place of respectability in the feudal order. With a utilitarian cynicism Christians sometimes encouraged Jews to undertake certain financial activities, which were regarded as unethical but as necessary to society. The Protestant Reformation, despite some preliminary gestures of understanding, generally continued to cultivate hostility towards the Jews.

Anti-Semitism has sometimes erupted in organized massacres of Jews, as in the *pogroms* in Czarist Russia. It has entered deeply into the ethos of the modern European-American civilization. The humanitarian spirit of modern liberal theology and of the secular Enlightenment has done much to overcome or moderate anti-Semitism. But the neo-paganism of Nazism brought in the twentieth century the most bitter, systematic persecution of the Jews in all history, with the deliberate extermination of some six million Jewish persons.

The Christian Church by the mid-twentieth century has formally renounced anti-Semitism on almost all levels of its organized life. Latent (and sometimes deliberate) anti-Semitism remains a continuing danger in modern civilization, but the Church can at last be expected to oppose it, except in some obscurantist church groups.

The First Assembly of the World Council of Churches (1948) denounced anti-Semitism as 'sin against God and man'. The Third Assembly (1961) specifically insisted that 'the historic events which led to the Crucifixion should not be so presented as to fasten upon the Jewish people of today responsibilities which belong to our corporate humanity and not to one race or community'. After a series of papal declarations against anti-Semitism, over a period of many years, the Vatican Council II condemned 'all hatred, persecutions and other manifestations of anti-Semitism, whatever the period and whoever was responsible; the Council further urged that Christians should never present the Jews "as rejected by God or accursed", as though this followed from Scripture' (*Declaration on the Relation of the Church to Non-Christian Religion*, 1966).

Jules Isaac, *The Teaching of Contempt: Christian Roots of Anti-Semitism*, 1964; Jacques Maritain, *A Christian Looks at the Jewish Question*, 1939; Peter G. G. Pulzer, *The Rise of Political Anti-Semitism in Germany and Austria*, 1964.

ROGER L. SHINN

Antony of Egypt, St

St Antony of Egypt was a famous Christian ascetic, died *c*. 356. The story of his renunciation of the world, his retirement to the desert, his famous battles with the demons and his counselling of those who came to seek his advice, is vividly told in the *Vita S. Antoni*, attributed to St Athanasius. *See* **Asceticism; Monasticism.**

Anxiety

Anxiety connotes, in common speech, a certain kind of feeling, ranging from jitteriness to terror. In several areas of knowledge it is used precisely but not always with the same meaning. In theology, Augustine made the first considerable use of it. It entered modern theology through Kierkegaard, who regarded anxiety as intimately related to freedom. When we confront all the undetermined choices yet to be made in our lives (our freedom), we properly become dizzy (or anxious). The anxiety is painful but necessary. If we react only to its pain, we draw back, and thus never quite become human. But if we see the worth of the freedom despite the pain, anxiety becomes a kind of tutor as we become human, use our creative powers, and confront life as it is. Among modern theologians, Reinhold Niebuhr presents substantially the same view as Kierkegaard. Paul Tillich, in partial contrast, distinguishes between ontological anxiety (like Kierkegaard) and pathological anxiety, but believes both are forms of the same phenomenon. Most continental theologians speak of anxiety sparingly, regarding it as mainly a subjective phenomenon not a proper topic for theology. In earlier American evangelicalism, 'anxious inquirers' were persons seriously concerned about the gospel but not yet committed to it.

Several modern fields of study have contributed to the understanding of anxiety including its pathologies, of which an excellent description is given in Rollo May, *The Meaning of Anxiety*, 1950. The seminal work from a psychological and psychiatric point of view was done by Freud. First identifying anxiety with the tensions produced by frustrated excitation within, and hence as a kind of feeling, he later set forth an understanding that roots anxiety in the process whereby we send and receive signals of danger or challenge. Thus the normative function of anxiety is to ring the alarm when there is peril or possibility. If the signal is properly heard and heeded, then the ego or person examines, identifies and protects itself against the peril; and the unpleasant feeling is dissipated. When the person is unable to mobilize himself relevantly, then pathologies appear, beginning with a continuing unease or jitteriness, extending in more severe cases to phobias (like fear of horses), and finally to symptoms which keep the alarm signal from producing pain but at the cost of adaptation to the situation. The danger about which anxiety rings the alarm may be small or large, may come from outside or inside. But in all cases, it is the ego or person who must interpret and mobilize to meet it. When its source is properly identified, then the feeling that persists until action has been taken is fear. Thus the primary phenomenon is anxiety, while fear is an aspect of it.

Authorities disagree on the extent to which there is a single phenomenon of anxiety, of which everything spoken of as anxiety is derivative, or whether there are two or three central phenomena all identified as anxiety in different contexts. With discussions contributed both by theologians and psychologists including psychiatrists, *Contructive Aspects of Anxiety*, 1963, by Karl Menninger and Seward Hiltner, presents several views on this question.

If anxiety is used to refer only to phenomena already judged pathological, then it would have a place in psychiatry and psychology but perhaps not in theology and philosophy. If it were used only as a kind of cognitive-type confrontation, for instance, of God, then it might be regarded suspiciously by psychiatrists who need some word to describe the painful feelings of some patients. Freud's theory of the signal offers a bridge.

The statement that creativity depends on anxiety is often asserted as if uncertainty or discomfort were the soil of creativity. This seems to be false. But if anxiety is understood either in the sense of Freud or Kierkegaard, then the capacity to experience its signals, interpret them aright, and act relevantly upon them, would indeed be closely related to capacity for creativity.

Ethics is concerned with anxiety as a motive for decision and action, or as a deterrent. Discriminating capacity to feel danger or challenge signals is an indispensable condition for relevant ethical decision. Conversely, if anxiety as affect or feeling is too strong, it paralyzes all decision and action. Thus, the reduction of capacity to deal with anxiety decreases initiative in moral decision; while an intact anxiety signalling system, although neither making nor guaranteeing moral decisions, is nevertheless a necessary base for them.

SEWARD HILTNER

Apartheid

Apartheid (literally 'apartness') designates the rigorous form of racial segregation in the Republic of South Africa. The word, introduced when the Nationalist Party came into power in 1948, stood for intensification of the traditionally racial policies of the white minority, seeking to perpetuate political and economic control. (The population of South Africa is approximately 19.5% white, 68% Bantu, 3.1% Asiatic, and 9.4% 'coloured' or mixed.)

The Group Areas Act of 1950 established forcible separation of races in 'white' areas. About 13% of the country has been set aside as reservations for the native Africans. In the crowded, impoverished areas the Africans are permitted some measure of local self-government, subject to approval of the national government. Those who are allowed to remain in the white-dominated areas, to perform menial work, have few legal rights. They must carry permits; their movements and occupations are controlled; and they are subject to expulsion.

Enforcement of apartheid has led to harshly repressive acts. The government may detain persons without trial for renewable periods of 90 days. It may forbid publications and political

meetings. It has punished opponents of apartheid for 'sabotage' or furthering 'Communism'. It has halted peaceful demonstrations by violence, most notably at Sharpeville in 1960, where 69 persons were killed and 186 wounded.

World opposition has embarrassed but not softened the government. In 1960 the Nobel Peace Prize went to Chief A. J. Luthuli, African political leader and churchman. The UN has repeatedly urged the government to abandon apartheid. The General Assembly has asked UN members to break diplomatic and trade relations, and the Security Council has asked for a cessation of shipment of arms to South Africa. But increasing foreign investments have contributed to prosperity of the dominant groups in South Africa. The government has substituted the phrase, 'separate development', for apartheid. It promises eventual 'political independence' to the Bantu on their reserves, but it assures its white constituency of 'domination', 'control' and 'supremacy'.

Apartheid has posed a grave problem for the Christian conscience in South Africa. Spokesmen of the Dutch Reformed Church traditionally offered biblical and theological arguments for apartheid. Now they have largely abandoned that position for a defence based on the practical necessities of preserving white civilization on a black continent.

The non-Dutch Reformed churches (especially Anglican, Methodist and Roman Catholic) have spoken against apartheid. In 1960 at the Cottesloe consultation officials of the World Council of Churches met with representatives of eight South African churches, including the Bantu and Dutch Reformed. Their agreement – that churches may not exclude Christians on grounds of race and that the state may not interfere with the church's proclamation of the gospel – led to the counterstatements from Dutch Reformed spokesmen and to withdrawal from the World Council of Churches of the three Dutch Reformed Synods that had been members. In succeeding years an increasing number of Dutch Reformed spokesmen have opposed apartheid, sometimes at the cost of heresy trial and conviction or removal from their pastoral or professorial posts.

A. S. Geyser, et al., *Delayed Action*, 1960; Leslie A. Hewson, ed., *Cottesloe Consultation, The Report*, 1961; Trevor Huddleston, *Naught for Your Comfort*, 1956; J. C. G. Kotze, *Principle and Practice in Race Relations according to Scripture*, 1961; United Nations Publications: *Apartheid in South Africa*, 1963; *A New Course in South Africa*, 1964.

ROGER L. SHINN

Appetites

Appetites are the basic desires and needs of man. The word has become somewhat old-fashioned in ethics, modern writers preferring to speak of drives or instincts (q.v.).

Aquinas. *see* Thomas Aquinas, Ethics of St.

Aristocracy

Aristocracy, in the strict sense, means government by the best element in the people. The best-known, though imaginary, example of such an aristocracy is provided in the *Republic* of Plato (q.v.). More commonly, an aristocracy is a country where the power lies with a class enjoying hereditary privileges, such as ownership of the land. The political power of a landowning aristocracy has long ceased to be a problem in industrialized countries, but it remains a factor to be reckoned with in the so-called 'underdeveloped countries' (q.v.). The Church has frequently been allied with aristocracy, but there is now a strong movement, for example, in Latin America, to throw the weight of the Church behind those seeking social reform.

Aristotle, Aristotelianism

One of the greatest of Greek philosophers, Aristotle (384–322 BC) has also had an incalculable influence on Christian theology and ethics. In this dictionary, his teaching is discussed in detail in the article **Plato and Aristotle.**

Armaments. *see* Peace and War.

Arnold, Matthew

Matthew Arnold (1822–1888), English poet, held views on religion and morality which are still being discussed. In his view, what constitutes the major part of religion is conduct and the pursuit of righteousness. His famous description of religion as 'morality touched with emotion' might seem to suggest that there is no cognitive content in religion at all, and that it is simply an auxiliary to the moral life. This, however, would not accurately represent his position. He does seem to have believed in a 'power making for righteousness', with which man co-operates. However, Arnold left the intellectual or dogmatic content of religion vague and minimal. The stories and dogmas of religion are valuable as literature (perhaps we would now say 'myth') having a formative power in the lives of the religion's adherents. A more recent view, having close affinities to Arnold's, is that of R. B. Braithwaite. Arnold's views are expounded in his *Literature and Dogma*, 1873; *God and the Bible*, 1875; *Last Essays on Church and Religion*, 1877.

EDITOR

Artificial Insemination

Somewhere between 8% and 10% of marriages are infertile. In biblical times it was assumed that childless marriages were always the fault of the wife, but we now know that in at least 25% of the cases it will be due to the husband. There may be some accidental or congenital deformity of the genital organs, or the husband's semen may lack density or motility. There may, however, be psychological causes leading to impotence in varying degrees, or premature ejaculation, or failure to ejaculate in spite of normal coitus. Artificial insemination from the husband (A.I.H.) is the artificial implantation of his semen in the uterine canal. There are two forms of it, one by a doctor when the wife gives him a specimen of the husband's semen obtained by masturbation, and the other is the use by the couple themselves of a self-insemination syringe to introduce the semen as far as possible into the uterine canal. Roman Catholic moral theologians consider the latter 'imperfect artificial insemination' and see no objection to it in principle, but they condemn the former because they hold the lawful desire to beget children in matrimony does not outweigh the unlawfulness of an act of masturbation, which is 'against nature'. Anglican and Protestant theologians have not agreed with this condemnation. If masturbation is to be condemned as a bodily expression of self love (and there are grounds for looking again at the whole matter) such a condemnation does not seem to apply in this case. A.I.H. may therefore be approved, though in cases where male infertility is due to psychogenic causes they may point to an instability in the marriage which could have bad effects on the child. For instance the wife might transfer her love possessively to the child and the husband reject it. In most cases, however, where A.I.H. is achieved it is successful.

In the last twenty-five years some doctors in some countries have carried out insemination from an anonymous married donor who is already a parent, by agreement with all parties. This is known as A.I.D. The doctor is the only one to know all the details and he does not disclose them. There is anonymity, secrecy and consent. For this reason it is difficult for the public to know the facts either of the conception or of the subsequent histories of the children and the families concerned. There is only occasional evidence disclosed by doctors, on which there is no empirical check. In law it would appear that such a conception is classed as adultery, though many of the usual features of adultery are missing, for example, unfaithful intentions. The argument for it (as against adoption) is that it gives the wife the actual experience of motherhood. It is difficult to see, however, that a Christian woman can *demand* such an experience (especially when adoption could be a boon to a child already born). As far as state policy is concerned there are many who think it should be made a crime, if only because of the web of deceit which is involved. A less stringent policy would be to make clear that, if not a crime, it is unlawful, as fornication is in some countries. The question of fertilizing spinsters in this way has also been raised on the argument that a woman is entitled to the experience of motherhood, if she wants, even if she is not married. But deliberately to produce children who would have no evident father is not likely to commend itself to many, and it is not likely any state will encourage it, stilll less any church.

The process of deep freezing may make possible the establishment of semen banks, like blood banks, protected from radiation hazards, and offering the possibility of selected breeding on eugenic grounds with parents of different generations, in a way which might hitherto have been thought the preserve of science fiction. The use of stored sperms, or telegenesis, like the transplantation or storage of fertilized ova (also a possibility and a variant of A.I.D.) is likely to be regarded by Christian moralists as unjustified, because they threaten the personal life of the family out of which the reproductions of persons should come.

It is perhaps surprising that doctors, who are not trained for this function, should be prepared to take upon themselves the immense psychological and pastoral responsibility involved in A.I.D. There is in fact no agreement revealed how to select donors, whether they should be paid, where responsibility lies and what factors each party ought to consider.

The most considerable investigation of A.I.D. is by a Dutch doctor, and he comes down heavily against it (A. Schellen, *Artificial Insemination in the Human*, 1957).

RONALD PRESTON

Ascetical Theology

Ascetical theology is concerned with the development of the Christian life, and in particular with training in self-discipline and prayer. It has often been distinguished from mystical theology on the grounds that ascetical theology deals with the 'ordinary' ways and mystical theology with the 'extraordinary' ways of prayer, but such a distinction is difficult to justify, either on theological or practical grounds. Here the term 'ascetical theology' is taken to include mystical theology. Closely connected with ascetical theology is sacramental theology, for it is evident that the development of the Christian life can only rightly take place within the sacramental fellowship of the Church. Since all these studies concern the basic attitudes and practices of a Christian, they must inevitably be closely linked with human behaviour, the special subject of ethics and moral theology.

In any study of one aspect of the Christian life certain dangers immediately occur. They arise from the artificiality of isolating one part of human life from the rest, when all is closely interconnected. It has been widely thought that the danger of approaching ethics or moral theology from the point of view of general principles is so great as to make it virtually useless. This view is held by those who lay stress on the need for 'situational ethics'. Human behaviour, they maintain, cannot be examined in general, except by setting up external standards, which do not take into account the individual conditions of different persons and situations. But the same objection might be brought against almost any general study. Nevertheless in practice it is necessary to make some generalizations, for it is in this way alone that the experience of the past, and of other situations, can be brought into relation with each particular problem. Such general principles are just as much a part of an actual situation as are its own peculiarities.

There remains a danger in all general studies that external principles may be adopted and imposed without distinction. A study of ethics or morals runs special risks of its own, in that it may be detached from the elements which from a Christian point of view give such a study its relevance, namely, an understanding of the relation of each person to God. It is this relationship which ascetical theology sets out to examine. In Christianity knowledge and life are one, and there is no such thing as intellectual knowledge of the truth, divorced from the living practice of religion. Christian truth is known only through commitment to Christ as the way and the life: 'I am the way, and the truth, and the life' (John 14.6). To know how a Christian ought to behave is not merely a question of making the right calculations, or of discovering the right principles: it depends on his unity with the Father through Christ. There cannot be any final distinction between external and internal elements, for the outward behaviour of a Christian springs from his inner belief and condition.

Therefore, in considering problems of Christian behaviour, the whole of a Christian's life must be taken into view, especially those aspects of it which affect his relationship to God and to the fellowship of the Church. It is here alone that he shares in the love of God and confronts its deepest demands. Since, according to Christian teaching, belief, faith and commitment precede their results in the form of behaviour, it is impossible without distortion to consider behaviour as though it were independent of these other factors, or as though it came first in importance. The aim of the Christian life is not in the first place to achieve Christian behaviour according to some discoverable pattern; its aim is union with God, from which true Christian behaviour can alone derive. It is only one who is living the Christian life as fully as possible who can rightly know what is and what is not Christian behaviour.

The power of convention in moral behaviour is such that the treatment of ethics and morals tends to take on too much of the colour of the prevailing atmosphere. His social and intellectual environment is bound to affect the student to some extent, but, if it does so too much, the result is a static and external approach to problems of morals, or its opposite, an attitude which is completely rootless. The best way to avoid these outlooks is to combine the study of ethics with that of ascetical and sacramental theology, since these studies correct erratic tendencies by emphasizing the central importance of personal commitment to and union with God and of fellowship in the Church.

Indeed the arguments put forward for 'situational ethics', when rightly valued, heighten the importance of ascetical theology. If ethical issues can only be settled and rightly judged in an actual situation, this can only be done from a Christian point of view when the person or persons involved in that situation are trying to live a Christian life, and when their conduct is related directly to the spiritual demand of God upon them. This is the subject of ascetical theology.

In manuals of moral theology by Roman Catholic writers a section is often included on sacramental theology. Part of the reason for such a combination may lie in the fact that moral theology is often closely associated with canon law in the Roman Catholic Church, and the administration and discipline of the sacraments fall under this heading. But from a minimal point of view it is sensible to include the sacraments in a study of moral theology, since without their use it is impossible to live a full Christian, and hence a full moral life. Fr B. Häring's book *The Law of Christ* (1961–2) has as titles for its three volumes (in the French edition) 'General Morals', 'Life in Communion with God' and 'Life in Fraternal Communion', thus clearly showing that moral theology cannot be rightly seen except in the light of Gospel and Church, that is, as part of a living relationship with God through Christ in his Body. K. E. Kirk, probably the best modern Anglican exponent of moral theology, showed himself keenly aware of the need to consider moral and ascetical questions side by side. In his best-known work *The Vision of God* he wrote: 'The first practical question for Christian ethics is, therefore, how is disinterestedness, or unselfishness, to be attained? Once grant that moralism, or formalism, cannot bring the soul nearer to it, and there remains only one way – the way of worship' (abridged edition, 1934, p. xii).

As we have seen, it is important to avoid the departmentalization of the various studies of the Christian life, but it can be avoided in the wrong way. While the link of ethics and moral theology with ascetical theology is important, it would be unfortunate if ascetical theology were to be regarded as part of moral theology, as is suggested by the *Dictionary of Moral Theology* (Pietro Palazzini, ed., 1962). If this occurs, it suggests that a certain kind of behaviour is the chief aim of the Christian life. It is true that the quality of Christian life can be tested by the way Christians behave, but to make a certain standard of behaviour the aim of the Christian life inevitably results in legalism and externalism with all their consequent evils. It would be more accurate to say that ethics and morals could be properly regarded as a part of ascetical theology, that is, as a subordinate element in the study of the Christian's relation to God.

Sacramental theology not only deals with the Christian's relation to God but with his relations to other Christians and other human beings. It is only in the true understanding of liturgy that Christians can find their right living relationships with others, and the experience of the Christian fellowship is the pattern and inspiration of the Christian's attitude to those outside the fellowship of the Church. This aspect of theology corrects the lack of balance of those who speak of ethics solely in a social context, as though it were a matter of individuals communing with others, or as if a solitary Christian had to find his way in a social setting independently of the Church. There should be no such thing as a Christian relating himself, or being related, to another except in and through the Body of Christ. Sacramental theology has a vital part to play in elucidating this aspect of the Christian's life. In the past sacramental theology has sometimes deteriorated into a study of an academic type, leaving on one side the question of personal relations within and without the community in favour of theories of grace and practice which, however interesting, can only be characterized as barren and lifeless.

One must therefore conclude that no study of Christian ethics or of moral theology should be undertaken without a corresponding study of ascetical (including mystical) theology and of the theology of the sacraments. Protestants ought naturally to decline to study behaviour apart from the work of grace in the soul, and Catholics (whether Roman, Orthodox, Anglican or others) should find in the ascetical and sacramental life the only framework in which moral theology can be seen in right perspective. At the same time such studies should expose the false character of those types of piety and 'churchiness' which are a form of escape from engagement with serious ethical issues, and should encourage Christians to relevant ethical action at a deeper spiritual level.

Gerard Gilleman, *The Primacy of Charity in Moral Theology*, 1959; B. Häring, *The Law of Christ*, 1961–2; Kenneth E. Kirk, *The Vision of God*, abridged edition, 1934; Herbert Waddams, *A New Introduction to Moral Theology*, 1965.

HERBERT WADDAMS

Asceticism

The Greek word *askesis* has as one of its meanings practice or discipline, and therefore came to be used for the disciplined way of life inculcated by Stoics and other philosophers. Greco-Roman observers called Judaism a 'barbarian philosophy', with reference as much to its rules of life as to its doctrines – and passed a similar judgment on the Brahmins of India. The community recently made known to us through the Dead Sea scrolls was an outstanding example of Jewish asceticism; other instances are described by Philo and Josephus, and in the Gospel accounts of John the Baptist. Asceticism may be considered as spiritual athletics; St Paul uses the figure in describing the Christian life as a race (or even a prize-fight) for the eternal prize (I Cor. 9.24–27). But the charter of Christian asceticism is to be found even further, in the teaching and example of Jesus. He was both humanist and ascetic, who 'came eating and drinking' (Luke 7.34), but called on his followers to deny themselves and take up the cross after him (Mark 8.34, etc.).

In the early centuries of the Church the threat of persecution and the pressure of surrounding paganism gave the whole Christian community an ascetic character. One can see this in the writings of Christian humanists such as Clement of Alexandria as well as those of rigorists like Tertullian. However, in addition to the common standard, dedication to virginity, whether by men or women, was a special ascetic renunciation (cf. I Cor. 7.8). In the early fourth century Methodius of Olympus, in his *Banquet of the Ten Virgins*, extols virginity as the perfect way of life. But 'Origen's rash act', the literal following of Matt. 19.12, was an extreme practice finally condemned by the Church (Canon 1 of the Council of Nicaea, 325). After the time of Constantine the Church came closer to the world, for good or ill, and those who wished to leave all for Christ fled into the desert, or its equivalent, as monks or hermits. *See* **Monasticism**. Many carried poverty to the greatest possible extreme, and engaged in competition in self-denial. A striking type were the stylites ('pillar-saints') who settled on pillars (*stylai*), where their simple needs were met by admiring pilgrims. Early monastic writers discuss whether the greater renunciation is that of the hermit who fights alone with the powers of evil, or that of the coenobite who renounces his own will in obedience to his Abbot; the asceticism of the

former was more visibly heroic, that of the latter perhaps more profound. Meanwhile devout Christians living 'in the world' were still expected to live up to a fairly ascetic discipline. Leo the Great (Bishop of Rome 440–61) in his Lenten sermons expounds ascetic principles in terms of the three 'notable good works' of Matt. 6 – prayer raises the mind to God, fasting disciplines the will, almsgiving expresses love of neighbour. In the next century St Benedict may be described as a humanist ascetic. The external regimen envisaged in his monastic *Rule* did not differ greatly from the life of a devout layman of moderate means – ascetic discipline was found in the common life of prayer, study, and work under obedience.

In the early Middle Ages, perhaps due to the rapid spread of the Church in northern Europe, there was an increasing difference between the minimum standard expected of the laymen and the ascetic practice of the monk – though disciplinary literature such as the Celtic Penitentials shows that strict standards were still held up at least in theory. But the layman often sank into the position of a spectator in the life of the Church, while the clergy performed its sacred rites and monastics accepted more intense obligations. A visible sign of this development was the decline of Communion among the laity, for whom the Fourth Lateran Council in 1215 was obliged to lay down a minimum rule of annual reception (Canon 21). Since monasticism itself could become worldly and comfortable, religious revivals took the form of a return to greater simplicity and austerity in the cloister. And the clergy generally adopted some features of monastic asceticism, such as celibacy (in the Eastern Church only for bishops) and rules of daily prayer.

The coming of the friars began to bridge the gap between secular and ascetic Christians. St Francis of Assisi (q.v.) challenged the standards of the world while still remaining closely connected with it; however, in his *Rule* the friars are bound to live in poverty, chastity, and obedience, the three 'evangelical counsels' of traditional asceticism, which in previous monastic rules are implied rather than formally stated. The 'Third Orders' of lay associates rather forced themselves on the friars as a result of their preaching than were organized by them. Their members combined a semi-monastic discipline with life in the world, still responsible for property, family and personal rights, thus beginning to bring asceticism out of the cloister into the home and the market place. Laymen as well as monks and clerics often lived strict and devout lives in the later Middle Ages – a famous example is Sir Thomas Moore, in England on the eve of the Reformation. On the other hand the older monastic orders were often stagnant if not actually corrupt. Humanists like Erasmus, as well as the Reformers, accused their members of falsely claiming superior merit before God for purely formal religious practices.

The Reformers generally attacked the traditional forms of asceticism – not that the call to a life of discipline and self-sacrifice was abandoned, but that it was proclaimed as something expected of all Christians, and as the result rather than the cause of their justification before God. Luther tended to leave this to the work of grace in the believer; while the Reformed tradition, especially in its Calvinist form, aimed to enforce generally what Ernst Troeltsch described as *innerweltliche Askese*, that is an ascetic life within the common orders of society. In its Anglo-American form we know this as the Puritan ideal, which aims to bring the whole social order into obedience to the law of Christ. Protestant asceticism faces the same problem as that of its Catholic precursor – the strict ideal will appeal only to an elite, which will either try to dominate the Church and the world, or will flee from worldliness into isolation. As Catholicism produced new ascetic Orders, so Protestantism has produced ascetic sects, a tendency illustrated in different ways by such groups as the Mennonites, the Quakers, the Moravians and the Salvation Army.

Parallel to the Protestant development is a similar urge within the Catholic tradition to bring the devout life out of the monastery into the world. In seventeenth-century France this is illustrated by the devout humanism of Francis de Sales (and the active ministry of Vincent de Paul), in eighteenth-century England by the work of William Law (with his influence on the Wesleys), in nineteenth-century Russia by the surprisingly down-to-earth spiritual guidance given by the monastic elders (*startsi*). In modern Catholic writing ascetical theology (q.v.) means the systematic discussion of the life of prayer and personal discipline, intermediate between the treatment of ethical duties in moral theology and that of intense forms of spiritual experience in mystical theology.

There is always in the Christian life some expression of the paradox of the cross. We are called to joy and to suffering, to freedom and to discipline, to love the world which God loves and yet to be ready to renounce everything, even our own selves (cf. the apparent contrast of John 3.16 and I John 2.15 ff.). With our contemporary concern for the outreach of the Gospel into the common life it has been suggested that the modern form of *innerweltliche Askese* is a call to 'holy worldliness'. A twentieth-century form of ascetic is the Christian who answers a call to witness at the peril of fortune or life for a social cause – against war, for instance, or for racial equality. The Reformers rightly opposed the dangerous idea of a more meritorious way of life which could be undertaken optionally. But some of their

followers have forgotten the principle of varying vocations (cf. I Cor. 7.7b), some of which are in external appearance more heroic than others. And wisdom is justified by all her children (Luke 7.35).

Two classical studies of the history of Christian asceticism are Ernst Troeltsch, *The Social Teaching of the Christian Churches*, 1911, ET, 1931, reprinted 1960; and K. E. Kirk, *The Vision of God, the Christian Doctrine of the Summum Bonum*, 1931. In its own immense literature cf. the works of John Cassian, *Institutes* and *Conferences;* Martin Luther, *Freedom of a Christian Man*; Francis de Sales, *Introduction to the Devout Life*, tr. and ed. by John K. Ryan, 1953; William Law, *Serious Call to a Devout and Holy Life*, ed. by J. Meister and others, 1955; O. Chadwick tr., *Western Asceticism*, Library of Christian Classics, XII, 1958; T. Tappert, ed., *Luther: of Spiritual Counsel*, Library of Christian Classics, XVIII, 1955.

E. R. HARDY

Aspiration

Aspiration is the desire to realize an ideal. Sometimes a 'morality of aspiration', that is, one motivated by pursuit of the good, is contrasted with a 'morality of obligation', that is, one that proceeds from a sense of duty.

Association, Right of.
see Industrial Relations; Rights.

Athanasius, St

Renowned as the resolute foe of Arianism under the successors of Constantine, Athanasius (*c.* 295–373) was born and educated in Alexandria, where as a young man he was deacon and assistant to the bishop Alexander, whom he accompanied to the Council of Nicea (325). On Alexander's death Athanasius succeeded to his episcopal Chair (328) as well as to his troubles with Meletianism and Arianism. The life of Athanasius after his elevation to the episcopate was a continuing struggle against imperial and ecclesiastical compromise with Arianism – a struggle in which he enjoyed the confidence and the alliance of the Roman Church, but which brought him repeated persecution and exile. By the time of his death, Athanasius had seen, and had contributed to, the beginnings of that settlement of the trinitarian controversy which was brought about under the Emperor Theodosius.

Throughout his life Athanasius was an advocate and ally of the ascetic-monastic movement which had its origins in the Egyptian Church. Friend, disciple and biographer of St Antony of Egypt, Athanasius favoured the monks of the desert and was instrumental in introducing the monastic ideal into the west. In his *Life of Antony* he exhibits his admiration for the ascetic ideal, and especially for the life of poverty and celibacy, which for him, as for others of his time, symbolized not merely rejection of the world or of the flesh, but also a positive conversion towards the invisible things of the Spirit.

The rationale of Athanasius' conception of the Christian life is provided by his idea of the purpose of the incarnation, which he understood to be not merely the provision of immortality to the flesh of fallen man, but also the restoration of the soul to its status as a participant in the Logos, the Image of God. Standing as he did in the Alexandrian tradition of a Platonistic Christianity, it was natural for Athanasius to understand the restoration of man to the Image in terms of man's deification through knowledge of the divine Logos himself. Thus for Athanasius, as for the whole tradition in which he stood, the Christian ethic was understood as an ascetic practice which, by purifying the soul of its attachment to visible and created things, freed it for the knowledge of God revealed in Christ – a knowledge, moreover, which is from the beginning more than intellectual, since it consists in the sharing of the soul in that divine life which is Christ's by nature. The purpose of the ascetic way was thus for Athanasius the realization, through the practice of detachment and of positive love of God, of the soul's true character as an *alter Christus*.

R. A. NORRIS, JR

Attrition. *see* Contrition.

Augustine of Hippo, St and Augustinian Ethics

St Augustine (354–430) tells in his *Confessions* (III. 4 f., VII. 9 f.) that his conversion to the Catholic faith was prepared by his readings in Stoic and Platonic philosophy. The dominant concern of philosophy in the Roman Empire was ethics. Naturally, then, Augustine the convert would look to find in Christian moral teachings the true answers to the questions raised by the pagan thinkers with whom he was previously acquainted. These questions centred in the problem of the good life, the 'chief end of man'. Augustine regularly takes as starting-point for ethical discussion the generally accepted proposition that 'all men desire to be happy' (*beati*). It is important to note that the 'happy life (*vita beata*)' does not in this connection mean 'happiness' in the sense of pleasant feeling: it means that fulfilment of human existence, that 'blessedness' which Christ defined in the Beatitudes. The 'desire for happiness' is innate in all of us in this sense: where men go wrong is in their beliefs about what will make them *beati*.

Augustine begins with the Platonist assumption that the Good for man must lie in the exercise of his highest endowment – the con-templative intellect. The practice of virtue is the means by which the soul is purified for contemplation – the vision of God. The maxim of Porphyry the Neoplatonist, 'Flee from all that is bodily', and the similar exhortations of St Ambrose, encouraged in Augustine the belief that this purification demands above all the suppression of the desires of the flesh; and the moral crisis of his conversion was a struggle between his sexual passions and the shaming examples of Christian asceticism. But the tendency to regard the 'flesh' – material exist-ence as such – as either evil in itself or the source of evil was soon checked by the polemic in which the convert became engaged against the Manichaean dualism to which he had for-merly adhered. Augustine had to confront this dualism with a Christian doctrine of creation, in which the changeless (eternal) being of the Creator was identified with goodness. The God who is absolute goodness alone truly and fully 'is'; but everything in his creation is good in virtue of its existence. The created universe presents a graded order of being and goodness, which all things possess in proportion to their degree of likeness to the Creator. In this order, the living is higher than the inanimate; among living creatures, thinking men are higher than brutes; in men themselves, the mind is higher than the body which was created to be its servant. All created things, including the living soul, are subject to change; it is the property of soul to be self-moved, the source of change in itself. In the human soul, free-will, the power of intelligent choice, constitutes a special degree of likeness to God; but it also makes possible a disturbance of the order of creation – the order which is the product of the divine will. For it enables men to choose and pursue what is beneath them in preference to what is above them, the lesser good in preference to the greater, the changing and perishable to the changeless and eternal; and the result of such perverted choice is that the soul whose blessed-ness consists in willing subjection to God becomes the servant of the body instead of its master.

According to the choices made in the exercise of its freedom, the soul can change either for the better or for the worse. The motive power of change, the dynamic which determines the direction of the soul's movement, is what Augustine calls sometimes 'will' (*voluntas*) and sometimes 'love' (*amor*), the terms used varying according as the conative or affective element is being emphasized. A rightly ordered love depends upon a right judgment of value, a recognition of the degree of goodness, and therefore of being, imparted to each particular creature by the Creator. Love is evoked by good, and there is *some* good in everything created, everything that has being. But the soul of man has the capacity for loving the supreme good which is God; and since all love has the effect of assimilating the lover to that which he loves, the love of God must tend to raise the soul towards the fullest likeness to God of which it is capable – in other words to that blessed state of existence called in the gospel eternal life. In the text, 'This is life eternal, to *know* thee', Augustine finds confirmation of his Platonist setting of contemplation above every other form of human activity, as the highest possible good for which man has been created – his 'chief end'.

But the commandment to love God not only with the mind but with the heart and soul means that the *whole* life of man, with all his powers of action and affection, must be devoted to God. How will this dictate our attitude to all those lesser goods which may become object of our action and affection? What is the relation of the love of neighbour as of self, enjoined in the second of the two great commands of the gospel, to the love of God in the first? Here Augustine takes up the distinction made in the Stoic ethics (learnt from Cicero) between the morally good (*honestum*) and the profitable (*utile*), and broadens it into the distinction between means and ends, objects of 'use' and objects of 'enjoyment'. God alone is to be 'enjoyed', which means loved for himself, as the final and complete satisfaction of all needs. All other goods are to be 'used', which means loved in the degree of their relevance to the love of God, their service of that ruling purpose.

It is this apparent degradation of Christian love for our fellowmen to a 'means' whereby the individual is aided to achieve his own perfection, which led Karl Holl to denounce Augustine as the 'corrupter of Christian morals', and Anders Nygren to conclude that his doctrine of love is a hopeless attempt to combine the egocentric pursuit of self-fulfilment through *eros* with the NT understanding of *agape* as the human imitation of God's outflowing goodness. Nygren admitted, however, that Augustine was well aware of the difference between the God of the philosophers, the *Summum Bonum* or perfect object of desire, and the God of Christian faith who is himself *Agape* and gives himself in creation and redemption. The goal of *eros* for Augustine is to be made like God, to share in the measure possible for creatures in his eternal being, which means in his nature as self-giving love. The Augustinian doctrine of grace means that only by self-surrender to the divine charity can we participate in it; and no reader of the impassioned Homilies on the First Epistle of St John can doubt that the preacher knew what charity means. Nor is Augustine so far astray in his understanding of the nature of the love enjoined in the two great commandments as might at first appear. *See* **Love**. The love that can be commanded is willing acceptance of the order of creation which is the expression of the divine will. It is the will of God that men should

know their dependence upon him for all good, and should exercise in due subordination the natural impulses which direct their life both as individuals and as sharers in a common humanity. In this aspect, the love of neighbour like the love of God must find its expression in service. In the last resort the categories of 'use' and 'enjoyment' prove inadequate: the love of use, when it is 'referred' to God, coalesces with the love of God and becomes a love of enjoyment. So Augustine will define the peace of the Heavenly City as 'the perfect union of hearts in the enjoyment of God *and of one another in God*' (*De Civitate Dei*, xix, 13).

The application of these theological principles to practical ethics in the various spheres of conduct is profoundly affected for Augustine by his conviction that in men *as they are* the order of creation has been confounded by transference of love from the highest good to goods that are inferior. The confusion began with pride, the desire of man to be as God, master instead of servant. It led to the enslavement of spirit to flesh in the perverse pursuit of 'enjoyment' of the material goods which should only be objects of 'use'. Augustine found the most glaring proof of this enslavement in the imperious nature of sexual desire. But instead of maintaining the goodness of the sexual instinct *in itself* as implanted by the Creator, his own experience of it as uncontrollable passion led him to pronounce it, in the fallen state in which we know it, an *evil*, only to be converted into good when treated not as an end, for the pleasure it gives, but as the means of procreation.

Neither the doctrine of original sin nor that of the superiority of virginity to the married state were Augustine's inventions. But his theory of the transmission of original sin by way of the sexual urge which is the typical form of 'concupiscence', the lusting of flesh against spirit, has had a most disastrous influence upon much of traditional Christian ethics. In Augustine's intention, his great drama of the Two Cities was not a conflict between flesh and spirit, but between 'the love of God extending to the contempt of self', and 'the love of self extending to the contempt of God'. (*De Civ. Dei*, XIV, 28.) But the *City of God* was too easily read as encouraging a rejection of all this world's good for the sake of the world to come; and that is a rejection which runs counter to the central principles of Augustinian ethics.

'The Nature of the Good', *Early Works of St Augustine*, Library of Christian Classics, VI, 1953; The Problem of Free Choice, *Ancient Christian Writers*, XXII, 1955; 'Letter 155 to Macedonius', *Writings of St. Augustine*, Fathers of the Church, XI, 1953; 'On Christian Doctrine', *Works of St. Augustine*, IX, 1873 (ed. Marcus Dods) and in Nicene and Post-

Nicene Fathers (various eds.) 'Homilies on the First Epistle of St John', *Later Works of St. Augustine*, Library of Christian Classics, VIII, 1955; *The City of God*, Books XIV and XIX, Healey's translation in Everyman's Library edition (1945) and many other versions; E. Gilson, *Christian Philosophy of St. Augustine*, 1960, part II, pp. 115–84.

JOHN BURNABY

Authenticity

Authenticity, in the terminology of some existentialist philosophers, denotes a style of existing in which the existent has become genuinely himself. The German equivalent is *Eigentlichkeit*, from the word *eigen*, 'own'. To be authentic is thus to be one's own self. This is not a moral conception in the usual sense, for authenticity has nothing to do with conforming to rules or fulfilling some universal ideal of humanity. However, authenticity acquires something of a moral connotation in the context of existentialist ethics (q.v.). The authentic existent is precisely the person who does not take refuge in rules or ready-made ideals, but accepts himself as the person that he is and seeks to realize the possibilities that are factically his. Thus the notion of authenticity would lead in the direction of a situational ethic (q.v.), not governed by rules or general principles but dependent on the unique circumstances and possibilities of each individual situation. Would one have to say then that for some persons an authentic existence might take forms that were condemned by conventional moral standards, for instance, that authenticity might mean for some people becoming committed Nazis? The more extreme exponents of this point of view would not hesitate to come to such conclusions. The error of such a view lies in its extreme individualism. No human existence can be authentic without a communal dimension, and a true conception of authenticity would need to take account of this. Among Christian existentialists, there can be no authenticity without love, and so no purely self-regarding authenticity that would be disruptive of the community. The notion of authenticity is related to that of self-realization ('Become what you are!') as this was used in idealist ethics (q.v.).

EDITOR

Authority

Claims to authority made on the basis of revelation or religious faith have been very much under fire in modern times, and perhaps this is nowhere more the case than it is in the field of ethics. Standards of conduct can no longer be upheld by a simple appeal to the authority of the Church or the Bible. In modern secular societies, Christian ethicists are agreed that it is unreasonable to try to legislate Christian standards for the whole body of citizens, for example, in such matters as marriage and divorce. Even members of the churches do not always follow the teaching of their churches on particular matters. If therefore we can still talk of an 'authority' in Christian ethics, it can hardly be thought of as an authority that is imposed, for it rests on the voluntary acceptance of those who profess themselves Christians. *See* **Discipline.** But when we ask about this authority, we find wide divergences of opinion. Are there, for instance, authoritative rules of conduct that the Christian undertakes to obey in all circumstances? Perhaps some biblical Protestants would recognize the Ten Commandments as laws having divine authority, and thus to be obeyed without question. Catholics would recognize as authoritative many pronouncements of the Church, even those regulating minute details of conduct. Perhaps most writers on Christian ethics nowadays insist on the primacy of charity, and avoid any rigid legalism. Whether any Christian community could get along without some minimum of rules is questionable, but even those who make a point of 'persons before principles' recognize an authority, namely, the demand of love. The ultimate authority for all Christian ethics is Jesus Christ himself. But this statement is not in itself very helpful when it comes to deciding about some actual situation, for we have to find some means of relating this situation to Christ. It would seem that the most indisputably authoritative statements in Christian ethics are also the most general, not to say jejune, and that the more specific we become, the more careful must we be about laying claim to 'authority'. Amid the complexities of contemporary society, a certain degree of modesty is desirable, and moral pronouncements by the churches should have some flexibility and be open to revision. While those who believe that Jesus Christ is God's revelation to men will accept him as their ultimate and authoritative guide on matters of conduct, they will also admit that it is not always clear what his mind on some particular question would have been, and this is obvious from the fact that sincere and learned Christians are often sharply divided over the 'Christian' thing to do in a given situation. In any case, there would always seem to be some 'mediate' authority between Christ and the particular situation, and this mediate authority could not have the ultimacy belonging to Christ himself. Perhaps we could visualize this mediate authority as a composite one, in which several factors have to be taken into account. First among these would be the teaching of the NT, especially any teaching of Christ directly relating to the matters about which guidance is being sought. But this biblical factor might not be decisive in itself – for instance, in such an important question as that of divorce, the evidence about Christ's teaching is ambiguous or even conflicting. The second factor would be the traditional teaching of the Church on any given matter. Especially where the NT teaching is unclear, the consensus of the Church's interpretation of it must be accorded a high degree of authority. The third factor would be one's own conscientious judgment in the concrete situation. To give a concrete illustration, it might be felt that the Church's traditional teaching about the just war, though representing the consensus of Christian opinion in interpreting the NT teaching, was no longer applicable in the current situation. There is a sense in which conscience has always an ultimate moral authority, for no one ought to be ordered or compelled to act against his conscience. But, on the other hand, conscience may be poorly educated, or it may be distorted in various ways. An appeal to conscience should not become an excuse for an irresponsible individualism. Thus, in admitting conscience into the composite authority, we are thinking of a Christian conscience that has been purged of individual idiosyncrasies and that has undergone Christian formation and illumination through prayer and study. Such a conscience, however, has its right to be heard after the NT and the Church when there is a question of authority in Christian ethics.

EDITOR

Autonomy of Ethics

Autonomy means the power of self-determination and freedom from alien domination and constraint. Autonomy stands opposed to heteronomy or subjection to the determination of another. A distinction may be drawn between the autonomy *of* ethics and autonomy *in* ethics. With regard to the latter the focus is upon the individual self and its capacity for self-determination; autonomy in ethics means freedom and the power to bind the self by a law which the self promulgates. By the autonomy of ethics is meant the doctrine that the moral dimension of human life has a form and structure of its own that is independent of religion, of custom and convention and indeed of any other sphere of life or form of authority. The autonomy of ethics has frequently meant the separation of ethics from religion, but there are other factors – mores and customs, psychological and cultural determinism – from which ethics is also to be free if it is to retain its autonomy.

The problem of the autonomy of ethics was focused for modern thought by the moral philosophy of Immanuel Kant in which autonomy figured as the central principle. Kant was attempting to root morality in practical reason independent of external influences and constraints. The problem underlying Kant's attempt is much older than his treatment of the issues involved. Plato raised the question in a dramatic way in the dialogue *Euthyphro* where Socrates discussed the question, 'Is the holy

(good) act holy because the gods love it? or do the gods love the holy (good) act because it is holy?' The alternatives are clear: in the first instance, the holy is being defined by the judgment of the gods and the ethical is made subject to the religious, whereas in the second case the standard of the holy exists beyond the gods and must be recognized by them no less than by mortal men. The second alternative marks the autonomy of ethics because the standard of the good is independent of all other factors in existence and requires only to be grasped by the knowing mind.

In recent decades the autonomy of ethics has been a central issue both in religious and in ethical thought. Those who are sceptical about the validity of religion in an age of science argue for the complete independence of ethics from religion in the belief that the good is not dependent on God and that values can be preserved even if a religious interpretation of morality is no longer tenable. On the other side, the proponents of the religious view claim that ethics can never be entirely independent of religion because religion supplies the insights from which moral ideals are framed and without the grace of God the moral self has insufficient power to perform its duty.

W. G. DeBurgh, *Towards a Religious Philosophy*, 1937; H. D. Lewis, *Morals and the New Theology*, 1947; W. G. MacLagan, *The Theological Frontier of Ethics*, 1959; J. E. Smith, *Reason and God*, 1961.

JOHN E. SMITH

Avarice

Avarice is usually considered as a particular form of covetousness – the desire to get and keep money. Persistent avarice kills generosity and breeds anxieties; e.g., anxieties about the safety of the hoard and possible danger of losing it. Money hidden away gives the avaricious one a sense of power and pride in his achievement; he is ready to enlarge his hiding place to find room for money, like the rich man in the parable (Luke 12.15–20).

In modern times the avaricious man is found looking at the statement of his bank balance rather than looking at his actual money. In our society people show avarice in small ways such as putting off the payment of bills and annual subscriptions as long as possible. Treasurers of many institutions will often suggest certain small economies and postpone payments of various sorts, thinking that the life of an institution depends on its financial resources.

People avaricious about money tend to be avaricious in their approach to other things as well, which is the practical result of belief that a man's life consists in the abundance of his possessions.

There is an avarice that is spiritual rather than material. It can be partly described as eagerness to possess knowledge, love, joy, peace, faith, and hope. The eagerness to possess spiritual things banishes them beyond human reach. All expressions of avarice expose the same error – a man cannot have the exclusive use of anything, he can only live 'as having nothing, and yet possessing all things'.

R. E. C. BROWNE

Babylonian Ethics

The law codes (Ešnunna, Lipit-Ištar and Hammurabi) might appear from their contents to deal with social contract rather than morality. (If man is to live in society, to marry, to inherit and bequeath, to practise agriculture and engage in trade, and generally to live a life which creates all kinds of relationships with other men, rules have to be laid down and punishments prescribed in order to bring continuity and stability into this traffic of man with man.) But there is a genuine humanitarian element in these laws and this humanitarianism which is already attested in the inscriptions of the Sumerian social reformer, Urukagina of Lagaš, is probably the earliest expression of ethical concern in Babylonian society. Hammurabi's intention is 'that the strong may not oppress the weak [and] so to give justice to the orphan [and] the widow' (Driver and Miles, II, p. 97). Moreover, in the prologue and epilogue Hammurabi relates his laws to a concept of moral order of which he is the executor, and the gods, particularly Marduk and Šamaš, the guarantors and upholders (Driver and Miles, II, pp. 13, 99, 103).

There are good reasons why the idea of theodicy did not come easily to the Babylonians and why the alliance of religious belief and morality (notwithstanding Hammurabi's bold statement) was tentative and uncertain. The old myths contain no basis for this marriage of religion and ethics, for the gods do not themselves have the moral stability to guarantee a moral order. They tend to reproduce all the foibles of man in his society on a larger scale and they differ from men principally in respect of superior power and freedom from death. It required the spur of adversity in the Cassite period (1500–1200 B C) to urge the necessity of a more intrinsic connection between religion and ethics, and even then this new ethical sensitivity hinges on the belief that there is a direct relationship between sin and suffering. It would be going too far to say that the conscience only becomes lively when suffering is experienced, but yet it is especially in adversity that a man searches his heart to discover what sin he has committed against the gods. This may be no more than a cultic technicality but it may also be a failure in justice or compassion; disloyalty or dishonesty.

What has been said above indicates that the element of self-interest was strong in Babylonian ethics. The belief in a moral order was not held rigorously and the function of the personal god on whom the individual Babylonian set such store was to secure for its patron preferential treatment with the great gods and to protect him from evil demons – a reminder of the tenacious power of magic over the Babylonian mind. Nor was there any sense of moral obligation, of morality as a thing to be pursued for its own sake. The gods made certain moral demands and men had better keep them if they wished to avoid disease and misfortune and to enjoy a long and prosperous life. This outlook is reflected in those wisdom precepts (Lambert, pp. 96 f.) which offer practical guidance on correct behaviour. Some of these are pragmatic, others inculcate the observance of religious duties, but all of them subserve a frank eudamonism which is undiluted by any belief in life after death, for the message of the Gilgameš epic is that immortality belongs to the gods and man cannot grasp it.

Two compositions, 'The Babylonian Theodicy' (Lambert, pp. 63 f.) and 'I Will Praise the Lord of Wisdom' (Lambert, pp. 21 f.), throw doubt in different ways on the existence of a moral order and even the possibility of intuiting ethical values. The latter describes the perplexity of a pietist, a devotee of Marduk, who cannot reconcile his sense of blamelessness with his experience of suffering and whose belief in a theodicy is subjected to strain, for the 'Šamaš Hymn' (Lambert, pp. 121 f.) teaches that the righteous are rewarded and the wicked punished *now*. The interest of this work lies not in the pious conclusion that the sufferings of the righteous man are temporary and that all will come right in the end (in a this-worldly sense), but in the suggestion which is thrown up that man may have no intuitive sense of sin and may have no access to those moral values which regulate the actions of the gods. 'Good' and 'bad', 'right' and 'wrong' may mean the opposite for gods and men and so the behaviour of the gods cannot be accounted for nor their theodicy challenged. The 'Theodicy', which is in dialogue form, is a robust social protest directed towards the actual conditions of oppression and moral chaos in human society and their incompatibility with the postulates of a theodicy. Here too the orthodox friend counters the rebel by drawing on teaching about the inscrutability of the gods, but the conclusion which they reach and which apparently satisfies the apologist no less than the rebel is that men are born liars and oppressors and that this is how the gods made them. In other words men are incapable of morality.

G. R. Driver and J. C. Miles, *The Babylonian Laws*, 2 vols., 1952–5; W. G. Lambert, *Babylonian Wisdom Literature*, 1960.

WILLIAM MCKANE

Barth, Karl

Ethics, like theology, for Karl Barth (1886–1968), indicates at one and the same time the total crisis in which man's existence is placed before God, and the total grace by which he is enabled to live in Jesus Christ. These two movements of his thought were consecutively emphasized in Barth's career though they have always been simultaneous in his basic thought. In his early writings ethics is understood as an attack upon man's existence. It exposes the hypocrisy of every ethical system and the self-justification of all moral conduct. 'The problem of ethics contains the secret that man as we know him in this life is an impossibility. This man in God's sight can only perish' (*The Word of God and the Word of Man*, p. 140). But the same God before whom we perish, is he who lends our life its possibility. The only hope for man then is to surrender himself to this doom joyfully, to give up the struggle for a goodness which is his own accomplishment, and to rejoice in the life he is given by forgiving grace alone. In this context human civilization and values will have a certain relative dignity and authority as profane expressions of a world which lives by the movement of God to man.

This negative movement remains assumed in all of Barth's later work. In the *Church Dogmatics*, however, the starting point changes. No longer total crisis but total grace becomes the basis of ethical knowledge and behaviour. The foundation of ethics is the divine determination of man in Jesus Christ. Ethics is the doctrine of God's commandment which 'explains the law as the form of the Gospel' (*Church Dogmatics*, II, 2). It is the structure which God's sanctifying election of man as his covenant partner in Jesus Christ assumes variously as conditions require in the history of this covenant relation. Ethics is therefore quite simply 'action in praise of the grace of Jesus Christ'. It is the form of man's freedom wherein he realizes himself in relation to Christ. God's commandment is essentially a permission, the 'granting of a quite definite freedom'. It is a dividing of that which fulfils from that which destroys. As such, ethics is also God's judgment on man whenever and wherever man does not accept the forgiveness offered him, but wishes to be good in his own right. Ethics is man's sanctification through judgment, wherein sin is recognized as such in repentance and prayer, and is pardoned.

This is Barth's general answer to the ethical question. He relates it to the particular problems of the common life in two quite different ways. In *Church Dogmatics*, III, 4, and in some occasional writings, his method is suggestive and analogical, depending primarily on the analogy of relation. Beginning with the creation of man and woman, expressing the image of God in their relation to one another,

he explores what this relation means for all men and women before turning to its particular intensification in marriage. Similarly in the family it is not the institution which is central but the relation of parents with children; and in culture and society the emphasis is on 'near and distant neighbours'. In shorter writings he suggests how political construction might be guided by the effort to create, in a relative and external way, parables and signs of the Kingdom of God. Rejecting the traditional Lutheran division of the two realms, he places the state firmly in the order of reconciliation under the control of Christ. The same spirit pervades his treatment of the protection, development and limitation of human life, in which his doctrine of work and vocation is included.

This is certainly the dominant methodology in Barth's 'special ethics', and that which conforms best to his general ethics of grace. There is, however, also a method of crisis and confession which is first found in his anti-Nazi writings and continues in his later occasional political works. The command of God, although it brings freedom, is always a call to concrete obedience in particular human relations. All of man's powers of analysis and discernment are summoned to search out the form which this free obedience should take, a form which, when it is found, is binding not only for the Christian who discovers it, but for all to whom he can make it known. There are false spirits abroad in the world which result in other analyses and other actions. The Christian therefore confesses his faith and rejects false gods in his ethical decision and action. Political and social decisions are theological matters in which faith or unfaith, obedience or apostasy, are involved. With this binding urgency they must be debated, and made.

It is not easy to reconcile these two methods. At times Barth suggests they should alternate. Not every ethical decision is a *status confessionis*. The Church is not always called to speak a direct political or social word. There are times when events should be watched and judgment reserved. 'The question of what is commanded and forbidden will always necessarily retain a certain breadth and openness' (*Church Dogmatics*, III, 4). On the other hand the fact that grace claims man wholly in Jesus Christ gives an urgency to the particular expressions of grace in every human relation which leaves no area of life unaffected. Christian ethics in Barth's understanding is always informed by the total gift and the total claim of the gospel, on the whole common life of man.

Karl Barth, *The Word of God and the Word of Man*, 1928; *The Church and the Political Problem of our Day*, 1939; *Against the Stream* (shorter post-war writings), 1954; *The Humanity of God*, 1960; *Church Dogmatics*, I, 2, Par. 22:3, 'Dogmatics and Ethics'; II, 2, Chap. 8,

'God's Commandment'; III, 4, 1936–62. *See also* for untranslated material *Eine schweizer Stimme* (anti-Nazi and wartime writings), 1945; *Die christliche Ethik* (Schriftenreihe 'Theologische Existenz Heute'), 1946; C. C. West, *Communism and the Theologians*, Chaps. 5 and 6, 1958.

C. C. WEST

Basil the Great, St

St Basil (*c.* 330–379), Metropolitan bishop of Cappadocian Caesarea after 370, was the son of a wealthy hellenistic-Christian family of Cappadocia. Educated in classical literature and philosophy at Constantinople and Athens, he turned after his baptism to the ascetic life, which he studied in the communities of Egypt and Syria and at the feet of Eustathius of Sebaste, the organizer of monasticism in Asia Minor. His sense of active responsibility in the affairs of the Church drew him from his retirement to become first presbyter and then bishop at Caesarea, where his theological writing and political activity contributed largely to the settlement of the Arian problem in the east.

Essentially, however, Basil was a moralist and a monk for whom the ascetic life represented the basic form of Christian discipleship whether in the world or in withdrawal from it. Educated in Neoplatonic philosophy, a disciple of Origen and of the Stoic moralists, Basil enunciated an ethic which grew out of the interaction between his thoroughgoing Christian biblicism and his Greek intellectual heritage. The Christian life for him is a life of absolute and sensitive obedience to the call of Christ, who portrays complete self-denial, humility and unworldliness as the one way to the Kingdom of God. Basil therefore sees the foundation of spiritual progress for the believer to lie in a love for God and neighbour which in its turn presupposes a doing-to-death of physical lusts and selfish interests, and a turning away from worldly entanglements: in a word, that ascetic life whereby the soul is purified from passion, freed from enslavement to the ephemeral goods of the visible world, and elevated to a love of things spiritual and eternal.

This programme obtains both for the monk and for the Christian living in the world: in the strict sense, Basil admits no 'double standard'. He sees the communal ascetic life as a revival of the authentic Christianity of the primitive Jerusalem Church, and therefore as a general norm for the life of all believers. Thus he insists on the one hand that the monastic life must be a life in community; the isolation of the hermit bespeaks an egotism inconsistent with Christ's commandment of neighbour-love. On the other hand, the Christian in the world must be supremely earnest in the systematic sharing of his wealth, in prayer, and in mortification – the more so since the married state (which Basil will just tolerate) and involvement in worldly

business are manifest and all-but-fatal obstacles to the cultivation of a pure and undistracted love of God. Christian life in the world is not, for Basil, an alternative and inferior form of discipleship. It is merely the practice of asceticism under dangerously adverse conditions.

It is with some justification therefore that Basil has been described as a rigorist, a pessimist, and (more sympathetically) 'a pilgrim of the Absolute'. Certainly his puritanism and his extension of the monastic ideal to all forms of Christian life justify these labels. But at the same time they testify to his earnestness in seeking a rebirth of costly discipleship in a time of confusion and laxity.

R. A. NORRIS, JR

Baxter, Richard

Richard Baxter (1615–1691), a representative of English Puritanism at its best, was born in Shropshire and ordained to the Anglican priesthood in 1638. He exercised a most influential ministry at Kidderminster for some nineteen years and also served for a time as chaplain to the Parliamentary Forces. Disapproving of the Act of Uniformity, he suffered in the Ejectment and thereafter became a writer and itinerant preacher.

Baxter was probably the most prolific of all English theological writers, since he published 141 volumes as well as contributing to forty others. His best-known works are *The Saints Everlasting Rest*, a devotional classic, and *The Reformed Pastor*, a manual of pastoral theology.

His own life was completely dedicated to God and his chief desire was to reform the Church according to what he believed to be the mind of Christ. As a biblical scholar, Baxter was before his time, for he discarded the literal in favour of the general interpretation of the Scriptures. Although he has been called a liberal Calvinist in theology, he still held firmly to the doctrine of election and emphasized the driving power of fear in bringing people to God as well as the drawing power of love. While he disapproved of separatism and deeply believed in a national church which had moderate episcopacy, few men influenced nonconformity more. Because of his incessant desire to avoid extremes, he has been called the first propagator of ecumenism in England.

As a political philosopher Baxter had a great influence, though his thinking in this sphere was not original since he is found repeating the mediaeval view which saw Church and State as two facets of the same community. He disapproved of democracy because he considered the majority of people vicious and stupid. His ideal was a Christian commonwealth or theocracy, the State existing for the glory of God and the welfare of souls.

H. Martin, *Puritanism and Richard Baxter*, 1954; F. J. Powicke, *A Life of the Reverend*

Richard Baxter, 1924; R. Schlatter, *Richard Baxter and Puritan Politics*, 1957.

S. J. KNOX

Beatitude. *see* Blessedness; Sermon on the Mount.

Behaviourism

Behaviourism is the doctrine which either denies mental events or reduces them to physiological processes such as movements of vocal organs. If taken seriously it is most difficult to see how it could leave any place for ethics, but most behaviourists would defend rather the behaviouristic method in psychology than behaviourism as a philosophical theory. The behaviouristic method has the advantage of avoiding the difficulties and uncertainties which arise through depending on introspective reports, but is is difficult to see how it could yield results which are genuinely psychological and not merely physiological without being supplemented at least implicitly by the introspections of the psychologist who uses the method.

A. C. EWING

Benedict, St

St Benedict (*c.* 480–550) is reckoned the father of western monasticism. Born at Nursia, he protested against the laxity of his times by becoming a hermit and living in a cave at Subacio. Here he founded a number of small monastic communities. After a disaffected monk had made an attempt on his life, Benedict moved to Monte Cassino and founded there the famous monastery that still remains on the hilltop. His great achievement was the composition of the Rule of St Benedict, *c.* 540, considered to be one of the great formative documents in the development of western Christianity. The Rule is distinguished for its simplicity and humanity, and commended itself to such later promoters of the monastic life as St Gregory the Great (q.v.). The Rule deals with the organization and government of a monastic community under an abbot. The abbot is to govern with unquestioned authority, but he is to consult the monks on matters of importance and is not to be overbearing. The Rule goes on to the monastic virtues, and to the regulations for the daily office or *opus Dei*, which is to have precedence over every other activity and is to be the centre and inspiration of everything that is done. The Rules, however, are not excessively austere, and there is a reasonable division of time among prayer, work and reading. According to Gregory the Great, the Rule is 'conspicuous for its discretion'. There is a Latin and English edition by O. Hunter-Blair, 4th edn., 1934. *See* **Monasticism.**

EDITOR

Bennett, John Coleman

John C. Bennett (1902–   ), one of the most influential contemporary interpreters of Christian social ethics, is Reinhold Niebuhr Professor of Social Ethics and President of Union Theological Seminary in New York City. He has been an active participant in ecumenical discussions of social issues since the Oxford Conference on Church, Community and State (1937) and a leader in the Amsterdam (1948), Evanston (1954), and New Delhi (1961) Assemblies of the World Council of Churches. *Christian Social Ethics in a Changing World*, which Bennett edited, was part of a four-volume series prepared for the World Council of Churches Conference on Church and Society (Geneva, 1966). In his writings – including both books and numerous articles in such periodicals as *Christianity and Crisis* – he was primarily concerned with the relationship of Christian faith to economics and politics, including the State, Communism, foreign policy and war.

Bennett has worked closely with the National Council of the Churches of Christ in the USA, participating in the preparation of a series of volumes sponsored by that body on the Ethics and Economics of Society. The chapters which he contributed to this series, 'A Theological Conception of Goals for Economic Life' (in *Goals of Economic Life*, ed. A. Dudley Ward, 1953) and 'Christian Ethics in Economic Life' (in *Christian Values and Economic Life*, 1954) reflect Bennett's realism in dealing with social issues and his effort to make clear the relevance of Christian faith for the decisions and choices involved in the economic life. Bennett has also dealt with this issue extensively elsewhere in his writings, including his early book, *Social Salvation* (1935); and it has occupied a major part of his attention in his work with the World Council of Churches.

Christianity and Communism (1949), the revised edition of that work entitled *Christianity and Communism Today* (1960), *Christians and the State* (1958), *Nuclear Weapons and the Conflict of Conscience* (1962, which he edited), and *Foreign Policy in Christian Perspective* (1966) reflect Bennett's concern with political issues and his realistic understanding of the complex and morally ambiguous nature of political decisions. In his writings about Communism, for example, he has called for an effort to understand the origins of this movement, the elements of social justice which it represents, and the changes which have taken place in the system itself. Such an understanding, he believes, is necessary as a corrective to the view, particularly common in the USA, that Communism represents a total and unchanging system of evil; and also to provide the basis for the openness, self-criticism and the restraint which are needed in international affairs if nuclear war is to be averted and peace is to be achieved.

Bennett has described his conception of the methodology of Christian social ethics most fully in *Christian Ethics and Social Policy*. The primary purpose of this series of lectures was to develop a strategy which would make it possible for Christian ethics to become more relevant to, and effective in, the formation of public policy. Bennett identified and rejected the following four strategies as inadequate: (1) the Catholic appeal both to the unquestioned authority of the Church and to natural law; (2) the method of withdrawal from the morally ambiguous aspects of public life; (3) the identification of Christianity with particular social programmes; and (4) the strategy of espousing a double standard for personal and public life. As an alternative to these four methods Bennett described a fifth, the major characteristics of which are its emphasis upon both the relevance and the transcendence of the Christian ethic of love, a recognition of the universality and persistence of sin, and the acceptance of certain elements of technical autonomy in the formation of social policy. The Christian social imperative of love for the neighbour requires, Bennett believes, a continuous effort to spell out the content of this demand in relation to social policy. This can be done through the formulation of a series of goals – guiding principles, middle axioms, and specific next steps – which represent the will of God in each generation. While such moral judgments become increasingly tentative as they are stated in increasingly specific terms, they also become more concrete and hence more relevant to the formation of public policy in this very process.

E. CLINTON GARDNER

Beneficence

Beneficence is active well-doing. Christian ethics recognizes a duty to do good to the neighbour and even to the enemy, but almost all ethical theories, religious or secular, teach a duty of beneficence. *See* **Altruism.**

Benevolence

Benevolence is an attitude of good will, and may be considered as the subjective disposition corresponding to the activity of beneficence (q.v.).

Bentham, Jeremy

Jeremy Bentham (1748–1832), the most rigorous of the thinkers grouped together under the titles 'hedonistic utilitarians' or 'philosophical radicals', belongs to the early period of the Industrial Revolution (the last part of the eighteenth and the early years of the nineteenth centuries). The school of which Bentham was the most powerful intellectual leader earned the title 'philosophical radicals' because of their deep involvement in movements for political, legal and social change characteristic of the age in which they lived. Indeed it could be claimed that Bentham's significance belongs to the history of jurisprudence rather than to that of ethics or political theory. Yet his voluminous writings reveal an attempt to establish a rigorously *objective* principle of human behaviour, that of utility. All human action could be assessed by reference to its tendency to increase or diminish satisfaction. For Bentham all satisfactions were completely homogeneous, though differring, for example, in duration, intensity, purity and above all in fecundity or fertility: in other words, their tendency to promote further satisfactions. Thus Benthamites were ready to undertake the role of defenders of economic laissez-faire on the ground that the distribution of satisfaction achieved by its adoption was likely to prove more fertile than that offered by the alternative policy of state regulation or direction of the economy. Other utilitarians have, of course, in equal fidelity to Bentham, been prepared in different circumstances to defend a measure of collectivism.

In ethics Bentham was hostile to all forms of moral sense theory, as well as to all forms of rational intuitionism. He insisted that the role in the justification of government, played by the notion of the promotion of natural right, could be far better fulfilled by his own principle of utility. This, he insisted, provided a yardstick whereby common law could be reformed and brought into conformity with the needs of human nature. Where punishment, for instance, was concerned, he espoused a thorough-going deterrent conception of its role, rejecting as mystical nonsense the idea of punishment as retribution. It was characteristic of his combination of remorseless faithfulness to a single principle, with minute attention to detail, that he devoted much attention to the problem of the proper organization of prison life. He designed a 'Panopticon' from which the activities of those undergoing a period of detention could be continuously supervised. Poetry he dismissed as misrepresentation and he allowed no significance to the life of the imagination. His confidence in the possibility of human betterment rested on a ready acceptance of the associationist psychology expounded by his fellow radical James Mill, the father of John Stuart Mill.

One can trace in his writings – especially in his insistence that the worth of actions depended upon their overt consequences and not upon the motives from which they were done or the agents' intentions in doing them – a sympathy with the tendencies we know today as behaviourist. From the point of view of technical philosophy the critical insight displayed in his theory of fictions (also reflected in some of the arguments in his *Book of Fallacies*) shows him in some respects an ancestor of later logical analysis. Although animated by a set of narrow, sharply articulated principles, whose power and limitations many-sided application of them continually reveals, he was on occasion capable of a sharp penetration, for example, into the actualities of government that seems to transcend the frontiers imposed upon him by his theory. As an instance of this, one may refer in conclusion to the extremely shrewd discussion of the four subordinate ends which in his *Theory of Legislation* he regards as foundations of the happiness of society. These ends are subsistence, abundance, equality and security, and whatever one's judgment on the conclusions Bentham draws concerning their relations, no reader can fail to be provoked by the shrewdness of his discussion – however hostile his opinion of the central principles to which Bentham was so unflinchingly committed. *See* **Utilitarianism.**

D. M. MACKINNON

Berdyaev, Nicholas A.

The unique contribution of Nicholas Berdyaev (1874–1948) to the problem of ethics is his insistence that ethics is not a pedantic scholastic cataloguing of virtues and sins, but an all-out spiritual endeavour to transform the world into its divine Image. Berdyaev's dissatisfaction with the world as it is has been mistakenly taken by many to mean his rejection of the world and a negative attitude to it. It is true that Berdyaev rejects the image of the world as conceived by naturalism, materialism, positivism and other purely immanentist philosophies precisely because, in his opinion, their world is not real, but an illusion, arrived at by what Berdyaev calls the process of objectivization; that is to say, a world conceived in terms of its external appearances and not in terms of the divine Spirit who creates it and without whose presence and activity the world would be both impossible and meaningless.

Ethics for Berdyaev is man's free and creative response to the theonomic character of the world, revealing its divine nature and illuminating human existence by it and thus assisting it to participate in the life of the divine Spirit. This divine Spirit and the world are conceived in a strictly Christian sense. Berdyaev is preoccupied with the problem of ethics because he is deeply concerned with the fact that human existence is meaningless without the assertion on man's part that God, who wills it, is also the creative principle in relation to which all existence must be lived. For Berdyaev it is the mission of man to reveal this creative Divine theonomy as the true principle of existence.

The basic issue of ethics for Berdyaev is the acceptance of God, for rejection of God means a rejection of man, man without God is unthinkable. Without an acceptance of God we do not accept man, but violate his true nature, man being created by God for fellowship with him.

The ethics of Berdyaev may be described as the ethics of Religious Humanism. The basic issue of this ethics is *human personality*. Personality in Berdyaev's use is theandric, a divine-human synthesis in man, by which he knows himself as a free spirit born of God in this world through God's creative act in order that together with other personalities he might reveal God and through his creativeness refashion the world in God's own image. For man as a personality to know the world, according to Berdyaev, means to be engaged in changing it in order to free it from the power of necessity which nature imposes upon it, making it 'an object', that is, a world deprived of spiritual character and significance – a fallen world. In this fallen world man is not known as a spiritual being to be loved, but an object to be used, exploited and eventually discarded. The good and the knowledge thereof consists in man's awareness of himself as a theocentric, spiritual being or personality, participating in the divine life, while evil and man's participation therein is the knowledge of one's self as being exclusively of this world, without any awareness of its transcendent spiritual nature and destiny.

For Berdyaev, all materialistic forms of philosophy, such as Communism and materialistic bourgeois philosophies, hide the spiritual depth of man and are to be completely discarded as enemies of man. Their ethical systems are fit for slaves only and not for free men. The only meaningful foundation of ethics is Christian personalism, that is, the ethics based on the revelation of God in Christ, through whom there is given to man the only possibility of authentic existence. Ethics, in short, is man's endeavour to bring about such a form of existence and all of Berdyaev's writings, especially his book, *The Destiny of Man*, are descriptions of it and a passionately argued plea for it.

Nicholas Berdyaev, *Dream and Reality*, 1950; *The Destiny of Man*, 1931; *Meaning of the Creative Act*, 1955; *Slavery and Freedom*, 1944; *Freedom and Spirit*, 1926; *Truth and Revelation*, 1953; *The Realm of Spirit and the Realm of Caeser*, 1952; Oliver Fielding Clarke, *Introduction to Berdyaev*, 1950; Donald Lowrie, *Rebellious Prophet, a Life of Nicolai Berdyaev*, 1960; Matthew Spinka, *Captive of Freedom*, 1950; Michael A. Vallon, *An Apostle of Freedom: Life and Teachings of Nicolas Berdyaev*, 1960.

C. B. ASHANIN

Bergson, Henri

Creative Evolution (1907), by Henri Bergson (1895–1941) startled and enchanted the general reading public by its rich allusions to science, the apparent novelty of its world-view, its delicate imaginativeness and the beauty of its writing. He had begun the technical exposition of his philosophy in 1889 and continued it for twenty years after 1907 without, to the impatience of his admirers, elucidating the bearing of his outlook, method and results on ethics. This he did not do until 1932 in *The Two Sources of Morality and Religion*. Few philosophers found this impressive. It retained as basis his long contention that reality springs from a living force, mental in nature, which in the animal realm took two divergent forms, one the rigidity of instinct, the other the mobility, sensitiveness and creativity of intelligence in its purest form, which is not analytic but intuitive. He found an analogous distinction in human conduct, a static and dynamic. What is usually called morality is conformity to the impersonal customs and laws of one's society, which have been developed for its protection, order and solidarity. This obedience to the fixed rules of a limited group has much of the rigidity and unintelligence of instinct, and is felt by the individual as an obligation that comes from outside him. It is a set of habits; the habits vary indeed from group to group, state to state, but common to all group-life is the basic habit of living by habits. This is the morality of 'closed society'. Authentic morality has shown itself in exceptional minds – in the sages of Greece, the prophets of Israel and Christian saints. Instead of being bounded by the interests of a group and conservative, it is universal, for all men yet intensely personal (springing from the appealing to intuition), and moves onwards to fresh insights and achievements. This is the morality of 'open society'. Bergson proceeded to draw a corresponding distinction in the sphere of religion, the sub-intellectual one of wishful fancy and security-seeking, and the superintellectual one of the mystics. The ultimate lifeforce is now called God or part of God. On the way he classified the usual types of theology with the sciences as analytic, detached and falsifying. Although in his last years inclined towards Christianity, when anti-Semitism revived under Nazi occupation he publicly asked not to be treated differently from his fellow-Jews. He died in 1941, aged eighty-two.

T. E. JESSOP

Bigamy

Bigamy is the marriage to a second wife or husband while a previous marriage is in force. Bigamy is a crime in western countries though in other parts of the world bigamy or polygamy (the marriage of many wives) is commonly practised.

HERBERT WADDAMS

Blasphemy

Blasphemy is defamatory speech against God. Sometimes the notion is extended to speech against persons, things or institutions accounted holy. In earlier times blasphemy was severely punished. The OT prescribes the death penalty (Lev. 24.16). In modern societies, even if there are laws against blasphemy, they are rarely enforced. This may be partly due to the fact, noted by St Thomas, that blasphemy cannot hurt God in the way that crimes damage one's neighbours. But it is due partly also to the modern democratic conviction that there should be freedom of expression in religious matters, including freedom to criticize and reject. What seems blasphemy to the believer may be considered legitimate polemic by the non-believer, and the principle of religious freedom would demand that the widest latitude of expression should be allowed. Accusations of blasphemy can be employed as an emotional way of repelling criticisms and innovations that ought to be considered on their merits, and we may recall that more than once Christ was accused of blasphemy (Mark 2.7; 14.64). On the other hand, every group, whether of believers or non-believers, has a right to be protected against vicious and slanderous attacks. True blasphemy is probably very rare indeed, for it could come only from one who genuinely believed in God but who had consciously and deliberately set himself against him. No atheist, but only a believer, could be in that state of revolt that finds expression in blasphemy.

EDITOR

Blessedness

The Sermon on the Mount (q.v.) gives a series of descriptions of blessedness. No single one of them can be treated separately; they are dependent on one another and illuminate one another. In the end people do not want to describe blessedness but to experience it; this experience is given to a person in the course of his loving God, the world, his neighbour and himself. But in saying this it should be noted that blessedness is not to be regarded as a deserved reward or wage for work being done; it is rather in the nature of a gift, unexpected at the time it is given.

Blessedness is not a state only to be achieved after death. It can be experienced in this world; *see* the first Beatitude – 'Blessed are the poor in spirit: for theirs is the kingdom of heaven' (Matt. 5.3). That is, blessed are those who are strong enough to recognize their limitations for they shall participate in the regal life of God – not at some distant point in time but now, not as servants but as sons. This Beatitude is dependent on each of the other Beatitudes for its fullest significance. 'Blessed are the poor in spirit' is richer in meaning when thought of in the light of all that is implied by the Beatitude 'Blessed are the pure in heart, for they shall see God' (Matt. 5.8). That is, blessed are the single-minded for they shall know God . . . not completely, not continuously, but in certain moments.

St Paul adds to our understanding of the way to think about blessedness in saying '... remembering the words of the Lord Jesus, how he said, "It is more blessed to give than to receive" ' (Acts 20.35). If the gift is refused then full blessedness is denied both to the one who offers and the one who refuses. Therefore, it is blessed to receive because the giver is blessed thereby, but it is always more blessed to give because it is taking the initiative in the development of a relationship, a step requiring much wisdom and bravery. As a relationship develops there is less awareness of giving and receiving as separate acts – gradually the giving and receiving are recognized only as parts of the single act of sharing. This blessedness is only possible because God blesses us richly. It is blessed to receive what God gives to us and more blessed to give it to others.

If a man desires blessedness with greedy insistence either for himself or for others he is creating the condition in which it cannot be given. It cannot be claimed as a right or requested as a favour. It belongs to those who even now are capable of being lost in wonder, love and praise; that is, to those whose private prayers and public worship are not so burdened with acts of penitence and intercession that rejoicing in the glory of God is prevented from being given its full expression.

R. E. C. BROWNE

Body

For the Christian, the body, as created by God, is good and not to be despised. Thus there can be no place in a Christian ethic for that hatred of the body found in Gnosticism and Manichaeism, systems in which the material universe was considered to be intrinsically evil and hostile to God. The NT, on the other hand, cannot visualize a human existence apart from the body, for even the life to come will be a resurrection of the body, albeit a 'spiritual' body. Reflection shows us that we can only be in a world and in relation to other persons in so far as we are embodied. Thus the NT can use the word 'body' almost in the sense of 'person' – it is the full individual existence in all its relationships. The body can be 'a temple of the Holy Spirit' (I Cor. 6.19) and Christians are enjoined to 'present your bodies as a living sacrifice, holy and acceptable to God' (Rom. 12.1). On the other hand, the body is to be disciplined (I Cor. 9.27). The Christian understanding of the body is further dignified by the place which the idea of the 'Body of Christ' occupies both in eucharistic theology and in the theology of the Church. In this article, however, we cannot follow up these theological themes but must restrict ourselves to the significance of the Christian understanding of the body for ethics. If the body has the dignity which the NT ascribes to it, then concern for men's physical well-being is already built into the Christian ethic. The NT makes clear the duty to relieve need and to heal sickness. More broadly speaking, the Christian ethic cannot be other-worldly. Yet because the Christian is incorporated into the 'Body of Christ' and is therefore subject to the law and discipline of Christ, concern for the conditions of bodily existence cannot degenerate into a pursuit of affluence and indulgence. The Christian attitude to the body, like the attitude to the world, is a dialectical one. If this attitude is designated 'holy worldliness', there may be times and situations when it is right to stress the worldliness, but other times and situations when holiness must be stressed. Thus there have been and probably will be periods in history or conditions in society where, when bodily indulgence and licentiousness have become widespread, the best interests of the body are served by a Christian ascetic witness to the need for discipline.

EDITOR

Bonhoeffer, Dietrich

Dietrich Bonhoeffer (1906–1945) is one of the seminal figures in modern theology. His most striking work, reflected in the *Letters and Papers from Prison*, and also in more extended form in many parts of the posthumously published *Gesammelte Schriften*, bears the marks of casual and fragmentary thought. This is especially true of his now well-known views on 'religionless Christianity', a world 'come of age', and the 'secret discipline'. Nevertheless, these views have proved immensely stimulating in the midst of a confused theological situation.

It is, however, in his earlier works, and not in the *Letters and Papers from Prison*, that his thought on the problems of Christian ethics is most penetrating. At the same time, the union of his ideas with his own bitter and in the end tragic struggle with the Nazi regime, must never be forgotten. He is rightly regarded as a Christian martyr.

Throughout his work there is a remarkable effort to combine, sometimes in almost prophetic strain, the various tendencies in theology which have been struggling for power over the past fifty years. In particular, these may be specified as the liberal, the neo-conservative, and the Bultmannian. Bonhoeffer was brought up with a fine regard for the bourgeois, civilized values of which his teacher Adolf Harnack in Berlin may be regarded as the theological exemplar. This regard he never lost, and it is as the forwarder of liberal values that he must basically be appraised. But the influence of Karl Barth played a major part in his thought, as well as in his relationships to the Church during the church struggle in Germany. Barth's piercing clarity of vision *vis-à-vis* the German Christians and the pretensions of Nazism was enthusiastically adopted by Bonhoeffer. His whole thought was changed by the theology of the 'Word'. Nevertheless, Bonhoeffer did not rest in a position which seemed to him in the end to be marked by what he called a 'positivism of revelation', and his final position may be described as one of regretful non-Barthianism. Under the influence of Bultmann (which recent discoveries among his correspondence – see, e.g., E. Bethge's introduction to the German edition of J. A. T. Robinson's *Honest to God, Gott ist anders* – show to have been less naive than the earlier published letters might lead us to suppose) Bonhoeffer was moving towards the end of his life into a much more radical position than that of, say, his rather jejune *Life Together*, or even than the intensely moving but not particularly original *Cost of Discipleship*.

This radical position is adumbrated in the volume which appeared posthumously with the title of *Ethics*. His ethical system was never completed, and what we have in this volume is the careful assemblage by his faithful friend Eberhard Bethge of all that was left when Bonhoeffer was killed.

The teaching of the *Ethics* is concerned with the relationship of Christianity to the world, and the clue to Bonhoeffer's view is to be found in his christology. But how this is elaborated, what the 'form' of Christ in the world is, can only be tentatively outlined; for Bonhoeffer was still struggling with new possibilities. These were undoubtedly moving in the direction of an inclusiveness, which struggled with his earlier, more positivist christological views. Basically, he was becoming aware of the unity of God and the world in Christ. 'There is a place at which God and man have become one . . . in Christ the Reconciler of the world. . . . Whoever sees Jesus Christ does indeed see God and the world in one' (*Ethics*, p. 8).

This unity meant that Bonhoeffer took seriously the structures of the world. His christology became more and more thoroughly historical. 'The concretion of Christology is Christ existing as the church.' Bonhoeffer's concern in the *Ethics* is to understand this earlier formulation in the light of his growing conviction that 'thinking in two spheres' was invalidated by the ultimate reality of Christ. 'Whoever professes to believe in the reality of Jesus Christ as the revelation of God must in the same breath profess his faith in both the reality of God and the reality of the world' (*Ethics*, p. 66). The Church still has a visible concrete 'space' in the world; but 'the only way in which the church can defend her own territory is by fighting not for it but for the salvation of the world' (*Ethics*, p. 69). This thought is the clue to the liberating power of the twofold movement of Christ 'taking form' in the world, and of man's conformation with Christ. In this movement the 'penultimate' situation comes to the fore. Man's life in the world, the whole civilized order, even, we may say, 'natural'

goodness, are not simply set under the ultimate judgment. How the concrete historical life of man is related to God is left unclear: the conception of *imitatio Christi* is undoubtedly of fresh and great significance. The concerns of the prison letters to some extent obscure this significance, since in these letters the striking things are Bonhoeffer's analyses of the penultimate situation, in which ecclesiology, and even the concept of God, seem to have been absorbed into the world in which men live 'as though God were not given'. But this penultimate situation does remain penultimate: Bonhoeffer has not, like some of his successors, entered an undialectical realm of sheer immediacy. On the contrary, it is because there is still present in his mind the dialectic established by God's transcendence that he is able to speak at all of 'this-worldly' transcendence.

In addition to the works now available in English, there are also the *Gesammelte Schriften* 1958ff., in four volumes, ed. by E. Bethge; four volumes of symposia, *Die Mündige Welt*, 1955–63; J. D. Godsey, *The Theology of Dietrich Bonhoeffer*, 1960; M. E. Marty, ed. *The Place of Bonhoeffer*, 1963; E. H. Robertson, ed., *No Rusty Swords*, 1965; *The Way to Freedom*, 1966; R. Gregor Smith, ed., *World Come of Age*, 1967; *The New Man*, 1956; W. A. Zimmermann and R. Gregor Smith, eds., *I Knew Dietrich Bonhoeffer*, 1966.

R. GREGOR SMITH

Boycott

The name is used for a collective refusal to have dealings with some individual or corporate group, and is derived from a certain Captain Boycott (1832–1897), a landlord's agent who was made the target for such collective action on the part of the landlord's tenants in Ireland. The boycott has been increasingly used in recent times as a method of bringing moral persuasion to bear on bodies that are allegedly guilty of malpractices and that have resisted verbal persuasion. The word 'boycott' should be restricted to the actions of private groups. Similar action by governments is better called a 'sanction' or 'embargo'. Examples of boycotts in which Christians have joined include the boycotting of South African produce as a protest against apartheid; the boycotting of schools in an attempt to obtain better education for underprivileged groups; the boycotting of commercial concerns in protest against their employment policies. In the complexity of modern society, it is extremely difficult to judge about the rightness or wrongness of particular boycotts. They do on the one hand provide a way of bringing pressures to bear in a society that is controlled by large corporate groups – industrial concerns, government agencies, trade unions and the like. On the other hand, the boycott is, like the strike and the atom bomb, a somewhat indiscriminate weapon and is bound to hurt a good many people other than those at whom it is aimed. The Christian must consider each case very carefully, and decide whether the harm that will be inflicted on innocent people will be outweighed by the eventual righting of wrongs through the pressure exerted. In practice, this will often amount to calculating whether the action can be swift and successful. In cases where there might be doubt, there would be the possibility of substituting for a full-scale boycott a token boycott, perhaps for a day or a week, simply as a demonstration for the purpose of bringing to the public notice the particular injustice against which the protest is being directed.

EDITOR

Bradley, F. H.

For the last fifty years of his life Bradley (1846–1924) was a Fellow of Merton College, Oxford, but because of ill-health could take no part in teaching. In consequence his considerable influence came through his writings. His first book, *Ethical Studies* (1876), was the earliest in which the recently transplanted Hegelian type of philosophizing reached an original English expression. It was not, however, through it that he came to be regarded in Britain as the most formidable of the idealists, but through his *Principles of Logic* (1883) and even more his *Appearance and Reality* (1893), these being thorough and obviously major works. His ethical book, unlike these, did not become an idol to be revered or overthrown, because, besides being shorter and plainly incomplete, it was never re-issued by him, so that copies soon became scarce, and when it was posthumously reprinted (1927) the philosophical climate was on the verge of one of its changes. It had been in any case overshadowed by Green's *Prolegomena to Ethics* (1883), which had a prepared circle of readers, the substance of it having been conveyed to many in his long years of teaching. The main formula of *Ethical Studies*, 'self-realization', was the same as Green's and rested on a broadly similar theory of knowledge and reality. For both, self-realization was a movement away from subjective privacy and separateness towards a social and even wider whole, and both therefore attacked hedonism in any form. Bradley's method was bolder and more sharply dialectical. Hedonism, he argued, sets up an impossible end, because pleasure, by itself a theorist's abstraction, can be got only by seeking objects, and because the shivering of the moral life into mere pleasures would turn it into a sequence that has no end in the sense of a goal, but only an ending. Nor is the extreme opposite of hedonism tenable, Kant's stern ethic of the good will, willing the universally right yet providing no guide to what is right in particular; his idea of duty taken apart from

duties is as theoretically abstract and as practically inapplicable as the hedonist's pleasure. Still, will is nearer to moral reality, for a moral act is not one that just happens but one with which the self identifies itself and thereby expresses and realizes itself. This is not selfishness, self-centred interest; the interest is objective. Besides, as in knowing, the self seeks not the punctual and merely sequent, but connection, and moves on towards self-identification with a system that will embrace all connections coherently, that is, a whole. The nearest whole is that of one's society, so that our immediate task is to ally ourselves with all that is best in its structure, practice and temper – this being the point of his famous chapter entitled 'My Station and Its Duties'. This, however, is for Bradley only an imperfect stage, beyond which his dialectic of noting contradictions and transcending them drives him; for it is a fact that every society has features which the developing self must criticize and which is therefore contrary to moral self-realization. The wider whole of humanity is to be recognized and worked for, the good of which requires and includes the good of one's own group. So far, Bradley's process of self-realization appears to be simply one of widening social outlook and service and could be stated apart from its idealist setting; but in this setting he cannot avoid presenting the process yet more inclusively, as the unfolding of all the distinctive potentialities of spirit, that is, the pursuit of truth, beauty and religion as well as of moral goodness in the usual sense, and he refuses to reduce the value of those three either wholly or chiefly to social usefulness. All through he detects contradictions to be resolved dialectically, for example, separate self and society, the self that is at any time actualized and the self that effects the actualizing; and conceives the ultimate resolution as one in which these are integrated and fulfilled in both inner intention and outer embodiment. From this ultimate point of view morality and religion, still riven with the inner contradiction and tension of perfect and imperfect (without which they could not be), are provisional stages or phases of the completely achieved life of Spirit, in which all oppositions are absorbed and overcome.

W. F. Lofthouse, *F. H. Bradley*, 1949, Chap. 4; R. Wollheim, *F. H. Bradley*, 1959, Chap. 6.

T. E. JESSOP

Brunner, Emil

Next to Barth, Emil Brunner (1889–1966) the Swiss theologian, was probably the best-known representative of dialectical theology in its early days, but later his influence declined. He had always a strong interest in ethics. Basic to his ethical position is his understanding of man, expounded in *Man in Revolt* (1937).

Brunner strongly emphasizes the uniquely personal nature of man, and acknowledges his indebtedness to writers such as Ebner and Buber who had explored the I-Thou relationship (q.v.). The uniquely personal nature of man comes from his being created in the *imago Dei*, which is not to be narrowly conceived as rationality but is rather man's full answerability before God. But man, created in the divine image, is in revolt against God; thus he is in revolt against himself. Faith in Jesus Christ creates a new relation to God, and this in turn empowers a new kind of human conduct. This was set forth in *The Divine Imperative* (1932). This statement of Brunner's ethic is organized around two notions. One is the divine command, which is the command to love. The other is that of the 'orders of creation' within which the command has to be applied. Five such orders are recognized: the family, the economic community, the State, culture and the Church. There is a strong Protestant emphasis in Brunner's teaching. This comes out strongly in his criticism of the institutional church; his critical attitude led him at one time to identify himself with the so-called 'Oxford Group Movement' (Buchmanites, later Moral Rearmament) and to develop an interest in the 'no-church' movement in Japan. One of the most important statements of his concern for ethical, social and political issues occurs in his Gifford Lectures, *Christianity and Civilization* (2 vols., 1948–9). Beginning from the observation that the NT has little to say directly on the broader issues of civilized society, and that, on the other side, great civilizations have arisen apart from Christianity, Brunner goes on to show the interpenetration of the two and to make many suggestions as to how Christianity can help to mould the institutions of modern society. Although he understood the Christian faith primarily in eschatological terms and although he was pessimistic about technology (which he sharply distinguished from science), Brunner showed, nevertheless, a very positive concern for the ordering of life in this world. His small book *Faith, Hope and Love* (1956) contains some lectures given in the USA.

EDITOR

Buber, Martin

Martin Buber (1878–1965), born and bred a Jew, has had an extraordinary influence on Christian thought, as well as in many spheres, including that of psychology, of education, and of theology. But he must always be understood against his Jewish background. His *Tales of the Hasidim* is perhaps his most revealing work. There we find the hallowing of the everyday, in concrete stories and simple language, which is perhaps the underlying element of all his ideas.

His most important work, however, so far as its general appeal is concerned, is undoubtedly the slender volume, *I and Thou* (German, 1923, English 1937). This book has had acknowledged influence on the thought, to name only a few, of Karl Heim in Germany, and H. H. Farmer, J. H. Oldham and Herbert Read in Britain. And its influence may be said to be all-pervasive in modern theology. Its basic teaching concerns the realms of I-Thou and I-It. The I-Thou realm is that of persons, the I-It realm that of things. But this simple distinction can be deceptive, especially if it is taken to divide the world into two quite distinct parts, one in which poetry, theology, and mysticism play their part, and the other in which science and the world of impersonal and mass thought is dominant. This is not how Buber envisages the matter. The world is one world, and it has two possibilities. These possibilities are not tied down in rigid forms. Even in relations with other persons, the Thou becomes an It: it must do so – this is 'the exalted melancholy of its fate'. And the world of science is not necessarily the impersonal world, for here the Thou may also be active, establishing a creative relation in which the scientist is brought into an I-Thou relation with his so-called 'object'.

In his later writings, such as *Between Man and Man*, *The Eclipse of God*, and his essays on 'Distance and Relation' and 'Elements of the Inter-Human', Buber develops both the practical application of his views and an ontology of human relationship which are of immense significance for modern ethical thinking. His basic thought may be described in terms of the 'dialogical principle', which is best understood not as a matter of language but as *action*. It is in the concrete realm, which is not divisible into 'sacred' and 'profane' but is one world, in which human possibilities in relation to the 'eternal Thou' are realized, and made present, that Buber's thought is most fruitful. It is here that the primary word I-Thou is spoken, which means the give-and-take between two persons, who are set in this primary word in the one relation of reciprocity, mutuality and presence. This is the world of 'between', in which experiencing and using and manipulating are far away. Full humanity is to be found only in the constant realization of the meeting between the I and the Thou.

The contribution of Buber's ideas to the field of ethics may therefore be summarized as a deepening of the awareness of the 'other', viewed not as an 'it' but as one who is encountered as another subject. Evil in the human situation is the predominance of the world of 'It', which in turn means the lack of the decision which makes the presence of the Thou and full interhuman relations possible. But these interhuman relations are always regarded as realities in which the 'breath' of the eternal Thou may also be present. Buber's understanding of grace is not in the least dogmatic, in the sense of overwhelming or replacing moral action, but is rather to be seen as thoroughly biblical, in the sense of a power which is met in and through the structures of historical action and concrete demands upon us in our everyday life.

In addition to *I and Thou*, 1923; *Between Man and Man*, 1947 and *Eclipse of God*, 1952, may be mentioned *Tales of the Hasidim*, 1956, a volume of essays, *Pointing the Way*, 1957; *The Knowledge of Man*, 1965; R. Gregor Smith, *Martin Buber*, Makers of Contemporary Theology, 1966. A full bibliography will be found in M. Friedman, *Martin Buber, The Life of Dialogue*, 1955.

R. GREGOR SMITH

Buddhist Ethics

Buddhist morality in part reflects the special spiritual aims of the faith. The Buddha's teaching included both a diagnosis of the condition of human beings and a prescription on how that condition could be alleviated and finally cured. The regimen he prescribed is known as the 'Noble Eightfold Path', which leads to nirvana, and moral perfection is considered to be part of the means for attaining that degree of peace and insight which will release a person from the round of rebirth. Thus the Path includes, as three of its eight aspects: right speech, right action and right livelihood. The last indicates that a good Buddhist should not pursue an occupation which is necessarily in conflict with the moral precepts of Buddhism – in particular, one which involves the taking of life, such as being a butcher.

The moral requirements of Buddhism are more fully, though negatively, explicated in the Five Precepts (*pañcasīla*), binding both on laymen and on monks. These are that one should refrain from: taking life, including non-human life; taking what is not given; sexual misconduct; wrong speech; and taking intoxicants. The ban on deliberately taking life partly flows from the sense of kinship with other living beings implicit in the doctrine of rebirth and partly from the non-violent attitude (*ahimsā*) of Buddhism. The ban on intoxicants (both drugs and liquor) fits in with the strong emphasis on mindfulness (*sati*) or psychological self-awareness which forms a vital ingredient in the training of oneself in serenity and perfection.

Further and more stringent rules are binding upon monks and nuns. These are designed to promote a moderate asceticism (the Buddha claimed to teach a 'middle way' between extreme self-mortification and self-indulgence). Thus monks' personal possessions are drastically limited. Some offences attract expulsion from the Order (*Sangha*), such as having sexual intercourse and falsely claiming to have attained nirvana. Since there is a strong stress on mental training, Buddhism teaches that one should restrain mental dispositions, such as lust and greed, which represent the psychological counterparts of prohibited actions. Various meditations are prescribed to uproot such dispositions. The stress on the mental side also means that a non-legalistic interpretation of the rules is offered: it is intentional infringement which counts.

Laymen have a central religious duty, that of giving food and alms to the members of the *Sangha* and in general of respecting and helping the community through pious works. Conversely, the monks have the duty of preaching and of instructing the laity in the doctrine (*Dhamma*). These duties are summed up as 'giving' (*dāna*), as distinguished from the cultivation of personal virtue (*sīla*) as defined by the Precepts. But the need for giving extends beyond the bounds of the adherents of the faith: preaching must extend to the unconverted, while the provision of shelter and care for men and animals is counted a meritorious act.

Behind the good behaviour delineated above, there should lie a general attitude of compassion (*karunā*), which holds a place in Buddhism comparable to that of *agape* in Christianity. Thus the scriptures record the legend of how the Buddha at the time of his enlightenment was tempted by the Evil One (Māra) to disappear into nirvana without teaching the saving truth. But out of compassion for living beings he rejected the temptation. This motif becomes prominent in the development of the Mahāyāna. The so-called Hīnayāna or 'Lesser Vehicle' (a term which was originally abusive), now represented by Theravāda Buddhism in Ceylon, Burma and parts of South-East Asia, was criticized by adherents of the Greater Vehicle as holding up an essentially selfish ideal – that of achieving one's own salvation. By contrast the Mahāyāna pointed to the pattern of life found in the career of the Bodhisattva or Buddha-to-be, who sacrifices himself through countless lives for the welfare of living beings and who puts off his own nirvana to do this. Thus the true Buddhist treads the path of the Bodhisattva (*bodhisattvayāna*). With this there went some reinterpretation of the doctrine of darma. Instead of the view that one had to work off the results of prior deeds through one's own efforts, there was substituted the belief that a Bodhisattva or Buddha can transfer some of the immense store of merit accruing to him as a result of his vast series of heroic lives. It can be transferred to the otherwise unworthy faithful who call upon the Buddha; thereby they are assured of rebirth in a Paradise (the 'Pure Lane') where the conditions for the attainment of nirvana are especially propitious. The extreme outcome of this trend was Pure Land Buddhism, which, in its Japanese form, even went so far as to deny the efficacy of any works in bringing salvation: thus Nichiren (1222–1282) could argue that celibacy, itself a 'work', was not required of monks.

The Bodhisattva ideal expressed the centrality of compassion, and became a new norm for religious conduct and self-sacrifice on behalf of others, which was built into the practice of a popular religion of worship (in the Theravāda, by contrast, the Buddha is not an object of worship).

But also, in the Theravāda, popular moral teaching of a not altogether similar kind is catered for through the *Jātakas* or 'Birth Stories': these are tales about previous lives of the Buddha, often incorporating, and giving a Buddhist form to, existing fables. Thus humility and self-sacrifice are commended in the story of the hare (the Buddha in a previous life) who immolates himself on the fire of a lonely and hungry holy man.

Because the Buddha rejected the claims of contemporary Brahminical religion, controlled by a priestly class, he was opposed to the religious inequality implicit in the social order later to develop into the fully articulated Hindu caste system. Thus anyone could join the *Sangha*, which transcended class and caste distinctions. The emphasis on non-violence in Buddhism also had some social effects, for example, through the conversion of the emperor Aśoka (268–*c*. 233 BC) from a career of martial aggrandisement. These facets of the Buddhist tradition, together with the ideal of compassion, provide the basis for modern Buddhist programmes of social justice. On the other hand, Buddhism has adapted itself in its long, widespread and complex history to a variety of social orders, and even military virtues, in mediaeval Japan, could come to be interpreted as a way towards liberation. This, however, was a rather exceptional application of the Buddhist way, which prides itself on the fact that it has not generated any religious wars.

Buddhaghosa, *Visuddhimagga*, tr. by Pe Maung Ting, 3 parts, 1923–31; Edward Conze, *Buddhism*, 1963; Har Dayal, *The Bodhisattva Doctrine in Buddhist Sanskrit Literature*, 1932; I. C. Sharma, *Ethical Philosophies of India*, 1965.

NINIAN SMART

Bultmann, Rudolf

For Rudolf Bultmann (1884–   ), German NT scholar and theologian, the decisive moment in the Christian life occurs when the individual, responding to the *kerygma* in faith, ceases to try and find his security on what lies within his power. Many things lie within a man's power and he may build his life on money and possessions (like the rich fool in the parable) or on his own achievements (like St Paul's Judaizing opponents). But decisive Christian living begins when a man ceases to rely on these, and instead begins, on the basis of faith in Christ, to build his life on what is unknown and outside his control, confident (through his faith) that it will meet him in love. For a man to take this step means that for the first time he is delivered from care about himself and is open to meet others in love.

Christian love thus becomes possible to us as a basic element in the new life, which in turn comes to us through acceptance of the *kerygma* in faith. 'Only he who has been loved can love' (*Kerygma und Mythos*, I, p. 43).

Bultmann is reluctant to lay down any pattern, which the love for others, thus set free, will take. Apart from the basic insistence on love, the tables of moral precepts found in the NT are influenced positively and negatively by a number of factors of a mainly contingent nature. Among these are the influence of the OT and of popular Stoic philosophy and the fact that for the early Christians political responsibility did not come within the bounds of possibility. So far from setting out a general programme, the Christian imperative refers me to my particular situation at the moment so that I may hear the claim of the other who meets me in it and, as one who loves, find out what to do.

Apart from this central point perhaps Bultmann's main ethical contribution to Christianity lies in the way in which he (in common with Barth) sets limits to the *Aufklärung*'s approach to life through the critical reason. Bultmann has not hesitated to push the conclusions of biblical research to their ultimate conclusions. Yet he remains convinced that it is the Christian *kerygma* which judges us, not we the *kerygma*.

Thomas C. Oden, *Radical Obedience*, 1964.

IAN HENDERSON

Bunyan, John

Born near Bedford, England, John Bunyan (1628–1688) was first a tinker like his father and then enlisted in the Parliamentary army, serving for two and a half years. From earliest days he was deeply conscious of his own sinfulness but after much reading of the Bible and other books on the religious life, he found peace of mind and in 1657 became the pastor of the Independent (Baptist) congregation in Bedford. Imprisoned with other dissenters three years later, he wrote in jail his spiritual autobiography, *Grace Abounding to the Chief of Sinners*, published in 1666. During a later imprisonment he composed his famous *Pilgrim's Progress* (1675). The last thirteen years of his life were spent in preaching and writing. In all he wrote some sixty works.

Although uninfluenced by contemporary currents of thought, his own influence was both immediate and lasting at home and abroad. Using a strong, simple, unadorned style, he can claim to be the greatest of all English allegorists and the most popular propagator of Puritan doctrine. For Bunyan religion and ethics were inseparable. While always emphasizing that salvation was of God, he stressed good works as the evidence of salvation. His *Holy War* shows that he regarded the Christian life as a struggle with the powers of darkness, but there was nothing gloomy in Bunyan's theology, for the goal of man's life was everlasting happiness and God's final triumph over evil was assured.

Probably because of his imprisonment, he was a great lover of home and family life and while not a believer in feminine equality, he regarded women as sharers with men in godly service. Although not deeply interested in the ethics of business, he did not hesitate to condemn usury, bankruptcy and the unfair distribution of possessions. The Christian merchantman must see all his dealings in the light of the divine law.

Equipped with a prodigious knowledge of the Bible, to which was added an original, witty and imaginative mind, Bunyan succeeded where many Puritans failed, in making the virtuous life seem both worthwhile and enjoyable.

Entire Works of John Bunyan, ed. by H. Stebbing, 4 vols., 1862; J. Brown, *John Bunyan, his life, times and work*, 1887; O. E. Winslow, *John Bunyan*, 1961.

S. J. KNOX

Bushnell, Horace

Horace Bushnell (1802–1876), Congregational minister and author, often called the father of liberal theology in America, was educated in his native Connecticut. A graduate of Yale College and Divinity School, he reacted against the blend of Edwardsean and Common-Sense theology taught by Nathaniel W. Taylor in favour of the romantic idealism of Coleridge. In 1833 he was called to the pastorate of the North Church in Hartford, where he served until his retirement because of ill health in 1859. Confronting a divided congregation, he worked out a method of comprehensiveness whereby a larger truth to comprehend the partial truths in conflicting party views would be sought. Troubled by the 'machinery system of revivals' then so strong in Protestant life, he stressed the view that children of Christian parents can grow up in the faith without the need of a revivalistic conversion experience. In 1847 he published his arguments for 'Christian nurture' in several forms; later he revised and enlarged this work as *Christian Nurture* (1861). It was highly influential in the Sunday School and later religious education movements.

Early in 1848 Bushnell had a significant religious experience, the theological fruit of which can be seen in his basic book, *God in Christ* (1849). In an important 'Preliminary Dissertation on Language' he discussed the inadequacy of language precisely to convey spiritual truth; it transmits such truth through images, analogies and paradoxes. The bulk of the book deals with three matters: (1) the Trinity, in which he presents an instrumental view, (2) the atonement, in which he elaborated a moral influence theory which nevertheless has an *objective* as well as a subjective side, and (3) 'Dogma and Spirit', in which he sought to loosen the hold of dogma and creed in church and theological life so that the deeper spirit of Christianity might be apprehended by heart as well as head. The work provoked intense controversy, but many who had found modern knowledge beclouding their faith felt themselves liberated by it. Bushnell continued his apologetic theology in *Nature and the Supernatural* (1858), in which he argued that nature and supernature are not antithetical but complementary. In later years he returned to the theme of atonement, writing *The Vicarious Sacrifice* (1866) and *Forgiveness and Law* (1874) – in 1877 they were published in two volumes under the first title. He also published a number of sermons, addresses and occasional writings, which often had influence where his theological treatises were resisted.

Bushnell's ethical views were much shaped by the Anglo-Saxon middle-class world of which he was a part. He rarely challenged the dominant individualistic ethics of trade or the familiar alliance of virtue with success, but often presented religious life as a temporary, freeing escape from the struggles of life. He was fearful of Roman Catholic influence; he opposed woman suffrage. He saw the Civil War as a costly baptism in blood which prepared the way for genuine national unity, destiny, and progress towards perfection.

Sharply opposed in his time, Bushnell's work was appropriated by the evangelical or christocentric liberal party as it emerged as a power in Protestantism in the last quarter of the nineteenth century. His influence was strong in the Social Gospel (q.v.) which was so closely related to liberalism. His work prepared the way for the reception of Schleiermacher and Ritschl in America. Though his theological work was unsystematic and unbalanced, it showed originality and was the most important single force in American Protestant thought at the close of the nineteenth century.

Mary A. Cheyney, ed., *Life and Letters of Horace Bushnell*, 1880; Barbara M. Cross, *Horace Bushnell: Minister to a Changing America*, 1958; H. Shelton Smith, ed., *Horace Bushnell*, 1965.

ROBERT T. HANDY

Business Ethics

In what sense can business ethics be thought of as different from personal ethics? Christian opinions on this have reflected varying views on the relationship between the Christian calling and the world in which it has to be lived out.

In NT times, when the emphasis was on the Church as a new creation, over and against a corrupt world, there was little concern for the economic order as such, apart from the obligation to work conscientiously and honestly to get one's living (cf. II Thess. 3.6–12; Col. 3.22–25; Eph. 6.5–9).

In the Middle Ages, business ethics formed part of a whole system of Christian ethics, in which an attempt was made to work out the duties and obligations of men in every walk of life. In a slow-changing, ordered and graded society, it was possible for theologians to go beyond general principles and lay down precepts governing actual conduct in the process of getting a living. Such doctrines as those of the just price and just wage were intended to ensure that everyone received the just reward for making his proper contribution to the general welfare.

As the economy became more complex, with the rise of commerce, finance and industry, and the breakdown of feudalism, Christian thinking did not keep pace with the changes. In the sixteenth century the tendency on the whole was to reiterate the old doctrines and to try to maintain the values of the older, more static society. This was true not only of Roman Catholic thinking, but also of Luther and of the early days of Calvinism at Geneva, as well as of England under Charles I's personal rule. With later Calvinism and Puritanism there came the more individualist emphasis on the doctrine of the calling and on the duty of industry and frugality which, as emphasized by Weber and Tawney, played their part in giving rise to the ethics of capitalism. There was little attempt at a theological critique of the changes which were taking place in the economic order and of the values and aspirations that went with them.

By the eighteenth and early nineteenth centuries the prevailing climate of thought was that of the acceptance of natural law, and of the 'invisible hand' that would ensure that through competition in the market the enlightened self-interest of each would lead to the greatest good of all. This did not go without protest from Christian thought, though at first mainly of a romantic and backward-looking type, which did not grapple with the opportunities and problems that industrialization was bringing with it. The prevailing Evangelical theology in Britain and the USA was too individualistic to be adequate for this task. Thus the modern industrial order was allowed to grow up without the development of an adequate economic ethic to act as a guide to responsible conduct by Christians in the business field.

The history of Christian social thinking ever since is largely one of attempts to catch up. There is the massive development of Roman Catholic thought, as inspired by the Encyclicals *Rerum Novarum* (1891), *Quadragesimo Anno* (1931) and *Mater et Magistra* (1961), and expressed in western Europe in a widespread growth of trade unions and workers' and professional groupings. The main emphasis here has been on the organization of industry and business into responsible communities at every level from the individual firm up to State. More characteristic of Britain and the USA has been an empirical concern for social justice, as seen in the Christian Socialists' ideal of producers' co-operatives, the leading part played by Free Churchmen in the growth of the trade unions and the Labour movement, and the use of state power to redress the injustices of the excessive power of business, from the days of the early Factory Acts up to the modern emphasis on the control of monopoly and the ensuring of full employment and planned growth of the economy.

There have also been more far-reaching attempts to undertake the type of theological critique of the ideals and achievements of the economic system which had been lacking for so long. The School of Christian Sociology associated with the Christendom Group of the 1930s may be mentioned, though some of its members had a romantic tendency towards idealizing the agrarian societies of the past and underrating the real achievements of modern industrialism in making possible the overcoming of poverty. Canon Demant's *Religion and the Decline of Capitalism* is the most profound example, exposing the inadequacy of any purely economic philosophy, whether of the market or of a collectivist type, which ignores men's deeper need for a satisfactory rooting in community.

More recently, Christian economists have been trying to look critically in the light of the faith at the actual working of the economy. We may mention the works of D. L. Munby and M. Fogarty and the series of studies of Ethics and Economic Life undertaken by the National Council of Churches in the United States. These examine the functions of business enterprise in the modern economy, how they are performed and how they should be performed if true welfare as understood by Christians is to be achieved.

One result has been to place greater emphasis on the social responsibility of those engaged in business and industry, as against reliance either on the impersonal regulation of competition in the market, or on deliberate regulation from outside by the State. Thus H. R. Bowen sees a movement towards the acceptance by businessmen of standards of responsibility which take account of the effects of their actions on their employees, customers and competitors, as well as on the community as a whole. Goyder and others have focused attention on the possibility of altering the legal structure of the Joint Stock Company, so as to make it formally responsible to its employees and customers, as well as to its shareholders. In Britain the Marlow Declaration (1963) by a group of business leaders, trade unionists and churchmen is along the same lines.

It is now generally accepted that questions of business ethics involve consideration of the effects of business decisions on the whole working of the economy, on costs and prices and technical progress, on income distribution and the level of employment and the location of industry, and so on. They cannot be considered merely in terms of individual honesty, diligence and frugality. But most of the issues are still unsolved, and it must suffice to list some of the more important.

What is the function of profits? How far is the pursuit of profit justified as an incentive to enterprise and efficiency and a criterion to judge the most economic use of resources, as against the dangers it involves of exploitation of those in a weaker bargaining position and strengthening the acquisitive motives, as against those of co-operation and stewardship?

How far is competition essential as a stimulus to economic efficiency even if it involves conflict? How far is co-operation possible, between firms, or between management and workers, without involving a danger of the protection of producers' interests at the expense of those of consumers, or of lack of enterprise in introducing new processes and products?

How far do the pressures of the struggle for commercial success lead to a lowering of standards, for example, of honesty in advertising, of quality of products, of consideration for competitors and employees?

Does the businessman in fact fulfil his functions in the economy, of initiating and co-ordinating production and undertaking the risks of enterprise? Is business as we know it, in which co-operation of a team within the firm takes place in a framework of competition between firms and regulation by State, an effective means of providing for the material needs of the community, while at the same time giving a meaningful and satisfying way of life to those who take part in it?

Questions such as these must be answered before satisfactory guidance can be given on the ethics of the decisions which Christians engaged in business and industry must take every day of their lives. The thinking necessary can only be done by those who are involved in the situations concerned, as industrial directors and managers, businessmen, trade unionists, politicians, economists, sociologists or moral theologians.

H. R. Bowen, *The Social Responsibilities of the Businessman*, 1953; V. A. Demant, *Religion and the Decline of Capitalism*, 1952; M. Fogarty, *The Just Wage*, 1961; *Christian Democracy in Western Europe*, 1957; D. L. Munby, *Christianity and Economic Problems*, 1956; *God and the Rich Society*, 1961; J. F. Sleeman, *Basic Economic Problems, A Christian Approach*, 1953; R. H. Tawney, *Religion and the Rise of Capitalism*, 1963.

                                          JOHN F. SLEEMAN

Butler, Joseph

Joseph Butler (1692–1752) was an eighteenth-century British moralist and divine; for the last two years of his life, Bishop of Durham. His best known works comprise a volume of *Fifteen Sermons* (1726), and the *Analogy of Religion*, published ten years later. The latter embodies a very subtle exploration of the relations of revealed and natural theology. This work is largely neglected today; but it has an importance in itself, apart from its influence on John Henry Newman, who in his *University Sermons* (1829–43), perhaps the *chef d'oeuvre* of his Anglican period and certainly one of his masterpieces, counted himself *inter alia* a nineteenth-century continuator of Butler's work.

Butler's moral philosophy is contained in the volume of *Sermons* and in his short Dissertation on the Nature of Virtue appended to the *Analogy of Religion*. As a moralist he stands alone. In his arguments he often shows himself a man of his century, ready to commend moral virtue on prudential grounds, but the bias of his thought was against Utilitarianism, as his criticism (in the Dissertation on the Nature of Virtue) of Shaftesbury's identification of benevolence with the whole of virtue clearly brings out. For him moral excellence consisted in fulfilling the demand made upon us by our whole nature in the *hic et nunc* of concrete situations. His empiricism is more of the temper of Edmund Burke than of the 'philosophical radicals'; and it is to concrete fact that he appeals against, for example, Hobbes' identification of sympathy for another with fear for oneself induced by the sight of that other's predicament. He argues for the actual complexity of human nature and criticizes those who argue in the manner of Shaftesbury for ignoring it. These people argue that virtue can be identified with a generalized concern for human welfare, ignoring the special pull of particular claims upon one's devotion, for instance, of members of one's family or one's friends. He was deeply aware of the conflict between the demands of compassion, even of the obligation to forgive, and those of a proper resentment against injury done to others or even to oneself. The fact that Butler draws inferences of a metaphysical character from his doctrine of the sovereignty of conscience, and adheres in an uncritical way to the principle of causality which he regards at once as self-evident and as employable in speculation concerning the ultimate origin of the world might suggest that he is putting forward a simpler and less sophisticated version of Kant's doctrine of the primacy of the practical reason. However, Butler's deep and subtle understanding of the different claims between which conscience must intervene as an arbiter, reveals him as superior to Kant in presenting the detail of his moral psychology. In this part of Butler's work we see him steadfastly refusing to subscribe to a dogmatic psychological egoism.

Butler's work illustrates in a remarkable way the extent to which moral insight of permanent value can be mediated in utterances of a style and form which frequently reveal very clearly the particular historical and cultural relativity to which they belong. He made, in fact, one of the most considerable contributions in the modern period to the effective re-activation of the tradition of natural law. In Butler's works we have a presentation of natural law which does proper justice to its inwardness, and which shows the extent to which in practice acknowledgement of a natural order of human conduct may issue in an insoluble and even tragic conflict of obligations. Yet, as we read him, we come to see how, flexibly interpreted, it is only this tradition of natural law, with its combined attention to general principle and human particularity, that provides the setting within which some of the fundamental moral problems of human existence (e.g., those touching the conflicting claims of mercy and justice) can be articulated.

In his *Sermons on the Love of God*, Butler shows himself familiar with the controversies raised by the doctrine of 'quietism'. If the bulk of his work is small, it is hard to dispute the claim of the sermons to be regarded as one of the masterpieces of English moral philosophy. To be appreciated they need to be read in their entirety. The student should not allow a faulty academic tradition to restrict his attention to the first three, with a brief glance at the Dissertation as the source for evidence of Butler's movement towards an intuitive as distinct from a descriptive, conception of the nature of conscience on its cognitive side. He has been rightly compared to Aristotle in that Aristotle criticized Plato's failure to do justice to the complexity of the moral life. But the discriminating reader of his work can extract suggestions of the way in which the insights characteristic of the utilitarian and the natural law traditions of moral theory can be fused and held together with those characteristic of a more existentialist, or situational, approach to ethical questions. In

the deepest sense of an over-worked term, he may be described as a 'seminal' moral philosopher.

D. M. MACKINNON

Calling. *see* Vocation.

Calvin, John and Calvinist Ethics

1. *Foundations.* The ethics of John Calvin (1509–1564) is grounded in the principle that man belongs not to himself but to God. 'Now the great thing is this: we are consecrated and dedicated to God in order that we may thereafter think, speak, meditate, and do, nothing except to his glory. . . . Let this therefore be the first step, that a man depart from himself in order that he may apply the whole force of his ability in the service of the Lord. . . . The Christian philosophy bids reason give way to, submit and subject itself to, the Holy Spirit, so that man himself may no longer live but hear Christ living and reigning within him.' (*Institutes*, III, 7, 1.)

According to Calvin, God's claim to the worship and obedience of man is clear in that he has created man 'in his own image and likeness, in which we see the bright refulgence of God's glory' ('Preface to Olivetan's New Testament', in *Calvin: Commentator*, ed. by Joseph Haroutunian and Luise P. Smith, 1958, p. 58). In this passionate early writing, Calvin treats of man's 'act of outrageous ingratitude' by which 'he set out to exalt himself in pride against his Maker and Author of all that is excellent in him' (ibid.); of God's mercy towards fallen man in the election of Israel and his covenant with them; of the Law and the Prophets, and finally of the Mediator, 'the great Ambassador of the Father sent here below to accomplish the salvation of mankind' (ibid., p. 66). 'It follows,' he says, 'that every good thing we could think or desire is to be found in this same Christ alone. For, he was sold, to buy us back; captive, to deliver us; condemned to absolve us.' (ibid., p. 69). In the ethics of Calvin, therefore, to be God's is also to be Christ's, and in this way not to be one's own.

But to be God's and Christ's is also to belong to the Church, or God's people. The basis of the Christian's life is gratitude to God who has in Christ revealed himself as the Father, and his having been engrafted into the body of Christ, which is the Church (*Institutes*, III, 6, 3). Therefore, the Christian life is altogether different from the Stoic ideal of life 'according to nature'. It is a consequence of reconciliation with God and 'the denial of ourselves'. By self-denial, Calvin understands dedication to the glory of God or doing all things to please God (ibid., III, 7, 2). But this means going against 'nature', in 'seeking to benefit one's neighbour', to make 'lawful use of all benefits . . . in a liberal and kindly sharing of them with others . . . for the common good of the Church' (ibid., III, 7, 5). Thus, Christians practise 'right stewardship' according to 'the rule of love'.

2. *The Law of God.* Since love is the sum of the Law of God, it is well to remember Calvin's treatment of the latter. In the Law, man confronts God himself. In it, he is presented with the character of God and with the demand that God makes upon him (ibid., II, 8, 1, 4, 51). In it, God has shown man how he may please him and fulfil his duty before him and his feilowman (ibid., II, 8, 2, 8, 48). In short, with regard to the Law, man's business is with God. The love of the neighbour is the fulfilment of a debt to God and its true ground is the claim of God upon man as Father.

The Law, summed up in the Great Commandment, is the gift of God to his people for their knowledge of him and his will, and for their guidance in obeying him. This famous 'third use' of the Law of God, given in Scripture, is the main thing in Calvin's teaching on the Law. He regarded the giving of the Law as an act of divine grace, as an expression of God's care and as a blessing. From this point of view, even the first use of the Law (that it shows man's inability to please God by his own virtue and convicts him of sin) and the second use of the Law (that it restrains the wicked and makes public life possible), are seen as due to divine favour and conducive both to his glory and man's well-being (ibid., II, 7, 2 f.).

The Law of God, according to Calvin, is contained in Scripture, and especially in the Ten Commandments and the Great Commandment. However, he sees the biblical Law not as an imposition upon man but as a clear and decisive statement of 'natural law', the law of human nature and one man must obey to attain his proper good. Natural law is implanted in man by his Creator, and it is known by man's conscience. But conscience is confused by sin, and its functions are to condemn man for his iniquity, rather than as a sure guide in his knowledge of his duty before God. Natural law is certainly necessary in enabling him to judge between right and wrong on the level of politics, and it underlies civil law which governs conduct in human societies. But, even here it needs the illumination of the written Law of God. When it comes to pleasing God and loving one's neighbour, 'self-denial' is of the essence of Calvin's ethics (ibid., III, 7, 52).

This does not mean that piety is irrelevant to the common life. In fact, it is the ground for a proper use of common goods. By self-denial, a man acknowledges that he is to share God's gifts of earthly goods with his neighbour (ibid., 7, 5). He is enabled to delight in, as well as use, food and raiment; and to enjoy the beauty of God's gifts as well as their usefulness. 'Let this be our main principle,' writes Calvin, 'that the use of God's gifts is not wrongly directed when it is referred to that end to which the Author himself created and destined them for us, since he created them for our good, and not for our ruin.' (ibid., III, 10, 2). Under this principle, God 'has greatly commanded abstinence, sobriety, frugality, and moderation, and has also abominated excess, pride, ostentation, and vanity . . . [and] approves no other distribution of good things than one joined with love' (ibid., 10, 5).

3. *Ethics and Economics.* Calvin's Geneva was a commercial city. It produced clothing, leather works, jewellery, watches and books. It was engaged in commerce and had bankers, and money was lent and borrowed with interest. All this provided a living to the populace, and created the problems of usury and exploitation; and the Church, beginning with Calvin, took an interest in these matters. The latter was concerned with the general prosperity of the city, with the employment and living of its citizens, and the prevention of poverty and its attendant evils. To these ends, prices were fixed, and so were pay and working hours. Calvin held to his basic purposes of public well-being and order, with justice and compassion as guiding principles.

It is in this context that we are to understand Calvin's ethics. He condemned interest and sought to limit it to 5%. He insisted that loans to the poor be made without interest. He opposed minimum wages and treating man's work as merchandise. Even though he saw prosperity as a sign of God's goodness, he refused to see poverty as a sign of God's displeasure. He insisted that the weak, the poor and strangers, be treated with compassion. He regarded a man's work as his calling, and for the sake of the stability of the community, he judged that 'it is not lawful to exceed its bounds' (ibid., III, 10, 6). In short, property, profit and work, under God's favour, were to be used for the common good, and in self-denial for the service of others. He said under 'Communion of Saints': 'It is as if one said that the saints are gathered into the society of Christ on the principle that whatever benefits God confers upon them, they should in turn share one with another. This does not, however, rule out diversity of graces. . . . Nor is civil order disturbed, which allows each individual to own his private possessions. . . . [Acts 4.32]. If truly convinced that God is the common Father of all and Christ the common Head, being united in brotherly love, they cannot but share their benefits with one another' (ibid., IV, 1, 3).

It is doubtless true that Calvin's doctrine of calling, together with his insistence upon work and frugality, contributed, at a distance of a century and more, to the development of 'capitalism' in western Europe and America. However, it did this through a process, long and complex, in which Calvinism was secularized and lost its basic principle of self-denial to the glory of God, which Calvin had firmly tied to the commandment, 'Thou shalt love thy neighbour as thyself'. The capitalistic thesis that riches as such are signs of election and poverty as such is a sign of divine rejection, was shared by non-Calvinists, and is a travesty of the ethics of Calvinism, both early and late.

André Biéler, *The Social Humanism of Calvin*, tr. by Paul T. Fuhrmann, 1964; Robert W. Green, ed., *Protestantism and Capitalism: The Weber Thesis and Its Critics*, 1959; John T. McNeill, *The History and Character of Calvinism*, 1954; Ronald S. Wallace, *Calvin's Doctrine of the Christian Life*, 1954; Max Weber, *The Protestant Ethic and the Spirit of Capitalism*, tr. by Talcott Parsons, 1958.

JOSEPH HAROUTUNIAN

Canon Law

Canon Law is the body of rules governing conduct in the Christian community. The word *kanon* is used by St Paul for such a rule (Gal. 6.6) and perhaps even the most enthusiastic champions of 'situational ethics' would hardly deny that the Church, like any other corporate body, needs some basic rules if it is to function or even to survive. We already read in the NT of the formulation of such rules by the college of Apostles. In the subsequent history of the Church, the number and scope of its rules have greatly multiplied, though from time to time attempts have been made to codify and simplify the accumulated canon law. The canon law of the Roman Catholic Church in particular is a vast affair, the revised Codex of 1917 containing 2,414 canons. Canon law in the Anglican and Eastern churches is much simpler and briefer. Since canon law belongs rather to the constitution and polity of the Church than to ethics, it will not receive any detailed treatment in this volume. *See* **Discipline; Law; Moral Theology.** It may be noted, however, that with the separation of Church and State, either in law or in fact, and with the subsequent divergence between the law of the Church and the law of the State, canon law has been acquiring a fresh ethical significance in certain fields. A good illustration is the whole area of marriage and sexual behaviour. If the Christian ideal of marriage is to be maintained, the Church may lay certain rules upon its members. These rules, however, cannot be imposed on society at large, where the Christian ideal of lifelong monogamous union is not accepted by many people, and where the civil laws, recognizing this situation, are much laxer than the laws of the Church.

In such cases therefore the authority of canon law depends on the free consent of the Christians who belong to the community in which this law prevails.

EDITOR

Capital Punishment

The Christian faith came into a world where capital punishment was an accepted feature of the legal system. When the Church came seriously to consider the problems and duties of the State it tended to take capital punishment for granted and to find biblical justification for it in certain texts, which need not concern us today, and in Rom. 13.4 which does not in fact bear directly on the matter. Lactantius was one of the few early Fathers to oppose it, and in this he has always been followed by a minority in the Church. Today more and more Christians are opposed to it, and in many Protestant circles the severity of the main Reformation teaching (largely based on naive biblicist reasons) is being called in question. The legitimacy and wisdom (not necessarily the same thing) of capital punishment can only be assessed in terms of the various Christian theories of punishment. Here it must suffice to point out that the status of capital punishment in Christian thought arises out of the Christian understanding of the place of the State as an institution ordained by God for the good of mankind. One of its tasks is to maintain the possibility of civilized life by protecting its citizens against crime. (Its duty to protect from aggression has led to treason usually being a capital offence.)

If *deterrence* is admitted as an element in a Christian theology of punishment, capital punishment must be allowed some place *if* it deters. Evidence shows, however, that there is a strong tendency to exaggerate the effects of deterrent punishments. Murder remains as practically the only capital crime in most countries. If the evidence shows that the death penalty greatly reduces the number of murders there is a good case for its unpleasant necessity. But the evidence does not show this, but rather that the number of murders varies very little whether there is a death penalty or not. One is most likely to be murdered, for instance, by a member of one's own family or relations as a result of some emotional crisis on which the question of the death penalty has little, if any, influence; calculations of rational self interest hardly enter. There is evidence, however, of the deterrent value of capital punishment in some circumstances, for example, to prevent looting after a disaster. That is why its use cannot be ruled out in principle. If *reformation* is an element in Christian approval of punishment, capital punishment cannot play much part in it, except on occasion to produce a death bed repentance. But few would justify such a drastic means of producing this possible result.

There remains the *retributive* theory of punishment. Christian opinion is divided whether this is a legitimate element at all. Assuming, however, that it is, it is difficult to justify the death sentence except on the grounds of an 'eye for an eye, and a tooth for a tooth', and this cannot be squared with a *Christian* understanding of the matter. If all these theories of punishment are denied on the ground that crime is a sickness to be cured not punished, requiring therapy not judicial proceedings (a position which has some truth in it in the light of modern psychiatry, even if it is often exaggerated), then the death penalty is obviously ruled out.

Capital punishment is unpleasant for those who have to carry it out, and it has a bad effect on the public which is apt to gloat morbidly over its victims. It has the further disadvantage that miscarriages of justice cannot be corrected, and a number of such cases are known. There are, therefore, strong grounds for opposing it, unless in a specific instance it can be shown to be an effective deterrent against grave crime. If it can, then it must be a Christian vocation to be a judge, warder or executioner to carry it out for the common good. The Christian view of the State and of punishment neither excludes capital punishment nor requires it, but it does require a strong case before approval can be given to it.

The minority of Christians who oppose the death penalty on principle may do so on equally naive biblicist lines as some of its defenders, or on pacifist grounds (q.v.), or because it has a weak doctrine of the State. There are also Christians who defend it on the grounds that a long prison sentence is worse than death. But (1) a prisoner is not given the choice, nor is it proper that he should be; (2) a civilized community should find a constructive punishment for grave crime which is not worse than death.

RONALD PRESTON

Capitalism

Every economic system requires capital, as one of the basic factors in the production of wealth. The name 'capitalism' is used for the system in which capital is, for the most part, privately owned and is operated for profit. From the Christian point of view, there is nothing inherently right or wrong about such a system. Where it functions efficiently, benefiting the majority of the people and not creating any injustices, there is no ethical question involved. The system, however, lends itself to some abuses. The profit motive may encourage sectional interests and lead to the exploitation of workers or to the unloading on consumers of inferior goods. The concentration of the means of production and distribution in the hands of a relatively few people leads to an abnormal concentration of power, with the consequent temptation to abuse it. From the NT onward, Christian ethics has tended to be critical of the rich and has regarded excessive economic power as an evil. Thus in modern times many Christian moralists have tended towards socialism. But an uncontrolled capitalism in which there is exploitation of workers and consumers by a few powerful profit-seekers is largely a thing of the past. State-regulation of industry and commerce protects both workers and consumers, as well as the community at large. Competition and incentives within a system of free enterprise provide built-in controls against some evils, such as the production of inferior goods. Capitalism, moreover, has its own virtues, for it demands the diligence and concern associated with risk, and encourages care for property. Socialism, on the other hand, may dull initiative and create contempt for public property, for what belongs to everybody is nobody's concern. Perhaps in modern society, a so-called 'mixed economy', with both private and public sectors, is the best arrangement. But this is not an ethical judgment. The Christian is not committed to any particular economic system. He is committed to seeking the economic well-being of all, and to fighting against injustice, poverty and waste; but in some countries this may be better achieved under a capitalist or mixed system than under socialism. *See* **Business Ethics; Communism, Ethics of Marxist; Property, Ethics of; Socialism.**

EDITOR

Cardinal Virtues

Mediaeval churchmen have made us familiar with a type of Christian living found in the understanding and the practice of the seven virtues. They held that faith, hope and love are the fundamental Christian virtues and that the cardinal virtues (prudence, justice, temperance, fortitude) are needed to express faith, hope and love in all the varying circumstances of life in the world. It was never stated that the practice of the virtues depended solely on either human effort or divine grace.

The concept of the Christian life as the practice of the virtues encouraged an individualistic view of behaviour and led many to care more for acquiring virtue than for their neighbours. In mediaeval times and since there is a certain disregard of the corporate nature of virtue seen in the neglect of such facts as: (1) a judge cannot administer justice when there is perjury; (2) a man cannot forgive another unless the other is willing to be forgiven; (3) a man cannot be generous if no one will accept his gifts.

In the twentieth century Christians continue to regard faith, hope and love as the fundamental Christian virtues but the place of the cardinal virtues is given to a consideration of the behaviour likely to make and maintain personal relationships. In explaining this required behaviour people make statements which could be used to describe the four cardinal virtues. Four such descriptive statements are made here noting the virtues which each describes: (1) an ability to discern what act is both necessary and possible in a given human situation and thus throw light on fulfilling obligations consequent on the relationship of those concerned (prudence); (2) treating each individual differently and all as human (justice); (3) being sufficiently self-controlled not to dominate or be dominated by others (temperance); (4) to withstand temptations which are inevitable in every human relationship and to endure the loneliness of being misunderstood (fortitude).

The cardinal virtues are also useful in answering the questions which are asked about the relationship of groups to one another: (1) How is a man to behave in the light of the fact that he belongs to several groups at the same time and each makes a complete demand on him? (2) What kind of behaviour problems are likely to arise for a man who belongs to a small group which is one of many within a large inclusive group – for example, university or engineering works? (3) What should be thought about a man who will not commit himself deeply to any group in case by doing so he finds that he is in opposition to himself as a member of other groups? (4) Does speaking of one's attitude to a group imply that a group has a life apart from its members? (5) What is meant by group action? Who is responsible for it? (6) How are formal and informal groups within the Church to be judged?

These questions have no simple answers. They are dealt with in the first place by clarifying the terms of the question as much as possible. Christian behaviour is not thought of as correct or incorrect but as truthful or untruthful, as loving or unloving – in the Christian meaning of loving.

R. E. C. BROWNE

Caroline Moral Theology

Caroline moral theology is an inexact but convenient term to denote the works on moral theology written in England during the seventeenth century when the subject was highly esteemed by men of all shades of churchmanship. After the upheavals of the Reformation the provision of a moral theology appropriate to the needs of a reformed Church of England had been delayed, primarily because those who were best qualified to give a lead had been immersed in doctrinal controversies. A few modest contributions appeared during the Elizabethan period, but the first notable work on the subject was William Perkins's *The Whole Treatise of the Cases of Conscience* (1606, posthumous). Other works of major importance included: William Ames's *De Conscientia et eius jure vel casibus* (1630); Robert Sanderson's *De Juramenti Promissorii Obligatione* (1647), and *De Obligatione Conscientiae* (1660);

Joseph Hall's *Resolutions and Decisions of Divers Practical Cases of Conscience* (1649); Jeremy Taylor's *Ductor Dubitantium* (1660); Richard Baxter's *A Christian Directory, or a Summ of Practical Theologie and Cases of Conscience, etc.* (1673); John Sharp's *A Discourse Concerning Conscience* (1683), and *The Case of a Doubting Conscience* (1684). It will be noted that among these authors were famous leaders of the 'puritan wing' of the Church of England as well as distinguished bishops. Further contributions were made by them and by many others in selective treatises and monographs, popular handbooks, lectures, occasional discourses, letters, devotional works and sermons. Indeed, the total relevant literature is enormous, and the fact that it is so heterogeneous in form, though perhaps a disadvantage to the modern student, only underlines how extensive was the demand for a sound moral theology (or 'casuistical' or 'practical' divinity as it was variously called) among all classes of men at that time. It was not regarded as a priestly pursuit alone, nor identified exclusively or even mainly with the confessional. The works of the English moralists were written in English, or quickly translated from Latin, for the benefit of all who could read them; and, though the need of personal guidance was never minimized, they wished to assist men as far as possible to resolve their own moral problems with confidence and safety. They were ready to benefit from the labours of their mediaeval predecessors and Roman contemporaries, but quick to criticize and reject whatever items they considered to be inconsistent with 'right reason', Scripture and early Christian teaching – though some required a weightier Scripture reference than others. Much of the terminology and many of the categories and distinctions familiar to mediaeval moralists reappeared in their pages, and (like Hooker) in their expositions on law and conscience they stood for the most part within the Thomist tradition. Accordingly, though they may have failed to adapt traditional teaching vigorously enough to the rapidly changing social, economic and political conditions, and though on some issues they were divided in their judgments, they sought to demonstrate by the range of their own studies that no area of human life, public or private, lies outside the orbit of Christian moral principles. On the other hand they reacted adversely to certain elements in contemporary Roman moral theology and (sometimes as the victims of ignorance or prejudice) they were inclined to pillory whatever might be labelled 'Jesuitry'. It was not simply a matter of Jesuit political theory or of devices like verbal equivocation and mental reservation. They dismissed *probabilism* and defended *probabiliorism* as the correct method to determine most cases of conscientious doubt. While dissociating themselves from any doctrine of the parity of sins, they rejected the distinction of mortal and venial as commonly taught. Dissatisfied with a doctrine of repentance that appeared to be inseparably linked with an alleged sacrament of penance, they insisted that only a sorrow for sin that is properly contrition (not 'attrition') will suffice for absolution, and emphasized the scriptural concept of repentance as a radical conversion to the life of obedient sonship. Their tendency towards rigorism was to some extent a comment on the real or alleged laxity of many continental Roman casuists. But it was also related to their own conception of the nature and function of moral theology. They saw it as a comprehensive science adequate to lead a heedful society in the ways of justice and the individual Christian in the path of holiness; as including not only the resolution of difficult cases of conscience and all the juristic side of moral theology, but also the entire range of what is sometimes thought of separately as ascetic theology: not a legalistic system but a body of teaching that would help men in all the circumstances of life to grow in grace and 'guide them safely in their walk with God, to life eternal' (Baxter).

H. R. McAdoo, *The Structure of Caroline Moral Theology*, 1949; Thomas Wood, *English Casuistical Divinity During the Seventeenth Century*, 1952; 'An Anglican Manual', *CQR*, cxlvi (1948), 150–78.

THOMAS WOOD

Casuistry

In its widest sense casuistry is the art of deciding what is right or wrong in particular cases where general norms are not precise enough. For example, shall I be strict or lenient towards this disobedient child on this occasion in order to be guided by the universal precept of love? Or, how shall I vote in this election in order to further the general good of justice? It is with this widest meaning that philosophical moralists have said that 'casuistry is undoubtedly the goal of ethics' (H. Rashdall, *The Theory of Good and Evil*, 1924, II, p. 420) or G. E. Moore: 'Casuistry may indeed be *more* particular and ethics *more* general; but that means that they differ in degree and not in kind. . . . Casuistry, not content with the general law that charity is a virtue must attempt to discover the relative merits of every different form of charity' (*Principia Ethica*, 1903, pp. 4, 5). Aristotle had expounded casuistry under the name of equity, a rectification of 'law where law is defective because of its generality' (*Nic. Ethics*, V.x.6). It operates through the virtue of prudence which takes account of particular facts (VI.vii. 7). The equitable man must be morally earnest, experienced in concrete situations and not use his art solely in his own interests. A contem-porary philosophical moralist expounds a casuistical argument, though not under that name, and defends it from the charge of laxity, when he says 'What we are doing in allowing classes of exceptions (to a principle) is to make the principle, not looser, but more rigorous'. The rule never to say what is false becomes more strict, not less, when exceptions are made, for example, 'Never say what is false, except in war-time to deceive the enemy' (R. M. Hare, *The Language of Morals*, 1952, p. 52). This kind of situation discloses the inevitability of casuistic judgments such as everybody makes. It also exposes the possibility of their perversion by generalizing the scope of the judgment beyond that of the exception and its kind.

In Christendom moralists have had to deal with several kinds of problem which, according to the assumptions of this article, come validly under the heading of casuistry. And in pre-Christian society solemn concern for the Law among the Jews and a germinal sense of conscience among the Stoics, demanded guidance when the general statement of an obligation failed to enlighten men in exceptional circumstances. Christ's endorsement of a breach of Sabbath observance (Mark 2.23 ff.) weighs the needs of life or healing against commands of worship and rest, giving those needs priority without abrogating the commands. In Christian history the two main kinds of casuistical questions have been the assessment of guilt for past faults and guidance for behaviour where the course of duty is unclear. Under the first, come inquiries as to the limits beyond which breaches of moral standards deserve exclusion from the church community. Persecution produced many cases of believers breaking vows and ceasing to observe conditions of church membership. It was a casuistic judgment to decide under what conditions such faithlessness had happened, and whether such lapses could be tolerated and offenders restored to communion. A form of the second question arose when those who were torn between deepening their spiritual life by flight to the desert and faithfulness to a promise that they would return to Palestine (cf. Cassian: *Coll.* xvii). A common problem with a large literature deals with conditions under which lying is morally justified. Augustine took a more rigorous view than most church moralists (*De Mendacio*; *Contra Mendacium*; *Ep.* XXVIII). On the whole one may lie to keep alive when threatened, to prevent homicide, or when the truth would involve innocent persons in disaster. Recent situations in resistance movements against tyrannous governments raise questions of the legitimacy of lying, cheating and terror in the cause of freedom. When may violence and compulsion be used by Christians, especially in view of the gospel precepts of non-resistance? Or again, what is one's duty when an unjust command is given by legitimate authority?

These are problems of casuistry. Further, if the needs of stability in society and state override individual conscience or lesser loyalties and church liberties, which has to give way? This kind of problem was faced by Catholics, Puritans and Anglicans in the seventeenth century (cf. G. L. Mosse, *The Holy Pretence*). Such are matters of casuistical judgment in that they concern action where there is a conflict of obligations, fulfilment of each of which is regarded as demanded by the conscience. In brief, the conscience is perplexed, that is, confronted with incompatibility in the demand of two approved moral courses.

A different kind of casuistical question arises with doubt whether a particular action is of moral obligation or not. If I belong to a church or club, membership of which requires the profession of certain convictions, can I honestly continue to belong, or seek adherence, if I reject one or a few of the conditions? Or, believing that life is a trust, is birth-control morally allowable, and if so when? Is gambling morally innocent or wrong? Is it lawful for a Christian to drink alcoholic liquor? Is artificial insemination by a donor a form of adultery or not? Am I deceiving myself in believing that it is my conscience which impels me to disobey my lawful ruler by, for example, objections to military service? Is it a moral offence to evade customs dues or taxes if I can? On such matters there is no conflict of duties, but uncertainty as to what is one's duty; and frequently doubt arises because all Christians are not agreed. If in doubt take the safe course, follow the strictest view, says one theory (tutiorism). You may with innocence follow the majority opinion (the more probable one) that an action is lawful, although a minority considers it sinful (probabiliorism). Or, if any reputable guide or guides declare it morally reputable you may follow them although they be in a minority (probabilism). This third position is rightly adopted by the majority of men who have never heard of the theory. But it is open to unscrupulous use which encourages moral laxity. It was for such abuse that the seventeenth-century Jesuits were castigated, albeit with some unfairness, by Pascal in his *Lettres Provinciales* (1656).

Casuistry not only seeks to convert a doubtful conscience into a certain one, to make clear whether an action is right or wrong in itself. It also envisages circumstances which may modify a general approval, for example, temperance does not demand total abstinence, but for a man with certain weaknesses it should be observed by him, and by his friends on occasions. The act of gambling may be morally innocent in itself, yet a widespread and frequent practice of it may be socially and personally detrimental. Scale as well as quality has to be considered.

Besides questions of perplexity and doubt as to the morality of contemplated actions, casuistry also deals with approval or disapproval of acts already committed. By the thirteenth century public discipline of sinners was replaced by auricular, private, acknowledgement of faults, and detailed guidance as to conditions of absolution and penance was required for confessors. While this opened the way for over refinement, it also trained consciences of penitents and minds of directors in sensitivity. Moral judgment thereby had to consider, besides the objective nature of an act (for example, to kill a man or to save a life), but also the circumstances which would increase or diminish the guilt or the virtue; and further the subjective end of the act, or the motive (for example, in the above mentioned examples, the killing might be to prevent worse evils or to remove a witness or for theft; the saving of a life may be done out of humanity or to retain an accomplice in crime). To judge the morality of an act by the motive alone had often been regarded as the specifically Christian contribution to ethics; but notice that if it is the sole criterion it becomes the warrant for doctrine that the end justifies the means, a doctrine rightly suspect in, say, Machiavelli, or in the laxist perversions of casuistry. A further casuistical task is to decide whether an objectively evil act is done in 'ignorance of law', not knowing that it is morally wrong; or in 'ignorance of fact', for example, executing a prisoner of war thinking in error that he is a terrorist. Again, a casuistical judgment seeks to discover whether ignorance of the moral law is vincible, that is, could have been overcome by a conscientious man, or whether it is invincible and therefore excusable.

The scope of casuistry as thus delineated discloses its logic, whereby a general universal norm is posited, and then a number of exceptions or modifications or extenuating circumstances are recognized as justifying departure from the strict unconditional letter of the norm. And it is only when such legitimate departures can be to any extent classified that it is possible to speak of casuistry. But there are also situations which cannot be regulated or judged as cases because they are so unique as to elude both the appropriate universal norm and the recognized category of exceptions. In such situations both an external judging authority and the conscience which is baffled have available the virtues of prudence and equity to decide an unclassifiable moral dilemma. These take us beyond the sphere of casuistry, strictly speaking, and have affinities perhaps with 'the weightier matters of the law' (Matt. 23.23). But it is a work of casuistry to distinguish the three moral realities: norm, classifiable exceptions and unclassifiable uniqueness.

Not to allow for exceptional modifications of the norm or for unique problems unamenable to rule, is to fall into the evil of rigorism.

Not to recognize the norms behind the casuistical adaptation (for example, honesty behind the allowable stealing of a loaf of bread by a starving man; or truthfulness behind justifying a statesman's ruse to prevent invasion) and to make the exceptions the ground of a general moral custom, is to encourage laxism. This latter has been the prevailing danger of casuistry when misused. But when responsibly handled casuistry aims at a more detailed charity and so far from being a necessary evil it is a good demanded by the imperfection of generalized knowledge. The contemporary call for 'situational' or 'contextual' ethics springs from dislike of any general or even relative standards and proclaims in faith that any situation can be morally handled *de novo* without categorizing it, and with a *morale du moment*. This call implicitly poses the question: Is there such a thing as situational ethics which is not either a refinement of the older casuistry or else a position which rejects every classifiable moral judgment, sometimes miscalled existentialist, and relies exclusively upon untutored decision and is therefore not ethics at all?

Articles in *HERE* and *Encyclopaedia Britannica*.
    Roman Catholic: J. C. Ford and Gerald Kelly, s.j., *Contemporary Moral Theology*, 1, 1960; Genicot and Salmans, *Casus Conscientiae*, various editions; Joseph Pieper, *Prudence*. 1959; Eduard Hamel, s.j., *Loi Naturelle et Loi du Christ*, 1964, Chaps. 2 and 3.
    Anglican: K. E. Kirk, *Ignorance, Faith and Conformity*, 1925; *Conscience and its Problems; Introduction to Casuistry*, 1927; Jeremy Taylor, *Ductor Dubitantium or The Rule of Conscience*, Works, XI–XIV; *The Serpent and the Dove* (Sermons 20, 21, 22), Works, VI; Thomas Wood, *English Casuistical Divinity during the Seventeenth Century*, 1952.
    Puritan: William Ames, *Conscience with the Power and Cases Thereof*, 1643; Richard Baxter, *A Christian Directory*, 1673; William Perkins, *The Whole Treatise of the Cases of Conscience*, Works, II, 1603.

                                                V. A. DEMANT

Categorical Imperative

Kant makes a distinction between hypothetical imperatives which command an action merely as a means to a given end and therefore have no validity for us unless we wish to attain the end, and categorical imperatives which command an act as good in itself and therefore as necessary if our will is to conform to reason. The latter only are held by him to be moral imperatives, so that the distinction leads to an ethical system which in opposition to all forms of Utilitarianism avoids basing our obligations on consequences. There is indeed one end which none of us can help desiring, happiness, thus giving rise to what he calls an 'assertoric

imperative', but even the fact that the end is actually pursued by everybody does not make the imperative to pursue it 'categorical'. *See* **Kant and Kantian Ethics.**

                                                A. C. EWING

Celibacy

Celibacy means originally simply the unmarried state – in Latin *coelebs* is 'bachelor', as in the imperial laws intended to encourage marriage. But the term is commonly used for acceptance of the single state as a religious duty, whether by vow or under some general obligation. Perhaps in view of God's approaching judgment, the early Church deprecated the marriage of adult converts (cf. I Cor. 7.20–27); some parts of the Syrian Church in the second and third centuries seem to have insisted on either marriage or commitment to celibacy before baptism. In some heretical sects, and semi-Christian groups such as the Manichaeans, only the celibate were considered full members, and others remained in a status similar to that of catechumens.

    What was once expected of the laity continued to be demanded of the clergy, and marriage after ordination was rare if not unknown – a rule further strengthened by the reverence for ascetics which made it natural to select celibates for the higher positions in the Church. In 451 the Council of Chalcedon (Canon 14) assumes that only the lesser clergy, such as readers and singers, are still marriageable. In 691 a Council at Constantinople (the so-called Quinisext) enforced the discipline which still prevails in the Eastern Church; priests and deacons may be married before ordination, but bishops, if not celibate, must separate from their wives – they are in fact almost invariably chosen from the monastic order.

    The Western Church was already moving towards a general enforcement of clerical celibacy, although practice varied in the early Middle Ages. The rule of celibacy was a main point of the Gregorian reform in the eleventh century – intended not only to encourage a semi-monastic standard for the clergy, but also to prevent their absorption in the feudal system (at least technically).

    The Reformers generally rejected compulsory celibacy as wrong in principle, and not merely because of the scandals which often accompanied it; and this has remained the general Protestant position. In England under Henry VIII the Act of Six Articles (1539) enforced clerical celibacy as required by divine law; but the marriage of the clergy was allowed by an Act of 1549 under Edward VI (repealed in 1553, re-enacted in 1559), and defended in Article 32 of the 39 Articles, 'Of the Marriage of Priests' (1553, revised 1563). There has always remained in Anglicanism, however, some recognition of a special call to the celibate state, some going as far as the seventeenth-century Bishop Ken:

A virgin priest the altar best attends,
A state the Lord commands not, but
commends.

Modern Roman Catholic theology considers clerical celibacy, however desirable, a matter of ecclesiastical rather than divine law, and hence subject to exceptions such as the recognition of the Eastern practice among Eastern Catholics. In the Latin rite ordination to the subdiaconate is held to involve acceptance of the obligation of celibacy; but there have been occasional exceptions, most recently in dispensations granted by Popes Pius XII and Paul VI for the ordination of former Lutheran ministers. Some modification of the Roman discipline is likely in the near future, as shown by the discussion at the Second Vatican Council of such possibilities as a married diaconate. *See also* **Virginity, Asceticism.**

On the history, H. R. Niebuhr and D. D. Williams, *The Ministry in Historical Perspectives*, 1956; on the theory of the celibate vocation, Lucien Legrand (Catholic), *The Biblical Doctrine of Virginity*, 1963; David P. O'Neill (Catholic), *Priestly Celibacy and Maturity*, 1966; Max Thurian (Reformed), *Marriage and Celibacy*, 1959.

E. R. HARDY

Censorship

Censorship is the scrutiny of material (literature, art, plays, films, etc.) before it is published, exhibited or performed. It acts therefore as a sieve to prevent what is undesirable from ever reaching the public. The censor must have some official standing, though he may in some cases be employed by a semi-official body, as, for example, the British Board of Film Censors. The prosecution of publishers and others after publication or performance is not, strictly speaking, censorship, but has the same ultimate effect of keeping the public from further access to the offending material, and may lead to more excessive timidity and caution in publishing, since successful prosecution involves serious financial loss.

Censorship is most commonly discussed today in terms of pornography, but it is possible that it has been more frequently used for political and religious than for moral ends. The Church itself has been the most ardent of censors, and the Bible the most censored book.

While the right of public authority to suppress material in certain circumstances (where it causes grave offence, or is a danger to the public good) can hardly be denied (even, for example, the censorship of letters in time of war) it is open to grave danger of abuse (for example, the suppression of news derogatory to one's own cause), and it is therefore axiomatic that severe censorship is a mark of

tyranny, spiritual or political, and that freedom of speech and expression is a mark of a mature community. But even the noblest defenders of liberty of speech, such as Milton and J. S. Mill, believe that it has limits.

Those who burn or suppress the writings of others believe in the power of these writings to influence or corrupt those who read them, and believe also that by suppressing or destroying the material they remove the danger caused by the opinions expressed. Both beliefs are probably much exaggerated. It is arguable that some forms of pornography act less as a stimulus to action than as an escape-valve, allowing socially unacceptable interests to be expressed in fantasy rather than in action. Other forms may reinforce and exploit tendencies already present in society, or in the individuals for example, the association of sex with violence. Strangely enough, the censors and would-be censors always believe themselves to be beyond corruption. But pornography and prudery share the same unhealthy attitude towards sex, as naughty or evil in itself. The prude dares not express his interest except through condemnation.

Censorship often operates through very arbitrary and rough and ready rules, and many anomalies could be cited. The effect of some recent legislation which insists that a work be considered as a whole, and allows account to be taken of literary merit, in any prosecution for obscenity, has been to encourage more intelligent discrimination. Unofficial censorship is often exercised by pressure-groups, religious and other, working upon library committees and the police, and organized protests against television presentations, etc. For lack of any other pressure, such groups can sometimes dictate policy. Since they are frequently fanatical and undiscriminating, they do not merit the unthinking support which they often receive from the churches. There is need for an enlightened Christian judgment to distinguish the trivial, the shoddy, the debasing from the authentic, the genuine, the human – not only in the field of pornography, for the corrupting influences in our society are by no means confined to that particular human interest. A society with the maturity to discriminate would have less need to be protected by censorship.

D. H. Lawrence, *Pornography and Obscenity*, 1929; J. S. Mill, *On Liberty*, 1859; Milton, *Areopagitica*, 1644; C. H. Rolph, ed., *Does Pornography Matter?* 1961; Denys Thompson, ed., *Discrimination and Popular Culture*, 1965.

JAMES A. WHYTE

Censure

Censure is the word used for a reprimand or punishment awarded by the Church for a breach of ecclesiastical discipline (q.v.).

Chalmers, Thomas

Thomas Chalmers (1780–1847), preacher, philanthropist, ecclesiastical leader, economist and theologian, became minister of the Tron parish, Glasgow, 1815, of St John's parish, Glasgow, 1819, professor of moral philosophy, St Andrews, 1823, professor of divinity, Edinburgh, 1828, leader of the Free Church of Scotland, 1843.

Chalmers believed that the uplift of the poor depended on the growth in them of strength of character based on Christian principle. Hence education, and primarily religious education, was the chief cure for social ills. In order to demonstrate how irreligion, demoralization and poverty could be overcome Chalmers divided the parish of St John's, Glasgow, with a population of some ten thousand persons, into twenty-five sections, to each of which he assigned an elder for spiritual oversight and a deacon whose duty it was to care for the material needs of the people. Day schools and Sunday schools were also established in the parish. The funds for the relief of the poor came from voluntary church offerings. As a poor-relief scheme this continued till 1837 when St John's parish was included in the city's normal scheme for poor relief. Its success in the initial stages was undoubted and Chalmers retained his faith in it to the end. Critics condemned the moral rigour of the sharp discrimination between deserving and undeserving poor, and suggested that the scheme tended rather to conceal than to relieve poverty since too much depended on the attention, judgment and humanity of the deacons. Chalmers certainly inspired a vast amount of personal service and showed what the Church could do for society when skilfully organized and enthusiastically led.

As an economist Chalmers was unduly deferential to the views of Adam Smith and still more of Malthus, and in his zeal to abolish pauperism and remedy the demoralization of the city masses he neglected the environmental and non-individual factors in their poverty. His great merit was his union of economic with religious and moral considerations. He was strongly opposed to any legal right of maintenance for the poor, but he believed in selecting and training his agents who should have knowledge of each case of need and make every effort to maintain family loyalties. Thus both directly, and also indirectly through his influence on the Elberfeld system in Germany, Chalmers inspired a school of thought which issued in the Charity Organization Society movement with its distinctive technique of social work.

DNB, IX, 1887, 449–54; S. Mechie, *The Church and Scottish Social Development, 1780–1870*, 1960, Chap. 4.

STEWART MECHIE

Character

Character means, generally speaking, a distinguishing mark, and hence when applied to human beings it denotes those qualities or traits that distinguish them from other human beings.

In psychology the meaning is slightly different; it is the basic behavioural pattern of the individual and its sub-structure, which gives a certain shape or bent to the personality, but is not the whole of it. Personality is thus the larger term. Character refers to the typical or 'characteristic' aspects of personality. *See* **Personality, Psychological Views of.** Character persists through time and manifests itself even when behaviour, for the time being, appears to be 'uncharacteristic' or inappropriate. Character in the psychological sense does help to distinguish one person from another, but it is not the unique mark of individuality. It may be identified by a system of traits which are often broadly shared.

Some psychologists, notably Gordon Allport, use the term as synonymous with 'personality', except that character has for them an *evaluative* connotation. This usage is more widespread in Europe than in the USA. Even here, however, the evaluative connotation persists in the diagnostic term 'character disorder', which originally referred to a volitional deficiency or disturbance, as distinguished from a cognitive or emotional disturbance. The term 'character disorder' has now largely fallen into disuse, and has been replaced by the term 'personality disorder', which is thought to be less evaluative when applied to such problems as alcoholism and delinquency.

The principle use of the term 'character' in present day psychology is in the phrase 'character types', a specialized version of the first, or narrow definition. Psychologists on the whole, and psychoanalysts in particular, have tended towards parsimony in character typology, as opposed to the literary tradition in which a large number of character types has been described (e.g., Plutarch and Bunyan).

In psychoanalytic thought, beginning with Freud and continued by Karl Abraham and Wilhelm Reich, and others, character types have been identified by the stages of psychosexual development – oral, anal and phallic. That is to say, the dominant personality pattern of adulthood, or character, is thought to be in large measure due to failure adequately to resolve conflicts during childhood stages of development. Hence character has a defensive quality about it, and responses typical of it may be evoked by real or imagined threats. Further some aspects become so ingrained or 'learned', that they appear constantly, even in the absence of threat. The phrase 'character armour' which means the outer defence which protects the more sensitive aspects of personality, indicates the basic quality of character. It also clearly shows the ambiguous nature of character as a defence. By enabling the individual to stand fast or move ahead during times of stress it has an adaptive function – hence the phrase in common speech 'strong character'. Such 'strength' of character may be a liability, however, in times which require flexible adaptation to changing circumstances. *See* **Psychoanalysis; Development**.

The character types described in the psychoanalytic literature are typified by behaviour originally associated with the so-called 'erotogenic' zones of the body, but which become displaced and generalized in adult life. Thus the oral character is optimistic, dependent, talkative and usually good-natured (he is seldom regarded as a 'strong character'). The anal character is retentive, meticulous, orderly, neat, and not overly communicative or outgoing. The phallic character (a term less frequently used) is aggressive, belligerent, often a braggart, and a 'lady-killer' (at least self-styled). These are normal defences. When these character types are severely threatened emotionally, other responses may appear, such as oral regression into panic or collapse, anal 'explosiveness', and phallic violence.

The stage of maturity is called the genital stage in psychoanalytic thought, but the term 'genital character', or one who has successfully resolved all psychosexual conflict, has not gained much currency.

Character types are not to be confused with the neurotic and psychotic syndromes also associated with the development stages, since these represent unsuccessful, regressive, defences against one's impulses and the environtiment. Character, on the other hand, is a relatively successful, that is, adaptive, defence.

Among other widely used character typologies is that devised by Karen Horney and presented in final form in her last book, *Neurosis and Human Growth* (1950). This character typology is based on a spatial-relational model, and consists of three fundamental types of 'movement' – towards people (dependency), away from people (fear of dependence), and against people (power).

Carl G. Jung set forth a famous typology in his *Psychological Types* (1923). Though the concepts 'introversion' and 'extroversion', which, form the bases of this typology, have come into common currency, the typology as a whole has not gained wide clinical acceptance.

Neither in the psychoanalytic types nor in Horney's or Jung's are character types thought to be found often in 'pure' form. Mixed types are the rule rather than the exception, but various segments of personality functioning may nevertheless be helpfully identified by means of a character typology.

Ethically speaking, two additional points are worth noting. The first is that character structure is regarded as relatively unalterable by psychologists. A response pattern may be modified to some extent, so as to be more adaptive, but the basic pattern cannot be radically changed.

The second point is that some character types have been much more highly prized in western culture in the past than have others – a fact which has sometimes unconsciously influenced moral judgments. The anal character has been valued in the recent industrial and commercial past; the phallic character was highly prized in the Middle Ages and Renaissance. Perhaps the oral character is coming to be valued more in our present age of communication. *See also* **Ego; Defence Mechanisms; Superego; Id**.

JAMES N. LAPSLEY

Chartism

Chartism is the name of the movement in Great Britain whose rallying point was the People's Charter (1838) which made six demands – manhood suffrage, vote by ballot, annual parliaments, abolition of the property qualification for members of parliament, payment of members of parliament and equal electoral districts. The impetus behind the movement was partly political, as these demands would suggest, and partly economic. There was disappointment among working men that the Reform Act of 1832 had failed to give them any political status and a swing-back to the method of political agitation after the triumph of the masters in the early 1830s, symbolized by the collapse of Owen's Grand National Trade Union and the transportation of the Tolpuddle martyrs. There was also economic pressure in the slump period after 1836, especially in the north of England, with unemployment and bitter resentment of the working classes against certain features of the English Poor Law of 1834. Similar factors operated in Scotland, but in several respects, for example, the temporary emergence of Chartist churches, Scottish Chartism may be regarded as almost an independent movement.

The main division among Chartists was between those who believed in moral force with the possibility of middle-class co-operation and those who were prepared to use physical force to gain the Charter's demands. Some of the leaders used language which went far beyond the six demands and seemed to imply measures like confiscation and bloodshed. Despite some sporadic outbreaks of violence, Chartism showed few of the features of a truly revolutionary movement, and after its inglorious failure at the presentation of a monster petition in 1848 it slowly died away. The energies it had engendered found expression in the co-operative and trade union movements, and in course of time all the demands of the Charter, with the exception of annual parliaments, were realized.

M. Hovell, *The Chartist Movement*, 2nd edn., 1925; L. C. Wright, *Scottish Chartism*, 1953.

STEWART MECHIE

Chastity

Chastity is the preservation of sexual purity according to one's state of life – virginity for the unmarried, continence for the widowed, loyalty to husband or wife for the married. Violation of chastity is fornication for the unmarried, adultery for the married (sometimes called double adultery if both parties are married). Perhaps in reaction against the laxity of the pagan world, the early Church tended to hold that sexual intercourse was permissible only with the positive intention of procreation (cf. Athenagoras, *Embassy on Behalf of the Christians*, 33). But with longer experience of human nature the Middle Ages recognized that it was at least 'a remedy against sin' for 'such persons as have not the gift of continency' and an expression and encouragement of the 'mutual society, help, and comfort' of the married couple. These three traditional purposes of matrimony, here quoted from the English *Book of Common Prayer* (Solemnization of Matrimony), are certainly in accordance with the teaching of the NT (cf. I Cor. 7.1–10 and Eph. 5.21–33). The reference in the latter passage to marriage as a 'great *mysterion* (Latin *sacramentum*)' related to Christ and the Church is probably responsible for the inclusion of marriage among the sacraments (Greek *mysteria*) in an age when the celibate life was highly esteemed. However, the Church has always taught, against such heretics as the Manichaeans, that salvation is open to the married as well as the continent (cf. Canon I of the Fourth Lateran Council, 1215).

As a virtue chastity is not merely, or even primarily, a matter of physical purity, but an aspect of the all-encompassing virtue of love. It is an expression of respect and honour for other human beings as children of God, and for one's own physical and psychical nature as the work of the Creator, redeemed in Christ (cf. I Cor. 6.9–20); and may be violated by other forms of indulgence besides the overtly sexual. (One may note that the *Rule* of St Benedict, which assumes monastic chastity, has to guard against temptations to indulgence in food and drink and personal possessions.) Hence the Sermon on the Mount applies the seventh Commandment, against adultery, to unlawful desires as well as the physical act (Matt. 5.27–28) – and the Prayer Book Catechism interprets it in the broad terms of 'to keep my body in temperance, soberness, and chastity' (American *Book of Common Prayer*, p. 289). Monastic chastity has a similar double meaning. Externally it means the preservation of the virgin (or widowed) state by the monk or nun; spiritually it is the devotion of all powers of body and soul to the service of God. For this reason, perhaps, it does not appear as a special vow in the oldest monastic customs, but as a necessary aspect of the monastic state – St Benedict, for instance, does not prescribe a separate promise of chastity, but includes it in the general promise of monastic behaviour (*conversatio*, or in later texts *conversio*; *Rule*, Chap. 58).

For a modern discussion, cf. J. A. T. Robinson, *Honest to God*, 1963, Chaps. 6 f.

E. R. HARDY

Childlikeness

Childlikeness and childishness are both terms in common use and need to be distinguished from one another. Childishness is used often to describe the habitually self-centred adult. This self-centredness can be seen in self-display, in making excessive demands on others for attention, affection and praise; it is seen in the man who considers everything he does to be of the utmost importance and judges every event and person in terms of benefit to himself. No-one finds it easy to free himself (and his associates) from all traces of childishness. Many would wish to make the Pauline words their own: 'When I was a child, I spoke like a child, I thought like a child, I reasoned like a child; when I became a man I put away childish ways' (1 Cor. 13.11).

After our Lord's example we take the image of a little child to symbolize the innocence, gaiety and trustfulness which should be found in a Christian life. The child has no ulterior motives; he does not want to be popular with all or accepted by some important power group. Childlikeness in an adult appears as foolishness to many when they see the cost of its generosity and truthfulness.

Childlikeness in an adult is known in a man who does not set out to turn events and persons to his own advantage; that is, he lives with an innocence associated with little children. The innocence of a child is largely due to ignorance and lack of experience; the innocence of an adult is maintained in spite of his knowledge of men and affairs and the ways to act for personal advantage. There is no such thing as a little child who is habitually innocent and admirable but there is much innocence seen in these four characteristics of childhood – trust, spontaneity, curiosity, growth. The childlike innocency of mature men and women is noted in these same characteristics. For example – philosophers go on trusting that human thinking is significant despite seemingly contradictory evidence; artists delight and enrich us with their spontaneous discoveries; scientists allow their love of truth to carry them into dark uncharted territory; theologians are ready to adjust their system of thought on account of growth in knowledge of the physical universe and on account of the changes in human behaviour brought about by the present urban civilization.

Churchmen are to protect the innocence (the childlikeness) of the Church. They must avoid giving by word and deed even the appearance that the Church has an ulterior motive in the interest taken in individuals and institutions. Childishness in church life is usually seen in either false church-centredness (i.e., when people are more concerned in preserving the institution than in the church's worship and mission) or in a false member-centredness (when the riches of corporate life are in danger through looking at church life from the individual member's point of view). Childlikeness is expressed in joyful worship and the ready acceptance of the church's mission in the wicked world which God loves.

R. E. C. BROWNE

Children

The Christian ethic regarding the child takes its start from the words of Jesus, 'Let the children come to me, . . . for to such belongs the Kingdom of God' (Mark 10.14, cf. 9.37). There follows a warning to those who cause 'one of these little ones' to sin. In the Epistles, children are commanded to honour and obey their parents (Col. 3.20); parents are commanded not to provoke their children (Col. 3.21) but to 'bring them up in the discipline and instruction of the Lord' (Eph. 6.4). These references support two basic concerns: the life and welfare of the child; and his spiritual and general nurture.

The concern for the life of the child began in the first century when the Church opposed the practices of abortion and of exposing the unwanted child. The Christian protest was the establishment of the orphanage, one of the earliest recorded charitable institutions. The practice of abandonment eventually disappeared. Abortion continues to be a problem, evidenced in debate over the question 'is it right that a child liable to severe birth defect should be brought to birth rather than the pregnancy terminated?'. The Roman Catholic Church affirms the right of all conception to issue in birth; Protestants vary in their positions.

The development of rural Europe seems to have presented little problem concerning the physical welfare of the child since overpopulation was prevented by high infant mortality and widespread plagues. Not until the rise of cities did the child become an economic problem, his plight becoming accentuated by the eighteenth century Industrial Revolution. Child labour became the lot of the poor. The Christian protest reached its height in the pleas of Maurice and his fellows in the Christian Socialist movement in England in the mid-nineteenth century. Slowly laws were enacted

limiting the hours and kind of work and protecting the safety of children at work. The USA still does not have a nationally effective law prohibiting child labour, and the neglect of migrant children working in the fields is as pathetic as that of the physically mature adolescent to whom society denies any satisfying work.

The crux of the problem in the enactment of child labour legislation has been the question of the right of the State to impose its will over the rights of the parent. In Thomistic theology, the parent has God-given rights and duties over the child, subject to the teaching of the Church but beyond the power of the State. Some religious adherents, notably Christian Scientists and Jehovah's Witnesses, refuse medical care for their children, thereby (in the eyes of other citizens) jeopardizing the right of the child to physical life.

An increasing problem, more often noticed in lower-socioeconomic groups, is the physical mistreatment of children by parents who themselves are under emotional stress. Mental cruelty, or emotional deprivation, is less easily discerned, even by the parent practising it, and therefore less easily treated. These deprivations point to an area in which Christian action is needed.

A second major concern is that of child-rearing. The Christian child is baptized under the new covenant and thereby belongs to Christ. The obligation is placed upon those who present him to bring him up as a Christian. Under 'nurture' comes the responsibility of parents for the discipline of the child. They are responsible for teaching him obedience, respect for adults, honour towards nation, and reverence for God.

Formal education did not affect the majority of people until the present century. The early Christians sent their children to pagan schools. The break-up of Roman culture and the slow development of northern Europe found learning preserved through the monasteries. The eighth-century educational edicts of Charlemagne had no more effect than the later letter of Luther to city magistrates urging them to establish schools. Education for the child began in Latin before the native language was used, and school teachers were sometimes brutal in their discipline. From Comenius (seventeenth century) to Froebel (nineteenth century) preceptive educators sought to bring more understanding of the child into the process of education. Today in the USA the questions concern education for special needs, and adequate as well as integrated education for Negro children.

Present problems in ethics stem from the various ways in which the child may be disadvantaged in the twentieth century. In many nations of the world this means sheer physical deprivation. The Christian community has addressed itself to this need through the relief programmes of the World Council of Churches and through its continuing world-wide mission of feeding, healing and teaching. In the USA the concern is largest (numerically) for the child in the city slums, usually deprived because of colour or national origin. Increasing adult unemployment, resulting from automation, will be reflected in both the physical and emotional neglect of children by one or both parents. Increasingly early maturation of girls combined with changing sexual mores brings more illegitimacy, the effects of which are less felt by the upper and middle classes where adoptive children are eagerly sought, than among lower income groups where children are now in the third generations of families receiving dependency help. The Church has faced these problems in terms of social settlement work, nurseries and counselling services of all kinds. Increasingly, it is stressing the centrality of the worshipping congregation as the centre from which the love of Christ is mediated to his children in their needs.

This brings up the ethical problems with which the culture faces the adolescent, restless and uncertain. who sees no future either with education or without it, and who escapes either into violence (gangs, destruction, robbery and violent sexual expression) or into despair expressed in dope addiction and alcoholism.

The child needs nurture through parents (or their surrogates) who love him, who give him a satisfying childhood and who help him to grow into maturity. He needs legal protection to safeguard life and health and he needs from his society the kind of education which will fit him for life therein.

IRIS V. CULLY

Chivalry

Originally meant a body of mounted warriors; then the qualities of the ideal warrior – valour and loyalty to both his lord and his own men; then the qualities of the ideal knight outside of battle – honour, disinterested justice tinctured with mercy, defence of the weak, and a great courtesy to women. The humanization of warriors was originally and largely the work of the Church, which linked the Germanic form of knighthood, conferred by prince or father, with religion and a moral code. By the end of the eleventh century it was becoming usual for the initiate to spend a whole night in solitary prayer in a church and on the next day to make his confession, receive communion, be publicly sermonized on his duties and be declared a knight in the name of the Trinity. The Crusades provided a broad outlet for such Christian chivalry. There was also a striking literary expression of it. Indeed, vernacular poetry as a contrived art began with epics of the famous knights, for example, Charlemagne, Roland, Arthur. In the twelfth century in southern France, which had more internal peace, a

legacy of Graeco-Roman culture, and a climate and leisure that encouraged refinement, the troubadours, singing in courts their own lyrics (of exquisite craftsmanship), virtually narrowed the notion of chivalry to the platonic love and devoted service of distinguished ladies. This celebration of 'courtly love', idealizing womanhood, was neither adopted nor condemned by the Church. It seems to have been influenced in some degree by the growing cult of the Mother of God, and by the preachers' theme of the beauty and purity of genuine love for God. Such poetry spread throughout France and into Italy, Germany and Austria; it helped to form the versification of Dante and his glorification of Beatrice. Some of it was wholly aesthetic, metrical variations on the *idea* of woman and the *idea* of love.

T. E. JESSOP

Choice

This is crucial for any theory of ethics, since moral action is in some sense choosing aright. Right choice depends on three factors: (1) a due appreciation of values and obligations, (2) right belief as to the facts, including the consequences of one's action, and (3) willingness to do what the agent thinks right. It has been held, for example, by Socrates, that it is impossible knowingly to choose what is wrong and that all wrong action is due to mistaken or confused belief, but this is hard to square with the facts that theologians have discussed under the heading of 'sin'. It does seem as if many wrong choices have to be explained by the fact that the strength of a person's desires are not always proportionate to the value he supposes their object to have. Most (perhaps even all) people want to do right, other things being equal, but they sometimes want other things much more and then they are tempted to sin.

According to one school of thought what we choose is always determined by the relative strength of our desires; but if more is meant by 'the strongest desire' than the desire that prevails, which would make the statement a tautology, this seems to imply too mechanical a view of the self and its determination by desires, as though the latter were a kind of physical force, and is hard to reconcile with the cases where a man seems after a struggle to act against his strongest desire. Here, if anywhere, it is supposed, we have the occurrence of free will (or choice not completely determined by antecedent causes). The self is regarded as something over and above its successive mental states which can, so to speak, stand apart from its desires and choose between them, and it is held that but for this undetermined intervention by the self we should always be governed by the desire felt most strongly at the time and there would be no such thing as moral action. It may be argued, however, that even on a determinist view we need not hold that we are always governed by the desire, or group of desires, felt most strongly, for we have no ground for saying that the causal efficacy of a desire needs always be in proportion to its felt strength. Determinism is the thesis that all our actions are determined, but it needs not imply that they are determined in any one particular way.

The whole idea of a mental action of volition has recently been questioned in some quarters, but while it is unreasonable to suppose that every voluntary act has to be preceded by a specific volition, one can hardly deny the occurrence as psychological events of decisions and efforts, and while we cannot limit voluntary action to action preceded by a choice, we can hardly regard an act as voluntary unless the agent would at least have done differently if he had chosen. Whether it could be regarded as free unless he could also have chosen differently without previous circumstances having been in any way different is a point in dispute between determinists and indeterminists.

A. C. EWING

Christendom Group

It is the designation of a group of Anglican thinkers and writers who produced a body of Christian social teaching in the years between 1930 and 1950. They inherited some of the tradition which stemmed from F. D. Maurice and the Christian socialists of the nineteenth century but they took an independent line both theologically and politically. The group was Anglo-Catholic in its religious allegiance and also had contacts with all Christian work for the radical re-ordering of social life and it had many avenues of expression and influence in non-religious movements.

The movement for which it stood and by which it became known could be epitomized in two main ideas. One was the recovery of a Christian judgment upon the structure of society and not only upon the behaviour of men within it. For this idea the phrase 'Christian Sociology' was coined, and in spite of some valid criticism directed to the validity of this hybrid term, it was stuck to for want of another which did justice to the group's aims. The other idea was expressed in the title of a precursor volume of essays, *The Return of Christendom*, introduced by Bishop Charles Gore in 1922. The group used the term 'Christendom' for its hope of a renewed Christian guidance in the secular spheres because it had some appreciation of the contribution of the Middle Ages in this field, and was in consequence often regarded as a backward looking body. The term also served to designate the quarterly journal *Christendom* which ran for twenty years with an editorial board composed, for most of its career, of M. B. Reckitt (editor), P. E. T. Widdrington, Ruth Kenyon, V. A. Demant and W. G. Peck. Later collaborators were David Peck, Patrick McLaughlin and Julian

Casserley. The journal had editorial links in the USA through Vida Scudder and Joseph Fletcher. The group also produced a volume of essays, *Prospect for Christendom* in 1945.

A further activity took the form of an annual summer school which continues to meet at this date (1966) after the demise of the journal in 1950. The group made an integral contribution to interdenominational church work for social justice – notably in the early Christian Social Council in England, and its members played a prominent part in the Malvern Conference during the second World War, presided over by Archbishop William Temple (*see* volume *Malvern*, 1941). Although the group is less influential than it was and has met with some resolute destructive criticism for its theological and sociological assumptions and is considered dead in many quarters, it still performs an unintentional service in providing students with a meagre addition to the rapidly diminishing stock of raw material for the thesis industry! This could mean either burial or hibernation.

For the historical background, *see* M. B. Reckitt, *From Maurice to Temple*, 1947.

V. A. DEMANT

Christian Social Movement

(England, nineteenth century. For the USA *see* **Social Gospel**.) The first phase is represented by the Christian Socialism of 1848–54. J. M. Ludlow, a layman acquainted with the Socialists and Social Catholics in France, was its founder; F. D. Maurice, its theologian and prophet; Charles Kingsley ('Parson Lot'), its popular interpreter. Closely associated were Thomas Hughes and E. V. Neale. While the official Church continued to tolerate prevailing utilitarian and laissez-faire doctrines, and seemed indifferent to the iniquitous social conditions and mounting discontent, this group sympathized with the aspirations of the unenfranchized working-class set forth in the People's Charter of 1838. They discerned potentially constructive ideas and forces in the agitation and revolutionary movements of the day, both in England and abroad. In the collapse of Chartism (1848) they saw a moment of opportunity, and in the Church's failure to seize it a betrayal of its faith and national responsibility. 'The Bible had been used,' said Kingsley, as 'an opium dose for keeping beasts of burden patient while they are being overburdened.' In taking the name Christian Socialist they propounded no precise economic doctrine. For them Socialism meant 'the science of partnership', and Christianity entailed a form of society in which men would work with and not against one another. Competition was not a law of the universe but a blasphemy. The Fatherhood of God, the incarnation and Christ's teaching about the Kingdom, indicate that human brotherhood is not a distant ideal but a present fact to be recognized and acted on. It is the Church's task to help men to see and become what they already are. Firmly rooted in theology, Christian Socialism demands something far more radical and comprehensive than a display of benevolence towards the less fortunate. The group, which met regularly for prayer and Bible study under Maurice, pleaded for truth and social justice in the spirit of a crusade. Their periodical *Politics for the People* (1848) was followed by *Tracts on Christian Socialism* (1850) and *The Christian Socialist* (1850–51). In one year (1850) Kingsley published two didactic novels, *Yeast* and *Alton Locke*, and a blistering denunciation of 'the political economy of mammon' in *Cheap Clothes and Nasty*. Meetings and conferences were held with Chartist workmen, and the way prepared for The Society for Promoting Working Men's Associations – in tailoring, building, iron founding, printing – visualized as a first step towards the extension of co-operation and profit-sharing in all industry. Since working men could not fairly be expected to exercise the greater responsibilities to which Christian Socialism pointed them without fuller educational opportunities, evening classes were organized and led to the founding of the Working Men's College in London. On the short view the movement was a failure. The popular journals were short-lived; the associations soon collapsed; the majority of church people continued to be either apathetic or hostile towards what they regarded as a group of cranks. On the long view it was not a failure. It initiated the Provident and Friendly Societies Act of 1852, exercised a formative influence on the Co-operative Movement and encouraged the growing trade unions. For a quarter of a century there was no organized group of Christian Socialists in the Church of England, but seeds which had been sown continued to grow. In 1877 S. D. Headlam founded the Guild of St Matthew which combined the theological outlook of Maurice with the high churchmanship of the Tractarians. Its members included Thomas Hancock, Charles Marson, H. C. Shuttleworth and Father Stanton. In 1899 (the year of *Lux Mundi*) the Christian Social Union was formed, a larger body with comparable standards and aims but devoted to a more protracted study and interpretation of fundamental Christian social principles. Bishop Westcott was its first president, and its leaders included Henry Scott Holland and Charles Gore. By the turn of the century one can speak not simply of the Christian Socialists of the Anglican Church but of the Christian Social Movement in England as a whole. For in 1893 (two years after *De rerum novarum*) the Catholic Social Union was inaugurated, followed by the Catholic Social Guild in 1909; in the late nineties Dr Clifford founded the Christian Socialist League; the first of the quasi-official 'social service unions' was formed by the Wesleyan Methodists in 1905; and by 1911 it was possible for representatives of all these denominational organizations to meet at Birmingham under the chairmanship of Bishop Gore to form the Interdenominational Conference of Social Service Unions. *See also* **Social Service of the Church.**

G. C. Binyon, *The Christian Socialist Movement in England*, 1931; N. C. Masterman, *John Malcolm Ludlow: The Builder of Christian Socialism*, 1963; C. E. Raven, *Christian Socialism, 1848–1854*, 1920; M. B. Reckitt, *Faith and Society*, 1932; *From Maurice to Temple*, 1947.

THOMAS WOOD

Church and State

'Church' here means a Christian community and its ecclesiastical organization; 'State' means a nation in its corporate capacity and organized for civil government. How ought these two institutions, and the claims that they make upon the allegiance of mankind, to be related? Every normal human being has to be a citizen of some State: a 'stateless' person is notoriously in an intolerable and pitiful condition. Although it is far from being the case that everyone has to belong to a church, yet, because churches exist in nearly every country in the world, relations between Church and State are a world-wide problem. The problem is an ancient one too, and it has been solved, in so far as it ever has been solved, in a variety of ways.

There have been many different kinds both of Church (papal, episcopalian, presbyterian, independent, etc.) and of State (monarchical, republican, democratic, totalitarian, etc.). These differences have affected the character and extent of their inter-relations. Then again, the problem has been posed differently according to whether the membership of a church was more or less coterminous with that of a state, or a church was a small minority within a state, or there were several churches or only one church in a state. Hence no simple description of, or prescription for, Church-State relations is possible.

Christians have naturally searched the Scriptures for guidance with regard to the circumstances in which they found themselves, but the Scriptures are not as helpful as might be wished. Scriptural authority has been claimed for many divergent doctrines. It may be that Christians have tended to extract from, or read into, the Bible what they wanted to find there. The OT, though it testifies that both civil government and ecclesiastical organization are divinely ordained, is not otherwise directly relevant, since Israel was both Church and State in one, not two distinct societies: there was no problem of the relation between them such as has arisen in the Christian era. After Pentecost the Church of Christ soon became a distinct society, but in the NT period it was never more than a small minority within the Roman Empire. All it looked for, so far as civil government was concerned, was freedom and security for its missionary work. There was no question yet of formal relations between civil government and ecclesiastical organization. Moreover, since history was not expected to endure for long, the Apostles had no occasion to theorize about future contingencies. They acknowledged that civil government was a necessary and beneficent institution and they prayed for the political authorities. It never occurred to them that Christians might one day have the opportunity of shouldering responsibility for the political order, that is, an opportunity of administering the State as well as the Church and a need to reconcile the two obligations. In spite of everything that commentators have said about a passage like Rom. 13.1–7, no one can say for certain what the Apostles would have thought if they had lived three centuries later than they did.

The relations of Church and State did not become as problematic, as in one way or another they have been ever since, until the Emperor Constantine, early in the fourth century, inaugurated between the two institutions an alliance which may have been too readily welcomed by the Church because of the relief it afforded from the threat of periodical persecutions. Before long, Christianity was made the official religion of the Empire.

From that time and right through the Middle Ages, the accepted idea was that Church and State, while in principle distinct societies, were united in one commonwealth (the *Corpus Christianum*): the distinction between them was to be seen chiefly in their separate hierarchies (pope and emperor, etc.) with their different functions and in the systems of law which they administered. After the schism between East and West there were *two* commonwealths of this kind: otherwise the main idea was not affected, except that in Byzantium the Emperor became the dominant partner. In the West there was ever-recurring tension or rivalry between the ecclesiastical and civil authorities, of which the Investiture Controversy is a famous example. All the same, there were in the Middle Ages undercurrents of misgiving about the accepted conjunction of Church and State. There were groups of enthusiastic Christians who alleged that, since the time of Constantine, the Church had succumbed, or been conformed, to the world, and had compromised its witness which should have been inspired by the Sermon on the Mount and the standards of the Primitive Church. There sprang up a number of non-conforming sects which were deemed to be heretical and were subjected to persecution, but they were

evidence that the post-Constantinian developments could be called in question on evangelical grounds.

At the Reformation the unity of the Western Church was broken up and there emerged a variety of national churches. Some continued to be in communion with the pope while claiming a considerable degree of national independence (e.g., Gallicanism in France); others – Lutheran, Reformed and Anglican – had rejected the papal suzerainty. The Lutherans and Anglicans, it may be noted, were much more willing than the Reformed (Calvinists) to let the civil power (the 'godly prince') manage the Church. Still the accepted idea was that in each country Church and State were one commonwealth: in England Richard Hooker was the classical exponent of this idea. Unity in religion was held to be necessary for the sake of the political coherence and stability of a nation.

On the other hand, the Reformation gave birth to new embodiments of the quite different idea that had found expression in the mediaeval sects, notably in the case of the Anabaptists. Their contention was that the true Church instead of veneering whole nations with a nominal Christianity, should consist of those who were called out of the world into separate communities – gathered churches instead of national churches. Churches therefore should not be established or depend on civil governments for support. Worldliness, compromise, even sacrilege, were inevitably entailed in establishment.

Nevertheless, until the French Revolution and the gradual disintegration of the *ancien régime* elsewhere, the union or alliance of Church and State was generally maintained in Europe, with a more or less precarious toleration of dissenting minorities. In the USA after some uncertainty, the separation of Church and State became an accepted principle. In European countries the civil and ecclesiastical authorities struggled for the upper hand. By the eighteenth century the former had the latter everywhere under control, as is strikingly illustrated by the fact that they induced the pope in 1773 to suppress the Society of Jesus.

The control of the Church by the civil power is known as 'Erastianism' among Protestants, as 'Josephism' or 'Febronianism' by Roman Catholics, and as 'Caesaro-papism' in the Eastern Church. When in the nineteenth century civil governments in Europe ceased to be professed upholders of the Church or recognizably Christian, perceptive churchmen began to wonder whether establishment was any longer tolerable, witness the Oxford Movement in England and the Disruption in Scotland. In fact, the idea of the union of Church and State was now being eroded, giving way to the pluralist or liberal idea of the State. According to this, the function of the State is to preserve law and order and the freedom of citizens to profess and practice any religion or none: in other words, its function is that of a policeman and not of a father, still less of a Father in God.

The logical outcome of this view would be the separation of Church and State, as in the USA or 'the free church in the free state' and no interference by either in the affairs of the other. But churches in Europe, which retained the allegiance of a majority of citizens, preserved much of their involvement with the State with their traditional prestige and privileges, or at least some of the signs and ceremonies of the old order were kept on in states for which in all vital matters pluralism had really become axiomatic.

It looked as though the coming norm for Church-State relations would be secular states, which would be religiously neutral, and churches, which would be voluntary societies left to their own devices. However, pluralism and liberalism, and the freedom of churches which they were supposed to secure, have been rudely shaken in the twentieth century by the growth of collectivism and the advent of totalitarianism. Totalitarian states seek to impose a secular faith on all their citizens, and tolerate churches only if they are content not to challenge or criticize it. Churches are expected to confine themselves to 'the salvation of souls' and preparation for the next world.

No self-respecting church can accept such limitations. 'A free church in a free state' is an attractive formula, but it leaves many questions unanswered and may be so interpreted as to be incompatible with the Christian duty to bear witness to God's will for the whole life of mankind. How can non-Christian statesmen be persuaded that churches have an inherent authority directly derived from God, that is, rights which the State does not confer but must be required to acknowledge? On what grounds can a church, whose freedom is being restricted by a state, convincingly and effectively base its resistance? Can the provinces of Church and State be so easily demarcated as liberalism presupposed? As soon as education, in which both Church and State have an essential interest, becomes universal and compulsory, either collaboration or conflict is inescapable. This is a particularly thorny subject even where Church and State are formally separate as in the USA.

Questions such as these have been driving Christians to do some fresh thinking. The novel characteristics of the modern state, the breakdown of the old forms of establishment, and the inadequacies of the liberal solution, mean that churches have to come to terms with an unprecedented situation and to articulate anew a doctrine of the Church and of the State and of their inter-relations. A critical reassessment of past attitudes and assumptions has been going on for some time both in the Roman Catholic Church and under the auspices of the World Council of Churches. A particular urgency is given to this undertaking by the uncertain prospects of churches in the new states of Africa and the East with their strongly nationalistic dispositions.

The claims of churches to unrestricted liberty will always be viewed with suspicion by statesmen who remember the attempts of churches in the past to monopolize power and influence, and also the intolerant and persecuting spirit with which their history has been compounded. Churches are unlikely to get accorded to them the freedom which they seek and which is necessary for their mission, until statesmen are satisfied that churches have irrevocably accepted the desirability of pluralist societies, wherever they may be had, and so can be depended on to defend the religious freedom of all citizens and not only their own. The Roman Catholic Church appeared to do this at Second Vatican Council. *See also* **State**.

Lord Acton, *Essays on Church and State*, 1952; K. Barth, *Church and State*, ET, 1939; J. C. Bennett, *Christians and the State*, 1958; D. A. Binchy, *Church and State in Fascist Italy*, 1941; W. Adams Brown, *Church and State in Contemporary America*, 1936; S. Parkes Cadman, *Christianity and the State*, 1924; A. J. Carlyle, *The Christian Church and Liberty*, 1924; *Church and State*, Report of the Archbishop's Commission, 2 vols, 1935; M. Cruikshank, *Church and State in English Education*, 1963; O. Cullmann, *The State in the New Testament*, 1957; C. Dawson, *Religion and the Modern State*, 1935; F. Dvornik, *National Churches and the Church Universal*, 1944; S. Z. Ehler and J. B. Morrall, *Church and State through the Centuries*, 1954; N. Ehrenström, *Christian Faith and the Modern State*, 1937; T. S. Eliot, *The Idea of a Christian Society*, 1939; J. N. Figgis, *Churches in the Modern State*, 1941; P. T. Forsyth, *Theology in Church and State*, 1915; C. F. Garbett, *Church and State in England*, 1950; F. Gavin, *Seven Centuries of the Problem of Church and State*, 1938; E. B. Greene, *Religion and the State: the Making of an American Tradition*, 1941; A. Keller, *Church and State on the European Continent*, 1936; J. Lecker, S. J., *Toleration and the Reformation*, ET, 1960; C. C. Marshall, *The Roman Catholic Church in the Modern State*, 1928; D. L. Munby, *The Idea of a Secular Society*, 1963; A. V. Murray, *The State and the Church in a Free Society*, 1958; J. C. Murray, S. J., ed., *Religious Liberty: an end of a Beginning*, 1966; T. M. Parker, *Christianity and the State in the Light of History*, 1955; H. M. Relton, *Religion and the State*, 1937; P. C. Simpson, *The Church and the State*, 1929; L. Sturzo, *Church and State*, ET, 1939; W. Temple, *Christianity and the State*, 1928; E. Troeltsch, *The Social Teaching of the Christian Churches*,

ET, 1931; A. R. Vidler, *The Orb and the Cross*, 1945; M. A. C. Warren, *The Functions of a National Church*, 1964.

A. R. VIDLER

Civilization. see Culture, Society and Community.

Classes, Social. see Social Class.

Clement of Alexandria

Clement of Alexandria (Titus Flavius Clemens d. *c*. 215) was head of a school of Christian philosophy at Alexandria where he began to teach *c*. 190. The son of pagan parents and apparently an Athenian by birth he received the regular rhetorical and philosophical education of his time, but only ceased his search for truth when at Alexandria he became a Christian under the tutelage of Pantaenus. A man of diverse and extensive learning, Clement was an apologist for Christianity and a teacher of Christian wisdom, whose inclination and circumstance alike led to interpret Christian teaching in terms of the philosophical culture of his time. He fled Alexandria during the persecution under Septimius Severus (*c*. 202), and died probably in Asia Minor.

Clement's moral teaching is based upon the idea that the Christian life is a growth of man into the likeness of God – a likeness inseparable from the contemplative knowledge of God in love. The preconditions of the achievement of this goal are twofold: the freedom of man, which Clement, like Origen later, upholds against the Gnostics; and the saving activity of God in his Logos, who is the Image of God and the universal Teacher and Saviour of men. The man who believes in the Logos-made-flesh sets his foot on the path of salvation; but this is fully realized only when faith turns into knowledge and man is himself divinized through participation in the Logos-Image.

The way to this goal – the state of the 'true gnostic' – lies in the cultivation of virtue as an habitual state. In his delineation of the virtuous life, Clement draws not only upon Scriptures and the tradition of Christian moral teaching, but also on the resources of Stoic, Platonic and Aristotelian moral philosophies. In his account of the qualities which mark the life of the believer – justice, temperance, kindness, purity, patience – Clement includes the Stoic ideal of exemption from passion (*apatheia*), and makes reference to the practical usefulness of the Aristotelian principle of the 'mean'. The Christian seeks a life which is harmonious and balanced in its accord with the truth of man's nature and destiny. This means, in the first instance, a turning towards spiritual reality and a detachment from externals. But Clement is no puritan, or rigorist: he speaks no condemnation of the good things of man's material and social life, but requires self-discipline and temperance in their use and enjoyment.

Clement's teaching has a rationale, but it is not, or does not give the impression of being, a system. His high conception of the Christian's calling is combined with a nice pastoral sense, and his method is always that of eloquent persuasion. His teaching represents the first systematic attempt to show that the Christian ideal is the fulfilment of the ideals and hopes of pagan wisdom; and at the same time it marks the beginnings of the ascetic-mystical tradition in Christian morals which Origen and the Cappadocians were to develop.

R. A. NORRIS, JR

Collective Bargaining.
see Industrial Relations; Power.

Collective Security.
see International Order.

Collectivism

Every society seeks to preserve itself. It expects to outlast the individuals within it. Society requires individuals to adjust, to fit in, to perform a social function, and to make sacrifices (e.g., taxation, willingness to die in military service).

Society finds ways to impose its values and enforce its will upon individuals. Such enforcement is most effective when it is unpremeditated and its sanctions are self-enforcing; individuals internalize the attitudes and mores of the society without realizing that they act under compulsion. When the social consensus is less than complete the society must rely upon law and punishment to enforce compliance.

Collectivism is thus one primary element in human experience. It appears to be the basic assumption of men in primitive tribes and ancient empires. Man's self-awareness comes through the tribal self, the corporate personality. The Bible includes many echoes of primitive collectivism: blood-guiltiness for crime falls upon the tribe, and vengeance is executed against the tribe of the offender; the sins of fathers are visited upon children; the misdeeds of kings bring retribution upon the people.

The individualistic protest against collectivism emerged in two major points of the western heritage: the Hebrew prophet and the Socratic questioner both challenged their societies and brought to mankind a new awareness of the person, whose freedom and responsibility transcend the demands of the society. *See* Individualism. Despite these protests, collectivist attitudes prevailed over individualism, to varying degrees, through the history of the Roman Empire and mediaeval feudalism.

Modern history has brought an increasing intensity to both individualism and collectivism. To the extent that individualism has cut off man from rootage in tradition and community, it has contributed to the rise of new collectivisms. These have been of three major types.

(1) *Nationalism*. The modern revolutions, which have overthrown old tyrannies for the sake of freedom, have often turned into new nationalisms, which have subjected man to the State. The movement from the French Revolution to the Napoleonic era is the most obvious example of a familiar pattern.

(2) *Communism*. Although the early Marx advocated a humanistic personalism, official Communism has submerged persons to the conflict of classes and parties. Particularly under Stalinism Communism became a fanatical collectivism.

(3) *Nazism*. Opposing bourgeois individualism and Communism alike, Nazism combined a romantic philosophy of blood-and-soil, a vicious racism, and a refined technique of tyranny to achieve a collectivism unsurpassed in history for ruthlessness and cynicism.

Any of these modern collectivisms may – and Nazism must – be totalitarian. Totalitarianism is the form of collectivism that uses modern technology and cruelty to extend its tyranny into the total life of man, demanding that family, church and inner attitudes of individuals serve its demands.

Collectivist impulses operate also in 'free societies'. Political forces, sometimes claiming to support individualism, seek to stifle freedom and dissent, by methods of propaganda and character defamation. In a quite different process the needs of a technical society require collective action in the corporation, the labour union, the military forces and civil government. The individualistic ethos may be transformed into the patterns of conformity that produce the 'other-directed social character' (David Riesmann) or 'the organization man' (W. H. Whyte, Jr).

Collectivism is a real threat to freedom and personal integrity, but it is not adequately answered by naive individualism. Contemporary social psychology and cultural anthropology have shown that the isolated individual is an unreal fiction. Yet both personal and social health require freedom from collective tyranny.

The Christian doctrine of man-in-community emphasizes that man becomes human only in personal relations, but that the person is a unique self, never simply a fragment of society. Persons can live in a responsible freedom that is not understood either by collectivism or by individualism.

Hannah Arendt, *The Origins of Totalitarianism*, rev. edn., 1963; John C. Bennett, *Christians and the State*, 1958; Karl Popper, *The Open Society and its Enemies*, 1954.

ROGER L. SHINN

Colonialism. *see* Imperialism.

Colour Bar

This is the prohibition against the participation of a racial group, identifiable by colour, in the institutions or social life of the dominant group. The term has been used primarily in colonial situations, although it can logically be used of any situation where segregation is based on colour. The colour bar may be applied to political, economic, professional, religious or social situations. Often it has been used by a privileged enclave of white men living in the midst of a largely coloured society. *See* **Race Relations; Segregation.**

ROGER L. SHINN

Communism, Ethics of Marxist

According to the modern textbooks of Marx-Leninism, ethics or morality has a clearly defined subordinate role to play in the promotion of social revolution and the construction of a socialist society. The source of this view is Lenin's application of the teachings of Marx to the Russian Revolution in 'The tasks of the Youth Leagues' and in numerous scattered references throughout his writings. Ethical standards in this view emerge from and serve the requirements of the particular economic conditions and structures which produce them. All morality therefore expresses the interests and struggles of a particular class. The idea of an eternal moral order whether based on human reason or the commandments of God is a deception practised by the possessing classes in defence of their privileged positions.

Communist ethics then is subordinate to the revolutionary struggle. It repudiates and condemns the capitalist and feudal social orders as based on exploitation and justifies all steps necessary to bring about their destruction and replacement by a socialist society. Morality is discipline and inner commitment in this struggle. Good and right actions are those which promote this end. Otherwise stated ethics and morality belong to the superstructure not to the basis of society. Effective social change takes place when the relations of production shift and economic power falls into new hands. Political structures, culture, philosophy and ethics rise from a new economic base as a reflection of it. In the words of Marx: 'It is not the consciousness of men which determines their existence but on the contrary it is their social existence which determines their consciousness.' Moral judgments are one of the areas in which men become conscious of conflicts of economic power and fight them out. This is regarded as necessary and right, but not fundamental.

Communist ethics then depend for their content on the stage of the working classes' progress towards socialism. In a capitalist society they correspond to the strategy and tactics of revolutionary activity leading towards the capture of power by the 'exploited classes' under the leadership of the Communist Party. In colonial or underdeveloped countries an ethic of collaboration with nationalist forces and a positive attitude towards liberal democratic ideals, cultural and even religious traditions may be called for. After the Communist seizure of power, however, primary moral obligation becomes constructive and defensive. This means first the conversion of the whole society to 'a spirit of collectivism, industry and humanism' (Programme of the XXII Congress of the Communist Party of the Soviet Union). This involves negatively a continual ideological struggle carried out by the Communist Party to eliminate 'individualist' or 'unscientific' attitudes and 'religious superstition'. Positively it calls for the creation in spirit of 'a new man who will harmoniously combine spiritual and moral purity and a perfect physique' (XXII Congress), for whose development the economic and political conditions are already present. This new man as recent literature describes him will be imbued with an ethos of unstinting labour, a primary concern for public life and welfare, a comradely solidarity with his fellow workers, and with working people everywhere, a love of his country and the entire community of socialist lands, a devotion to the building of Communism in the whole world, and 'an uncompromising attitude to the enemies of Communism, peace, and the freedom of nations' (XXII Congress). The content of this ethic is in many ways similar to the democratic idealism of many western lands. Honesty, modesty, family loyalty and responsibility are all given their due place along with the virtues named above. Early adventures with relaxed marriage and divorce laws have given way to an almost Puritan discipline more accentuated in China than elsewhere, which emphasizes comradely equality and plays down sexual differences. The purpose and direction of this whole ethic, however, is the building of a Communist society. All else is subordinate to this.

This official ideological picture of Communist ethics, however, leaves certain elements out which belong to the dynamic of Marxism as it has influenced modern society. One of these is the problem of freedom and authority, of resistance and submission, within the framework of a Communist Party or a Communist-dominated state. Marxist theory avoids this question; Marxist practice is constantly preoccupied with it. Marx and Engels in *The Communist Manifesto* proclaimed that the Communist Party is nothing but the vanguard of the whole proletariat, that its task is only to bring into focus and express in action the actual interests of this class as a whole. The question arose immediately then in the First International to what extent the will of the proletariat should be determined democratically. Marx

chose the way of theoretical discipline at the cost of democracy. His political thought in his later years moved more toward the tactics of power conquest than toward the building of a community of mind and will with the working classes. Nevertheless the vision of an aroused revolutionary proletariat forming its mind in open meeting and fighting for a better society through mass action dominated a large part of the movement which called itself Marxist in succeeding generations. Social democratic parties the world over have worked successful, if partial, revolutions in the Marxist spirit and on the basis of a Marxist analysis, although these parties have specifically rejected Leninist Communism.

The extreme form of party discipline from which the Communist movement has suffered is due, however, primarily to Lenin although it is being attacked in a number of Communist countries today as Stalinism. Lenin limited democracy in the party to the provisional discusion of tactical matters. He openly argued that the proletariat would never develop a revolutionary consciousness if left to its own devices. The Party alone governed by the theories of Marx was capable of bringing the working classes to a proper understanding of their revolutionary destiny and the steps necessary to achieve it. Dogmatic unity in the interpretation of Marx was therefore essential in Lenin's scheme. Free debate was in order about immediate steps in Party policy but once the Party had decided rigorous unity was in order. Recalcitrant opponents in the organization were for Lenin dangers to the success of the cause.

Under Stalin and the Chinese Communists this Party discipline was further refined. The Chinese theoretician Liu Shao-Ch'i raised 'intra-party struggle' to a basic principle of operation although he tried to protect it from being directed against personalities. This struggle for Liu is the continuing effort of the Party to define the central line of its policy against errors to the left and right, to help comrades to purge themselves of such errors and to expose enemies within the Party. Liu combines this with a concept of the personal self-discipline and development of a Communist Party member. The initial decision, he points out, does not make a man a good Communist. It is only in the course of ceaseless struggle against counter-revolutionaries that he learns to know his enemy, himself, and the laws of social development and revolution. In the process he himself develops into a more effective and humble servant and leader of the masses.

All of this is expressed in the Chinese Communist Party and formerly in the Soviet Union by the process of criticism, self-criticism and confession. This takes place usually in small groups where the members examine each other's attitudes, actions and thoughts and are encouraged to confess any faults of which they may have been guilty. It is here that the most intimate ethos of the Communist Party is formed and deviation most thoroughly rooted out. Confessions may be written and rewritten many times until they satisfy the group and its leader. Innermost attitudes are expected to be bared and corrected. A variant form of this collective discipline of the spirit is described by Arthur Koestler in his story of the Moscow purge trials, *Darkness at Noon* (E T, 1946).

Outside of China since the death of Stalin this whole concept of Party discipline has, however, been called in question. Khrushchev's denunciation of Stalin's crimes dealt a body blow to a concept of the infallible correctness of Party leadership in matters of tactic and policy. Resisters have been rehabilitated and have become heroes. Even a single strategic direction for the socialist revolution as a whole has become problematic in a polycentric Communist world. The problem of developing an ethic of legitimate resistance and structures for its recognition within the Party has become urgent for the Communist future.

A second basic problem in Communist ethics concerns the role of the Marxist understanding of man. Although Marx throughout his life passionately rejected every appeal to standards of justice and right on the grounds that they were ineffectual and abstract, the starting point of his earliest works was the outraged conviction that man has been alienated from his true humanity by the conditions of society in which he lives. To discern and serve the laws of history whereby this alienation could be overcome was his life's work. Marx's humanism was generic rather than personal. In this he differed from his older colleague, Feuerbach, whose understanding of religion as illusory compensation for man's alienation he adopted. Collective man was intended in Marx's view to dominate nature and overcome all obstacles to his 'free conscious self-activity'. He found in the idea of a creator God an intolerable limitation upon this collective man. To be free man must have created himself through his own labour and owe his existence to no outside reality. To become free the most completely dehumanized portion of mankind must overthrow completely the existing order of things. Religion is a hindrance to this revolutionary self-liberation because it provides an imaginary fulfilment which dulls the will of man to work for change. It is the people's opium.

This humanism is still a basic motivation of the Communist movement however obscured it may be beneath a dialectical materialist jargon. Lenin expressed its paradox most radically when in *State and Revolution* he refused to plan for or speculate about the time when the State would wither away in a Com-munist society, and yet expressed his absolute faith that this time would come. Lenin's whole policy moved toward dictatorship, centralism and bureaucratic control. And yet he believed that man in the new society he was creating would be so transformed that the necessity for State control would disappear with the certainty of a scientific prediction.

This paradox also was driven to its extreme and discredited in the policies of Stalin. The glorification of collective human achievement went hand in hand with the grossest inhumanities. The result has been in the post-Stalin era in Russia and Eastern Europe a new search for the meaning of humanity which has been forced to question the adequacy even of Marx himself. The rising popularity of existentialist writers in Eastern Europe outside of Russia and the signs of a new dialogue with the Christian Church constitute admission that human nature is not the product of social existence but shows dimensions both of greatness and of bestiality which are constant in capitalist and socialist societies. Soviet and other writers are re-emphasizing the subtlety and variety of personal relations over against the collective. The one overriding end which justified every means – the building of the socialist society – is being slowly and subtly modified by recognition that the goals of human life are various and that some inhumanities are justified by no end they seek. Marx's protest against inhumanity plus long experience with the limitations of his vision for man are raising anew for Communists everywhere the question which Marx thought he had answered: What is truly human?

Ernst Bloch, *Das Prinzip Hoffnung*, 1954–7; F. Engels, *Ludwig Feuerbach and the End of German Classical Philosophy*, E T, 1934; and *The Origin of the Family, Private Property and the State*, E T, 1902; R. Garaudy, *From Anathema to Dialogue*, 1966; V. I. Lenin, *What is to be Done?* E T, 1933; *State and Revolution*, E T, 1919; and *Materialism and Empirio-criticism*, E T, 1947; Karl Marx, Economic and Philosophical Manuscripts (in *Marx's Concept of Man*, by Erich Fromm, 1961); K. Marx and F. Engels, *The German Ideology*, E T, 1947; and *The Communist Manifesto*, ed. by D. Ryazanoff, 1963; Liu Shao-Ch'i, *On the Party*, E T, 1950; *On Inner-Party Struggle*, E T, 1951; and *How to be a Good Communist*, E T, 1951; Mao Tse-Tung, *The New Democracy*, E T, 1954; *On Contradiction*, E T, 1952; and *On Democratic Dictatorship*, E T, 1951; The Programme of the XXII Congress of the Communist Party of the Soviet Union, 1962.

C. C. WEST

Community. *see* **Culture, Society and Community.**

Compensationism

This is a moral system which resembles tutiorism in favouring the safer course where there is doubt the obligatoriness of an act. The name indicates that the doubt whether the law applies must be weighed against the person's imperfect understanding of the law, and suitable compensation made for the latter.

Compromise

Anyone acquainted with Roman Catholic moral theology might expect to find under this heading a discussion of the process of making mutual concessions in a question of litigation to avoid a law suit, and the attitude taken to it by Common Law. But for a Protestant the problem of compromise may arise when he first wonders whether the ethical teaching of Jesus (which depends for its cogency on acceptance of his ministry as bringing near the rule or Kingdom of God, and his ethic as therefore one of grace) can be 'applied' directly to the tangled structures of life in economics, industry and politics where a Christian is placed by God cheek by jowl with men of all faiths and none, and has to act with them and not as an isolated individual.

This problem can be avoided by those who think that timeless rules of conduct can be extracted from the Bible by extrapolating texts from their contexts and applying them directly to current situations. Or there are those who assume that there is a simple will of God for any situation which can be certainly known by the 'inner light', or guidance of the Holy Spirit, a position characteristic of many Quakers and others. A variant of this is the four absolutes preached by the Moral Re-armament movement – absolute honesty, love, truthfulness and purity – as simple possibilities in any situation. Another one is what the ethical teaching of Bultmann amounts to, namely, the assertion that by radical obedience we may know in each situation what we would like for ourselves and therefore how to love our neighbour in it, for we are commanded to love him as ourselves. All these positions in effect look at life in a purely personal way; they result in a Christian taking a simple personal stand on a narrow range of issues which in turn have been over simplified, and having little or nothing to contribute to the problems of Christian obedience in the daily life of the world's work and politics.

To take these collective structures or orders of creation seriously is to be concerned with the facts of the empirical situation and an estimate of the likely consequences of possible lines of action. It is to evaluate these possible consequences by Christian criteria, and to choose what line of action, all things considered, is the best *in the circumstances*. This is what casuistry tries to do. It is not content to say

that it is the spirit in which something is done that matters; it wants to find out what is the right thing to do in the circumstances. It is to this that much recent Protestant theology has addressed itself, particularly through the Ecumenical Movement. But to call the result *compromise* is misleading. It could only be that if one was trying to evade obvious Christian duties, and find out the minimum one must do to avoid 'mortal sin'. This is precisely what at the Counter-Reformation casuistry did do, and it has never quite recovered from the bad name it got then. In fact every Christian must be a casuist unless he thinks that he can be guided by divine inspiration without the use of his moral reasoning powers and without having to be concerned with empirical facts. If he succeeds in finding out what to do, it is the right thing to do in the circumstances and not a compromise. He may err in judgment about the facts, his judgment may be distorted by sin, he may fail to achieve or practise what he knows in theory he ought to do. The Christian is not infallible or sinless. That is why he knows he is justified by faith not by moral achievement. That is the point of Luther's well-known *pecce fortiter*. But it is still true that in principle to find the right action in a particular situation is not a compromise but a fulfilling of the will of God in that situation. To think otherwise is to assume that the Christian ethic applies only to a perfect world and cannot be brought to bear, however tangentially, on the intricate structures of life, with their entail of achievement, frustration and sin in which human life is set.

On 'compromises' necessary in every historical decision, *see* F. Le Roy Long, Jr, *Conscience and Compromise*, 1954; and R. Ullmann, *Between God and History*, 1959, a Quaker criticism of Quaker theology on this point.

RONALD PRESTON

Concubinage

Concubinage is the habitual practice of sexual intercourse between a man and a woman who are not married to one another. Co-habitation may or may not be associated with it. Concubinage of the clergy was a problem for many centuries after clerical celibacy had been made compulsory in the Church of the West.

HERBERT WADDAMS

Concupiscence

The word 'concupiscence' is most frequently used as meaning the immoderate desire to satisfy the sexual physical appetite. The word is also used to denote desires which are satisfied by the things of this world. Christians, in all ages, stress the danger of allowing any desire to become strong enough to dull sensitiveness to the divine promptings and awareness of the needs of fellow human beings. In western Christianity there has always been an undue fear of fleshly and worldly desires. In consequence of this fear warnings against concupiscence have been frequent, and warnings of this sort are spiritually bad for those who give them too often and for those who hear them too often. Desires are mastered by a mature Christian love for the objects which would satisfy them.

R. E. C. BROWNE

Conduct. *see* Act, Action, Agent.

Confession

Confession is the acknowledgement of one's guilt to others, or to God. NT enjoins the practice: 'Confess your sins to one another, and pray for one another, that you may be healed' (James 5.16). In this passage, as is usual in the NT, forgiveness and healing are closely associated. Modern psychotherapy has rediscovered the healing effects of confession. To make confession and to hear words of forgiveness can be a release from guilt-feelings and from the moral paralysis that sometimes goes with them. On the other hand, an over concern about confessing one's sins can be a mark of scrupulosity (q.v.) and there can even be a kind of perverted boasting of one's sins. The Church provides for confession in various ways: (1) general confession is provided for in public worship, and is designed to promote self-examination, repentance and the assurance of absolution; (2) the sacrament of penance provides for private confession to a priest, who gives to the penitent counsel, penance and absolution; (3) sometimes ecclesiastical discipline has required a public confession from an offender, but this would be rare nowadays. *See* Absolution; Forgiveness; Penance.

EDITOR

Conflict of Duties

Strictly speaking this phrase is a misnomer because, if something really is our duty, it cannot conflict with any other duty, but the phrase is used to signify cases where there are moral reasons in favour of each of two or more incompatible actions. I think this is best discussed in terms of a phrase coined by Sir David Ross, *prima facie duties*. A *prima facie* duty is a possible action for which there would be a compelling moral reason in the absence of any moral reason against it, so that it is always obligatory to fulfil a *prima facie* duty if it does not conflict with any other. Thus it is a *prima facie* duty not to lie, but this may conflict with a *prima facie* duty to save a man from being murdered. The *prima facie* duties are sometimes regarded as ultimate, sometimes as dependent on the good they produce; also we think of ourselves as having *prima facie* duties which put us under special obligations to further the good of, for example, relatives rather than the equal good of a stranger. It is

arguable that they can all ultimately be explained on utilitarian grounds, but even if this is true – and it would be much disputed – the above account comes much nearer the way in which we usually think in practical life than does pure Utilitarianism (even if the good is conceived as wider than pleasure). No philosopher has succeeded in producing adequate general rules for dealing with conflicts of duties, probably because this is intrinsically impossible. Sometimes we can see quite clearly that one obligation is more weighty than another, but in many cases it is a matter of difficult individual judgment where one could not venture to condemn anybody who disagreed with one. The sharpest and most obvious cases of conflict of duties occur in war, but they are present in a lesser degree throughout life if only because time and resources devoted to furthering one end have to be taken from the time and resources devoted to furthering another.

A. C. EWING

Confucian Ethics

Even after considering variations and eras of decline, Confucian ethics, in range of time and numbers of persons influenced, is perhaps the most extensive system known to history. Moreover, its interlocking with significant structures of the family and of the State, its centrality in a millennial culture and education intimately related both to the family and to the State, added to the majestic continuity of Confucian ethics and its awesome pervasiveness within Chinese society. Confucius, working in the sixth century BC, took the stand of a compiler, even a restorationist, of principles already dimmed in contemporary confusion. Confucianism's supremacy and official status broke down only from 1905. About 1928 it was displaced, in sociopolitical and educational realms, by Sun Yat-Sen's *Three People's Principles*; and utterly, about 1949, by Marxist-Leninist ideology and texts.

We attend centrally to the major thinker-authors of 'orthodox' Confucianism: Confucius and early followers whose work blended with his own in the Classics, so thoroughly familiar to every official whose status was derived from knowledge of them and to every literate person austerely taught to read from them until about 1920; then Chu Hsi and the Neo-Confucianists who from the eleventh century onward provided on the one hand a more substantial metaphysical background, on the other a somewhat more specific pattern of conduct for a larger range of persons in the historic Empire. But the continuity of basic ideas and of social tradition was massive, and the early Classics remained basic, even if seen by intellectuals in a new philosophic perspective and applied by Neo-Confucian teachers in restated prescriptions for daily behaviour.

To this day Chinese and other scholars in this field confute one another, now by boasts or accusations that Confucian ethics is both rationalistic and humanistic, again by claims or praise that it is cosmically and quasi-religiously supported. The problem arises radically in fundamental terminology and explication, and is rooted in the contrasting cultural backgrounds of Confucian and of Christian (or other religious) concepts and language. Is the first, comprehensive, supreme virtue of *Jên* – which is, indeed, the essence of man and *a fortiori* of the good man – to be understood and therefore translated as benevolence, magnanimity, love in the sense of *agape*; or as human-heartedness, man-to-man-ness, true humanity? Does *T'ien*, the Heaven which is in the background of man's existence and is more specifically related to his moral life, carry the meaning of Nature, of the Universe, or of God? Content and tone of great terms like these may vary even more in the Chinese language than in the English, if that is possible. But a timorous generalization must be attempted. The human concern overwhelmingly predominant in *Jên* tends to be social and practical, though at its highest the quality is spiritual, with origin and sanction ascribed to a moral cosmos. *T'ien* is Nature, comprehensive and ultimate, linked with human life and considered often to possess qualities of the philosopher's or moralist's deity, infrequently those of God in a Christian or broadly religious sense.

Let Confucius and his disciples speak for themselves, in translations slightly adapted from Lin Yu-T'ang: '*Jen* is the denial of self and response to the right and proper.' (Specifications of 'the right and proper' abound in rigorous subordination of the common man to the ruler and his officials, juniors to seniors, females to males; and in ritualization of moral behaviour.) '*Jên* is to love your fellow-men.' 'Repay kindness (good) with kindness (good), but evil with firm justice.' 'What you do not wish others to do to you, do not unto them.' (The principle of reciprocity is prominent in Confucius' formulas for the practice of *Jên*. Its calculating quality is contrasted by Chu Hsi with the naturalness of *Jên*, though not devalued.) Chu Hsi wrote, in language here slightly modified from that of his translator and expositor J. P. Bruce, whose mind was fully formed in the western tradition: '*Jên* is the principle of origin, one of the divine attributes . . . the positive and active mode of the Supreme ultimate.' '*Jên* is the vital impulse. It is after we have received this vital impulse, and are thereby in possession of life, that we have righteousness, reverence, wisdom, and sincerity. From the point of view of priority, *Jên* is first; from the point of view of greatness, *Jên* is greatest.' '. . . all evil is good originally, but it has lapsed.' 'The object of the sages was to

teach men to reverse the evil, attain to the Mean, and rest therein.' '*Jên* is man.' 'The Mind of the Universe is *Jên*.'

There is no recent treatise on Confucian ethics as such. Indeed, ethics was hardly a distinct category in Chinese life and thought, despite the strongly moral and didactic factors in Chinese society and letters. The tradition combined general thought and philosophy, ethics, history, statesmanship, in one indeterminate *corpus*, even comprising belles-lettres composed by Confucian scholars. Among convenient doors of approach are the following: J. P. Bruce, *Chu Hsi and His Masters*, 1923; Chu Hsi, *The Philosophy of Human Nature*, tr. by J. Percy Bruce, 1922; Clarence Day, *The Philosophers of China*, 1962; Ernest R. Hughes, *Chinese Philosophy in Classical Times*, 1942; Lin Yu-T'ang, *The Wisdom of Confucius*, 1938.

M. SEARLE BATES

Conscience

This is a key term in Christian ethics, a foundation of traditional moral theology, and a word familiar in popular speech. Traditionally it has not been thought of by Christians as a special faculty, or as an intuitive 'voice of God within us', but simply as 'the mind of man making moral judgments'. This is how St Thomas Aquinas (q.v.) classically defined it. Strictly speaking conscience decides in a particular case what is to be done or avoided in the light of a grasp of general moral principles which St Thomas called *Synderesis*. Conscience, then, is a judgment of the practical reason at work on matters of right and wrong. There is an element of emotion in the workings of conscience because when the reason decides what *ought to be* done we feel emotionally drawn towards it, or emotionally divided if we partly shrink from doing it. In the same way if the moral reason passes judgment on what *has been* done we feel either 'pangs of conscience' or feelings of approval, whichever way the judgment goes. Because man is a 'fallen' creature the pains of conscience are very familiar and, paradoxically, the more sensitive in conscience we become the less we are likely to enjoy a 'good' conscience. This has been the clear testimony of those whom we think of as the most saintly.

The traditional Christian teaching is that it is a Christian's absolute duty to obey his conscience. This does not mean that the conscience is infallibly right. It can err because judgment may be corrupted by interest, because it makes errors of fact, or because it wrongly estimates tendencies and possible consequences of action (and there can be no certainty in advance about these). But the traditional Christian view is that an erring conscience (objectively considered) must be followed. We must take responsibility for our own decisions before God and follow what at the time our moral reason prescribes. We may, of course, decide to give someone else the duty of deciding for us (as, for instance, when someone takes a vow of poverty, chastity and obedience), but that decision itself must be a conscientious one. Even then if subsequently we are ordered to do something against our conscientious judgement, we should disobey.

None of this teaching is meant to absolutize prejudices. It is assumed that the judgment is a conscientious one, and that reasonable care has been taken to consider the relevant factors in arriving at it. It follows that we have a duty to educate our conscience. If we make mistakes because we have not troubled to put our consciences to the school of Christ we are blameworthy. To educate conscience is to allow the mind of Christ to be formed in us (I Cor. 2.16) so that it grows in sensitivity. The right environment for the education of conscience is life in the fellowship of the Church. Here we shall draw on the resources of prayer, sacramental grace and Bible study. Here we shall have for our guidance what wisdom the Church has accumulated on questions of conduct in nearly two-thousand years. Here, too, we may learn from the mistakes of the past. Here we may get corporate or personal counsel from our fellow Christians in general, and from our clergy and ministers in particular. But these Christian aids do not exhaust the sources of education for the conscience. We cannot afford to ignore the whole sweep of human knowledge wherever it is relevant. And when we come to consider the precise facts of particular cases of conscience, as soon as they go beyond domestic concerns of the Church and raise public issues the fact are not peculiarly Christian but must be obtained in the same way as anyone else obtains them. There ought, however, to be much more discussion of moral problems in groups among Christians.

In living the Christian life we have many helps from the past and the present. We do not face the burden of decision naked and bereft. Nevertheless the decision finally must be ours. This might be a daunting prospect if the basis of the Christian life was not justification or acceptance by faith in Christ and not as a reward for a high record of conscientious moral achievement. Indeed it is precisely because the Christian is secure in the knowledge of what Christ has *already* done for him that he is able to face unafraid the inevitable uncertainties of moral decisions in the present.

To bring to bear moral judgments on the facts of a particular case is known as casuistry (q.v.). There is much in its history which is dubious and has been questioned, but there is no escape from every Christian being a casuist once he admits that acting from the right motive is not enough; he must also seek to do what is right in the particular circumstances. The training of motive is a matter of ascetic theology;

the training of the moral judgment in the situation is the education of conscience.

It follows of course from this discussion that conscience belongs to man as man. It is not the peculiar possession of the Christian. Having the capacity to recognize moral distinctions and apply them in particular cases is part of what we mean by a man. It belongs to all who are not insane. The actual deliverances of conscience are profoundly (and rightly) influenced by time and circumstance, though they are not *determined* by them, as the Marxist would want to say. The Christian has the advantage of a more adequate understanding of human life and destiny, and a deeper grasp of goodness, through Jesus Christ, than can be found elsewhere. He has also greater resources through the Holy Spirit in the Church on which to draw. He therefore has the greater responsibilities. But all men, whether they have heard the gospel or not, whether they believe it or not, are responsible before God for acting according to their conscience, and for educating their conscience according to their circumstances and possibilities.

This is the position implied in the Bible. The word is not found in the OT but what it stands for is presupposed in the whole prophetic movement in the light of which our OT has been edited. So we find it underlying the Genesis sagas, the historical books, the prophetic books and the wisdom literature. A striking instance is the story of Nathan and David (II Sam. 12). The word is not found in the Gospels either, but is presupposed in the whole of Jesus' parabolic and gnomic teaching (cf. Luke 12.57). The word conscience or *suneidesis* occurs twice in Acts, and twenty-seven times in the NT Letters, chiefly in those of St Paul. The word was used in popular Greek ethical vocabulary, but mostly in the sense of an adverse judgment on acts committed by the self in the past, leading to remorse. St Paul took up the term and used it in a wider sense. He does use it in the old sense of an interior judge of past actions, though he says it not only condemns but may approve (cf. Rom. 2.14 f.). But he also uses it to cover decisions in advance on what should be done. He holds that, though it may err in doing so, it should still be obeyed (cf. I Cor. 8 and 10 on food offered to idols). This is what St Thomas Aquinas followed. The word, therefore, is used in extended senses in the NT and a good conspectus of them can be found in the five occurrences in Hebrews (9.9; 9.14; 10.2; 10.22; 13.18).

This exegesis has been challenged by C. A. Pierce (*Conscience in the New Testament*, 1955), who maintains that St Paul used the word only in the previous Greek negative and retrospective sense. This involves a strained interpretation of some texts in which the word appears to have a positive sense (cf. II Cor.

1.12). The practical effect of the discussion is small because it clearly has a good sense in some cases in the Pastoral Epistles (e.g., I Tim. 1.19), and because at the end Pierce brings in the unbiblical term *proairesis* (choice) to cover what he has excluded from the traditional understanding of conscience, and says this must be educated. This exegesis, however, accords with some continental Protestant theologians who interpret conscience only in a negative sense. Brunner (q.v.), for instance, in *The Divine Imperative* (1932) treats it only as the experience of the wrath of God (pp. 156 ff.). Apart from the dubious exegetical basis of this, it leaves unsolved the question of the nature and authority of Christian moral judgments. The only way to avoid the traditional understanding of conscience is to assume that one knows what to do in a particular situation by direct guidance from God without the use of the moral reason. This is the position, for example, of Moral Re-armament and is fraught with extreme danger. To follow it would make all rational discussion of Christian ethics impossible.

The traditional Christian position is akin to the one taken up by much traditional moral philosophy. For example, Butler (q.v.) in the eighteenth century writes: 'There is a principle of reflection in men by which they distinguish between approval and disapproval of their own actions ... this principle in man ... is conscience' (*Sermon* 1; cf. *Sermon* 2). In this he has been widely followed. The term is not widely used by moral philosophers today but in fact they do not stray far from it. Confusion is caused by a quite different use of the term in Freudian psychoanalytic theory. Freud finds the seat of conscience in the (necessarily) repressive super-ego. What Christians mean by conscience he calls 'the reality principle' and it is by this he wants people to live. Whether, therefore, Freud's theories are sound or not they do not contradict Christian teaching. Indeed they throw light on the well-known phenomenon of the 'scrupulous conscience'. He has confused the terminology by being unaware of the usual Christian understanding of the term.

Eric d'Arcy, *Conscience and its Right to Freedom*, 1961, Parts 1 and 2.

RONALD PRESTON

Consent

Consent is voluntary acquiescence. The notion is an important one in several areas of ethics. A valid marriage requires the consent of the partners, though it becomes an extremely complex matter to say in detail just what are the conditions for consent. *See* **Marriage**. According to John Locke, a civil government requires the consent of the governed, though this certainly does not mean according an unlimited power to the political authority. *See* **State**.

Conservatism

Conservatism is a fairly vague term used to designate the political attitude that resists change and seeks to maintain the *status quo*. Actually, in the modern world so-called 'Conservative' parties (as in Britain) may inaugurate social changes that would once have been considered 'progressive', and they would not seek to turn back social change. In some countries, however, the term 'conservative' still denotes those who seek to maintain the privileges of wealth and social status and who are opposed to either political or economic democratization. In the past, the churches have frequently been allied with conservative political forces, perhaps because ecclesiastical privileges have sometimes been at stake in the course of social change. Nowadays it is widely recognized that the 'extreme right' in politics is just as hostile to Christian ethical ideals as is the 'extreme left', and that Christians who are continually exploiting the fear of Communism are presenting a distorted and one-sided view of the situation, for rightist views can be just as degrading to a genuine humanity as the excesses of the left. The Christian should find the extreme right just as abhorrent as Marxism. But there may be situations where a Christian feels it a duty to support a moderate conservatism, especially where some stability or even some breathing space is required in the face of the threat of runaway change.

EDITOR

Contemplation

Contemplation, in the sense of the intellectual vision of the highest good or the highest reality, is undisturbed by feeling or striving, and represented for Plato and for classical philosophy in general the summit of human possibility. This view passed over into Christianity, and such outstanding Christian thinkers as St Augustine and St Thomas (qq.v.) have maintained the superiority of the so-called 'intellectual' virtues. In modern times, there has been a reaction against the place formerly given to contemplation. Critics of the contemplative ideal see it as reflecting the notion that the soul must escape from the encumbrance of the body, and so as other-worldly and quietist. The modern temper calls for an ethic that is activist and this-worldly. Some of the criticisms are doubtless justified, but one should not underestimate the place of contemplation or brush it aside. The ancient Christian writers did not advocate contemplation in isolation, but saw it within the context of the whole Christian life. But more importantly, there can be no sustained and intelligent Christian action, properly so-called, unless it is guided by Christian understanding; and this in turn arises from the immersion of the Christian mind in the contemplation of the vision of God, granted in Jesus Christ. *See* **Ascetical Theology.**

EDITOR

Contemporary Society, Ethical Problems of

Our discussion deals with problems created by social change which call into question traditional moral perspectives (for entries on specific social vices, see **Addiction; Alcoholism; Crime; Divorce,** etc.). The dynamics of social change in America provide clues to the ethical problems facing an increasingly industrialized world community. Despite political cleavages, similarity of change in the more industrial societies of East and West is startling. Though the rapid transition from traditional to modern society is a major development in international politics, social change within so-called 'developed' societies is equally dramatic.

Always critical and decisive, social change produces tremendous upheavals in the ethos of a people. It is ethically dangerous to assume that the kind of change taking place in contemporary society either brings its own happy solutions or calls for complete condemnation. The organic nature of social life implies a built-in tendency toward equilibrium. More appropriate for our day than the analogy of organic evolution, however, is that of a series of cultural explosions throwing off new patterns. Thus the ethical problems of contemporary society may be viewed as cultural explosions in these areas of life: population, metropolitan, technological, cybernetic, organizational, leisure, knowledge, automation and the human rights explosion.

The future 'ain't what it used to be', for now it explodes upon us. A concern for survival alone will only support devastation. Ethical reflection begins with the hope that there is sufficient human resilience and responsibility to harness these tremendous forces. Social forces cannot be rejected as inhuman *per se*, lest one reject the genuinely human impulses which have created these cultural explosions. One such genuine human impulse is the drive to create and to master creation. Nothing is more dramatic than the instant creation by which technological ingenuity transforms modern life. Equally important, however, is the desire to understand and to master what human ingenuity has either created or co-operated in creating. Barring a final nuclear spasm, powerful new creations demand ever more ingenious forms of social organization and human response.

Some of the issues which seem to cut across various of the cultural explosions will now be listed:

(1) The ambiguity of planning and policy for the public good is a major ethical problem made more dramatic by the exploding metropolis. In a 'participant society' where everyone is urged to be free and responsible – at the same time that the bigness of modern bureaucracy overwhelms the concerned individual – outmoded political ideologies have tragic consequences for the fate of the common good. Thus we find resistance to effective metropolitan planning in the name of constitutional rights and in the image of Jeffersonian democracy. Here in microcosm, one perceives the same ideology that pits state rights against federal responsibility, or national isolationism against global interdependence. The Republic is safe, but our cities may go to hell.

The political image of the city-state, the sociological image of planned ecological balance, and the economic image of centralized production and business all betray the heavy hand of nineteenth-century liberalism. In contrast, the 'organizational demiurge' at the centre of metropolitan development dictates, in the foreseeable future, continued dispersion of human activites in huge urban regions ('megalopolis') with multiple nuclei of power. This massive pattern will supersede the culture, folklore, life styles and democratic ideology identified with the 'city'. So Scott Greer has surmised that the contemporary metropolitan community is without a moral and legal father, without a stable hierarchy, without obedient estates, without simple policy questions of right *or* wrong. It is, in this sense, the large-scale society in miniature.

Meanwhile we extol the mystique of grass-roots democracy. Small municipalities refuse to give up their jurisdictions. The middle-class public resists planned inclusiveness in housing or in education and prefers to spawn an endless proliferation of homogeneous suburbs. The lower class and minority groups get what's left over from the exodus, but ironically, not fast enough, so that the word 'now' (justice *now*, freedom *now*) implies a new sense of urgency. Resisting plans for urban renewal that may displace them, the underprivileged have adopted a little grass-roots democratic movement of protest on their own. And the community power elites play a game of musical chairs with the panoply of urban problems. The chief actors change positions as the issues revolve, and sometimes the pyramids of power cancel each other out. Sometimes they produce genuinely 'utopian' plans, such as the effort to 'suburbanize' the city.

Whose goals for urban life deserve preference? Most plans for the city prefer the interests of business and educational elites. Lower-class community organization tends also to be parochial. Democracy in the exploding metropolis is defective, despite technological skills and egalitarian traditions. Sub-communities with their specialized interests will have to turn in their weapons of war to an organization with common representation and a mandate to shape broader policy. Such a suggestion is still somewhat utopian, but the need for more viable forms of urban democracy cannot be ignored. Modern society cannot indulge itself with the dreams of gentle evolution, but must confront the accelerated process by which today's uto-pian hopes and nightmares become tomorrow's realities.

(2) The dynamism of contemporary society revolutionizes not only political life, but also styles of personal morality and life goals. The sense of moral responsibility is being reshaped by the organizational, metropolitan and leisure explosions. A decided shift may be discerned in basic life style, moving from asceticism to hed-onism. Both styles of life have always been somewhat intermixed, but the recipe has now changed. Thus, Max Weber's thesis (*see* **Weber, Max**), that the Puritan ascetic ethic has moulded the behaviour of the *entrepreneur*, dies hard for those in the Protestant tradition, but the new ingredient is orientated to consumption and pleasure. An economy of scarcity has shifted to an expense account and credit society. We live with a new mentality of happily wasteful indul-gence quite foreign to the traditional Protestant ethics. Whereas once the national temperament was to make all and save all, today the national purpose encourages everyone to make and to spend as much as possible in order to keep the economy moving.

Given the self-reinforcing pattern of dedi-cated hedonism, are there other moral straws in the wind? Certainly we are not devoid of oppor-tunities created by the new leisure society, the explosion in knowledge and information, mass communications and automation explosions. These developments precipitate a crisis of meaning, forcing affluent man to face the *ennui* of the prevailing life style. Some segments of society are entering a post-affluent era. But this opportunity still poses a crisis. A sense of im-morality – which is our legacy from traditional ethics – will not be a sufficient guide in a posi-tive exploration of leisure, education, machine-controlled work or the kaleidoscope of the mass media. And a policing conscience, which is an asset to the elementary equilibrium of society, focuses moral instincts only on the most blatant threats to existence, as in the struggle against totalitarian laws or threats to subsistence. A benevolent society, on the other hand, tranquillizes us while decisively reshaping the total ethos of life. In general, the greater the margin of subsistence and social justice, the broader the segments of daily life given free play outside of normative controls. Men are thrown more than ever on their own sense of meaning and choice of values, with more time and opportunity available to explore the quality of life in leisure pursuits. Given more freedom from controls, the search for happiness and the good life could lead to an abdication of social responsibility, or, on the other hand, it could lead to deeper social involvement and community responsibility.

(3) A third critical problem is the need for deeper value consensus in decision-making. Contemporary society reflects extensive orga-nizational elaboration and skill. Its distinctive attribute is increasing scope of functional co-ordination with two corollary tendencies: to nucleate (bureaucratize) and to differentiate (compartmentalize). The machinery and con-text of decision-making, despite great variety, suffer a certain social rigidity.

The vicissitudes of bureaucratization and compartmentalization are not limited to public agencies and business enterprises, but also directly affect the family, play groups, schools, churches, community and professional groups, all of which are caught up in the organizational explosion. The weakness of this development is *formalism*; its strength is the extension of pro-fessional resources to all areas of social life. From this perspective, decentralized organiza-tion and intermediate groups afford promise – if their efforts are directed to strengthening basic social institutions and if they allow meaningful fellowship and feedback to over-come formalism.

Even if structural opportunities for increas-ing social responsibility exist, even with a special willingness to apply effort in the handicapped areas (blighted neighbourhoods, school drop-outs, unemployed and the unemployable, delinquents and disturbed elderly individuals) – given all this, problem solving still depends on value consensus. Anomic, mobile masses and expedient elites too often share in patterns of value evasion. A sense of the dignity of the per-son or of social justice becomes less and less tangible. Between the aberrations of mass hedonism, rugged individualism, and organiza-tional formalism, contemporary society must grasp the meaning of *responsible freedom*. Often justice remains a function of imagination, or freedom is reduced to the desire to be left alone in pursuit of licence. And desire for political power by various interest groups often short-circuits the process of freedom in the name of preserving freedom. In a mass society both freedom and responsibility tend to shrivel.

(4) One final problem area in our listing: the urgent need for civilizing conflict. Common usage seldom shows any relationship between civility and conflict. Yet civility can be des-cribed as the civilizing effort of men locked to-gether in conflict, a dialogue of many 'con-spiring' for just social organization and cultural opportunity. Though democracy can-not allow violent subversion, it can encourage diversity. Here too is a point of common interest that has come to the foreground in discussions of pluralism and national purpose. Since no tradition or group has the inside track to civility, a pluralistic society thrives on conflict within a broad framework of consensus as the only method of extending responsible freedom. Two responses particularly undermine this process of creative conflict: cultural funda-mentalism and confusions of security with justice.

Cultural fundamentalism is the response of the older middle class to the process of cultural change shaped by contemporary 'explosions'. Traditional values identified with the middle class of the nineteenth century are symbolically threatened, leading to status conflict of a reactionary type. Piety, thrift, parental discipline and individualism are superseded by a normative valuation of secular rationality, indulgence, equalitarian family relationships and economic dependence upon public agencies. The reaction as exemplified in the radical right, is an anti-pluralistic political fundamentalism. This extreme opposition tries to circumvent the ground rules – such as civil liberties – of civilizing conflict in a pluralistic society.

The other response is to make 'security' normative. From this perspective nearly all facets of change can only be construed as unjust, 'unconstitutional', or an encroachment upon freedom. Thus in the civil rights explosion, the middle class sometimes confuses justice with the security mentality.

The civilizing process calls for vast changes in the *status quo* as expressions of dynamic justice. Civilizing conflict is the contemporary alternative to violent revolution. Can contemporary society have its revolutionary cake and eat it too? Can we have both the advantages of swift change and the *status quo*? Will we have the human sanity, ethical idealism and public understanding to adapt to new forces and to harness them in the continual shaping of the common good?

Harvey Cox, *The Secular City*, 1965; Harry K. Girvetz, ed., *Contemporary Moral Issues*, 1963; Robert Lee, *Religion and Leisure in America*, 1964; Walter G. Muelder, *Foundations of the Responsible Society*, 1959; Robert A. Nisbet and Robert K. Merton, eds., *Contemporary Social Problems*, 1961; David M. Potter, *People of Plenty*, 1954; David Riesman, Nathan Glazer, and Reul Denney, *The Lonely Crowd*, 1950.

ROBERT LEE

Contextual Ethics

The phrase refers to a way of thinking about the method and content of ethics. Characteristic of this way of thinking is the importance given to the perspectives, relations and functions of human behaviour as the concrete setting of action. Behaviour is *ethical* and *in context* when the perspectives, relations and functions relate to the motives, goals and structures of behaviour in such a way as to exhibit the human reality and meaning of an act or acts. The context of behaviour and the ethical significance of behaviour are congruent. The merit of contextual ethics lies in the clarity and thoroughness with which the human meaning of the connection between the perspectives and the circumstances of action are maintained and explored.

Motives and goals, directives and structures, relations and functions have occupied a central place in ethical theory, since men began to think about ethical matters at all. The etymology of the word, 'ethics', itself makes plain that the fundamental connection between what is 'ethical' and what is 'human' has always been recognized. Aristotle's dictum, moreover, that 'in ethical matters, absolute certainty is very difficult to attain' (EN, 1094b), epitomizes the haunting disparity between the norms and the activities of human behaviour from which no ethical theory has escaped. Aristotle also recognized, however, that ethical reflection must seek 'as much clearness as the subject matter admits of' (EN, 1094b). Hence it has come about that ethical thought has both advanced in clarity and differed in the interpretation of a largely common subject matter according to the *method* of analysis employed. The contextual method is a twentieth-century case in point. Like pragmatism, or positivism, or utilitarianism, or idealism, or empiricism, or entelechism before it, contextual ethics undertakes to analyze and interpret ethical reality, but unlike its predecessors, contextual ethics proceeds in a *contextual* way.

Careful attention to the factor of method makes it possible and desirable, to distinguish *contextual ethics* from two ways of thinking about ethics with which contextual ethics is often identified or confused. One of these is *ethical relativism*; the other is, *situational ethics*. In common with *ethical relativism*, contextualism recognizes the dynamic and changing character of ethical reality, the pluralism and inter-relatedness of motives and goals, of directives and structures, which are a major part of the content of ethics, and that there is no single principle, which can be identified and applied as the criterion of what is 'ethical'. In distinction from ethical relativism, a contextual ethic seeks to show that the dynamics of behaviour always exhibits a context of circumstance and meaning which informs and shapes decisions. All these factors are at once *relative* to each other and *related* to whatever is recognized *in actu* as pointing to the human significance of behaviour. In common with *situational* ethics, contextualism recognizes the primary importance of the concrete environment of decision. It is this 'situation' which functions as the immediate matrix of ethical action. An analysis which fails to take full account of this matrix can only end in abstraction. Under the mistaken notion that 'in situational ethics the moral judgment is measured only by the subjective, immanent light of the individual in question' (Robert Gleason, s.j., *Situational Morality*, Thought, 32, 555, 1957), the movement was condemned by Pope Pius XII in 1952. A contextual ethic, however, is to be distinguished from *situational* ethics because contextualism regards the connection between the dynamic and the directional factors in behaviour, as being given *with* the situation, to be sure, but not *by* the situation. It is not the *situation* which makes the *context* ethical; but the *context* which makes the *situation* ethical.

The distinctive meaning and importance of contextual ethics can, perhaps, be further clarified by contrasting contextual ethics with its opposite number, that is, *ethical absolutism*. The absolutist position in ethics is the view that what makes an action *ethical* is its conformity, in greater or lesser degree, with a standard of conduct which can be applied to all people, in all situations, in the same way. The standard may be the highest good, however defined; or a law; a virtue; a value; or the will of God .The most influential instance in western ethical theory, is the *natural law* (q.v.). The important point, in each case, is that however much the 'standard', or 'principle', or 'law', may be refined in the course of its application to the diversity and complexity of ethical decision, the 'standard' et al., functions as a 'rule of reason', the ethical meaning of which is its *absolute* validity, that is, that it can be applied to all people, in all situations, in the same way. The gap between the ethical claim and the ethical act is, thus, never closed. Instead, it is bridged by a 'counsel of prudence'. A contextual ethic, by contrast, takes with primary seriousness, the gap which cannot be bridged. It tries to hold the dynamic and the directional aspects of ethical reality together by describing as accurately and completely as possible the *context* in which behaviour arrives at the point of decision. And it identifies the *ethical* factor in the context, not with the *context* itself, but with the concrete exposure of the *human significance* of action. Thus, the criterion of action functions rather as a 'frame-of-reference' for behaviour which applies to different people, in different situations, in different ways. *Sensitivity* to the *human significance* of action not *consistency* of action is the measure of ethical reality.

The contextual method of ethical analysis became recognized as a distinct, though debatable, way of thinking about the method and content of ethics, chiefly owing to the collapse of idealism and the rising incidence of ethical perplexity, occasioned by the complex and uncertain decisions with which sensitive minds and consciences were confronted by political totalitarianism and the second World War. These circumstances severely challenged the adequacy of traditional ethical standards, on the one hand, and of relativism, on the other. The normative effectiveness of absolutism in ethics seemed more and more impotent and remote. Relativism, as an alternative, tended towards nihilism. The question of a *tertium quid*, a creative option, which might somehow guide ethical sensitivity and responsibility through the impasse posed by absolutism and relativism, seemed long overdue.

It is not surprising, therefore, that contextualism as a *method* should have been variously applied and that the *content* of its application should have varied accordingly. Some contextualists have stressed the contextual importance of social relations and structures, others have stressed the self as a centre of value, still others, have stressed theological perspectives. Clearly each of these contexts affects differently one's interpretation of motives and goals, of values and virtues, of criteria and their application. Indeed, this variety has led to the suggestion, that the term 'contextual ethics' has been overtaken by such a wide diversity of usage and interpretation, as to make it desirable to abandon the phrase altogether. The present interpreter, however, does not share this assessment of contextual ethics, chiefly, for three reasons. The first is that diversity of usage and interpretation is a commonplace of the intellectual tradition which, if seriously espoused, as a ground for abandonment, would undermine the intellectual enterprise as such. The second reason is that it is quite possible to explain and to understand the sense in which 'context' is used as a key to the method and content of ethical thinking. The third reason is that the contextual analysis of ethics has compelled a searching reappraisal of the normative tradition, with its standards, principles and rules, so that ethical discussion is increasingly beginning to move beyond the polarization of 'context' over against 'principles' in the search for a more concrete and persuasive account of ethical reality. When that search shall have reached its own creative option, contextual ethics may well lose its urgency but scarcely its importance. Meanwhile, as a way of thinking about *Christian ethics*, contextual ethics offers one way at least of describing what God is doing in the world to give what man is doing in the world the human shape of action.

The interpretation of Christian ethics is particularly well-suited to the contextual method. However, the relative clarity, importance, and expendability of a contextual approach to ethics in general may be judged, Christian ethics is intrinsically contextual. This means, on the one hand, that the content of Christian ethics is most appropriately described, and most adequately understood, by taking up the contextual method. On the other hand, the meaning and significance of contextualism in ethics are both evident from and confirmed by a Christian interpretation of ethical reality. Christian ethics requires a contextual method. Contextualism, as a way of thinking about ethics from a Christian perspective, is itself a response to this perspective; it is not derived from a general theory of contextualism, but arrived at on other grounds.

A Christian interpretation of ethical reality is an attempt to describe the implications for human behaviour of God's self-identifying self-disclosure in Jesus of Nazareth. The point of departure for such a description is neither the highest Good nor 'the general will', nor 'the imperative of duty' with its universal moral maxims. The point of departure for Christian thinking about ethics is the concrete reality in the world of a community, a *koinonia*, called into being and action by Jesus of Nazareth. In this community, what God is doing in the world, is clearly discerned as exposing the human meaning of behaviour by giving human shape to action. God is doing in the world what it takes to make and to keep human life human. This understanding of God's action is derived from the biblical description of God's messianic will and purpose in covenant and creation, in deliverance and Decalogue, in the first Advent and the second, in the fulfilment of the 'old Israel' by the 'new Israel', and in the consummation of the 'new Israel' in a 'new heaven and a new earth' in which 'God will be everything to every one' (I Cor. 15.28).

Owing to this expectation of human fulfilment, behaviour is being shaped and may be evaluated according to the will and purpose of God identified in Jesus of Nazareth, the Christ (Messiah). This expectation involves the transformation of human motivation and of human inter-relatedness in *this* world, as well as in the next. The goal of this transformation is human whole-ness or maturity. God's action involves man in an environment of dynamic change and direction towards fulfilment in which the ethical meaning and significance of behaviour are identified with the human thrust and sense of action. Thus, the *koinonia* is a kind of laboratory of humanization in the world. Here, an experiment is continually going on in bringing the concrete stuff of action into dynamic and concrete relation to a perspective upon action. The perspective is God's action in the world to make men free to be the selves whom God intended them to be, through the humanizing results of the way men behave. In short, the *koinonia* is the context for the doing on earth, as it is in heaven, of the will of God. In the *koinonia*, the possibility and the power of ethical action are always being contextually appropriated and behaviourally expressed – as surely as 'he who does what is true comes to the light' (John 3.21).

The best available survey of the method, content, problems and literature of contextual ethics is by James M. Gustafson in an essay entitled 'Christian Ethics', in *Religion*, 1965, edited by Paul Ramsey, and in an article entitled 'Context versus Principles' in the *Harvard Theological Review*, 58, 1965, pp. 171–202. Mention may also be made of the monograph by Paul Ramsey, *Deeds and Rules in Christian Ethics*, Scottish Journal of Theology, Occasional Papers, No. 11, 1965; also a little pamphlet by John A. T. Robinson,

Christian Morals Today, 1964. For a contextual analysis of Christian Ethics, *see* Paul Lehmann, *Ethics in a Christian Context*, 1963.

PAUL LEHMANN

Continence

St Thomas Aquinas (*Summa Theologaie*. II.9, 155) says: 'The word *continence* is taken by various people in two ways. For some understand continence to denote abstention from all venereal pleasure. In this sense perfect continence is virginity in the first place and widowhood in the second. Others, however, understand continence as signifying that whereby a man resists evil desires, which in him are vehement.' (Continence for Thomas, as a virtue of the will, is distinct from temperance, which moderates the desires themselves.)

The distinction between perfects continence (*continentia virginalis, vidualis*) and marital continence (*continentia coniugalis*) is not formally maintained in Reformed thought, but *continence* is used in the same sense. Calvin (*Institutes*, III.8) interprets the seventh Commandment as meaning 'that every part of our lives ought to be regulated by chastity and continence'. 'Virginity, I acknowledge, is a virtue not to be despised. But as this is denied to some and to others is granted only for a season, let those who are troubled with incontinence and cannot succeed in resisting it avail themselves of the help of marriage, that they may preserve their chastity according to the degree of their calling.'

Great stress was laid on continence in some early Christian writings. II Clement is not untypical in regarding perfect continence as an important part of the perfect way. 'Keep the flesh pure and the seal unstained to the end that we may receive life.' (II Clement, 8; cf. 12–15). The virgins (*parthenoi*) of Rev. 14.4 may show the same emphasis within the NT itself. St Augustine (*Confessions*, VII) seems to have regarded his 'conversion' largely as an embracing of continence. The Church, however, consistently defended marriage against philosophical and gnostic sects which repudiated it altogether.

Christian writers adopted the current philosophical viewpoint that the agitation, physical and emotional, associated with sexual activity was peculiarly contrary to the calm self-control of the life ruled by reason. Pleasure was suspect, even within marriage. 'The marriage act that is done out of sensuous pleasure is a lesser sin than fornication' (Thomas, *Summa Theologiae*, II.9,154). Augustine's view that the violence of the passions in sexual activity is consequent of the Fall came to be widely held (*see* Calvin, op.cit.) and coloured Christian thinking about chastity and continence within marriage.

If Christian writers today can find within their faith and its biblical source grounds for a more positive evaluation of sex, it is largely because the secular attitude has radically changed. In a post-Freudian age it may be necessary to distinguish in a new way two kinds of continence; that which springs from a neurotic fear or hatred of sex and the sex impulses, and that self-control, responsibility of action, which is compatible with freedom and self-understanding.

Traditional Christian thinking was male-centred. Continence meant resisting desires, and for those without the gift, marriage afforded a remedy. Such a view is open to the objection that it makes marriage legalized prostitution; an argument reinforced by the doctine of the *debitum coniugale*, the marriage duty. It was the Puritans who first understood the marriage relationship in terms of companionship and personal love. A modern reinterpretation of the virtue of continence must be in *relational* terms, in which continence is a part of Christian love, acting responsibly and in genuine concern for the other.

                                    JAMES A. WHYTE

Contraception. *see* Procreation.

Contrition

Contrition is perfect sorrow for sin, arising from inner conviction and from the love of God. It is distinguished from attrition (q.v.).

Conventional Morality

In any stable society there will be (almost by definition of 'stable') a substantial measure of agreement on matters of moral principle – on what makes conduct right or wrong, a man good or bad, etc. This will mean that the 'descriptive meaning' of the moral terms (*see* Ethics) will be constant as between one speaker and another; and some degree of constancy of this sort is necessary, if such terms are to have the use which they typically do have. We expect, when a man calls another a good man, to receive some idea of what qualities the man has; if he is being called good for very eccentric reasons, we may be seriously misled. Thus all stable societies have a 'conventional morality'; and within the confines of this, moral words can be used to give information, in just the same way as descriptive words like 'red'. It is this fact which lends plausibility to naturalist and descriptivist ethical theories. *see* Naturalistic Ethics. As a result of exclusive attention to the conventional aspect of morality, a use of moral words can grow up in which their 'action-guiding' force is lost; in calling a man a good man we are no longer holding him up for imitation, but merely attributing to him certain properties.

In such a situation, moral reformers of various kinds can attack the dead morality of convention (cf. Christ's attack on the Pharisees, and the Communists' on 'bourgeois morality') and attempt to restore the action-guiding function of the moral words while altering their descriptive content. For example, a fifth-century Athenian could have said 'Nicias is a bad man because he is a ruthless slave-owner', although according to the conventional morality of the time Nicias was a typically good man, and slave-owning was held no bar to being called 'good'. The logical possibility of doing this is the strongest argument against descriptivism; if the descriptivism were true – that is, if the moral words had their meaning determined by the properties in virtue of which they are applied, the supporter of conventional morality could always say to the moral reformer: 'In saying that a man is bad whose character is well known and whom everybody except you calls good, you are just misusing the language; for we *mean* by "good man" a man like him.' The very fact that they understand what the moral reformer is saying to them shows that this is not what they mean by 'good man'.

                                    R. M. HARE

Conversion

Early studies in the psychology of religion tended to deal mainly with conversion as a sudden and radical acceptance of Christian faith. William James' *Varieties of Religious Experience* (1902) contains the best early account and draws extensively on the reflections of G. Stanley Hall and the pioneering direct observation studies of Edwin D. Starbuck. All subsequent general works on the psychology of religion have continued to deal with these sudden conversions, particularly in adolescence. For recent accounts *see* Walter H. Clark, *Psychology of Religion* (1958) or Paul E. Johnson, *Psychology of Religion* (revised edn., 1959). *See also* Conviction of Sin.

The incidence of sudden conversions seems to be less today than it was fifty years ago and recently more attention has been given to the processes underlying gradual changes which culminate in a decisive turning point. Both 'sudden' and 'gradual' conversions are now normally regarded as having a history in the life experience of the concerned individual which extends back beyond the crisis experience itself. Recent studies have also paid more attention to adult conversions and some have dealt with conversions to other than religious faith, for example, to political positions. *See*, e.g., William Sargant, *Battle for the Mind* (1957). A representative sample of different kinds of traditional and contemporary treatments of conversion is found in Orlo Strunk, *Readings in the Psychology of Religion* (1959).

Beginning with psychoanalysis, some forms of dynamic psychology have tended to regard all kinds of conversions as symptomatic efforts to resolve inner conflicts. These efforts are not necessarily healthy or constructive. The value of the conversion would seem to depend largely upon the nature of the original conflict and the freedom of the person to continue to develop beyond the point arrived at in the immediate conversion experience. Carl Jung has introduced the notion that some conversions may be important positive attempts initiated in the unconscious (q.v.) to redress an imbalance or one-sidedness which has developed in the person's conscious psychic life.

To date there have been relatively few empirical studies of conversion and those that have been made have dealt only with small samples or limited aspeccts of the situation. Most of the literature deals in general theories and discussion. It becomes aparent, however, that the role of unconscious psychic mechanisms in the conversion process cannot lightly be dismissed.

GRAEME M. GRIFFIN

Conviction of Sin

It refers to the affective state of mind, frequently regarded in an earlier age as the normative antecedent of a crisis experience of conversion (q.v.), characterized by feelings of general wretchedness and unworthiness, self-blame and contempt, and frequently compounded by fears of eternal punishment. This state of mind could extend over days, months or even years; it could be extremely intense and productive of deep despair but after conversion crisis normally gave place to a sense of release, peace and joy. Revivalist preaching, such as that of the early Methodist movement and the Great Awakening, consciously attempted to secure conviction of sin in the belief that the person so affected would better appreciate, and more willingly accept, the proffered mercy of God. One of the most perceptive apologists for this approach, who also recognized some of its dangers, was Jonathan Edwards. See, for example, his A Treatise Concerning Religious Affections (1746).

John Calvin, especially, recognized that it was some kind of awareness of the work of grace that permitted one to be convicted of sin. Thus, conviction of sin and acknowledgement of grace were not to be seen in simple chronological sequence. Modern modes of thought provide better vehicles for conveying this insight than did those available to Calvin.

Early students of the psychology of religion were aware that there was frequently no direct relation between the intensity of the conviction of sin and the extent of any actual transgressions. Fear and suggestibility were seen as major factors contributing to a conviction of sin. Orlo Strunk, Readings in the Psychology of Religion (1959), includes a summary statement of this early work written by Edward S. Ames.

It is now recognized that striving for the production of feelings of worthlessness may confirm neurotic tendencies (e.g., to self-punishment) in some persons and actually render them less capable of hearing the gospel message. Most forms of contemporary dynamic psychology acknowledge that accepting realistic responsibility for one's own past is a necessary preliminary to responsible facing of the future, but insist that the proper emphasis is upon the future rather than the past. Some existentialists go even further and tend to denigrate the importance of the past and to concentrate upon the present as the basis for future responsibility. Changing theological emphases, together with these psychological insights and the further awareness of the difficulties that can be created for the personality when feelings of guilt (q.v.) are dissociated from their appropriate objects, have tended to devalue the concept of conviction of sin in its traditional form. Responsible Christian teaching and preaching still insists, however, that in appropriating the gift of God's salvation, man should become aware of his own sin in his awareness of redemption in Christ.

GRAEME M. GRIFFIN

Corporal Punishment

Judicially this usually takes the form of flogging, and may be the penalty for such crimes as robbery with violence and sexual assault. Similar arguments apply as to capital punishment (q.v.). Does it deter? There is a widespread tendency to exaggerate its deterrent effect. Changes in the law on flogging bear little relation to the volume of crimes for which it may be the penalty. Does it reform? The more abnormal the offender, the less effective flogging is as a means of reformation. Is it a suitable retribution (if retribution be allowed on a Christian theory of punishment)? If only behaving in a physically unpleasant way to those who themselves have behaved in such a way is thought to be proper, it is hard to sustain this on Christian grounds.

Fairly stable characters may be brought up sharp by a physical punishment when they have committed an offence, and it may do them no harm. This is why most of those who are thrashed on occasion by their parents, provided that they are sure of their love, are not likely to come to much harm, though it is questionable whether such punishments are often necessary. But the circumstances of a judicial flogging are quite different, and the chances of harm much greater. Elements of eroticism and flagellation can easily enter. In any case the less stable the character the less point there is in flogging. Those who have already suffered from the unpredictable and perhaps violent behaviour of their parents need patient re-training, not flogging. Those whose unpleasant conduct represents a conscious or unconscious reaction to their upbringing by asserting themselves, need self-understanding, and flogging will not achieve this. Those who are so excitable that their conduct is not a rational choice but a relief of tension need a sheltered environment, and those who are clearly mentally ill need hospital treatment. (For those who are moved by rational choice it is the certainty of detection rather than unpleasant physical punishment which is the more important factor.)

Parents who love their children need not be afraid of short, sharp physical punishments, provided they are administered consistently, though they are not likely to find many occasions for them. The same reasoning may apply to a school, if it has a wholesome atmosphere, but again such punishments will have but a minor role. Corporal punishment is rarely a remedy for serious disorders.

RONALD PRESTON

Counsels

Counsels, in moral theology, are exhortations which are helpful toward the attaining of the good life, but are not binding, as precepts are. The 'counsels of perfection', also called the 'evangelical counsels', are the exhortations to poverty, chastity and obedience (qq.v.). This way of talking seems to suggest that the 'religious' life is 'higher' or 'more perfect' than the life of involvement in the world, and this would be challenged by Protestant moralists. But it is a mistake to talk of 'higher' and 'lower', and it is a misunderstanding of the expression 'counsels of perfection'. The Christian social ethic demands that many persons should involve themselves in the life of the world, but especially in an age of affluence and of the overprizing of comfort and wealth, this same ethic equally demands that some should hear the evangelical counsels and witness to the realities of prayer, aspiration and true holiness. This is far from being 'escape' or 'withdrawal', but it demands non-attachment and self-renunciation.

EDITOR

Courage

Courage cannot be explained with reference solely to itself. A courageous man is one who has courage to do something, to be something. That is, he believes that there is more to be done with life than prolong it. It is said that a man must have the courage of his convictions, but he can have no courage unless he has convictions.

The NT in general, and the Sermon on the Mount in particular, makes it clear that the courageous man's first victory is a conquest over anxiety. Anxiety can be described under these headings: (1) *Material* – Fear of increased prices, inflation, unemployment, changes in trade, nationally and internationally, illness, infirmity. These might be summarized as a general, though vague, feeling of political and economic insecurity. (2) *Spiritual* – Fear of

loss of freedom and power to keep one's identity. Fear of being a hypocrite or incapable of significant action. Fear of being inadequate in personal relationships especially in the family. (3) *Religious* – Fear of the failure and disappearance of the church on account of the small number of practising members. Fear through a reluctance to think and live in the light of the fact that Christians walk by faith and not by sight and therefore cannot answer all the questions men may ask. Christians do not claim that only Christians can be courageous but that a man, or woman, requires courage to be a Christian in any century – whether in facing violence, torture and death or enduring the constant battle to be fought out against anxiety.

It is brave to accept dangers oneself but it is even braver to allow and even exhort others to be courageous in their particular spheres of living – for example, a bishop ordaining clergy, parents encouraging their sons and daughters to leave home and take full responsibility for themselves, friend helping friend to make a decision where one should be made no matter at what cost.

Christians learn that courage is a necessity rather than a virtue through their frequent meditation on the passion and triumph of our Lord. In every generation orthodox doctrine and individual piety are most clearly expressed in the compassion and courage of church members. Where there is no courage, compassion dwindles and where compassion is absent courage tends to become arrogant self-display.

R. E. C. BROWNE

Courtesy

Courtesy should be unobtrusive and therefore demands unself-consciousness in the courteous. It is the reverence due to every individual as a unique person born to fulfil a unique destiny, and a being made in the image of God. This reverence for people is part of a man's worship of God.

The courteous man listens to others without impatience; he never monopolizes conversations; he does not ask embarrassing questions and treats members of his family as courteously in private as he does in the presence of friends and acquaintances. He welcomes guests warmly but never overwhelms them with his greetings. He is particularly careful to treat children with such courtesy as is appropriate to their age.

Christians are enjoined to be courteous to one another, specially where there are acute differences of opinion, and to those who are of different religion, race or class. Care must be taken lest condescension and a patronizing spirit adorned with good manners be mistaken for courtesy.

It is recorded (Luke 7.36 ff.) that our Lord rebuked Simon the Pharisee for discourtesy and courteously accepted the ministrations of the woman described as a sinner when she set out to supply what Simon had rudely omitted.

R. E. C. BROWNE

Covetousness

The last of the Ten Commandments is the only one of them that deals directly with sins of thought as distinct from sins of word and overt deeds. It is concerned with covetousness: 'You shall not covet your neighbour's house; you shall not covet your neighbour's wife, or his manservant, or his maidservant, or his ox, or his ass, or anything that is your neighbour's' (Ex. 20.17). Covetousness is a dynamic state which is liable to explode into violent action but more often it stimulates plans to get the things so much desired. That is the course of covetousness in strong men. Covetousness in timid people shows itself in resentment, discontent, irritability and a readiness to belittle the possessor of the coveted thing or things.

Covetousness is in complete contradiction of the Christian doctrine of man and his possessions. Our Lord says: 'Take heed, and beware of all covetousness; for a man's life does not consist in the abundance of his possessions' (Luke 12.15).

Covetousness could be called an obsession: St Paul spoke of it as idolatry because he thought of it as a thing-centred religion with an interior pattern of wishes, thoughts and characteristic behaviour forms.

R. E. C. BROWNE

Creativity

Creativity is the capacity to produce new forms of expression in the arts and novel expressions of old forms which reflect aspects of universal human experience, and the capacity in the sciences to provide new solutions to problems or new ways of understanding problems.

The factors which combine to produce creativity have long been sought by the social sciences, and in particular by psychology. Yet they remain only partially understood. Factors which command a measure of agreement among psychologists are the following: (1) A relatively high drive or energy level: There is no consensus regarding the respective roles of constitutional or acquired factors producing this, though constitutional factors are widely regarded as playing some part. (2) A high degree of control of drives by ego structures: Such control allows for concentration and perseverance, and also, in the case of the artist, for a flexibility in repression, so that the ego can be in touch with unconscious instinctual elements in the personality without being overwhelmed by them. See Repression. In the case of the physical scientist and mathematician the control probably rather serves in part to prevent the unconscious from disturbing concentration on the external problem. (3) Restlessness or dissatisfaction: Such dissatisfaction is regarded as partly due to external problems and situations which stimulate the motivation toward mastery of the environment, and partly due to unconscious conflict which the creative behaviour is an attempt to resolve. Psychoanalysts have held in the past that such conflict is similar to neurotic conflict, if not identical with it. Recently, ego psychologists such as Ernst Kris have stressed the universality of such conflict and its role in normal development processes, and especially in creative processes. The recurrence of themes of incest, aggression, guilt and dependency in the literature of the West reflects the universal concerns of childhood experience. Viewed this way the creative artist portrays universal problems and their solutions, and is assisted by psychotherapy rather than hindered by it, as some persons have thought, since through it he may become better able to tolerate contact with unconscious processes.

These factors illuminate the creative process to some extent, but they do not explain the roots of creativity, or even why some artists and scientists are creative and some only journeymen. Psychology can, thus, in the broadest sense, show why a person may choose a career in science or art, but it cannot predict who will be a great scientist or artist.

Creativity appears at present to be too dependent upon special endowment to become an ethical norm of universal applicability, though its encouragement by all persons when the signs of it appear may well become such a norm, even though such encouragement conflicts at points with traditional controls of behaviour.

For a treatment of the problem in art from the psychoanalytic viewpoint, see Ernst Kris, *Psychoanalytic Explorations in Art*, 1952. For a treatment of creativity in science, see Charles A. Thomas, *Creativity in Science*, 1955. Abraham Maslow has presented a strong case for viewing creativity as 'self-actualization' in his *Motivation and Personality*, 1954. See also Eric Fromm's *The Sane Society*, 1955.

JAMES N. LAPSLEY

Crime

In the broad sense, crime is an offence against the laws of right, an act against morality and the common good. Since culture patterns vary, what is considered a crime may also vary from society to society, but behaviour such as parricide, treason and incest tend to be uniformly condemned.

Taken in its legal sense, crime is an act committed or omitted to which a law attaches a penalty or punishment. The concept of crime involves intervention between the offending and the injured parties by an agency representing the public. Criminal acts are broadly categorized as felonies or misdemeanours. A felony is punishable by loss of life or incarceration and/or deprivation of civil rights. A misdemeanour is punishable by fine and/or imprisonment.

On a given day in the USA, there are approximately 220,000 men and women in state and federal prisons. Another estimated 100,000 are in local and county jails. Over 2,500,000 offences occur annually. The majority of those sentenced to local jails are drunks, vagrants or social misfits of some kind. Of those sentenced to the federal and state penitentiaries, the majority have been convicted of non-violent crimes, such as car theft, larceny, etc. Less than 10% have been convicted of homicide, rape or kidnapping. The general prison population in the USA has declined since 1930 (from 8.9 per 100,000 population in 1930 to 5.1 per 100,000 in 1962).

Many variables have been associated with criminality. Incidences of crime vary according to the social and cultural characteristics of a community. A common assumption is that more crimes are committed by lower-class inhabitants of overcrowded, deteriorating inner city areas where there may be a greater accumulation of social problems, such as slums, broken families, addiction, prostitution and poverty. However, this finding must be qualified, for official crime statistics are more likely to reflect lower-class violations and overlook offences committed by members of middle and upper classes.

'Crime as a way of life' refers to the patterns of culture adopted by criminals – the language, ethical codes, traditions, values, manners and behaviour shared by career criminals.

'Organized crime' refers to a network of collaboration among criminals, varying from simple partnership to a highly organized large-scale operation which may be international in scope and have clandestine ties with police officers and public officials. Organized crime flourished during the 1930s, expressing itself in bootlegging, the numbers racket and other gambling enterprises. Organized crime is still a present reality.

'White collar crime' is to be distinguished as those crimes committed by persons of respected professional, business or social status in pursuit of occupational activities or financial advancement. White collar crimes frequently go undetected and usually centre around financial dealings, such as swindles or frauds.

Criminology, the study of the causation, correction and prevention of criminal behaviour, reveals numerous theories, as to the cause of crime, beginning with an Italian, Cesare Lombroso in the nineteenth century, who associated heredity with crime. His theory centred on peculiarities of physical appearance (especially skull deformities) supposedly indicative of a criminal type. Gabriel Tarde, a French psychologist later advocated the theory that crime was learned in association with other criminals. The nineteenth-century European socialist writers attributed crime to poverty. Early in the twentieth century, Charles Goring in England ascribed criminality to mental deficiency without correlation to the physical peculiarities of Lombroso. Still another theory, that of an American psychiatrist, William Healy, maintains that crime results from many factors operating together – the multi-causal theory. More recently, psychoanalysts have suggested that crime is a symptom of disturbing experiences occurring within the family during a child's formative years. Finally, there is the differential association theory of Edwin Sutherland, an American sociologist, which holds that crime is normally learned behaviour of individuals who are exposed more thoroughly and earlier to pro-criminal behaviour that it overcomes the influence of anticriminal behaviour. The variety of theories illustrates that one all-inclusive cause of crime cannot be easily advocated.

Criminal laws of the USA are regarded as the most severe in the world. The American criminal serves about twice as long as his counterpart elsewhere in the world. There is also a great disparity in the sentences handed down by the courts – a convicted murderer in Texas is apt to get a shorter sentence than the man convicted of the same crime in Illinois.

There is a continuing debate over the issue of capital punishment (q.v.), and in certain places this debate has political repercussions. Some feel that the death penalty is the only protection that society has against criminals, while others contend that the electric chair, gas chamber and gallows are a reflection of a punitive and primitive society. The debate is further reflected in the differing views of penology between those who feel that punishment and imprisonment are effective deterrents to crime and those who view prison life as detrimental and encouraging recidivism. On moral grounds, there are those who contend that no human being has the right to take away the life of another, while others argue that the punishment must fit the crime for the sake of social order and control.

Crime prevention and the rehabilitation of criminals is not solely the responsibility of law enforcement agencies. Individuals, communities and society as a whole must develop a concept of social responsibility for crime and for the criminal offender; all must work for crime prevention, legal reforms and measures for constructive rehabilitation.

Harry Elmer Barnes and Negley K. Teeters, *New Horizons in Criminology*, 3rd edn., 1959; Marshall B. Clinard, *Sociology of Deviant Behaviour*, 1957; Edwin H. Sutherland and Donald R. Cressey, *Principles of Criminology*.

6th edn., 1960; Gus Tyler, ed., *Organized Crime in America*, 1962.

ROBERT LEE

Cruelty

Cruelty can be described as the unnecessary infliction of pain by one person on another or others. A distinction can be made between pain consciously and unconsciously inflicted. *Consciously inflicted pain* includes among other things: (1) the infliction of physical pain in one or more of the countless ways possible; (2) the calculated humiliation of a person in public by exposing his ignorance, lack of social experience or general incompetence in living; and (3) the steady attempt to undermine another's confidence in himself by whatever means seem most effective. *Unconsciously inflicted pain* includes: (1) constant questioning, nagging, fussing, reminding; (2) the frequent repetition of anecdotes and reminiscences; (3) readiness to give advice on all occasions; (4) dominating conversations and assuming that all thinking people agree absolutely with the speaker's religious, political, aesthetic and moral tenets; (5) a consistent ability to bore others on all subjects; (6) incessant noise from immoderate use of television, radio, record players, etc.

There are those who find perverted satisfaction in the actual physical excitement of inflicting or bearing bodily pain, while others enjoy a different excitement in either inflicting or bearing non-physical pain, for example, humiliating another or being humiliated.

R. E. C. BROWNE

Culture, Society and Community

1. *Introduction*. Each of the words treated in this article has a history of its own, a history filled with ambiguities of meaning and reversals of connotation. An account of the differing usages characteristic of different authors would require several volumes. We have chosen, therefore, to focus attention on a few of the most widely accepted meanings of the terms, and on the various levels of sociological analysis which need to be differentiated from one another, and which often have been and fruitfully can be designated by the terms culture, society and community.

Any human collectivity which has an orderly existence over a period of time must have at least minimal consensus on the values, norms and role-expectations appropriate for its members. There must also be at least minimal acceptance of the legitimacy of the institutional structures by means of which resources are allocated and utilized, decisions regarding the interpretation of the consensus in specific situations are made, and social direction and control are enforced.

Following Parsons' postulation of the four 'functional imperatives' of social organization, we may assign the following meanings to the terms: *Culture* is the province of *values*, those elements in a world-view which reflect a collectivity's notions of the *ends* appropriate for it and its individual members. Culture is concerned with *patterns* of norms and aspirations above and beyond concrete role-expectations in specific situations where specific purposes are sought; it is concerned, furthermore, with the maintenance of these patterns. *Society* is the province of *goals*, the division of labour employed as a means of attaining these goals, and the institutions – laws, arrangements governing production of economic goods, family structures – by means of which behaviour is organized for particular purposes and regulated in their pursuit. Collectivities which are separate politically are sometimes spoken of as belonging to the same society because of the fact that the *organization* of political, economic and social life is similar in each nation – for example, it is frequently said that 'Western Society' is 'mass society' because technology, bureaucracy and popular entertainment are similar (both in extent and in effect) in the nations included in this category – yet because *laws* are of such crucial importance in the integration and adaptation of social behaviour, a society is typically a distinct political entity, and it is always in quest of the highest degree of economic self-sufficiency possible for it. *Community* is normally used to refer to a geographically defined collectivity (usually a relatively small area). Sometimes, however, especially when used by theologians, the term refers to a collectivity characterized by an unusually high degree of consensus and a very strong 'we-feeling' among members; often, indeed, community refers to the *sentiments* of strong mutual affection, devotion to common ideals and self-sacrificial concern that are characteristic of some closely-knit collectivities.

2. *Culture*. Words such as agriculture and horticulture, and use of the word 'culture' in connection with bacilli grown in laboratories, preserve the earliest meaning of the word in regard to man: the cultivation or nurture of desirable human capacities. This essentially aristocratic Greek understanding of the term accompanied its introduction into German by Kant and its early elaboration by Herder, and is adhered to by modern classicists such as Matthew Arnold, John Cowper, Werner Jaeger and T. S. Eliot. Lester F. Ward introduced in America a variant of this meaning absorbed from P. Barth and Tonnies, for example, the concept of culture as control of nature in science and art, in contrast with civilization, the control of human nature in politics and morals. An important contrary current is that best represented in Germany by Alfred Weber and in America by Robert MacIver, Talcott Parsons, Robert Merton and Howard Odum: these writers use the concept of culture to refer to the

non-material treasures of a people (values, principles and ideals – the ends toward which they strive), in contrast with civilization, the knowledge and technical skills – the means – that determine the scientific and material level achieved by a people. Another group of writers follow Voltaire in using the term culture to mean 'the spirit of a people'.

Anthropology reads a more general, more descriptive and less normative meaning into the term. After an initial period in which culture was thought of as just a collocation of unrelated customs, it gained currency as a term meaning the 'social heritage' or the 'way' characteristic of a particular group. The generally accepted modern anthropological meaning ascribed to the term began with E. Tylor, who declared that 'Culture, or civilization . . . is that complex whole which includes knowledge, belief, art, law, morals, custom, and any other capabilities and habits acquired by man as a member of society'. As elaborated by other scholars, culture is a descriptive *concept* based on characteristics which seem to be present in all known cultures (that is, in the configuration of value-orientation, institutions and patterns of thought or behaviour in a particular human collectivity where this onfiguration governs attitudes and influences action). Most scholars now describe culture as having the following attributes:

(*a*) It is not the result of biological or other natural factors; it is the work of human hands and minds. It may be heavily influenced by biological and environmental conditions, but it is 'man-made', a human *response* to these conditions rather than an inevitable consequence of them.

(*b*) It is not just a collocation of customs or attitudes which are unrelated to each other; it is a patterned whole in which, to a greater or lesser degree, each cultural trait is interlocked with and functionally related to many other traits. (Contemporary functional theorists, notably Robert K. Merton, contend that early functionalists, such as Malinowski and others who based their conclusions on study of primitive societies, erred in assuming that *all* cultural traits are inter-related with all other traits – but modern analysts agree that a high degree of inter-relationship and integration is necessary if a culture is to maintain itself.) As Ruth Benedict emphasized in her seminal work, *Patterns of Culture*, this viewpoint is also held by philosophers of history who are influenced by Dilthey or Gestalt psychology.

(*c*) Culture implies continuity in time as well as comprehensiveness in scope, for it is not only shared by all members of a society (even those who reveal its impact upon them by challenging certain aspects of it, perhaps aspects regarded by them as dysfunctional in terms of the culture's own values) but it is transmitted to future generations and to new-comers through appropriate rituals and institutionalized processes. Ralph Linton stresses this characteristic of culture by asserting that it must be thought of as a *continuum*; he insists that 'the sharing which justifies the inclusion of a particular item in the culture configuration' cannot be established at only one point in time; this question can only be answered by examining the culture over a substantial period of time.

(*d*) The values, the worldview, the overall orientation of a society are especially important elements of its culture. The focus of concern on values which is so typical of contemporary sociologists and anthropologists began with W. I. Thomas and F. Znaniecki's *The Polish Peasant*, which was published in 1918–20, and it is especially pronounced in the work of Talcott Parsons and his students today.

3. *Society and Community*. The best known and probably the most important meaning attaching itself to these terms is derived from their use as the English equivalents of *Gesellschaft* and *Gemeinschaft*, concepts of abiding significance in sociology which were introduced by F. Tönnies. *Gemeinschaft* (community) is the ideal-type of a human collectivity in which all members 'love and understand each other . . . and dwell together and organize their common life'. In contrast to *Gesellschaft* (society), in which relationships are contractual and interaction is 'business-like', community relationships are based on sentiments of warmth and respect for tradition, and community interaction is characterized by organic unity. 'The real foundation of unity, and consequently the possibility of *Gemeinschaft*, is in the first place closeness of blood relationships and mixture of blood, secondly physical proximity, and finally – for human beings – intellectual proximity.' Society 'is conceived as mere co-existence of people independent of each other', who relate to one another only because it is in the interests of the members to relate segmentally in particular areas of life where they are, for functional reasons, interdependent. Apart from 'transactions' there would be no 'common values', and the latter disappear when the former have been concluded.

The importance of these ideal-typical concepts in a civilization where the relatively simple harmonies of rural or small town life are being replaced by the complexities of urban life is obvious; it is hardly surprising, therefore, that many writers have endeavoured to refine these concepts as applicable to their own time and place – and that many reflect a bias different from that of Tönnies, or make explicit a value-judgment more favourable to societal (associational) than to communal tendencies in modern western culture! A host of contemporary social analysts have accepted the notion that life in a technological bureaucratic, mobile age is bound to be characterized by rootlessness, anomie, depersonalization, segmentation of human relationships, development of an inhumane 'marketing orientation', etc., as a result of (in the title of a recent work by Maurice Stein) 'the eclipse of community'. Others, while accepting much that is valid and illuminating in this dominant school of thought, have followed the lead of Durkheim in showing that society is not as devoid of the communal traits as Tönnies suggested, nor is community as simply harmonious (or desirable!) as many of his intellectual offspring imply in their quest for 'neighbourliness' and 'belonging' in metropolitan areas. As Durkheim pointed out, the solidarity of the community was due largely to lack of imagination and a parochial vision of life possibilities; moreover, he called attention to the fact that societal relationships are not purely contractual, since arrangements for division of labour, trade and government would break down except for the fact that these utilitarian arrangements also generate sentiments of loyalty and warmth that go beyond contractual obligations and serve to promote social cohesion. (Durkheim even reversed the terminology of Tönnies – he called the solidarity of the community 'mechanical' and that of the society 'organic'.) Durkheim's observations are confirmed by the findings of psychology, which emphasized the ambiguity of individuals and groups which function as a 'mother' and the ambivalence of those who are the 'children' of such individuals or groups. On the one hand, the acceptance and love of an intimate group are necessary for the emotional well-being of every person; on the other hand, however, the arms which nourish and sustain the spiritual life of the individual can also confine, stunt and even suffocate him.

One of the most interesting refinements of theory regarding associational and communal ties is that of Hans Schmalenbach, who proposes that the term 'communion' (*Bund*) be added to those of society and community in order to explain certain paradoxes evident in earlier presentations of the polarity. Declaring that the three terms are not designations of 'species of concrete structures' but rather characterizations of tone, 'forms of being that may or may not be assumed by such concrete structures', he goes on to suggest the following ideal-typical schema: on basis of relationship, contract for society, custom for community and devotion for communion; on nature of ties, good faith (momentary, specific, yet with a continuity based on self-interest) for society, obedience (enduring relationships of obligation and privilege, but with sentiments of duty rather than of warmth) for community and passionate attachment (inevitably unstable because of the intensity of emotion) for communion; on prototype, economic and juridical relations for society, family for community

and friendship for communion; on spirit of interaction, rational-purposeful acts for both society and community and value-rational (but purposeless, non-calculating) for communion. According to Schmalenbach, the history of most collectivities is partly the story of their efforts to routinize the charisma of communion into the dependability of community or society. Countervailing tendencies are apparent within religious groups, for again and again (as the recurring outbursts of sectarian vitality indicate) the attempt is made within churches to rekindle the intensity of love rather than rely on the rigidities of order of the calculations of justice. Countervailing desires are also manifested in individuals who, counting insecurity a small price to pay for the joys of communion, eschew all permanent liaisons that might harden into community.

Ruth Benedict, *Patterns of Culture*, 1934; Emile Durkheim, *The Elementary Forms of the Religious Life*, 1912; *The Division of Labour in Society*, 2nd edn., 1902; *Suicide*, 1897; Alfred L. Kroeber and Clyde Kluckhohn, *Culture: A Critical Review of Concepts and Definitions*, 1952; Ralph Linton, *The Study of Man*, 1936; Bronislaw Malinowski, *A Scientific Theory of Culture*, 1944; Robert K. Merton, *Social Theory and Social Structure*, 2nd edn., rev., 1957; Talcott Parsons, *Essays in Sociological Theory*, 1949; *The Social System*, 1951; Ferdinand Tönnies, *Community and Society*, 1887; Max Weber, *The Theory of Social and Economic Organization*, 1922.

HENRY B. CLARK

Custom

Custom refers to the habitual behaviour of a society. It represents the normal, typical, response of any social group to the normal conditions of life, interpersonal relationships, and environment. It is the daily, immediate working out of the effects of tradition, ethics, religion, values and world-view. The American who turns a piece of pie so that the point is towards him when he eats it, or who looks automatically to his left for oncoming traffic when he crosses the street (whereas the Britisher looks to his right), or who becomes excited over World Series games, or who feels repulsed by the thought of eating fried caterpillars, or who feels that a distance of 12–20 inches between people engaged in conversation is 'intimate' (whereas for a Latin American anything greater is cold and withdrawn), is following the customs of his group.

The customs of any group are not a collection of oddities, or of odds and ends of unrelated behaviour, however. A people's customs, no matter how diverse and unrelated they may seem to the observer, are to varying degrees interwoven into a network of behaviour, personality, emotion and value system, which is unique for every society, and which constitutes its culture. Customs are the individual habitual traits of behaviour by which people act out their culture, but a culture is far more than a listing of customs. It is a dynamic force rooted in a people's psychology, values and history. Customs are part of its manifestation.

Most customs, or *folkways*, exist only on the level of the unconscious, unsophisticated ways of daily life. People act as they do because of their cultural pre-conditioning without ever giving it a thought or dreaming of being critical of what seems so 'natural'. Some customs, particularly those which are threatened by change or by the example of some other intruding culture may shift to the level of *mores*, of prescriptive behaviour, but prescriptive behaviour simply accepted as right, not formulated into law. Laws and taboos may then eventually derive from such customary behaviour when even greater sanction is required to keep it from being changed.

Once a custom is called to the attention of the people who practise it by being threatened in some way, it may be quickly rationalized, given a pseudo-historical explanation, or a mythological reason for existence. Anthropologists, on the other hand, have set themselves to find the historical, functional and psychological factors within the culture which provide the basis for significant individual custom.

People's tendency to accept the greatest bulk of their own customs as right, natural and comfortable leads to ethnocentricity when they look at the customs of other people. These seem odd, difficult, cumbersome, embarrassing, primitive, stupid, dangerous, or (on the other hand) glamorous, powerful or exotic. In either case foreign customs may be copied and assimilated into the receiving cultural system, thus modifying the culture, but on the other hand massive influence from another culture may be seen as a threat to be opposed bitterly.

Custom, therefore, can be understood in any non-superficial way only relative to other custom, and to the culture as a whole. It can also best be understood cross-culturally, that is relative to other people's ways of meeting the same kinds of problems with other customs which are the manifestations of other cultural configuration.

WILLIAM A. SMALLEY

Cybernetics

Cybernetics is defined as the study of control and communication processes in animals and machines. The word seems to have been first used in 1948 by Professor Norbert Wiener of the Massachusetts Institute of Technology. The aspect of cybernetics which has attracted most attention is the comparison between the functioning of electronic machines and nervous systems, including the nervous system of man and the mental life associated with it. Two very different questions are raised by cybernetics for the student of ethics. The first question is whether man can be understood as analogous, in his mental life, to an electronic machine, and whether one could then continue to regard him as a moral agent. The notion of man as a machine is not, of course, a new one. What is new is the extent to which it is now possible to show that such activities as speech, memory, counting and the like are explicable in terms of the way these new machines work, and that many of these activities can be more efficiently performed by machines. So far, of course, only the lower mental activities, like calculation, can be done by machines, and one could argue that just as man has largely relieved himself of heavy manual labour by inventing machines to do it for him, so he may relieve himself of routine mental processes and be freed for creative ones. But to this it might be replied that there is no obvious limit to what machines may be able to do, and that perhaps they will take over our supposedly creative and imaginative activities too. But let us suppose (and according to C. von Weizsacker, the supposition is not entirely idle) that a 'machine' was built that could do everything that man can do, including the initiation of spontaneous and intelligent action. This would not prove that man was at bottom a machine, but rather we would have to say that the 'machine' that had been built was no longer a machine. A new kind of entity would have emerged, a kind of quasi-person which would be itself a moral agent if indeed it was capable of exercising all the faculties that man possesses. The second moral problem raised by cybernetics is a much more practical one. As the use of control and communication mechanisms increases, the whole structure of society may be very profoundly affected. In particular, there may be an elimination of a great many unskilled or semi-skilled jobs, that will be better done by machines. Already there are programmes for retraining workers left behind in such developments. Yet there would seem to be a limit to the possibilities for retraining and reabsorption. Some economists are already talking in terms of a time when work will be optional, and when our automated industries will be able to provide a guaranteed income for all, whether they work or not. But no one has yet considered the very serious moral and social problems of such a situation. The persons displaced from work and maintained in an enforced idleness would be the least intelligent and least educable elements of the population, and so those least fitted to make any creative use of leisure. To put it bluntly, they would be the discards for which society could find no use. Their lives might well be intolerably boring and frustrating. Moreover, we would have a society more sharply and dangerously divided and polarized than ever before in history. There would, however, be a strange reversal of roles and transvaluation of values. The workers would constitute the new aristocracy. Perhaps some of the speculations and questions now being raised by economists and sociologists will not be realized, just as the fears that the Industrial Revolution would lead to widespread idleness were mistaken. Nevertheless, as the cybernation process speeds up, moralists of all persuasions must set their minds to the question of how the dignity and sense of worth in human life can be maintained for those who will be least able to cope with the changes. Most of the schemes so far envisaged seem to be aimed only at 'keeping the natives quiet'.

EDITOR

Cyrenaics

Of all the hellenistic schools of philosophy that of the Cyrenaics was the simplest and the most uncomplicated. Its founder Aristippus held that pleasure is the supreme good and the highest aim in life (Diogenes Laertius ii.85,87; Cicero, *Academics* ii.xiii.131). And the pleasure in question is the pleasure of the body, for bodily pleasures are the most vivid and intense (Diogenes Laertius ii.87,90). Still further, the pleasure in question is the pleasure of the moment, for the past is gone and the future is quite uncertain (Diogenes Laertius ii.66; Athenaeus, *Deipnoposphistae* 544). The aim of the Cyrenaics was not *eudaimonia*, happiness, but *hēdonē*, pleasure, so that they were sometimes called the hedonists.

The Cyrenaic theory of perception adds still something else to the picture. The Cyrenaics held that the only thing a man can know is sensation. He may have the sensation that something is sweet; the sensation he does know, but of the thing itself he knows nothing. It follows that there is no possible knowledge of anyone else's sensations; all that a man can know is his own. There are therefore no absolute criteria; the only possible guides are convention and tradition (Diogenes Laertius ii.93).

If there are no absolute criteria and if individual sensation is the criterion, then it is difficult to see how ethics enters into the Cyrenaic scheme at all. But the Cyrenaics did study moral philosophy under five parts – what to avoid and what to seek, passions, actions, causes, proofs (Sextus Empiricus, *Against the Logicians* i.11).

The Cyrenaics admitted that in common sense the consequences of any pleasure must be taken into account. Simply to get the greatest pleasure out of pleasure the Cyrenaics respected prudence and wisdom, and simply to avoid unpleasantness they abstained from what law and convention regard as evil (Diogenes Laertius ii.87,90,93). No one denied that a man could leave the school of Aristippus a profligate (Cicero, *De Nat. Deorum* iii.xxxi.77), but if he

did so it simply meant that he was not having pleasure at its most pleasant.

One thing remains to be added. The Cyrenaics insisted that a man must be master of pleasure and not pleasure master of him. In regard to his relationships with Lais, the famous courtesan, Aristippus spoke his most famous epigram, *echō, ouk echomai*, 'I possess, but I am not possessed'.

For the Cyrenaics ethics existed simply to make pleasure more pleasant, and the odd consequence was that Aristippus and many of his followers were far better than their creed. It was Plato who paid Aristippus the greatest compliment: 'You alone are endowed with the gift to flaunt in robes or walk in rags' (Diogenes Laertius ii.67).

WILLIAM BARCLAY

Cynics

The Cynic preacher was a familiar wanderer in the ancient world, shaggy and unkempt, always uncompromising and sometimes heroic to the point of martyrdom.

Epictetus (*Discourses* iii.xxii.1–10) paints the picture of the Cynic saint. He cannot start without God. He has no desire but the desire for goodness. His self-respect is his only protection and his only guardian. He is the ambassador of God and the preacher of righteousness. He may be naked and penniless but he knows true freedom and true happiness. He will be flogged and he will love the man who flogs him. His governing principle, waking and sleeping, will be purer than the sun.

For the Cynic virtue is all that matters. Ethics is the one and only science. And ethics is not theory; it is action (Diogenes Laertius vi.11). Virtue is something that can be taught and it can be achieved only in one way, by putting your mind to it.

Happiness to be real must be inalienable. The one thing a man can never lose is his mind. Therefore virtue consists in a certain attitude to life. What is that attitude? It is complete self-sufficiency, complete independence of all material things and all external happenings.

Wealth must be abandoned, for wealth and virtue cannot exist together. 'The love of money is the metropolis of all evils', Diogenes said (Diogenes Laertius vi.50). Pleasure must be abandoned. Antisthenes, the founder of the school, said that he would rather be mad than pleased (Diogenes Laertius vi.3). 'May the sons of your enemies live in luxury,' he said (Diogenes Laertius vi.8). Pleasure is the supreme enemy of life and *ponos*, toil, is the supreme good. Love must be abandoned for it makes a man the slave of his passions. 'If I could lay my hands on Aphrodite,' said Antisthenes, 'I would shoot her' (E. Gomperz, *The Greek Thinkers* ii.143). But the Cynics were no ascetics, and took their pleasure where they found it.

Zeller sees cynicism as a series of renunciations (*Socrates and the Socratic Schools*, pp. 316 ff.). It is a renunciation of civilization and a return to simplicity. Diogenes even tried eating his food raw (Diogenes Laertius vi.34, 76). It is a renunciation of social and political life. Diogenes called himself a citizen of the world. He may have coined the word *kosmopolitēs* (Diogenes Laertius vi.63). The Cynics were the first thinkers to declare slavery unnatural, and to insist that the only difference between man and man is the difference in virtue and vice. It was for the Cynic the renunciation of modesty and shame. The Cynics notoriously did the most private things in the most public places, believing that, if it was right to do a thing anywhere, it was right to do it anywhere (Diogenes Laertius vi.69). It was a renunciation of the gods. Dill holds that the Cynics were 'probably the purest monotheists that classical antiquity produced' (*Roman Society from Nero to Marcus Aurelius*, p. 363). They believed that the only true sacrifice was a life of goodness and virtue (Julian, *Orations* vi.199,200; Xenophon, *Memorabilia* i.iv.9–15). Virtue was for them the only worship.

The Cynics believed that goodness was everything, worth any renunciation, and open to any man who would pay the price in toil.

WILLIAM BARCLAY

Dante

Dante (1265–1321) was born at Florence, surnamed Alighieri. Dante's ethical views received their most mature expression in *The Divine Comedy*, a poetic 'vision' or 'seeing into' the 'state of souls after death' and the great issues of this life. It is in the form of an imaginary journey, the aim of which is the attainment of human perfection. The *Comedy* has three 'canticles' – *Hell*, *Purgatory* and *Paradise*. Other works in which ethics are important are *The Banquet* (in Italian) and *On the Monarchy* (in Latin). The most important influences on Dante's ethical views were Aristotle, especially the *Ethics*, and St Thomas Aquinas both as writers of the *Summae* and as a commentator on Aristotle. Nevertheless Dante retains a personal emphasis and is not always in agreement with St Thomas.

The basis of all Dante's ethical thought is the belief that man is made for the vision of God and can find perfect peace in nothing else. Everything should be ordered to this end, even though the end, with very rare exceptions, can only be reached in Paradise. The true path to human maturity is a progress from a 'confused' seeing of God in bodily things, to a clearer knowing of him in scientific and philosophical speculation, and finally to true contemplation through divine illumination. For most people life here should be both active and contemplative.

Dante's *Hell* is a showing up of the evil which can cause an unrepentant sinner to miss the goal. Sins of intemperance – lust, gluttony, avarice (with prodigality), and wrath – are the least serious, being looked on as a failure to subject passion to the guidance of reason. All other sins involve deliberate evil will and are called malice. Malice is subdivided into sins of violence and deceit. Violence may be directed against God, one's neighbour or oneself, in person or property. Violence against God includes cursing God, sexual perversion as a despising of God's ordering of creation, and usury as a violation of the law of creative work implied in Genesis. Deceit is treated as more serious than violence because it is not only a deliberate injuring of one's neighbour, but is a perversion of man's noblest faculty, his mind. It is subdivided into simple deceit, such as flattery, seduction, stealing, coining, simony, political corruption and counselling deceitful actions – and treachery, which not only breaks the natural bond between each man and his neighbour as in simple deceit, but in addition breaks the special bond created by another's trust and perhaps love.

In the *Purgatory* the repentant sinner learns goodness, which means learning perfect love as a preparation for Paradise. The arrangement of Purgatory is based on the seven deadly sins in the order pride (the worst), envy, wrath, sloth, avarice, gluttony, lust, all being treated as imperfections of love. The first three are a loving of evil towards one's neighbour, sloth is insufficient love of the supreme good, the remaining three are excessive love of objects less than God. Dante lays great stress on the freedom of the will to choose what is discerned as good and to reject evil, even though heredity and the influences of the heavenly bodies make good choice more difficult for some than for others. To restrain greed and to correct natural human error Dante advocates one supreme earthly ruler (the Holy Roman Emperor) to establish order, and one supreme spiritual guide, the pope, without temporal power.

In the *Paradise* all souls are completely blessed, though in degrees varying with the capacity of each one. This depends both on endowment at birth and on the use made of this endowment during life.

The Divine Comedy, ed. by J. Sinclair, 1948, has the Italian text with a good English translation and notes; K. Foster, *God's Tree*, 1957, esp. Chap. 4, 'The Theology of the Inferno'.

SHEILA RALPHS

Darwin, Charles Robert

Darwin (1809–1882) is famous as the scientist who provided a firm empirical basis for the hypothesis of biological evolution. The new theory had its impact upon ethics, as on almost every other study related to human behaviour. It suggested that the 'moral sense' (to use the expression common in Darwin's time) needs no special explanation to account for its origin and presence in man, but, like other human characteristics, can be accounted for naturalistically. Darwin held that 'of all the differences between man and the lower animals, the moral sense or conscience is by far the most important'. He regarded it as 'in a high degree probable that any animal whatever, endowed with well-marked social instincts, the parental and filial affections being here included, would inevitably acquire a moral sense or conscience as soon as its intellectual powers had become as well, or nearly as well, developed, as in man'. He also suggested that different animals would develop different notions of morality according to their biological needs, and that man's moral standards are therefore not absolutes but relative to his condition. Ethics, however, was not a major concern of Darwin himself, and it was left to such writers as Huxley and Spencer to work out the consequences of evolution for ethics. *See The Descent of Man*, Chap. 4. *See also* **Evolutionary Ethics; Naturalistic Ethics.**

EDITOR

Decalogue

The Decalogue or Ten Commandments is perhaps the most famous basic code of moral law in the world. Traditionally, it was revealed by God to Moses, and it is given in two similar versions in the Old Testament (Ex. 20.1–17 and Deut. 5.6–21). The Commandments are differently divided among Roman Catholics on the one hand, and Protestants, Anglicans and some Orthodox on the other. The former take as a single Commandment the prohibition of other gods and of images, whereas the latter count these as two Commandments; conversely, the coveting of the neighbour's wife and goods can be reckoned as two Commandments or one. This makes a practical difference when the Commandments are mentioned by number: for the Protestant, the seventh Commandment has to do with adultery, but for the Roman Catholic it prohibits stealing. Because of their almost universal applicability, the Ten Commandments have been regarded as a kind of fundamental morality, and have been widely taught to children and used as a standard for self-examination. At one time they were commonly displayed in parish churches. Yet even so simple a code as the Decalogue is historically conditioned, notably in the matter of Sabbath observance. *See* **Old Testament Ethics.**

EDITOR

Decision

In the most general sense, to decide is to give an answer (not necessarily in words) to any question; for example, logicians speak of 'decision-procedures' for deciding whether propositions are true or false. Most commonly, however, the word is used of answering, for oneself or another, the question 'Shall I do this (or that)?', in the sense in which asking that question is deliberation (q.v.). It is commonly supposed that every voluntary action is preceded by a decision; but this is not so. To decide, or answer the question 'Shall I do this?', I have first to *ask* this question (deliberate); if I act without having asked the question, I have made no decision. We sometimes act without having decided, because we have not had time to ask the question. For although it cannot be said that the actual deciding always takes time (it may be the mere boundary between being undecided and being decided) nevertheless there has to be time for asking the question before we can answer it. Additional time may be, but need not be, spent on considering this question; when we say that a man took a long time to decide, our meaning could otherwise be expressed by saying that he took a long time before deciding. But lack of time is not the only possible reason for acting without deciding; a man may (voluntarily) enter holy orders, to whom it has never occurred to do anything else (the youngest son, say, of an aristocratic family in which it is taken for granted that the youngest son becomes a clergyman). We might say: 'He never *decided* to enter the ministry; he had always intended to.'

Therefore decision is not a necessary constituent of voluntary action, nor of the forming of an intention (q.v.). Nevertheless, a being who in principle could not make decisions (that is, ask himself, and answer, the question 'Shall I do this?') could hardly be said to act voluntarily or to be a free agent in the fullest sense.

R. M. HARE

Defence Mechanisms

Defence mechanism is used generally of any adjustment adopted automatically to avoid having to come to grip directly with painful facts or situations, but having adaptive intent. Technically it is employed in psychoanalysis (q.v.) to describe measures by which the ego (q.v.) resists unwanted impulses from the id (q.v.) and unwanted feelings, both positive and negative. These measures are carried out below the level of conscious awareness and hence can never be observed directly but are reconstructed in retrospect. Defence mechanisms are in part accompaniments of neurosis and in part substitutes for it. Individual persons tend to be relatively consistent in the sort of defences they employ.

The most significant of the defence mechanisms, *repression*, will be dealt with in a separate article. Other common mechanisms are: *regression*, in which the person reverts to an earlier level of thinking, feeling, or behaving, to escape the threat inherent in increasing responsibility and complexity; *reaction-formation* in which an impulse or conflict is rejected and a new personality characteristic (frequently embodying the exact opposite) is developed in lieu as, for example, where an intolerable hatred is disguised in an excess of love. In such instances the new characteristic frequently subtly achieves the aims of the original impulse as, for example, where the excessive love cripples and destroys the hated person; *projection*, in which one's own feelings, attitudes or desires, are attributed to other persons; *introjection*, or identification, in which the attributes or attitudes of others are taken over as one's own; *sublimation*, in which instinctual aims which cannot be directly gratified are re-directed into other and more acceptable channels. This last has been much disputed, particularly in relation to interpretations of creativity as sublimated sexuality. A complete treatment is contained in Anna Freud, *The Ego and the Mechanisms of Defence* (1937).

The popular tendency is to treat all defence mechanisms as uniformly bad. While they do have in common a distortion of reality, some forms of defence may be necessary for the survival of the ego. There are forms of regression, for example, which are extremely helpful if they permit the individual concerned to re-group his resources better to move forward again in the developmental process. Defence mechanisms are common both to normal persons and to neurotics. They become neurotic symptoms when re-inforced by constant use against the same stimuli. It is possible for strong defensive measures to become independent of the original conflict and to result in bodily changes (e.g., rigidity or stiffness) or personality characteristics (e.g., the fixed smile or an arrogant attitude). Mobility can frequently be recovered with proper psychotherapeutic treatment.

GRAEME M. GRIFFIN

Deliberation

Deliberation is the name given to the process of asking and considering the question 'Shall I do this?'; to answer this question is to make a decision (q.v.). The minimal form of deliberation is the mere asking of the question; but since normally we decide for reasons, deliberation is usually concerned with the consideration of reasons for or against some action. The two types of reason most commonly discussed by philosophers are: (1) that the action is of a certain kind; (2) that the action is a means to a certain end. Since (2) is a sub-case of (1), an account of deliberation in terms of (1) is likely to be more complete than one which is confined to (2). Another reason for rejecting accounts of deliberation solely in terms of means and ends is the following: it is usually said that means precede their ends in time, and are causes or conditions of attaining them. But often we decide to do *a*, *although* it has the

consequence c_1, *because* it has the consequence c_2. If c_1 precedes c_2 in time, and is the cause or condition of it, c_1 can in most cases be called the means and c_2 the end. But suppose that c_1 succeeds c_2 in time, as when we order oysters because they will give us pleasure (c_2), although they will give us indigestion (c_1); nobody in that case would call getting indigestion tomorrow a means to getting pleasure today; yet there is a close analogy between this sort of case and the preceding, which the means-end terminology obscures. In morals it is most important to realize that the relative position in time of the various things that we bring about by an action is normally irrelevant to the morality of the action. It is as bad to bring about a small good today at the cost of a greater evil tomorrow (both being equally certain) as to bring about a small good tomorrow at the cost of a greater evil today.

The following schema of deliberation is adequate to cover most cases. Faced with the necessity of doing one of several alternative actions, we consider in detail what we should be doing if we did each of them (including the consequences we should be bringing about). It will be found that certain of these details bring the actions under various moral or other principles (the word 'principle' is here to be understood in its Aristotelian sense, to include, e.g., desires): if I did a_1, I should be transgressing principle p_1; to do a_2 is required in order to observe principle p_2; if I do a_3 I shall (or shall not) fulfil my desire for x, etc. In the simplest case it will turn out that only one of the alternative actions is consistent with our principles; if so, then unless we have in the process been led to reconsider the principles themselves, we shall do that action. In other cases there is a conflict of principle and we cannot, as things are, observe or obey all our principles; this forces us to reconsider them and to qualify one of them so as to admit an exception in this type of case, if the principles are moral ones. If, however, a moral principle is in conflict with a non-moral one, the latter may be merely overridden, not qualified. A moral principle, in one sense of the word, is one which cannot be overridden in this way. Therefore, if two moral principles are in conflict, one of them has to be qualified, unless we are content to say that whatever we do in certain situations is bound to be wrong – a conclusion which offends against the principle that it is always possible to avoid doing wrong, or that 'ought' implies 'can'.

It is the finding of principles which will resolve such moral conflicts that constitutes the substance and the difficulty of moral thought, and is the source of most moral progress.

R. M. HARE

Democracy

The primary meaning of democracy is government by the people either directly or, as in most cases, through their elected representatives, but there are important differences between the democratic tradition that tends to absolutize the general will, however this may be expressed, and the democratic tradition which limits what the majority may do by protecting the rights of individuals and of limited groups under the rule of law. The first of these traditions is generally associated with the French revolution and the second with the growth of Anglo-Saxon institutions under the influence of the Puritan revolutionary ferment in the seventeenth century and of John Locke. The second type of democracy is more often defended on Christian grounds for it makes room more clearly for divine sovereignty above the State, for freedom of conscience and for checks upon the power of the people because of the recognition of the pervasiveness of sin.

It would be a mistake to assume that Christians in general have historically shown a preference for democracy in either form. Churches have often lived with despotic regimes without basic protest though Christian reflection has often been favourable to some form of constitutional aristocracy. Both Thomas Aquinas and John Calvin illustrate the latter tendency. In spite of the record of many churches, there are sources of deep conflict between Christian faith and ethics on the one hand and political tyranny, on the other, for the latter tends to defy the authority of God or to deny the claims of the individual conscience or of the Church.

The widespread revolutions of the recent past have swept away the authoritarian regimes with which some churches had learned to live and today there is a very common tendency for Christians to recognize that there is a kinship between their faith and political democracy of the constitutional type. It is often realized by Christians that unless the suffrage is open to all classes and races great injustice is usually done to the people who have no voice, that a nation that does not encourage wide participation in political life fails to develop its human resources, that unless there are constitutional protections for individuals and minorities a nation can easily slide towards tyranny of the totalitarian type and the State may become an idol. Such considerations do predispose Christians in many countries to prefer democracy. The concept of 'the responsible society' developed by the World Council of Churches points towards constitutional democracy. The two most recent popes, Pius XII and John XXIII, have opened the way to an acceptance of democracy without prescribing any form of government as mandatory. (*See* especially *Pacem in Terris*, par. 52.) Protestant liberalism of the Social Gospel type took democracy for granted as an expression of Christian faith and did so on the basis of a highly optimistic view of man. Reinhold Niebuhr has restated the

Christian case for democracy on the basis of a realistic view of man. (*See* his *Children of Light and Children of Darkness*, 1944.) Karl Barth has also developed a Christian basis for democracy. (*See* especially his essay, 'The Christian Community and the Civil Community' in *Against the Stream*, 1954.)

The great variety of historical experience makes it important to avoid a legalistic identification of Christianity with any of the established western democratic structures. This is clearly seen when Christian spokesmen from Asia, Africa and Latin America are heard. There are situations in which the chief priority may often be order, or a revolutionary breakthrough to greater justice and experiments with governments that are more authoritarian than democratic may seem to be necessary. To those who feel the need of revolutionary change, established democratic structures often seem to provide the form rather than the substance of freedom for the vast majority. On the other hand, the Christian concern for all the people including those who are weak and disadvantaged and the Christian concern for freedom from arbitrary power point towards institutions which in ways, old or new, express the impulses behind constitutional democracy.

JOHN C. BENNETT

Deontology

Deontology means literally the 'science of duty'. The word is used in several distinct senses: (1) the expression 'deontology' seems to have been first used by Jeremy Bentham (q.v.) to designate his own utilitarian ethics, but it would not commonly be understood in this way nowadays; (2) among Roman Catholic moral theologians, 'deontology' is used for the special ethics associated with a particular profession or vocation. *See* **Medical Ethics; Professional Ethics;** and (3) perhaps most commonly, 'deontology' denotes a view of morality which takes as its fundamental categories the notions of 'obligation' or 'duty', and the 'rightness' of acts. This deontological view of morality may be contrasted with the view which stresses the end of action (the 'good'), sometimes called 'agathology'.

Depravity, Total. *see* Total Depravity.

Descriptivism

Descriptivism is a name sometimes given to the view that the meaning of moral terms is exhausted by their descriptive functions: for example, that 'He is a good man' serves solely to describe a man as having a certain property or properties – so that to know the meaning of 'good' is simply to know what property or properties objects have to have in order to be called 'good'. Often contrasted with prescriptivism. Naturalism is currently the most popular variety of descriptivism (*see* **Naturalistic Ethics**) others are intuitionism and (in some senses) subjectivism (qq.v.). *See also* **Ethics; Conventional Morality.**

R. M. HARE

Destiny

We confine ourselves to the ethical significance of this idea. Many nations or communities have believed themselves to have a 'destiny', in the sense that a certain goal had been set before them. The use of the word 'destiny' usually implies that this goal has been set by some transhuman agency, perhaps God; but the notion need not be fatalistic, since the community may have to strive to fulfil its destiny. The word 'destiny' is not biblical, though one does find related terms, such as 'determinate' and 'predestinate'. However, something like the idea of destiny is contained in the biblical doctrine of God's providence and his sovereign disposal of history. From an early time, the people of Israel were conscious of having a destiny, and it was this consciousness which held them together and gave them their identity. In the NT the Church appears as the eschatological community, and such a community may be said to be conscious of a destiny. In modern times, the word has often had more sinister associations. German philosophy in the nineteenth and twentieth centuries has made a good deal of the destiny (*Geschick*) of the German people, and there can be no doubt that this notion contributed to German nationalism. The notion of having a destiny is found also in the USA. There it takes the relatively harmless form of supposing that God has specially favoured America and conferred on it the mission of leading the rest of the world to freedom and affluence. The pervasiveness of such ideas is evident from the habit of American politicians of decorating their speeches with pious references. A much more baneful conception of destiny is found among the white population of South Africa. From these few illustrations, it becomes apparent that the conception of destiny has very ambiguous implications for ethics. A sense of destiny can bring cohesion to a community, can invest its life with meaning and dignity, can inspire noble aspirations and ideals, and give courage to endure hardships in the pursuit of them. But it can also induce feelings of superiority and it has in fact contributed to aggressiveness, racism, nationalism and fanaticism. *See also* **Fate and Fatalism.**

EDITOR

Determinism. *see* Freewill and Determinism.

Development

Development means literally 'unfolding' or 'unwrapping', but has come to mean the sequence of more or less gradual changes, both structural and functional, which take place during the life of the organism from the beginning of life to maturity or death. By analogy the term is also applied to changes in nonorganic phenomena – such as minerals, human societies and cultures and abstract ideas.

Although the primary model of the current conception of development is biological, and is specifically derived from changes which take place in the embryo, development is conceived to be due not only to biological, or hereditary factors, but also to environmental factors, including in the development of human beings learning and other cultural influences.

The basic processes of development are: (1) differentiation of relatively diffuse structures and (2) their re-integration into more complex wholes. Growth, which is included in development, but is not identical with it (in spite of much current usage), takes place in spurts, and may occur during either differentiation or integration (for example, the marked differences in growth and development of human beings at puberty). These processes are repeated many times during the life of an individual, resulting in ever more complex integrative systems.

Timing and sequence of development have been shown to be crucial by experimental embryology. If proper internal and external conditions are not present when the biological potential is maximal, deficiencies and abnormalities result. Structures already developed become a part of these conditions, and hence must be 'evoked' in proper sequence. For a technical discussion of the embryo-logical aspects of development, *see* Hans Spemann, *Embryonic Development and Induction* (1938), and for a more general discussion, *see* L. von Bertalanffy, *Problems of Life* (1952).

Evolution through natural selection and mutation has provided a secondary model for understanding development. This model has illuminated the adaptive aspects of development. *See* T. Dobshansky, *Mankind Evolving* (1962).

These points applied to human development are illuminated by the following perspectives of interest from the standpoint of ethics:

(1) *Development as the result of nurture.* Given a biological potential within normal range, the human infant and young child is dependent upon stable, warm, firm parental relationships for development without undue defect or distortion of personality. Freud was the first to provide a systematic understanding of the processes involved. He designated three developmental stages of childhood: oral, anal and phallic, according to the bodily focus of primary psycho-biological needs. Rejection, absence, inconsistency and binding the child too close, can result in less than optimal development at any or all of these stages. The last, or phallic stage, is thought to be difficult, if not

impossible, to pass through without some un-conscious personality conflict residuals being carried into adult life. It takes place ordinarily from three to five years of age, involves the rivalry of the child with the parent of the same sex for the affection of the parent of the opposite sex, and its consequent ambivalence of feeling. See **Psychoanalysis; Oedipus Complex; Character; Instincts or Drives.**

(2) *The developmental task*. Developmental tasks as defined by Robert J. Havighurst, originator of the term, are those functions which a human being in a given culture should be able to perform at a certain age. Some are more biologically determined, such as walking and talking, others are more culturally deter-mined with regard to timing and specificity – such as marriage and vocational choice. Havig-hurst holds that many developmental tasks have great influence on subsequent develop-ment, and therefore must be learned in proper sequence. This point can readily be seen when applied to such 'tasks' as walking, talking and reading, but Havighurst also has shown that such 'tasks' as learning social interaction with age mates of both sexes after puberty are im-portant for moral and intellectual development. *See* Havighurst's *Human Development and Education* (1953). *See also The Psychology of Character Development*, by Havighurst and R. J. Peck (1960) for a detailed exposition of the ethical implications of this viewpoint, though it includes factors other than those associated with conscious effort.

(3) *Development as response to conflict.* Though this idea is rooted in the Freudian tradition already mentioned, it has been systematically expounded by Erik H. Erikson as a combination of psychoanalytic ideas and concepts derived from cultural anthropology. 'Conflict' thus means intra-psychic and social conflict. Erikson's basic idea is that each developmental stage presents the individual with a core problem which he must solve or overcome. Thus the core problem for the infant is trust versus mistrust, that of the anal stage is shame versus autonomy, etc. Failure to solve the problem adequately leads to distorted development.

Though there are eight stages developed by Erikson, covering the entire life cycle, his treatment of adolescence has won him most renown. He conceived the core crisis of adoles-cence to be that of identity – in the sense of gaining a sense of self-sameness and continuity in various roles which adequately assimilate the instinctual drives, and which corresponds at least roughly to the image that others have of one. This is particularly acute in a multi-faceted culture such as ours which does not prescribe roles rigidly. Erikson further pointed out that adolescence tends to be prolonged in our culture because of its complexity. This pro-longation may result in eventual mastery, or in

adults who are adolescents in their interests, emotional instability and personality con-striction. Erikson's principal work is *Child-hood and Society* (1950).

(4) *Development as continuing beyond physical maturity*. Erikson and C. G. Jung have pointed out that development of capacities and func-tions continue until old age. Jung in particular has emphasized the importance of intra-psychic development in later years. *See* **Jung, Carl Gustav.**

There are two principal general implications for ethics to be drawn from the study of develop-ment. The first is the regulative principle that conduct cannot be judged by a static norm. Expectations of persons must take account of developmental factors, including functions which fail to develop because of earlier diffi-culties. Secondly, development has been taken by some as a constitutive principle of ethics, in the sense of the promotion and encourage-ment of development of persons and societies. Though this is a useful principle, it is not adequate of itself, since development brings increasing complexity, and consequently more possibilities for both good and evil.

JAMES N. LAPSLEY

Dewey, John

John Dewey (1859–1952), is fully discussed under **Pragmatism.**

Direction, Spiritual

It is an absolute necessity that you who are haughty and powerful and rich should appoint for yourself some man as trainer and pilot. Let there be at all events one whom you respect, one whom you fear, one whom you accustom yourself to listen to when he is outspoken and severe, though all the while at your service.

This early reference to spiritual direction comes from the end of the second century (Clement of Alexandria, *The Rich Man's Salvation*, chap. 41). The classical world and the Eastern civilizations knew the value of a director (*guru* among the Hindus) to reverence and obey. In the Christian Church this function was largely exercised in the confessional, though it is quite separate from ministering absolution. Guidance was also given outside the ecclesiastical setting, both verbally and by epistolatory correspondence. 'Spiritual Letters' take an important place in Catholic and Reformed *pastoralia* like those of Fenelon or Charles Simeon.

Individual Christians whose personal situa-tions cannot be dealt with in sermons or general instruction need spiritual direction in these kinds of problem: (1) to become aware of one's faults, to overcome one's besetting sins and avoid self-deception; (2) to convert a doubting conscience which does not know whether a course of action is right or wrong, into a certain and reliable one; (3) to learn how to make a decision in perplexity, i.e., when faced with a choice of conflicting duties; (4) to meet adversity courageously and profitably; (5) to find out what discipline and *ascesis* is called for; and (6) to learn humility.

Beyond these questions the field in which spiritual direction is best known and welcomed is the life of prayer, especially when it goes beyond 'saying one's prayers'. Guidance is needed, for instance, about the purgative, the illuminative and the unitive ways, and about the signs of passage from one to the other; also about the impossibility for some people of meditative prayer and the opportunities of other forms like contemplation or inner acts directing the feelings (affective prayer); again, about 'the dark nights' of the senses and the spirit which are daunting unless understood as a passage from a presence of God one can feel, to one in our very being; finally in order that one may 'test the spirits to see whether they are of God' (I John 4.1), so as to avoid mistaking one's own spiritual vibrations for the action of the Holy Ghost.

All the authorities lay it down that the spiritual director must be experienced and wise, and ready to detach the disciple from dependence upon the director and so learn to stand on his own. cf. *John of the Cross, The Dark Night of the Soul* (I.viii.3); *Ascent of Mount Carmel* (Prologue 3). For general reference: J. T. McNeill, *A History of the Cure of Souls* (1951).

V. A. DEMANT

Discipline

Discipline has two related meanings. It may mean the maintenance of certain standards of conduct through the enforcement of them by appropriate penalties; or it may mean the training of persons so that they will conduct themselves according to given standards. When one talks of 'ecclesiastical discipline', unfortunately one thinks too readily of only the first of these two meanings. It is true that from the beginning the Church had to enforce some minimal standards for its members, otherwise it would have lost its distinctiveness and been rendered ineffectual for its mission. At some times in its history, the Church has been very rigorous in its discipline, and has even invoked the civil authorities for the enforcement of its standards. Nowadays the strict discipline that was once enforced is neither practicable nor desirable. It may well be, however, that the decay of discipline is due as much as anything to indifference. In any case, the discipline of the Church should never be harsh. The Church must find room within itself for 'weaker' members, as St Paul called them, and its aim must be to sustain these and eventually strengthen them. This is not to say that its standards are to be weakened, but that whatever is done must aim eventually at reconciliation and at the

rehabilitation of those who have injured the community. This is where discipline, as the maintenance of standards, passes into the more important kind of discipline which has to do with the forming of disciples and their training in the Christian life. *See* **Ascetical Theology.**

EDITOR

Dispensation

Dispensation is permission by an ecclesiastical authority to perform an act which would normally be against some rule of the Church, or the waiving of the penalty due for having done such an act. A dispensation would be granted because of some special circumstances obtaining in a particular situation. While this conception of dispensation undoubtedly lends itself to abuses, it has a legitimate function as mitigating the rigour of rules and introducing a situational element.

Divine Right of Kings

In the later Middle Ages this was intended as a restriction of papal claims; the lay ruler should be the sole ruler of temporal affairs. Luther and Calvin went further. Besides seeking the entire abolition of papal authority even in spiritual matters they preached absolute obedience to the lay ruler – with the different results that Luther, conceiving the spiritual as wholly inward (apart from the behaviour of individuals to one another), encouraged the authority of State over Church, while Calvin, more aware of the intertwining of religion, morality and civil order, made his church at Geneva controller of the State, and was followed by the English Puritans under Cromwell and in New England. The next stage was concerned wholly with the relation of the ruler and his subjects. In France the wearing series of civil wars between king and Huguenots in the second half of the sixteenth century threw the problem of civil order into prominence. The disorder being as much religious as political, a religious ground for order was desirable. That any disobedience to the king was sinful was secured by the view, first clearly formulated by Pierre de Bélloy in 1587, that kingship was instituted by God and that therefore his authority over his subjects is absolute. In England this view entered with James I, who in Scotland had suffered from unruly nobles and strong Calvinist resistance to his episcopalianism. On inheriting the firm throne of England (1603) he put into practice his sense of kingship as the fount of all civil authority and power, and passed on to his son both that conviction and the antagonism of the House of Commons which he had begun to arouse. With the defeat and execution of Charles I, the assertion of divine right disappeared from actual government, lingering on only in the more ardent devotees of the two later Stuart kings and in the Jacobites of the Hanoverian period. In its French and English form the idea of divine right had sharp boundaries; it was applicable not to any legitimate government but to single royal princes only, legitimated by succession through primogeniture, and it grounded royal absolutism not on God's providential willing of order as the causal condition of human welfare but on a special divine decree creating kingship as his sole mode of vicarious rule over men. In this sharp form it is not covered by Rom. 13. It fell outside of public discussion because it was a thought-form which neither jurists nor philosophers could use, as is evident in James I's reference to 'them that sit in the throne of God' and his dictum 'that which concerns the mystery [here meaning sacrament] of the king's power is not lawful to be disputed'.

T. E. JESSOP

Divini Redemptoris. see Pontifical Social Encyclicals.

Divorce

The term 'divorce' is used for two different conditions. The first is divorce *a mensa et thoro*, from table and bed, more accurately defined as separation. In this case the partners to a marriage live separately and cease to cohabit, but neither is free to remarry another person while the partner is living. It is a condition recognized by the law and allowed by Christian tradition in marriages where it is no longer possible for the partners to live together for an adequate reason.

The second sense of divorce is divorce *a vinculo*, by which is meant the dissolution of the bond of marriage, leaving the partners free to marry again as if they have never married in the first place. Such divorce is incompatible with the doctrine of the indissolubility of marriage as it has been traditionally held in western Christendom.

Since the Reformation, however, Protestant churches have for the most part permitted divorce and remarriage to those who can prove adultery on the part of one of the partners, in accordance with Matt. 5.32, though the exact meaning of the passage is obscure. This passage is known as the 'Matthean exception'. In recent years the facilities for divorce in the civil courts of many western countries have been widely extended, and many Protestant churches do in fact recognize the decisions of the civil courts as adequate to permit remarriage in church of those concerned. The Anglican Church, generally speaking, often refuses to allow second marriages in church during the lifetime of a partner of a previous marriage, though, after such remarriage elsewhere, pastoral needs may be met by the admission to communion of those concerned with the approval of the bishop.

The Eastern Orthodox Church has a much easier attitude to divorce and remarriage, springing from earlier close connection with the State in the Byzantine Empire, which, for example, under Justinian permitted divorce of the wife for indulging in mixed bathing. The Eastern Orthodox permissions for divorce reflect the inferior position of women, who do not have the same rights as men. All Christians agree that marriage is dissolved by death, and the Eastern Orthodox have introduced the concept of moral death to permit divorce. Many reasons are allowed including treachery against the life of one by the other, adultery and bigamy, and even frivolous conduct leading to suspicion of adultery, intentional abortion without the husband's consent, impotence, abandonment by the husband for two years, incurable lunacy for four years, prolonged disappearance, and leprosy.

Among Roman Catholics there are two cases in which a marriage which is otherwise indissoluble can be dissolved in special circumstances. If two unbaptized persons are lawfully married and one of them becomes a Roman Catholic, the other refusing to live 'without offence to God', the marriage can be dissolved according to what is known as the 'Pauline privilege' (I Cor. 7.15; Canons. 1120–7). The second case is that of two baptized persons whose marriage has never been consummated. 'This union can be dissolved either by solemn profession of one of the parties or by a dispensation of the Supreme Pontiff for good and just reasons' (Canon 1119). These decisions are quite different from declarations of nullity (q.v.).

There is thus great variety among Christians with regard to the matter of divorce. Modern developments have created a situation in which Christians are faced with difficult moral decisions about divorce, since the teaching of the Churches and the practice of civil legislatures have more and more diverged. There can be no doubt that Christian teaching from NT times onwards has been that marriage between Christians is a lifelong union to the exclusion of all others, and almost all Christian services of marriage stress this aspect of marriage. There is also a strong Christian tradition that this concept of marriage is not merely a Christian ordinance but that it derives from the natural moral law. The Roman Catholic Church because of its structure and discipline has succeeded in maintaining a discipline among its members, which most other Christian churches have been unable to secure. But even in the case of the Roman Catholics there have been actions which seem to outside observers to be stretching their own principles rather further than they ought to go.

Strict laws in a Christian community are impossible to maintain unless there is a workable system of dispensation for cases where this is needed. Most of the Christian churches must depend on the free readiness of their people to live according to their teaching, though in the conduct of the marriage service by ministers an opportunity exists to establish rules which uphold to some extent the Christian belief as to the intrinsic nature of the marriage bond.

The Church and the Law of Nullity of Marriage. Report of the Commission Appointed by the Archbishops of Canterbury and York, 1955; *Putting Asunder*, Report of the Group Appointed by the Archbishop of Canterbury, 1966.

HERBERT WADDAMS

Dreams

Although widely regarded as important media of divine inspiration and revelation in ancient civilizations and in contemporary 'primitive' cultures, dreams tended to be dismissed as meaningless and of no scientific significance in the West until the publication of Freud's *The Interpretation of Dreams* (1899). Freud contended that dreams are symbolic expressions of unconscious processes in the human mind and that careful dream interpretation could yield insight into unconscious wishes and desires. They take their shape both from the events of the waking day and from the impulses of the unconscious (q.v.). He distinguished between 'manifest dream content' and 'latent dream thoughts'. The manifest consists of the actual events, images, sequences and feelings admitted into consciousness through the dream and susceptible to recall when awake. These contents he regarded as symbolic masks or disguises for the basic feelings, desires and wishes (the latent dream thought), which could only be tolerated in consciousness in disguised form. The movement from latent dream thought to manifest dream content proceeds unconsciously, as a sort of internal censorship, and is characterized by all manner of distortions, condensations, displacements, reversals and omissions. A wide range of common symbols is used in this process. The latent dream thought can be recovered through the interpretative techniques of psychoanalysis (q.v.) and in so doing the unconscious impulses of the id (q.v.) can be discerned. Most subsequent psychological work on dreams has built on these foundations.

Carl Jung added three things to Freud's theory. He maintained that dreams could only be interpreted in series; that sexuality was not the sole basis for the unconscious contributions to dream contents; and that some dream symbols arise from the collective unconscious and are extremely important for personal wholeness and religious maturity. *See*, for example, *Two Essays on Analytical Psychology* (1953). Other researchers have indicated the relationships between dream contents and the physical needs or environmental situation of the sleeper. A good and brief summary is in Gardner Murphy, *Personality: A Biosocial Approach to Origins and Structure* (1947).

When properly interpreted, and that requires technical skill, dreams can yield important insights into motivations that exist below the level of consciousness. Dream work may also, on occasion, be a relatively efficient alternative to the destructive discharge of hostilities and aggressions, as in dealing with the Oedipus complex (q.v.), for example. Similarly, dreams may be allowed to substitute for acts which properly should be performed in fact, and not merely dreamed of. There is still much confusion of claim and counter-claim on the role of dreams in anticipating future events.

GRAEME M. GRIFFIN

Drives. *see* Instincts or Drives.

Drugs

The manufacture and substitution of synthetic for natural drugs on a large scale today has intensified the ethical problems involved in drugs. Drug addiction in Britain, although not on the same scale as in the USA, has increased since 1961. Keith Bill has written on the problem in Britain and Larner and Tefferteller in the USA. The use of certain drugs during the War to keep bomber pilots and others awake does not seem to have led to addiction, so it looks as if some factor has crept in since 1961. The manufacture and storing of chloral, benzedrine, barbiturates and derivatives is a constant temptation to crime. There has always been a demand for sedatives to sooth, narcotics to induce sleep, euphorics for a sense of well-being, and hallucinogens to escape reality. The tranquillizers have had a long history. T. R. Glover mentions an Egyptian compound called *kyphi* which, when inhaled, calmed the mind and reduced anxiety.

Addictive drugs are easy to procure. Dr Peter Chapple has described a schoolboy's financial gain from the sale among his chums of purple hearts (containing dexedrine but no longer purple nor heart shaped). The addicts may get a supply (on prescription from a doctor who is afraid of the results of withdrawal) at the all-night drug store, or a youth may get it at a Youth Club. This is serious, for heroin which is a derivative of morphia can cause undesirable behaviour-structures. The personality structure of the adolescent is still too fluid to be exposed in this way. Weekends seem to be the time for indulging in doses of amphetamine drugs.

It is seldom easy to know where use ends and abuse begins. The use of stilboestrol (synthetic oestrogen) for cases of homosexuality is questioned by an expert like D. J. West on the ethical grounds that it is questionable to interfere with the endocrine system of an otherwise perfectly healthy man. The use of pills to prevent conception will remain an ethical issue for a long time to come and, whatever the use, will still be subject to abuse.

Certain drugs as distinct from medicines develop a dependence, a demand for increasing doses, and show withdrawal symptoms. With some people even nicotine has one or more of those aspects. Drugs do not, except in a few cases, lead to mental disease (Henderson and Gillespie). Their evil results show in moral deterioration and psychological and social symptoms. Drug addiction can be a symptom of mental disease. Owing to the misuse of LSD–25, the phantasy drug, the British Government is going to ensure a stricter control. Psilocybin and mescaline are also to be controlled. Even children are said to be getting 'hooked' on hard drugs.

The general view is that for addiction there must be a disintegrated personality. A time may come when the drug addict does not wish his dose because of the ultimate misery but the will in such a personality is weak. Even a brilliant American surgeon was reported to be a cocaine addict. Kraepelin regarded fatigue as inducing susceptibility, and H. L. Hollingworth would add other factors like temperature, hour of the day, habit and tolerance (physiological) cumulative effect and the idiosyncrasy of the person.

The formal use of addictive drugs is to induce sleep and give relief from pain. Thus a special responsibility rests with the doctor who makes the prescription. It is easier to know who can be hypnotized than to discern the potential drug addict. Trial and error is a risky business at any time.

To appreciate the problem an ethical approach rather than a statistical one has to be made, for it is not a matter of cold logic that the number of addicts has risen but that each case is a tragedy in itself.

An addict has often to act as a hawker to obtain the drugs he cannot do without and which he could not afford to buy. Those wretches are often in the hands of unscrupulous persons who specialize in narcotics. Because of the withdrawal symptoms those tragic individuals must continue their consumption or face those dreadful symptoms.

One must look at the question of the use of drugs in experiments. Researchers in extra-sensory perception used sodium amytal to be safe. Aldous Huxley allowed an experiment on himself with mescaline which is the ancient Mexican drug, of which the active principle is peyotl. It is claimed that peyotl should not demand increased amounts. As a result Aldous Huxley regards the intellect as unchanged, the will as weakened but the sense of vision much intensified. Before him Jaensch, Havelock Ellis and Weir Mitchell had experimented with mescaline. More serious was Jane Dunlap's experiment with LSD–25 the new hallucinogen from which she tried to get a spiritual 'boost'. Admittedly religion and drugs are two ways of transcending our personal limitations but religion is to be preferred as it keeps us nearer to reality. The heightening of forms and colours is of doubtful utility. It is well known that amounts as small as 30–50 micrograms if taken by mouth can produce hallucinations.

We have the old but useful record of De Quincey who consumed considerable amounts of opium over many years both for pleasure and later to alleviate the pain of what looks like a 'grumbling' appendix. 'For nearly ten years I did occasionally take opium for the sake of the exquisite pleasure it gave me, etc. – it was not for the purpose of creating pleasure but of mitigating pain in the severest degree that I first began to use opium as an article of daily diet' (*The Confessions*, p. 5). He broke away from his addiction leaving us a record of how he unwound the chain by reducing (not uniformly) his intake from 130 drops of laudanum on June 24 to none on July 27.

In his biography of Freud, Ernest Jones gives a chapter on the 'Cocaine Episode'. Freud was excited about the possibilities of cocaine and found that 1/20 of a gramme turned a bad mood into cheerfulness. Freud himself seemed to be immune to addiction but his friend Fleischl was not, and Freud later regretted giving him cocaine although it was to wean him from his addiction to morphia. In Fleischl's case addiction was to more than one specific drug.

The present day doping of horses, dogs and athletes shows the importance of the effect on efficiency. H. L. Hollingworth found that small doses of caffein quickened typewriting speed whereas large doses did the oposite. Drugs may have varying effects if administered orally, subcutaneously or intravenously. So many factors are involved that in experiments on the effects of drugs scientific precision is essential (Munn). There is often the 'placebo' effect. A drug may increase efficiency for a short period and in the long run cancel the initial benefit. After reading confessions from addicts one sees how necessary it is to depend on objective tests.

Regarding help for addicts the modern view is that drugs which lead to addiction have to be withdrawn gradually because of the severe withdrawal effects. Some form of psycho-analysis may be necessary to get at the root of the trouble which may be due to heredity or a sense of inferiority, or even extreme introversion. Also, the drugs may have hidden the basic inner conflict.

Peter Hays insists on the necessity of education because 'probably no sedative drug known at the present time is without addictive risk'. Yet he would not include hemp (hashish) in the list because adolescents finding no miserable results from this might think that the dangers of other drugs on the list had been exaggerated.

H. L. Hollingworth maintains that therapy must be threefold, involving the physiological, social and psychological fields, and to this W. S. Brown would add the religious field, believing that here is the power to break the habit. The minister or doctor should know when the addict is dodging reality and help him to face up to it. Faith in God is a better prop than drugs.

With life tending to become more and more monotonous in this technological age, the Church and other institutions need to encourage the creative arts if adolescents and others are to be kept from artificial forms of excitement such as drugs offer.

The problem is being attacked along lines similar to those used by the Alcoholics Anonymous. If the Narcotics Anonymous is as successful as the other group many will be profoundly grateful.

Keith Bill, *The Needle, the Pill and the Saviour*, 1966; Jane Dunlap, *Exploring Inner Space, Personal Experiences under LSD-25*, 1961; Peter Hays, *New Horizons in Psychiatry*, 1964; D. K. Henderson and R. D. Gillespie, *A Text Book of Psychiatry*, 1936; H. L. Hollingworth, *Abnormal Psychology*, 1931; Aldous Huxley, *The Doors of Perception*, 1960; E. Jones, *The Life and Work of Sigmund Freud*, 1964; Jeremy Larner and Ralph Tefferteller, *The Addict in the Street*, 1966; Thomas De Quincey, *Confessions of an English Opium Eater*, n.d.

ARTHUR MCNAUGHTAN

Duty

Duty, especially in modern moral philosophy, means primarily a motive or principle of conduct that serves as an indication of the individual person's moral quality. The meaning of duty is inseparable from that of obligation, the acknowledgement of what ought to be done, of what we are bound to do, of what we are 'under orders' to perform. Immanuel Kant made the apprehension of duty the fundamental principle of his ethics and he took man's capacity for respecting and subjecting himself to a moral law to be the mark of his dignity as a moral person. In Kant's analysis, duty as a motive implies the existence in the moral self of counter-factors or temptations that stand opposed to, or in some way obstruct, the performance of duty. Kant spoke of inclinations or self-regarding springs of action which must be opposed, redirected or out-witted if the moral law is to be obeyed and our duty performed. The moral law of conduct confronts us in the form of duty just because we are imperfect beings and not fully able to determine ourselves through the dictates of practical reason. God, by contrast, embodies the moral law in his holy will so that the idea of action out of duty in relation to a holy will becomes irrelevant.

Duty as a motive for action is generally regarded as 'unconditional' and not subject to external qualifications. Here the term 'unconditional' does not mean that we are allowed to ignore the actual situation and the conditions of action in determining what we are to do, but rather that once our duty becomes clear we must perform regardless of our personal inclinations and without calculating the advantages or disadvantages to ourselves based on the anticipated consequences of the act. If we fail to acknowledge our obligation and act in accordance with it, we are morally without excuse.

Appeal to duty as a basic moral principle defines a morality of motives and locates the moral quality of the person in the character of his willing. Opposed to such a view is the utilitarian position in ethics according to which all human conduct is to be judged and evaluated not by its motive but by the extent to which the consequences of our actions contribute to or prevent the realization of happiness or well-being. According to the morality of duty, on the other hand, the good man is the man whose will is good solely in virtue of the motive it expresses and who is judged by references to his ability to do not only *as* duty requires but *because* duty requires.

While the religious man may regard his performance of duty as conduct based on a duty to God and thus be motivated by the love of God, the main aim of duty or obligation theories in ethics has been to ground duty in reason alone and thus to establish it as a self-sufficient spring of action. Human freedom and the autonomy of morality are said to reside in the fact that nothing beyond the acknowledgement of obligation or duty is required for moral motivation. This point can be seen most clearly if we consider the questions that have frequently been raised in connection with the idea of obligation, Why should I perform my duty? or, Why should I be obligated? From the standpoint of the morality of duty, these questions themselves are fundamentally immoral because they presuppose some further end beyond obligation or some good that entices me to obey. The acknowledgement of obligation is the essence of morality; duty can have no ground or further reason beyond itself if its moral import is to be preserved. In Kant's thought, for example, respect for the law that obligates us is the fundamental moral spring of action; there is no thought of being motivated by the anticipated consequences of an action or the attainment of some good as an end.

It is important to notice the close connection that exists between the concept of duty and a community of moral persons as expressed, for instance, in Kant's idea of a Kingdom of Ends.

Acknowledgement of duty is at the same time acknowledgement of a universal law that is binding on all other beings capable of understanding their nature as moral persons. In one formulation of duty prescribed by the moral law, Kant held that I must so act as to treat every other rational being as an end in himself and never merely as a means. The universal import of the duty principle can best be seen by attending to the fact that the principle is intended to exclude any conduct based on a maxim that is peculiar to myself; the morality of duty is set against my making an exception in my own case and it marks off as immoral any deed based exclusively on my own self-interest or on an 'ulterior' motive which means a form of personal gain. Thus Kant would say that the good man is one who, for example, is honest not because it is the best 'policy', for that means calculation of consequences and advantages, but the one who acknowledges his obligation to speaking the truth without regard to 'policy'. Only if entirely self-regarding moral principles are excluded is it possible to have a community of moral persons.

In addition to duty understood as a motive or ground of action, we also speak as well of particular duties by which we mean specific actions which we ought to perform. It has sometimes been debated whether a 'duty' and a 'right action' are always the same; the reason why such a question would arise is not difficult to find. Insofar as saying that some particular action is our duty also means that we have inclinations or predispositions against performing it, identifying right action with duty is questionable, for it would leave out of account right actions that we perform either habitually or without any clear sense of their being against our inclination. While it seems that duty can never be other than an obligation to perform the act that is right, there are right actions, for example, eating the proper food and resting adequately in order to maintain our health, that would not generally be regarded as duties in the sense that they confront us as obligatory over against natural inclination. And yet even in these cases we can see that should neglect of proper food and rest lead to illness jeopardizing both our own lives and the lives of others, it would be legitimate to say that it is our *duty* to obtain proper food and rest.

The ethics of duty has often been the subject of criticism on the ground that it is abstract and formal, leaving no place for action motivated by love. Thus the poet Schiller chided Kant by saying that whereas he wanted and liked to help his friends in distress such action would be without moral worth on Kant's view because only what is done from a sense of duty is in accord with the moral law. There are, to be sure, profound and difficult problems connected with the relation between law and love, disposition and command, but these cannot be treated in brief compass. It is, nevertheless, important to notice that while Kant's morality of duty has often been cast in the legalistic form of 'duty for duty's sake' it was actually intended to be a transcendence of law and not a form of legalism at all. Kant found the essence of morality in the person for whom morality means *respect* for a law that expresses the dignity of the moral person, the willingness to be bound by a universal principle. The good man is the one who has this respect and who needs no determining ground beyond it as a spring of action. By denying the moral standing of all self-regarding motives and reasons, Kant was excluding the possibility that, as he expressed it, the 'dear self' could become a valid determining ground for the good act.

F. H. Bradley, *Ethical Studies*, 2nd edn., 1927; H. R. Niebuhr, *The Responsible Self*, 1963; Hastings Rashdall, *The Theory of Good and Evil*, 2 vols., 2nd edn., 1924; S. Toulmin, *The Place of Reason in Ethics*, 1950.

JOHN E. SMITH

Ebionites

The Ebionites may be described as Jewish Christians, or rather as a sect who wished to accept Christianity without ceasing to be basically Jewish in their religion. Beveridge (*HERE*, V, p. 141) speaks of Ebionism as 'simply the residuum of the struggles and heart-burnings of the age when the religion of Jesus Christ shook off the trammels of Judaism'. They are therefore a sect which had a Christianity which stopped short of full development. In the end they therefore became what Weiss (*Earliest Christianity*, II, p. 730, Torchbooks edn.) called a 'fossilised relic', and by the fifth century they were extinct (Theodoret, *Haer. Fab.* 2.II).

They existed in three forms. There were those of them who were called the Nazarenes, and who themselves rigidly practised the Jewish law, but who did not wish to impose this law on others, and who had no objections to associating with non-Jews. There were what may be called the Ebionites proper, who made the observance of the Mosaic Law a condition of salvation, who would not associate with Gentiles, and who regarded Paul as a dangerous heretic, who indeed had only become a renegade from Judaism because he was disappointed in his attempt to marry the daughter of the high priest (Epiphanius 30.16). There were lastly the syncretistic Ebionites, who were fairly strongly tinged with gnostic ideas.

In ethics the first two types of Ebionites were strongly legalists. They based everything on the Law of Moses, although they did not accept the scribal and oral law. They believed that Jesus became the Christ because of the virtue of his life in obeying this Law, and they went the length of saying that all who do perfectly obey that Law can also become Christs (Eusebius, H.E.3.27; Hippolytus, *Phil.* 7.34; Epiphanius, *Haer.* 30.18). They naturally strongly insisted on the observance of the Sabbath, on circumcision and on ablutions (Epiphanius, 30.32).

The ethic of the syncretistic Ebionites was markedly ascetic. They ate no flesh and drank no wine (Ephiphanius 30.15; *Clem. Hom.* 12.6). They were even said to observe the Lord's Supper in bread and water (Epiphanius 30.16). They abandoned animal sacrifice, and they despised marriage, although their opposition to marriage was later relaxed (*Clem. Hom.* 3.68).

Their name gives a good idea of their religious and ethical position. In later times they were supplied with a founder called Ebion (Epiphanius 30.1). But the name undoubtedly comes from the Hebrew word for *poor*. Origen took this to be a reference to the poverty of their doctrine and belief (*C. Cels.* 2.1; *De Princ.* 4.22). But they themselves took to themselves all the blessings on the poor in the NT (e.g., Luke 6.34), and in the OT (e.g., Psalm 34.6). At its simplest their ethic was that of the devout Jew, and at its more elaborate it was that ethic tinged with gnostic asceticism.

WILLIAM BARCLAY

Economic Aid

In expressing the inclusive concern of Christian love for underdeveloped countries, economic assistance is basically important. Economic growth is a prerequisite to other forms of social development. Ethical imperatives supporting such aid are discussed in the article on **Underdeveloped Countries.** There are also moral considerations involved in shaping concrete programmes. We ought to be as wise in selecting means as we are clear about defining ends.

Foreign aid needs to be of such types as to provide foundations for permanent self-help, rather than merely providing emergency relief. The criterion of freedom requires minimizing interference in the internal affairs of receiving nations, reducing controls to such essentials as integrity in the administration of approved projects. There is a strong argument for government grants supplementing private funds. Many basic projects, such as sanitation or disease control, do not return monetary profits, and the total magnitude of need exceeds private philanthropy and investment. There are also strong considerations favouring international administration of much of the aid given, the more easily to encourage mutuality instead of paternalism, and to enforce standards with less resentment. Policies facilitating trade are important re-enforcements for grants in aid. Total assistance given must be sufficient to allow economies to become self-propelling. Too little aid may leave recipients comparatively worse off.

The Christian of all men should advocate more generous policies than are customary. God's material creation is a gift to the entire human family. We do not give thanks when we manage physical resources only for private ends. In the economy of God, need anywhere constitutes a claim on resources everywhere. Devotion to God requires the dedication of possessions to the greatest social needs.

HARVEY SEIFERT

Ecumenical Movement, Ethics in

The Ecumenical Movement, expressed in the twentieth century by the multitude of contacts among Christians which have produced the World Council of Churches, the World Student Christian Federation, instruments of co-operations and dialogue between Roman Catholics and other churches, and many other channels, is difficult to separate into its biblical, theological and ethical components. Its activities have tended to be functional, seeking the form of the mission, the unity, and the responsibility of the Church in the world, rather than analytical, on the model of a theological school curriculum. There are, however, three distinguishable strands of ecumenical work with special significance for the student of ethics. They arose separately out of the life and mission of the churches, and are today being woven into a common pattern of what might be called an ecumenical experience of the ethical problem.

The first of these is the effort of the churches to understand their missionary task through the Student Volunteer Movement, the great World Mission Conferences in Edinburgh (1910), Jerusalem (1928), Madras (1938), Whitby (1947), Willingen (1952) and Ghana (1958), the International Missionary Council, and the whole intellectual ferment to which the foreign missionary enterprise of the nineteenth and twentieth centuries has given rise. The central ethical issue in all of these has been the question of the faithfulness of a missionary church in the forms of its life to the gospel it seeks to communicate to a non-Christian society. Self-critical repentance and the urgency of proclamation stand in inevitable tension here. The experience of churches in ecumenical mission during the twentieth century has been one of ever deeper discovery of each of these poles and the dialectic of their interaction.

Awareness of this dialectic was present in some form from the beginning. John R. Mott, setting forth for the Student Volunteer Movement his call for *The Evangelization of the World in This Generation* (1900), found the greatest hindrances to this goal in the home church itself – in its 'secularized, self-centred' conformity to its own society. The point was underlined in the Edinburgh Conference of 1910 where the success of the urgent missionary task was linked continually with the renewal of the sending churches and the reform of un-

Christian aspects of European and American society, not least its political imperialism and rapacious trade relations with non-Christian lands. The Jerusalem Conference in 1928 acknowledged explicitly that Christianity was not wholly accepted in the western world, and proclaimed the missionary task as a world-wide one, in which every nation's 'pride of national heritage or religious tradition' would be humbled before Christ. The burden of its deliberations concerned the proper appreciation of non-Christian systems of life and thought, both religious and secularist, in order to bring the gospel to them as fulfilment, not destruction, of their proper values.

In the years that followed two ethical issues dominated ecumenical missions: (1) The question whether the exclusive claim of Christ over the life of the world is in itself an expression of Christian pride and domination. Such a position was suggested by Dr William Ernest Hocking, under whose direction *Rethinking Missions, a Laymen's Inquiry after 100 Years* was produced in 1932. Dr Hocking's alternative was an emphasis on non-evangelistic forms of service, and the pursuit of ultimate truth with and through all religions. This point of view has been expounded in recent years by Arnold Toynbee and many others. In contrast Hendrik Kraemer, drawing on the inspiration of Karl Barth, argued in *The Christian Message in a Non-Christian World* (1937) that human religion itself is a double phenomenon, partly man's recognition of, and reaching for, God, and partly his effort to make his own interests, dreams and cultural ideals divine in defiance of God. The Christian message is about historical events in which God reveals his judgment on all religions, including the religious habits and hopes of Christians, and subjects living men to the saving claim of Christ in the whole of their lives and cultures. Kraemer's point of view was the central issue, which remained unresolved, of the World Mission Conference at Tambaram near Madras, 1938. (2) The question which has dominated missions since second World War is still more radical. Political and social revolution, driven by rising nationalism and often nourished by the earlier work of Christian missions themselves, have faced the Church in every part of the world with the question of its own indigenous integrity, as a witness to the power of God alone, and not to the influence of European or American culture, funds and personnel. In one country after another a transfer of power has taken place from missionary to indigenous leadership, often only after an indigenous church revolt, or a political upheaval, as in China. But this is only the first step, for an aggressive non-Christian nation then challenges the indigenous church to make known its reason for existence. The Church's repentance for worldliness and its discovery of the mission of Christ to his world are two parts of the same

response to God. The issue, as was explicitly recognized at Willingen in 1952, at Ghana in 1958, and in the missionary concern of the World Council of Churches since its merger with the International Missionary Council in 1961, is basically the same for churches in what once was Christendom and in the so-called non-Christian world.

The second strand of ecumenism is Christendom's counterpart of the first: the recognition of the estrangement of large classes in modern society from Christianity and the Church, as a problem for evangelism. Pre-second World War pioneers in this discovery were a Scottish Presbyterian, George MacLeod, from whose work in the slums of Glasgow the Iona Community arose, and a French Roman Catholic Henri Godin, the first of Paris' worker priests. Since the War, such experiments have mutiplied, in missions to industry and industrial workers in Mainz-Kastel, Germany (H. Symanowski), Sheffield, England (E. R. Wickham), Detroit, Michigan and elsewhere; in new forms of urban parish life of which East Harlem in New York (G. W. Webber), Halton, Leeds (E. Southcott) and Colombes, Paris (G. Michonneau) are among the best known; and in thousands of less known evangelists who have made identification with some estranged and needy social group the starting point for a rediscovery of the Christian message. All of this ferment has been focused and cultivated by the World Council of Churches' Department on Studies in Evangelism, under the leadership of Hans Hoekendjik, D. T. Niles, Hans Margull, and lately Walter Hollenweger, and by the Department on the Laity under the leadership of Hans Ruedi Weber. The publications of these departments and the writings of these men are the best sources for the study of it.

Theological, ethical and sociological factors have interacted in this new evangelism. The challenge of Marxism has made the Church acutely aware of the extent to which its forms of community life, its social ethic, and its basic understanding of the relation of man to God in the drama of salvation, are conditioned by its roots in rural or upper- and middle-class urban society. Other sociologists also have goaded the Church to repentance, with analyses of the forms of its social bias in particular countries. Experimentation in ecumenical evangelism has therefore taken the form of identification with those social groups which reproach the Church with its provincialism, and of rediscovery of the form of the Church, reflecting the action of God and the presence of Christ in new forms of community and new structures.

The problem, both theological and ethical, of modern evangelism is to discern and express in life, the form of Christ's Church which will confront both religious and secularized, complacent and troubled forms of modern society with judgment and hope.

The third ecumenical strand of ethical significance is that represented first by the Universal Christian Conference on Life and Work through its conferences in Stockholm 1925 and Oxford 1937, and since the formation of the World Council of Churches, in its Department on Church and Society, and the studies and statements which World Council Assemblies and other conferences have produced. In this ecumenical study and action nearly all the significant lines of Christian social thought and action in recent generations have come together. The Stockholm Conference was conceived, following five years of preparatory study, in the spirit of the Social Gospel, but already in its sessions this anti-theological optimism was challenged. The Oxford Conference, with its seven preparatory volumes and forty-seven contributors, brought into conversation leading representatives of social thought in every branch of Christendom. Its report remains to this day the most comprehensive ecumenical statement on problems of Church and society ever produced, covering the responsibility of the Church in relation to (1) other human communities of nation and race, (2) the function, authority and limits of the State, (3) the economic order and its reform, (4) public and private education, (5) war, peace and the international order, and (6) the general disintegration of social order.

Between Oxford and the First Assembly of the World Council of Churches at Amsterdam in 1948 intervened the shattering experience of the second World War. Ecumenical social thought turned naturally therefore to diagnosis of the dynamics of a world which had proved uncontrollable by the best of Christian principles and to the task of the Church's witness and obedience in that world. The problem, as Amsterdam understood it, was to find ways of creative living for 'little men in big societies', to plan for personal responsibility and community life in a world increasingly dominated by large aggregations of power having a momentum of their own. This was the context of the concept 'responsible society', 'one where freedom is the freedom of men who acknowledge responsibility to justice and public order, and where those who hold political authority or economic power are responsible for its exercise to God and to the people whose welfare is affected by it' (Section III Report, p. 200).

On the basis of this understanding Amsterdam condemned both Communism and laissez-faire capitalism, and initiated a period of search for those forms of balance between freedom and planning in the economic order, efficient production and equitable distribution of goods, effective centralization of political power and constitutional limits in the interests of free personal relations and local responsibility, which lasted through and after the World

Council's Second Assembly in Evanston 1954. Section III of the Evanston Report is an effort to explore this balance pragmatically in the midst of the powers and pressures of (1) western technologically developed society, (2) Communist-dominated areas, and (3) the social revolution in Asia, Africa and Latin America.

It has proved impossible since, however (as it was at Evanston), to hold these three areas together with one analysis and social programme. In 1956 therefore the World Council initiated a study of Christian responsibility in countries undergoing rapid social change. The term was understood to apply not to the rapid changes in relatively stable societies such as Europe or North America, but to those nations where the whole structure of political, social and economic order is in upheaval. This study was diverse and detailed. Its primary purpose was to stimulate the churches on the spot to examine their own ministry to their changing world. Most of its results were published locally or in occasional papers by the Department of Church and Society in Geneva. Some common findings were drawn together, however, in P. Abrecht's *The Churches in Rapid Social Change*, and in an international conference in Thessalonika, Greece in 1959. Among the emphases of these reports were: (1) a more positive, hopeful attitude towards centrally planned technology and industrialization than in the West, despite the human costs involved; (2) an affirmation of nationalism as a creative force, despite the moral dangers of political idolatry, and of nation-building as a basic Christian responsibility; and (3) an urgently future-oriented ethic, prepared in principle to take chances with the unknown consequences of radical change rather than rest with known, but unpromising securities.

Since the World Council's Third Assembly in New Delhi 1961 world-wide problems have again come into focus. The third World Conference on Church and Society in Geneva, 1966, was in every way broader than the second in Oxford nearly thirty years before. Its four preparatory volumes with eighty four contributors from every part of the world and, for the first time, full Roman Catholic and Orthodox as well as Protestant and secular participation, give a good picture of its scope. *Christian Social Ethics in a Changing World* (ed. by J. C. Bennett, 1966) raises the basic issues of theology in revolution, biblical bases of ethics, responsible society and natural law vs. contextual ethics which underlay the whole conference. *Economic Growth in World Perspective* (ed. by Denys Mumby, 1966) provided the material for a special section on the ethics of technological change in developed societies, special problems of developing countries and world economic relations. *Responsible Government in a Revolutionary Age* (ed. by Z. K. Matthews, 1966) underlay two section reports on the nature and function of the State and the structures of international co-operation. *Man in Community* (ed. by E. de Vries, 1966) dealt with the basic problems of ideology, secularization, cultural and ethnic tensions and change, and the bases of human community as a whole. Some of these were also taken up in a section report from the Conference. Geneva 1966 was portentous for the ecumenical movement in two respects: First, it was the first major ecumenical conference in which laymen not clergy were in the majority and theology was not the integrating universe of discourse. Nor did sociology, economics or any other discipline dominate the field. The material of analysis was delivered by several sciences, of society in radical social change, and many individual ethical insights were formulated. But integration and new theological insight is the task of the future. Second, it witnessed the sharpest confrontation so far, of the technological development expertize of the industrialized world with the revolutionary politics especially of Africa and Latin America. This conflict superseded the earlier tension between the Communist and the western world as the basic crisis which will claim the attention and ministry of the Church in its ecumenical expressions during the next few years.

It is the combination and interaction of the three strands above, which forms the web of ecumenical ethics. Ecumenical work in Church and society is peculiarly difficult to summarize because, like missions and evangelism, its heart is in dialogue. This dialogue may lead to consensus in a given conference and influence action in a given church or nation. But this consensus is itself a moment in the ongoing relation of God with man in Christ, and of men from different churches, nations and cultures with one another in his presence. The Ecumenical Movement therefore is characterized by a continual direction of repentance which honest dialogue brings forth, responsibility of which it makes the Christian aware, and witness in action to the work of Christ in the world in both judgment and promise for Christian and non-Christian alike.

In addition to items mentioned in the text: E. Duff, *The Social Thought of the World Council of Churches*, 1956; H. Godin, *France Pagan?*, 1949; Visser 't Hooft and J. H. Oldham, *The Church and its Function in Society*, 1937; *The Church and the Disorder of Society*, Amsterdam Assembly Series, III, 1948; *Dilemmas and Opportunitities:* Report of International Study Conference, 1959; G. MacLeod, *We Shall Rebuild. The Work of the Iona Community on Mainland and on Island*, 1945; G. Michonneau, *Revolution in a City Parish*, 1949; D. T. Niles, *Upon the Earth*, 1962; E. Southcott, *The Parish Comes Alive*, 1956; H. Symanowski, *The*

Christian Witness in an Industrial Society, 1966; G. W. Webber, *God's Colony in Man's World*, 1960; *World Conference on Church and Society*: Official Report, 1967.

C. C. WEST

Education, Christian Moral

There is universal agreement among educators that education should be moral. There is disagreement as to how education can create moral character. Some believe that the family is the major determinant of morals; others hold to the possibility of an individual's slowly working out his own moral code; and others affirm that the Church or general cultural influences determine morality.

There is wide agreement that morals are relative to the demands of a particular culture or to the subculture to which a person belongs. Cultural anthropologists have shown that almost any behaviour condemned in one society is approved or tolerated in another. When this relativity of moral codes first came into prominence, many intellectuals were led to assume that there could be no moral code better than another. Now we tend to infer that the relativity of moral codes proves that morals are learned and that one must judge the value of any moral code by the quality of life it produces. Our problem, therefore, is to understand the process by which morals are incorporated within a person and to suggest ways in which this process can be fostered and guided by the Church.

1. *Social Context.* A person absorbs the moral code of the people who raise him and to whom he belongs. Normally, this process of transmitting morality is the function of the family and other adults who are close to the child. Moral values are communicated to the growing child by the way these adults structure and interpret hundreds of little events that shape the child's life. Community values are often incorporated by the child through his experiences in school and through the various media of mass communication to which he is exposed.

It is difficult to know the precise relationship of religion to morals. *See* **Religion and Morality.** The Christian and Jewish religions are highly moral in their teachings; in addition to regular worship services, they sponsor many agencies such as parish and synagogue schools and adult education programmes which include lectures and sermons on moral topics. But various empirical studies beginning with the famous *Studies in Deceit* by Hartshorne and May (1931) have shown that there is little, if any, correlation between knowledge of biblical and other religious material, and observable moral behaviour. A child who has no religious connection, for example, could be just as honest as one who could recite a considerable number of Bible verses. However, it is thought that where honesty is practised as well as taught in the home, there is a high expectation that the child will develop the trait of honesty. There is some indication that participation in a religious community creates a difference in moral behaviour. The Kinsey Report (*Sexual Behaviour in the Human Male*) shows that sexual immorality is significantly less among people who have a strong religious connection; this is also shown by Strommen's study (1965) of Lutheran young people. We can conclude, therefore, that when religion is considered as a person's close relation to a believing community – rather than just a knowledge about religion – its adherents do display moral behaviour different from that of the surrounding culture.

The social context of morality has been intensely studied by scholars interested in juvenile delinquency. Out of all of these studies it has been found that no one factor such as home, intelligence, income, etc., is closely correlated with delinquency. Rather, there are a number of social forces that produce delinquency: at the centre of the delinquent's life is a feeling that he is not appreciated, that he is not loved, and that he is not being treated fairly. These feelings, according to Glueck and Glueck, began early in life and are related to the type of discipline exercised by the father, the quality of supervision of the mother, the quality of the affection between parents and between parents and the child.

2. *Conscience* (q.v.) Environment is first in influencing moral conduct, but environment does not automatically shape every person to a predetermined end. The person as he grows can transcend and modify his social conditioning. The struggle takes place in an area of our being which we call conscience. Conscience is created in a baby over a long period of time. At first, he experiences life through restrictions and a schedule related to feeding and bodily processes imposed by adults, usually his mother. He soon learns that he must obey this 'order' that is imposed so that he may obtain love and approval and may avoid punishment. The baby's morality is based on external authority; as he grows, he internalizes the rules so that the super-ego is formed, much of it being unconscious. He accepts more and more of the positive principles by which his parents live, and he more consciously tries to do some of the things they want him to do. Out of his desire to incorporate within himself conduct that he genuinely wants is formed the ego ideal.

Since the superego was formed out of things the child was not allowed to do and for which he was punished, he feels guilty when he breaks the rules. Guilt, when felt by a person, is a powerful emotion that forces him to do something to regain his emotional equilibrium. Usually he hurts himself or lets someone else hurt him until the punishment equals the guilty feeling. Sometimes he projects his guilt on to another person or institution and then blames them for his uneasy conscience. By this process he absolves his own inner feeling of guilt. Some people assuage guilt by buying gifts or working hard for a cause or by confessing their sins in corporate worship or personally to a priest.

Since the ego ideal was formed out of a relationship to a person he liked and represents things which he voluntarily accepted, the reaction to a failure to live up to that image is shame. However, shame is different from guilt. All guilt wants is enough satisfaction to return the person to his normal state of being. Shame, however, causes a person to want to do better; it forces him to rethink his situation to see how he must change in order not to grieve the internal image he has of himself or the person whose memory he reverences. Shame, therefore, is a more constructive emotion than guilt, but both are often intermingled when a person violates his conscience.

3. *Stages of Moral Development.* Conscience begins to be formed as soon as the baby is required to conform to a schedule, and it continues to be shaped and modified throughout life. According to Havinghurst, there are five stages of moral development: (*a*) The amoral impulsive stage characterizes the first year of a baby's life when he follows his impulses, and his well-being is mainly based on physical comforts. There is little or no morality at this stage because self-consciousness has not developed. (*b*) The egocentric expedient stage is from two to four years of age. During this time the child learns to control his impulses. The child still wants his own satisfactions, but he learns to adjust in order to please his parents and to get what he wants. During this stage he becomes conscious of the specific things he is not allowed to do, thus beginning to give content to his superego. (*c*) The conforming stage extends from about age five to ten. During this time the child learns the moral code of the adults around him and internalizes a great deal of the style of life he experiences. By the age of ten the normal child has pretty well established himself in relation to external rules. (*d*) The irrational conscientious stage is identical with early puberty. During this time the person is more conscious of other ways of life, diverse moral codes, and alternate ways of interpreting moral conduct. However, he does not try to think his way through new situations but rather tries to apply the code that he internalized during the conforming stage in a doctrinaire manner. (*e*) The rational conscientious stage extends from middle adolescence on into adulthood. During this time the person becomes more emotionally free from his parents and has opportunity to experiment on his own with the moral code he has been taught. Although he has a stable set of moral principles, he realizes that morality must be related to human conditions and therefore

must often be modified and redefined in the light of new human problems.

It must not be assumed that everyone moves through these five stages. Some people are arrested in their moral development at each stage, and many never go beyond the conforming stage. Perhaps it would be more accurate to say that as a person goes through these stages, he seldom leaves the early stages completely behind. Most adults are impulsive about some things, egocentric about others, and yet capable of rational adaptation of morality in still other areas of their lives.

4. *Moral Education.* The goals of Christian moral education are shared by the Jewish faith because both share the OT as a revelation from God for man's conduct. Moreover, the moral teachings of Jesus have been shown to be a reiteration of the best of Hebrew teachers. The uniqueness of Christianity lies not in its morality but in its belief about the person of Christ and his resurrection. Therefore, the methods of moral education, in so far as they relate to family and Church, are similar to those used in the Jewish faith. The differences between Roman Catholics and Protestants in moral education would be primarily in their different view of the authority of the Church, the Protestants taking a more individualistic view of authority in relationship to God. Roman Catholics with their penitential system have a method of assigning acts of penance to the believer in relationship to his sin, whereas Protestants believe that forgiveness can be determined only by an individual in his faith-relationship to God.

Apart from these theological differences, many Protestants, Catholics and Jews would today agree on the way moral education functions within religious groups and at various developmental levels. Using Havighurst's stages, we would comment on them as follows: (*a*) during the amoral impulsive stage, religion is represented almost exclusively by the parents. At this time, 'basic trust' is learned. If the baby learns to love and trust his parents, a foundation is laid for all future development of love. If love is not learned or is distorted during this time, the baby will probably have emotional and moral problems later on in life. (*b*) During the egocentric stage, the child continues to gain most of his morality from his parents and begins to associate morality with religion. As the child plays with other children, he learns some of the limits to his impulsive actions, and these limits are often given moral sanctions by supervising adults. (*c*) The conforming stage is the period in which the child absorbs the major moral affirmations of the Church, the church school and the community. He learns the specific meaning of honesty, of kindness, of respect for others, and the proper use of other people's property. This does not mean that he

follows these precepts exactly; but he knows what the common morals are and he learns the extent to which his family, school, and community enforce the moral laws. Much of the direct religious instruction by church and synagogue is concentrated in this period of the child's life and is correlated with, and supports, the moral code.

Since most people do not go much beyond the conforming stage of moral development, a church's major task is to help young people and adults move into the latter stages of moral development. Although a certain amount of moral development may come as a person participates in corporate worship and listens to sermons and lectures in church, significant growth will come only as young people and adults engage in face-to-face discussion over a period of time that focuses the morality of the Bible on concrete problems about which contemporary decisions must be made. Church groups which foster such a process will be training adults to move on to the rational conscientious stage of moral development as they live out their lives, performing roles as officers of the church, parents in the home, and Christian laymen in their work. Since morality is carried in the church by means of stories, maxims, commands, injunctions and theology, all of which are verbal generalizations, it can become meaningful to children only through human tutors who explain and apply these generalizations to human conditions as they arise. Adults must therefore continue their own moral growth in order to communicate properly to home, church school and community the meaning of morality. Otherwise, they will be able only to moralistically repeat what was taught them when they were children.

E. B. Castle, *Moral Education in Christian Times*, 1958; Lindsay Dewar, *Moral Theology in the Modern World*, 1964; Emile Durkheim, *Moral Education*, ET, 1961; Sheldon Glueck and Eleanor Glueck, *Unravelling Juvenile Delinquency*, 1950; Hugh Hartshorne and Mark A. May, *Studies in the Nature of Character*, 3 vols., 1928–30; Robert F. Peck and Robert J. Havighurst, *The Psychology of Character Development*, 1960; Merton P. Strommen, *Profiles of Church Youth*, 1963.

C. ELLIS NELSON

Edwards, Jonathan

Jonathan Edwards (1703–1758), generally reckoned as America's greatest theologian, was a champion of strict or consistent Calvinism, a leader in the Great Awakening, and the founder of the New England school of theology. A profound and original thinker, thoroughly acquainted with Lockean psychology, Newtonian science, Cambridge Platonism and Puritan theology, Edwards was grasped by the vision of the universe as an inter-related, unified system of being. Though he planned to produce a large systematic work, his early death following a smallpox innoculation just after he accepted the presidency of Princeton prevented it. His writings thus consisted chiefly of a large body of notes (now at last being published in full), sermons preached while he was pastor at Northampton, Massachusetts (1727–50) and missionary to the Indians at Stockbridge (1751–8), and theological treatises originating in the issue of the day but devoted to themes of perennial concern. His ethical thought was a very important part of his total vision of God, the world and man and was expressed in many of his works, but of particular importance are *Charity and Its Fruits* (or *Christian Love*, based on sermons preached in 1738 but not published until 1851), *A Treatise Concerning Religious Affections* (1746), *Freedom of the Will* (1754), *The Great Christian Doctrine of Original Sin Defended* (1758), and especially *The Nature of True Virtue* (posthumously published, 1765).

Edwards believed that the affections, or emotions, directed towards objective goods are the springs of human action. As long as a man is free from external compulsion to do what he wills, then he is morally responsible for his acts, even though he is not free to choose his emotions, not free to select what he hates or turn from what he loves. Since the Fall natural man is caught in the bonds of self-interest, he is trapped by self-love and cannot love another for the other's sake. But some men are through no merit of their own elected and moved by divine grace; they are the saints enabled to love God and men for their own sakes and empowered to live truly virtuous lives. No affection limited to something less than God, or focused on any private system that is not dependent on or subordinate to God, is truly virtuous. One cannot rise from self-love to divine love, nor can one build from such natural ethical principles as self-interest, conscience or moral sense (important and necessary as these are in the natural order) to universal good and disinterested benevolence. The ethics of the love of God come as a gift of the Spirit, which motivates love of all being as united in God and by him, and which transforms such particular loves as that of family and nation into divine love. The possibility of true virtue for man rests on the redemption wrought by Christ. Those only who have been given by grace the joy of universal benevolence have a sense and a taste for the beauty of God's holiness, and will surely be guided 'to the best purposes'.

ROBERT T. HANDY

Egalitarianism. *see* Equality.

Ego

In Freud's later topographical model of the human mind the ego is the institution responsible for perception, thinking, memory and judgment. It develops out of the id (q.v.) and endeavours to modify the id-impulses to conform to the demands of reality. It is partly conscious and partly unconscious and in general performs the controlling and integrating functions in the human personality. The conscious ego tends to act rationally and logically and is prepared to postpone immediate pleasure for the sake of anticipated future pleasures. Psychoanalytic theory regards the conflicts between id, ego and superego (qq.v.) as basic in the development of personality. Ego structure may also be influenced by external factors and an ego is said to be strong when it is capable of dealing realistically with a wide variety of pressures both from within and without.

Little attention was paid to the ego in the early years of psychoanalysis (q.v.) but this trend was reversed with Freud, *The Ego and the Id*, 4th edn., (1947). *See also* Anna Freud, *The Ego and the Mechanisms of Defence* (1937). In recent years there has developed an 'ego-psychology' (particularly associated with Heinz Hartmann and David Rapaport) which claims that the ego is somewhat autonomous of the id and has both its own sources of energy and its own aims and purposes. This position has found widespread, but not universal, acceptance among psychoanalysts. Gordon Allport, *Pattern and Growth in Personality* (1961), espouses a modified form of ego-psychology.

There is no general agreement in psychology on the relation of the term 'ego' to the term 'self'. Some theorists use them interchangeably, others insist that there is a difference but some of these use both terms in a manner directly opposite to their use by others. C. S. Hall and G. Lindzey, *Theories of Personality* (1965). present a brief but comprehensive summary of the different usages. It is abundantly clear, however, that there is no warrant in the best contemporary psychology for the common misapprehension (from which even theologians are not exempt) that any considerations of ego or of self constitute a pandering to man's pride, egoism or self-centredness. The simple fact is that man could not survive as man without an adequate ego, that is, without some central integrating structure and function in the personality. The traditional issues in ethics about egoism versus altruism focus around a different concern.

Among the more notable contributors to the long-standing philosophical disputes on the existence, nature and standing of an ego in man are Descartes, Hume, Spinoza and Kant.

GRAEME M. GRIFFIN

Egoism

Egoism is self-centredness. Of course, man could not be human or a moral agent unless he was a centred self or ego (q.v.). However, the word 'egoism' is used in a pejorative sense to mean excessive self-regard. It may be the case that true self-regard does not conflict with regard for others, for genuine selfhood is attainable only in a community of selves. In many particular situations, whatever may be true in general about the ultimate coincidence of self-regarding and other-regarding conduct, the moral decision presents itself as one between one's own interests and the interests of other persons. The Christian ethic stresses the claim of the other and teaches that true selfhood can be gained only through willingness to lose oneself. More subtle than the egoism of the individual is what may be called 'group egoism', the unrelenting pursuit of its own interests by, let us say, a family, a social class, a nation, without regard to the damage or injustice inflicted on others. Reinhold Niebuhr's contrast between 'moral man' and 'immoral society' points to the curbing of egoism in the individual and its relatively unrestrained exercise by the group; and also makes clear that the Christian ethic cannot be thought of merely in terms of individual integrity but must seek to permeate the larger social structures as well. *See* **Altruism; Persons and Personality.**

EDITOR

Egyptian Ethics, Ancient

Maat ('order', 'justice') is both a cosmological and ethical concept and presupposes the integration of the order of nature with the order of Egyptian society. This harmony is achieved in the person of the Pharaoh who is a god and kingship dates from the time of creation and belongs to the basic order of existence. Nature does not confront Egyptian society as threatening or unpredictable, but is a complex harmony alive with the gods who all have their allotted place and such changes as are seen are predetermined rhythms which declare the utter stability of the created order. The Egyptian therefore lives in a world which was perfect from the day of creation and this static view extends to Egyptian society so that history is no more than the inevitable working-out of the original constitution of that society. The Egyptian state is the Pharaoh who is the source of *Maat* and who preserves through the derivative powers of his officials that immutable order of society which derives from his person.

Akhenaton, the heretic king of the eighteenth dynasty, claimed that he lived on *Maat* (as his food), but his successor, Tutankhamen, declared that 'His Majesty drove out disorder (or falsehood) from the Two Lands so that order (or truth) was again established in its place; he made disorder (falsehood) an abomination of the land as at "the first time" (creation)' (*AER*, p. 54). From this point of view Akhenaton threatened to destroy the harmony of the created order and to reinstate chaos. Akhenaton's use of *Maat* is somewhat specialized; in art it meant something like truth to life, while in other spheres (literature, social manners) it indicated a revolt against traditionalism and a zest for experiment. The god of the monotheistic cult which he established at his new capital, Tell-el-Amarna, was the sun disk, Aton, and this reform certainly involved the suppression of the Amon cult and the other Egyptian gods, although it should not be forgotten that Akhenaton himself was a god and that it is on the unique relationship of Aton to his person that the reform hinges. Its most important religious document is the *Hymn to the Sun* (*LAE*, p. 288) which has aesthetic and intellectual merit and which adores Aton for his creative, ordering and sustaining work in nature, but in which there is little evidence of ethical emphasis. The so-called universalism of the Aton cult was not an entirely new departure (cf. *The Hymn to Amon, LAE*, p. 282) and its significance should not be exaggerated, for, although parochialism was transcended the favoured relationship of Egypt with the God was still asserted (see *LAE*, p. 292, n. 3).

'Order' or 'justice' was not so much a concern of the private Egyptian as of the Pharaoh and his officials as is evident from the 'Instructions' genre. These 'Instructions' (*LAE*, pp. 54 f., 234 f.; *ANET*, pp. 412–25) are manuals on the art of statesmanship compiled for the benefit of those who are to serve the Pharaoh in the upholding of *Maat*. They contain a vocational ethic and were used in the schools where apprentice statesmen were trained. Their authors are sometimes seasoned statesmen who at the end of a successful life conserve their stores of wisdom for those who are to succeed them in office. The 'Instruction' for the most part inculcates a hard-headed wisdom and warns against intellectual rather than ethical flaws. One who is to succeed in affairs of State should bridle his tongue, cultivate silence, stifle impetuosity and speak only when he has something weighty to say. He ought to avoid quarrels and make as few enemies as possible and it is essential that he should know his limitations and not imagine himself to be more important than he is. Pride in a statesman leads to disaster. There is, however, a great variety of maxims in these instructions; they deal with matters of etiquette and they rise to genuine ethical injunctions. Probity and incorruptibility are demanded of the official and he must take great pains to see that justice is done (this is perhaps the point of *The Complaints of the Peasant, LAE*, p. 116; *AER*, pp. 46, 146 f.) and be ready to help the less fortunate members of the community. Frankfort and others have objected to the description of these maxims as 'pragmatic' and have held that they are overarched by religious belief and that *Maat* is everywhere presupposed. Nevertheless Frankfort agrees that they are empirical wisdom and that they do not have the moral fervour which accompanies the concepts of Law and sin in biblical thinking (*AER*, pp. 73 f.). The Egyptian gods do not 'reveal' a social ethic to men nor do they give extraordinary 'guidance' on matters of State. Religion thus makes room for statecraft based on a bank of experience accumulated over many generations and the native intelligence coupled with a rigorous educational process is part of the *Maat* which guarantees harmony to the created order. Empiricism is attuned to the divine order.

A. Erman, *The Literature of the Ancient Egyptians*, tr. by A. M. Blackman, 1927; H. Frankfort, *Ancient Egyptian Religion*, 1948, Chaps. 2 and 3; J. B. Pritchard, *Ancient Near Eastern Texts*, 1955; John A. Wilson, *Before Philosophy*, 1949, Chap. 4; *The Burden of Egypt*, 1951, Chap. 6, Akhenaton.

WILLIAM MCKANE

Emotion

Emotion is the general term for the whole range of feeling states (affects) and the physiological changes accompanying them. It has been a major subject of investigation in experimental psychology since its beginnings with Wundt. Emotions are usually classified according to the type of dominant feeling tone (pleasant or unpleasant). Freud and subsequent depth psychologists have shown how emotional feelings may be inhibited (*see* **Repression**) and the damage that can result to the personality through either over-emphasis or neglect of the emotional dimensions of life. *See also* Carl Jung, *Psychological Types*, 1923.

An important normative function of emotion (and the one which makes it most relevant for ethics) is to motivate appropriate reactions to a wide variety of circumstances. Too high an emotional level may paralyze one for action; too low a level may leave one indifferent and fail to stimulate the needed response. *See* **Anxiety**. Walter B. Cannon, *Bodily Changes in Pain, Hunger, Fear and Rage* (1915), has persuasively argued that the emotional mechanisms were originally designed for the primitive conditions of the life of early man. In the tremendously increased complexity of modern living in which, for example, flight or fight are no longer the simple alternatives in face of a situation of danger, the emotional mechanisms may inhibit rather than facilitate appropriate action.

William James, *Varieties of Religious Experience* (1902), suggested that emotions with a religious object were not different in kind from those with non-religious objects. In our day Gordon Allport, *The Individual and His Religion: A Psychological Interpretation* (1951), adopts a similar position. In arguing for a specifically religious emotion, Paul E. Johnson, *Psychology of Religion* (rev. edn., 1959), invokes the extremely important discussion by Rudolf Otto, *The Idea of the Holy* (1923), of the awe and reverence evoked by experience of the numinous. Emotion is involved in almost all practices and attitudes of healthy religion. One of the functions of religious ritual seems to be a patterning of emotional experience so that one is neither overwhelmed by it, nor deprived of it. The power of emotion to influence attitudes and action makes its responsible use imperative in worship and in Christian living. *See* **Guilt; Motives and Motivation**.

GRAEME M. GRIFFIN

Emotivism

Emotivism is the view that the primary element in the meaning of moral judgments consists in their function of expressing the emotions or attitudes of the speaker, or arousing similar emotions or attitudes in his audience. It is to be distinguished from prescriptivism, subjectivism, relativism (qq.v.).

R. M. HARE

Empathy

Empathy is the term used to denote the human capacity to apprehend directly the state of mind and feeling of another person. It involves, in effect, putting oneself in the place of the other to experience his feelings and to see his world as he himself sees it. The line between empathy and sympathy cannot be drawn rigidly but in general terms the sharing of the other's feelings involved in empathy is a sharing in quality rather than quantity, in kind but not in degree. This difference in degree makes it possible for one to enter into the emotional situation of the other without oneself being ruled by the emotions involved. The most comprehensive discussion is in *Empathy: Its Nature and Uses* (1963) by Robert L. Katz.

Empathy on the part of the therapist is regarded as very important in all systems of psychotherapy. It is a valuable tool for gaining insight into the other person and thus for assessing his capacity to deal with given situations. But perhaps even more important is the fact that an attitude of empathy, particularly when coupled with a non-judgmental approach to the other person, comes to be perceived by the other party as genuine understanding. This perception in itself can be very liberating and makes possible real growth in the relationship. This combination of empathy and acceptance on the part of the therapist is particularly stressed by Carl R. Rogers in his *Client-Centred Therapy* (1951).

The term empathy is used in a particular sense in the interpersonal theory associated with Harry Stack Sullivan. Here it denotes the 'emotional contagion' by means of which an infant perceives and responds to the emotional state of his mother. Anxiety in the mother, for example, is transmitted to the child in a way which does not seem to involve any of the known sense organs. This anxiety 'caught' from the mother results in feelings of insecurity.

The capacity to empathize is obviously valuable in all forms of human relationship. Its absence usually indicates that the person concerned is caught up in personal conflicts and difficulties which do not allow him freely to enter the thought worlds of others. The removal of these inhibitory factors is sometimes possible, enabling a recovery of the ability to empathize. This capacity can be developed to a high degree and when present markedly facilitates communication with others.

GRAEME M. GRIFFIN

Encyclicals. *see* Pontifical Social Encyclicals.

Endogamy

Endogamy is the custom of marrying within the tribe. *See* **Anthropology; Custom.**

Enlightenment

Immanuel Kant (1724–1804), in the opening sentences of his essay, *What is Enlightenment?* (1784), gives this definition:

Enlightenment (*Aufklärung*) is the movement of man out of his minority state, which was brought about by his own fault. The minority state means the incapacity to make use of one's understanding without the guidance of another. This minority state is brought about by a man's own fault if it is caused by a deficiency not of understanding, but of the resolution and the courage to make use of it without the guidance of another. *Sapere aude!* Have the courage to make use of your own understanding is thus the motto of Enlightenment.

This definition implies the autonomy of the rational self-consciousness. Human reason possesses the power to find the truth about man, the world, and God, and to live in accordance with this truth. The authoritarian claim of positive religion to possess special supernatural powers and evidences for the understanding and realization of the truth is denied. Sometimes it is tacitly excluded, sometimes (as with Lessing) it is modified to mean that while 'revelation does not give man anything which human reason left to itself would not also discover', nevertheless revelation 'gave and is giving man the most important of these things sooner' (*Education of the Human Race*, section 4). But in general it may be said that the Enlightenment works with an intramundane conception of morality in which the concept of grace has no place. Morality is therefore secularized. Religion is esteemed (if at all) simply as a buttress of morality.

Leibniz (1646–1716) is the great figure of the Enlightenment. In him may be seen the distinct connections with earlier movements (especially with Descartes and the sixteenth-century Renaissance), and the manifold powers and problems of the Enlightenment itself, which to this day have not been exhausted or resolved. Thus the principle of individuation leads to the conception of man as a microcosm, and to the cardinal importance of the individual conscience. Again, the doctrine of pre-established harmony between man and the outer world establishes a cosmos which is basically the product of human thought. But it is insufficient to describe his ethical position as 'Stoicism' (Karl Barth, *From Rousseau to Ritschl*, 1959, p. 57). For in Leibniz's view true piety consisted in the recognition of the divine providence behind the pre-established harmony.

But the Enlightenment took many different forms; in Britain empiricism (Hume), in France positivism (Voltaire), in Germany both literary and critical metaphysical forms (Lessing, Kant), leading to idealism. In general, so far as ethics are concerned, the view of the Enlightenment may be summarized as intramundane, with the stress on the autonomy of the human reason, humanitarian, tolerant and optimistic. Man could discover for himself what the good was, and he could achieve it. Thus the stress lay upon the continuity of cultural goods, and the means for maintaining and developing this continuity lay in education.

The effects of these views upon the traditional Christian teachings were immense, and have not yet been completely worked out. The Enlightenment may be regarded as the first deliberate effort of the human spirit to think through the consequences of the break-up of the mediaeval synthesis. The doctrines of sin and atonement were re-interpreted in moral terms. The religion of Christ is preferred io the Christian religion. The teaching of Jesus replaces the dogmas concerning Christ. God is even regarded as a principle immanent in man.

From the standpoint of Christian ethics the emphasis was laid upon Jesus as a teacher of eternal truths, upon the fatherly love of God, upon human brotherhood, and upon immortality and freedom. 'The goal and measure of history is to be seen in the self-produced progress of the truth' (W. Anz, *Religion in Geschichte und Gegenwart*[3], I, 716). While it is easy to dismiss much Enlightenment teaching as shallow and pretentious, especially in the notion of the progress and perfectibility of society, the autonomy of the human reason as propounded by Leibniz, and the sense of the significance of history as expressed by Lessing, are contributions of central importance for a creative assessment of ethics. The views of the Enlightenment, in general, represent a release from the heteronomies of authoritarian dogma.

R. GREGOR SMITH

Entertainments. *see* Amusements.

Enthusiasm

Enthusiasm is employed religiously in a number of different, but imprecisely defined, ways. It is used originally by late Greek writers for effect of divine indwelling in poets, mystics, seers and philosophers (e.g., in Plutarch and Plato), subsequently for any claims to direct divine inspiration, including Christian prophecy in the first two centuries (*see*, e.g., *Revelation* of John and *Shepherd of Hermas*), most commonly as a pejorative term implying doubt of the authenticity of the claimed inspiration. In this sense it has been used at various times of individuals and of such disparate movements as Montanism, Donatism, the Anabaptists, Jansenism, Quietism, the Society of Friends, the Moravian movement, the early Methodist movement, the Shakers, Revivalism, the Irvingites, Seventh Day Adventism, Christian Science, Pentecostalism and neo-Pentecostalism and many others of lesser consequence. By extension the term has also come to mean any extravagant manifestation of religious devotion or practice and was thus discussed by early writers on the psychology of religion such as William James. The best descriptive account of enthusiasm, concentrating on the luxuriant period from the mid-seventeenth through the eighteenth centuries, is found in Ronald A. Knox, *Enthusiasm: A Chapter in the History of Religion with Special Reference to the XVII and XVIII Centuries* (1950). Umphrey Lee, *The Historical Backgrounds of Early Methodist Enthusiasm* (1931), includes an extensive bibliography of works by enthusiasts and on enthusiasm up to 1930.

The emphasis in enthusiasm has been consistently soteriological (and frequently in intensely individualistic terms), accompanied by some form of theoretical or actual separation of the 'elect' from others. Expectation of an immanent return of Christ is not uncommon and enthusiasts have usually attacked the ecclesiastical status quo of their times.

Much attention has been focused on the spectacular psychic or physical phenomena accompanying some enthusiastic groups. These are usually interpreted (by adherents) as evidences or seals of the divine favour and activity. Phenomena include speaking in strange tongues (glossolalia), involuntary jerking movements of head, body or limbs, trance states, visual and auditory hallucinations, involuntary cries and ejaculations, barking, etc. Viewed from the standpoint of dynamic psychology, many of these suggest the presence of intra-psychic conflicts of a substantial order. It appears that the group expectations exercise some control over the forms of expression adopted for the release of tensions, fears, etc. This very factor of having a socially acceptable (within the group) mode of expression may, in some instances at least, act constructively as an alternative to complete or partial psychic disintegration.

GRAEME M. GRIFFIN

Environment and Heredity

Environment and heredity, taken together, exhaust the factors which determine and/or influence development and behaviour. Strictly speaking, heredity is limited to factors transmitted through the genes. All other pre-natal events are regarded as environmental factors, though all factors present at birth whether actual or potential, are commonly regarded as a part of the individual's constitution, whether due to genetic or determinants or pre-natal conditions.

The controversy concerning whether hereditary or environmental factors are most important in shaping the individual is a very old one. In aristocratic societies in the past heredity has been emphasized, and in more recent democratic and socialist societies (exclusive of communist societies influenced by Soviet genetics) environmental factors have been stressed.

The following factors are now known to be determined or influenced by heredity, with the degree of susceptibility to environmental influences increasing in rough parallel to the progression of the list: (1) blood groups, including type and other factors; (2) physiological defects, such as colour blindness; (3) quantitative differences, such as stature and degree of skin pigmentation; (4) resistance and susceptibility to some disease; and (5) mental and emotional characteristics.

The fifth mentioned factors are generally regarded as much less determined by heredity than the four preceding factors – and emotional factors less than mental factors. Studies of identical twins, the primary source of data concerning the relative importance of heredity and environment, show wide variations in mental and emotional traits in twins reared in separate environments. There are apparent hereditary limits to mental variability, however, as no study has shown more than 25% difference between identical twins. *See* H. H. Newman, F. N. Freeman, and K. Holzinger, *Twins: A Study of Heredity and Environment* (1954).

Anthropological and educational studies have shown that race, as a genetic factor, is not determinative of mental ability and temperament in all cases. Difficulties presented by separating hereditary from cultural and social factors have so far made it impossible to determine whether and to what extent race may directly or indirectly influence these factors in some individuals, but the bulk of scientific opinion is against such influence.

There is little evidence that a programme of eugenics can be justified on the basis of the inheritability of 'higher' functions alone, even aside from ethical considerations of individual rights. Examples of phenotypes of wide degrees of genetic determination are known for men. Yet the potential for behaviour provided by heredity sets limits on man's malleability and control by his fellow man.

JAMES N. LAPSLEY

Envy

It is said in the Gospels that Pilate knew the chief priests had delivered Jesus up for trial out of envy (Matt. 27.18; Mark 15.10). They had many reasons for their envy, particularly on account of his authority and his refusal to dictate or be dictated to; his power over the people whom he would neither exploit nor flatter; his refusal to bribe or be bribed; and his disregard for his own safety. Like all envious men the chief priests set out to destroy what they could not possess. Some people are as envious of spiritual qualities such as wisdom, truthfulness, courage or sanctity as of riches, power and the prestige of high office. They would find less reason to envy Pilate than to envy his prisoner.

Preachers and pastors unknowingly tempt people to envy by frequent exhortation to have more faith and more courage, giving vivid examples of men and women in every generation who live with the virtues that most people lack. Envy of material things is much easier to detect in oneself than envy of others' spiritual qualities such as faithfulness or devoutness. Parents often, without knowing it, produce conditions which help to make children envy one another, for example, by stressing the cleverness of one and the kindness of another. The members of any group can encourage one another to be envious without knowing what they do.

The Anglican litany groups envy, hatred and malice in that order, perhaps because envy leads to hatred and hatred, together with envy, gives birth to malice. The familiar table of the seven deadly sins (pride, envy, anger, sloth, avarice, gluttony, lust) indicates that pride gives rise to envy – the proud man wants to be rich and adorned with all qualities and honours; when he fails to achieve this his envy kindles anger.

There is no single virtue which can be pitted against envy: rather it is the whole quality of devout living which enables a man to rejoice in the good fortune, sanctity and abilities of others instead of being envious.

R. E. C. BROWNE

Epictetus

Epictetus (c. 50–125 AD), Stoic philosopher. See Stoicism.

Epicureanism

It might at first sight look as if Epicureanism had no ethics at all. Or, if Epicureanism had an ethic, it might seem bound to be the 'ethic of the pig-sty'. This is so for a variety of reasons.

Epicureanism reduced man – and everything else – to 'a fortuitous conglomeration of atoms', which came together by chance to form man, and which at death simply disintegrated. Epicureanism banished religion, which it held to be the chief curse of man (Lucretius i.62–79), and removed the gods to a lonely isolation in which they had not the slightest interest in mankind. The word epicureanism has become a synonym for the worship of pleasure, and for Epicurus pleasure was the supreme good (Lucian, Hermotimus 36). Pleasure is 'the alpha and omega of the blessed life', 'the first and native good' (Diogenes Laertius x.128,129). Epicureanism is therefore admittedly the pursuit of pleasure.

Sometimes the Epicureans did speak as if they meant bodily and sensual pleasure, but the fact was that in the ancient world the Epicureans were notorious, not for their indulgence in physical pleasure, but for the austerity of their lives. Clement of Alexandria quotes a saying from a play of Philemon: 'This fellow (Epicurus) is bringing in a new philosophy; he preaches hunger and his disciples follow him. They get but a single roll, a dried fig to relish it, and water to wash it down' (Clement of Alexandria, Strom. ii.493; cf. Seneca, De Vita Beata xiii.1; Aelian, Var. Hist. iv.13; Athenaeus, Deipnosophistae iv.163; Diogenes Laertius x.11). How does this come about? It comes about because for the Epicurean the supreme pleasure is ataraxia, the calm serenity when the soul is at peace. The Epicurean definition is: 'By pleasure we mean the absence of pain in the body and trouble in the mind' (Diogenes Laertius x.131). This meant that it was always the long view of pleasure that had to be taken, and therefore the sensual pleasures which brought pain to follow were the very things the Epicurean avoided.

So for the happy life content is necessary. 'If you want to make Pythocles happy, add not to his possessions but take away from his desires' (Epicurus, Fragment 28). The real necessities are all the simplest things (Fragment 67,71). Physical love is to be avoided. The wise man will not fall in love because it disturbs his peace (Diogenes Laertius x.118,119). Envy must be banished as injurious (Fragment 53). Ambition must have no place in life. Epicureans strenuously avoided politics and public affairs. Their motto was: 'Live unseen' (Fragment 68).

The Epicurean believed in the necessity of virtue, but only from the purely selfish point of view that without virtue happiness is not possible. Epicurus advocated justice, for instance, not because justice is absolutely good, but because, if we do wrong, we may be found out, and, even if we are not found out, we cannot be at peace, because we will always be afraid that we may be (Fragment 2,7; Seneca, Letters xcvii.13).

Epicureanism had a high ethic but its motive was prudent selfishness and enlightened self-interest.

WILLIAM BARCLAY

Equality

It is obvious that all men are *not* created equal. They differ among themselves in innumerable ways, and in particular some are more gifted and more able to cope with the demands of life than others. But it is just as obvious that justice requires that in a great many regards, men should receive equal treatment. This is certainly in accordance with the Christian ethic, and is rooted in some fundamental Christian doctrines: the doctrine of creation, whereby all men are created by God for his good purpose, and are loved and valued by him; the doctrine of sin, whereby all men are said to have sinned and fallen short, so that they are all equally under judgment; the doctrine of reconciliation, Christ's work being for all; and the doctrine of the Church, which is declared in the NT to be the community within which the worldly differences of sex, race, nationality and social status are transcended. An interpretation of equality must have regard both to the fact of diversity (inequality) and to the demands of justice; and a Christian interpretation will have regard further to the doctrines mentioned above. The most obvious demand for equality is equality before the law, and this was in fact one of the first kinds of equality to be achieved in any substantial measure. Privileges of wealth or position, or their absence, should confer neither advantage nor disadvantage in the operation of the law. Equal say in the government of the community (the principle of 'one man, one vote', irrespective of sex, race or status) took longer to achieve, but now obtains to a substantial degree in countries which have developed democracy (q.v.). Equality of opportunity, that is to say, the opportunity to develop to their fullest capacity and to make use of one's talents and opportunities is the most difficult kind of equality to achieve, and can be only partially achieved by legislation. There can be no doubt that race in the USA and the 'old school tie' in Great Britain, as well as many other factors, subtly operate to the detriment of some individuals, who are discriminated against in education, employment and promotion, although in terms of ability they may be very well qualified. On the other hand, the rightful demand for equality of opportunity should not be confused with a false egalitarianism which, sometimes springing from an understandable resentment against past abuses of privilege, seek to level everyone down to mediocrity, for instance, in the field of education. A modern technological society has imperative need for excellence as well as for equality, and if increased affluence makes possible a fuller development than has hitherto

been possible of the potentialities of the masses of the people, this should not prevent a special investment in those in the top bracket of ability, provided that their ability alone is the determining factor.

EDITOR

Equiprobabilism

The system in moral theology which attempts to meet objections to probabilism and probabiliorism by holding, as against the latter, that the benefit of the doubt may be taken where the arguments for and against the *existence* of a law are roughly equal, but, as against the former, that it may not be taken where the doubt concerns whether a law, known for certain to have existed, has *ceased to exist*.

R. C. MORTIMER

Erastianism

Erastianism is the type of relationship between Church and State whereby the former is subjected to the latter. See **Church and State**.

Eros. see Love.

Error. see Ignorance.

Eschatological Ethics

As the result of the work of a large number of NT scholars beginning with Johannes Weiss and Albert Schweitzer, it is generally recognized that Jesus' conception of the Kingdom of God presupposes an eschatological and apocalyptic world-view. In the teaching of Jesus the Kingdom of God was essentially an eschatological event and its coming was conceived to be imminent. Its advent would be marked by a radical transformation of the present world order and the inauguration of a new aeon in which evil would be completely overthrown and the righteous rule of God would be fully manifest.

Recognition of the eschatological and apocalyptic presuppositions which underlay Jesus' understanding of the Kingdom of God called for a re-examination of the nature and purpose of his ethic. In *The Quest of the Historical Jesus* Schweitzer urged that the purpose of Jesus' ethical teachings was to show men what they must do in order to prepare themselves to enter the Kingdom, the coming of which he believed to be imminent. Since it was intended only for a relatively brief interval between the proclamation of the Kingdom and the actual advent of the latter, Jesus' ethic was in reality an *interim-sethik*. Its content was so conditioned by the expectation of an imminent end to the present historical order, Schweitzer believed, that it is inapplicable to life in a radically different cultural situation in which a much longer chronological future is anticipated.

Subsequent biblical scholarship has modified Schweitzer's thorough-going eschatology at a number of important points. It is now generally recognized, for example, that Jesus' conception of the Kingdom had a present as well as a future dimension. Moreover, it is also generally acknowledged, as we shall see, that Jesus' ethic cannot be adequately understood simply as an 'interim ethic' even though it is also agreed that his ethic cannot be properly understood apart from its eschatological setting. But the basic question raised by Weiss and Schweitzer was not whether there was such an eschatological element in Jesus' teaching; rather, the fundamental question which they raised concerned the *meaning* of Jesus' proclamation of the imminent end of the present age. In so far as Christian ethics is concerned, the basic question in this regard is this: To what extent did eschatology condition Jesus' ethic? To what extent did the former determine both the sanction and the content of the latter? Does Jesus' ethic lose its entire validity once the expectation of the immediacy of the *eschaton* is no longer held?

As previously noted, Schweitzer argued that Jesus' entire ethic was an 'interim ethic', the purpose of which was to summon men to repentance in preparation for the advent of the Kingdom of God. In this respect he went farther than Weiss who had acknowledged that some of Jesus' teachings – especially the commandments to love God and one's neighbour – do not seem to have been directly affected by his expectation of the imminent advent of the new age. Since Schweitzer some NT scholars have sought to distinguish in various ways between one set of Jesus' ethical teachings which appear to be eschatologically conditioned on the one hand and the remainder of his ethical teachings which seem to presuppose a relatively long continuation of the present historical order. Thus, Hans Windisch in *The Meaning of the Sermon on the Mount* distinguishes between the following two main streams in the ethical thought of the Sermon on the Mount: (1) radicalized wisdom teachings which had their origin in the non-dualistic wisdom tradition of Judaism and hence were not basically affected by Jesus eschatological beliefs and (2) prophetic-eschatological announcements of salvation and judgment, the content of this was directly related to his eschatological expectations. The content of the wisdom teachings – for example, the counsel to love one's enemy, the warning against anxiety, and the admonition that one about to go to court should make friends with his accuser – was not determined by the nearness of the judgment; nevertheless these sayings are given a radical eschatological interpretation as they appear in Matthew in contrast to Luke.

While it is possible to discern at least two types of ethical counsel in the teachings of Jesus – one reflecting the wisdom, or law, tradition and the other reflecting a more prophetic, eschatologically-conditioned demand and while the former may be more directly applicable to a non-apocalyptic setting than the latter, it is difficult to make a sharp, clear-cut distinction between these two types of teachings. Moreover, the most distinctive ethical counsel of Jesus is couched in the form of certain stringent demands which he places upon his followers in view of the impending apocalyptic crisis. At the deepest level, therefore, the fundamental question concerning the relationship of eschatology to Christian ethics must be raised in connection with the prophetic. radically eschatological demands of the gospel, And, finally, the question arises as to whether there is any unifying element underlying the whole of Jesus' ethical teaching which may provide a basis for placing the questions of eschatology and an 'interim ethic' in a larger perspective. In an attempt to indicate some of the most important interpretations of the significance of eschatology for Jesus' ethic which have been set forth in opposition to Schweitzer's concept of an 'interim ethic', we shall briefly consider the following: Rudolf Bultmann's existentialized eschatology, C. H. Dodd's 'realized eschatology', Martin Dibelius' concept of an 'eschatological stimulus', and Amos Wilder's distinction between the secondary and primary sanctions of Jesus' ethic.

In *Jesus and the Word* Bultmann argues that, despite the apocalyptic character of Jesus' teaching concerning the Kingdom of God, the validity of his ethic is not affected in the least by the failure of this expectation. Bultmann characterizes Jesus' ethic as one of 'radical obedience', involving the claim of God upon the whole man to do the divine will in each present moment of decision. The basic significance of the eschatological element in Jesus' teaching is to be found in the fact that the proclamation of the coming of the Kingdom points men to '*the present moment as the final hour* in the sense of the hour of decision' and that this 'now' is always for them their last hour in the sense that in it a man is confronted with the necessity of making an existential decision for or against total obedience to the divine claim. Hence, it is a matter of indifference whether or not the specific content of certain of Jesus' specific ethical teachings was derived from his eschatological expectations; for that which is permanently valid about his ethic is the demand which it makes for radical obedience to the demand of God, the precise content of which must be existentially heard in each new moment of decision. Jesus' ethic cannot, therefore, be dismissed as an 'interim ethic'; moreover, his proclamation of the coming of the Kingdom and his ethical teaching about the will of God have an indissoluble unity in the 'word' of God – that is, in the event in which man is confronted with the message of God's forgiveness and with the necessity of making a decision either for or against obedience to God.

While Bultmann maintains that for Jesus the coming of the Kingdom of God lay wholly in the future, C. H. Dodd argues that Jesus viewed the Kingdom as having arrived both as judgment and as grace in his ministry. In *The Parables of the Kingdom* Dodd acknowledges that certain sayings of Jesus apparently imply a future coming of the Kingdom, but he holds that such sayings refer, not to a future coming of the Kingdom in this world, but to a 'transcendent order beyond time and space' – an order in which 'many who are not yet "in the Kingdom of God" in its earthly manifestation, will enjoy its ultimate fulfilment in a world beyond this'. The eschatological hope for the coming of the Kingdom was thus being 'realized' in Jesus' own lifetime, and he did not look for it to come again or in any fuller sense in this earthly order. Hence, Jesus' ethic cannot have been intended as an 'interim ethic'. Rather, Dodd believes, it was intended as 'a moral ideal' for men who are even now living in the new age. Or, as Dodd puts the matter in *Gospel and Law*, they are intended 'as the new law which supersedes the law of the Old Testament'; they are intended, in short, as 'the law of the Kingdom of God', As such the ethical precepts of the Gospels have two purposes: on the one hand they serve as an aid to repentance, and on the other hand they serve as a guide for positive moral action for those who have received the Kingdom and seek to live their lives in the presence of God's judgment and grace.

According to Martin Dibelius in *The Sermon on the Mount*, Jesus looked for the end of the present age to come soon but his ethic was not for this reason intended as an 'interim-ethic'. On the contrary, the commandments of Jesus represent the eternal will of God, and as such they 'were given for eternity'. Indeed, all of the commandments in the Gospels, and not just those with an explicit reference to the coming of the new age, are eschatological in that their starting point is the absolute will of God, not human ability and the conditions of earthly life in the present age. Jesus' ethical teachings as well as his deeds are, therefore, 'signs of God's Kingdom'. They were not intended as law but rather as 'radical examples of what God demands' of those who want to be children of the Kingdom even now in the present age. It is impossible for modern man, who does not share Jesus' apocalyptic expectations, to be fully obedient to the will of God since he cannot escape responsibility for the social problems of today; nevertheless, the ethic of the Gospels is just as relevant to life in the modern world as it was to Jesus' hearers. The primary purpose of this ethic then and its essential function today is to 'make men well acquainted with the pure will of God' to the end that, although they

are 'not able to *perform* it in its full scope', they may 'be *transformed* by it'. Jesus taught neither an ethical ideal which men might seek to attain as the goal of their social life nor a law for moral conduct either before or after the arrival of the new age; rather, his ethic serves as an 'eschatological stimulus' which, because it is completely focused upon the reality of the Kingdom of God and because it is intended as a sign of the Kingdom's presence, confronts men with the pure and eternal will of God in a way in which it is impossible for either a set of laws or any other system of ethics to do.

In *Eschatology and Ethics in the Teaching of Jesus*, Amos N. Wilder recognizes that eschatology provided the 'dominant sanction' for Jesus' ethic, but he argues that this appeal to rewards and punishments was for Jesus only a formal and secondary sanction and that it was based upon his religious-prophetic apprehension of the divine will. Hence, the essential and fundamental motivation for righteousness is found in the appeals which Jesus made to man's discernment of the nature of God, of man, and of the world; to intuition; to gratitude; to obedience; and to the desire to be children of the heavenly Father. The eschatological appeal to rewards and punishments is thus basically a mythological albeit pedagogically necessary formulation of the consequences of human conduct in a world in which man's primary relationship is the personal one which he bears to the righteous and sovereign Lord of history.

Eschatology has three main functions in relation to Jesus' ethical teachings according to Wilder. In the first place, in so far as the coming of the Kingdom is conceived of in futuristic terms the appeal to eschatology provides 'the motive for repentance and for urgency in doing righteousness, and the particular demands are looked on as conditions of entrance to the future Kingdom'. In the second place, in so far as Jesus teaches that the Kingdom is already present he recognizes that a new ethical situation has been created by its presence; his ethical teaching points, therefore, to the new possibilities of life made possible by the presence of the Kingdom, and his ethic may be described as 'an ethic of the present Kingdom of God or a new-covenant ethic'. Finally, eschatology is related to Jesus' ethical teachings in a third way; for the crisis associated with the coming of the Kingdom, which Jesus identified with his own work, placed special claims upon his followers during this period. Particularly stringent acts of loyalty, witness and sacrifice were required of his disciples during this time of conflict. This 'discipleship-ethic' was thus conditioned in a special way by the eschatological expectations of Jesus, but even here as elsewhere the fundamental sanction is Jesus' apprehension of the divine will.

While his emphasis upon the historical nature of Christian faith, the present character of the

Kingdom, and the responsive nature of Jesus' ethic provides a needed corrective both to Bultmann's highly individualistic, existentialist interpretation of Jesus' ethic and also to C. H. Dodd's essentially legalistic interpretation of the latter as a new law, it appears that Wilder gives too large a place in Jesus' thought to the on-going character of the present socio-historical order. His interpretation would be more cogent if the mythological character of eschatology were taken more seriously so that attention were focused more exclusively upon its essential meaning – namely, that God will ultimately triumph over all his foes and that the reign of God will finally prevail. Such a modification would not fundamentally alter the relevance of Jesus' ethic for life today; nor would it weaken either the religious base, the urgency of the essential sanction, or the free, responsive character of this ethic. Not only would Jesus' ethic still represent the radical will of God which will finally be done when his Kingdom is fully come, but it would also still represent – by signs more than by law – the divine will for men in the present socio-historical order.

R. Bultmann, *Jesus and the Word*, 1934; M. Dibelius, *The Sermon on the Mount*, 1940; C. H. Dodd, *Gospel and Law*, 1951; *The Parables of the Kingdom*, 1936; N. Perrin, *The Kingdom of God in the Teaching of Jesus*, 1963; Albert Schweitzer, *The Quest of the Historical Jesus*, 1910; Amos N. Wilder, *Eschatology and Ethics in the Teaching of Jesus*, rev. edn., 1950; Hans Windisch, *The Meaning of the Sermon on the Mount*, 1951.

E. CLINTON GARDNER

Essenes

Our information about the Essenes comes from four main sources. It comes from Josephus, *Antiquities* 18.15; 15.10,4,5; *Wars of the Jews* 2.8.2–13; from Philo, *Quod omnis probus Liber* 13–14; from Pliny, *Natural History* 5.17.4; from Eusebius, *Praeparatio Evangelii* 8.11.

The Essenes were deeply devoted to the Jewish law. To them Moses came second only to God, and to blaspheme the name of Moses was a crime punishable by death. Their ethic was therefore basically the ethic of devout Jews. But in more than one direction they carried their ethic beyond the ethics of Judaism. Schurer (*History of the Jewish People* 2.2.198) calls them 'connoisseurs in morality'.

(1) Their ethic was a community ethic. They held everything in common. Food, clothes, money, even their tools were the property of the community. There was therefore among them no such thing as poverty, and they were famous for their treatment of the sick and the aged, who in the Essene community received such care that they had nothing to fear.

(2) They worked for the community, but they had certain views regarding work. They would only work in villages and in the country, for they would not share in the immoralities of towns and cities. They were forbidden to make a weapon of any sort, or to manufacture anything that would hurt or harm any other human being.

(3) They were abstemious and even ascetic. They ate only enough to keep them alive, and were content with one dish and with no variety in their food. They wore the simplest clothes, and wore them until they were completely worn out. Unlike normal Jewish practice, they forbade marriage, and practised celibacy, although some seem to have married, perhaps for the sake of the continuance of the community.

(4) In certain things they were in advance of their time, and different from normal Judaism. They refused all oaths, on the grounds that a statement which required an oath was already condemned. They rejected animal sacrifice, although they sent incense to the Temple. They had no slaves, and believed slavery as an institution to be wrong.

It may fairly be said that they practised the ethics of Judaism, but intensified them in a community which was in character monastic.

WILLIAM BARCLAY

Ethical Language

As the philosophical concern with language has developed over the last half-century, so have there been correspondingly different views of the character of ethical language; and in recent years this interest in language has made possible a novel approach to old problems and controversial distinctions. In discussing the three different attitudes to ethical language which have broadly characterized the present century – attitudes associated respectively with G. E. Moore; with R. Carnap, A. J. Ayer and C. L. Stevenson; and with R. Braithwaite and R. M. Hare – their relevance to four well-known controversies will be mentioned: (1) *The distinction between 'fact' and 'value'*: Here the question is whether a rigid distinction can be drawn as, for example, David Hume supposed, between judgments of fact and judgments of value, usually expressed as a contrast between 'is' and 'ought'; (2) *the distinction between 'normative' and 'descriptive'*: This is the traditional distinction between 'normative' and 'descriptive' sciences, and it is not altogether unrelated to (1) above; (3) *the objectivity of morals*: In what sense (or senses) can morality be said to be 'objective'? And (4) *the possibility of theologically-based ethics*: Here the problem is whether we can speak of *duty* as 'the will of God' or 'what God commands' in a way which neither (*a*) compromises the 'autonomy' of ethics, as is done when there is a claim to *derive* ethics from theology nor (*b*) commits the believer to a crude anthropomorphism, talking of God as if he were a celestial Sergeant-Major.

On G. E. Moore's view, to talk of an action, for example, benevolence being 'good', was to describe a quality – goodness – possessed by that action, just as to speak of a certain rose being 'yellow' is to describe a quality – yellowness – possessed by the rose. In this way, Moore assimilated 'that action is good' and 'that rose is yellow'. 'Goodness' was an indefinable characteristic and one which had to be known by being directly recognized. Since, however, 'goodness' is plainly not a visible quality, he spoke of it as a *non-natural* quality. No doubt the appeal to non-natural qualities enabled Moore to distinguish the non-natural 'ought' from the natural 'is', but his assimilation of goodness and yellowness inevitably suggested that the language of morals was purely descriptive and did no justice whatever to its normative character. Further, while Moore argued for the objectivity of morals in the sense that moral judgments, being concerned with non-natural qualities, were not merely a matter of my feelings or emotions, nor yet of the feelings or emotions of any group or groups of people, it was an objectivity which, like the 'objectivity' of scientific reporting, was so detached as to call forth no sort of moral commitment, and so descriptively independent as to fail to account for the moral concern which moral judgments express. Finally, for Moore 'duty' could not mean nor be defined as 'the will of God' any more than it meant or could be defined as, for example, 'maximizing pleasure'; on Moore's view both translations – the metaphysical phrase as much as the hedonistic phrase – committed the 'naturalistic fallacy' by professing to regard as synonymous, phrases which evidently differed in their use. *See* **Conventional Morality.**

The empiricism of Moore was succeeded by that of the logical positivists. The logical positivist of the middle-thirties had no time for non-natural qualities, qualities which *a fortiori* were not verifiable by sense-experience. On such a view, Moore had entirely misread the logical grammar of moral assertions; he had been misled by the *verbal* similarly of 'That rose is yellow' and 'That action is good'. For the positivist, moral assertions, whatever their verbal appearance, were logically identifiable as exclamations; they were merely complex expressions of emotions, of feelings of delight or repugnance. So to speak of some act of benevolence as 'good' was logically equivalent to grading some act as 'benevolent', and accompanying such grading with an approval word like 'Hurrah!' or 'Splendid!' or 'Cheers!'. To speak of stealing as 'wicked' was to accompany the grading of a certain act, that is, taking something without the permission of its known owner and with no intention of returning it, as 'stealing' with a disapproval word such as 'Bad!', 'Offensive!' or 'Deplorable!'. Here was the 'Hurrah – Boo' theory of ethics according

to which the language of morals had to be construed, partly and characteristically in terms of the logic of exclamations, and partly, of course, in terms of the logic of descriptions in so far as ethical language necessarily specifies and so describes features of those situations which it characterizes as 'good' or 'wrong'. All that now remains, on this view, of the distinction between fact and value is the distinction between descriptions and exclamations; nothing remains of the idea of ethics as 'normative', and in so far as exclamations are supposed to be subjective emotional utterances, expressing nothing but the private psychological reactions of whoever utters them, nothing remains of the objectivity of ethics. As for talk of duty or goodness in terms of God's will, this could only and at best be a colourful, picturesque way of talking about one's private feelings or emotions. But, undoubtedly, the major weakness of this theory is that it cannot allow for the irreducible disagreements which in fact occur between those who make moral judgments.

We saw that Moore's account of the language of morals did no justice whatever to the element of personal concern and involvement which ethical language expresses; and if by contrast the Hurrah-Boo theory did give some account of this personal involvement, it was an account which did not go beyond the utterance of an exclamation, and so was hardly adequate. While, no doubt, there are, for each of us, specific feelings directed towards patterns of behaviour said to be 'good' or 'evil', 'right' or 'wrong', our moral judgments are not distinctive merely in having the logical force of exclamations; it is now recognized that they rather declare our intentions to perform a certain action, or to abstain from another, when the appropriate occasion arises. Further, because we share in a common humanity, not only do we commend good behaviour to ourselves, the implication is that we also commend it to others, that is, to other human beings, and we equally condemn bad behaviour for everyone, not merely for ourselves. So ethical language not only *describes* certain circumstances; it is also *evaluative*, and in being evaluative is declaratory of a behaviour policy to which we are committed, and which we thereby commend to others, who are human beings like ourselves.

On this view, the traditional distinction between 'fact' or 'value' is rather a logical distinction between 'descriptive' and 'evaluative' language. In the case of scientific assertions, for example, 'blue copper sulphate turns white on heating', their most characteristic logic is descriptive, and we then talk about the 'descriptive' sciences, and 'facts'; in ethical assertions, it is their evaluative logic by which such an assertion is expressive of a policy or an attitude to the world, which is more evident, as it is, for example, in 'love your enemies'. It is because of this feature of ethical judgments whereby they are determinative of thought and action, that such judgments have been spoken of as 'normative'. Plainly this view of the language of morals does far more justice than its predecessors to the element of personal commitment which characterizes moral judgments. What account, however, does it give of the 'objectivity' of morals, or of the traditional interpretation of moral judgments in terms of God's will?

Undoubtedly, the objectivity of morals would be interpreted in terms of the universalizable character of moral judgments which arises from our common humanity. Moral judgments are not merely prescriptive – like an isolated exclamation or imperative – they are universalizable, and in this way there emerge moral principles as relatively stable guides to conduct. R. M. Hare remarks that it is because of this complete universalism which belongs to moral judgments that these judgments are sometimes invested with a quasi-factual character, when the 'objectivity' of moral judgments runs the risk of being interpreted in descriptive terms. This would be objectivity bought at the price of ruin, for if any judgments were in this sense 'objective' they would have exchanged an evaluative logic for a descriptive logic, and so would have ceased to be moral judgments (see comment on G. E. Moore above).

Even so it might be argued that in fact these defenders of objectivity, in no matter how disastrous a way, have been endeavouring to do justice to another logical feature of the language of morals and one which can be overlooked and even denied. When someone says: 'You ought to do x'; or 'It was good of you to do y'; they are certainly talking descriptively, in specifying those relevant features which characterize the behaviour patterns x and y. Further, these moral judgments, as moral judgments, are prescriptive and universalizable; they are declaratory of a policy, or a way of life, which embodies the behaviour patterns x and y, and such a policy or way of life is morally appropriate for all of us in similar circumstances. But that is not all. In order to be the topics of moral assertions, x and y must also be *claim-possessing* circumstances, and it is such claims as these which I and others acknowledge in the very making the moral judgments we do. In other words, there is a feature of every moral situation which involves no new 'facts' of a perceptual or scientific sort, but it is precisely that which gives moral judgments the prescriptivity they need to have to be moral judgments. This feature is a claim which arises around and out of a behaviour pattern as a condition of that behaviour pattern becoming the topic of a moral judgment. In this way a 'moral' claim is disclosed around a pattern of behaviour whenever this becomes the topic of a moral judgment, and it is to such a disclosed claim that the

prescriptivity, of which Hare speaks, arises as a response. To evaluate is to respond to a claim, and prescriptivity is not so much something that arises out of human decisions, it rather relates to that moral claim which certain circumstances possess, a claim which human decisions acknowledge and to which they register a response. From one point of view what I am suggesting might be expressed by saying that Hare's concept of prescriptivity needs to be further analyzed so as to allow for both the claim-element as well as the response-element in moral assertions, though we may readily grant that prescriptivity, as Hare speaks of it, arises as part of the response. Defenders of 'objectivity', disastrous though their accounts have been when they have spoken of this objectivity descriptively as a quality, have nevertheless rightly endeavoured to preserve the logical priority of this claim element. On this modified version of Hare's theory the language of morals must be regarded as not only descriptive and prescriptive, but as responsive.

If Hare's view is developed in this way there can then arise a possible theological interpretation of ethics. With the more restricted view, belief in God becomes no more, though no less, than the expression of an attitude to the Universe; theism specifies a particular policy for human behaviour. This is the view of R. B. Braithwaite, and it has sometimes been called theism without God. On the other hand, without in any way compromising the autonomy of ethics, theological interpretations can be offered of those claim-possessing features of a situation which a moral judgment implies. Theological phrases can be used as currency for what is prescriptivity in a logically prior sense, the prior prescriptivity which, by *our* response and acknowledgement, is converted into that derived prescriptivity which is the prescriptivity of which Hare speaks. This is no derivation of ethics from theology; it is merely meeting what is a logical necessity for any adequate language of morals, viz. to give an account of the moral *claim* which moral assertions presuppose, by using terms or phrases which have also a use in theology. Hence, Maclagan can speak of theology providing a 'lateral enrichment' of ethical language. On this view, the use of theological terms to talk of the claim element in a moral judgment no more compromises the autonomy of ethics than does the use of scientific terms to talk of the equally necessary descriptive elements of a moral judgment.

Since any such theological term must be currency for a moral claim and must in this sense be prescriptive, it can be seen how a phrase like 'God's will' becomes used as the basis of the theological interpretation, for 'will' readily articulates a claim which we acknowledge and to which we respond. At the same time, like any other characterization of God, 'will' is no more than a model or analogy or way of speaking, and any further theological articulation, for example, in terms of commands, can be developed only with the greatest logical circumspection. *See* **Ethics**.

A. J. Ayer, *Language, Truth and Logic*, 2nd edn., 1946; Paul Edwards, *The Logic of Moral Discourse*, 1955; A. C. Ewing, *Second Thoughts in Moral Philosophy*, 1959; R. M. Hare, *The Language of Morals*, 1952; *Freedom and Reason*, 1963; W. G. Maclagan, *Theological Frontier of Ethics*, 1961; G. E. Moore, *Principia Ethics*, 1903; *Ethics*, 1912; P. Nowell-Smith, *Ethics*, 1954; A. N. Prior, *Logic and the Basis of Ethics*, 1949; I. T. Ramsey, ed., *Prospect for Metaphysics*, 1961; esp. Chaps. 1 and 2; *Christian Ethics and Contemporary Philosophy*, 1966; W. D. Ross, *The Right and the Good*, 1931; C. L. Stevenson, *Ethics and Language*, 1943; S. Toulmin, *The Place of Reason in Ethics*, 1950; J. Wilson, *Reason and Morals*, 1961.

IAN T. RAMSEY

Ethics

The word 'ethics' is used in a variety of ways, and confusions between these uses are common. At least three main types of question are called 'ethical' in different senses: (1) questions as to what is right, good, etc., or of how we ought to behave (normative ethics, morals); (2) questions as to the answers given by particular societies and people to questions of type (1) (descriptive ethics or comparative ethics, a branch of moral sociology or anthropology); and (3) questions as to the meanings or uses of the words used in answering questions of type (1), or the nature or logical character of the moral concepts, or, in older language, of what goodness, etc., are (theoretical ethics, philosophical ethics, moral philosophy). It is perhaps best, in philosophical writing, to reserve the word 'ethics' (unqualified) for inquiries of type (3). The motive for undertaking them has, however, often been the hope that their results might bear on questions of type (1); whether and in what ways this is possible is the question that above all others vexes students of philosophical ethics, and divides the supporters of naturalism, intuitionism, emotivism, descriptivism, prescriptivism (qq.v.), etc.

The simplest answer is given by naturalism and related theories, which hold that to understand the meanings of moral terms is already to be assured of the truth of certain general moral principles, from which, in conjunction with statements of fact, particular moral judgments can be derived. Against this it has been objected by the followers of G. E. Moore that moral principles are matters of substance, or synthetic, and therefore cannot be established by appeal to the meanings of words. More recent writers (prescriptivists) have added to

this objection another, that, since moral judgments are prescriptive or action-guiding, they cannot be derived by logical deduction (with or without the use of definitions of terms) from merely factual premisses. The substance of this objection goes back to Hume and Kant. Both these objections rely on the general logical principle (itself not undisputed) that the conclusion of an inference can contain nothing that is not there, at any rate implicitly, in the premisses.

In a religious context, this controversy is most aptly illustrated by considering the suggestion that 'wrong' *means* 'contrary to God's will'. If this were so, then we should at once be assured of the general moral principle that what is contrary to God's will is wrong (it would, indeed, be a veiled tautology); and from this, in conjunction with factual premisses about what, in particular, God wills, we could deduce particular moral judgments about what is wrong. If objections about the difficulty of ascertaining God's will are ignored, there remain the objections: (1) that it must be matter of substance, not a mere tautology, that what is contrary to God's will is wrong; and (2) that no mere definition of terms could enable us to deduce the prescriptive judgment that something is wrong from the factual statement that it is contrary to God's will. It is further objected that it must be possible for a sufficiently perverse man to maintain without self-contradiction that an act is contrary to God's will but not wrong, or *vice versa*. Moreover, the word 'wrong' is used, and apparently understood, by atheists, and it is not obvious that they are using it in a different sense from theists. For these reasons most philosophers would now reject the view that 'wrong' *means* 'contrary to God's will'; but this does not imply a refutation of the view that what (and only what) is contrary to God's will is wrong. The latter view (an answer to a question of type (1) rather than of type (3) above) is held by most Christians. It does not follow that Christians will agree with one another about all moral questions; for issues which among non-Christians would be treated as disputes about what is wrong, simply, will often be treated among Christians as 'factual' disputes about what God's will is, being assumed that, whatever it is, what is contrary to it is wrong. Often, there being no independent way of ascertaining God's will, it gets accommodated to the moral views of particular disputants. It is perhaps only when a speaker is prepared in this way freely to 'tailor' what he calls 'God's will' to his own moral opinions, that the expressions 'contrary to God's will' and 'wrong' can be said to be equivalents.

If we ask more positively what *are* the meanings, functions, natures, uses, etc., of moral words or concepts, we are, naturally, on controversial ground; but there are some points on which, perhaps, a majority of moral philosophers would agree, their differences lying in matters of emphasis and interpretation. (1) It is a widely accepted view that moral judgments containing such words are in some strong and special sense action-guiding (for example, that there is a more than merely contingent connection between thinking an act the best in the circumstances and being disposed to choose it). This is the feature of moral words which is most emphasized by prescriptivists. (2) Most thinkers would agree that when words like 'right', 'wrong', 'good' and 'bad' are used, they are applied to acts, etc., in virtue of some feature or features of them (apart from their mere rightness, etc.) which is the *reason* for using these words of them. It is held by many to follow from this that to call one act, for example, wrong, is to commit oneself to call any other act wrong which resembles it in all, or in the relevant, particulars. This thesis has been called 'the universalizability of moral judgments'.

These two theses, (1) and (2), are not inconsistent, though they can be made to appear so by mistaken interpretation, thus giving rise to needless disputes. This in turn has led to the rejection of one of the theses as incompatible with the other. For example some naturalists have rejected (1), holding that moral judgments are action-guiding only in the sense in which any factual judgment whatever may be; the information that an act is the best in the circumstances will lead me to do that act, *if* I want to do what is best, just as the information that a stone is the flattest available will lead me to choose it, *if* I want the flattest stone; the effect of this is to turn moral judgments into something like Kant's 'hypothetical imperatives'. They have done this because they thought that, if thesis (2) is correct, the only thing that we can be doing in calling an act the best act is to inform our hearers that it possesses those features which entitle it to this name. If this were so, then the information would guide action only given a prior disposition (which might be absent) to do acts which have those features.

Against this, adherents of Thomism on the one hand, and many modern prescriptivists on the other, have insisted, in different ways, on thesis (1). This doctrine is summed up in the maxim, which goes back in substance to Socrates, '*quicquid appetitur, appetitur sub specie boni* (whatever is desired, is desired under the appearance of its being good)'.

Thesis (2) is incompatible with thesis (1) only if we take (2) as implying that when we call an act, for example, the best, and do so in virtue of something about it, we are doing the same sort of thing as when we call, for example, a surface red in virtue of something about it (its visual appearance under normal conditions). In the latter case to know the meaning of 'red' is to know that we are entitled to call a surface red if, and only if, it appears *thus* under normal conditions. If 'best' functioned like 'red', then, once its meaning was known, there would be no choice left as to what sorts of acts we could call best. And this would lead to a dilemma. Either we should have to reject thesis (1); or else we should have to maintain that to think some act the best is, indeed, to be disposed to do it, but that, once we know the meaning of 'best', what sorts of thing we are disposed to do becomes unalterably fixed; and this runs counter both to our common understanding of the meaning of 'best', and to our feeling that to know the meaning of a word can never restrict our freedom of choice in this way.

Faced with this dilemma, some have felt that, sooner than reject thesis (1), it is best to reject thesis (2), and deny that acts are necessarily called 'the best' in virtue of *anything* about them. But we can avoid this implausible conclusion by interpreting thesis (2) more carefully; it can be taken as implying, not that the meaning of words like 'best' ties them to *particular* features of, for example, acts (the same for all users of the word) but rather that whenever anybody uses the word, he must have in mind, as his reason for using it, *some* features of the act in question (which, if repeated in any other acts in relevantly similar situations, would oblige him to call them, too, the best in their respective situations, or else to withdraw his judgment about this present situation); but these features might differ from speaker to speaker, depending on their various moral opinions, without thereby the *meaning* (in one sense) of the word 'best', as used by them, altering. In other words, the user of the word 'best' thereby commits himself to *some* rule for its application, but there is no single rule to which all users of the word are committed by its meaning. The rule followed by any speaker will depend on his own moral principles as to what is best in this type of situation. For certain necessary qualifications to this statement, *see* **Conventional Morality**.

This issue has sometimes been stated in terms of the distinction between the descriptive and the prescriptive (or evaluative) meaning of moral words. The descriptive meaning is the features in virtue of which an act, for example, is called the best; the prescriptive meaning is the conceptual link whereby a judgment that such and such an act is the best is logically tied to a disposition to choose it. Most current controversies in ethics are essentially about the relations between these two sorts of 'meaning', and the extent to which one or the other of them is properly called 'meaning'. It may safely be said that any ethical theory which ignores either of them is bound to be incomplete; if the prescriptive meaning is ignored, the action-guiding character of moral judgments, which alone gives them their importance and even their use, is lost; if, on the other hand, thesis (2) is denied, then the basis of the rationality of moral judgments, viz. that they are made for reasons, that is, because of *something about* their objects, is destroyed.

The issue just discussed has a bearing on the question of the so-called 'objectivity' of moral principles, which has been the 'philosopher's stone' of ethics. It is possible to interpret 'objectivity' in such a strong sense that it can be established only by some form of naturalism – that is, by saying that the *meaning* of the moral words is such that, once it is known, there is no option left as to what we call, for example, right. Those who reject naturalism cannot in consistency seek to establish this sort of objectivity. However, it is likely that what most 'objectivists' are really after is not so direct a link between the meanings of the moral words and the features of things in virtue of which the words are applied to them, but rather some way or other of establishing the rationality of moral thinking. Much recent controvery in ethics has been between those who think that it cannot be established without adopting some sort of descriptivism (that is, by denying thesis (1) above, in practice usually by espousing some kind of naturalism), and those who think, on the contrary, that thesis (1) is not incompatible with the rationality of moral thought, and may even be essential to it. The word 'objectivism' and its opposites subjectivism and relativism (qq.v.) have been used in so many different senses (often without the realization that they are different) that clarity would be furthered by abandoning the terms altogether and characterizing the disputants in the current controversy by new terms such as 'descriptivists' and 'non-descriptivists'. But, if this is done, it is important to realize that a non-descriptivist does not necessarily deny that moral terms have descriptive meaning; he merely affirms that this is not the only element in their meaning.

For amplification of the argument of this article, the reader is referred to the author's articles 'Ethics' in *Encyclopedia of Western Philosophy and Philosophers*, 1960, ed. by J. O. Urmson, and 'Descriptivism' in *Proceedings of British Academy*, 1963, and to his books *The Language of Morals*, 1952, and *Freedom and Reason*, 1963. For a general survey of the field of ethics from a different standpoint, with further references, *see* R. B. Brandt, *Ethical Theory*, 1959.

R. M. HARE

Ethics, History of

1. *Greek.* Moral reflection, long expressed in maxims, took philosophical form in Socrates, when he inquired into the meaning of such terms as good, just and temperate, and practised a method of testing suggested definitions,

viz. comparing each with the kind of instances it claimed to cover, to make sure that it did cover all instances of that kind and no others; so that ethics began with an intellectual awareness of the need to put precise questions and seek answers with a conscious technique. Plato went further, sketching the first outline of the moral life, as in particular the realization of the four cardinal virtues (justness, courage, moderation of desire and practical insight), and in general a movement from the sensory and the sensual towards a perfection eternally there behind our only half-real world. Aristotle, as much a scientist as a philosopher and therefore less hurriedly soaring than Plato, considered human life more concretely: its raw stuff of appetites and emotions are not in us to be mortified but to be humanized by reason. He worked out a sober moral scheme of fourteen virtues, reserving the highest virtue of pure contemplation of the eternal to philosophers (as Plato had done). Another line of succession started more from Socrates the man than from his teaching, and set going the post-classical tradition that placed him apart as the ideal wise man. One of his immediate pupils, Aristippus, picked out his controlled use of pleasure, and founded the so-called Cyrenaic school; another, Antisthenes, fastened on Socrates' contentment with few wants, his rigorous sense of duty and his serene self-possession in all circumstances. These two opposed viewpoints were represented again, with more intellectual breadth, by the Epicurean and Stoic schools respectively, founded about 300 BC and enduring for centuries. For both the end to be aimed at was tranquillity. For the Epicureans this meant the calm pleasures of intellect and friendship, the avoidance of pleasures that trail pains behind them, and reasoned emancipation from religious dread. For the Stoics it meant reducing moral concern to what is entirely within our control, viz. our judgments and decisions (being 'self-sufficient', the Stoic term translated 'content' in Phil. 4.11 AV, *see also* RSV), and conceiving the external natural order as under the control of divine providence, this religious note being strong. Stoicism is known most fully in the writings of Seneca and Epictetus in the first century AD and of Marcus Aurelius in the second. With the first and third of these we are in Rome, where the best families found it congenial. In the first century BC the moral writings of Cicero had already been largely Stoic.

2. *Christian.* A morality unified from its base to its peaks by love, and made possible by a communicated grace (thus tied to religion as the morality of the redeemed), was a revolutionary change. Its application to converts in a pagan environment, begun by Paul and continued by the clergy, was a practical pre-occupation, the intellectuals turning their mind chiefly on theology. The first powerful mind to

grapple with the general problem of the Christian moral life theoretically was Augustine; but in his controversy with Pelagianism what he was fighting for was the reality of original sin and the utter necessity of grace for salvation, that is, not strictly ethical but theological issues. In the twelfth century Abelard, besides re-affirming something very like the Pelagian view, contended that moral goodness and badness lie in intention, not in outer act. Not until Thomas Aquinas does an ethical system appear, super-ficially Greek, with Paul's faith, hope and love added as theological virtues, these, however, being seen to modify the lower natural virtues. In the succeeding centuries the system was rigidified rather than developed, though there was built on it and on earlier pronouncements of 'doctors' a detailed body of rules and exam-ples for pastoral guidance (casuistry). At the Reformation Luther and Calvin rejected the mediaeval dualism of a lower morality for those whose life lay in the world and a higher for those devoted to the spiritual life: the higher has to be expressed at home, in neighbourhood, at work. There was a short public dispute, echoing the old Pelagian controversy, between Luther, contending for our natural impotence for good because of the entail of Adam, and Erasmus standing for a fair degree of freedom of will. Within both Romanism and Protes-tantism Christian ethics has tended to remain a preserve of theological and biblical scholars.

3. *Modern.* Here we return to purely philos-ophical ethics. The Renaissance loosened in-veterate habits of thought; it produced scarcely any systematic thought about morality. In the seventeenth century the European continent had but one original and weighty ethical thinker, the Dutch Jew Spinoza, whose writings, however, were shunned until towards the end of the next century on the odd supposition that he was an atheist. In England his contempor-aries, the Cambridge Platonists, latitudinarian divines, started the rationalist line, which Locke followed, that moral principles are as self-evident to reason as mathematical axioms, a line continued at the beginning of the next century by S. Clarke and towards the end of it by R. Price. Hobbes slightly preceded the Cambridge group with the postulate that every man willy-nilly seeks his own pleasure, and claimed to show that supposedly altruistic motives can be analyzed into egoistic ones; and on this basis erected his political theory that only fear of the pains of anarchy brought man into organized society and can keep him there. The Enlightenment may be taken to mean the eighteenth century in time, western Europe in place, and in character that part of reflective culture that was then distinctive in the sense of being expressed by famous writers and opera-tive in the outlook and conduct of the leading sections of society. It is often labelled the Age

of Reason (which philosophers apply more fitly to the seventeenth century), partly to indicate its anti-authoritarianism and partly to mark it off from a contemporary recoil called the Age of Sentiment (which some historians include within it). The instigation came from England, practically from its example of political freedom secured without bloodshed, in the realm of ideas from Locke and Newton. Locke had developed an empiricist theory of knowledge, and Newton, drawing into one grand explana-tory scheme the recent physics and astronomy, had established these as assured sciences. The powerful impact of these two thinkers spread to France and Germany, was there modified by local temper and circumstance, and became part of the culture of the Continent. The general effects were a more empirical approach to all philosophical problems, an acceptance of the new scientific world-view, and an emphasis on reasonableness in inferential thinking instead of the seventeenth-century trust in the power of abstract reasoning to spin truth out of supposed axioms, which was replaced with over-confident generalizations about man and his affairs.

In Britain one result was a deistic tendency, claiming that religion reduced to its essentials – alleged to be personal worship, devotion to morality and belief in reward and punishment hereafter – is independent of revelation. The leader of the church were able to counter that, but some of them were contemporary enough to lighten the load of dogma and to present Christian morality as having happiness as its ultimate motive, not merely its ultimate conse-quence. A more theoretical result was the turn-ing of philosophical ethics into a psychological study of the mental nature and source of moral awareness: for example, Shaftesbury, Hutche-son and Hume defined it as not rational insight but a spontaneous sense of what is appropriate or excellent, analogous to taste as the sense of beauty, and characterized it further as a 'dis-interested' attitude, here retorting on Hobbes' egoistic analysis (e.g., of pity as self-pity). For all these, then, morality was an immediate out-flow from human nature, so that even atheists can be held to it, though the first two did recognize a metaphysical ground in God, which Hume declared to be unprovable. Whether Butler is to be assigned to the Enlightenment is doubtful; his deeper probing and his conviction of the difficulty of inducing men to be moral seem to exclude him. Late in the century an *a priori* rationalist strain appeared among the 'enlightened': Godwin announced that human nature is so responsive to rational education that men could live, and live better, without any political controls ('anarchism', the acme of moral optimism), Paine championed the notion of absolute rights of man, and Bentham, deny-ing this notion, neatly reduced morality to the calculated pursuit of pleasure. In America the Enlightenment passed to the framers of the ideals and structure of the new republic chiefly through Hume (his political writings), Paine, and such independent minds as Franklin.

Voltaire was the chief carrier of Locke and Newton to France, the country commonly thought of as the most typical scene of the Enlightenment. France had a more vivacious intelligentsia than elsewhere, and these men had two advantages: they were welcomed into the salons of the aristocracy, and most of them could talk and write in the clearest of clear French. Consequently what they said and wrote was widely noted. Further, they were subjects of a very despotic monarchy, and members of a society over whose beliefs and conduct the Roman Church claimed, with royal support, an immense authority. Hence they learned eagerly from Locke the language of political liberalism, and from Locke and Newton together the principle that thinking, applied as well as pure, can recognize the authority of nothing but experience and reason. They turned their weapons against the king rather than the aristocracy, and many of them more against the Church, priests and imposed dogma than against religion. Their ablest leaders, besides Voltaire, were Diderot and d'Alembert, who directed the remarkable 'Encyclopaedia'. This work (35 volumes, 1751–80) was both a trumpet and a campaign: scientific, technological, humanistic and socially oriented, it aimed at the improvement of life by propagating the new knowledge of man and his world and by rousing hope in large and sure progress by such means. They neither preached nor intended violence. Few of them followed philosophy in its technical forms, though they could handle its ideas with much intelligence. None of them shaped a system of ethics, an ordered clarification and grounding of moral notions. Their interest in morals was practical, and the morality they recommended was benevolence and good taste; some of them were practical philanthropists. What distinguished them was their naturalistic approach to all human questions, seeing them on the worldly plane, not relating them to a metaphysical or religious perspective, even when they acknowledged one; their stress on the right of every individual to happiness *now* (suffering being wrong as unnatural, not to be accepted as one's lot), and on the causal necessity of securing it socially; and a lively faith that such happiness could be secured fairly soon, a faith based on the supposition (drawn by analogy from Locke's theory that we begin our knowing with a clean sheet) that we start life with neither a bias to goodness nor an entail of wickedness, but are fashionable either way according to the manner of our upbringing and the temper of our society. It was the second and third of these features that led some Frenchmen before the end of the century to begin the study of backward children, and Beccaria in Italy to initiate the view that criminals could be scientifically diagnosed and treated, not merely punished. Germany had wide areas of Protestantism into which the Enlightenment could enter. In Prussia, one aspect of the 'enlightened despotism' of Frederick the Great was his drawing of French modernizing scholars and writers to Berlin. Philosophy stepped out of Latin into the vernacular, Wolff's scholastic systematization of Leibniz was slackened, emphasized on its empirical side with some additions from Locke, and made plainer. Religion without revelation reared its head in the Jew Mendelssohn and the Protestant scholar Reimarus; and Lessing brought other religions besides Christianity into view, leaned towards Spinoza's notion of an immanent God, and renewed Spinoza's fine plea for liberty of thought. Kant put an end to both a native German pedantic form of rationalism and echoes of British empiricism by defining morality as an absolute command given by reason (in its practical function) to the will, no feeling except reverence for that command being relevant; and by making that absolute command the only lever by which we can philosophically break through the world of appearance to the world of reality ('the primacy of the practical reason') he gave us the moral way of arguing to God.

The nineteenth century opened with the emergence of two incompatible schools, of utilitarianism in England, of idealism in Germany, the former largely psychological, ethical and political in interest, and regarding man as a social animal, the latter ambitiously and boldly speculative and viewing man in the context of his entire cultural history and of the universe as a whole. Idealism, the doctrine of the supremacy of an immanent world-spirit, assumed different forms in its leaders, Fichte, Schelling, Hegel and Schopenhauer, but its monism had the common implication for ethics that individuality is an abstraction so that moral individualism was ruled out. The great wave of idealism was stopped in Germany in mid-century by a reaction against its immense claims, by a materialism based on a renewed enthusiasm for physics, and by the startling new current of evolutionist biology. Utilitarianism, initiated very bluntly by Bentham and given a more persuasive form by J. S. Mill, was a form of hedonism: happiness, understood as the planned predominance of pleasure over pain, is the only good, and the goal to be aimed at is 'public utility' (hence the name of the school) understood as 'the greatest happiness of the greatest number'. Evolutionism as a philosophy of man came near to hedonism in some of its English writers, and virtually all of them took a purely naturalistic view of human life. It thus became, with Utilitarianism and all philosophy based on either subjective natural feelings or natural science, the common enemy of thinkers who in the 1870s revived in Britain the Idealism that had risen and fallen in Germany, Green and Bradley being specially interested in its ethical aspect. A similar revival with the same direction of antagonism occurred in America, with W. T. Harris as its first leader and Royce as its later and most distinguished representative; also, with perhaps less moral emphasis, in Italy under Gentile and Croce. All this Germanic idealism declined swiftly, except in Italy, after 1918. Since then strictly ethical thought has had few distinguished mouthpieces, for example, the pragmatist or instrumentalist Dewey in America, the analyst Moore in England, and Nicolai Hartmann in Germany; Bergson's long awaited book on ethics (1932) evoked little response. In the distinctively recent philosophizing, Logical Positivism has expelled ethics as non-philosophical, and Linguistic Analysis, denying the specific tasks and therefore the boundaries of the traditional branches of philosophy, deals with moral terms as with any others that interest it, viz. analyzes the ways they are in fact used in everyday language. For these two schools the quest for prescriptions of how we ought to behave fall outside the business of the philosopher.

C. Becker, *The Heavenly City of the 18th Cent. Philosophers*, 1932, repr. 1959; Woodbridge Riley, *Men and Morals: the Story of Ethics*, 1929; A. K. Rogers, *Morals in Review*, 1927; H. Sidgwick, *Outlines of the History of Ethics*, 1931.

T. E. JESSOP

Eudaemonism

Eudaemonism is the theory which holds happiness (q.v.) to be the highest good.

Eugenics

It has long been known that selective breeding of animals and plants may lead to the development of better and stronger strains, and the practice is now universal in agriculture, with beneficial results. But whenever one considers the extension of this practice to human procreation, grave moral problems arise. Some of these problems are more easily resolved than others. Believing as he does in the personal and sacramental character of marriage, the Christian could never countenance the disregarding of marriage ties for the sake of producing superior individuals 'for the public good'; for he would hold that the public good would be more damaged than benefited, especially by the disregard of the personal character of marriage and the family, and the treatment of human sexual relations as if they were on the level of the breeding of animals. This would be true even if (and perhaps especially if) techniques of artificial insemination (q.v.) were employed, as has been advocated, for the continuation of

desirable strains; for the separation of procreation from the personal relation of marriage, and the further separation of the marriage relationship from family life, would be intolerable blows at the Christian understanding of marriage and the family. On the other hand, the Christian moralist would have to look much more sympathetically at measures to discourage or prevent the continuation of weak and defective strains, or the birth of defective children. Here it is a case of weighing the right of the individual to marry and reproduce against the suffering which such a course might produce in the children of the union, or the damage that might be inflicted on society. Here one would have to take cognizance of the advice of experts on heredity. *see* **Environment and Heredity**. Even if one were assured that a particular union might be very dangerous, voluntary restraint on the part of the marriage-partners would be preferable to any forcible measures to prevent reproduction. It is possible that in the near future, this whole subject may become much more urgent. As the nuclear structures of the living cell come to be better understood, the possibility will emerge of what is called 'genetic engineering', that is, techniques by which it may become possible to determine characteristics of the as yet unborn (or unconceived) child. It is futile to think of such techniques as somehow an invasion by man of what properly belongs to God, or a usurpation of godlike prerogatives. Every way in which man has brought nature under control is an instance of the same tendency in man – perhaps even the destiny for which he was created. The only difference is that as he goes on, his responsibilities become more frightening. Genetic engineering might make possible the elimination of many scourges. On the other hand, it bristles with moral problems, and calls now for serious study by Christian experts, so that when it comes along we shall have some idea of what to do. See **Family; Marriage; Procreation; Sex,** etc.

EDITOR

Euthanasia

From the Greek words *eu* and *thanatos*, the literal meaning is easy or gentle death. In pre-Christian times euthanasia was practised in some primitive and in some civilized countries, usually in the form of exposure of the very young and abandonment of the aged. Modern interest in the question dates from the nineteenth century. Perhaps few would defend it today in terms of a crudely utilitarian ethic as a sensible means of disposing of those members of the community who, because of disease, mental deficiency or physical uselessness, are regarded as burdensome. This argument for compulsory euthanasia was given a logical extension in Nazi Germany during the second World War to include those who were regarded as politically and racially as well as economically an embarrassment to the State. As advocated today it is usually understood in a narrower context as the theory or doctrine that when a person's life has become a burden to him as a result of incurable and painful illness, death should be anticipated by some painless method approved by science to shorten his sufferings. In this sense it might take a compulsory or a voluntary form: (1) *Compulsory*, that is, the giving of euthanasia by someone acting in a private or official capacity without the knowledge or consent of the sick person. This has been defended in terms of 'mercy killing' with special reference to seriously deformed or mentally defective children (*see* **Infanticide**) or adults who are thought to be incurably ill and perhaps in great pain. It is argued that to give them a speedy and gentle release would be an act of merciful kindness both to them and to others, particularly members of their family. This conflicts with Christian teaching. The right to life is God-given, and it is not within the moral competence of man deliberately and directly to take the life of any innocent human being either with or without his consent. Thus to do so in the circumstances envisaged would be to commit an act of injustice towards the sick person and an act of impiety towards God who gave him his life. True compassion there should be, but it is incompatible with injustice and impiety. We have a duty to relieve suffering, but not at any price. It is one thing to deaden or reduce pain by an injection that may also have the effect of shortening life, and quite another to give an injection with the direct object of terminating life. To take with deliberate intent the life of any innocent person, whether incurably sick or in good health, with or without the aid of medical science, is to commit the grave sin of murder; and (2) *Voluntary*, that is, the request by an incurably sick person for the easy and gentle death which euthanasia will bring. It is argued by the Voluntary Euthanasia Legalization Societies in Britain and America that, with various safeguards, the law should permit a man in these circumstances to terminate his own life or request a doctor to do it for him. A few Christians are known to support this view, arguing that a good man may conclude that he has already reached a stage when he can no longer do anything more to serve God or his fellow men by remaining alive. But this conflicts with the overwhelming weight of Christian opinion. A man is not the absolute owner of his life. It belongs to God who gave it. A man has the right to preserve and prolong it, but not the right wilfully to destroy it. Is it not a denial of God's loving providence to assert at any given time that one's life can serve no good purpose? It is true that suffering can sometimes seem meaningless to us; it is never to be sought or endured simply for its own sake, and so far

as possible it should be eased. It can be very terrible, but it is not the worst evil. Sometimes it is the occasion of spiritual growth. The manner in which it is endured can have moral effects of great value upon those who are privileged to be in attendance. Deliberately to take (or request another to take) one's life for any self-regarding motive, even that of escaping from the burden of what is at present an incurable disease, is to commit the grave sin of suicide. Euthanasia was condemned by the pope in 1943 and 1948; by the Archbishops of Canterbury in 1936, and York in 1950; and by the Protestant Episcopal Church in America in 1952.

Joseph Fletcher, *Morals and Medicine*, 1954; Norman St John-Stevas, *Life, Death and the Law*, 1961; Thomas Wood, *Some Moral Problems*, 1961.

THOMAS WOOD

Evangelical Counsels. *see* Counsels.

Evil

Evil can be considered in terms of its nature, explanation and remedy (or cure). Inevitably the Christian view of it coincides at many points with the views adopted by non-Christian thinkers. But the gospel provides a wholly new answer to the problem of its cure.

1. *The nature of evil.* Most theologians distinguish between moral and non-moral evil. Moral evil consists in transgression of the moral law or, when faith is present, disobedience to the will of God. Non-moral evils comprise those ills which do not proceed directly from man's sin.

Moral evil, or sin, will be analyzed in the other articles. Here it is enough to state that a human act can have evil effects without being itself evil in the moral sense. An act is morally evil only if it is a voluntary infringement of a moral law that is known to the agent. When the agent is invincibly ignorant of a law, or when he acts involuntarily, his act is not morally wrong, or sinful; so that any evil effects it may produce fall within the non-moral category.

Non-moral evils are various. One thinks chiefly of the human suffering produced by physical disorders – by earthquakes, famine or disease. (Whether the wastage in the evolutionary process, or the pain endured by sub-human animals, is to be judged evil is a disputable question. But nature is unquestionably often evil in relation to its highest product – man.)

Yet what is the nature of evil in itself? What is its ontological character or status? Aquinas held that it is wholly negative – a 'privation of good'. His aim was to exclude a Manichaean dualism that would be incompatible with the Christian doctrine of creation. Since everything is made by God, and since God is holy, evil cannot possess independent being. It is therefore a defect in a person or a thing. Just as blindness is lack of sight, so vice is lack of virtue. In both cases the human organism fails to actualize its nature and achieve its good.

If we are to understand this theory we must note two distinctions. Firstly, while Aquinas denied that evil is a positive entity he did not assert that it is unreal. It is a *real* privation. Secondly we must distinguish between an act *qua* evil and the effects which its evil character produces. While the effects are positive the evil is negative. Let us take the example of cruelty. The harm which a cruel person does is manifestly positive; but the evil nature of his act consists in the fact that it is contrary to the moral law.

The theory has two further merits. Firstly, it does justice to the spiritual truth (stated by both Plato and St Paul) that sin diminishes and corrupts the soul at the centre of its being. Secondly, it explains why we include both moral and non-moral ills within the single category 'evil', and why we view both with equal horror. We do so because they both distort reality. Both represent a declension from the creature's good and thereby from the perfect, loving, will of the Creator.

2. *The explanation of evil.* Even if we accept the view that evil is negative we still have to explain how it can occur in a world created by a holy God. Two general 'explanations' must be rejected.

The first rests on the denial that God is omnipotent. He is limited, if not in wisdom, then in power. He is faced either by recalcitrant material or by other, malign, agencies that coexist with him. Such a view (which was held by many gnostics) is incompatible with Christian theism which asserts that God made the world *ex nihilo*. God is not omnipotent in the sense that he can do anything; for some things are contrary to reason or morality. But he is omnipotent in the sense that he controls all things by his creative Word.

Some, again, have taken refuge in the contrast between God's 'absolute' and 'permissive' will. God does not will evil absolutely (by a direct expression of his nature), as he wills good. He merely permits it for a higher end. But this is an evasion, not a solution; for since God is simple he wills everything by a single, undivided, act of power. If we say that he merely 'permits' evil – and perhaps we are driven to say this in order to make his action intelligible – we must add that his will in permitting it is absolute.

Having rejected these 'solutions' we can explain evil, in its two main forms, along the following lines:

(a) *Sin.* According to the doctrine of the Fall, sin entered the human race through Adam's disobedience. But even if the Genesis-myth is taken literally it only pushes the problem a stage farther back. How could Adam (or any man in Adam's place) make a sinful choice if he was made in the image of a good Creator? Furthermore, it is impossible to see how human sin could be responsible for nature's disordered state, especially since this disorder (in many of its aspects) preceded man's arrival on the cosmic scene. If we explain this disorder by the fall of a World-Soul we cannot further explain how this soul could have departed from the will of its Creator.

(b) *Human suffering.* This has always been regarded as a powerful obstacle to belief in the Christian God. Nothing can be said which is both new and true. Some suffering is caused by the prior sin of the sufferer. But (as Job's experience and Christ's explicit teaching show) some suffering is unmerited. Unmerited suffering is often justified on two grounds. Firstly, it 'purifies' the sufferer by affording him an opportunity to strengthen his character. Secondly, the sufferings of others provide us with an opportunity to exhibit sympathy and deepen prayer. But (it could be replied) the first of these justifications is inapplicable to many cases. How could a child who knows nothing of Christian faith and who is brought up in a depraved environment be 'purified' by starvation and disease with those degrees of torment which, if they were inflicted by a *human* agent, would merit the death-penalty? Furthermore, is it not unjust that the innocent should descend to the depths of degradation and despair in order to be of spiritual benefit to others who are more fortunate?

At this point theists frequently invoke the idea of immortality. The miseries of earth will be outweighed by the joys of heaven. But the miseries are still evil. If God has the power to put wrongs right at a future day of reckoning why does he permit the wrongs at all?

Every explanation fails to satisfy the speculative intellect. Von Hügel pronounced the last word when he wrote: 'Let us quietly and deliberately admit that no man has yet explained the reality of evil in a world created and sustained by an all-powerful, all-wise, all-good Spirit, by God' (*The Reality of God*, 1931, p. 17).

3. *The cure of evil.* Although Christians cannot explain the fact of evil they possess the secret of its cure. God in Christ has saved them from the ravages of sin and suffering through his perfect sacrifice whereby he made of both a pathway to the heavenly world.

Hence, for the Christian, evil is characterized by a double paradox. On the one hand, its presence in a world created by a holy God cannot be explained. On the other hand, God himself, in his incarnate Son, has conquered evil and enabled us to share (by grace, not merit) in his victory. Again, evil is fully real – a terrible cancer at the heart of things. Yet we believe that, through the Spirit of the risen Christ, the greatest evil can become the occasion of the greatest good – if not of a good that is manifest here and now, then of a good that will be manifest hereafter.

Christians can, and must, face evil in its full reality and inexplicability. But their reaction to it is distinctive. They do not seek escape from it (as the Buddhist seeks escape in a passionless nirvana). They do not preach a Stoic 'indifference' to it. Still less do they make it an excuse for a pessimistic *Weltanschauung*. They have two duties: firstly, to combat it by every means, and secondly to believe that God will vanquish it according to the perfect (but hidden) wisdom of his providence.

St Thomas Aquinas, *Philosophical Texts*, selected and translated by Thomas Gilby, 1956, pp. 163–80; John Hick, *Evil and the God of Love*, 1966; C. S. Lewis, *The Problem of Pain*, 1944; F. Petit, *The Problem of Evil*, ET, 1959.

H. P. OWEN

Evolutionary Ethics

The notion that ethical conduct should be seen as an extension of biological evolution was popularized by Herbert Spencer (*see especially* his *Data of Ethics* [1879], Chap. II, 'The Evolution of Conduct'). 'Evolutionary' views of the development of cultures were prevalent among anthropologists of the late nineteenth century, assuming a pattern of stages of development from simple primitive forms to the complex rational forms of western civilization. That social and ethical conduct should be looked on as a direct continuation of biological evolution, to be described in similar categories, was challenged by Thomas Huxley in his Romanes Lectures of 1893, 'Evolution and Ethics', in which he maintained that ethical life, particularly insofar as it involved consideration for the weak, prescribed conduct directly opposed to the cosmic struggle for existence described by biological evolution. A version of the older view of ethical development as a further stage of evolution was given in 1943 in another Romanes Lecture, under the title 'Evolutionary Ethics' by his grandson, Sir Julian Huxley. Sir Julian Huxley is the best known contemporary exponent of this view. He sees ethical and cultural development as a new stage of evolution, where the human mind can deliberately shape the future course of evolution through purposive action. The continuity of this with earlier stages is seen by presenting the latter stages as development of potentialities inherent in the earlier.

A difficulty about this way of looking on ethics is to know just how the notion of evolution should be understood. Biological evolution is a theory of the differentiation of a number of species from a common ancestor, and the survival of some of these. The elimination of large numbers of species and the survival of others makes for a gradual change through the accumulative effect of small genetic variations. Whether or not the term 'evolution' should be restricted to biological evolution in this sense, it can be broadly said to stand for processes of large scale change over long periods through the accretions of small changes not attributive to the purpose or intention of individuals or to special creation. To use the term 'evolution' as equally applicable to ethical and social development may obscure differences between the characteristics of purposive human actions and the mechanisms of biological change. It may also suggest a single line of human social development, and even an inevitable line of progress. The notion of 'potentialities' can also be used to reinforce the metaphor contained in the word 'evolution': the unwinding of something implicitly already contained in what is already there. In *moral conduct*, on the other hand, while a number of different courses of action may all be 'potential' in the sense of 'possibilities', to decide which human potentialities – for instance those making for aggression or those making for co-operation – should be encouraged and which inhibited is a matter for decision in the light of value judgments. When Sir Julian Huxley speaks of cultural development as evolution directed by the human mind and also as the realization of potentialities, he blunts the fact that 'potentiality' as such is a neutral term: there may be all sorts of potentialities, good, bad and indifferent, and ethical conduct will be concerned with choosing between them.

The strength of evolutionary theories of ethics lies in their attempt to show human beings as living in a natural environment, and also in bringing out the fact that, like all living things, they are dependent on adapting themselves to their environment. There can also be an incentive to moral effort in the idea that human life, as it emerges from nature, and has developed over long stretches of time, is still incomplete: that 'the gates of the future are open', to use a phrase from Bergson's *Creative Evolution*. The weakness in this type of view consists in the slurring of the distinction between what is and what ought to be, between judgments of fact and judgments of value. If there are indeed natural tendencies in biological nature making for, for example, love and co-operation, and if human ethical behaviour directed to furthering these qualities can draw on the energies such instinctive drives may supply, this is a matter for which those who value these qualities may be grateful. But, if not, ought we to drop the conviction that these are qualities to be encouraged? If there are tendencies in nature strengthening ethical propensities, moral development will thereby be easier, but if not, we are not bound to take our moral cues from nature. Moreover, to hold that moral behaviour must be deducible from natural facts is likely to lead to an unduly moral interpretation for instance of phenomena of 'mutual aid' in animal behaviour. It is also likely to lead to bad logic in that no proposition prescribing what *ought to be done* can be deduced from propositions which simply state facts.

It should no doubt be conceded that theories of evolutionary ethics do not simply make this kind of deduction. The belief that ethical conduct is conduct in accordance with the direction of evolutionary change, and that 'good' means 'more evolved', rests on a valuationally loaded view of evolution, by which it is seen as change in a line of direction, so that what follows is held to be more 'advanced' and not only subsequent to what went before. There is some empirical support for this without making an assumption of universal progress, insofar as more complex stages make possible the achievement of a greater range of possible types and activity and of relationships and these more complex stages have generally been preceded by simpler and less differentiated stages. But the ethical question can still be raised whether, in human activies, the achievement of all 'possibilities' is desirable.

On the whole it is likely to make for greater clarity to speak of processes of social and cultural change in terms of 'development' rather than 'evolution'. This is of course a matter of recommendation; there is no authoritative legislation in matters of terminology and definition. But if the term 'evolution' is used of social and ethical development, it is essential to be aware of the differences between this kind of change and biological evolution.

There is, however, a sense in which the term 'evolutionary ethics' may be used, not as a view in which the standards and criteria of moral conduct are thought of as derivable from a process of change continuous with biological evolution, but as a theory that would be better described as 'the evolution of ethics'. This would be the view that ethical beliefs and principles have 'evolved', in the sense that they have taken different forms at different times as ways in which human beings in societies have met their biological and social needs. So long as this view is not taken to imply some single pattern of successive stages through which all cultures must pass (a view which nowadays has little support among anthropologists), there is considerable empirical support for this. Its main limitation is that it fails to express the extent to which the institutions through which human beings seek to satisfy social needs may be matters of contrivance as well as of piecemeal and even unconscious adaptation. It also makes little allowance for aspirations after non-utilitarian ideals of moral excellence and for the purposive work of reformers.

A sustained attempt to present a view of evolutionary ethics in both these senses was L. T. Hobhouse's *Morals in Evolution*. Hobhouse was concerned with 'the advance of the ethical consciousness to the full understanding of its own origin and function, viz. that it has arisen out of the conditions under which mind evolves and that its purpose is to further and perfect that evolution'. Hobhouse's view was a sophisticated one, in that he did not assume automatic progress, and saw that there was a need for criteria for evaluating social changes which were not drawn up simply in naturalistic terms. His own criteria were qualities making for the achievement of 'rational good', such as the increasing control over the conditions of life and the harmonious development of human potentialities. (Some of the question-begging character of the term 'potentiality' is here corrected by introducing the qualification 'harmonious'.) Morris Ginsberg, in his *Evolution and Progress*, has a sympathetic discussion of Hobhouse's work, along with a judicious estimate of the present standing of this kind of thinking.

M. Ginsberg, *Evolution and Progress*, 1961; L. T. Hobhouse, *Morals in Evolution*, 2 vols., 1906; J. Huxley, *Evolution and Ethics, 1893–1943*, 1947 (this is a publication of the Romanes Lectures of both the Huxleys, with an introduction by Sir Julian Huxley); T. Huxley, *Evolution and Ethics*, 1893; H. Spencer, *The Data of Ethics*, 1879; C. H. Waddington, *Science and Ethics*, 1942 (a discussion of some of the problems raised by 'evolutionary ethics' from a number of points of view).

DOROTHY EMMET

Excellence

The person who excels is the person who is superior to his fellows in ability and achievement. It is a simple fact of life that there must always be some persons who are above the average, and a very small group who are much above it. In *The Republic* of Plato, provision was made for this group to have special privileges and training, counterbalanced by special responsibilities laid upon them. Perhaps Nietzsche (q.v.), with his doctrine of the superman (*Übermensch*), carried the ethic of excellence to its furthest extreme and also showed the dangers inherent in it – dangers which manifested themselves in the rise of fascist and racist movements, rooted in this whole tradition. But there is also the danger that in modern egalitarian societies, excellence may be stifled and all reduced to a monotonous mediocrity. The immense complexities of a technological society demand an increasing number of very highly qualified and able people. That such persons should have full opportunity to develop and exercise their superior talents is not only their due but is also necessary for the health of society. This may mean that there must be provided for them such advantages in education and such rewards and incentives as will ensure their optimal development and functioning. This sets up a tension between the claims of excellence and the claims of equality (q.v.) which is not always easy to decide and which may become more acute as the technological revolution goes on.

EDITOR

Existentialist Ethics

In his famous lecture on Existentialism, Jean-Paul Sartre, the last existentialist to avow the title, tells of his refusal to advise a young man facing an ethical dilemma. In the subsequent discussion with the philosophers who heard the lecture, two criticized him. 'You should have told him what to do,' they said. One of these was a Christian, the other a Communist.

Existentialists make a virtue of not knowing what to do. They are not thereby as remote from Christian thought as some have judged. Basic concepts in Christian ethics are taken up into the viewpoint, especially in the attitude towards law and towards human freedom. Even the alleged acosmism, individualism and atheism of Existentialism have meanings which are closer to the Christian position than the casual observer generally concedes.

Living by laws, which is a way of knowing what to do, is regarded by existentialists as 'bad faith' (Sartre and Simone de Beauvoir). Any abridgment of human freedom is 'bad faith'. A legalistic ethic abridges freedom by taking decisions out of the hands of responsible selves. Søren Kierkegaard's treatise, *Fear and Trembling*, anticipated this view. Abraham was a knight of faith because he remained open to God's word. His willingness to murder his son out of obedience to God is higher than ethics because it does not force the future to conform to revelations of God given for the past.

In contemporary Existentialism what Kierkegaard called 'the teleological suspension of the ethical' is itself ethics. Openness to the future has primacy over conformity to the past. Not that one annihilates the past. To use Sartre's term, one simply 'nihilates', which is to say, 'suspends' it, in order to let the demands of the future emerge. The past tells a man what he ought to do. The future is a more reliable guide simply because it does not tell a man what to do, but appeals to him to 'invent' or 'create' in the light of the emerging situation.

Christian ethic has accomplished the same movement away from legalism. When the apostle Paul interpreted the preaching of Jesus as a reducing of the whole law to the one word, 'love', he rooted Christian behaviour in 'the trans-moral conscience' (Paul Tillich), 'an ethic without laws' (Paul Ramsey), an ethic of 'creativity' (Nicholas Berdyaev) or 'responsivity' (H. Richard Niebuhr). The transcendence

of laws does not mean, however, the abrogation of norms. For existential ethics, freedom, by which one transcends laws in the direction of creative action, is itself the norm for freedom. Man is freedom. Freedom is the source of man's possibility to act ethically, because freedom is nothing – a lack to be filled, a power of resoluteness which lets situations reveal their needs. And what is the norm by which to discern in any situation what is needful? One must so act as to let others be free while oneself remaining free (Sartre).

In fulfilling this ethical programme existentialists are known to be atheistic. What is less evident is that they are also acosmic. That is, they do not accept the world sponsored by cosmologists. If one could know why Existentialism is acosmic, he would have important clues to why existential atheism is quite benign. The world of the cosmologist is an out-there world into which a man is invited to fit as a coin fits in a box. Existentialists, however, believe the world is not something one is *in*. Worlds are modes of *being-in*. There is the world of politics, of sports, of religion, of art. There is no 'world' of ethics because ethics is the study of modes of being-in which results in revealing the possibilities for the worlds one creates through his modes of being-in.

The model from art comes the closest to exemplifying how an existential ethic works. The artist does not record a world that exists. He creates, through his aesthetic behaviour, the possibility for a world one may not previously have known (Martin Heidegger and Maurice Merleau-Ponty). The Acropolis mobilized the earth, sea and sky of Periclean Athens into a significant human world. Whether it still does so is questionable, so that artists continue to develop possibilities for today's world at the risk of reducing previous art works to the status of museum pieces. Ethics, like art, nihilates the world as cosmos (earth, sea and sky) in order to create the world as a mode of being-in (the Acropolis). Now it can be seen why it is a mistake to call Existentialism an individualism, implying that it has no social ethic. The primary term for existentialist ethics is neither 'individual' nor 'social' but 'world', a reality in which the distinction between individual and social disappears, for 'world' embraces *all* modes of being-in.

By analogy to acosmism, atheism does not mean the annihilation of God, but only his nihilation. God as a static reality is put in parentheses in order to let the world of man emerge as it is possible. Atheism has sometimes meant that men have killed God. In Existentialism it means that men have used a static concept of God in order to endorse effete causes whose prolongation is murderous to men. Such a god is not simply dead; he is an executioner. Kierkegaard was a theist for the very same reason that existentialists today are atheists.

Why is it that for Kierkegaard Abraham's willingness to slay Isaac was not a deficiency in his moral sense, so that he could be called a pioneer of faith? Because if there is a God, nothing else can be absolutized. All one's relations will be relative. Old worlds, like Isaac, must be allowed to die in order for new worlds to be born. In this case relativism does not mean the absence of standards, but the freedom, that is, the responsibility for creating in one's time the relevant mode of being-in.

Simone de Beauvoir, *The Ethics of Ambiguity*, 1948; Søren Kierkegaard, *Fear and Trembling*, 1941; H. Richard Niebuhr, *The Responsible Self*, 1963; Jean-Paul Sartre, *Critique de la Raison Dialectique*, I, 1960.

CARL MICHALSON

Exogamy

Exogamy is the custom which prevents a man from taking a wife from within his own tribe. The opposite is endogamy. *See* **Anthropology; Custom; Taboo.**

Exposition

Exposition of infants, that is to say, their exposure and abandonment, was a cruel form of population control, condemned by the early Church. *See* **Abandonment; Population Policy.**

Faith

Wittgenstein frequently emphasized the extent to which a pervasive habit of supposing that 'the meaning of a word was an object' was the occasion of grave intellectual confusion. It would certainly seem that discussion of the nature of faith has been vitiated by the assumption that there is some one thing called 'faith', an assumption to which a detailed study of the NT use of *pistis*, *pisteuo* and their cognates gives no encouragement. We have no reason to suppose that the faith which St Paul contrasts with works and the faith which the Fourth Evangelist contrasts with sight are identical in the sense they would be if the two writers by the language which they use were referring to identical acts or dispositions. Between the faith of which Paul writes and the believing (John does not use the noun *pistis*) to which John refers there is indeed resemblance; but it may be a resemblance of the kind that we are led to notice between baseball, shinty, shove-ha'penny, poker, tig and chess, which we bring out when we treat them all as games.

Such considerations may well be important when attention is directed to contemporary controversies concerning the cognitive element in faith. If in this article notice is particularly taken of this issue to the exclusion of much else, it is because of its extreme contemporary importance. From the work of Rudolf Bultmann there has sprung a whole series of essays which would seem in the end to evacuate faith of all intentionality, viz. direction upon an object outside itself. The *fides qua creditur* (to use the traditional language) has become constitutive of the *fides quae creditur*. While it is readily conceded that the ministry of Jesus and the 'happening' of the Easter-faith are *causally* necessary conditions of the emergence of the characteristic faith-attitude, their relation to that attitude is sometimes described in language which recalls, for example, the tracing back of the dissemination of syphilis in Europe to its introduction into that continent by returning Crusaders who had lightened the burden of their service of the cross with promiscuous sexual indulgence. Bultmann himself is far too considerable and complex a writer to be guilty of such crudity; but those who follow him in his scepticism in respect of the historical records in the NT, while eschewing his meticulous scholarship, and showing themselves hardly capable of his occasional deep spiritual insight, have committed themselves, in the belief that they are also continuing his programme of 'demythologization', to views of which the above is a justifiable caricature. Thus it is not uncommon to hear it said that faith in its autonomy creates facts, and is in no way to be judged true or false by the extent to which it embodies in its fundamental assents an adherence to what is or what is not the case. Although these views are frequently described as existentialist, the historian of philosophy must note in them an affinity in their more absurd forms to extreme Fichtean idealism. The factors to which they owe their popularity are various. There is the deep scepticism concerning the information we have about Christian origins, and especially the central figure of the gospel story, inevitably encouraged not only by recent NT criticism, but by a healthy reaction against the over-confident and uncritical blending of an intellectually naive acceptance of the mythological with a disregard of the detailed difficulties of the NT books, recently marketed under the name of 'biblical theology'. There is also the fact that the kind of analysis of the nature of faith as constitutive of the spiritual life of the individual which the best writers of this school have achieved is an impressive continuation of the work of Kierkegaard, even though that most remarkable Christian thinker (whose influence can clearly be discerned on Bultmann's treatment of John in his large commentary on the Fourth Gospel, perhaps his greatest work) must be acquitted of the kind of indifference to the concrete figure of Jesus as object of faith, of which the moderns are too often guilty. But it is in the detail of their analysis that their greatest strength lies. Yet even those who avoid the absurdities mentioned above seem to be in bondage to the illusion that reference to the contingent, and in consequence to the empirically vulnerable, must be expelled from the world of faith, as if faith could only be concerned with that which can be represented as necessary in the sense in which logicians speak of, for example, tautologies of the two-valued propositional calculus as necessary. Yet it requires hardly any reflection to see that such an aspiration is incompatible with acceptance of the incarnation as the central Christian verity. For if Jesus be indeed the eternal Son of God incarnate, what we learn of his earthly career must be contingent in the sense in which historical propositions are contingent, and as such must be vulnerable to empirical criticism. But such a paradox in faith epistemologically regarded is (as indeed Kierkegaard saw) the necessary counterpart in the way of our believing of the one to whom our faith is given, in whom, in the language of the ancient formula, Godhead and manhood are joined without possibility of confusion or conversion the one into the other, yet also without possibility of separation or division the one from the other. It should further be noted that to suppose that even if advance from the contingent to the necessary, from the precarious to the invulnerable, were theologically compatible with the nature of faith, as the theologian must understand it, to suppose that the transition could be effected by concentration on the inward at the expense of the outward, is to land oneself in a morass of confusion of which a slight knowledge of critical philosophy would soon make one vividly aware.

What is needed is a treatment of faith which will eschew from the outset the sort of confusions into which an ill-considered subjectivism must necessarily plunge the theologian, but which will do justice to the extraordinary complexity and many-sidedness of believing, of which the NT itself made us aware, as it was suggested at the outset of this article. We badly need the sort of exploration that Newman undertook in his pioneer work, *A Grammar of Assent* (1870). If his conclusions do not stand, he at least saw that the explorer of the nature and grounds of belief must thread his way in a territory where logical and psychological, epistemological, metaphysical and theological considerations jostle each other. Moreover, such work must pay the very closest attention to the apologetic question of the grounds of belief. It is quite illegitimate to dodge this issue by reference to a leap of faith, made in response to the hearing of the *kerygma*. It is greatly to Bultmann's credit that because, for all his philosophical shortcomings, he is alert to the reality of the epistemological problem, he has seen dimly the related issue of the validity and status of apologetic in general and the nature of contemporary apologetic in particular. It is ironic that in this matter he

has reverted to issues raised in Karl Barth's great *Commentary on the Epistle to the Romans* (1933), a work whose perceptions were primarily epistemological but from whose concerns its author turned aside when, under the influence of his rediscovery of the genius of Anselm, he began to prepare the massive structure of his *Church Dogmatics* according to a different plan, and in acceptance of a much more naive philosophical realism.

D. M. MACKINNON

Fall of Man, *see* Man, Doctrine of ; Sin.

False Witness

This is forbidden in the ninth Commandment and throughout the OT; the NT echoes the OT on it. The prohibition was of vital importance in legal cases in days when there was no Counsel to protect the accused. His fate could be determined, perhaps his life jeopardized, by false witness. Today the prohibition can readily be extended to cover slander, detraction and gossip. *See* Lying.

RONALD PRESTON

Family /

The family has played a central role in the Christian view of human life, and it has been universally regarded as the most important social unit of education and stability in the life of mankind. The Christian attitude to the family derives from that of the OT in which the importance of the male head of the family was determinative of the social structure and regulations of the Hebrews. Throughout the OT the Patriarch is paramount, although there may have been other earlier practices. The position of women is decided by their relationship to husband or father, and the woman becomes a member of the tribe of her husband. The determining factor in inheritance and kinship is always the man.

Throughout the OT we find that the family is supported by customs and laws, and the Jews were notable for the strength of their family feeling, a characteristic which has remained with them throughout history. The head of the household, the father, was considered to have a spiritual basis for his authority, and his wife was his possession.

The perpetuation of the family name was thought to be of great importance: this attitude was reflected in the question asked of Jesus by those who tried to entrap him regarding the wife who was married successively to seven brothers who died one after the other before an heir was born (Luke 20.27–33).

The history related in the OT shows a gradual progress towards monogamy in the practice of the Jews. The influence of the prophets was exercised towards this end, and the attempts of Hosea to redeem a faithless wife is perhaps the most striking example of such teaching.

Although the position of women was depressed, judging by modern standards, it was better among the Jews than among other religions of the eastern world. Among the Jews, moreover, the position of children born out of wedlock was more favourable than in Christian civilizations. So long as they were acknowledged by their father, the status of their mother was ignored, and the children were regarded as legitimate. The bastard (Deut. 23.2) was a child born as a result of incest, not one born outside the marriage bond.

It was against this background that the teaching of Jesus was given, and the concept of the family plays a large part in his recorded words. He used the family in its best sense as the clearest parallel of the relations between men and God. He took the positive elements of Jewish tradition with regard to the family and extended them so as to deepen their meaning and to apply them more widely.

Marriage was to be regarded, according to Jesus, as a sacred relationship whose centre was the complete union of the man and the woman. In Mark 10.6–8 Jesus seemed to base this on a principle of creation, a passage which has been widely used in Christian theology as a basis for regarding monogamous marriage as a part of the natural moral law. Divorce and remarriage is a sin against the very nature of marriage and involves adultery. Whether or not Jesus was intending to lay down a general law in these passages is a matter of dispute, but it cannot be doubted that he was plainly expressing the view that a true marriage which is based on a right relationship cannot contemplate such behaviour. These words, assuming them to be authentic, do not give answers to present-day problems which arise because a family has already broken up, and the interests of the younger members of a family are not always best served by holding together externally a family which has already lost its inner cohesion and life.

The effect of the teaching of Jesus was to enhance the position of women, for in the Gospels women played an important part, and in his parables and sayings no distinction was made between the status of men and women. This element in Christianity was to have marked effects on the life of the family, and developments have not yet come to an end. The attitude of Jesus to children also introduced a principle of loving relationships between parents and children and the way in which he used children as examples to his hearers was calculated to give them an added status in the family.

Yet Jesus also taught that the family was not the final end to which everything else had to be subordinated, but that, on the contrary, the family itself could only be rightly valued when seen as a means of serving God and doing his will. Moreover, the concept of the family was extended to cover all those who were faithful children of his heavenly Father (Mark 3.35).

Jesus used the family in his parables, such as the Prodigal Son, to teach men about God, but the teaching contained in them also had the effect of introducing into men's ideas of the family concepts derived from God himself. The Christian family during the succeeding centuries was deeply affected by the language which Jesus himself used in addressing the Father, especially as we find it in the Gospel of St John.

Roman Catholic teaching holds that the Christian family is a supernatural unit created by its origin in the sacrament of marriage (q.v.), having as its primary end the procreation and nurture of children. Its constitutive elements are the complete freedom of choice of the spouses, and the permanency of their union which derives from its nature. From these premisses Roman Catholics argue that the family is the fundamental condition for 'the physical, moral, social, and economic existence of human society'.

This point of view has practical consequences in social and political life, since it results in a firm conviction that it is the family which should alone decide the vital educational choices for its children, and that the State has no right to interfere with such choices. The function of the State in the matter of education is, according to Roman Catholic teaching, subsidiary to the function of the parents. It is therefore the duty of the State to protect and otherwise to support the family, to encourage its stability, and to refrain in any way from interfering with its freedom, except where this is clearly necessary for the safety of the community.

It is in pursuance of these tenets that Roman Catholics insist wherever possible on maintaining their own schools, in which they alone have control of the religious instruction, and approve the character and outlook of those who are appointed in them to be teachers.

There are a number of features of modern life which tend to disrupt the family, in which the State is necessarily involved, and which provide areas where clashes between Church and State may occur, especially in cases in which the church holds views identical with or similar to those of Roman Catholic teaching. Such areas are created by the increasing ease with which divorce can be secured, by the decline of parental authority, and by the increasing number of mothers who are engaged in full-time work. In none of these categories does the State and the Church come into direct conflict in most cases, but the tendency for the modern industrialized State to assume greater powers is apt to undermine the independence of family life to a degree not known in earlier and less complicated societies.

In recent years a new threat to family life has

appeared from the growth in the science of the human personality, both physical and psychical. This may be illustrated from a speech made in 1966 in California by a biologist, reported in the *New York Times* (October 30, 1966). Addressing a scientific gathering he pointed out that the family was an excellent method of passing on conventional wisdom in a static society, but not at all good at dealing with new ideas in today's society. He thought that progress in human genetics would weaken the family as 'the basic unit of human reproduction'. He foresaw an increasing invasion of the independence of the home in the interests of providing equal opportunity for all children, and pointed out that it was idle to suppose that equality of opportunity could be secured if children were left to the mercy of their families during their most impressionable years.

This attitude raises ethical questions which Christians must face and grapple with in the second half of the twentieth century. It is hardly too much to say that the traditional view of the family has to be re-thought by Christians if it is to survive and play a positive role in the society of the future.

G. R. Dunstan, *The Family Is not Broken*, 1962; *The Family in Contemporary Society*, Report of the Group Convened at the Behest of the Archbishop of Canterbury, 1958.

HERBERT WADDAMS

Family Planning. *see* Procreation.

Fascism

The name belongs specifically to the movement, headed by Mussolini, that ruled Italy in the period before and during the second World War, and is derived from *fasces*, the bundle of rods that symbolized civil power in Roman times. More generally, the name is applied to similar movements, such as the National Socialism of Hitler's Germany, the small parties of Sir Oswald Moseley in Britain and of Lincoln Rockwell in America, and others. Like Communism, fascism is more than a political theory. It is a complete ideology, and behind it lies a *melange* of philosophical ideas. These come from such diverse sources as Plato's *Republic*, German idealism and romanticism, Nietzsche's teaching on the will to power and the superman, pseudo-scientific theories about racial and ethnic superiority, notions of destiny, and so on. A fascist party is organized on quasi-military lines and is prepared to use violent methods if necessary to attain power. Fascist governments display some well marked characteristics. Power is concentrated in the hands of a party *elite*, or even of one man. Opposition parties are suppressed. The Church, the universities, the Labour unions and other associations are, so far as possible, transformed into agencies of the organic and omnicompetent State. Economic policy aims at the ideal of autarky or self-sufficiency. A strong propaganda machine, utilizing the schools, the press and the mass media, rigidly controls public opinion and the dissemination of information. Racial and ethnic minority groups, since they cannot be given a place within the organic, homogeneous state, are subjected to disadvantages, perhaps even to open persecution and attempted extinction. Foreign policy is aggressive, warlike and expansionist. From a Christian point of view, fascism is to be condemned because of its idolatrous absolutizing of the state or nation, and because of its denial of the personal rights of those who do not belong to the favoured group.

EDITOR

Fasting

Abstention from food as a religious exercise is found in many parts of the world, either as an expression of humiliation before deity or as producing a state suitable for religious impressions; as such it is often part of primitive initiation rites (cf. the Isiac initiation described in Apuleius, *Golden Ass*, Book XI,23). Both ideas appear in the OT, for example, in Ps. 35.13 and Deut. 9.9,18. Penitential fasting became more common after the exile (cf. Zech. 7–8), but the one universal fast of Israel was (and is) the Day of Atonement, from sunset to sunset (referred to in Acts 27.9 as 'the fast'). Pious souls might fast more often, even twice a week (Luke 18.12); the practice is assumed rather than directed in Matt. 6.16–18. By the second century Christians prepared for Easter by a fast of one or two days, which also prepared candidates for the Easter baptisms; not until the fourth century was the idea of a historical memory of the passion on Good Friday emphasized. A fast to the ninth hour (the common Roman dinner hour in midafternoon) or later was widely observed on the 'Station Days', Wednesday and Friday, at Rome also on Saturday. (Buddhist monks traditionally follow a converse practice, eating only before noon.) Roman and Anglican rites preserve a relic of stations in the Ember Days at the four seasons. The pre-Easter fast came from the fourth century to be extended over the Lenten season, necessarily less intensely; it often, however, was kept until broken by communion at the time of vespers in the late afternoon – in the Middle Ages this was gradually relaxed by anticipating vespers in the morning, a custom still common in the Eastern Orthodox Church, and assumed in the Roman rite till 1960. The mediaeval Latin Church also fasted on Christmas Eve and the Vigils of a number of other festivals. By the thirteenth century the observance of a fast day was defined as one main meal at noon or night, with one or two other slight refections permitted.

The Reformers generally objected to the legalism which they saw in the traditional fasts – though in the Church of England they were kept up by custom, and since 1662 have been listed in the Prayer Book, which also recommends fasting before adult baptism. But fasting out of private devotion or by special order of the Church was common in Reformed circles and not unknown in Lutheran – cf. the austerity still expected in Finland on the quarterly national days of prayer. In New England the Puritan colonies developed the custom of an annual fast day in the spring – this still survives formally in New Hampshire and in Connecticut (where since 1797 traditions have been combined by proclaiming the civic fast day on Good Friday).

In our time prescribed fasting seems to be obsolescent, except for such symbolic gestures as the Friday abstinence. In 1949 Pope Pius XII simplified the Roman Catholic rules, which had been complicated by many special exemptions; but even his rules are often further reduced by local dispensations. In 1966 Pope Paul VI reduced the canonical requirement to abstinence on Fridays, and fasting on Good Friday and the first day of Lent (the American hierarchy has decreed that abstinence from meat is no longer legally required on Fridays, though it is encouraged on a voluntary basis, or 'good works' may be done instead). Modern Anglicanism has followed a similar course – for example, the American Prayer Book designates Ash Wednesday and Good Friday as fasts, and calls for abstinence (q.v., but not precisely defined) in Lent, on Fridays (except between Christmas and Twelfth Night), and on Ember Days. The fast before communion was often observed in the Reformed churches – in Scotland for some time in the form of preparatory fast days – and was revived among Anglicans under the influence of the Oxford Movement. But it also seems to be obsolescent in view of the complex time-schedule of modern life and the widespread desire for more frequent communion. For Roman Catholics Pius XII reduced the obligation in 1957 to three hours, and Paul VI in 1964 reduced it to one.

But the call for temperance and discipline which fasting expresses still remains. Early Christian preachers often stressed that the true fast must include abstinence from sin (cf. Isa. 58), and that what was saved by fasting should relieve the needs of the poor. A modern form of fast has been developed in Great Britain and America since the second World War by which a simple meal is served at a church gathering (or at home) and the price of a full meal given to refugee relief or other special causes. 'Let us conduct ourselves becomingly as in the day, not in revelling and drunkenness . . . but put on the Lord Jesus Christ' (Rom. 13.13–14) as St Paul bids us in his name.

E. R. HARDY

Fate and Fatalism

The idea of fate, with variations in various cultures, is that of a force (sometimes half-personified) or law governing some or all of human affairs. The concept has sometimes been connected with an attitude to life known as fatalism – a kind of passivity in the face of the future. Fatalism has also appeared as a philosophical doctrine, as apparently entailed by determinism.

Paradoxically, fate can cover both what is thought of as necessitated by some inner law working in the universe and what is thought of as due to chance. Thus the relevant cluster of concepts in ancient Greek thought include both *anagke* (necessity) and *tyche* (chance). The reason for this ambivalence is that fate is invoked to account for occurrences to human beings, in particular where these events (such as death) are regarded as striking and inscrutable. Thus a personal disaster may appear an accident (mere chance), and yet may be assigned a deep-seated cause. The most comprehensive pattern of such thinking is the Indian doctrine of *karma*, which in principle explains all events to living beings in terms of a law (though theistic thought in mediaeval India saw this as an expression of God's will) and of an invisible force (*adrsta*). However, the necessity is normally thought of as conditional: there are ways in which one's future fate may be changed – through meditation, austerity, moral effort, faith in God, etc. Analogous to this is the way in which the Greek gods, and even men, might interfere with otherwise fore-ordained destinies. Thus Zeus (*Iliad*, Book XVI) contemplates saving Sarpedon from his doom, long since fixed by fate. Similarly the determinism implicit in Qur'ānic teachings is held in conjunction with the doctrine of the capacity of the individual to perform the duties laid upon him by faith.

On the other hand, in Islam and elsewhere, there have been attempts to interpret destiny as unconditional and universal. Thus the Ājivikas (a movement contemporary with the Buddha) held a doctrine of fate (*niyati*) as wholly determining the future. Hence the good works (such as austerity) associated with a liberated life are symptoms, not causes, of salvation. A similar conclusion, not based, however, on the concept of fate, but rather on that of the will of God, is found in Muslim and Christian predestinationism.

Fatalism as an attitude involves resignation to one's future lot, together with a sense of its unalterability. The first of these elements can appear, in theistic religions, as faith in providence. The second is a deduction sometimes made from determinism, whether the latter is conceived in terms of God's governance of events or in terms of empirical causation.

The standard reply to fatalism is that it

depends on an invalid inference. Thus 'Either I shall be alive in 1984 or I shall not; and suppose that I shall be: then I shall be whatever I do. Consequently, I can smoke fifty cigarettes a day'. This is invalid reasoning, because my actions enter into the causation of future events. Even if my actions are determined, this gives no ground for doing A rather than B, unless I know which way I am determined to act. But even here the very knowledge of the future gives me an opportunity to avoid disasters, etc.

A. J. Ayer, *The Concept of a Person*, 1964; S. G. F. Brandon, *Man and his Destiny in the Great Religions*, 1962; *History, Time and Deity*, 1965.

NINIAN SMART

Feminism. *see* Women, Status of.

Fidelity. *see* Loyalty.

Filial Piety. *see* Family.

Flagellation

Flagellation (from *flagellum*, scourge), self-scourging as a religious exercise, is related to the practice of self-torture as a form of abasement before deity found in various religions – as found among Hindu ascetics, and exemplified in the Semitic world by the prophets of Baal referred to in I Kings 18.28 (and noted in the second century by Lucian, *On the Syrian Goddess*, 50). It has aspects of sympathetic magic, as well as of the psychological perversity, with sexual overtones, which leads some people to find a certain enjoyment in suffering pain. Sometimes endurance of beatings is considered a proof of heroism, as in the initiation rites of ancient Spartans and some modern primitive tribes.

Christian asceticism properly stops short of such abnormalities, though some of the early monks approached them, taking with excessive literalness the command to take up the cross, or St Paul's words 'I pommel my body and subdue it' (I Cor. 9.27). When corporal punishment (q.v.) was an accepted form of penalty, as even in the generally humane rules of St Caesarius and St Benedict, self-scourging as an expression of penitence seemed a natural idea. We hear of it in some Byzantine monasteries; and in the ascetic revival of the eleventh century St Peter Damian (d. 1072) strongly recommended the practice, though obliged to moderate the excessive zeal of some of his disciples. The 'discipline', a small whip used for flagellation in private or together has continued to be used by individuals and in the customs of several monastic Orders; but it has little if any place in the teaching of the greater spiritual guides of the Church. *See* **Asceticism; Mortification**.

The public flagellant movement was an outgrowth of the stresses and strains of the later Middle Ages, first appearing at Perugia in 1260. Lay confraternities assembled for spiritual exercises which came to a climax in corporate flagellation at their meetings or in penitential processions. At the time of the Black Death the flagellants claimed the authority of a 'Letter from Heaven', alleged to have appeared on the altar of St Peter's; but in 1349 Pope Clement VI condemned the movement as heretical. Nevertheless some preachers of the late Middle Ages and the Counter-Reformation welcomed it as an assistance in their appeals for repentance and reform, and some flagellant practices have continued to be associated with the penitential confraternities which take an important part in Spanish Holy Week processions. In extreme forms, which have led to ecclesiastical condemnation, flagellation has survived in areas where Spanish piety is in contact with primitive religion, such as New Mexico and the Philippines.

Louis Gougaud, *Devotional and Ascetic Practices in the Middle Ages*, 1927, pp. 179–204.

E. R. HARDY

Flesh. *see* Ascetism; Body.

Forgiveness

Forgiveness, strictly considered, is a religious rather than an ethical idea and experience. The accent falls upon a certain relation between God and man. This relation is marked by the awesome holiness of God, by man's offence against this holiness, by man's guilt, and by man's need for assurance that his sin against God has been pardoned and that right relations between God and man have been restored. From the earliest apprehensions of the numinous to the classical Christian doctrine of justification by faith, the experience of forgiveness has been the setting aside of enmity between man and God and the restoration of right relations between them. In primitive religions, this transformation is an experience of ritual cleansing. In more highly developed religions, ritual undergoes the more conscious and symbolic refinement of liturgy, together with a theological clarification of the initiative of God in restoring man, despite his sin, to fellowship with God. Forgiveness, in this context, tends often to be loosely interchanged with justification, and/or with reconciliation.

More carefully considered, however, forgiveness, as a religious experience and idea, may be distinguished from justification, as well as from reconciliation. Such a distinction differentiates between an offense against God, set right by God's action (justification) and the consequent restored relation between man and God (forgiveness). Forgiveness expresses the *fact* of a restored relation between God and man and reconciliation expresses the result of this restored relation in behaviour, namely, the overcoming of enmity. Thus, forgiveness is a middle term between justification and reconciliation.

The ethical consideration of forgiveness requires a careful differentiation between forgiveness and love. One way of meeting this requirement is to deny to forgiveness any significant ethical meaning at all and to reserve it strictly for the religious relation between God and man already described. Such an interpretation would then find in love, the ethical correlate of the strictly religious term, 'forgiveness'. 'Forgiveness' would refer to restored relations between God and man; 'love' would refer to restored relations between man and man, particularly to the sincere and active willing of the neighbour's good. Did such a restoration involve the overcoming of enmity, love would be expressed as reconciliation. Thus, love would be the ethical correlate of forgiveness.

Such a differentiation has the merit of tidiness. But the price of such a neat arrangement is at best a formalism of thought; at worst, an abstraction from the reality of religious and ethical experience. Most notably, it would be difficult to apply such abstract formalism to the Christian understanding of forgiveness in the NT sense of the word. To be sure, the Bible, in common with the history of religion generally, exhibits a correlation between forgiveness and love. But the correlation is not one which reserves for forgiveness a religious meaning, for love an ethical one. The relations between the divine and the human, between God and man, involve both forgiveness and love, in a religious as well as in an ethical sense. In view of the formative importance of NT thought for Christian ethical interpretation, we may, with the aid of the NT, move beyond the obscurities which have deprived the ethical meaning of forgiveness of adequate clarity.

According to the NT, God both forgives and loves; and man is enjoined both to forgive and to love. The philology of the matter identifies as central to forgiveness, an act of 'sending away'; as central to love, an act of good will. These acts of God are *religious* because they exhibit God's free initiative towards man. In forgiveness, God 'sends away', or 'pardons' or 'covers' what man has done in violation or disavowal of this initiative. In love, God faithfully favours man with his good will. Forgiveness and love are *ethical* acts of God which exhibit God's sustaining and fulfilling fellowship with man. In forgiveness, God receives man into uninhibited fellowship with himself. In love, God actively sustains man in this fellowship. Forgiveness and love are *religious* acts of man in so far as they exhibit man's doing with abandon towards his fellow man what God has done towards him. Forgiveness means 'sending away' or 'pardoning' or 'covering' what has come between man and his neighbour. Love, means an insistent good-will between man and man. Forgiveness and love are *ethical* acts of man which express man's uninhibited fellowship with his neighbour and the active removal or transformation of whatever prevents good will between man and man.

The critical instance of the religious and ethical meanings of forgiveness and love in behaviour is exhibited in the relation between justification by faith and justice. In the tradition of Christian theology and ethics, justification and justice have largely failed creatively to intersect. The consequence has been an unhappy divorce between soteriology and ethics, between the religious and the ethical practice of forgiveness and love. When justice is understood as the setting right of what is not right in man's relationship to man, both private and public, then, the struggle for justice becomes the concrete expression, in behaviour, of man's response to what God has done, and is doing, to set things right between man and himself. The faith by which man is justified becomes what Luther called 'a busy, living, active thing' by which men learn, in the struggle for justice, what it means concretely to forgive and to be forgiven, to love God and one another. In the struggle for justice, the ethical meaning of forgiveness emerges as the practice of reconciliation.

It is noteworthy, especially in this connection, that the discussion of forgiveness in the literature of Christian theology and ethics is conspicuously slight. The grounds for this neglect are, perhaps mainly traceable to the obscurities mentioned above. There are, of course, exegetical discussions and those which find their way into theologies of the OT and the NT. As for systematic theology and ethics, Albrecht Ritchl's three-volume work on *Justification and Reconciliation*, 1882–3, English translation by H. R. Mackintosh, 1902, is still the most extensive and instructive. Ritchl's attention to forgiveness lies behind the moving, personal treatment by Wilhelm Herrman in *The Communion of the Christian with God*, translated from the 4th German edition of 1903 by R. S. Stewart, 1906; and also behind their influential treatment of the subject by H. R. Mackintosh, *The Christian Experience of Forgiveness*, 1927. Mention may also be made of Karl Barth's extensive discussion in *Church Dogmatics*, Volume IV/1, translated by G. T. Bromiley, 1956, latest reprinting 1961; of an admirable chapter on forgiveness and love, 'Love as Forgiveness' in Reinhold Niebuhr's *An Interpretation of Christian Ethics*, 1935; and of a small volume by Alexander Miller, *The Renewal of Man*, 1956.

PAUL LEHMANN

Formalism

Formalism is an excessive insistence on the outward observances of religion at the expense of a due regard to their inward spirit and meaning. It involves a pre-occupation with the formal correctness of rites and ceremonies together with a neglect of their inward content. Similarly in the sphere of morals it is an undue insistence on the form or letter of a moral code or a code of law and neglect of the spirit and purpose of the code.

R. C. MORTIMER

Fornication

In the AV the word is used in a very general way for sexual offences. Nowadays it usually means sexual intercourse between unmarried persons. *See* **Sex.**

Fortitude. *see* Courage.

Francis of Assissi, St

St Francis of Assisi (1181–1226) is in our time the best-known and most popular of mediaeval saints. The troubadour of Christ, who loved God in all his creatures, adorns many a Protestant garden as well as many a Catholic church. Less understood is the lover of Lady Poverty, that strange bride, as Dante put it (*Paradise*, Canto xi; *see* **Poverty**), who aimed to follow the naked Christ to the cross – and whose life ended in a sharing of the cross as he lost control of his own Little Brothers (Friars Minor) when they became an organized Order, received in his own body the mysterious stigmata of the wounds of the crucifixion, and died in joy and pain outside the walls of his native town. He remains a judgment and a challenge to all those whose following of Jesus is less literal, less joyful and less costly.

Francis was a loyal son of the Church, but no theologian – and ordained only to the diaconate, which he accepted because it carried the privilege of singing the Gospel at Mass. Nevertheless his principles have important implications for the history of Christian ethics. A son of the rising merchant class, he challenged the nascent capitalist age in the name of the call of Christ to leave all and follow him. But on the other hand the Friars Minor, having renounced endowments and property, were dependent for support on daily contacts with the world around them, through work or alms, in a way that older monastic communities were not. They thus express the paradox that the Christian who is most anxious to defy the standards of the secular world is least able to cut himself off from it. Symbolically, the Friars soon established themselves not only in the country hermitages which Francis loved, but also in great cities, where their churches became

centres of the Church's ministry to all classes – and in the universities, in spite of the anti-intellectualism of Francis himself. This was partly due to the influence of the Dominicans, who were from the start committed to fighting the battles of the Church in the intellectual arena. Moreover, in contrast to the highly corporate character of early mediaeval religion, the Franciscan appeal was strongly individual, calling for an individual response both from recruits to the Order and from those reached by its preaching and witness. Perhaps the first modern missionary effort, as distinct from the early mediaeval approach to nations and tribes, was Francis' bold attempt during a crusading war to preach directly to the Sultan of Egypt (who received him with respect as a strange dervish and sent him back safely to the Christian camp). By 1300 Franciscan missionaries, working primarily as individual explorers for Christ, had reached as far as China, where under the tolerant Kublai Khan Brother John of Montecorvino became the first Archbishop of Cambaluc (Pekin). In the West Ramon Lull, a lay Tertiary (see below) attempted to replace the military attack on the Moslems with a personal preaching which would use the best in their religion as a point of contact. Franciscan piety followed established forms of prayer and sacrament – but laid most stress on personal and evangelical elements, such as devotion to the Holy Infant (cf. Francis' invention of the Christmas crib) and the crucified Christ, and the cult of the Blessed Virgin. The Second Order of Poor Clares (so called from their foundress) for women followed Francis' principles, as far as conventual enclosure allowed: and by the mid-century the laity who desired to follow the Franciscan ideal in their state of life were organized, as Brothers and Sisters of Penitence, into the Third Order (secular Tertiaries). Ascetism (q.v.) thus began to come out of the cloisters into the life of the world. In many ways St Francis, the most demanding of mediaeval ascetics, is also the first modern Christian man.

Father Cuthbert, O.F.M.C., *The Romanticism of St Francis*, 2nd edn., 1924; David Knowles, *The Religious Orders in England*, I, 1948.

E. R. HARDY

Free Will and Determinism

Together with the problems of God and immortality, the problem of the freedom of the will is one of the three great metaphysical problems named by Kant as lying beyond the powers of the human intellect. By its very nature, free will would seem to be something that could neither be proved nor be disproved. The observable, external happenings belonging to any human act might be seen as constituting a chain of causally linked physical events, while even the internal states of mind of the agent might be explicated in terms of a determinist psychology, or assigned to influences arising from environment or heredity (qq.v.). Yet the agent himself may have been aware of deliberating between different policies of action, and of choosing one in preference to the other. *See* **Deliberation; Choice.** A great many ingenious arguments have been put forward in the history of philosophy, aimed either at establishing the reality of free choice, or at showing that the sense of freedom is an illusion and that all action is determined in advance by factors other than a conscious choice between alternatives. This determinism may be represented as physical, psychological or even, as in the case of Calvin's doctrine of providence, theological. But whatever the arguments, it would seem that none of them is conclusive. The case for free will (like the case for the reality of the external world or the reality of other selves) does not rest on demonstration, but on the fact that it is a presupposition of all our everyday thinking and acting. We warn and advise, we praise and we blame, we reward and we punish, we set goals and strive after them, and all this makes sense only on the supposition that there is some freedom of choice and action. Such freedom is never unlimited (never a *libertas indifferentiae*). It is always circumscribed by a great many 'givens', such as environmental circumstances, the past acts of the agent or of others, traits of personality, and the like. These limit freedom of choice at any given moment, and perhaps sometimes freedom is reduced to near the vanishing-point. Yet it would be senseless to talk of ethics and morality at all unless some human action enjoyed some range of freedom, however restricted.

The question of freedom in relation to a specifically Christian ethic becomes acute at two points especially – where it impinges on the doctrines of original sin and of grace. The awareness of this tension found its classic expression in the controversy between Augustinianism and Pelagianism. In practice, however, the Church would seem to have settled for a doctrine midway between these extremes. Even if we allow that man's fallen nature pulls him towards bad choices, he is not absolutely determined by this pull; and the very fact that there is a 'natural' awareness of sin is a sufficient refutation of any doctrine of total depravity, for such awareness is itself a breach in the domination of sin. On the other hand, even if we allow that man needs enabling grace, it cannot be supposed that such grace is 'irresistible' or imposed, so that man is a mere marionette. The dialectic of sin and grace is the theological counterpart of the ethical dialectic between freedom and determinism. In both cases, the dialectic must be maintained and explicated in fully personal terms.

EDITOR

Freedom

Freedom in the NT and most often in the context of Christian theology is a category not of social or political ethics but of the ultimate relationship between the Christian and Christ. Freedom is seen as freedom from sin and freedom for obedience to God. Paul emphasized freedom in these terms in Romans and Galatians especially, and always freedom as spontaneous loyalty and obedience to God in Christ is ultimate for Christian understanding. Deliverance from all hindrances to this loyalty and obedience is the negative dimension of freedom in this religious context. There has always been a problem in relating freedom understood in these terms to the specific social and political forms of freedom. For one thing it is possible to think of the freedom of the Christian as being independent of all external circumstances such as political tyranny or imprisonment. In this spirit Paul could say: 'in any and all circumstances I have learned the secret of facing plenty and hunger, abundance and want' (Phil. 4.12).

There is a relationship even between this exalted form of Christian freedom and freedom for the citizen when the Christian feels obliged by his obedience to God to take freedom to speak and act in the world. It sometimes becomes necessary to disobey the powers that seek to limit this freedom. 'We must obey God rather than men' (Acts 5.29). Here we can see how Christian freedom in the most distinctive sense may become a source of political ferment. Those who take freedom to obey God in the world, as they understand this obedience, often break through the structures that limit their freedom to speak and act they have in western history opened the r to political forms of freedom.

Until the seventeenth century in Christendom it was generally taken for granted that either to protect souls from the spiritually deadly effects of heresy or to preserve social unity by permitting only one religious allegiance within a political community it was right for Catholic or Protestant Christians to limit the freedom of those whom they believed to be in error. Gradually over a period of three centuries this assumption has been eroded until today it is explicitly abandoned by nearly all Christians. Today there is a very broad ethical consensus in the Church not only that it is bad public policy in pluralistic societies to use the power of the State to enforce religious uniformity but also that it is a sin against Christian love to 'force consciences', to tempt persons to hypocrisy by intimidating them when they fail to conform in their religious life and witness (R. H. Bainton, *The Travail of Religious Liberty*, 1951). The Declaration on Religious Freedom of the Second Vatican Council puts the Roman Catholic Church on record in favour of religious freedom for all on principle.

There has been interaction in western nations between the struggles for religious freedom and the struggles for other forms of freedom in the social order. Today it is widely recognized that such other freedoms as freedom of speech, freedom of assembly, freedom to organize political movements and religious freedom are interdependent and that efforts to stamp out political minorities may take the form of associating them with the religious heresies. Any ordered society, no matter how much it may be committed to all of the forms of freedom of expression contained in the American Bill of Rights or similar affirmations must set limits to freedom in the interests of order or national security or some aspects of public morality. Societies that are basically stable can take more risks at this point than those that are threatened by serious disunity or subversion. There is no universally acceptable line to be drawn here but governments do have to take seriously what the United States Supreme Court calls a 'clear and present danger'. Even practices that have a religious connection will be limited or forbidden at times in societies that generally guarantee religious freedom. Examples of this are the banning of 'suttee' in India by the British authorities, the outlawing of polygamy in the USA when it was regarded as a religiously sanctioned practice by the Mormons, and the compulsory vaccination for the sake of public health that may be against some religious scruples. How far a government should censor artistic productions is one of the most controversial issues ... liberal societies that prize cultural freed...

The relatio... ...tween the various forms of 'civil liberty' and freedom of private initiative in economic life varies from country to country and there is no one Christian view of the matter. The issue is settled in favour of the dominance of public initiative and planning in Communist nations and this is not in itself rejected in principle by churches in those countries. Elsewhere there is preference for a mixed economy which, while emphasizing the State's responsibility for welfare, allows considerable scope for private enterprise. Both the encyclicals of recent popes and the reports of the Assemblies of the World Council of Churches agree in presenting a flexible position in this context leaving much room for both private and public initiative. In the USA there remains a strong current of economic individualism that insists that freedom is indivisible and that the various forms of civil liberty or of cultural freedom depend upon the maintenance of a laissez-faire economic system. Corporate teaching in the American churches, while influenced by this tendency, expresses the concern for the flexibility that characterizes the ecumenical

social pronouncements. The State can be both a threat to freedom and a protection of the real freedom of choice of economically disadvantaged people. It is also often a check on the power of free economic institutions to control the community in their own interests.

At one time the Church may have been the chief threat to freedom but with a few marginal exceptions this is no longer the case. Today the State is usually the most powerful and the most obvious threat to the spiritual and cultural freedom of the person. In recent decades under both Hitler and Stalin the use of terror by the State to prevent any public expressions of dissent and to intimidate whole populations have shown how far the State can go to restrict not only the political but also the personal and cultural freedom of its citizens. To a lesser extent many states show this same tendency when there is no strong belief in personal freedom in their national tradition or in times of revolution or political instability. Against this kind of threat there is considerable clarity in Christian social thinking except where churches are themselves under tyrannical political authorities. It is much more difficult for Christians or anyone else concerned with freedom to deal with the more intangible threats to freedom in the culture controlled by mass media and by the pressures of public opinion. All modern societies face these threats though some still maintain considerable diversity. The distinctive feature of totalitarian systems has been the extent to which cultural forces are mobilized by the State explicitly to create uniformity.

Freedom in this article has been considered chiefly in terms of freedom *from* many forms of external hindrance to the person as he seeks to make his own choices, to express his own convictions, to be true in the public sphere to his own conscience. (The same considerations apply to groups and institutions especially when they respect the freedom of conscience among their members.) But Christian thinking about freedom does return full circle to freedom in the positive sense, freedom to be bound by loyalty to God's will revealed in Christ. Those who do not share the commitment of Christian faith may have the same form of positive freedom which consists in a commitment that both limits the freedom of the person and expresses it. Freedom *from* external hindrance, may be understood as opportunity for the person to speak and act as one bound by his deepest commitments.

JOHN C. BENNETT

Freud, Sigmund

Freud (1856–1939), the Vienese psychiatrist and neurologist, was the founder of psychoanalysis, and the seminal figure in the development of all contemporary dynamic psychology, that is, psychology which places emphasis upon the unconscious motivation of human behaviour.

See **Psychoanalysis** for a general treatment of Freud's thought and contributions. For more detailed treatment of particular ideas *see* **Unconscious; Repression; Id; Ego; Superego; Defence Mechanisms; Oedipus Complex; Dreams;** *and* **Transference. Character** *and* **Development** are partially devoted to discussion of Freud's contribution, as are **Anxiety** *and* **Guilt.**

JAMES N. LAPSLEY

Gambling

Gambling may be defined as the determination of the possession of money, or money-value, by an appeal to an artificially created chance, where the gains of the winners are made at the expense of the losers and the gain is secured without rendering in service or in value an equivalent of the gains obtained. Thus the playing of a game of chance wholly for amusement is not gambling. Insurance, which is a statistical reduction of the risks of chance is not gambling. The acceptance of a gift, though it is literally 'money for nothing', is not gambling because there is no appeal to chance. Gambling may be *gaming*, that is, playing for money in a game of chance; *betting*, that is, staking money on an event of which the outcome is doubtful; *lotteries*, that is, the distribution of prizes by lot or chance; and *pools*, which combine the latter two.

The habit of gambling is deeply rooted in human history. The huckle bone, the original of the dice, was used for this purpose in the sixteenth century B C. Many ivory, porcelain or stone dice – some of them loaded – were found in the ruins of Pompeii. Twice the Apostle Paul uses words which in their literal meaning refer to gambling (Eph. 4.14; Phil. 2.30). It is generally agreed that immoderate addiction to gambling is to be condemned. An individual or a community in whose life gambling plays too prominent a part betrays a false sense of values which cannot but impair the full development of the personality or the society. It should therefore be the concern of the State to control the indulgence within reasonable bounds.

Most Christian moralists who accept this general judgment assert that the danger lies in the excess. It is extremely difficult, they contend, to establish by abstract arguments that all gambling is inherently immoral without adopting views on the nature of good and evil that do not commend general acceptance. A small stake in a raffle for a worthy cause, for example, inflicts no conceivable hardship on the purchaser of the ticket and is motivated more by generous desire to help than by anticipatory greed. In much actual gambling, the element of amusement or harmless excitement is not dominated by cupidity. If a number of people join together in a competition in which, by completely voluntary agreement, some will win and others lose, those who win need not be ashamed. In short, when the gambler firmly controls his indulgence, and is not dominated by it, he may obtain from it legitimate enjoyment which adds colour and modest excitement to his life. The essence of this argument is that gambling is not wrong in itself. It may reveal, but does not cause, defects of character in the participants.

The answer of the minority of moralists who take a stricter view is that 'gambling in itself' is a meaningless phrase. Every gamble is a particular and concrete action. They contend that in no circumstances is any gamble morally justified. The essence of their argument is that the command to love one's neighbour rules out gain at his inevitable loss, even if he is a willing partner. The decisive consideration should not be the ability of the bettor to risk a loss, but his willingness to an undeserved gain. In the totality of transactions, large sums of money are transferred by the random operations of chance from one set of pockets to another set. To all the other tensions of economic life – the consequences of exploitation, mismanagement, waste and social injustice – is added an arbitrary, unpredictable and unnecessary tension. It is further argued that the moralistic condonation of small-scale gambling weakens the case against commercial exploitation on a large scale, and so puts a stumbling block in one's brother's way. Finally, it is contended that resort to gambling is a virtual denial of faith in God and an ordered universe, putting in its place an appeal to blind chance, prompted neither by love nor rectitude.

The two positions cannot be reconciled. They illustrate clearly two distinct ethical approaches. The 'Catholic' approach deprecates what is regarded as an exaggerated scrupulosity concerning acts and notions which can be reasonably argued to be harmless in their effects on the individual and on the community. The 'dominical' approach deprecates what is regarded as the condonation of acts which can reasonably be held to conflict with the law of love to one's neighbour. One is basically sociological, the other basically theological.

The undoubted fact, however, that the great majority of Christian moralists condemn excessive addiction, commercial exploitation, and government participation in the provision of facilities for gambling, suggests that there may be a considerable measure of rationalization in the less rigorous approach.

W. Douglas Mackenzie, *The Ethics of Gambling*, 1895; R. C. Mortimer, *Gambling*, 1933; E. Benson Perkins, *Gambling in English Life*, 1950; *Report of Royal Commission on Betting, Lotteries, and Gaming, 1949–1951*, 1951.

EDWARD ROGERS

Gluttony

Gluttony is said to be one of the seven deadly sins. No one can say that a hungry man's desire to eat is sinful. The glutton's desire for more food than he needs is sinful; his heavy dull state after a meal is more than a symbol of gluttony. To dull oneself by over-eating brings about a temporary inability to live fully in mind, words and actions; it cuts a man off from his fellows because he cannot pay sufficient attention to them; it deadens his general awareness of what is happening within his immediate relationships. Persistent gluttony makes concentration, thinking, prayer almost impossible.

Gluttony is not to be described as merely an individual's failure to control a fleshly appetite. The gluttonous man, knowingly or unknowingly, uses food as others use drugs to give him pleasurable sensations which can help him, for the time, to ignore the parts of his life which are boring, disturbing or terrifying. Gluttony, like all sins of the flesh, must be considered spiritually. That is, while over-eating is a defect, the spiritual condition which permits it is very much more serious as it reveals the glutton's urgent need to escape reality.

R. E. C. BROWNE

Gnosticism

Gnosticism is a somewhat vague term used to denote a whole family of religious movements that flourished in the Near Eastern countries around the beginning of the Christian era. Some forms of Gnosticism incorporated Christian elements, and may be regarded as Christian heresies; examples are the doctrines of Cerinthus, Marcion and Valentinus. Other forms of Gnosticism, like the gospel of Poimandres, were non-Christian or pre-Christian. Until recently, Gnosticism was known chiefly, though not exclusively, through the accounts of it given by Christian opponents, such as St Irenaeus. In 1947, however, a large gnostic library was discovered at Nag Hammadi in Egypt, and as the material from this library has become available, our understanding of Gnosticism has been greatly increased. The basic mood of Gnosticism was one of alienation coupled with a longing for salvation. Hans Jonas has seen a parallel between this mood and the one that lies behind modern existentialism and nihilism. The sense of alienation and lostness found expression in myths which represented the world in fundamentally dualistic terms. The true God was thought to be utterly remote, transcendent and unknown. The material world was no creation of his, but the work of demonic powers, who hold the world in subjection. The soul of man derives from God, but it has become imprisoned in the physical body. Man is now ignorant of his true being. He is like one asleep or drunk, and the first step is to rouse him to knowledge of himself, and to kindle the nostalgic desire to escape from the material world to the world of light or where he truly belongs. To accomplish this escape, man needs the *gnosis* or secret knowledge, brought to him in most of the myths by a Redeemer who comes down from the transcendent sphere. Thus the gnostic ethic is an other-worldly one. The physical world, as the creation and dominion of the demonic powers, is taken to be evil. The aim of the moral life is withdrawal from earthy entanglements, and eventually escape from the body itself. Hence fasting, celibacy and ascetic practices are typical. Among some gnostic groups, however, it seems that a libertine ethic prevailed, presumably on the assumption that since the body is not really part of the self, what happens to the body or in the body is unimportant. Bultmann and other scholars have drawn attention to resemblances between the gnostic myths and some elements of NT teaching. This may be conceded, but there is a fundamental difference between the gnostic and Christian points of view because of the latter's rejection of dualism. The Christian doctrine of creation recognizes that the material world and the body have value, and that these too must have their place in any scheme of redemption and salvation. But Christianity agrees with Gnosticism in recognizing that man, in his actual condition, is alienated from his best potentialities and needs to be awakened and redirected towards genuine selfhood and community.

EDITOR

Golden Rule

'So whatever you wish that men would do to you, do so to them' (Matt. 7.12; Luke 6.31) has been designated as the Golden Rule or Golden Law at least since the seventeenth century. Since it occurs both in Matthew's Sermon on the Mount and Luke's Sermon on the Plain it may be presumed to have belonged to the earlier tradition of Jesus' sayings which the two Gospels had in common, that is, the 'Q' document. Probably Matthew added the clause 'for this is the law and the prophets'. It has long been recognized that this principle, at least in its negative form, had been enunciated prior to and apart from the teaching of Jesus. For example in Judaism it appears in Tobit 4.15; Test. Naphtali (Hebrew) 1.6; *B. Shabbath* 31a; Aristeas 207; Philo, *Hypothetica* 7.6; and *Ahikar* (Armenian text) 2.88. Again an approximation to this saying is found in Confucius, *Analects* XV 23; Li-Ki 39.23; the Zoroastrian *Dâdistân-Î Dinîk* 94.5; Herodotus III 142.3; Aristotle, *Nic. Ethics* IX 4 (though only with respect to a 'friend'); Thales (reported in Diog. Laer. I 36); Isocrates, *Nicocles* 61; Seneca, *Epistles* 47.11; and, according to Lampridius in the *Life of Severus* 51.7 f., the latter wrote this axiom on his palace wall.

Apart from the Gospel references all others present a negative version of the Rule with the possible exception of Aristeas 207 which approximates a formulation of both negative and positive versions (cf. also *M. Aboth* II, 10 and 12). Debate has centred around the respective merits of the two versions: some scholars contending that the positive is superior since it makes greater demands on the altruism of the obedient hearer, while others have praised the negative version on the grounds that it 'goes deeper into the heart of the problem' (Abrahams). Chrysostom, *Concerning the Statues*, XIII 7, quotes both versions, commenting that one requires 'a departure from iniquity', the other 'the exercise of virtue'. Despite the positive form in the Gospels a negative version circulated in the Christian tradition. *See* the Western text of Acts 15.20,29; *Didache* 1.2; Clement, *Strom.* II 23; Pope Fabian, *Epistles* II 2; Cyprian, *To Quirinius* III 119. However the principle was even more frequently quoted in the form given by the Evangelists, e.g., *Clementine Homilies* XII 32; Tertullian, *Scorpiace* X; Cyprian, *Treatises* IV 28; Augustine, *On Christian Doctrine* III 14; Chrysostom, *Homilies on St John* LXXVII 1, etc.

As a principle of conduct the Golden Rule is another way of stating 'You shall love your neighbour as yourself', and the Jer. Targum on Lev. 19.18 adds the negative Golden Rule to the other precept. But neither statement represents a universally applicable norm; our desires for ourselves may or may not be commendable. It is no accident that some texts and quotations of the Golden Rule qualified it to read 'Whatever *good things* you wish . . .' (Augustine, *City of God*, XIV 8). However, the function of the Golden Rule or of 'You shall love your neighbour as yourself' is not to provide a rule of thumb for all interpersonal relations, but rather to shatter the radical self-centredness which obscures our awareness of the needs or rights of others.

I. Abrahams, *Studies in Pharisaism and the Gospel* (First Series), 1917, pp. 18–29; D. M. Beck, 'Golden Rule', *Interpreter's Dictionary of the Bible*, II, 1962, p. 438; G. B. King, 'The "Negative" Golden Rule', *Journal of Religion*, VIII, 1928, pp. 268–79; J. G. Tasker, 'Golden Rule' in J. Hastings, ed., *Dictionary of Christ and the Gospels*, I, 1906, p. 653 ff.

HARVEY K. MCARTHUR

Good Works

The phrase is used in controversy about justification and the place in it of faith and works. The debate runs into the question of the fruits of justification, as to whether it conveys righteousness or merely imputes it; whether it removes only guilt or also some unrighteousness. Further, whether good works before justification have any merit and even whether good works of the redeemed aid their salvation.

St Paul's writings contain some antinomies on the question. His emphasis on the primacy of faith as against works (Rom. 3.27; 4; 11.6; Gal. 2.16,21) seems to have been a protest against the excessive legalism of Judaism. He also recognized the value of good works (II Cor. 8; Phil. 2.12; II Thess. 2.17). There is no ultimate opposition between his teaching and that of St James who, in his Letter, maintained that the evidence of faith is the doing of good works (2.14,17,18,22).

The differences of Catholics and Protestants in the Reformation period were round the question whether reconciliation was a matter of faith alone or whether the faithful signify their faith by their good works. None doubted that the grace of God, accepted by faith, was the efficient cause of justification. Aquinas, who is credited with maximum concession to the necessity of good works, nevertheless is more Pauline than Jamesean in ascribing the first movement of salvation to the believer's faith in God's justifying initiative (*Summa Theologica*, Part II, First Section, q.13, arts., 8,9). But he also said that faith without works is *fides informis* and faith which leads to loving works is *fides formata* (Part II, Second Section, q.4, arts., 3,4,5). Augustine had taught that good works established merit, but that grace alone enabled man to perform them (*Enchir.* cvii, Ep. cxciv. 19). Calvin combatted the Catholics for holding that 'a man once reconciled to God through faith in Christ is accounted righteous on account of his good works' but added that 'there is no controversy between us and the schoolmen as to the beginning of justification' (*Institutes*, III. xiv. 11). In some respects the Puritans brought in a more moralistic belief in good works than the earlier Reformers had, while Liberal Christianity with its Pelagian bias almost made good works the beginning as well as the end of salvation, one sect even setting up a formula of belief: 'salvation by character'.

For fuller treatment of the differences between Catholics and Protestants, *see* A. Ritschl, *The Christian Doctrine of Justification and Reconciliation*, 1900, from an ethical Lutheran point of view; and J. A. Moehler, *Symbolism*, 1843, Part I, Chap. 5, section 'Of Good Works', for a Catholic interpretation of the controversy. *See also* articles 'Merit', 'Introductory' and 'Christian', in *HERE*.

V. A. DEMANT

Goodness

In ethics goodness has two main senses.

1. *Moral goodness.* The aim of this article is to state the *Christian* view of goodness. But one must begin by affirming two principles that fall within the scope of secular philosophy.

(a) Moral goodness is irreducible, or unique. Many attempts have been made to equate it with a non-moral factor. Thus hedonists have equated it with 'pleasure'. A good action is one that produces pleasure (or happiness) either for the agent or for someone else. Others (for example, Julian Huxley and C. H. Waddington) have equated it with the direction of the evolutionary process. A good action is one which satisfies the criteria which a morally neutral study of evolution can provide. All these attempts to reduce moral to non-moral terms were brought under the heading of the Naturalistic Fallacy by G. E. Moore whose refutation of them in his *Principia Ethica* (1903) is widely accepted by philosophers of every school.

This fallacy can take a religious form. Thus Occam held that an act is good simply because God wills it. But it is obvious that 'the good' cannot be equivalent to 'divinely willed' unless God's will is good and unless we know that it is good. It is obvious too that we could not know this unless we had a prior knowledge of the good as a purely moral, non-religious, category.

(b) Moral goodness is objective. It actually inheres in the object of which it is predicated. Whether it so inheres in things and circumstances may well be doubted. But most of us have no doubt that it inheres in those *persons* to whom we attribute it. It is (we think) a spiritual property of them. Yet modern empiricists (such as Ayer and Nowell-Smith) hold that goodness is entirely subjective. In calling a person 'good' we are merely expressing our 'approval' of him.

The purely philosophical objections to subjectivism are well stated by Brand Blanshard in his *Reason and Goodness* (1961). These are confirmed by Christian theism. It is absurd to say that when we call God good we are simply expressing our approval of him. He *is* goodness; for in him essence and existence are identical; so that creatures are good to the extent that they mirror him.

2. *Teleological goodness.* In this sense 'the good' signifies an end or goal in which a person, or thing, fulfils his, or its, nature or specific form. While this sense can include the first it need not do so. It is logically possible to maintain that the good life for man is one devoted to the pursuit of (let us say) wealth or fame.

The Christian and the non-Christian can reach a large measure of agreement in their views on goodness. They can agree on many of the qualities that make a person good (for instance, the cardinal virtues). Also they can agree on many of the values which constitute the good life. This area of agreement is part of the *lex naturae*.

The specifically Christian contribution consists in the following elements:

1. *Moral goodness.*

(a) The ideal of goodness is the character of God. Jesus sums up his moral teaching in the words: 'You, therefore, must be perfect, as your heavenly Father is perfect' (Matt. 5.48). The context makes it clear that the element in divine perfection which disciples are to copy is self-giving love. (The NT calls God 'love', not 'goodness'. But since his goodness is by nature self-diffusing, it is identical with his love.)

The view that moral goodness consists in the imitation of God's attributes was not original. The Jewish law was summed up in the precept, 'You must be holy, for I am holy'. Plato and the Stoics also regarded God as the model for human excellence. The originality of the gospel on this score consists in two facts: the incarnation and the gift of the Spirit.

The incarnation is primary. The apostolic writers urge converts to imitate the love, gentleness, patience and humility of *Christ* who is the Word and Image of the Father. Furthermore, we participate in Christ through the Holy Spirit who is his 'other self'. Christian goodness is thus doubly *supernatural* (that is, beyond the scope of the natural intellect and will).

(b) Through Christ the *content* of moral goodness is transformed. It is dominated by three virtues: faith, hope and charity. Each of these exhibits the dependence of Christian ethics on Christian revelation. Human goodness consists in the imitation of God's love through faith and hope in Christ. The Church did not reject the natural virtues described by pagan moralists. But two of its greatest thinkers – St Augustine and Aquinas – insisted that in the Christian life these virtues must be governed and transformed by charity.

Love (*agape*) distinguished, and continues to distinguish, Christian from non-Christian forms of goodness. Although Graeco-Roman moralists sometimes commended selfless generosity, they did not give it the prominence it had in Christianity. Thus Aristotle's ethics rested on the ideal of prudence (as the prerequisite of contemplation), while the Stoics preached self-sufficiency. Moreover, even the closest parallels to *agape* – such as Buddhist 'compassion' – lack the example and motive-power of God Incarnate.

(c) Christian goodness is unmerited. We cannot achieve it by our works; it is a gift of grace. Even if we were wholly virtuous on the plane of nature we could not claim supernatural perfection as our due. As it is, we fail even to enact the *lex naturae*. We all know the inner conflict that St Paul described: 'I do not do what I want, but I do the very thing I hate' (Rom. 7.15).

As D. M. Baillie noted, there is a paradox in acquiring goodness, just as there is in acquiring happiness. If we make happiness (in the sense of 'pleasure') an end that we deliberately pursue, it will evade us. Similarly if we make goodness a goal which we try to reach by our unaided strength we shall both fail to achieve it fully (on account of our inherent sinfulness) and stand in danger of falling into the further sin of pride by taking credit for the limited moral victories we may win. Hence growth in humility is always a constituent in, and sign of, moral progress.

(*d*) Christian goodness is essentially corporate in two ways. Firstly, each Christian is indebted to the guidance and encouragement afforded by both past and present fellow-Christians. Secondly, it is God's purpose to establish, not merely good individuals, but a holy Church – a community united by his triune love.

2. *Teleological goodness.* St Augustine and Aquinas followed Plato and Aristotle in basing their ethics on the concept of man's 'good' or 'end'. What can fulfil human nature and be the cause of permanent beatitude? Not riches, fame or pleasure; not even human friendship or the natural activity of the human mind in seeking beauty, truth and moral goodness. Man's final end is the vision of God. Nothing less can satisfy our deepest longings.

This vision is related to moral goodness in two complementary ways. On the one hand, it is through this vision (received partially and indirectly now, but fully and 'face to face' hereafter) that we grow in goodness. On the other hand, the holier we become the more clearly we see God. From the merely human standpoint goodness in the second sense is wider than goodness in the first; for God exceeds any moral goodness we are able to conceive. Yet in reality the senses coincide; for the God who is our 'good' *is* goodness (or holiness); so that in our perfect vision of him *per connaturalitatem* morality is, not abolished, but transformed.

Teleology is overlapped by eschatology. According to the NT, our end (*telos*) will not be reached immediately after death. It will be part of the 'last stage' (*eschaton*) in God's purpose for his whole creation. We shall not be perfected – we shall not fully possess our moral good and reach our final end (the Beatific Vision) – until all things are summed up in the Word by whom they were created.

The Christian's attitude to the world is therefore 'dialectical'. On the one hand, he accepts it as the sphere in which he can grow in goodness through submission to the will of God. On the other hand, he knows that God's will cannot now be embodied fully either in himself or in society. But he hopes for a fulfilment in the Kingdom that is yet to come.

Charles Gore, *The Philosophy of the Good Life*, 1930; A. E. Taylor, *The Faith of a Moralist*, I, 1930; G. F. Thomas, *Christian Ethics and Moral Philosophy*, Part 4, 1955.

H. P. OWEN

Grace

Grace, *charis*, in its Greek religious usage means 'divine gift' or 'favour'. Thus a 'grace' was a quality or power usually bestowed by the gods, a quality which could be exhibited by a mortal. The English word 'graceful' reflects this meaning.

Here as in so many cases the Christians used the Greek word in such a way as to make it express a special meaning in the context of the biblical understanding of the relationship of God and man. The foundation of the NT meaning of grace is given in the Hebrew *hesed*, God's mercy and love through which he overcomes and redeems the sin of his covenanted people. The Septuagint usually renders *hesed* by *eleos*, pity. There is evidence, however, that there was an increasing tendency in the hellenistic period to use *charis*. Thus the way is prepared for the NT use of *charis* to express the specific redemptive action of God in Jesus Christ. Grace thus means the divine forgiveness of sin constituting the new creation, and it also means the power of God communicated to those who enter upon the new life of faith, hope and love. Thus Paul says, we 'are justified by his grace as a gift, through the redemption which is in Christ Jesus' (Rom. 3.24), where grace is the quality and power of the divine action which redeems man from sin. Paul also speaks of grace as the continuing action of God which enables the Christian to live the new life. 'God is able to provide you with every blessing (grace) in abundance' (II Cor. 9.8). Thus also the writer of the letter to the Hebrews appeals to his hearers to have grace whereby we may serve God acceptably with reverance and godly fear (Heb. 12.28).

Christian theologians have made distinctions with respect to the different functions or relationships in which grace is manifest. The central meaning remains always the mercy and forgiveness of God given freely to sinners along with the empowerment to meet the demands of the new life, and to resist temptation. The power of grace always remains God's power but it becomes operative in man and thus fulfils, sustains, and renews human nature.

In the biblical view all God's action is ultimately gracious for it expresses his love towards the world. Hence there is an inevitable extension of the use of the term grace to cover all the divine action from creation to last things. Catholic theology has been based upon the foundation of the distinction between prevenient grace and saving grace. The former is God's sovereign will establishing the world and electing his people to redemption. The latter is God's forgiveness mediated to those who are brought within the company of the saved, and mediated through the Church and the sacraments.

The Protestant Reformers tend to confine the

use of the term grace more strictly to the forgiveness given in Christ. For them grace does not so much complete a human nature which has lost its endowment of faith and hope and love, as it recreates an almost totally fallen nature. At the same time Protestants developed a doctrine of common grace which pointed to the uncovenanted mercies of God manifest in his provision for man in the orders of creation and in the unexpected and creative events in life which sustain and renew the human spirit.

The doctrine of grace has always raised questions about the relation of the divine power and mercy to man's moral situation. The distinction between grace as forgiveness and grace as empowerment sets the terms of the problem, for grace is asserted to deal with the problem of sin which has a moral dimension, and it enables the person to love God and his neighbour. Hence there has been a continual discussion in theology of the relation of grace to human freedom and action, and there are perennial tensions in various theological standpoints.

Certain major areas of concern can be distinguished:

1. Grace is understood in the Christian tradition as the mercy of God which solves the ultimate moral problem of man, that is, his inability to fulfil the requirements of perfect love and obedience to the divine will. Grace as forgiveness transcends all ethical categories for it resolves the moral problem at another level than that of moral justification or fulfilment. The doctrine of justification by faith (q.v.) must be understood as meaning justification, that is, being made righteous, by grace which is received and grasped by faith, not by moral effort. It is true that grace so understood deals with more than ethical failure for sin is also a transmoral category. The sins of pride and idolatry cannot be classified simply as immoralities. Yet sin as violation of the divine law, and as specific acts of injury to self or neighbour is moral wrong-doing, and the affirmation of the grace of God has always included its power to restore the morally right relationship between man and God, and between man and man.

2. The assertion of grace as empowerment to live the moral life raises the question of human freedom and moral responsibility. Ethical systems which assert that only the free act can be understood as within the realm of moral behaviour, have rejected the conception of man as dependent on grace for the power to act rightly. Kant asserts that the structure of moral obligation implies man's power to fulfil the moral requirement else it is meaningless. A strong argument for this point of view is made by W. G. Maclagan in *The Theological Frontier of Ethics* (1961). He holds that moral action must be self-wrought to be moral action 'even though there are environmental pressures and solicitations which "render the will's" action to an indefinite extent easier or more difficult'

(p. 131). His position is that 'It is a condition of the very being of a moral personality that a man's willing, in its goodness as in its badness, should be absolutely his own, into which in neither case does God's action enter constitutively' (p. 118). This would appear to mean that grace operates wholly in a transmoral dimension of life. But from another theological standpoint the situation is more complex for it is asserted that man can recognize an obligation without being able of his own will to fulfil it, and that the actual moral experience is that of discovering a power beyond the self which enables man to make a right response. Grace is sometimes described as having a co-operating function once the initial restoration to right relationship is achieved by God's action.

The issue here has divided Augustinians and Pelagians through the centuries. It appears not only in the theological debate but also between all those who find man's moral situation that of being bound to powers he cannot control and those who assert man's freedom to direct his action. The issue has appeared, for example, between schools of psychology in the modern period.

The Augustinian position and all its followers have tried to interpret the actual situation of the person who is not free to become what he ought to become, or what he wants to become. His empowerment must come from outside himself. The problem of the position is to make clear in what sense there is moral accountability for man in this situation. The Pelagian theological tradition, as in Pelagius himself, never rejected the concept of grace. But it asserted that man as accountable must retain some freedom and power of action towards moral growth and that the function of grace, therefore, is educative and co-operative.

3. In the twentieth century many Christian theologians have attempted to show by an analysis of the ethical problem how the search for meaning in man's moral experience leads to the need for grace not only as forgiveness for individual guilt, but as the redemptive power of the divine working in history. This argument has been prompted by the increasing secularization of man's life and the resulting questioning of the need for or relevance of grace as conceived in the religious tradition. Autonomous man has no need of grace. Christian apologists, many under the direct influence of Kierkegaard, such as Gogarten, Tillich, Barth, Bonhoeffer, H. Richard Niebuhr and Reinhold Niebuhr, have sought to show through an analysis of man's moral existence and its ambiguities and failures that a meaningful human existence cannot be secured through ethical principle and action alone. Realization of the wholeness of life amidst the tragedies of history is possible only through reliance upon the divine redemptive working which can best be designated by the word grace. The mediation

of the divine mercy is present in communities of acceptance and forgiveness, within the recognized Church and beyond it, in which grace is present as the spirit of forgiving love transcending the demand for moral rectitude as the sole justification for human action. Thus the concept of grace set alongside the ultimate ethical dilemmas leads to a reconsideration of the theology of history and of the doctrine of the Church.

W. G. Maclagan, *The Theological Frontier of Ethics*, 1961; James Moffat, *Grace in the New Testament*, 1931; Reinhold Niebuhr, *The Nature and Destiny of Man*, 2 vols., 1941–3, especially II; John Oman, *Grace and Personality*, 1931; W. T. Whitley, ed. *The Doctrine of Grace*, 1932.

DANIEL D. WILLIAMS

Gratitude

The correlative of grace is gratitude. The words are basically the same (Hebrew *barak*, Greek *charis*) and it is natural that a theology of grace should issue in an ethic whose basic motive is gratitude. There is ample evidence for this in the NT, the most notable passage being Rom. 12.1,2, where the transition to the ethical section of the Epistle is made on the grounds of gratitude, looking back to the theological exposition of justification by grace. 'I appeal to you therefore, brethren, by the mercies of God, to present your bodies as a living sacrifice . . .' Christians are to show forth the praises of him who hath called them out of darkness into his marvellous light (I Peter 2.9) and in everything to give thanks (I Thess. 5.18. *See also* C. E. B. Cranfield, 'Thank', *A Theological Word Book of the Bible*, ed. by A. Richardson, 1957).

By contrast, the note of gratitude is not prominent in many of the early Christian writings, for neither is the note of grace. Where formalism or rigorism regards the Christian life as an earnest moral striving for a future reward, it is the hope of salvation and the fear of perdition that is held out as a motive, rather than gratitude. The early sermon known as II Clement begins with gratitude. 'And how many mercies do we owe to him? For he bestowed the light upon us; he spake unto us as a father unto his sons; he saved us when we were perishing. What praise then shall we give to him?' (II Clement 1.) But since the work of Christ is thought of here in terms of knowledge rather than of redemption, the Christian life is described in terms of stern moral achievement rather than of freedom and gratitude.

In Augustine, with the recovery of the Pauline doctrine of grace there is also a recovery of the significance of gratitude (*de Spiritu et Littera*, 18), which Augustine more commonly expressed in terms of love, 'which is shed abroad in our hearts' (op. cit., 29). When Calvin speaks of 'the sacrifice of thanksgiving' (*Institutes* IV. xviii.16) he includes in it 'all the office of charity, which when we perform to our brethren, we honour the Lord himself in his members; and likewise all our prayers, praises, thanksgiving and everything that we do in the service of God'. His exposition of the Christian life as self-denial (based on Rom. 12. 1,2) makes, however, no explicit mention of gratitude (*Institutes* III, vii). A notable and fine use of the idea is in the Heidelberg Catechism (1563) which subsumes its exposition of the Christian life under the theme 'How I am to be grateful to God for such redemption'.

'A true Christian is a man who never for a moment forgets what God has done for him in Christ, and whose whole comportment and whole activity have their root in the sentiment of gratitude' (John Baillie, *The sense of the Presence of God*, 1962, p. 237).

JAMES A. WHYTE

Green, Thomas Hill

Thomas Green (1836–1882), in a short life of forty-six years, exerted, chiefly in his oral work as a tutor at Oxford, a wide and long influence. It was he who secured the effective entrance of German idealism into British academic circles, breaching the long tradition of empiricism. He used the German outlook and method to attack naturalism in any of its forms, humean, utilitarian or evolutionist. His primary interest was social and moral, but he set his ethics in the context of a theory of knowledge and reality. Nothing can be known in isolation; knowing *is* relating; relating is the activity of a mind that has the unity of a self; and the order and unity of the world is the product of a cosmic self, in which we participate and of which we are organs. In these terms he formulated his view of morality. As in knowing mere sensations have to be changed into objects, so for conduct raw impulses have to be changed from feelings into desires directed towards objects (things or actions), and by this transformation they cease to be purely natural events. Further we have to look at them in order to see which to adopt as our motives for action, for only then is a desire and the resulting action our own in the strict sense of expressing the unitary self. This is Green's general definition of morality, one of its points being that pleasure is always bound up with an object, is in itself an unreal abstraction and therefore cannot, as it is in hedonism, be treated as itself an end. The end of all morality, the principle which should rule our adoption of desires, is self-realization, the balanced actualization of our distinctively human potentialities, not the meaningless chase of fleeting satisfactions. The principle is not to be read selfishly; it prescribes seeking also the self-realization of others. So far it remains vaguely general, not giving specific guidance. Metaphysically Green defines self-realization as approximation to the perfect nature of the cosmic self, God. This nature is evident, incompletely of course yet directively, in the spiritual efforts and achievements of men, especially the collective ones. This pointer enables Green to proceed from the general to the specific by referring to the Greek and Christian systems of moral virtues. It also leads him, Hegelianwise, to a high valuation of the tested social institutions, though his strong sense of the reality and responsibility of the individual and of the general brotherhood of man kept him from Hegel's exaltation of the state as the supreme and final human fact. *See* **Idealist Ethics.**

T. E. JESSOP

Gregory of Nyssa, St

Gregory (*c.* 330–395), a younger brother of St Basil the Great, was born in Cappadocia. He received the customary classical education, married, and became a teacher of rhetoric. In 372 Basil, in need of support against the forces of Arianism, had his brother named Bishop of Nyssa. Gregory resided in his see for two years, and in 374 was exiled. It was only after this exile that he entered with enthusiasm into Basil's theological and ecclesiastical programme, and only after Basil's death (379) that his full stature as a thinker, a polemicist and a statesman was revealed. Like his elder brother, Gregory was learned in the literary and philosophical heritage of the later Empire, being closely acquainted both with the Neoplatonism of the schools and with the Christian Platonism of Clement of Alexandria and Origen. Unlike Basil, however, Gregory had the gifts and the inclination for systematic speculative thought; and in his exegetical, theological and ascetic works, he expanded, deepened and rationalized the positions which his brother had sketched out, becoming one of the architects of the trinitarian settlement under the Emperor Theodosius.

Quite apart from his contribution to the formalities of the classical doctrines of the Trinity and the incarnation, Gregory in effect reconstructed the ascetical and mystical theology of the Christian Platonist tradition, through what amounts to a criticism of his master, Origen. For Gregory, the Christian life is a process by which the unity of mankind in and with Christ is progressively realized through an entrance, sacramental and moral, into the mysteries of his death and resurrection. In this unification with Christ, involving an interior death and rebirth, the soul is restored to the image of God and enters into the knowledge of God. For Gregory as for Origen the way to this goal is threefold, and the first step is essentially negative: a death to the life of the passions, to all those lusts, interests and emotions which distract the soul and alienate it from its true self. Of this renunciation the celibate life is, for Gregory the married man, the inclusive symbol. The fruit of this detachment is a new freedom

for God, an apprehension of God which is not a grasp of God in himself, but an acknowledgement of his gracious presence to the soul. This for Gregory is the second stage in the soul's assimilation to Christ: the way of illumination.

But the ultimate knowledge of God is achieved only as the soul moves from light into darkness: as, in faith and love, it moves eternally towards the infinite God whom it can never grasp. Thus for Gregory the highest knowledge of God consists in the existential apprehension of his inaccessibility; and in this vision of God which is an acknowledgement of his unknowability, the soul attains the highest degree of likeness to God, just as it realizes most fully in its own life the mystery of the rebirth which comes through death. In this doctrine Gregory, while building on Origen's foundations, passes beyond the limits of Origen's intellectualism.

R. A. NORRIS, JR

Guidance. *see* Casuistry ; Conscience ; Direction, Spiritual.

Gregory the Great, St

Gregory (*c.* 540–604), son of an ancient Roman senatorial family, rose to be Prefect of the City of Rome before he deserted public life to join the brotherhood of one of seven monasteries he had founded. His preference for the austerity and retirement of monastic life was shortly frustrated, and he was called into the service of the church, first as one of the seven deacons of Rome, then as papal representative at Constantinople. Elected pope in 590, he continued to live as an ascetic while dealing with the manifold political, economic and ecclesiastical problems which devolved upon the Roman bishop in this era of crisis, confusion and decline. Widely regarded as 'founder' of the mediaeval papacy, Gregory's practical and popular interpretation of the theology of Augustine provided the foundation of later mediaeval theology and won him the style of 'Doctor of the Church'.

Gregory was not a thinker of any originality. He was a pastor and preacher, whose writings and sermons reveal his conviction that he and his flock were living in a time of judgment, when the end of the world was at hand. Gregory's ethical teaching, therefore, while invariably informed by his native practicality and good sense, breathes a spirit of austerity and renunciation. For him, the Christian life is an extended act of penance, of self-inflicted rigour by which compensation is made for sin, self is humiliated in obedience, and God is glorified by good works. 'The perfect life is an imitation of death.'

The root of the Christian life is interior faith and love, which express themselves in outward good works: prayer, fasting, benevolence and service. By his works (which are good only as they flow from a grace-given inward conversion), the believer obeys God and makes himself pleasing to God. Gregory thinks in terms of the same ideas of merit and satisfaction which are found in earlier western writers, for example, Tertullian. Good works are meritorious for Gregory because they spring from the co-operation of the human will with divine grace. Thus by extraordinary good works in the present, the believer may make satisfaction for past sins. By the same token, he may seek to render himself more pleasing to God by doing more than is strictly commanded – by rigorous fasting, or almsgiving, or the perfect chastity of the celibate life.

The theological framework of this ethic is Gregory's doctrine of baptism and penance. The grace and forgiveness of baptism find their supplement – necessary in view of the actual sin of baptized persons – in the confession, contrition and satisfaction which together constitute penance, and by which both the guilt and the punishment of sin may be cancelled. The theory which lies behind Gregory's ethic of renunciation is thus moralistic and legalistic in character, and interprets the relation between God and man in terms of the relations of creditor and debtor: an image which was to have vast influence in later western religion.

R. A. NORRIS, JR

Guilt

It is important to distinguish at the outset between guilt as a moral or legal concept, and guilt as a feeling. The former has a primary objective reference to the breaking of some law or commandment, or some accepted code or standard of values. One does not have to acknowledge culpability to be adjudged guilty in this sense. Roman Catholic moral theology makes a further distinction between 'formal' guilt (the wilful commission of a transgression) and 'material' guilt (which involves no act of will). Persons who are guilty of some actual transgression may experience feelings of distress – self-reproach, self-blame, anxiety, remorse, etc. – unpleasant enough to stimulate remedial or expiatory action. A common sequence of such action is repentance, confession, seeking of forgiveness, reparation. Here the guilt feelings (the sense of guilt) are performing their normative function. If there were no capacity for guilt in man there could be no sense of responsibility in personal relationships.

But guilt feelings may also be expressed by persons who are, in the objective sense, not guilty of any transgression. And guilt feelings may persist after all appropriate remedial measures have been taken. These feelings are also unpleasant, and sometimes intensely so, but the feeling tone is subtly but definitely different from that obtaining in the guilt which is an acknowledgement of true accountability. It is now recognized that guilt may be a potent

motivating factor in human behaviour but not be felt as guilt at all. Dynamic psychology, following Sigmund Freud, has demonstrated that guilt feelings are very frequently displaced. That is to say, the feelings are aroused by something quite different from whatever it is the person says he is guilty of. Roman Catholic studies of scrupulosity have confirmed this general finding. Many guilt feelings amount to an obsessive pre-occupation with one type of responsibility as a defensive measure to avoid having to come to terms with other deeper, and even more threatening, problems. Since the guilt feelings are painful, the 'inner avenging forces' of the personality are satisfied, but at the price of concealing the true conflict. One consequence is that the measures of atonement adopted are largely ineffective to assuage the guilt feelings.

Feelings of guilt seem to be rooted in hostility, and Lewis J. Sherrill suggests, in his very perceptive *Guilt and Redemption* (rev. edn., 1957), that a vicious circularity develops in feelings of hostility, anxiety and guilt. Orthodox Freudian thinkers trace these guilt feelings to the disproportionate operation of the superego (q.v.). Guilt in this form can play a significant role in seriously disturbed neurotic and psychotic conditions. Some thinkers in the Freudian tradition have attempted an historical analysis of the origins of guilt in mankind (*see*, e.g., Theodore Reik, *Myth and Guilt*, 1957), but this work must be regarded as descriptive rather than explanatory. It seems now that a sociological change has taken place in contemporary US society regarding the way in which problems involving guilt are manifested. Perhaps because of increasing understanding of psychic mechanisms, fewer disturbed persons are developing the symptoms with which psychoanalysis (q.v.) was originally concerned, and more are developing character disorders (the acting-out behaviour patterns) which commonly exhibit a comparative absence of felt guilt and which are less amenable to therapy.

The Christian understanding of sinful man's guilt before God begins at the point where that guilt is effectively dealt with, the cross of Jesus Christ. In consequence, this real guilt is not felt by the experiencing person as guilt. What is felt is this other symptomatic or distorted guilt arising from inner problems or difficulties.

The new insights into guilt raise some acute questions for ethics and for theology generally. There are ways, for example, of proclaiming forgiveness which play into the helplessness which underlies some of the hostility element in guilt feelings and which therefore compounds the problem. The doctrine of redemption needs to be formulated in such a way that the forgiveness offered is truly freeing and not constricting. The whole matter of the punishment of offenders against the law and the relation of punishment to rehabilitation has been inadequately explored in ethics. It seems now that neither undue leniency nor harshness increase the chances of rehabilitation, whereas a structured firmness flexible enough to permit different attitudes to persons with differing internal situations does so. The criminal who gets caught accidentally, for example, poses a different question to the criminal who unconsciously arranges things so that he will be caught. The question of the role of guilt in such matters as race relations, sex, contraception, childlessness, medical and political ethics, euthanasia, etc., has yet to be resolved satisfactorily from a Christian point of view open to the best insights of contemporary psychology. *See* **Psychology and Ethics.**

GRAEME M. GRIFFIN

Habit

Habit is used generally of well-defined patterns of behaviour or modes of thought in which a person engages without his having consciously to initiate the process on each occasion or to give assent to each step in the process. Explicit decisions, trial-and-error judgments, and conscious acts of will may well have been necessary to establish the pattern, but once it has become established, it assumes a certain autonomy. One need not even be aware that the habitual action takes place – in the common phrase, it is done 'without thinking'. The formation of habits is essential to enable life to proceed. If one had to weigh judgments and make decisions about every separate activity of life, the whole day could be consumed in such trivia as the buttoning of one's clothes or the eating of one's food. The important thing is that the habits actually developed will free the person for the responsible discharge of his obligations.

Patterned readiness or disposition to respond emotionally in certain ways are also evidences of habit-formation, as in the person easily angered, or he who retreats, or one who becomes unctuous, etc. Such readinesses are sometimes referred to as emotional habit-patterns, or as characterological patterns. While not independent of what triggers them, they are far from being simple responses to environment.

Specific theories as to how habits are formed, modified or broken are related closely to particular understandings of the learning process. Many experimental .psychologists follow the lead of William James, *Psychology* (1892) and John B. Watson, *Behaviorism* (1925), and regard habits as consequences of the establishment of certain definite pathways in the nervous system which are reinforced by repetition (conditioning) and which tend to fade if not repeated. Other investigators have been more concerned with the development and maintenance of habits as stereotyped forms of reaction to internal stresses and conflicts. The emphasis in dynamic psychology generally has been on such 'habit-disorders' as nail-biting, enuresis (bed-wetting), masturbation, temper tantrums, etc. These are regarded in broad terms as manifestations of feelings of insecurity, anxiety (q.v.), confusion about identity, etc. Psychoanalysis (q.v.) has stressed the importance of the psycho-sexual developmental stages in personality in the formation of habits – *see* John Rickman, ed., *On the Bringing up of Children*, 1936. Others have stressed the role of social forces, and of imitation.

These different emphases are important to ethics. To oversimplify, the James-Watson position speaks of the overthrow of bad habits by the reinforced substitution of good ones, that is, by an effort of will. The dynamic position, in its various forms, warns that even the best intentioned will is ultimately powerless if the internal conditions which led to the formation of the habit are not effectively dealt with.

GRAEME M. GRIFFIN

Hamann, Johann Georg

Johann Georg Hamann (1730–1788) was born in Könisgberg, studied there, and on a business trip to London experienced a thorough-going conversion, from which stemmed the form of the rest of his life, 'serving from below'. His ethical position is characterized by a revolt against the narrow rationalism of the Enlightenment, as typified in his view by Immanuel Kant, a strong sense of the historicity of Christianity, and a deep awareness of the condescension of God in Christ. Added to this is a lively, but neither mythological nor pietistic, eschatological faith. His writings are brief, enigmatic, occasional pieces, and it is in his letters that he is clearest. His thought had a great influence on Kierkegaard, as well as upon the writers of the *Sturm und Drang*, especially Herder. His life was his best composition. In the words of Amalie, Princess Gallitzin, 'He shuns nothing so much as to appear virtuous or learned. . . . He speaks proudly, and shows himself to be humble.' In his own words, 'A strict morality seems to me to be more contemptible and shallower than the most wilful scoffing and mockery. To drive the good deep inside, to drive the evil to the outside, to seem worse than one really is, to be really better than one seems: this I consider to be both a duty and an art' (*Werke*, ed. Roth, VI, p. 339). His views have had a liberating effect upon ethical attitudes, and at the same time have linked them firmly to the historical, contingent realities of Christianity.

Sämtliche Werke, 6 vols, ed. by Nadler, 1949–57; *Briefwechsel*, ed. by Ziesemer and Henkel, 1955- ; R. Gregor Smith, *J. G. Hamann, a Study in Christian Existence*, 1960.

R. GREGOR SMITH

Hammurabi. *see* Babylonian Ethics.

Happiness

The distinction between happiness and pleasure (q.v.) is frequently blurred. In ordinary language happiness is frequently used to indicate a more stable, less intense state than pleasure; for instance, one speaks of the happiness of a marriage, but of the pleasure of an orgasm. Yet one could hardly predicate happiness of a life that was altogether without pleasure. While those teleological moralists who have favoured utilitarian conceptions of moral obligation have (apart from the late Professor G. E. Moore and his followers) usually adopted a hedonist conception of the end of moral action, those moralists who have combined teleological ideas with the rejection of Utilitarianism have inclined to speak of a happy life as the end of man, happiness being found in, and sometimes identified with, a life of fulfilment and harmony both within the individual and in that individual's relations with his fellows.

In much contemporary thinking about ethics notion of happiness is frequently invoked in criticism of moral conceptions which exalt such ideas as duty, obedience to superiors and established traditions, heroic engagement, even commitment, and at least by implication depreciate the significance of the individual's concern for his own and his fellows' welfare. Against such views (not without their representatives among *avant-garde* theologians) the importance of happiness as an unsophisticated, but comprehensive, human end receives justified and intelligible emphasis.

D. M. MACKINNON

Harnack, Adolf

Adolf Harnack (1851–1930), German scholar. *See* **Ritschl and Ritschlianism**.

Hartmann, Eduard von

Eduard von Hartmann (1842–1906) was an independent follower of Schopenhauer, modified the latter's metaphysics and ethics with views from Hegel. On the ground that Schopenhauer's irrationalism could not account for the order in the actual world, nor Hegel's rationalism for the disorder (especially suffering), he held that the Absolute must be a compound of will and reason. Will, being the active factor, created the world. In this every process works towards something that cannot be attained. In human life this failure shows itself in the futility of all our desires: there is far more pain than pleasure; and hope for happiness in the near future, or in a future life, or in a remotely future perfected civilization, is all vain. The cosmic reason that evolves into consciousness in man cannot change this worst of all possible worlds, but simply exposes its futility. What,

then, can we do? Not, as Schopenhauer had urged, suppress, each of us in himself, the will to live, but play our part socially in the furthering of the natural process of civilization to the very distant stage where its maximal development will make pain utterly rampant and, by intensifying our sensibility to it, intolerable. With this grand defeat of will cosmic and human, the cosmic will ceases to will, and in consequence its creature the world will go out of existence. In the prospect of this eschatological end Hartmann brings in his philosophical religion: in helping to bring about that final defeat we have the ideal not only of ending the misery of man but also of rescuing the reason in the Absolute or God from its long bondage to the will-factor, so ending the suffering of God. Hartmann, who had a considerable vogue in Germany in the 1870s and '80s, was working out the inevitability of pessimism when the standard of worthwhileness is taken to be happiness.

T. E. JESSOP

Hartmann, Nicolai

Nicolai Hartmann (1882–1950) was one of the very few imposing metaphysicians of his century. He was against all subjectivism: knowledge is the apprehension of something independent of the knowing. In his *Ethics* (1926, ET, 1932) he applies this viewpoint to moral values: these are known, are therefore objectively real. Natural facts can be contemplated coolly – they merely *are*, and operate according to causal laws; but ideals are commands or demands, require a feelingful attitude (e.g., respect and sense of responsibility), and determine nothing, that is, cannot realize themselves in the realm of fact. This impotence of ideals of goodness is the very condition of morality: they can be realized in the realm of fact only by beings in this realm and able to apprehend them, to decide to obey them, and able also freely to alter the state of fact by their own actions – and men are such beings. Any metaphysics that regards values as self-realizing or as realized by the purpose and power of a universal spirit makes moral responsibility impossible and the struggle of moral experience meaningless. It is to save morality that Hartmann rules out a metaphysics of either causal or teleological determinism, which latter, he believes, includes theism. He gives a thorough account of the system of moral values, but insists that the system cannot be completed: in man's unfinished career new forms of goodness manifest themselves from time to time.

T. E. JESSOP

Hatred

There is no one activity, or group of activities, which expresses an individual's hate. Few people in any generation love or hate deeply – the majority tend to suppress their feelings in the interest of keeping an uneasy peace within and around them. This refusal to feel deeply and live fully is the result of an unrecognized hatred for life itself.

The man who constantly loves is still capable of hating and the hater can still love. At times it is difficult to know if a deed is an expression of love or hate – even the doer of the deed may not know, for men often destroy the thing they love and preserve what they say they hate.

Hate and love are two ways of living: to hate is to break and attempt to destroy; to love is to bring new things into being.

At the centre of the Christian religion is a threefold injunction to love: 'Thou shalt love the Lord thy God . . . Thou shalt love thy neighbour as thyself'. That is, love God, love others, love yourself; act constructively, creatively. You cannot love God unless you love your neighbour and yourself; you cannot love your neighbour unless you love God and yourself; you cannot love yourself unless you love God and your neighbour. Loving yourself is losing sight of your own interests in loving God and your neighbour, or it is finding that your interests are becoming large enough to include the things of God and the things of all men. If you hate God you hate your neighbour and yourself; if you hate your neighbour you hate God and yourself, and if you hate yourself you hate God and your neighbour.

The causes of hatred are many and complex and the cure does not depend on finding the cause. Some of the causes are indicated under three headings, as follows: (1) *Hatred of God* – Men doubt and hate God because (*a*) the most necessary truths cannot be proved; (*b*) men cannot understand and control the physical universe any more than they can completely understand and control themselves; (*c*) events in the world appear to be a meaningless chaos in which some get more and some less than they deserve; and (*d*) men want freedom and at the same time long, unconsciously, to be prevented from misusing it. (2) *Hatred of Others* – A man hates others when he sees in everyone a threat to his own safety or importance; when he, knowing his own corruptibility, finds people who are impervious to threats, bribes or flattery; when he realizes that someone has become too dependent upon him or that he has become too dependent on someone. (3) *Hatred of Self* – A man hates himself for his inability to forgive himself for failure to achieve the successes in life which he had hoped for; when he sees the results of trying to possess or be possessed by one whom he loves; and when he cannot reconcile himself to his inability to overcome temptation and the power of sin by his own unaided efforts.

In any human relationship disordered love can banish love and replace it with one of love's counterfeits, for example, possessiveness or dominance, both of which are forms of hate even if not recognized as such.

In misplaced zeal for Christianity some Christians encourage their fellow members to hate the world that God loves; but to hate what he loves is to hate him.

R. E. C. BROWNE

Heaven

The traditional picture of heaven portrays the universal human aspiration to reach a highest good in this world and to achieve its lasting consummation in a cosmic and hierarchical order. The modern world-view, however, has not only abolished the literal equation, heaven = sky, but also calls into question the famous Kantian dictum that the moral law within has its sanction in the eternal order. The denial of the Christian tradition of heaven derives from political and cultural hostility, especially the Marxist-Leninist attack upon the idea of eternal life. Religious teachers, too, dislike the mystical other-worldliness which they associate with an escape from 'real' life. Modern ethical systems distrust a system of celestial incentives and the implicit self-interest which such a system encourages. Moreover, whereas heaven is a concept which presupposed that there is perfect truth and goodness as a transcendental fact related to God, moral empiricism denies its existence on the grounds of patent contradictions. The evidence taken from contemporary experience leads to the formulation of a moral relativism, in which all actions are seen and evaluated in the light of a complexity of motives. The sceptic uses this evidence as proof for the absence of the providential moral order.

Nevertheless a strong case can be made out for the traditional belief on empirical lines, such as the survival of the naive belief in 'the other world' among the less sophisticated, the revelations of 'the above' in dreams, the data of para-psychology, the self-transcendent properties found among ecstatics. The relevance of aesthetic activity to celestialism lies in its 'unearthly' quality and serves as evidence that man is not wholly self-enclosed. Most important for Christian moralists is heaven as the goal of ascetic practice, for it asserts that the discipline of desires in this world brings not only strength of character in this life but also sows the seeds of eternal life. Asceticism, positive in purpose and balanced in accord with reason, denies the gratification of appetites in order to secure the gradual ascent to heaven. The peculiar Christian emphasis on all mortifications lies in their connection with positive loving and a way of sacrifice which reflects Christ and the indwelling of the Holy Spirit. Heaven comes to stand thus for the glorious future and mystical union and eternal bliss, which God initiates among men to be made perfect, the 'There and Then' of virtuous conduct 'Here and Now'. *See* **Rewards and Punishments.**

John Baillie, *And the Life Everlasting*, 1950; F. H. Brabant, *The Everlasting Reward*, 1961; E. Brunner, *Eternal Hope*, 1954; Ulrich Simon, *Heaven in the Christian Tradition*, 1958; *The Ascent to Heaven*, 1961.

ULRICH SIMON

Hebrew Ethics. *see* Jewish Ethics; Old Testament Ethics.

Hedonism

Hedonism is the doctrine that pleasure (q.v.) is the chief good. *See* **Utilitarianism.**

Hegel, Georg Wilhelm Friedrich

The ethics of Hegel (1770–1831) is part of a rounded philosophy in which the universe is set forth as unfolding mind, essentially reason, which objectivizes itself in the creation and regular processes of the physical world and in the mind of man. His general method is to move from part to whole, from the incomplete to the completely developed, in which alone can the real nature of anything lesser be seen. In man the cosmic mind rises to consciousness of itself, our business being to express it in its universality or rationality, not to follow that which is peculiar in each of us, which includes what individualists call conscience. It is in that sense, not merely by reference to gregarious instinct and our obvious mutual dependence, that Hegel asserts the essential sociality of men. The individual as such is an unreal abstraction. The only human whole is a state: this is neither a sum of individuals nor an organizational device for the protection of individual interests alleged to be rights, but the highest form of objectivization of the cosmic reason, and the source of values that are truly common. The State is therefore that for which the individuals exist, so that their relation to it is one of entire subordination. Hegel thus virtually obliterates ethics as the study of the right relations of individuals to one another, leaving little more than a morality of political solidarity. Also, by maintaining that this form of solidarity is the widest and tightest achievable, the only real human whole, and that each state has its own local and temporal reason for its existence, he excludes moral relations among states. What political system is the best will become evident only in the one that eventually triumphs, this being the point of his famous saying that 'world-history is the world-tribunal'. His rationalism here seems to mean that what in the end is actualized is what must be called reason, whereas in some other parts of his system he seems to mean that what we can see to be reason is what will be actualized. The Hegelian elements taken over by Marx and given a materi-

alistic twist are the postulation of an inevitable goal of history, the process as a successive swinging from opposite to opposite with temporary conciliations to a stage that is final because tension within it is impossible, and the complete subordination of the individual to the social whole. *See* **Idealist Ethics.**

T. E. JESSOP

Hell

The conception of hell as a place under the earth where the damned receive everlasting punishment derives from mythology. The realm of the dead, Hades, beyond the Styx, the pit of destruction called Abaddon, the valley of Hinnon (Gehenna) where the people of Jerusalem burned their rubbish, the anonymity and oblivion of Sheol, became fused in the picture of the final destination of the unredeemed. With the rise of lurid portrayals of the end of the world and literal interpretations of apocalyptic teaching hell assumed proportions similar to that of heaven. This symmetrical arrangement features popular belief and is best to be studied in the iconography and sculpture of the Middle Ages (e.g., Bourges). Hell is ruled by the enemy Satan or Antichrist and governed by a hierarchy of evil powers and demonic angels. Hell stands for the permanent enclosure of evil, an enclave in God's universe. The best authorities, among them St Thomas Aquinas, refused to regard its fire and pains as metaphors and insist on the reality of the tortures of the wicked which are endless. They make up in endlessness that which they lack in severity.

The modern liberal reaction against this dogma has been sharp and is largely based upon ethical refutations. Hell is felt to be an offence against man's deepest moral convictions in as much as it sets up an eternal state of evil. In assigning reality to evil hell conflicts with the Christian apprehension of the character of God and his purpose for the world. Hell surrounds human responsibility with a web of mythological speculations. The argument that it sanctions goodness and grants emotional satisfaction to the victims of evil is to misread the experiences of martyrs and the sufferers of contemporary crimes. It is said that no one gassed at Auschwitz would have wished the perpetrators of the crime to continue to exist in an eternal concentration camp.

A way out of this very serious impasse may be found by a psychological understanding of hell. Men are demonically bent upon destruction and every virtue has its shadow and a heaven-hell dialectic governs human conduct. C. G. Jung shows with the aid of his archetypes that such an evaluation of evil gets to the root of human deviations. The imagery of hell is part of our existence. C. S. Lewis, too, corrects the balance in the moralists' too easy dismissal of Satan and outside demonic forces. Spiritual conflict without the antagonist and the symbol of perdition becomes meaningless. This new understanding of hell as a present reality recovers the essential strands of ancient thought without committing us to its eternal torments. See **Rewards and Punishments.**

Dante, *The Divine Comedy*; Karl Barth, *Church Dogmatics*, III, 3, 1961; A. Huxley, *Heaven and Hell*, 1956; C. S. Lewis, *The Screwtape Letters*, 1942; *The Great Divorce*, 1945; A. Winklhofer, *The Coming of His Kingdom*, 1963.

ULRICH SIMON

Heredity. see Environment and Heredity.

Heteronomy

Kant condemns as 'heteronomous' (as opposed to 'autonomous') any system which tries to derive ethics from anything but the nature of the rational will as such. He includes under 'heteronomous' systems egoistic hedonism, the moral sense theory, the metaphysical theory which derives morality from the concept of perfection and any theological theory of ethics. They are considered heteronomous because they all derive ethics from something else, thus destroying its unique character. Kant thus rejects them for a similar reason to that for which Moore rejects 'naturalism'. *See* **Kant and Kantian Ethics.**

A. C. EWING

Hindu Ethics

Ethical attitudes within Hinduism possess a complex diversity. Hinduism or the 'Everlasting Law' (*sanātana dharma*) is the result of the synthesis of a whole variety of religious and cultural elements in the Indian sub-continent. Since it contains within it a spectrum of theologies and customs, its unity is in certain respects rather formal. Thus on the theological side, Hindus look to the Veda or sacred revelation, but the interpretations placed thereon differ very widely; while the unity of customs is provided by the framework of the caste system, in which diversities are related through a complex of exclusive social categories. Certain motifs, however, in Hindu ethical thinking can be picked out; and it happens that in the modern period (from about the beginning of the nineteenth century) there is an increasing consensus on doctrinal and moral beliefs among educated Hindus.

In the principal Upaniṣads (eighth to fifth centuries BC) there is to be found the beginnings of a theory, later to become commonly accepted in Indian philosophy, about the ends of human life. These ends are: wealth (*artha*), desire (*karma*) and duty (*dharma*) – all of which should in principle subserve the supreme end of liberation or salvation (*mokṣa*). Since much, though not all, of Hindu thought has conceived of the means of liberation as involving the practice of meditation (*yoga*) and of withdrawal from wordly concerns, this theory of ends has been made practically consistent by a theory about stages of life (*āśramas*), which assigns different pursuits to different phases of the individual's career (by extension, the doctrine of reincarnatoin performs a rather similar function). Thus wealth, desire and duty are ends for the family man or householder; one graduates to this position after a period as a celibate student. Gradually the householder, as his children reach maturity, withdraws from these concerns; and the highest ideal is to reach the fourth *āśrama*, that of the wandering recluse or *sannyāsin*, bent solely upon spiritual knowledge and attainment. Since the realm of caste is defined by *dharma*, and since the recluse has left *dharma* behind, he is beyond caste and beyond social custom. This human arrangement is reflected in the doctrine sometimes stated in the Hindu tradition that likewise the Divine Being is 'beyond good and evil'.

The particular duties falling upon a person are defined by his social station. Certain rules (vegetarianism and abstention from liquor) apply to Brahmins, but not necessarily to other classes. The tensions created by such an ethical pluralism are expressed in the problem facing Arjuna in the *Bhagavadgītā*, before the battle to which he was committed and in which he would have to fight against, and perhaps kill, relatives and friends. Krishna, in the guise of Arjuna's charioteer, tells him that inactive detachment from the world is impossible. It remains Arjuna's duty to fight, for this duty belongs to his station in life. On the other hand he should practise a kind of active detachment – by renouncing the fruits of the deeds which he performs, and by performing them for the sake of the Lord. In this way liberation (*mokṣa*) will be granted by God. This teaching in the *Gītā* is in opposition to a widely held belief in ancient India – that any action (even a good one) is liable to bind one to the world and to the process of rebirth. It also expresses the relationship between faith in God and action which was to be worked out more fully in mediaeval Indian theism, with its stress on self-surrender to the Lord.

The *Gītā* encourages the warrior to fight on the ground that 'there is more happiness in doing one's own duty badly than in doing another's well'; but paradoxically it was the favourite spiritual reading of Gandhi (1869–1948), who was deeply committed to *ahiṁsā* or non-violence. He was giving a political dimension to another ancient motif in Indian ethics – the careful reverence for all forms of life, and by consequence the refraining from slaughter and cruelty to animals. On the other hand, the provisions of the ancient legal code could make applications of this sense of the sacredness of both human and non-human life which effectively cheapened the former. Thus the killing of a *śūdra* (a person belonging to the lowest of the four recognized classes) by a Brahmin attracted the same penalty as the killing of a dog or cat.

The last two centuries have seen a renaissance of Hinduism, partly under the stimulus of the challenge presented by western culture and Christianity. Reformers, beginning with Ram Mohan Roy (1772–1833), advocated social changes, social service was seen as flowing from the principles of religion, as in the teaching and practical endeavours of the Ramakrishna Mission, expressed most articulately by Swami Vivekananda (1862–1902). Gandhi, on the basis of the Hindu tradition itself, attacked castism, and in particular the exclusion of untouchables (whom he renamed *Larijans*, 'sons of God') from social and religious life. In addition, modern Hindus have seen as central to religious attitudes the virtue of tolerance, which reflects the all-embracing nature of Hinduism, together with the long, at least partial, emphasis on non-violence in the tradition. It is thus a common criticism of western Christianity that it often seems (to Indian eyes) to be exclusive and intolerant. These modern developments have given a new dynamic to the Upanisadic text that stresses the centrality of self-control (*dama*), giving (*dāna*) and mercy (*daya*).

The first of these is a reminder that the religious path in Hinduism has often been conceived as involving austerity and withdrawal, elements present in Gandhi's programme, which has helped to reinforce the puritanism of contemporary Indian society. Yet in terms of the total fabric of Hindu life it would be misleading to regard its ethic as 'world-negating'.

J. N. Farquhar, *Modern Religious Movements in India*, 1919; S. K. Maitra, *Ethics of Hindus*, 1958; William R. Miller, *Non-Violence, a Christian Interpretation*, 1965; I. C. Sharma, *Ethical Philosophies of India*, 1965; R. C. Zaehner, *Hinduism*, 1962.

NINIAN SMART

Hippocratic Oath

Hippocrates of Cos, *c.* 500 BC, has long been thought to have formulated the oath that bears his name, but modern scholarship has discredited the tradition. As the 'Father of Medicine' he remains an almost ghostly figure about whom much legend has gathered. Literary and historical criticism have also shown that the earliest extant version of the Oath is of the ninth century AD. The Greek pioneer in experimental physiology, Galen, who about 200 AD edited the Hippocratic Collection of treatises on medical subjects (for which no 'canon' is any longer possible), appears to have done something with the Oath. There is a considerable literature dealing with the

critical problems involved, comparable to studies of parts of the biblical materials. Investigation by modern methods shows that the Oath, along with other parts of the 'Hippocratic' *corpus*, have gone through untraceable and myriad changes at the hands of scribes, booksellers or manuscript merchants and expositors.

Its earliest versions appear to have been indenture agreements between master physicians and their apprentice-pupils, probably at the point of their becoming independent practitioners. Thus the opening promises were to be loyal to the master and to hand on medical knowledge to his descendants free of charge, if they want it. This part has been generally dropped from current versions, as schools of medicine have replaced apprentice training and as their graduation rituals have taken to administering the Oath as a corporate promise, *en bloc*, in the second personal plural. Physicians are nowadays asked in each case to swear their professional oath 'by whatever he holds most sacred', thus allowing for the religious and non-religious pluralism of modern culture. The very earliest versions may have had no vow at all, not even to Aesculapius (son of Apollo and father of Panacea, medicine's god-sponsor, and Hygeia, health's). There are grounds for viewing the Oath as ethically archaic.

A logical reduction of the Oath yields four promises of ethical importance for medicine: (1) to make the patient's interests supreme (my work will be 'for the benefit of my patients' and 'not for their hurt or any wrong'); (2) to refuse to give a 'deadly drug to any, though it be asked of me'; (3) to refuse to terminate any pregnancies, that is, 'aid a woman to procure an abortion'; and (4) to preserve professional secrets and the patients' privilege of communication ('whatsoever things I see or hear' in medical attendance 'which ought not to be noised abroad' will be kept as 'sacred secrets').

The *first* promise is undisputed as an ideal, but nevertheless is constantly infringed by the increase of direct human medical experimentation with new drugs and procedures. Sometimes these experiments and tests are carried out without the patients' knowledge and could not practically be revealed or interpreted, their moral defence being rested on claims of the general welfare. Issues arise around a fair interpretation of 'benefit' and 'hurt' and 'wrong'. The *second* promise has commonly been broadened to mean a repudiation of euthanasia. But this vow is thought to have been originally aimed against physicians becoming accessories to poison murders and assassination, especially political and familial. Some scholars have reasoned that the Pythagoreans, with their mystical doctrine of escape from this life to another, were the targets aimed at, but disciples of Hippocrates actually engaged in direct medical euthanasia. (Indirect euthanasia, 'letting the patient go' *in extremis*, is not in question.)

The *third* promise, if taken to be against abortion as such, runs into trouble with the modern acceptance of voluntary medical or 'therapeutic' abortion, and with voluntary terminations for 'non-medical' causes (mental health and social welfare). But there is good ground for taking the promise to have been against the unsafe and medically unsound use of *aborti-facients* in ancient Greece. The *fourth* promise, like the first, is an undisputed principle of medical respect for professional confidences, and has considerable (but not universal or constant) support in civil law; moral and legal exceptions are taken when the preservation of such secrets would victimize innocent third parties, as in the case of a seaside lifeguard suffering from serious cardiac failure and unwilling to let it be known. *See* **Medical Ethics.**

JOSEPH FLETCHER

History of Ethics.
see Ethics, History of.

Hobbes, Thomas

The textbook tradition is that Thomas Hobbes (1588–1679) was an atheist in religion, a materialist in metaphysics, and in ethics a determinist and egoist, holding also that good and evil are what civil law enjoins and forbids respectively. These labels have to be interpreted in the light of his general theoretical aim, viz., to construct a system in which the behaviour of matter, of men individually, and of men in politically organized communities could all be explained by the same principles. He took these from the new mechanics of his day – matter, and motion as the only process and the only and inexorable cause – because he thought that these alone were wholly clear and definite and therefore alone amenable to logical treatment; he expressly excluded God and historical events as not so amenable, but not denying their existence. In extending those principles analogically to man's mental life he conceived this as a play of forces, in which the strongest always wins. Taking desires thus as quantitative, he defined an act of will as the desire that happens to be the strongest. His dogma that every desire is basically for self-preservation (though sometimes for selfish power) was probably an analogue drawn from the mechanical principle of inertia as well as his reading of human nature in that age of civic strife; for, having a low estimate of empirical proof, the evidence he offered for it was scanty and loose, for example, his definition of compassion as fear at the sight of another's misfortune that a like lot may befall oneself is an unsupported epigram. That, of course, is moral psychology of a sort, not ethics. He applies it to the problem of political

government, practically to show how this could be made effective, theoretically to define the ground and scope of ruling power and civic obedience. The immediate application is that 'every man is enemy to every man', since everybody cannot help seeing that everybody else is as egoistic as himself, seeking his own by any means within his power. Such are men in their 'natural condition'. How, then, is the fact of politically shaped society to be explained? By the dreadful consequences of lawless egoism, viz. 'the life of man (is) solitary, poor, nasty, brutish and short', so intolerable that even selfish interest demands a change, the form of which intelligence prescribes: all individuals clashing in a given area shall surrender their way of living as they please to one person (or several) and give him absolute authority along with whatever armed power he may need to enforce it irresistibly. This is not history, but the logical implicate of Hobbes's egoistic psychology. The sovereign's rule shall cover all externals, therefore the Church's rules of discipline, rites, and statements of dogma, and what he commands is to be counted good and what he forbids bad. It was Hobbes's urgent concern with the political problem that made him throw into prominence that stark line of thought. Having made this clear he shows that it is an initial methodological abstraction by proceeding to additions and qualifications. (1) Human nature is not in fact only a bundle of desires seeking satisfaction by hook or crook. It includes 'right reason', awareness of moral distinctions and imperatives, for example, justice, fidelity to covenants, mercy, gratitude. These oblige internally, but are so contrary to our raw passions that we can be brought to follow them only when each of us is externally coerced and knows that everybody else is; that is, the properly moral laws can become operative in conduct only under the security against exploiting selfishness which absolute political authority alone can ensure. The full justification of this absoluteness is, then, that it is the sole condition of peace and of morality and all other constituents of civilization. (2) The moral laws of reason or conscience come from God, to whom subjects and sovereign are indefeasibly responsible internally. (3) In external conduct citizens remain wholly subject to the sovereign, the latter not to them but to God alone, in which relation he is obliged to respect the moral laws as far as the citizens' obedience makes that possible. (4) The better citizens will sometimes have the agony of having to choose between obeying God 'too much', so disobeying the sovereign, and obeying the sovereign 'too much', so offending God – a dilemma which Hobbes left unresolved. Although he was fashioning what he took to be a universally valid political philosophy, he was arguing throughout in particular against the contemporary Puritan claims that the sovereign is responsible to the citizens, that his laws should always be consonant with the moral laws, and that every citizen has the right to judge by his own conscience the *particular external applications* of moral laws and to *behave* accordingly: the result, he thought, would be anarchy, the worst of all evils. There is no reason for doubting the sincerity of Hobbes's appeal to moral laws and God, but he could not integrate them into his materialistic system.

R. Peters, *Hobbes*, 1956; A. E. Taylor, *Hobbes*, 1908.

T. E. JESSOP

Holiness

Recognition of holiness as that which belongs to sacred things and acts is the raw material of all religions, whether theistic or not. It implies a separation between the sacred and the profane or ordinary, the sacred having a mysterious, supernatural power which induces feelings of awe, fear, reverence and attraction.

The predominant OT emphasis is that holiness is not a quality of things and actions in themselves, but a characteristic of God alone; words, places, cults, people, receiving holiness solely from their dedicated relationships to the all holy Lord. Also, in OT holiness acquires the quality of moral righteousness (Lev. 19 and the eighth-century prophets) as well as retaining a sense of the numinous and that of cosmic transcendence characteristic of the Book of Job

In NT the Scripture (Rom. 1.2), the Christian's self-offering (Rom. 12.1), the brethren (Heb. 3.1), angels (Mark 8.38) are called holy. Supremely, Christ is addressed as the holy one of God (Mark 1.24); and his atoning death is figured in the imagery of the holy sacrifice (Heb. 7.26). The triune God is adored as thrice holy (Rev. 4.8) and the heavenly Jerusalem is the holy city (Rev. 21.2).

Out of this biblical background the Church has ascribed holiness to worship, to places, to words, to names, when they are connected directly with God from whom their holiness derives; for example, Augustine speaks of 'an external offering being a visible sacrament of an invisible sacrifice, that is, a holy sign' (*De Civ. Dei*, X.5). Holy communion is the Lord's own service; holy days are the representative offering for sanctifying the whole of time on the principle 'if the . . . first fruits is holy, so is the whole lump' (Rom. 11.16).

By a further delegation of the divine holiness certain kinds of human life are deemed holy. The baptized are a holy people. But in a more specialized usage, holiness is the quality of the holy man whose goodness has a fervour and an interior centre which gives it an impressiveness lacking in more creaking obedience to moral law. Such holiness is equivalent to sanctity. It appears sometimes as a spontaneous religious phenomenon and occasionally as an abnor-

mality (cf. W. James, *The Varieties of Religious Experience* (1902), Lectures XI–XV, Saintliness). Mostly it is a religious achievement cultivated by that growth in purity and stability prescribed by the masters of the spiritual life. This requires some ascesis, self-denial, curbing of self-will, abandonment to divine providence, and sometimes mystical union with God through the dark nights of senses and spirit. At least it requires a genuine desire to become what God intends one to be, prompted and sustained by that power of the divine action known as the Holy Spirit. If one book is to be mentioned it must be *The Imitation of Christ*.

M. Eliade, *Patterns in Comparative Religion*, 1958, Chap. 1; R. Otto, *The Idea of the Holy*, 1923; N. Sdöerblom and R. H. Coats, 'Holiness', *HERE*.

V. A. DEMANT

Homicide

It is necessary to distinguish between homicide that is accidental, culpable, and justifiable. (1) *Accidental*. It is not difficult to think of situations in which a person has been killed as a result of actions which have been in no sense willed either by the dead man or by others. A mountaineer might slip and knock a colleague who falls to his death as the rope snaps which links him with his companions. Let it be assumed that he and his friends were fit and qualified to make the climb, and that there had been no negligence when checking the serviceableness of the climbing gear. It is evident that in this and all comparable instances neither the victim nor his associates are blameworthy. (2) *Culpable*. A man's right to life is conferred upon him not by other men but by God the Lord and Giver of all life. A man's life is his to use but God remains the absolute owner of it and man is answerable to him for the use he makes of it. Since it does not belong to man absolutely, it is not within the moral competence of any man deliberately to destroy it. Thus it is never permissible to make any deliberate attack upon the life of oneself or of another person (even at his invitation), whether such an attack be the immediate effect or the inevitable, foreseen and directly intended consequence of one's action (or inaction). When such an attack is made and death ensues, it is an instance of culpable homicide. This is the act of murder to which the sixth Commandment refers. Examples of culpable homicide include the directly induced abortion of a human foetus, compulsory and voluntary euthanasia, infanticide, and suicide ('self-murder') (qq.v.). In any particular case the degree of culpability will depend upon all the circumstances in which the act was committed, including the mental condition of the offender(s). (3) *Justifiable*. It has been claimed that in no circumstances can an action be justified which involves the taking of human life. This is not the traditional Christian view. The right to life implies the right to defend one's own life or the life of another person against an unjust attack. Since the defence can only be effective if it is in proportion to the violence of the unjust attack, it is possible that in the act of defending himself (or another) the victim may kill his assailant. Assuming that any appeal to public justice was at that time out of the question, the defendant acted justifiably and was in no sense guilty of homicide. His purpose was *not* to kill his adversary but only to preserve his own (or another person's) life against an unjust attack. It would be an act of culpable homicide only if the victim could have been adequately defended without causing the assailant's death. It is by this same principle of self-defence against unjust aggression that capital punishment and killing in war may be justified. Under God the State is responsible for the maintenance of law and order and the protection of its citizens as a whole. This implies the right to adopt the extreme measure of the capital punishment of particular offenders *when the State cannot otherwise fulfil its general duty of defence.* When, however, the State finds it no longer necessary to exercise this right it cannot justly continue to do so and it should revise its criminal code accordingly. At any given period opinions may differ about the correct interpretation of the available relevant information; but many countries have already concluded that with them capital punishment can safely be abolished. The State is also responsible under God for the protection of the lives and property of its citizens against unjust attack from without. The fulfilment of this duty may involve the extreme measure of resorting to war. Thus in a just war (which is, by definition, essentially a 'defensive' war) a soldier cannot be accused of culpable homicide when the taking of an enemy's life becomes an unavoidable act in the performance of his military duty. Whether in any particular instance a country may truly be said to be engaged in a just war is another question; and it is a matter of present debate whether the defending country could continue to claim that it was engaged in an otherwise just war the moment it resorted to the use of nuclear bombs which are by their nature weapons of indiscriminate destruction.

Norman St John-Stevas, *Life, Death and the Law*, 1961; Thomas Wood, *Some Moral Problems*, 1961.

THOMAS WOOD

Homosexuality and Homosexualism

Homosexuality is a personal condition, not a kind of behaviour (for which the term *homo-sexualism* is used here). It consists in a general propensity towards members of the same sex and is found in both men and women. Its cause is not certainly known, but there are psychological indications that it is probably a form of inadequacy due to environmental conditions in early childhood (faulty parent-child relationship, disharmony between the subject's father and mother, etc.). But the possibility cannot be excluded that in some cases it may be due to genetic or hormonic factors. Homosexuality seems to vary in intensity in different individuals, and when it is deeply rooted reorientation is usually impossible; then the most effective help is to assist the subject to accept his handicap in a positive spirit.

As a handicapped person the homosexual presents society with peculiar and neglected problems; but moralists and legislators have usually shown more concern with homosexualism than with the adjustment of the homosexual. Homosexuality generally disposes the subject to self-expression in physical acts with others of the same sex, and when moral or social restraints are weak or absent there may be occasional or habitual indulgence in some kind of homosexualism. In certain circumstances, for example, segregation in a single-sex environment, heterosexuals may resort to substitutive acts of homosexualism; or they may do so viciously, experimentally, or as prostitutes. Such ambisexual behaviour by heterosexuals further complicates the problem of homosexuality and has led to confusion of its metaphysical aspect by the postulating of a hypothetical 'bisexual' or intermediate state.

There is no historical evidence of the incidence of the homosexual condition, though we may assume that it has been fairly constant. But from earliest times there is abundant evidence of homosexualism, and anthropology has established proof of its widespread occurrence among many peoples and cultures. It has not been consistently treated, however, by law, society or religion. Some cultures have tolerated or even institutionalized it; others have ignored it; and others again have penalized it or attempted to suppress it.

Biblical references to homosexualism are few. The OT condemns sodomy (?) as typical of the ethos of heathenism (*tōʿēbhāh*) and prescribes the death penalty (Lev. 18.22; 20.13). The NT denounces male and female homosexualism (Rom. 1.26–27) and specifies catamites and sodomists (I Cor. 6.9–10; I Tim. 1.9–10). But there is no foundation for the prevalent belief that Sodom and Gomorrah (Gen. 19) were destroyed for homosexualism; their sin is otherwise described in Ezek. 16.49–50, Wisd. 10.8; 19.8, Ecclus. 16.8. The 'homosexual' conception of this sin first appeared in the second century BC among Palestinian rigorists and patriots and seems to have been inspired by hatred of the Greek way of life; its emergence and development can be traced in the Pseud-epigrapha (*see* D. S. Bailey, *Homosexuality and the Western Christian Tradition*, pp. 9–28). This reinterpretation of the sin of Sodom is reflected in Philo, *de Abr.* 26 and Josephus, *Ant.*, I.xi.1 and 3, and left its mark upon the NT (Jude 6–7, cf. II Peter 2.4,6–8), whence it influenced Christian thought.

Roman law also moulded Christian attitudes. Homosexualism was apparently punishable under the obscure *lex Scantinia* (*c.* 226 BC), but legal interest in the matter properly dates from the third century, when jurists began to extend the *lex Julia de adulteriis* (*c.* 17 BC) by interpretative commentary aimed at protecting minors (*Dig.* XLVII.xi.1 § 2 imposing the death penalty if the offence was *perfectus*) and preventing loan of premises for the purpose of committing *stuprum cum masculo* (*Dig.* XLVIII. v.8). Under the later emperors there was further legislation. A curious edict of Constantius and Constans (342) may be aimed at male prostitu-tion (*Cod. Just.*, IX.ix.31) but more notable is that of Theodosius, Arcadius, and Valentinian (390) which prescribed death by burning for sodomy (*Cod. Theod.*, IX.vii.6). Some mediaeval systems of customary law preserved this penalty but it is doubtful whether it was ever inflicted. Justinian issued two *novellae* (77,141) against homosexualism in 538 and 544, which are remarkable because for the first time the Sodom story is invoked, and because his aim was not so much to punish as to bring offenders to repentance; legal penalties are reserved for the obdurate.

Scattered allusions in the literature and canons show that the early Church regarded male homosexualism as gravely sinful but not as deserving exemplary treatment. Penalties varied from nine years penance (Greg. Nyss., *epist. can.*, 4) to perpetual excommunication (*Conc. Illib.*, 71); political considerations may account for some of the severer enactments in Gothic Spain in the seventh century. (*Lex. Vis.*, III.v.4,7; *Conc. XVI.Tolet.*, 3). The Penitentials (especially Cummean's) contain a comprehen-sive treatment of homosexual sin; they recog-nize female practices, they distinguish between different acts, and they attempt to fit penances to the supposed gravity of the offence. In one instance in the Middle Ages there is an apparent connection between homosexualism and heresy. In the tenth and eleventh centuries Manichaean ideas infiltrated from Bulgaria into the West and became established in Provence, and there is little doubt that allegations of sodomy made against certain of the Albigensians were justi-fied; this explains in part the gradual transfer-ence of the epithet *bougre* (Bulgarian) from heresy to sodomy. In general the Middle Ages regarded homosexualism as properly cognizable by the Church, which imposed spiritual penal-ties but rarely surrendered offenders to the civil magistrate.

There is little useful consideration of the morality of homosexualism until Aquinas's discussion of *peccata contra naturam* (*Summa Theologica*, Part II, Second Section, qq. 152–4). He argues that the sexual organs must not be used for acts which preclude generation; there-fore *concubitus ad non debitum sexum* is a sin next in gravity to bestiality. Today an assess-ment of this question would be less narrowly based, but Christian moralists would at least restrict relational non-generative use of the sexual organs to heterosexual relationships in marriage. It would therefore be held that homo-sexualism is always materially sinful but that its formal sinfulness (and therefore blame-worthiness) must depend upon such factors as the knowledge or ignorance of the agent. Some would consider such 'traditional' moral judgments inadequate, however, and would contend that relational integrity should also be an important determinant of the morality of homosexualism.

Should homosexualism be regarded as criminal? This question involves legal con-siderations affecting other forms of sexual behaviour, including the attitude of society to female homosexualism. Current legal provisions in regard to private homosexualism between consenting adult males vary between tolerance in France (under the *Code Napoleon*) and severe treatment in Britain (under statutes of 1861 and 1885, modifying laws of 1533 and 1828 which made sodomy a felony punishable by death); and between these extremes there is a wide range of enactment. In Britain the Wolfenden Committee (*Report*, 1957) recom-mended that homosexualism should not in any form be cognizable by law unless it infringed public order and decency, offended or injured the citizen, or exploited or corrupted others (particularly the young and persons in special positions of dependence). This may be re-garded as representative of liberal opinion which advocates repeal of laws which are held to be barbarous legacies from the past; but strong emotional factors, social and personal, impede reform.

D. S. Bailey, *Homosexuality and the Western Christian Tradition*, 1955; *Sexual Offenders and Social Punishment*, 1956; D. J. West, *Homo-sexuality*, 1955.

SHERWIN BAILEY

Honesty

Honesty for honesty's sake can only appeal to a person who worships and serves his own virtue and not almighty God. An honest man must be honest about something and about the circumstances in which he is acting. A Christian holds that honesty is a necessary element in the expression of a man's love for God, his neigh-bours and himself.

Christianity teaches that a man is to be honest

in thought, word and deed. Some suggestions about what honesty implies in these spheres are as follows: (1) *Honesty in Thought*: (*a*) continually distinguishing between opinions which may be changed and beliefs which are to be held; (*b*) neither falsifying nor ignoring facts which disturb established opinions or appear to undermine beliefs; (*c*) examination of the obligations arising from relationships and reflection on the need to avoid the hasty formation of relationships; continually remembering that no man, knowingly or unknowingly, having begun a relationship can ever completely control its course; and (*d*) never judging wrongdoers on insufficient evidence. (2) *Honesty in Word:* (*a*) accuracy in giving information; (*b*) making contracts and promises in clear terms; (*c*) in argument no pretence of establishing by proof what can only be perceived by faith; (*d*) being ready to talk to anyone but unwilling to prolong a conversation unnecessarily; (*e*) listening carefully to others and replying as truth and love require; and (*f*) not claiming anyone's time and attention under false pretences. Salesmen, copywriters, politicians, publicity agents, journalists and other writers and speakers have their special temptations to dishonesty in the use of words. These temptations will be most fully understood by those churchmen, lay and clerical, who are called on to make public statements about church life and their own particular work in the church. (3) *Honesty in Deed:* (*a*) in all money transactions being as accurate as a trained accountant; (*b*) in public affairs being as precise as a dependable secretary; (*c*) being equally careful of private and public property; (*d*) being appropriate in deeds which truthfully express the doer's care for those who benefit by them.

R. E. C. BROWNE

Honour

The fifth of the Ten Commandments is 'honour your father and your mother' (Ex. 20.12). Not 'obey', but 'honour'; it can be necessary to disobey parents, but this can be done without dishonouring them. The Christian Scriptures explain our concept of honour with its injunctions: 'honour to whom honour is due' (Rom. 13.7) and 'honour all men' (I Peter 2.17). (1) *Honour to whom honour is due:* In our situation, to whom is honour due? Church office bearers, officials in the government, universities, schools, city corporations and international organizations are honoured as officials who would have no power at all were it not given them. This power is given to each by his institution. Institutions would have no power unless it were given them by God. The gross behaviour of some institutions may hide but cannot alter this fact. Christians in honouring institutions and officials should continue to do so in spite

of the justified criticisms they must make, recognizing the ways an institution opposes the Church deliberately or unkowingly. The honouring consists in being a good member without losing the ability to criticize and in bearing the burden of being a member of several institutions at the same time. (2) *Honour all men:* Honour all men because each man is born with the dignity of being human, an individual made in the image of God. He may hide this dignity by wilful ignorance, indiscipline and self-will. No matter how low a man may sink he continues to be capable of honouring and being honoured. Honouring men means the keeping of a right attitude towards those near us and to associate ourselves actively with all movements, sponsored by Church or not, concerned with the making of conditions more fit for human living.

It is important that individuals receive the honour paid to them as officials and as men. Men honour themselves by honouring others. At the same time people must be protected from thinking that they enlarge the office by their personality; rather they must realize that it is the office which enlarges them.

R. E. C. BROWNE

Hooker, Richard

Richard Hooker (*c*. 1554–1600) was the classical exponent of the Anglican *via media*. His *Treatise of the Laws of Ecclesiastical Polity* (Books. I–IV, 1594; V, 1597; VI and VIII, 1648; VII, 1662) was an eirenic attempt to resolve, within the framework of a coherent theological system, the issues raised in his controversy (when Master of the Temple, 1585–91) with Walter Travers, spokesman of those who wished to reform the English Church on the Geneva pattern. Rejecting 'Scripture only', Hooker appealed to reason, Scripture and tradition as complementary authoritative guides in morals as in belief and worship. The key to his teaching lies in his theory of law (Book I) which, with minor modifications, follows closely the *De Legibus* of Aquinas (*Summa Theologica*, Part II, First Section, qq. 90–108). All the laws of the universe find their ground in the eternal law of God's own being. Man participates in this eternal law and perceives his chief moral duties by the law of reason (natural law). This is confirmed, interpreted and amplified by divine positive law revealed in Scripture, without which sinful man cannot attain to his supernatural end. In so far as human laws (civil and ecclesiastical, national and international, public and private) are deduced from or consistent with natural and divine positive law, they are just and obligatory. He thought of Church and State as two aspects of one and the same Christian society. But, unlike the Caroline high churchmen who were to defend the divine right of kings, he favoured an essentially contractual theory of political government. Book VIII, which appears to replace a lost original but is 'authentic Hooker' (Sisson), treats of the doctrine and practice of repentance and argues, against Rome, that auricular confession must be voluntary and that priestly absolution is declarative and not judicial.

Works, ed. J. Keble, 3 vols., 1836. (There is an edition of *E.P.* in Everyman's Library, 2 vols.); J. S. Marshall, *Hooker and the Anglican Tradition*, 1963; P. Muntz, *The Place of Hooker in the History of Thought*, 1952; F. J. Shirley, *Richard Hooker and Contemporary Political Ideas*, 1949; C. J. Sisson, *The Judicious Marriage of Mr Hooker and the Birth of the Laws of Ecclesiastical Polity*, 1940; L. S. Thornton, *Richard Hooker*, 1924.

THOMAS WOOD

Hope

In common speech the word 'hope' states an uncertainty – 'He is very forgetful, I hope he remembers to come.' In the language of the Christian religion the word is used in statements of certainty. The Christian uses the word 'hope' to express his belief in the measureless power and love of God who is never idle but active in every movement of life, never living for men but always with them. Hope is the fruit of believing in the ceaseless creative activity of God even when living seems no more than being tangled in conflicts with others and within oneself, between and within groups. The psalmist knew this experience when he wrote 'I should utterly have fainted but that I believe verily to see the goodness of the Lord in the land of the living'. This phrase assumes, rightly, that men cannot see exactly what God will do or is doing. They do know that he works with them and through them and therefore they know that all genuine human work has genuine results whether men discern them or not.

It is said that we walk by faith and not by sight. The walking (that is, the thoughts, words and deeds of day-to-day living) generates and is generated by faith. Faith is not a substitute for knowledge and thinking: it is the acceptance of the facts that all human knowledge is fragmentary and all human thinking incomplete, but that men have sufficient knowledge and power of thought to live coherently and significantly. This kind of living is an expression of faith, hope and love.

Christians regard faith, hope and love as the three fundamental virtues (*see* I Cor. 12.27–13.13). They cannot be treated separately though they may be distinguished from one another. Thought about them always shows that love depends on faith and hope; faith, on hope and love; hope, on faith and love. No action can be described as the sole expression of any one of these three virtues. These virtues are not static commodities as implied in such remarks as – 'If only we had more hope. . . .' Hope, like faith and love, is a dynamic quality of living which is discernible, spasmodically, in the complex, ceaselessly moving pattern of human behaviour.

Hope is not to be confused with optimism's assurance that all will be well in the end. *See* **Optimism**. Hope is the style of living which proclaims that all is well here and now despite alarms, dangers and anxiety.

R. E. C. BROWNE

Hosea

Hosea, one of the early Hebrew prophets, taught in the eighth century BC. Like the other prophets, he stressed ethical action as against mere cultic observance, though he seems to have left a place for a reformed worship that would be tied to the quality of life. His most important ethical contribution was his development of the ideals of love and mercy. Equally important is the way in which he links these qualities in man and God. This is done through the parallel which he draws (Chaps. 1–3) between his love for an unfaithful bride whom he seeks to win back, and God's continuing love for apostate Israel. Through this teaching, the way is opened for a wider role for the virtues of love, mercy and faithfulness, alongside the sterner virtues of justice and righteousness, stressed by Hosea's contemporary, Amos. More than this, it is suggested that these virtues, as we meet them in man, have their prototype in God, and in God's dealings with man. *See* **Old Testament Ethics**.

EDITOR

Hospitality

Christian Scriptures (*see specially* Matt. 25, Luke 14 and John 12) make many references to hospitality. The essence of hospitality is a readiness to accept people as members of the household, temporarily, for short or long periods as the circumstances indicate. Hospitable people welcome guests without drawing attention to all the preparations that have been made, and guests are grateful and show it without expressing surprise at the host's thoughtful consideration. Before there can be hospitality there must be both hosts and guests; to be a good guest requires as much generosity, liveliness and imagination as it does to be a good host. Hospitality graciously offered and graciously received enriches the household that provides it as well as the guest who enjoys it. In present conditions, the field of hospitality is widened to include entertaining others at hotels, restaurants and cafes as well as numerous kinds of hospitality offered in the business world, in schools, universities, factories, etc.

Hospitality is more than kindness and friendship. The Church, government, university and other institutions depend on it because it makes for the informal conversations which stimulate creative thinking and action. Such conversations nourish the genius, the prophet, the saint or the artist. Hospitality has enabled countless people (as guests and hosts) to recognize their own ability as well as the abilities of others.

The Church is strong where those who worship together are at ease in enjoying each other's hospitality. Christians believe that it is not merely the entertaining of fellow members but that non-Christians are also to be welcomed, not patronizingly, but mindful that the poorest people are not only the materially poor but also the spiritually destitute. In short, hospitality can be a means of grace where it is freely given and freely received.

R. E. C. BROWNE

Hospitals. see Medical Ethics; Social Service of the Church.

Household Codes

At least since the days of Luther the term *Haustafeln* has been applied to Eph. 5.22–6.9 and Col. 3.18–4.1 in which exhortations are given *ad seriatim* to the various members of a household, that is, wives, husbands, children, fathers, slaves and masters. The term is sometimes used more widely to include similar NT passages, for example, I Peter 2.(13)18–3.7(8 ff.); I Tim. 2.8 ff.–3.13; 5.1–22; Titus 2.1–10. It is commonly noted that this parenetic form was characteristic of Hellenism (Plutarch, *On the Training of Children*, 10; Seneca, *Epistles*, 94.1; 95.45; Diogenes Laertius, VII 108; Epictetus, II, 10, II 14.8, II 17.31; Marcus Aurelius, V 31) but also of Jewish literature (Ecclus. 7.18–36; Philo, *On the Decalogue*, 165–7; Josephus, *Against Apion*, II 24–28; Ps. Phocylides, 175 ff.). However, a majority of these passages refer to the attitudes an individual should take towards various groups rather than to the behaviour of those groups themselves. Early Christian literature continued this form of parenesis (*Didache*, 4.9–11; *Barnabas*, 19.5–8; I *Clement*, 1.3; 21.6–9; Ignatius, *To Polycarp*, 4.1–6.3; Polycarp, *To the Philippians*, 4.1–6.3). It has been argued that a common, catechetical tradition stands behind the various versions of the Household Codes extant in Christian literature. There is need for further research in this area.

'Near to the church stood the Christian home' (Schlier). The leaders were anxious to bring the relations of the home and of the total life into the obedience of Christ. Their specific injunctions were neither novel nor distinctively Christian. It is scarcely revolutionary to suggest that wives, children and slaves should be obedient to husbands, fathers and masters respectively. (However, Ephesians has a distinctive digression on the husband-wife relationship as a parallel to Christ and his Church; Colossians has a disproportionately long exhortation to the slaves.) The distinctive Christian element is to be found in the repeated references to the 'Lord' which indicate that for the believer Christ is the master of family as well as of all other relationships. There is no doctrine of legal equality, for example, between husbands and wives, but it is made clear that the legal relationship is transcended in Christ.

The eschatological expectations of the early Christian community might have led to a rejection of all the patterns by which ancient life was held together, but the Household Codes are one of the evidences that this did not occur. The Christian community, while recognizing that all earthly relationships were subordinate to the coming Kingdom, expected those relationships to continue not only decently and in order but also 'in the Lord'. This was the beginning of the long struggle through which the Church has attempted to bring group and institutional patterns into obedience with the will of Christ.

In addition to commentaries on the passages mentioned *see* D. Daube, *The New Testament and Rabbinic Judaism*, 1956, pp. 90–105; E. G. Selwyn, *The First Epistle of St Peter*, 1947, pp. 363–488; K. Weidinger, *Die Haustafeln*, 1928; O. J. F. Seitz, 'Lists, Ethical', *Interpreter's Dictionary of the Bible*, III, 1962, pp. 137–9.

HARVEY K. MCARTHUR

Huguenots

The Reformation in France, while subject to Lutheran influence, naturally followed the teaching of the Picardy-born John Calvin. The first Reformed congregation was organized in Paris in 1555 and four years later seventy-two congregations constituted the first national synod of the Reformed Church in France. It was about this time that the French Calvinists were given the nickname of 'Huguenots'.

Varied explanations have been given for the origin of this nickname. It is said that a monk in a sermon first used the term in a derogatory sense because it was alleged that the Protestants at Tours frequented by night the gate of King Hugo who in a mediaeval romance was depicted as a ghost. Another explanation is that there was once a diminutive coin of that name and their enemies applied it to the Huguenots because they were of little significance. A more satisfactory interpretation is that when the bilingual city of Geneva was beseiged by the Roman Catholic Duke of Savoy in 1550, the French Protestants within the city had a leader called 'Hugues' and to his followers the German population applied the name 'Hugues genossen' which was contracted to 'Huguenots'. In France it was first applied to the followers of De la Renaudie, a reckless, brilliant adventurer who gathered around him a group of varied people, some from Geneva, in order to rebel against the persecution of the Calvinists.

The Huguenots can be regadred as the Puritans of France. Their sole code of conduct was the Bible and because of their devotion to it as the Word of God they developed a strong and sturdy character as a people with a faith that proved unshakable in the face of much persecution at the hands of successive kings of France. Those that were forced to emigrate invariably displayed in each of their adopted countries the Calvinistic spirit of consecration, work and talents being dedicated to the glory of God. They were the most gifted people that France ever produced.

Those that remained at home continued the struggle for freedom until in 1787 and 1789 civil and religious liberty was granted. By 1801 their legal rights as a church body were recognized. They divided into two groups in 1848, the moderates who accepted state aid and the traditionalists who refused it, but since all state subsidies to churches were abolished in 1905, both groups now belong to the Protestant Federation of France.

H. M. Baird, *History of the Rise of the Huguenots*, 2 vols., 1880; A. J. Grant, *The Huguenots*, 1934; C. Weiss, *Histoire des Réfugiés protestants de France*, 1853, English translation with American supplement, 1854.

S. J. KNOX

Humanism and Humanitarianism

Discussions of the term 'humanism' usually begin with an apology for not defining it. Humanism has indeed undergone so many mutations in the history of western thought that precise definition is not to be expected. Despite the attempts made in this direction by such American thinkers as Oliver Reiser, Corliss Lamont, and Ralph Barton Perry, 'humanism' remains what Perry calls a very versatile word. Yet its tenacity no less than its versatility needs to be accounted for; one may say that however indefinable, humanism is also an indispensable term for characterizing certain recurring stresses within modern and especially contemporary thought.

In the nineteenth century, as Henri de Lubac has reminded us, humanism makes its appearance in at least three forms – the Nietzschean, the Comtean or positivist, and the Marxist. Their ancestry is dubious at many points, but like their Renaissance and classical counterparts they lay down the principle that man is the measure of things. They are similar, however at variance with each other, in their common rejection of belief in God as either explaining or sanctioning human conduct, and in their common insistence that man must seek his ground and goal within his own intrinsic nature. Humanism therefore, in all three of these forms, takes the 'death of God' seriously

as freeing man once for all from his ancient bondage to whatever has hitherto seemed transcendent or supernatural; it regards man as the summit of the evolutionary process and the sufficient reason of his own existence; and it places upon man the sole responsibility for his betterment and fulfilment. As a matter of fact, the dignitative use of the word 'man' is one of the hallmarks of the humanist mode of thought.

In the twentieth century humanism acquires further connotations without abandoning its basic premisses. It becomes institutionalized in Communism. It finds academic expression in the aristocratic social and moral philosophies of men like Paul Elmer More and Irving Babbitt. It is enunciated as the platform of a group of religious liberals, mostly left-wing Unitarians, who would offer man or humanity as a God-substitute. It becomes the more or less explicit battle-cry of scholars and teachers of the humanities who wish to protect the wholeness and uniqueness of human experience against the encroaching effects of scientific naturalism.

Such contradictory variety makes a general interpretation difficult, but also necessary. Towards such an interpretation there are some observations which may certainly be advanced. It may be said that in our century humanism takes on greater depth and density because of the tragic and untimely situations to which thoughtful response must be made. As its former optimism regarding human amelioration and perfectability recedes sharply, its character as anguished protest against the widespread dehumanizing of man gathers strength. It assumes a darker, more defensive posture. New elements are introduced: a more drastic sense of human precariousness and ambiguity, a heightened anxiety over growing threats of technology, nuclear warfare or social conflict to the 'values' treasured in our western culture, and a greater willingness to entertain and deal with questions of 'ontology' or the *being* of man. At the same time the older stresses also persist: preoccupation with the silent, absent God, repeated programmatic efforts to cope responsibly with human ills chiefly through political engagement and the issuing of manifestos, and renewed affirmations of the ultimate dignity or worth of the human self *vis-à-vis* what are deemed reductive or destructive tendencies at work in science, philosophy, the arts and structures of public life.

Humanism, as we meet it in the contemporary world, is no longer a single pattern of thought but an accompanying feature of many diverse patterns. It is prominent in existentialist philosophies, as when Heidegger maintains that natural science cannot disclose the true nature of man, Sartre tells us that 'existentialism is a humanism' or Jaspers insists that all transcendence is self-transcendence. There is obviously a powerful humanist element in much contemporary literature; the novels of Kafka, Camus and Faulkner, or the plays of Arthur Miller, provide conspicuous examples. That God is dead and men must save themselves is the underlying axiom of most psychoanalysis and psychotherapy; it becomes most explicit perhaps in the essays of Erich Fromm directed against our 'humanoid' culture. The same assumption appears in discussions and procedures carried on within the academic community, as also in what is sometimes called the 'practical atheism' of problem-solving in both private and public spheres of life.

Most humanists, though not all, are also humanitarians. That is, they are in person and in principle committed to improving the human condition with a special care for the disadvantaged or exploited members of society. Fundamental to their thought and action alike is the conviction of human solidarity and mutuality. This may be expressed in various ways, such as the *unanimisme* of Romain Rolland, the Marxist phase of Sartre or the liberal-democratic faith of John Dewey and his circle of influence. Within this broad spectrum there are of course special doubtful cases and sharp differences, like those between individualists and collectivists, utilitarians and absolutists, but the basically humanitarian persuasion remains. Even totalitarian or authoritarian states justify repressive measures on the ground that social welfare will be thereby furthered.

Some defenders of explicit humanitarianism hold that it is not to be restricted to mankind but to all sentient beings. Anti-vivisection, for example, has been justified on these grounds. Here the signature of humanitarianism is found not only in concern with human welfare but also in humaneness towards all kinds of life. It is based, as with Rousseau and Schopenhauer, in what is called an instinct or sentiment or compassion or fellow-feeling evoked in the presence of deliberate cruelty or avoidable suffering. Transposed to the ethical plane, humanitarianism holds that such humaneness is a principle which ought to motivate all moral action. Some humanists, on the other hand, have ventured to attack humanitarianism on the ground of its sentimentality and lack of precise definition of the sphere of moral responsibility. It is true that the humanitarian impulse is often at odds with itself and can yield no single rational imperative for ethical purposes; yet it must be admitted that humaneness towards one's fellow-creatures constitutes an enhancement, not a debasement, of humanism itself.

The effort of humanist thought to find in man his own centre and sanction, displacing God, has left its mark both negatively and positively upon contemporary versions of the Christian faith. Jacques Maritain has even tried to reinstate an 'integral' humanism within Christian theology, maintaining in essence that whatever humanism can do Christianity can do better. Other thinkers such as Gabriel Marcel and Paul Tillich have sought to demonstrate that existential analysis of the situation of man only serves to raise the old question about God in a new and unavoidable way. According to them, we do not effectively dismiss God merely by exalting the prerogatives and potentialities of man. But it is clear that their conception of God is not the one which humanists reject; the issues therefore are not sharply drawn and the prospects for their resolution on these terms are very slight indeed.

Thus the opposition between humanist and Christian interpretations of what human being means is still with us and is far from being overcome. This is especially the case where ethical questions are involved, and above all in those regarding freedom and responsibility.

Humanist ethics sees in freedom the signal instance of man's unique, even 'absurd' standing in the total universe, as known in natural science. It seeks to preserve and protect that freedom by asserting man's independence from natural conditioning on the one hand, and from supernatural or divine sovereignty on the other. In Comte's words, man has his highest being, his 'God', in himself; in Sartre's, human life just happens and remains absurd. Freedom here is taken to mean self-motivation, non-accountability to any higher or lower power. That man can know, seek, and realize his own good without reliance upon any standard external to himself, is the hallmark of humanist ethics.

Christian ethics, far from denying the truth of human freedom, the power of effective choice, wishes to affirm it, since all moral obligation would be meaningless without it. But it regards such freedom as a gift of divine grace, a created good which man has abused and which God must therefore act to redeem. This freedom is the ambiguous source in man of both his alienation from and reconciliation to God; yet it is God and not man's freedom which makes the final difference. For the Christian, freedom is correlative with responsibility, not antithetical to it. Whatever obligation men may have to seek and serve the good of others – an obligation, as we have seen, which is characteristically proclaimed by humanists – is owed to a more-than-human source and standard, creative and redemptive with respect to all human good.

Is the growth of modern and contemporary humanism only the fruit of a 'tragic misunderstanding', as de Lubac holds? That is, can it be shown that humanism, instead of being inimical to Christian faith, is actually its corollary and derivative? Is it reasonable to declare that humanism requires and can profit from the correction of biblical and theological insights concerning man? Humanists themselves would be likely to retort that Christian modes of thought represent a continuing threat to their efforts and an outright denial of their beliefs. This is because they view all faith in God as illusory, defeatist and an obstacle to human progress all along the line. Why look to God for what unaided, disenchanted man can accomplish on his own?

Perhaps humanism itself, however, in its strong desire to rid men of their religious preconceptions and inhibitions, is unable to give an adequate accounting on its own terms of what is truly human in humanity. The best defence of Christian truth would then not be a contradicting anti-humanism, but rather a reassessment of the human situation and enterprise in the perspective furnished by our faith. From this vantage-point it becomes plain, at all events, that man is really much more mysterious in what Pascal called his 'greatness and wretchedness' than the humanists have been generally willing to grant.

The Christian estimate of humanism cannot be either a simple rejection or a straightforward acclamation. One may rejoice in the fact that humane values are indeed great and claim a high measure of devotion without presuming that they are self-explaining and self-justifying. The Christian doctrine of man is not the mere transcription of despair; and Christianity no longer can be thought to have any monopoly on the tragic sense of life. Man's greatness and his wretchedness are but two sides of the same truth. This truth comes to Christian expression with singular clarity in Berdyaev's statement that 'God is the meaning of human existence'. But this declaration from the side of faith can only be made good if Christians are willing to confess and rectify those perversions of their faith which have made the humanist protest possible and its critique at many points cogent. In order to show that belief in man and belief in God belong together, Christian thinkers must advance sounder interpretations and stronger motivations with respect to what being human means than humanism has thus far been able to provide.

Erich Fromm, *Man for Himself*, 1947; Corliss Lamont, *Humanism as a Philosophy*, 1949; Henri de Lubac, *Le Drame de l'Humanisme Athée*, 1959; Ralph Barton Perry, *The Humanity of Man*, 1956; Paul Tillich, *The Courage to Be*, 1952; Wilbur Marshall Urban, *Humanity and Deity*, 1951.

ROGER HAZELTON

Hume, David

All the philosophy of David Hume (1711–1776) was a protest against the claim that reason can construct a metaphysic of reality and values: we only lose ourselves in vague ideas and unverifiable propositions when we leave first-hand experience, which consists of sensations, memories and feelings, linked together in regular ways, and in beliefs that are 'natural' in the sense that we cannot help having them and cannot reason them away. Hence for him moral philosophy takes the form of inquiring what mental qualities in others we do in fact, at times irrepressibly and usually in our calm moments, approve as good, and what the grounds of such approvals are. He finds four classes of qualities. (1) Those that are immediately *attractive* to the spectator, for example, good manners, modesty, cleanliness. Why are they attractive? We do not know; they just are so. Here, as in his theory of knowledge, Hume enjoys pin-pointing a belief for which no reason can be given, and declaring that it is none the worse for that. (2) Attractive to the persons who have them, for example, cheerfulness, benevolence. The approval of what others in their self-experience find agreeable must spring from a 'natural sympathy' with others. This is a factual disproof of any egoistic ethic. (3) What a spectator recognizes as *useful* to the persons who have them, for example, frugality, diligence, discretion, another proof that as spectators we are not by nature egoistic. (4) What the spectator sees in a person to be useful to those who come into the company of that person, or to society generally, for example, justice, benevolence, that is, we naturally approve the social virtues, even when we are not ourselves being benefited by the particular actions we are approving, yet another disproof of egoism. Confining himself to what in fact we cannot help approving, he ignores the question of what we *ought* to approve and why. His radical empiricism precludes even the modest conclusion that we ought habitually to make those four kinds of approval, though this was clearly his personal conviction. In short, his treatment was psychological, not properly ethical. The above outline follows his *Enquiry Concerning the Principle of Morals* (1751), which he judged to be the best of all his works. He showed his practical moral concern in many of his essays and in his famous *History of England* (1754–62).

T. E. JESSOP

Humility

Humility is not self-abnegation; it is self-affirmation made possible by the calling and power of Christians to be the light of the world and the salt of the earth. This work cannot be done by the habitually self-centred even if they are concerned with fulfilling a wish to be humble. The humble man loses his self-centredness by his habitual attempts to proclaim the gospel with his whole being. In essence, humility is exposing oneself by a wholehearted attempt to express deep feelings and beliefs in a manner neither uncontrolled nor self-conscious. This is what the apostle means when he says '. . . we have the mind of Christ' (I Cor. 2.16).

One of the most familiar Christian images of humility is found in Phil. 2: 'Have this mind among yourselves, which you have in Christ Jesus, who, though he was in the form of God, did not count equality with God a thing to be grasped, but emptied himself, taking the form of a servant, being born in the likeness of men. And being found in human form he humbled himself and became obedient unto death, even death on a cross.'

In the mediaeval attempt to describe the good life by use of the table of the seven virtues humility is omitted. The omission may presuppose either that the practice of the seven virtues makes for humility or that only the humble man could practise them. In the second half of the twentieth century people tend to explain the good life in terms of human relationships and would think of humility in that context. The humble would be described as neither boastful nor domineering, not given to self display, always prepared to do well what he can do well and, as occasion demands, to attempt what he cannot do well. If an official of an institution he will think more of the work pertaining to his office than of his own importance as an official.

No man can make himself humble by acts of will; continued attempts to do so produce a condition which is not humility. Others cannot make him humble though they may humiliate him, and yet humiliation is part of the raw material out of which humility is so mysteriously made. There is no single activity which could be called being humble; it is rather a quality which flavours what a man does. Humility is given to men obliquely; it is, as it were, a by-product of the Christian style of living. This style is made through the consistent attempt to love God, neighbour and self in thought, word and deed – aware that each individual is at the same time first, a creature limited in knowledge and power; secondly, a being made in the image of God, capable of a relationship with God; thirdly, a sinner in constant need of repentance.

R. E. C. BROWNE

Hunting. see Animals.

Huxley, Thomas H.

Thomas Huxley (1825–1895), English biologist and writer, was a champion of Darwin's evolutionary theories, and sought to relate them to ethical and social questions. Credited with inventing the word 'agnosticism' (from the 'unknown God' of Acts 17.23), Huxley contended that we cannot know ultimate reality and that mankind's proper business is to improve his own lot upon the earth. Like many other writers of the nineteenth century, he claimed that the time had come for ethics to

be disengaged from its religious and Christian associations, and based instead upon the methods of science, and especially on the biological and anthropological sciences. His view on these matters found expression in his Romanes Lecture of 1893, entitled 'Ethics and Evolution'. His grandson, Sir Julian Huxley, has continued and updated the tradition by his advocacy of a humanistic and evolutionary ethic. *See* Evolutionary Ethics; Science and Ethics.

EDITOR

Hybris

Hybris is a Greek term taken over by Christians with its Greek meaning. It is used to denote the madness of human pride arrogantly setting out to defy the gods. Christians would describe *hybris* as the sinful folly of men setting out to control what human beings cannot control, even if they wish to do this for the glory of God, the furtherence of the gospel and the welfare of all men.

R. E. C. BROWNE

Hypocrisy

Hypocrisy is common among Christians whenever and wherever, consciously or unconsciously, they are more concerned about the importance of good behaviour than with the worship of almighty God. The Christian who tries hard to set an example very easily, and unknowingly, begins and continues to play a part. This can happen to parents, teachers, evangelists, no matter how good their intentions seem to be. The group of Pharisees described in the Gospels encouraged one another to be hypocrites in ways described with such force by our Lord. As in all such groups, the more conscientious the member, the more he is caught up in the group hypocrisies. The Sermon on the Mount (Matt. 6) teaches Christians not to be as the hypocrites who give alms, fast and pray ostentatiously that they may be seen of men. Our Lord says 'they have their reward' – a falsely earned public reputation for righteousness.

Conscious hypocrisy is relatively uncommon; it is pretending deliberately to be what one is not for immediate or distant advantage. Unconscious hypocrisy is much more common. A man's family and his circle of friends and acquaintances continually suggest to him what feelings, ambitions, amusements, loves and hates he should have. The suggestions made by family and by his circle of friends conflict and he tends to be one sort of person with his family and a different sort with his friends. This form of unconscious hypocrisy is found wherever group members are sufficiently with one another to make an image of the desirable life and encourage one another to speak and act as they fancy the image dictates. This group influence cannot be broken up but a man can free himself from it if he makes and keeps sufficient independence to criticize the groups to which he belongs while retaining his membership of them. Groups within the church are not immune from the dangers of group life. A church group is in danger of encouraging hypocrisy when members talk too well about the basis, aims and achievements of the group, because such talking encourages group members to hold a false view of the actual things done in the name of the group. It is easier to be content with moving descriptions of the group's aims than to make the costly effort of putting them into practice.

The unhappy individual who dislikes himself tends to be an unconscious hypocrite. For instance, the man who cannot forgive himself for being a coward will tell others how brave he is by making legends and myths about his bravery; in doing this his primary interest is not to deceive others but to secure their co-operation in his attempts to think well of himself.

Fear of hypocrisy haunts many people. When anyone struggles against this fear he becomes so obsessed with it that he is prone to end in the state he was most anxious to avoid. Hypocrisy is not to be feared, hated nor fought; it is overcome by love of the truth that sets men free.

R. E. C. BROWNE

Id

Id is the Latin form used in psychological literature in English to render Sigmund Freud's term *das Es* (literally 'the It'). In psychoanalytic theory id designates one of the three levels, orders, structures or institutions into which the human mind is divided. The other two are ego and superego which are defined elsewhere in this dictionary. Id, Freud's second topographical model of the human mind, has not found wide acceptance outside the psychoanalytic school, but the terms for the three component parts have come into general popular usage, frequently with very loose meanings.

The id is said to be the most primitive level of psychic organization. The instinctual impulses which reside in the id and relate to such matters as hunger, sex, self-preservation, love, etc., are said to be invested with large quantities of psychic energy which constantly seek discharge. In the id, the so-called *primary process* prevails; the contents are chaotically organized so that opposites are not mutually exclusive, ideas lack synthesis, affects may be related to inappropriate objects, and the whole process is governed by the over-riding principle of obtaining gratification or pleasure. The id is fundamentally amoral, is not concerned with considerations of reality, and seeks blindly to fulfil its own purposes and discharge its energies. It is also ineluctable.

According to Freud, the individual ego develops in due course from part of the id. The id cannot be directly observed. Its continuing existence beyond infancy is inferred from the apparent conflicts between deep-rooted instinctual impulses and the dictates of reality, morality and ethics. In psychoanalytic terms, its effects are seen in its conflicts with the ego and the superego. Freud postulated id-ego conflict as a major source of neurosis. The defences of the ego against the id are discussed in detail in Anna Freud, *The Ego and the Mechanisms of Defence* (1937). *See also* Sigmund Freud, *The Ego and the Id* (1927).

The id represents a continuing factor in human psychic life. Contrary to some popular misconceptions, Freudian theory does not advocate the uninhibited expression of id impulses. It clearly recognizes that this would be intolerable both for the individual and for society. Freud's own dictum was 'Where id was, there shall ego be'. *See also* **Instincts or Drives; Psychoanalysis; Unconscious.**

GRAEME M. GRIFFIN

Idealist Ethics

'Idealist ethics' is usually restricted to the sort of ethics that is bound up with the kind of idealistic metaphysics distinguished as objective idealism. This sprang up in Germany at the very end of the eighteenth century, with Fichte, Schelling and Hegel as its originators, and flourished there for several decades. In Britain it was imbibed at once by Coleridge and Carlyle, but made no impact on the philosophers until the publication of Stirling's *The Secret of Hegel* (1865); it was absorbed and modified at Oxford by Green and Bradley and carried from there to Scotland by E. Caird. In America also it was a man of letters, Emerson, who first responded to it; among the philosophers W. T. Harris propagated it from the 60s onwards, and Royce became its leading figure. Its most general characteristic was a heavy emphasis on mind or spirit. To specify it as the doctrine of the supremacy of spirit would be too wide, for that would cover any form of theism; as the doctrine that reality is mental, too narrow, for none of the idealists who believed that there really are blocks of stone would say that these are mental. We must specify it as the principle that mind is our fullest clue to the nature of the universe; or that everything that is not mind is inseparable from mind, as logically unthinkable apart from it or as a creature or embodiment of it. Another general feature is that mind is not restricted to what we can observe by introspection, to such evanescent facts of consciousness as impulses, feelings or ideas, but is also and far more importantly what observes these, takes them up into patterns that are not given, and uses them for the public actualization of its ideals; that is, mind reveals and realizes itself in its impersonal objective achievements.

Described negatively, this kind of idealism was a protest against the tendency of scientists to suppose that matter is the really real in terms of which all else is to be explained, or, more formally, that the concepts and methods used in the natural sciences are the only ones that lead to knowledge of the nature of anything. It was a protest also against the view of the subjective empiricists of the eighteenth and nineteenth centuries, and more searchingly of Kant, that reality as it is in itself cannot be known; and in rejecting *such* a duality between knowledge and reality, and between values and reality, objective idealism had a strongly constructive, uniting, monistic note. That kind of metaphysical outlook obviously had to take ethics seriously. Since each leading thinker devised his own system only a few very general statements, not all of them equally true of all the systems, can be made here. (1) They did not incline to moralism, that is, to regarding moral virtue as the only, or always the highest, excellence for which man is fitted and destined. The full range of the mind's possibilities is kept in view; we are to think of one Spirit immanent in the universe and working through finite minds towards the full externalization or realization of its versatile nature. The formula of Green and Bradley, 'self-realization', is to be understood in that context: it is the universal self in us, that in virtue of which each of us is (not Smith or Jones, but) spirit as such that is to be realized. (2) In consequence, although the form of idealist exposition is often abstract, the direction of the thinking is concrete: the nature, scope, evolution and culmination of mind are neither spun out of *a priori* definitions nor framed out of the subjectivities of introspection, but are elicited from the objective expressions of mind in its civilized feats – the creation of knowledge, art, society as politically organized, law, religion, and of course morality. That interest in the definition and history of these great cultural achievements which was one of the striking marks of the nineteenth century was caught from, and in some of those fields led by, thinkers of the idealist movement. (3) The relation of morality to religion was kept close, precisely because the outlook was metaphysical and spiritual (the breath of Platonism was in it). Indeed, the idea of a Spirit evolving towards complete cosmic fulfilment could be called a philosophical eschatology. The Spirit being regarded as immanent, objective idealism led most easily to pantheism or to panentheism; but some philosophers and (seeking a metaphysical ground for orthodox Christian doctrine) philosophical theologians stopped short of these two extremes and reserved a real separateness for finite minds. *See* **Bradley, F. H.; Green, Thomas Hill; Hegel, Georg Wilhelm Friedrich; Hartmann, Eduard von; Royce, Josiah.**

T. E. JESSOP

Ignorance

Strictly speaking, ignorance is the state of not knowing something, whether one could or ought to know it or not. In the moral sphere, however, the word is used to denote a lack of knowledge which one ought to have. The word error is used by some moral theologians in the same sense, and no distinction from ignorance is intended.

From the point of view of that which is not known, there can be ignorance of a fact and ignorance of the law. One may mistakenly think that this root is horse-radish when it is actually aconite. Or one may mistakenly think this is a two-way street, when in fact a by-law has declared it to be one way.

From the point of view of the person who is ignorant, ignorance may be '*invincible*' or '*vincible*'. Invincible ignorance is that which persists after all reasonable efforts have been made to dispel it. Vincible ignorance is that which a reasonable effort could and should overcome. What is reasonable depends on the circumstances, for example, the importance of the subject matter, and the opportunities afforded for inquiry or reflection. Vincible ignorance, since it is in some degree a man's own fault, does not excuse from blame any action to which it may lead. Invincible ignorance, on the other hand, does excuse.

The textbooks sub-divide vincible ignorance into 'simple', 'crass' and 'affected' or 'deliberate'. 'Simple' is where some effort has been made to overcome the ignorance, greater effort might have been made, but failure to do so is not very blameworthy. 'Crass' is where virtually no attempt has been made to dispel it, and there is little or no excuse for the omission to do so. 'Affected' ignorance is a deliberate act of will by which a man determines to make no effort to find out the truth in order that he may feel free to do whatever it is he wants to do.

From the point of view of the action which follows from the ignorance, the textbooks distinguish between 'antecedent', 'concomitant' and 'consequent'. Antecedent ignorance is an involuntary ignorance which is the cause of an action which, but for it, the agent would not have performed. For example, a motorist driving with all reasonable caution runs over a man whom he does not know to be in the road. Concomitant ignorance is also an involuntary ignorance, but is not the cause of the action which follows, in the sense that the agent would still have performed the action even if he had not been ignorant. For example, a murderer intent on killing his enemy 'accidentally' runs him over in his car. Such a man is morally guilty of murder, though technically and in law probably only of homicide or at worst manslaughter. Consequent ignorance is wilful ignorance and therefore the same as affected ignorance, if directly willed, or crass ignorance if indirectly willed, that is, the result of gross negligence.

The relevance of ignorance to a judgment on the culpability of an action, and the importance of an accurate understanding of the different kinds of ignorance are obvious. It is not surprising that moral theologians devote considerable space to the subject.

R. C. MORTIMER

Illegitimacy

An illegitimate child is one born out of marriage, not being the child of validly married parents. Legitimacy is an important element in most laws of inheritance. The Roman Catholic Church has clear definitions of legitimacy, and illegitimate children can be legitimated by the Holy See. English law has in recent years removed some of the disabilities of illegitimate children.

HERBERT WADDAMS

Imitation of Christ

Christian theologians have shown an ambivalent attitude towards the 'imitation of Christ' as an ethical ideal especially since the Reformation. Until then it had been taken, generally speaking, to be the distinctive motive of Christian behaviour.

The imitation of Christ has a place in the NT and is explicitly presented as an ethical ideal by St Paul, where it is not an endeavour to copy the historical Christ but a case of the Holy Spirit moulding the life of the Christian into some likeness of Christ. Hence Paul describes the life of the Christian in such a way as to suggest that behind it are the rhythm (humiliation/glory; suffering/triumph) of the way of the historical Jesus. The Spirit, in the Christian, imitates the image (*eikon*) of God, Christ. A similar function of the Spirit lies behind the Johannine idea of *paraclete*.

The germ of the ethical ideal of the imitation of Christ may be seen in the distinctive idea of discipleship discernible in the teaching and practice of Jesus himself, especially in the implications of 'following' in 'the way' of the 'Son of Man'.

In Christian history the ideal of the imitation of Christ has affected ascetical practices in particular. In the patristic period it was the driving force behind the ideal of martyrdom, celibacy and virginity. Later, especially in the period dominated by Bernard of Clairvaux and Francis of Assisi, there was a move towards a literal reproducing of the poverty of Jesus in personal life and (among the Cistercians particularly) in architectural ideals (*nudum Christum nudus sequere*).

Luther was critical of the ideal, partly because he was repelled by the puerilities of certain sects which were attempting a literal reproduction of the teaching of Jesus, and partly because he came to believe that it inevitably concealed a doctrine of works. He preferred to use the word *conformitas*, which he interpreted along Pauline lines, rather than *imitatio*, believing that the latter suggested emulation. In a not dissimilar way Kierkegaard distinguished between heroic 'admiration' of Christ as a great and good teacher and personal self-giving in 'imitation' which need not, as Luther contended, issue in a doctrine of works.

In the twentieth century, with the loss of confidence in the possibility of constructing a 'Life of Jesus', the imitation of Christ has been interpreted to mean repeating the faith-decisions of Jesus (E. Fuchs, G. Ebeling). Apart from the question whether there is warranty for this thorough-going scepticism about the possibility of knowing something of the historical shape of Jesus' mission, and even of what used to be called his 'selfconsciousness', Jesus is more in NT christology than pattern-believer, although he is certainly that (e.g., *Hebrews*). Bonhoeffer's presentation of Christian ethics as 'formation' is much nearer to NT, especially Pauline, teaching.

Psychology has demonstrated the primary role of imitation in the development of human personality. Growth in moral sensitivity is largely the result of the, conscious or unconscious, imitation of others (parents, teachers, etc.). There remains in adult life an important imitative element (e.g., of one's own ego ideal). The difference between a slavish imitation and one that is creative is that the latter produces ever new patterns, according to the personality concerned, that have a genuine individual stamp within a generic likeness. The history of art furnishes many examples of this kind of creative imitation. In the Christian life the Holy Spirit is '*creator* spirit' and this is the safeguard against a moribund archaism or literalism.

D. Bonhoeffer, *Ethics*, 1955; S. Kierkegaard, *Journals*, ed. and tr. by A. Dru, 1938; *Stages on Life's Way*, tr. by W. Lowrie, 1940; *Training in Christianity*, tr. by W. Lowrie, 1941; E. J. Tinsley, *The Imitation of God in Christ*, 1960.

E. J. TINSLEY

Imperialism

Imperialism involves domination or control by a nation of territories outside its own boundaries. It may be defined as serious infringement of the independence of a people by an outside power in pursuit of its own interests. Such control in its thorough-going classical form is colonialism, or the actual rule of another territory. Imperialism also includes lesser forms of domination within spheres of influence. A modern form of neo-imperialism exhibits less violent suppression or direct exploitation, while relying on subtler forms of economic and political pressure.

A complex of contradictory motives and consequences are associated with imperialism.

Genuine good will has led some to seek dominance that they might better share what they regarded as a superior culture or religious faith. Gross forms of economic nationalism have also been among the incentives towards imperialism. Nations have been driven by a desire for profits or prestige and by the requirements of expanding industrial economies to establish privileged access to raw materials, markets, investment opportunities or population outlets.

Colonial peoples have reaped genuine advantages from imperialism, in education, industrial development or social welfare. Any charity done is by definition, however, of a paternalistic variety. Paternalism is always an imperfect expression of love because it links benevolence to autocratic control. Some restrictions on freedom are necessary for immature populations, but imperialists tend to overestimate both extent and duration of immaturity. Varying degrees of exploitation are typically involved, since important ends of imperialist policy are the interests of the dominant power.

Imperialism has been a serious cause of war. In competition for spheres of influence, trade wars may become shooting wars. Friction between imperialists and colonies may explode into violence, or dependent areas may become pawns in the hands of great powers in their game of power politics.

Christian concern for freedom, integrity and justice demands that dominant nations adopt the attitude of trusteeship, making the welfare of subject peoples a paramount aim. Preparations for full self-determination need maximum possible acceleration. Empires have recently been disintegrating. Yet justice too long delayed is still an expression of defiance towards God. Moving in the right direction too slowly can also be disastrous. As the lot of subjugated peoples tardily improves, they may become even more frustrated, resentful and infected by extremism. Clinging too long to special privilege intensifies hostility and destroys the chance of developing an early relationship of trust among equals.

HARVEY SEIFERT

Indeterminism. see Free Will and Determinism.

Individualism

The Christian belief in the person-in-community is easily polarized into two heresies, individualism and collectivism (q.v.). Each expresses a partial truth and a partial distortion of the Christian understanding.

Individualism represents the outlook in which the person exists for himself. Society is the aggregate of individuals, and social institutions have the purpose of serving individuals. The individualist glories in freedom and autonomy. He has little interest in tradition, social solidarity and authority.

Individuality is not, in actual fact, the primary datum in human experience. Primitive tribes and ancient empires have usually been more impressed with the social unit than with the individual (see Collectivism). But individualism, like so many of the major themes of western society, emerged in the history of both the Greeks and the Hebrews.

In Hellenic society individualism appeared in the Promethean myth, in the celebrated Periclean oration in Thucydides, in the tragic heroes of drama, in the satire on personalities in comedy. The Sophists of the fifth century BC included radical individualists, highly critical of society and tradition. Socrates appeared in the Athenian tradition as the relentless questioner, who insisted upon thinking for himself and whose martyrdom in 399 BC demonstrated the power of a conscience that refused to surrender itself to society. Although Plato advocated an organic society, the Cynics claimed to follow the Socratic logic to its consequences in a stubborn, eccentric individualism. Epicurus, with an atomistic doctrine of nature and of the self, minimized the importance of society.

The Bible took a different path in the discovery of the person. The early sources emphasize the 'corporate personality' of the tribe or of Israel. But the call for fidelity and personal decision came to distinguish the individual from the society. The hope for the nation shifted to a hope for the remnant. The punishment of the family or tribe for the sins of some of its members gave way to law that fixed guilt and punishment upon individuals (e.g., Deut. 24.16). The prophets, while feeling solidarity with their people, became lonely in their alienation from their kin. 'I sat alone,' wrote Jeremiah (15.17); and his writings showed a quality of self-awareness never before expressed. Ezekiel emphasized personal responsibility to the extent of an unreal denial of social solidarity (18.1–4). The exilic and post-exilic psalmists frequently showed a penetrating quality of introspection and recognition of the inner life of the person. The late Jewish eschatology transferred the locus of future hope from the historical society, in which the individual found gratification by anticipation, to a consummation in which each person would participate and be judged.

The NT developed this Hebrew consciousness of the person to the highest possible pitch. Jesus taught that God numbers the hairs of man's heads, that there is more joy in heaven over one sinner who repents than over ninety-nine people who need no repentance. Jesus himself went to his lonely death on the Cross. Yet the NT interprets this solitary man as representative man, suffering and conquering sin for all men. Instead of individualism, he teaches and exemplifies love. He calls man, not into solitary devotion, but into a community of faith. His followers understand themselves as the household of God, as the body of Christ, as a holy nation.

In subsequent years Christians brought to society both an intense concern for persons and a commitment to community. The towering figure of St Augustine is an example of both. His *Confessions* (*c.* 400 AD) were a genre of writing hitherto unknown in their probing of selfhood. Yet he had an overwhelming sense of the solidarity of mankind in its sin and of the redeemed in the city of God. The mediaeval society accented man's social awareness in an organic, hierarchical society. Mystics and rebels kept alive the Christian awareness of personal experience; and the ordinary man knew that his sin, judgment and redemption were highly personal. But the mediaeval culture was not dominantly individualistic.

The modern world has seen the emergence of an individualism that has both Christian and heretical roots. What is commonly called 'Protestant individualism' has little to do with Christian faith or the Reformation. Yet it remains true that, just as the Renaissance awakened an exultant appreciation of human powers, the Reformation put a heightened emphasis upon personal responsibility. Luther taught that every man must do his own believing as he must do his own dying. Repentance and faith are personal, not institutional. Luther sought to recover the NT sense of the person-in-community when he said that all Christians are called to be priests and Christs to their neighbours. The Anabaptists, claiming to follow Luther's principles more consistently than Luther, emphasized the personal nature of faith in their insistence upon believer's baptism. They tended to see the Church as the community of those persons who have made decisions for Christ rather than as the organic community that nurtures persons in the faith. The later English Independents and Quakers emphasized in various ways the importance of personal decision and responsibility, the value of freedom, the significance of conscience and the inadequacy of external authorities.

These Christian movements, however, kept an awareness of the work of faith and love in creating community. Other streams of thought had to arise in order to bring about modern individualism, with its glorification of the autonomy of the self. Hobbes and Descartes, in the seventeenth century, separated man from the meaningful social nexus – Hobbes by reviving an ancient atomism and Descartes by defining man as 'a thing that thinks'. (Incidentally, Hobbes shows how easy it is to start with individualism and end with collectivism.) Defoe's *Robinson Crusoe* (1719) depicted the autonomous man fictionally. Locke, Hume, Adam Smith, Bentham and Mill in the eighteenth and nineteenth centuries described him philosophically.

This list of names suggests the importance of the modern economy in fostering individualism. It is in an industrial economy, where men and wealth are mobile and interchangeable, that individualism can develop. Such an economy may also esteem individual initiative, free enterprise and the doctrine of laissez-faire.

Curiously this very individualism has seemed to many to destroy the significance of the individual person. Industrial society, often substituting a process or system of production for personal relations, has fostered an abstract rather than a personal individualism. It tends to deal with masses rather than persons, to value individuals for their functions rather than for their selfhood, and therefore to make persons expendable.

One result has been the existentialist movement - a rebellion against Enlightenment rationalism in the name of an appreciation of authentic selfhood. Whether Christian, agnostic, or atheistic, existentialism has emphasized the individual person. Kierkegaard, with his emphasis upon self-exploration and decision, and Nietzsche, with his exultancy in the uniqueness of every person, were the early leaders of the movement. Heidegger and Sartre have carried it further.

It may be asked whether these men, in their concern for the individual and his freedom, have not lost the significance of community. But it is noteworthy to see them reassert the importance of the individual in the face of the very society that had so often stifled the person while flying the banners of individualism.

Individualism is the development of one aspect of the Christian understanding of the person-in-community. In itself it needs constant correction from those who understand that the self lives only in relation with others. But it is itself a correction of any doctrine of society or community that submerges persons.

St Augustine, *Confessions, c.* 400 AD; Martin Buber, *I and Thou*, 2nd edn., 1958; John Dewey, *Individualism, Old and New*, 1930; John Maynard Keynes, *The End of Laissez-faire*, 1926; John Stuart Mill, *On Liberty*, 1859; Reinhold Niebuhr, *The Self and the Dramas of History*, 1955.

ROGER L. SHINN

Industrial Relations

Industrial relations involves the conduct of, and the theories analyzing, relationships among men working for large organizations in a modern industrial setting. Until recently the term was limited to the interactions between employers and workers or managers and employees, particularly in business corporations. Now it is also applied to the relations among all those who contribute to the activities of any large organization, private or public, profit or non-profit, and manufacturing or service.

The problems with which industrial relations is concerned are those encountered by people dealing with others in hierarchical, bureaucratic, collegial or other systematic organizations. An issue of central importance is the kind of responsibilities superiors have in directing their subordinates and the nature of the obligations owed by subordinates to those above them in performance of their tasks. Another major issue is the amount of freedom an individual may assume within his work or occupational group and the extent to which individual and group goals can diverge from those of the larger organization. These issues arise in various forms, posed as problems of special conditions, circumstances and time. What people are to be hired and by what standards are they to be judged? How will their tasks be assigned and by whom? Why should special communications devices be used and for what purpose? How will work standards be defined? Who will enforce the performance and carry out any disciplining? When will promotions, lay-offs, or discharges be effected and for what reasons? Determination of the rates of pay, hours of work and job conditions along with the introduction of technological change are among the most difficult problems.

Industrial relations as an area of systematic study did not develop until the twentieth century. Before then scholars generally assumed and businessmen believed that the market automatically and appropriately governed the relations of employers and workers. Employers relied upon the market to regulate their dealings with workers; but they also looked to the tradition and law of the master-servant relationship to define the role of each party. Classical economists argued that individuals seeking work in a free market could not be injured since competition would force employers to pay the highest wages and provide the best conditions possible. While the argument possesses some validity experience has not always confirmed it. Workers all too often enjoyed little choice of employment and thus gained none of the protection a competitive market was supposed to offer.

To their considerable market power, employers added the traditional 'rights' of a master's prerogatives and of an owner's property. Socially superior as proven by his position – the chosen of God or Nature – his authority was reinforced by the law which warded off all attacks upon his arbitrary directives and absolute rules because it guaranteed him the right to dispose of his property and to manage it as he saw fit. Though today managers seldom appeal to the old traditions to bolster their prerogative claims, many still insist that they do and ought to possess at least some unquestioned rights in directing or administering the organization.

In the mid-nineteenth century, **Karl Marx** (q.v.) powerfully criticized the capitalistic market system which gave overwhelming power to employers. He argued that it allowed exploitation which impoverished labourers and that it degraded men by alienating them from their works. Some employers, of which Robert Owen is an outstanding example, recognized the inadequacy of the market in providing healthful conditions of work and living standards conducive to an efficient, effective labour force. Interested as well in social reforms, Owen established a model industrial town, New Lanark, in 1800, encouraging education, productiveness and moral behaviour. Throughout the nineteenth century other employers experimented with programmes similar to Owen's. They provided conditions for their workers superior to those which the market would have provided, but the improvements usually depended upon the paternalistic concern or 'enlightened' self-interest of the employer, not upon the right of workers. Neither their voices or views were allowed free expression, initiative and decisive role. The employers' values were almost always served first, and in time of depression or low profits the workers' interests were disregarded completely.

Employers were tempted to puff up their concern for their workers into the presumptiousness of the President of the Philadelphia and Reading Railroad Company in 1902 when he declared that 'the rights and interests of the labouring man will be protected and cared for, not by labour agitators, but by the Christian men to whom God in his infinite wisdom has given the control of the property interests of the country'. A more common temptation today is for managers to assume a new paternalism, asserting that they can comprehend the needs of their employees and serve them equitably and justly. For the past twenty years the executives of the General Electric Company, for example, have tried to legitimize their managerial control by claiming that they can 'Do Right Voluntarily in the Unified Best Interests of All'.

Beginning around the turn of the century and reaching full flower after the first World War, the theories and movement of scientific management proposed a new kind of industrial relations. Specially trained, naturally talented managers were to determine the one best way of performing job tasks; workers were to be chosen rationally on the basis of tests that revealed their individual aptitudes and willingness to follow the minute rules and regulations imposed upon them. Advocates argued that all concerned would benefit, both workers and employers sharing the assured productivity increases.

While it contributed greatly to improving work efficiency, scientific management wrongly assumed that there was only one best way of performing a task and expected a rationality in organizations that probably does not exist. The diversity of abilities, talents and temperaments among people allow different workers to achieve the same efficiency in their job in a variety of ways; and selection, direction and administration continue to involve a great deal of art and subjective evaluation despite the use of tests, objective measurements and rigorously defined standards. Moreover, groups of employees seldom remain passive instruments to be ordered about or manipulated to fulfil the needs and demands of even a scientific manager. They have continued to insist upon their own approach to their work, on occasion subverting the purpose of scientific management. Under piece rate systems, for example, work groups not infrequently learn to use its techniques to serve their purposes of maintaining or raising earnings without a corresponding change in production.

The recognition by social scientists that employees in factory, shop or office formed social groups, imposing work norms upon their members, led to the development of a new approach to industrial workers – that of human relations. Managers were urged to listen to their employees' problems and complaints, not simply to act upon their own diagnoses. They were told to make workers *feel* they were important and to convince them that their interests were carefully and seriously considered when solutions and remedies were proposed. The heart of human relations is an open unimpeded channel of communications between manager and employees through which managers learn the foibles, weaknesses and needs of their employees. Managers can then help employees solve their problems, teach them the necessities of business and encourage them to develop socially useful (that is, business oriented) attitudes and habits.

At its best, human relations can give employees a sense of participating in the governing of their work lives. At its worst, human relations degenerates into attempts to manipulate employees as instruments solely to serve managerial purposes. It is seldom helpful in confronting conflicts of interests and values among employees or between employees and managers, however. Improved communications resolve conflicts only insofar as they arose from misunderstandings. Conflicts of interests and values may be left unresolved or even heightened. If employees possess no organization of their own or method of forcefully supporting their interests, the superior position and power of the managers will, of course, tend to resolve these conflicts in favour of management.

To insure themselves the right to participate in managerial decisions and to help resolve conflicts of interest in their favour, some workers have striven for recognition of collective bargaining as a lawful, regular means of conducting industrial relations.

Collective bargaining is seldom a process of unilateral imposition of demands; usually it involves mutual accommodation and adjustment on both sides. The very success of collective bargaining in the industries where it is prevalent has brought about the growth of large, bureaucratic unions and raised the same issues and problems for workers that the rise of the large factories did. The worker on the job now finds that he may have exchanged one master for two – management and the union. To guarantee his rights as a worker and protect his job interests he must also insure his rights and interests as a union member.

While collective bargaining receives the most public attention because of its contentious procedure and the dramatic strikes that sometimes accompany it, only a minority of those in the labour force use it to determine the rules under which they work. In the USA, for example, less than one-fourth of the labour force is covered by collective agreements. Not all workers desire to use collective bargaining. Some believe that the individual bargaining they enjoy is appropriate and adequate to their demands. Others, such as many professionals and white collar workers, find that the labour market protects and rewards them satisfactorily. Workers democratically choose representatives to bargain for them. The collective strength of the union allows workers to deal with managers on the basis of some equality. If managers will not agree to conditions of work which workers feel they must have, they can impose sanctions, disrupting production, interfering with distribution or cutting off sales of the product. Through such exercise of economic power unions can sometimes force managers to act in ways they might not otherwise have chosen. Collective bargaining thus allows workers to help establish and administer through representatives the rules and regulations that govern their work lives.

All the several varieties of industrial relations mentioned above can be found in any of the western industrial nations. An organization may follow several of them at the same time depending upon the kinds of workers and occupations involved. No one of them excludes the other, nor should one expect it to do so. Each can be useful to both manager and worker, depending upon circumstances. And each can be injurious to the parties and problematical for society.

JAMES KUHN

Industrial Revolution

Industrial Revolution is the term commonly used for the first phase of the industrialization of Great Britain which is dated approximately 1760 to 1820 or 1830. The term seems to have originated in France early in the nineteenth century and in its original use there was an implied comparison with the French Revolution. The currency of the term in Britain can be traced to Arnold Toynbee (1852–83) who in 1881–2 gave a course of lectures, published after his death, entitled *Lectures on the Industrial Revolution of the Eighteenth Century in England*. Toynbee and his successors stressed the social losses through industrialization rather than the technical advances and economic gains, while recent writers tend to do the opposite.

The term has come in for criticism and has been largely abandoned by economic historians owing to its lack of precision. Some writers have applied it to the process of industrialization that has taken place in country after country down to the present day, while others have used it loosely for any sudden and striking technological change in even a single industry. In this way many industrial revolutions may be detected by the historian, for example, economic changes in the woollen industry in England in the thirteenth century, and even by the prehistorian who has found an industrial revolution in the late Bronze Age. Moreover, the term suggests greater suddenness than the facts warrant. While Britain saw a rise in population, the industrial use of many important new inventions and a concentration of population near sources of power in the later eighteenth century, the way to these changes had been pointed by developments in the previous century. Further, no reason can be assigned for regarding the revolution as ended early in the nineteenth century. To all appearance it is still in progress.

Nevertheless the vagueness of the term should not blind us to the unique and decisive character of what happened in Britain's classic period of industrial revolution when a new relationship emerged between men, machines and resources. It was then that the economic and social pattern of the contemporary world, with the ethical problems involved, began to command attention.

T. S. Ashton, *The Industrial Revolution*, 1948; G. N. Clark, *The Idea of the Industrial Revolution*, 1953.

STEWART MECHIE

Infanticide

Infanticide is the killing of a new born child either by the parents or with their consent. Many primitive and non-Christian peoples (including the Greeks and Romans) are known to have approved the practice (by direct killing or abandonment), as a form of religious sacrifice (rarely), as a means of population control, or as a matter of domestic convenience. In Christian teaching it has been consistently condemned. In modern times three arguments have been used by way of defence or mitigation in the case of infants known to have some gross physical or mental handicap: (1) the interests not only of their own family but of society as a whole is best served by the painless killing of such infants, because they would otherwise become an increasing social and economic burden to the community; (2) they should be put to death painlessly for their own good as an act of compassion: they cannot expect to enjoy the pleasures and opportunities available to normal children and adults, and it is kinder to spare them the frustrations and hardships they must otherwise inevitably experience; (3) though infanticide may not be morally permissible, it should be regarded as a less heinous offence than the murder of a grown child or adult, because an infant cannot experience fear or terror or even pain in a comparable degree, nor does its removal impose any significant hardship or loss on the family circle. From a Christian standpoint all three arguments are unsatisfactory: (1) every human being derives his essential value not from society but from God who gave him his life and to whom he is infinitely precious; and society itself is judged by the manner in which it does or does not care for its weaker members; (2) the parents may feel profoundly sorry for their handicapped child (and not only sorry for themselves, as is sometimes the case), but the decision to kill him even for what they consider to be 'his own good' is one that they are not morally competent to make. The right to life is the infant's, and on what grounds other than their own subjective feelings can they claim to know that it would be 'better for him to die', or that he would not wish to live if he were given the opportunity? There are in fact many grievously handicapped children and adults who rejoice that they are alive, who know happiness despite their sufferings, and give joy and sometimes service to others despite their limitations; (3) legally the question can be one of some complexity (and varies from country to country), but factors like age and physical or mental handicap have no bearing upon the right to life. It is never morally permissible deliberately and directly to kill any innocent person. Morally the distinction between infanticide and murder has no significance, though it may be a convenient one in some systems of criminal law. This is not to deny, however, that in any particular instance of infanticide there may be extenuating circumstances. The mother may be virtually inculpable because of her mental condition at the time (though the same is unlikely to be true of any of her accomplices); and she may be in urgent need of medical and spiritual care.

N. St John-Stevas, *The Right to Life*, 1963; Glanville Williams, *The Sanctity of Life and The Criminal Law*, 1958.

THOMAS WOOD

Inhibition

Inhibition literally means a 'holding in', used generally of habitual or occasional restraint in behaviour, movement, thought, etc. It can refer either to restraint imposed by some external condition, force or authority, or to restraint which is imposed from within, either consciously or unconsciously. In psychology, inhibition is largely confined to the internal imposition of restraint but the term is frequently used without precise definition. In psychobiology it denotes the blocking of one set of processes by another as, for example, when the sympathetic division of the autonomic nervous system inhibits the para-sympathetic division in a situation of fear (*see* W. B. Cannon, *The Wisdom of the Body*, rev. edn., 1963).

In dynamically-oriented psychology, inhibition is used generally of the operation of mental mechanisms which curtail the free recognition or expression of thoughts, impulses, etc. A distinction is sometimes drawn between inhibition and self-control on the grounds that self-control is an essentially conscious restraint imposed by the ego whereas inhibitions are largely automatically functioning, unconscious mechanisms. Franz Alexander uses the term specifically of the activity of the superego (q.v.) in preventing impulses from the id (q.v.) from coming into conflict with the ego (q.v.). In this sense inhibition is a mechanism which operates to forestall the necessity for repression (q.v.) or other ego-instituted defences.

Freud suggested that inhibitions can arise when the developmental process is, for whatever reason, arrested in a particular direction, or fixated, at one of the major psychosexual stages in personality development. These fixations he regarded as the origin of the predisposition to particular forms of neurosis (*see* his *A General Introduction to Psychoanalysis*, rev. edn., 1920). The aim of psychoanalysis and other psychotherapies is not to remove inhibitions indiscriminately but rather to replace psychically destructive forms of control with other forms which are more flexible and more responsive to the complex demands of reality.

In yet another usage of the term, most conflict theories of personality regard the inhibition, or blocking, of natural growth tendencies as a root cause of later psychic distresses.

GRAEME M. GRIFFIN

Innocence

Older theology tended to identify innocence and perfection, to see in Aristotle the ruins of an Adam. More recent study has tended to distinguish between the two. Thus F. R. Tennant has pointed out that a child could be sinless but could not be morally perfect: 'There are heights of considerateness and courtesy, for instance, which are inevitably beyond the compass of a child's nature, in that they involve knowledge of ourselves and of our fellows derived from experience such as cannot lie within the child's reach' (*Concept of Sin*, 1912, p. 28).

On its positive side innocence has been analyzed most acutely by Kierkegaard in his *Concept of Dread* (first published in 1844). Innocence, says Kierkegaard, is ignorance. Consequently when God said to Adam, 'Of the tree of the knowledge of good and evil you shall not eat, for in the day that you eat of it you shall die' (Gen. 2.17), Adam understood neither the command nor the threat. But both command and threat open out possibilities to Adam, possibilities which may follow on his actions, possibilities which he does not understand and which for that reason make him anxious. This state of anxiety or dread is thus a product of that situation of freedom and finitude in which man finds himself. This state of dread is an unpleasant one and it is inevitable that innocent man should try and escape from it, and it is in this escape that the leap into sin – ultimately inexplicable – takes place. Innocence therefore involves this state in which man is overcome by dizziness at the thought of his own finite freedom. When he emerges from it, he finds that his freedom is real enough, but that its reality has been shown forth in sinful action. In theory, the dread could have been resolved by faith – why it is not is the enigma of sin, which Kierkegaard never professes to resolve. But in fact what happens is that the soul, caught up in this state of dread, attempts to escape from it by flying from either the finitude or the freedom, which are its two constituent elements. In the one case, man treats himself as a god. In the other, he surrenders his freedom in exchange for servitude to his own lusts or the will of a dictator. In either event innocence has been lost.

IAN HENDERSON

Instincts or Drives

The basic notion denoted by the term instinct is that of an enduring tendency or disposition to act in an organized way without previous performance or foresight. The term drive, though sometimes equated with instinct, usually refers to a motive with an intense 'demand' character which must be met by the organism in some way. Drives are generally instinctual, but some writers speak of secondary or acquired drives which are partly learned.

The concept of instinct has long been a controversial one in psychology, and many psychologists prefer not to use it on grounds that it is too vague and inferential. For those who do use it, it has the following major connotations.

1. Instinct refers to innate hereditary, potentials for behaviour, as opposed to learned or acquired motives. Although some psychologists deny that it is possible to discriminate between innate and learned behaviour, the work of the ethologists, such as Konrad Lorenz (*see On Aggression*, 1966), has shown that much animal behaviour is not learned, in the sense of

learned by trial and error or conditioning, but is activated by *imprinting* the response on the young of the species at an appropriate time by an adult of the species of a particular sex. Lorenz has demonstrated, for instance, that sexual responses are not completely innate in geese, but that young male geese will develop as homosexuals unless exposed to an adult male at the appropriate stage of development. Instinct is, then, an innate potential which must be developed. *See* **Development.**

2. Instincts in man refer generally to the irrational aspects of his personality, and as such may cause difficulty or distress, while in the lower animals instincts are generally adaptive in character, facilitating life and not hindering it. The adaptive nature of instincts formerly aroused controversy over their presumed teleological implications. They were regarded by many as evidence of purpose, and frequently instinct theories were accepted or rejected for that reason. Now instincts are not widely regarded as evidence of purpose, but as the result of mutation and natural selection.

The instinctual behaviour of animals is more highly developed and pervasive than in man, which results in the relatively fixed character of their adaptive pattern, as, for example, in the ant. Man is more flexible because of the less specific determinants of his instinctual life.

3. The number of instincts in man has been a subject of dispute. William McDougall, a prominent instinct theorist of a generation ago, tended to posit relatively large numbers, which fluctuated to some extent. In his *Outline of Psychology* (1923) he listed fourteen: escape, combat, repulsion, parental, appearance, mating, curiosity, submission, assertion, social or gregariousness, food seeking, acquisition, construction and laughter. These embrace all dimensions of the psychic life. While Freud, taking a more genetic approach, emphasized the drive-like quality of the instincts and their small number. He first held to one basic drive or instinct, the sexual, but later changed his view to include a second drive – the aggressive. There is considerable ambiguity in translating Freud at this point, as he used the word *Trieb* to indicate both the drive quality and the instinct quality at least in the phrases translated 'life instinct' and 'death instinct' by which he meant basic tendencies rather than immediately demanding motivations. *See* his *Beyond the Pleasure Principle*, 1920; *see also* **Id.**

While one may speak of strong or weak instincts, drives are strong by definition. They may, of course, diminish in intensity, as does the sex drive with passing of years, but in such instances it is perhaps not appropriate to speak of a drive. Drives may be displaced, as in animals sexual frustration sometimes results in overeating. The principle of displacement was also used by Freud to account for the substitute character of much human gratification, and formed the basis of his view that the man who could love and work was the optimal man, having displaced his primitive sexual and aggressive drives. Drives may also be frustrated, turned back on the self, or inadequately expressed. In such cases mental illness develops.

Acquired drives develop according to the laws of learning through conditioning and reward, though partly through unconscious displacement. Alcoholism is an example of an acquired drive. Such drives can be 'extinguished', though with difficulty.

The present climate in psychology favours minimizing the role of instincts, and maximizing the role of learning in the development of motivational drives. An instinctual base is acknowledged, but it is regarded as relatively vague and inaccessible for study, while secondary drives can be more easily studied and controlled. Recently, however, specific drive centres for eating have been discovered in the brain of rats, giving promise of behaviour control through cortical stimulation. Other 'pain-pleasure' centres are being searched out, so that sex and aggressive needs may also soon be met through the medium of electrodes placed in the brain.

Studies of drives and instincts, then, afford some comfort for those interested in man's flexible capability for higher functioning. They also suggest that man's drives do not have to be thwarted to produce ethical behaviour, but rather sometimes displaced through regulation by the ego. The drives serve the positive social function of limiting the malleability of man at the hand of man, though the cortical stimulation experiments mentioned above warn that even the drives may become subject to control by others. *See also* **Motives and Motivation** for a more general treatment of these issues.

JAMES N. LAPSLEY

Intention

The concept of intention has been thought to be important for ethics mainly because whether a man is blamed for an act can sometimes depend on whether he did it intentionally. It belongs to the same group of 'mental concepts', whose nature is still very obscure, as belief and desire; two people who had the same belief or desire or intention could in all cases be said to be 'of like mind'. It is characteristic of these states of mind that they have what are called 'intentional objects'; that is to say, what is the object of my intention is determined, not by what actually takes place, but by a certain description of it (true or false) which I 'have in mind'. Thus I may intend to dial ABBey 4520 (if asked what I was doing, I should say 'Dialling ABBey 4520'), but in fact be dialling ABBey 4250. A man who intends to do what he does under one description may not intend to do it under another description; he may intend to wound a man, but not to kill him, though the act of wounding does kill him. Similarly, I may believe that I am wounding a man, but not that I am killing him, although by wounding him I am in fact killing him.

The fact that we can intend to do what we do not actually do shows that intention is not any sort of knowledge of the future or the present. Nor is it any sort of belief. It is more akin to the kind of thought that is expressed by commands and requests; indeed, when I tell somebody to shut the door, I might be said to express the intention that he should shut the door. It is therefore tempting to compare intentions with self-addressed commands – but this remains an obscure metaphor.

If the genus to which intention belongs is 'being of a certain mind', the species is to be sought by asking what counts as 'having the same intention' or 'having a different intention'. Suppose that at a certain time I intend to do *a* at time *t* in the future. If, when time *t* comes, and I know that it has come, and am not forgetful of my intention, and can do *a*, I shall be said to have changed my intention (changed my mind) if I do not do *a*. An attractive definition of 'intention' (though not a complete one) is: 'A man is said to have an intention to do *a* if and only if he is of such a mind that he will have changed his mind if he fails, other than through inability or mistake or forgetfulness, etc., to do *a*.' If the 'etc.' could be satisfactorily filled out, this definition would at any rate differentiate intention from belief, though not without a perhaps unavoidable circularity, in that, by the reference to mistake, a prior definition of 'belief' is presupposed.

The definition, however, requires at least the following qualifications: (1) We do many acts intentionally without having had, *previously*, an intention to do them; (2) it must not be thought that to have an intention (any more than to have a belief) is to have something going on currently in one's mind (a man whose mind is at the moment a complete blank, or who is thinking solely about the game of football he is watching, can still be truly said to intend, or even to be intending, to return to London tonight); and (3) at the same time, a definition of intention solely in terms of dispositions to action will have difficulty in distinguishing between intentional and unintentional actions.

It has recently been disputed whether all foreseen consequences of an action must be intended, even if not desired. That this is so is suggested by the legal maxim that a man must be presumed to intend the natural consequences of his actions; for this is arrived at by deduction from the two premisses, 'A man must be presumed to foresee the natural consequences of his actions' and 'All foreseen consequences of actions are intended'. The maxim would lose its basis if either of these

premisses were false. Some, however, reject the second, on the ground that there are always many foreseen consequences of my actions which I should not properly be said to intend: for example, when I dive into the pool, I know that I shall make a splash, but I do not dive in with the intention of making a splash. Nor is the making of a splash *un*intentional; but on this view 'intentional' and 'unintentional' are not contradictory terms but only contrary – a consequence of an action may be neither.

If this view be accepted, it alters the relation, with which we started, between intention and blame; for, if I foresaw a consequence of my action, I shall be blamed for it, whether or not I intended it in the narrow sense proposed. Thus absence of intention, in this narrow sense, does not excuse. This has a bearing on the so-called 'Law of Double Effect'. The Law is sometimes put in the following way: if an act, not sinful in itself, has two consequences; and if one of these consequences is something which it is normally sinful to bring about, and is a necessary condition of the other, which is good, it may not be sinful to do the original act, because only the good consequence is intended, the other not. It may be that this doctrine rests upon an equivocation between wider and narrower senses of 'intend': in the sense in which absence of intention excuses, we intend all the foreseen consequences of our actions, bad as well as good; but in the sense in which undesired consequences are not intended, the absence of intention is no excuse, but only the absence of knowledge. *See also* **Negligence**.

R. M. HARE

Interest. *see* **Usury and Interest.**

Interim Ethic

The expression was used by Albert Schweitzer (q.v.) for the ethic of Jesus. This teaching was given in the expectation that there would be an almost immediate end to the age. It is to be understood therefore in relation to the situation of the imminent end and not as applying universally to any and every situation. *See* **Eschatological Ethics; Jesus, Ethical Teaching of.**

International Order

Relationships between nations, no less than between individuals, are subject to God's judgment. International order may be viewed as applying to the world criteria of justice and order similar to those traditionally assigned as functions to the national state. International order requires the effective structuring of the relationships of states and the harmonious functioning of international processes towards adequate goals. Under a sovereign God the world is to be regarded as a unity. In international society the closest possible approximation to the full requirement of love is expressed as opportunity for the individual and co-operation for the community.

A major end of international order is the preservation of peace, in the negative sense of the absence of war. In the words of the Amsterdam Assembly of the World Council of Churches, 'War as a method of settling disputes is incompatible with the teaching and example of our Lord Jesus Christ'. Yet mere cessation from military conflict is not sufficient. Nations may refrain from physical aggression and yet not live in peace. In its fullest sense peace also involves co-operative pursuit of the common welfare.

Justice, security and freedom are also among the goals of international society. Order is disrupted not only by war, but also by tyranny or exploitation. Each state tends to seek international arrangements which conform to its interests or purposes. The basic political problem of relating freedom for individuals or small groups and control by larger groups must be solved on a world scale as well as on the national level.

International order does not necessarily mean the absence of all forms of conflict. Differences in policy or ideology may contribute to mutual enrichment rather than to physical hostility or destructive rivalry. Within a framework of basic agreements, procedures can be worked out for the creative handling of conflict and for deeper reconciliation after differences have been openly faced.

Neither will coercion be completely absent from an international order in a world of imperfect men. Given the power of self-interest and the lure of evil, order cannot rest on consent alone. Power is always necessary to implement purpose. Because of the irrational impulses of men that power can never be solely persuasive. If human society is to continue, however, we must also find substitutes for the grosser forms of violence available to the modern State. Procedures of police power need to supersede reliance on international war. This involves both disarmament as a goal and the development of more redemptive and less punitive forms of force, as has been attempted, for example, by the practitioners of non-violent resistance.

A dynamic dimension must be introduced into any viable world order. No established social arrangement has eternal legitimacy. As changes occur in accepted values, technological processes, national purposes, or groups in power, so must international policies be correspondingly altered. There are always revisionist as well as *status quo* forces in society. Too firmly to solidify existing custom is to invite revolutionary explosion. What was once accepted as justice comes to be regarded as injustice. Appeals to law and order may then become advocacy of injustice and exploitation. Essential to international order, therefore, are procedures for the peaceful settlement of disputes, and for amending international law.

A more concrete description of the requirements for international order in our time leads to consideration of technological, political, economic and spiritual aspects. The first of these, developments in technology and applied science, provides both an imperative and a resource. Perhaps the most important social event of the past century was the birthday of the world. In terms of transportation, communication and common technological processes nations are tied together in an intimate web of interaction. What happens in one country immediately affects others. It is the more urgent therefore that humanity be protected against destructive uses of technology by necessary political controls. It is also important that the constructive possibilities of the modern technological revolution be fully released and made available everywhere on earth. This involves the cultivation of an even more active interaction among the nations in the free exchange of persons, ideas, cultural factors and economic resources.

The political features of international order would take us beyond narrow nationalism and the irresponsible exercise of national sovereignty. Order must be expressed in structural terms in social institutions. This requires organized co-operation and a rule of law in strengthened agencies like the United Nations. Unless such a form of democratic group decision can replace the anarchical conflict of independent national forces, war cannot be prevented. Furthermore, without such international structures, the realization of the great promise in modern technological and economic developments will be severely limited. Developing internationalism in other fields is running into the vestigial fetters of an antiquated international political system. *See* **United Nations; World Government.**

An economic programme supporting international order must deal with the great inequalities in the modern world and the self-interested policies which lead to conflict. Both these evils are challenged by Christian altruism with its thrust towards sharing opportunity. Economic measures to implement this motivation should include the lowering of barriers to world trade. A freer flow of goods is essential to improved economic opportunity. International political organization should also provide channels for the economic agreements necessary for smooth conduct of business across national boundary lines, for the protection of material resources, and for providing access by all responsible nations to adequate raw materials, markets and investment opportunities. A world strategy of development also demands the liquidation of empires and equality of racial opportunity. Wealthier nations need to provide economic aid both as justice to the disprivileged and as means towards developing stable governments, able to resist subversion and to play a responsible role in international life. *See* **Economic Aid; Imperialism.**

Even more fundamental are spiritual factors in world order. Without such non-material and non-institutional foundations, even the best political structures and economic practices are weak and transitory. A common groundwork of social understanding and ethical principles strengthens every superstructure. In a dynamic society there will continue to be differing economic and political ideologies. Yet a truly international ethos should at least provide similar general goals, such as peace, opportunity and freedom. Every effort needs to be made to widen the extent of consensus to include more specific matters such as procedures for diplomacy, the rights of small nations, the undesirability of a nation being sole judge in its own cause, or a sense of obligation to a more ultimate ground of national being. While mankind can go a long way towards peace and justice without such a developed consensus, the full concept of international order requires also a common basic ethos.

In all these fields, the political and economic as well as the spiritual, the Church has a special responsibility for world order. The international sphere in its full range is an area for obedience to God. The Lord of the nations calls all men to repentance, faith and compassionate concern for fellow men everywhere. Both the biblical message and the historical experience of a supra-national church show the possibilities in a new fellowship of new men. The Church as the body of Christ has a ministry of reconciliation and of proclamation. It is to heal wounds and foster fellowship. It is also to judge evil and promote justice. Rooted in worship and informed by study, churchmen have access to guidance which is more incisive and motivation which is more powerful. Theological grounding provides a sharper focus for ethical insight. In the light of God's love the limitations of political nationalism and economic egoism become clearer manifestations of sinful greed and pride. An international ethos orientated towards peace, justice and freedom becomes even more urgent for those moved by deeper dimensions of religious faith.

John C. Bennett, ed., *Nuclear Weapons and the Conflict of Conscience*, 1962; *Foreign Policy in Christian Perspective*, 1966; Alfred DeSoras, *International Morality*, 1963; Helmut Gollwitzer, *The Demands of Freedom*, 1965; Ernest W. Lefever, *Ethics and United States Foreign Policy*, 1957; Denys Munby, ed., *Economic Growth in World Perspective*, 1966; William J. Nagle, ed., *Morality and Modern Warfare*, 1960; Reinhold Niebuhr, *The Structure of Nations and Empires*, 1959; Paul Ramsey, *War and the Christian Conscience*, 1961; Edward Rogers, *Poverty on a Small Planet*, 1964; Harvey Seifert, *Ethical Resources for International Relations*, 1964; Papal Encyclical, *Pacem in Terris*, 1963.

HARVEY SEIFERT

Internationalism

The technological development of communications and the growth of large, complex structures of political and economic power has forged a network of interdependence around the nations of the world. Major social events anywhere affect men everywhere. Economic and political ties now provide a basis for internationalism, or commitment to international co-operation in realizing as far as possible the interests of all nations.

This spirit is supported by the all-inclusive emphasis of Christian love, extending to the farthest extreme of social distance to include even enemies. Love is non-preferential in the sense of recognizing no boundaries which exclude the distant, the different, or the distasteful. Every person is a focal point for concern. God is his Creator. Even while men are yet sinners God encircles them with the full intensity of his love.

God created man not in isolation, but in relationship. It is the will of God that man should live in creative community. Any disruption of fellowship strikes at the heart of God's intention for man. This has implications for both the quality and the range of community. To the fact of God's unification of mankind in his universal concern must now be added also the fact of man's acceptance of a social policy aimed at the closer unity of all humanity.

Any fragmentation of mankind by artificial barriers or any favouritism granting arbitrary privilege is foreign to the central articles of our faith. From the Christian standpoint every war is a civil war. Estrangement from neighbour is at the same time alienation within oneself. Exploitation of another constitutes self-deprivation also.

Immediate choices are limited by the ambiguities of existing situations. Yet important goals continue to be: world patterns for security in which safety for one is also safety for all, procedures for economic welfare gained not at the expense of others but by serving the mutual advantage, and protections for freedom not by the subordination of others, but in the democratic acceptance of status for all. The spirit to be embodied as fully as possible into international life is not that of antagonistic search for diverse ends but of full co-operation for the general welfare. *See* **Nationalism.**

HARVEY SEIFERT

Intuition

Intuition is the name given to supposed direct knowledge by rational insight of states of affairs; for example, in the ages when Euclid's axioms were thought to be absolute (in spite of the criticism of the 'parallels postulate', which goes back at least as far as Proclus) and believed to obtain in respect of the space of the physical world, these axioms and the theorems deduced from them were thought to embody universal and necessary truths concerning the structure of configurations in actual space. The axioms were believed to be established by immediate inspection of their terms, or by construction of these terms in an ideal medium. Thus one only had to think what one meant by a straight line to see, by a kind of direct intellectual insight, that it was the shortest distance between two points. The development of non-Euclidean systems of geometry, beginning with the work of the Russian geometer Lobachewski (who numbered Lenin's father among his outstanding pupils) and Bolyai and culminating in the use of such systems for the effective correlation of measurements in actual space in Einsteinian physics, constituted an intellectual revolution of the greatest importance, in that the claim made on behalf of geometry, viz. that it was a non-inductive study, giving us incorrigible insight into necessary relations within the actual world, must be regarded as invalidated, although philosophers of mathematics are by no means agreed in their understanding of the nature of pure geometry, the logical character of its proofs, etc. This revolution is particularly significant where moral philosophy is concerned. Thus many philosophers (e.g., John Locke in the seventeenth century and Professor H. A. Prichard in the twentieth) had supposed an analogous insight where the first principles of conduct were concerned, to that supposedly enjoyed where the axioms of Euclidean space were at issue. It is not for nothing that several moralists, who like Prichard would be regarded as intuitionists, fought a sustained, if somewhat pathetic, rearguard action against the claims made for non-Euclidean geometry. But the sort of apologetic for moral absolutism that has relied on the supposed analogy of geometry must be judged finally invalidated. The moralist, therefore, who is convinced that the intuitionist tradition embodies genuine perceptions concerning the nature of moral experience, is faced with the task of presenting alternative models of the direct insight into the moral universe he claims that we enjoy.

Other uses of the term which may be distinguished carefully from the foregoing and from one another which should be noticed include the following: The term is sometimes used to refer to the synoptic vision of all forms in the light of the 'Idea of the Good', which Plato distinguishes from the preceding grasp of individual forms. It occurs also in exposition of Bergson's opposition between two sorts of temporal succession of which we are differently aware. In common parlance it is used to refer to allegedly feminine quick perception concerning, for example, human motives sometimes hardly defensible by inductive argument but often disquietingly correct.

Finally in Kant's theory of knowledge in the *Critique of Pure Reason* (1781) the term is used to refer to the passive sense-awareness by which the subject receives the temporarily successive, and spatially discrete, data which through the co-operation of imagination and discursive understanding yield us knowledge of the single world of space and time, whose detailed causal order it is the task of the physical sciences to establish. In his third *Critique* Kant makes use for purposes of illustration of an important distinction between such an understanding as ours, which is inherently discursive and relies for the possibility of objective knowledge on resources (viz. a sensible intuition) extraneous to itself, and one which he calls intuitive such as the understanding enjoyed by God, if he exists, which posits its own object, and to which therefore all things are transparent. Kant develops this distinction in order further to elaborate his fundamental awareness of the limitations of characteristically human knowledge; he is not in any sense arguing for the existence of God; but in his discussion of the notion of an intuitive understanding and the contrast he draws between its condition and that of a human being relying on perception, theory-building (itself dependent on the elaboration of more powerful forms of mathematics), experiment (bound to the state of technical aparatus available as well as to the inventive genius of the experimenter), induction, observational invalidation, etc., he threw an enormous amount of light on the nature of that omniscience predicated of God in traditional metaphysical theology.

D. M. MACKINNON

Isaiah

Isaiah, one of the most famous of the Hebrew prophets, flourished in Judah *c.* 700 BC. He was apparently influential at court, and played an active part in shaping the foreign policy of his country. Like the other Hebrew prophets, he stressed the ethical demands of God upon the people, and criticized religious rites that were divorced from conduct. Perhaps his most characteristic ethical contribution was his development of the idea of holiness. As Rudolf Otto has shown, the most primitive sense of the holy has no ethical content, but points to a felt mystery, to something that is separate from the everyday and profane. Isaiah, to use Otto's expression, 'schematized' this primitive sense of the numinous by introducing moral and rational content into it. The *locus classicus* is the account of his vision in Chap. 6, where the holy God is the utterly pure and righteous God, the very sense of whose presence is a judgment upon the sins of men. The expression 'ethical theism' is perhaps too metaphysical to describe Isaiah's faith, but he must be reckoned a pioneer of the kind of religion that thinks of God in moral terms and that believes the worship of God to be inseparable from right conduct. *See* **Old Testament Ethics.**

EDITOR

I-Thou Relationships. *see* Buber, Martin.

James, William

William James (1842–1910), American philosopher. *See* **Pragmatism.**

Jealousy

The second of the Ten Commandments (Ex. 20.5) describes God as being a jealous God, that is, not tolerating people who find satisfaction in relationship with any being other than himself. Christian revelation has broken up this primitive conception of God as jealous and vengeful.

People do not decide to behave jealously, they drift into such behaviour with little or no conscious knowledge of what is happening until they find themselves imprisoned. The detection of jealousy is usually difficult because it is often born of the warmth of a generous love – thus parents in their protective love for their children will try to limit their companionships, thereby robbing them of their human birthright of independence and ability to develop freely. Jealousy in an engaged couple is a sign of danger, in marriage a sign of disaster because jealousy breeds suspicion, distrust and deception.

Churchmen, in the name of the Church, are often jealous of social institutions because of the amount of time given by church members to them and the place and power they hold in society. To alter St Paul's words, the institutions that be are ordained of God, to be accepted, loved and criticized but never to be ignored destroyed or regarded as permanent.

There is no simple cure for jealousy, no sure way of stopping it at its first sign. Its absence is a tribute to a loving disposition which feeds and is fed by a regard for the individuality of each person and a sense of responsibility for his, or her, full human development which requires a width of relationship far beyond a limited companionship. The masters of spirituality continually remind us, century by century, of the beauty of ordinate affection where people share a love of God which is greater than their love for one another.

R. E. C. BROWNE

Jeremiah

Jeremiah, Hebrew prophet, was born at Anathoth near Jerusalem in the second half of the seventh century BC, and was active in Judah in the decades preceding the fall of Jerusalem in 586 BC. He lived through the reformation of Josiah, and his ethical and social teaching resembles that of Deuteronomy. *See* **Old Testament Ethics.** Jeremiah is distinguished among the prophets for the depth of his spiritual life and his personal faith. His response to the divine call to a prophetic career meant for him the renunciation of marriage and family life, and the subordination of personal ambitions to the demands of his vocation. He seems to have suffered much from the authorities and from the common people alike, but was sustained through his experiences by his communing with God. We get a glimpse of this Hebrew spirituality in the passages known as the 'confessions' of Jeremiah.

EDITOR

Jesus, Ethical Teachings of

1. *Sources.* The ethical teaching of Jesus must be derived almost entirely from the Synoptic Gospels, Matthew, Mark and Luke. Even these Gospels present the tradition in its second generation form but the central thrust of the material may be assumed to reflect the intention of Jesus. The Fourth Gospel presents a distinctive emphasis and will be considered separately in the final section of this article. Undoubtedly some of the ethical teaching in the Epistles and Acts (*see* **Paul, Ethical Teaching of St**) is derived from the ministry of Jesus but here the admixture from other sources is considerable. The extra-canonical literature is even more distant from the historical Jesus and is of minimal value in determining his original teaching.

2. *Relation to Judaism.* Since Jesus was a Jew it is to be assumed that his ethical teaching was, in the main, a form of Jewish ethics. Sayings ascribed to him, particularly in Matthew (cf. Matt. 5.17–20; 23.2–3), affirm his solidarity with the Mosaic Law and there is no reason to doubt his commitment to the inherited tradition. Furthermore it has frequently been pointed out that practically all of his individual ethical statements have approximate parallels in Jewish and Rabbinic literature. This does not mean that his teaching was identical with that of his contemporaries, but rather that the materials he used were from the common Jewish stock. Jesus differed from his predecessors in the *radical* character of his demand, in his ignoring of the problem of practicability for the majority, and in his willingness to 'legislate' on the authority of his own relationship with God.

In this connection a crucial question concerns the understanding of the *Antitheses* in Matt. 5.21–48. They are introduced with the formula: 'You have heard that it was said . . . but I say unto you . . .'. On one interpretation the contrast in the formula reflects a consciousness on the part of Jesus that he was the bearer of a new or additional law. On another, and perhaps more probable, interpretation the formula implied 'You have understood that the Mosaic Law meant . . . but now I am telling you that its true significance is . . .'. Even if this latter view is correct there were still some points at which his teaching implicitly abrogated the established Law. This is true in connection with divorce (Mark 10.1–12; Matt. 19.1–9; 5.31–32; Luke 16.18), oaths (Matt. 5.33–37), clean and unclean foods (Mark 7.1–23; Matt. 15.1–20), retaliation (Matt. 5.38–48; Luke 6.27–36), and, possibly, sabbath observance (Mark 2.23–3.6; Matt. 12.1–14; Luke 6.1–11; 13.10–17; 14.1–6). In some of these areas Jesus' teaching appears clearly to abrogate portions of the Pentateuchal law, even though this may not have been his conscious purpose. Probably this fact cannot be escaped by arguing that Jesus fulfilled the 'intention' of the older law.

3. *Principles*. The central principle of Jesus' ethical teaching was a demand for radical obedience to and trust in God. This teaching normally found expression not in abstract statements about total obedience but in concrete injunctions in which allegiance to God was placed above other possible commitments such as family or possessions. For the contrast with allegiance to family *see* Mark 3.35 (Matt. 12.50; Luke 8.21); Luke 14.26 (Matt. 10.37); Luke 9.59 f. (Matt. 8.21 f.); Luke 12.51–53 (Matt. 10.34–36); Luke 9.61 f.; Matt. 19.10–12. For the contrast with possessions *see* Matt. 6.19–34 (Luke 12.22–31, 33 f.; 11.34–36; 16.13); Mark 10.17–31 (Matt. 19.16–30; Luke 18.18–30); Luke 12.13–21; 16.19–31.

Under the concept of radical obedience to God may be placed also the passages which insist that obedience includes inner attitudes as well as outward acts (cf. Matt. 5.21–30 on anger and lust), passages which indicate the ruthlessness with which sinful propensities must be eradicated (cf. Mark 9.43–48; Matt. 18.8–9; 5.29–30 'If your right eye causes you to sin, pluck it out and throw it away . . .'), and passages which stress that acts of piety must be done for God's sake and not for man's approval (Matt. 6.1–6, 16–18 almsgiving, prayer, fasting).

The second principle of Jesus' ethical teaching was a demand for radical concern for the good of the neighbour, and neighbour was understood in the broadest possible sense, cf. Luke 10.25–37; Matt. 5.43–48; Luke 6.27 f., 32–36. This principle came to expression in the Golden Rule (q.v.), Matt. 7.12; Luke 6.31, and in his repetition and application of the command from Lev. 19.18 'You shall love your neighbour as yourself' (Mark 12.31; Matt. 22. 39; Luke 10.27; Matt. 19.19). In these last passages the command for love to neighbour is combined with love for God thus articulating the two central principles of Jesus' ethic. Since both of these commands are taken from the OT it is again demonstrated that Jesus' ethic was essentially 'Jewish'. Its distinctiveness lay in the radical application of these two principles. With respect to concern for neighbour it may be argued that in some passages requiring unlimited surrender to the demands of others (cf. Matt. 5.39–42; Luke 6.29–30), the motive of Jesus may not have been so much concern for the good of the other as a desire to shatter the self-concern of the individual confronted by these demands. (Is it really always in the interest of the 'other' to give him what he asks?) But this shattering of the self-concern is finally for the sake of the obligation to God and the neighbour.

Some parenetic passages which do not seem initially to be motivated by a concern for God or 'the other' are nevertheless extensions of these concerns. Thus the prohibition of oaths and the insistence on a simple 'Yes' or 'No' (Matt. 5.33–37) expresses the passion for total truthfulness before God and the neighbour.

The ethic of Jesus attacked the self-centredness of the individual but it did not deny his immense value. On the contrary Jesus' ministry witnessed to the concern of God for each individual. This is revealed in his attitude towards the religious outcasts of his culture. His estimate of God's concern for a single individual is perhaps best expressed in the parable of the Lost Sheep, Luke 15.1–7 (Matt. 18.12–14). This same concern for human beings was also expressed in his subordination of the demands of the sabbath to human need (cf. Mark 2.27, 'The sabbath was made for man, not man for the sabbath'; Luke 13.15 f.; 14.1–6). Presumably this was also his attitude with respect to other facets of the ceremonial or ritual law – although the evidence is negligible (Matthew is the most legalistic in his presentation of Jesus, but he is also the one to quote 'I desire mercy and not sacrifice', 9.13; 12.7).

Like his contemporaries Jesus took the reward motif for granted. It is perhaps most prominent in Matthew (cf. 6.1–18; 10.41 f.; 16.27; 18.23–35), but it appears also in the other Synoptics (Mark 9.41; 10.29–31; Luke 6.23, 32–35; 12.47 f.). However, it is noticeable that the promised rewards are not material, probably not even in Mark 10.29 f. Furthermore the term 'reward' may be a misnomer since it is clear that these come more from the grace of God than from the 'merit' of the man involved (cf. Luke 7.36–50; 17.10, 'We are unworthy servants; we have done only what was our duty'; Matt. 18.23–35, The Unmerciful Servant; 20.1–16, Labourers in the Vineyard).

If a non-dialectical statement of this teaching is possible, it would be that, for Jesus, the blessings of God are proffered to all men (Matt. 5.45; Luke 6.35) but the behaviour of some prevents the reception of the proffered gifts (Matt. 18.32–35).

4. *Problems.* Numerous theoretical and practical problems exist in connection with the ethical teaching of Jesus.

Did he assume that his demands had a universal or only a limited application? Were they intended for all men or for disciples only? Were they for all times, or for the brief interim before the expected arrival of the Kingdom (Interim Ethic, q.v.), or for the Kingdom age which was thought to have arrived already, or for the Kingdom which was still expected?

In view of the element of hyperbole in Semitic thought and in Jesus' own teaching (Luke 14.26; Matt. 10.37; Luke 16.13; Matt. 6.24; 6.6) how absolutely did he expect his instructions, for example, Matt. 5.34, 39–42; Luke 16.18, to be taken?

What was the relation between achievement and grace in his thought? The paradox of his teaching is that on the one hand he made demands on human life even more stringent than those of his contemporaries (Matt. 5.20), while, on the other hand, he declared God's love and forgiveness to individuals who had not obeyed even the lesser demands, for example, 'tax-collectors and sinners'. Did he share the Pauline assumption of the universal need for grace? Some of his teaching seems to presuppose a universal sinfulness, notably his general demand for repentance or Luke 11.13; Matt. 7.11; but did he regard 'repentance' and a new will as human possibilities?

His ethic appears to be aimed at the individual. Was there any concern on his part for 'social order' or 'world order'? Can his teachings be applied in the same way to 'Moral Man' and to 'Immoral Society'? Or is it possible that his principles are directly applicable *neither* to individuals *nor* to society, that is, that his demands remain as a North Star for human conduct but the application both to personal and to collective life requires adaptation according to the situation?

What was the connection between his ethic and his person? Was obedience to his ethic adequate apart from personal commitment to him – as would be suggested by Luke 6.46; Matt. 7.21; Mark 3.31–35; Luke 11.27 f.? Or was a personal commitment to himself a part of his demands, for example, Mark 8.38; 10.21b? To put it differently: was the ethic of Jesus an expression of his messianic consciousness and claim, or was it a part of the traditional prophetic task to make clear the will of God?

5. *Johannine Ethic.* The Fourth Gospel presents a distinctive formulation of the ethical teaching of Jesus, and this formulation is repeated in I John. This may be seen in three ways. *First*, instead of a series of diverse, ethical imperatives – as in the Synoptics, especially Matthew – there is only one imperative, 'A new commandment I give to you, that you love one another; even as I have loved you, that you also love one another' (John 13. 34–35; cf. 15.12,17; I John 3.11,14,23; 4.7,19–21; 5.2). The details disappear and this single, all-embracing command is highlighted. *Second*, in the Synoptics the norm for the love commanded is that we should love the neighbour as we love ourselves; but in John the norm is 'as I have loved you'. The abstract command has disappeared, being swallowed up by the life which had reflected that command in word and in deed. The norm is no longer human self-love but the life which had embodied the divine self-giving. *Third*, the Fourth Gospel is so concerned to stress the fellow-Christian as the object of the love commandment that love for those outside is almost entirely ignored. Note the 'one another' of John 13.34 (twice), 15.12, 17 (cf. I John 3.11,23; 4.7,11,12; II John 5) and the 'brother(s)' of I John 2.10; 3.10,14; 4.20,21. Probably this does not mean John denied the earlier teaching of love for the 'enemy' or the outsider, but rather that he was concerned to stress *either* the special love which is possible only when it is reciprocated, *or* the distinctive love which the believing community was called upon to show as a sign to the outside world (John 13.35).

While the Johannine formulation is certainly that of the Christian community, it underlines an indispensable characteristic of the Christian ethic, namely, that it is a response ethic, an ethic of gratitude. The life of joyous obedience is the normal, spontaneous response to the gifts of God in creation and in the Christ.

In addition to the standard studies of Jesus and his thought *see* the following: C. H. Dodd, *Gospel and Law*, 1951; R. N. Flew, *Jesus and his Way*, 1963; John Knox, *The Ethic of Jesus in the Teaching of the Church*, 1961; William Lillie, *Studies in New Testament Ethics*, 1963; T. W. Manson, *Ethics and the Gospel*, 1960; L. H. Marshall, *The Challenge of New Testament Ethics*, 1948; C. A. A. Scott, *New Testament Ethics*, 1930.

HARVEY K. MCARTHUR

Jewish Ethics

If the unity of God is the central affirmation of the Jewish religion, the unity of man is the central theme of Jewish ethics. Indeed, a good case could be made for the thesis that the theological doctrine was a reflection on the metaphysical plane of the Jewish concept of human nature. In its most basic form, this concept asserts that man must strive to become a fully harmonious being – one in himself, one with mankind, one before God.

The first principle is therefore an act of faith. For, in our experience, man is pulled in opposite directions by the conflicting forces within his being. The good desire, *yezer tov*, and the *yezer hora*, the evil desire, are perpetually at war within our breast (Berochot 5a). On the plane of philosophy, this conflict is reflected in the polarity between the concept of man as a self sufficient entity and the view of him as a dependent creature inherently related to a metaphysical realm or being. Then, as we turn to the realm of social relations, we encounter the opposition between man as a political animal, who discovers his identity in the State, and man as an independent source of judgment, whose conscience is perpetually and properly in polar tension with the laws and judgments of the community.

In our experience, then, man is in tension, in the three dimensions of existence – psychologically, metaphysically and sociologically. The fundamental assertion of Jewish ethics is that man can and ought to achieve a harmonious resolution of these tensions, for they derive from God, who is One. 'And be ye holy; for I, the Lord, am holy' (Lev. 19.2). Man is to *become* holy, while God *is* holy.

Psychologically, it is the function of the good desire, not to overcome and crush the evil desire, but to embrace and sublimate it. Commenting on the divine assertion that 'man is very good', the Sages affirm, 'good is the Good Desire, "very good" is the Evil Desire' (Gen. 1.31; Yalkut Shimeoni, ad loc.). For the depths of passion within us make possible superlative levels of achievement, levels which must be transcended almost as soon as they are attained. So, it is our duty to guard our personal well-being, to enjoy the legitimate pleasures of life, including the normal delights of food, family and company and take delight in all the gifts of life. But, we must also know that we belong to God, not to ourselves, and voluntarily deny ourselves some permissible indulgences – 'sanctify yourself by means of that which is permitted to you' (Yebamot 20a).

Philosophically, man is a thinking being. It is his task and destiny to reflect on the whole of creation, assigning 'names' to all creatures and discovering their essences. Wisdom consists in classifying all things, putting them into their respective categories. In human relations, the quest of philosophy is to achieve a design of life, in which every impulse and every ideal is accorded its proper place (Abot 4.3). This quest is opposed by our numinous feeling, or our metaphysical intuition, which insists that the essence of our being eludes the meshes of reason. Human nature cannot be fitted into the System, because it contains a dimension that transcends the knowable world. And in this polarity, too, Jewish ethics embraces both horns of the dilemma, asserting both the rightness of humanism and the need of transcending

it. 'Complete, ye shall be *with* the Lord, your God' (Deut. 18.13). To render justice to the whole of human nature is right, but this task is infinite in nature, since, apart from his reference to the Supreme Being, man is not complete.

Sociologically, man is a 'political animal', incapable of self-fulfilment in isolation. Hence, it is his duty to submit to the laws of the community and to obey the law, even if his life be required. But, man may also discover the divine will in his heart, the inner depths of which are beyond the reach of the State. Every man faces God directly, and when the commands of God collide with those of the State, the latter must yield. 'The words of the Master, and the words of the disciple – whose word shall be followed?' (Kiddushin 42b).

Some scholars describe the central motif of Jewish ethics as being the 'sanctification of life'. This phrase is extremely suggestive, but also ambiguous. Is life holy, or must it be made holy? In reality, both answers are given. Human life, in all its many-sidedness, is good, but not as it is in the raw – only insofar as it is directed towards God. And the task of so directing it is never completed.

In the pagan world, man's yearning for ethical perfection was fragmentized, since the deity was conceived under the aspect of many and warring gods. Certainly, the promptings of conscience were reflected in the literatures of ancient Egypt and Babylonia (Breasted 'Dawn of Conscience'). Wisdom, or philosophy, was cultivated by Sages and formulated in memorable maxims. The priests of the 'official' religions and of the private, 'mystery' cults, catered to man's sense of the numinous. And the law of the land was proclaimed with all the authority of gods and kings. But, these disparate ideals were not fused into one flame of idealism. The priests plied their trade, the ecstatics impressed the populace, the men of wisdom trained the bureaucrats, and the kings proclaimed their laws in the names of the gods. Since the diverse disciplines were not related to one source, there was no dynamic dialectic. And when philosophy emerged in full bloom in the schools of Athens, its principles and practice were quite independent of the rituals of the city-cult and the laws of the civil government.

In the biblical world, the wholeness of human nature and its transcendent dimension were affirmed. Hence, the tension arises between instinct and ideal, between the rituals of tradition and the individual's awareness of the divine word, between the laws of State and Temple and the insights of human wisdom. This tension is not between the divine and the demonic, but between the several embodiments of the divine. Therefore, the tension is resolved only through a series of compromises, which extend throughout man's history, attaining the perfection of peace only in the end of days.

In the Hebrew Bible, we are given many examples of the creative character of this on-going tension. The life of Abraham is paradigmatic. He is represented as the great ancestor, 'the father of a multitude of nations'; yet, by divine command, he leaves his aged father in search of a new destiny. Like the good and pious men of his age, he is prepared to offer his son, Isaac, as a sacrifice, but, in advance of his time, he affirms that God abhors human sacrifice and demands only man's inner obedience; hence animal sacrifices are quite sufficient. He is not merely the 'knight of faith' but, what is far more significant, the defender of a faith that is rational and moral, even as it is a commitment to the transcendent God. He preaches the justice of God, in behalf of the individual, and in his plea for the Sodomites, he insists that God must not destroy the just along with the wicked. Yet, in behalf of his descendants, he accepts the state of slavery and torment for four hundred years, so long as this period of trial will eventuate in the emergence of a 'great nation'.

The Jewish faith unites man's moral and rational faculties with the mystical feelings of surrender to the divine will. Hence its inner dialectic. The very concept of a covenant implies a realm of existence in which God and men enjoy a fundamental mutuality. It is true that God lays down the law for his creatures, but not as a wilful autocrat. The purpose of his laws is to enhance life, and to bestow wisdom (Lev. 18.5; Deut. 4.6). The 'way of the Lord' is not a mystical *Tao*, but it is 'to do justice and righteousness' (Gen. 18.19). In his God-given freedom man rethinks the thought of God, in respect of the True, the Good and the Holy.

Some scholars have maintained that Judaism is a 'classical faith', in the sense of harmonizing all of man's faculties (Leo Baeck, *Judaism and Christianity*, 1958). But this classicism is balanced by the non-classical recognition that human nature points beyond itself to the divine Being, whose thoughts are not our thoughts. Hence not man in himself, but 'man as he stands before God', is 'the measure of all things'. And to face the divine is to remain open to new insights, even as one bows to his will, which is revealed in Torah and Wisdom.

The Hebrew Bible is the work of three religious personalities – the priest, the prophet and the sage. This is how Jeremiah envisaged the sacred tradition, 'for there shall not cease Torah from the priest, the word from the prophet, and counsel from the sage' (Jer. 18.18). In all religions, the priest is the guardian of the tradition. He performs the sacred rites, which symbolize man's dependence upon the divine Being. Priestly rites are non-rational and even irrational, for their function is to minister to man's sense of the numinous. But the Torah of the priests is balanced in Scripture by the living word of the prophet, who confronts the social realities of his day with a fresh awareness of the divine will. The prophet is a moralist insisting that the core of the divine will is goodness and mercy. And the Sage adds his 'counsel', which consists of the lessons of human experience and reflection. But though they speak with different voices, the priest, the prophet and the Sage together reflect the will of God. The wisdom of the Sage is divine in origin, along with the admonitions of the prophets and the teachings of the priests (Prov. 2.6). The basic virtue of the Sage is justice in society and temperance in personal life – 'giving all things their due', and refraining from 'excess' in all the spheres of life. The central virtue of priestly piety is charity or love – the love of God and the love of man – self-surrender to God, and self-giving to man. The prophet accepts both counsels, and he fuses them in the mystical fire of divine confrontation – hence the entire tradition becomes problematical to him. He adds the quality of humility, which derives from the awareness of the infinite dimension of man's task. Hence there emerges Micah's summation – 'to do justly, to love mercy and to walk humbly with the Lord, thy God' (Micah 6.8).

In the post-biblical era, the nature of Jewish ethics could best be described as loyalty to the teachings of 'the law and the prophets'. It was not sufficient to comply with the requisites of the law; one had to embrace also 'the prophets', who represented the heritage of critical and inspired reflection on the *meaning* of the law. While the law set the norms of conduct for the community, the pious individual was bidden to go 'beyond the line of the law' and to meditate on its governing principles. He was also commanded to defer to the conscience of civilized humanity (*derech erez*), for Torah is founded on the obligations of humanity (Abot 2.3; Leviticus Rabba, 9). The Jew was therefore expected to share in the virtues of priesthood, prophecy and universal wisdom.

Out of the blending of these three biblical hero-images, there emerged the rabbinic hero-image, the disciple of the wise. He took upon himself the obligation to abide by the priestly regulations of purity (Tossefta, Demai 2), to the extent that he merited it, 'the Holy Spirit' directed his Torah-reasoning (Yoma 9b). It was his responsibility to care for the sick, the widows and the orphans (Moed Koton 6a). He was the judge, the teacher, the social service worker and the preacher, doing the Lord's work without pay, 'even as the Lord takes care of our needs without any compensation' (Hilchot Talmud Torah 3.10). He practised his trade for so many hours a day, in order to provide for his wife and children, but he set fixed hours for prayer and Torah-study. He was an athlete of the spirit, endeavouring to climb the ladder of forty-eight virtues, whereby the Torah was acquired and the gift of the Holy Spirit was merited (Abot 6.6). But, he was not an ascetic. To be sure, he 'sanctified himself by denying himself the things that were permitted', but only with moderation. Like the ancient philosophers, he esteemed learning as his chief pleasure, but his learning was inseparable from the practice of charity, the pursuit of 'the ways of peace' in the community and the raising of his family. 'A man whose wisdom exceeds his deeds, to what may be he compared? – to a tree, the branches of which are large and the roots of which are small. When the Southern wind comes, it is uprooted and turned over' (Abot 3.22).

Above all, in his quest of the vision of perfection, his ultimate goal was beyond time itself. While no more was required of him than to follow the way of the Torah, as it was formulated in the oral law, he required of himself the unrelenting endeavour to achieve perfection. Every day he was to say to himself – 'when will my deeds reach the level of Abraham, Isaac and Jacob?' In the face of the infinite demand, he could not but be humble and discontented with his spiritual attainments – 'the disciples of the wise cannot rest, either in this world or in the next one' (Berochot 64a). Yet he knew that in 'matters of the heart', achievements could not be calculated mechanically. For in pride, all may be lost, and in true repentance and humility, a 'person may acquire his world in one hour' (Aboda Zara 10b).

The disciple of the wise was not distinguished from the people by any formal ordination. To be a disciple was the popular ideal in rabbinic Judaism, an ideal that was 'professionalized' in part only in the later Middle Ages. At different times one or other aspects of this ideal personality was emphasized. Saadia Gaon stressed the need of balance and harmony – we must not allow any one ideal to distort our personality, not even 'the love of God'. Bahya was far more singleminded, assenting even to the virtues of the monastic life. Maimonides was more even-handed. He retained the polarity of 'the golden mean' on the one hand, and the 'intellectual love of God' on the other hand.

On the threshold of the modern age, the Hassidim emphasized the virtues of religious enthusiasm, of unquestioning piety and limitless zeal in the practice of charity. They revived and adapted the ancient pharisaic *Haburah*, binding themselves by special covenants to be loyal to a saintly leader. In their fellowships joy and piety were inseparable, as they sang and danced and drank 'for the sake of heaven'. Their motto was the psalmist's injunction – 'serve the Lord in joy, but rejoice in trembling' (Ps. 100.2).

The *Mithnagdim* (opponents) stressed the intellectual component in the hero-image of disciple of the wise. To them the noblest virtue

was diligence in learning. The ethical movement which arose in their midst (Mussar) sought to achieve ever higher levels of perfection through the regular practice of self-criticism and self-examination.

When the boundaries of orthodoxy were breached by the impact of modern thought, the impetus of the ethical ideal was directed largely toward classicism. This tendency was enhanced by the circumstance that the friends of Jewish emancipation were generally liberals. Nevertheless various romantic currents exerted a powerful pull in the past century.

Under the joint influence of Zionism and utopian socialism, there emerged the hero-image of the *Halutz*. Both Martin Buber, with his theory of interpersonal relations, and A. D. Gordon, with his romantic glorification of agricultural labour, contributed to the emergence of this ideal. The *Halutz* achieves 'self-realization' by the surrender of any personal ambition for gain or fame; he fulfils himself in the service of the nation and as a servant of the life-giving soil; yet he does not 'retreat' from the world; he marries, and his children are given a good education in the *Kibbutz*; he overcomes the 'self-alienation' of bourgeois society by becoming part of a collective, which is the nucleus of the ultimate, world-wide socialist society. He shares in the cultural as well as the political aspirations of the nation. He is a peasant-scholar-soldier and man of culture. He is a disciple of the wise in a new guise.

Jacob B. Agus, *The Vision and the Way, An Interpretation of Jewish Ethics*, 1966; Martin Buber, *Tales of the Hassidim*, 1947; A. J. Heschel, *Who is Man?*, 1966; Max Kaduslim, *The Rabbinic Mind*, 1952; Maurice Lazarus, *Jewish Ethics*, 1901.

JACOB B. AGUS

John XXIII, Pope.
see Pontifical Social Encyclicals.

John Chrysostom, St
John (*c*. 354–407), the most eminent representative of the so-called 'Antiochene' school, was born and educated in the metropolis of Syrian Antioch, where, after his ordination to the priesthood in 386, he gave himself to the ministry of preaching which won him the name 'Chrysostom', 'golden-mouthed'. With his eloquence he combined remarkable gifts in the exposition of Scripture, and a profound moral earnestness. The burden of his preaching was less dogmatic than hortatory. His aim was to reawaken in his hearers a sense of the magnitude of their Christian vocation to simplicity of life and to love for God and man. When in 398 he was made Patriarch of Constantinople, he brought to his new post in the capital the same passion for moral reform

which had guided his ministry at Antioch. At the imperial court, however, neither his monastic habits of life, nor his moral severity, nor his more than occasional lack of tact won him any friends; and the emnity of the Empress Eudoxia, assisted by the intrigues of the jealous Patriarch of Alexandria, Theophilus, brought about his ultimate deposition and banishment (404). Chrysostom died in 407, as the result of the rigours of a journey on foot to a new place of exile.

Prior to his ordination, Chrysostom had lived the monastic life; and his moral teaching reflects in its severity and elevation the ascetic ideal of the monk. The object of his teaching was the practical one of converting his flock from a merely conventional Christianity to a faith which expressed itself in inward and outward dedication of life. He emphasized repeatedly the necessity of good works, of love for God bearing fruit in active obedience. In part, such obedience was understood as abstention from worldly values and preoccupations. Chrysostom warns his people against the snares of life in a great metropolis; against theatre and circus, the frivolities of the social round, vanity in dress, the dangers of lust, avarice and ambition.

Most characteristic of Chrysostom, however, is his emphasis on the positive practice of love in the conduct of public as well as private life. His criticism of the semi-Christian society of Antioch and Constantinople is directed particularly at what seems to him a scandalous neglect of the poor and underprivileged, whose champion he constitutes himself. He points repeatedly to the injustice in the coexistence of superfluous riches for the few and poverty for the many. He insists upon the duty of sacrificial and sympathetic almsgiving and relief. He sees the economic contrasts in Roman society as the products of avarice and envy, and demands that Christian faith shows itself in a love which proceeds deliberately to set such wrongs right. Chrysostom, therefore, is a witness to the social criticism, and the cry for social justice, implicit in the ethical tradition of the fourth-century Church.

R. A. NORRIS, JR

Jung, Carl Gustav

Jung (1875–1961) was a Swiss psychiatrist. Early in his professional work he read some of Freud's early writings, and found the dynamic emphasis similar to that which he was himself developing. He entered the psychoanalytic movement, and for a time it seemed that he would become its leader following Freud. But the men developed disagreement on some theories, which also involved personal feelings, and parted company about 1913 (when Jung was still under forty). The therapeutic movement, akin to psychoanalysis, that collected itself around Jung is usually called 'analytical

psychology', although some other terms, including 'complex psychology', have been used.

The analytical psychology movement, especially in relation to psychotherapeutic work, has always been much smaller than the Freudian movement, and in the USA has had little influence on psychiatry generally. Yet some of Jung's therapeutic writings of thirty or forty years ago sound surprisingly modern today, as in the collection of papers, *The Practice of Psychotherapy* (1954). A considerable proportion of the 'Jungian analysts' today are not trained medically but rather in psychology and related fields.

During his lifetime Jung would not write an autobiography, nor would he release material for a biography. However, he did help to edit *Memories, Dreams, Reflections*, published soon after his death. In the prologue he wrote, 'Recollection of the outward events of my life has largely faded or disappeared'. But the book is astonishing for the insight afforded into Jung's inner life, even far back into dreams of his early childhood. His interest in religion was strong throughout childhood and the teens; but he felt all his life that this interest was clear and immediate to him, in contrast to the laboured faith of his pastor-father.

Because of Jung's early relation to Freud and psychoanalysis, and the subsequent break, for a long time it was suggested that one had to take either Freud or Jung. It now becomes clearer that Jung's permanent contributions are mostly of a different kind from Freud's. Jung never ceased to credit Freud with the discovery of the dynamic unconscious, with the development of a dynamic psychotherapy, and with other discoveries. Feeling that he was moving on from Freud, Jung pioneered in understanding the human psyche through a 'theory of opposites' applied to every level of psychic life. Examples are the concepts of anima, the sub-dominant female principle in a man, and the animus, the sub-dominant male principle in a woman.

A great deal of Jung's study and research was in seeking data in unlikely records of human culture for their correlative significance with what he was turning up in therapeutic work. He studied religions of many kinds, both oriental and occidental; he studied alchemy and Gnosticism; and even, finally, flying saucers. He saw all such things (as he felt proper to a psychologist) as psychic facts giving important insight into the human mind. He was especially impressed by the emergence of 'archetypal images' in many different contexts, demonstrating, he felt, the existence of 'collective' as well as 'personal' dimensions to man's unconscious psychic life. It is in terms of his many brilliant correlations of such data that Jung's permanent contribution to science will eventually be chiefly based.

Although scholarly study has not yet been done on Jung's contribution to ethics, the centre of this contribution lies in his methodology of 'opposites', especially in the conception of psychic compensation. When a man becomes fixed rigidly along some particular line (his favourite example was the man who tries to handle everything by thinking, even when a bit of feeling or intuition would be appropriate), something in his psyche tries to signal him, warn him, and re-direct him so he may get things in better balance. Thus Jung did not believe in a rationalistic control by clear consciousness; but neither did he believe in letting the unconscious take over, for it could destroy the psyche altogether if unchecked. Thus, his theory not only calls for expanded awareness of inner and collective as well as personal contents of the unconscious, but also holds that many devices of culture (especially religion) through the ages were precisely to foster this kind of relationship.

The function of religion, he held, was to keep man open to the depths within him (which also transcend him), but at the same time to prevent his being overwhelmed by them. For lonely and over-intellectualized western man, he felt religions could not perform this function automatically as before. Thus, his conception of morals is related to the way in which a man deals with his conscious and unconscious mind together, and his using the result for his proper 'individuation'. To Jung a man's self is, empirically, just what we can now see as his centre; but the self is also the goal of his individuation.

Jung resisted the efforts of many theologians to get him to speak of 'objective reality'. He felt a psychiatrist and psychologist should show only that psychic reality is also reality. He articulated very little of the philosophical premisses of his thought. Kantian modes of thought seem strong, but there are also fundamental points akin to existentialism, to process philosophy, and perhaps others.

The best beginning in reading Jung himself is *Two Essays in Analytical Psychology*, 1928, available in paperback. The religious and ethical student will be especially interested in *Psychology and Religion: West and East*, 1958, in *Aion*, 1959, and in *Memories, Dreams, Reflections*, 1963. The Modern Library's *Basic Writings of C. G. Jung*, 1959, is also a good starting point. A comprehensive, well-translated, and beautifully printed *Collected Works* of Jung is now being published by Pantheon Books. About two-thirds of the twenty-odd volumes are now available. Several brief collections of writings by Jung are also available now in paperback form.

SEWARD HILTNER

Jurisprudence. *see* Law.

Just Price and Just Wage

The doctrine of the just price, and that of the just wage, which is a special case of it, arose out of the mediaeval attempt to apply a detailed system of Christian ethics to every aspect of life. In any transaction, it was held, justice requires that the seller receive a value equivalent to that of the goods or services which he provides to the buyer. In practice, this price was taken to be that arrived at by common evaluation, as reflected in prevailing market prices. Hence it was recognized that it must reflect changes in the general conditions of demand and supply, though it was also strongly maintained that a buyer's exceptional necessity did not give a seller the right to exact a higher return. Taking advantage of temporary shortages to extort high prices was regularly condemned.

The just wage, similarly, was a price for labour fairly equal to the value of the service provided by the seller to the buyer. Hence it was held to imply equal pay for equal working capacity and that in each type of occupation the pay should be adequate to enable the worker to maintain the status associated with his position in life.

The detailed application of these principles to actual prices and wage rates was obviously easier in a slow-changing society, where customary rates were known and accepted over long periods, than it could be amid at the rapid technological and social changes of the present day. When new products are always appearing and when technical innovation is constantly changing costs of production, creating a demand for new jobs, and destroying the demand for others, it is very difficult to say in practice just what a just price or a just wage should be. Modern economic theory, being thoroughly positivistic, does not use such terms, but seeks rather to analyze the forces which lead to actual market prices. Yet the idea of fairness or justice still underlies much or our thinking on such matters as opposition to high prices charged by monopolies, or to resale price maintenance, as against the desire of traders not to cut prices below what is felt to be a 'fair' level. Similarly, trade unions insist on the 'rate for the job' and on the maintenance of comparability with other occupations. M. P. Fogarty in *The Just Wage* (1961) makes an interesting attempt at a critique of modern British wage and income policy in the light of the doctrine.

JOHN F. SLEEMAN

Just War

The doctrine of the just war attempted to set forth the minimal conditions that must obtain to permit of a Christian's participating in war. We should be perfectly clear that a 'just' war is entirely different from the notion of a 'holy' war. The latter has never had a place in Christian thought, though perhaps the Crusades and wars of religion were, in practice, holy wars. But for Christian theologians, war was from the beginning essentially unholy, and participation in it must be considered problematical. The doctrine of the just war, as developed gradually in the thought of St Augustine, St Thomas and others, was never intended to glorify war or to assign to war some affirmative character, but rather to indicate cases where the evil of war might or even must be accepted in preference to some greater evil of injustice, oppression or inhumanity that would take place if not stopped by an act of war. The conditions for a just war, according to St Thomas, are: (1) it must be waged by constituted authority; (2) the cause must be just; (3) there must be the intention of establishing good or rectifying evil. To these conditions is usually added a fourth, taken from Francisco de Vitoria: (4) the war must be waged by proper means. For many centuries, this doctrine served very well, and although it has come under much criticism in recent times, we ought to recognize that it is a fair and realistic way of trying to contain the evil of war in a society which knew worse evils. The question today is not about the essential moral validity of the doctrine for the circumstances which its authors envisaged, but whether it still makes sense in the very changed circumstances of our times. Concerning the first condition, for instance, it might be argued that wars of liberation (e.g., the guerrilla wars of Algerians against French or Cypriots against British), though not waged by sovereign powers, were just, and quite different from the private wars of mediaeval noblemen, which St Thomas presumably had in mind. More importantly, it might be asked whether, in view of the great destructiveness of modern weapons, the third condition can still hold. Would not a nuclear war blot out all the parties engaged, so that there could not be any righting of wrongs as a result? Actually, not only a just war but any war must envisage some result, and if nuclear conflict must lead to universal destruction, then strictly speaking it is not 'war' any more. However, the most competent authorities seem to suppose that, however great the destruction, survival of nuclear war is possible. The question would seem to be whether one could visualize an injustice so overwhelmingly great that the massive losses of nuclear war would be worth paying for its removal. The fourth point, about using 'proper means', has been questioned chiefly on the grounds that the methods of modern warfare, especially aerial bombing, cannot be brought within the category of 'proper means'. This question, however, is not a simple one. The old distinction between 'military' and 'civilian' has become blurred and may well disappear as war becomes increasingly mechanized and automated. It may well be a civilian who pushes the button, so to speak, and no war could be fought nowadays that did not strike at the armaments production and administrative network of the enemy. The very problems of war have become so overwhelming that no nation will ever lightly embark upon war. It is in the face of these problems that there has emerged the concept of the 'limited war', and in some respects this is almost a secular counterpart of the traditional theological idea of the 'just war'. *See* **Peace and War.**

EDITOR

Justice

Justice is a fundamental ethical concept, but because the word gets used in a number of senses, it is hard to pin down. Justice was one of the four cardinal virtues of the ancients, and it also appears prominently in the OT. In modern times, the quest for social justice has been a major ethical concern. In the widest sense (for instance, when we talk of the 'just man'), justice is hardly to be distinguished from integrity or moral excellence. It is in this wide sense that the word is mostly used in the OT. *See* **Righteousness.** In the narrowest sense, justice is conformity to the law. The just person or the just act has regard to the law, and the enforcement of justice means the insuring by the civil authority that the laws are obeyed, or their infraction punished. *See* **Law; State.** Perhaps the most interesting ethical sense lies somewhere between the two already noted. We can talk about an 'unjust law', and in doing so, we recognize a criterion of justice beyond the law itself. Yet this is something more definite than just a general righteousness or moral excellence. There is a notion of fairness, of a balancing or harmonizing of rights and claims – hence the traditional symbolism of the balances of justice. In the most famous treatise on justice ever written, Plato's *Republic*, justice is depicted as the harmonious functioning of the constituent parts – either, in the individual, the constituent parts of the soul, or, in the State, the constituent classes of which it is made up. In this complex matter of maintaining different rights and claims, many different kinds of justice have been distinguished. One of the commonest distinctions is between retributive justice, which aims at punishing the infringement of a right (*see* **Rewards and Punishments**) or at restoring the enjoyment of the right, and distributive justice, which attempts to ensure the fair distribution of rights and privileges, on the maxim: 'to every man his due'. There have been many theories of justice. The OT story of Moses receiving the law from God saw (in common with other ancient religions) the basis of justice in the will or *fiat* of God. The Stoics (q.v.) thought of justice as rooted in the natural (rational) order of things. This is something like a doctrine of natural law (q.v.); while in turn the natural law may be conceived as approximating to a divinely given law, or may be thought of in a more secular way as belonging to man's universal rationality. From the sophists down through Hume to the pragmatists of modern times, still another view of justice has prevailed. It has been thought of as a convention which may change with changing circumstances, as men devise the most suitable ways for regulating conflicting claims in an orderly fashion. It is a false disjunction that suggests an opposition between justice and love. In an imperfect world, justice must be maintained and enforced in face of the constant threats of injustice, and the Christian has a duty to uphold justice as well as to exercise love. *See also* **Rights.**

EDITOR

Justification by Faith

Justification by faith, or more fully, justification by grace through faith has been called 'the article by which the Church will stand or fall'. The usual designation, 'justification by faith', is subject to such misunderstanding that the fuller statement, 'justification by grace alone, for Christ's sake, through faith active in good works' is preferable. Faith then is to be regarded as 'the comprehensive name for the Christian God-relationship' (Gustav Aulen).

For St Paul, the only righteousness which saves is the active righteousness of God which is imparted to men (especially, Rom. 1.16–17; Eph. 2.8–10). The agent in justification is entirely the gracious God, who covers man's sin, thus justifying the ungodly (Rom. 5.6–11) and at the same time creating the 'new man' in Christ, that is, sanctification (II Cor. 5.17–21). This view is abundantly substantiated by the total biblical witness.

Luther understood 'justification' comprehensively: 'Where there is forgiveness of sins, there is life and salvation.' In distinction from the Roman conception of justification as a gradual process of growth in sainthood *via* sacramental infusions of grace employed in good works, he affirmed the all-at-once, gracious act of justification, which is at one and the same time a forensic act and an act of renewal. Grace is not a power infused by God himself in his gracious disposition. It is the *sinner* who is *declared* righteous and at the same time *made* righteous. A man does not become good by doing good, but he must first *be* good, before he can *do* good. Only a good tree brings forth good fruit (Matt. 7.16–20). At the beginning of the life of the Christian stands the once and for all, complete act of justification, which makes the sinner fully the forgiven child of God and heir of all the blessings of salvation. Full assurance of salvation thus rests wholly upon God's word which accomplishes what it says and not on man's faith in his own faith or on his good works. The Christian remains always

'simultaneously righteous and a sinner' and, therefore, in need of daily repentance and renewal.

This has profound implications for the Christian life, for it is only when man's pride and egocentricity, in which he seeks himself in all he does, are broken by the act of justification, that he is free not to use his neighbour as a means to his own salvation. Then he becomes, by God's grace, the channel through which God's *agape* flows through him out to the neighbour. The direction is altogether from God down to man and out to the world's needs. There is a genuine 'life-together' based on openness to the neighbour where each one knows himself equally sinful yet equally beloved and accepted. This rules out false 'perfectionism'. In all respects and at all times, in his thoughts, words and deeds a man is justified only by grace through faith which is never a meritorious work on man's part since it is the work of God in man.

Thus it is invalid to object to 'by faith alone'. Works are not added to faith as its consequence, because faith is present only as it is alive in works, just as the sun is present only in its shining. Therefore, also, there is no contradiction when James says that faith without works is dead (James 2.17) or when, in the final judgment, it is the deed of love which is decisive (Matt. 25.31–45).

Thus the quality of the Christian life can always be judged by whether or not there is the realization that a man lives only by forgiveness and is thereby freed and empowered to do God's will of love in service to the neighbour in his particular standing place. But it does not follow that this must at all times be put in terms of 'justification'. The NT is rich in variety of expressions and different times demand different emphases, just so the substance of the gospel, which is the 'justification of the sinner by grace alone' is preserved.

H. F. Lovell Cocks, *By Faith Alone*, 1943; William H. Lazareth, *Luther on the Christian Home, An Application of the Social Ethics of the Reformation*, 1960, especially pp. 34–165; Alexander Miller, *The Renewal of Man*, 1956; G. Quell and G. Schrenk, *Righteousness*, Bible Key Words from Gerhard Kittel's *Theologisches Wörterbuch zum Neuen Testament*, IV, 1951.

MARTIN J. HEINECKEN

Juvenile Delinquency

By legal definition, a delinquent is any juvenile who has committed an offence in violation of the law. State laws vary in defining the juvenile age range, although such a person is in most States between the ages of ten and seventeen. In some States the upper range limit has been raised to eighteen and even twenty-one years. Nor are State laws uniform in their delinquency statutes: offences vary from petty theft to vandalism, from homicide to sexual misconduct. A statistical code guide of the New York City Children's Court lists nine categories: (1) wrongful appropriation of property; (2) ungovernable behaviour; (3) act of carelessness or mischief; (4) sex offences; (5) habitual truancy; (6) running away; (7) injury to person; (8) peddling; and (9) other. Broadly speaking, no child is a juvenile delinquent until a court has declared him to be such on the basis of established guilt.

Statistics indicate that juvenile delinquency in the USA has increased dramatically since the second World War. Arrests doubled between 1950 and 1960. In 1961, 1,750,000 juveniles were arrested and 50,000 were wards of the juvenile courts. Incidences of recidivism indicate that nearly one-half of those brought before the juvenile courts will become criminals in adult life. It should be noted that delinquency is not solely an American phenomenon, but is found in all nations and all cultures.

The official agencies dealing with juvenile delinquency include the police, detention homes, juvenile courts and correctional institutions. In addition, there are numerous non-legal agencies, such as child-guidance clinics, family service agencies, welfare agencies, etc.

Basically, delinquents are divided into four groups: the essentially healthy adolescent whose behaviour is not an unexpected reaction to a bad environment; the sound adolescent whose behaviour has grown out of excessive inner emotional conflict; the neurotic delinquent; the *true* delinquent (sociopath) who has little strength of personality. That types of delinquents are identifiable leads to the conclusion that delinquency may be a form of adjustive behaviour. Thus where socially accepted channels have been closed or are unattainable, delinquent behaviour becomes the vehicle of self-expression.

Four major approaches to delinquency are discernible: (1) The psychoanalytic approach, which is concerned with personality formation, accounts for delinquency on the premiss that identity is achieved through relationship to proper role models. 'Ego diffusion' or uncertain identity occurs where a child has not attained selfhood in relation to those who mean the most to him. While 'ego identity' provides ego strength to manage increased drive, 'ego diffusion' leaves youth open to drives and conflicts. The youth who has not achieved adequate ego identity may turn to delinquent acts as a compensatory means of fulfilment. (2) The ecological approach accounts for delinquency on the basis of its geographic distribution or the tendency of delinquency to be concentrated in certain areas, such as slums. (3) The socio-psychological approach places the emphasis on the influence of experiences the individual has had in acquiring role or status in social groups. According to this approach, the delinquent is a socially disattached individual with fewer group identifications than the average non-delinquent. (4) The socio-cultural approach focuses on the aspects of society which cause an individual to become disturbed and disorganized, such as conflicting values. This approach stresses that there is a relationship between adjustive problems of youth and the type of social framework in which he was reared.

No single cause of delinquency can be isolated. Research has indicated that in each case of delinquent behaviour, many factors have been at work. Some contributory factors are:

(1) *Society*. Modern society is in a state of transition. Rapid technological change, greater mobility and specialization, have resulted in increased anonymity. Overstimulation has occurred in mass media where crime, violence and sexuality are often exploited. Society also presents conflicting values. A premium is put on success, status and wealth. This very stress tends towards 'anomie' or normlessness, whereby discrepancy in the capacity to achieve this cultural goal may be overcome through deviant behaviour.

(2) *Community*. There are certain community conditions which may influence delinquency: overcrowded or dilapidated housing, lack of or limited recreational facilities, class or racial segregation which accentuate hostility and antagonism, a deficient educational system, inadequate community agencies, including churches, guidance centres, etc.

(3) *Family*. The family as an institution has been caught up in the changes occurring in society at large. Traditional functions assumed by the family have been reduced. Traditional patterns of authority are being revised: the trend is from the patriarchal to democratic type. Intergenerational conflict is common between immigrant parents and their native-born children. Confusion of the feminine role is reflected first in the trend towards more women seeking employment outside the home and secondly in the phenomenon of the middle-class male, especially the commuter, who spends a great amount of time away from the home leaving the mother to fulfil both masculine and feminine roles. A child may later rebel either against the substitute parent or the imposed femininity.

(4) *Individual*. The basic need of all children is for personal identity and acceptance. To achieve this they need adequate and meaningful relationships, proper models, and obtainable realistic goals. When deprived of such things, the tendency is towards the adoption of short-range goals or joining a sub-group which meets these needs. Such a group may be a delinquent sub-culture in which deviant behaviour is the norm.

Besides the legal agencies for delinquency prevention and control, there are other non-legal agencies of importance. There are slum clearance programmes, public health programmes, recreational services, public school improvement, economic assistance programmes and Church involvement with the problem. A key measure in delinquency prevention is to clear up misconceptions, that is, that there is one definable cause of delinquency, that blame can be attributed to one source, and that delinquents differ radically from non-delinquents. By far the best preventive measure is a concerned and aware community.

Albert K. Cohen, *Delinquent Boys*, 1955; Haskill M. Miller, *Understanding and Preventing Juvenile Delinquency*, 1958; D. H. Stott, *Delinquency and Human Nature*, 1950; Frederic M. Thrasher, *The Gang*, 1927; Helen Witmer and Ruth Kotinsky, eds., 'New Perspectives for Research on Juvenile Delinquency'. Washington, D.C., Department of Health, Education and Welfare, 1956.

ROBERT LEE

Kant and Kantian Ethics

Immanuel Kant (1724–1803), a native of East Prussia, is generally regarded as the greatest modern philosopher. Brought up in the rationalist (Leibnizian) school, he nevertheless became convinced of the impossibility of justifying 'metaphysics' (*a priori* theoretical knowledge of reality). In his major work, *The Critique of Pure Reason* (1781, 2nd edn., 1787), he maintained that all judgments capable of giving new information about matters of fact must include both an empirical and an *a priori* element, the former providing matter or content and the latter form or organization. This enabled him to furnish a justification of causality and other *a priori* categories against philosophers like Hume, on the ground that they were necessary if we were to make any judgments at all, but also to refute theoretical metaphysics on the ground that it depended for its arguments on using the categories illegitimately beyond the realm of experience.

But he took a quite different view of judgments as to moral principles, regarding these as essentially *a priori*. This enabled him to produce ethical arguments for the objective validity of the only metaphysical ideas which he considered of practical interest to man, namely God, freedom and immortality. For according to his view an ethical proposition could say something new (be 'synthetic') without being dependent on empirical facts and therefore could yield conclusions which went beyond the realm of experience, thus escaping his objections to *a priori* arguments in theoretical metaphysics. The general principle behind his argument for God and immortality is that the moral law bids us pursue the supreme good as attainable. It cannot, however, be attained in this life or in any finite time, hence immortality, and since the possibility of realizing it depends not only on ourselves but on external circumstances we must think of the latter as ordered for the greatest good, which we can only do by envisaging everything as created and controlled by a being who is both perfectly good and omnipotent. (This is the essence of the argument, but its actual form would have been improved if Kant had not restricted his idea of the good to 'good will' and happiness, *see below*.) The argument is held by him to give indeed not theoretical knowledge but sufficent evidence to justify a subjectively certain practical belief. It occurs in *The Critique of Practical Reason* (1788). He not only regards religious belief as justifiable solely by ethical arguments, but takes the view that religion is of value only as a means to leading a good moral life, and in *Religion within the Bounds of Reason Alone* (1793) he reinterprets the dogmas of Christianity in terms simply of ethics and of a belief in the moral government of the world.

Kant's view of freedom is very difficult, and he admits that the concept, though we must accept it, is unintelligible to us. As the result chiefly of various epistemological arguments and the antinomies about infinity he had come to the conclusion that everything in space and time is appearance and not reality. This he applied even to our view of ourselves in introspection. The appearance self, he thought, must be like everything in time completely subject to causation by previous events, but the real self was timeless and so could be free, not being determined by previous events. Its freedom consisted in the possibility of moral action, 'ought' implying 'can'.

Kant's best known work on ethics is his *Groundwork of the Metaphysic of Morals* (1785), though we must remember that it was intended as the introduction to a work which would develop ethics more in detail, as he did in the *Metaphysic of Morals* (1797). ('Metaphysic' is here used not in the sense in which Kant denied its possibility, that is, *a priori* theoretical knowledge of reality, but simply to mean a systematic investigation of the *a priori* elements in our moral thinking.) His ethics, as already suggested, is noted for its *a priori* character. He holds that only 'hypothetical' and not 'categorical' (genuinely moral) imperatives can be derived from considering the consequences of actions. If I am to attain a certain end I am subject to a hypothetical imperative to adopt the means needed for this purpose, but the imperative is binding on me only in so far as I desire the end, and even so it is only a prudential and not a moral 'ought'. A categorical imperative on the other hand is concerned with the principle ('maxim') of an action and not with its consequences.

This is connected with Kant's view of what is good in itself. The *Groundwork* opens with a statement that the only thing unconditionally good is the *good will*, by which is meant the will to do our duty just because it is our duty. This is not the same as saying that the good will is the only thing good otherwise than as a means. Kant regards happiness also as good in itself but only if the happiness is deserved by the exercise of the good will, and so only conditionally on the other higher good being attained. He does, however, seem to deny the value of anything else besides good will and happiness, even of intelligence and knowledge, love, aesthetic and religious experiences, except as a means. He points out that the goodness of the good will does not depend on its being successful in its endeavours or on its actual consequences. He denies any merit to action which is not morally motivated, however well it conforms outwardly with the moral law, and this has aroused criticism on the ground that many acts are better done out of love than out of a sense of duty. It is, however, doubtful whether Kant meant to deny moral value to an action that was done both from love or some other (good) desire and from a sense of duty, provided the latter was strong enough to bring about the action of itself even if the other motive had not been present also. And he insists that, if we are really moral, we will do our duty gladly despite the *prima facie* opposition between duty and desire. His rather rigorous attitude is to be understood as a reaction against the view, very common in his day, that the reason for doing our duty was ultimately to be found in the agent's own happiness.

Since the good will is a feature of the action itself and its motives and not of its consequences, and happiness, although an end which could serve as a ground for action, is regarded by him as of comparatively subordinate importance, his view of the good debarred him from setting up an ethic which derived our obligations mainly from an appeal to consequences. Instead he uses universalizability as his main criterion. He does not indeed hold that we ought to act according to every principle which could be universalized, but he does hold that we ought not to act according to any principle which could not be universalized. What the cheat wants is not that everybody else should cheat him, but that an exception should be made in his own case. And Kant thinks there are certain principles such that it would be impossible for us to will their universalization. Thus we could not have a state of affairs in which everybody always made any promise he chose without any intention of keeping it because there would be then no point in making the promises since they would

not be believed. Similarly he tries to base the obligation to help others in need on the argument that we could not will the universalization of the opposite principle since we ourselves might need help from others. This must be distinguished from the merely prudential argument that we ought to help others because we are then more likely to be helped ourselves. Kant is appealing not to the actual consequences of any kindness we may show but to the purely hypothetical situation which would arise if kindness were never shown. I think his contention is in essence that it would be unfair to break ourselves a general rule which we cannot help expecting others to obey in their dealings with us. Kant assumes that the moral principles which he establishes hold universally, as one would indeed expect an *a priori* principle to do, but then the question arises what we are to do if two of them clash in a particular case. Kant expressly defended the view that one ought never to tell a lie even to save the life of a man pursued by a would-be murderer, but it is not clear why the principle of truthfulness should be given priority over the principle of preserving life. But Kant has the merit of being the first moral philosopher to realize the immense importance of the concept of universality for ethics. It is an essential part of the moral attitude that any reason for or against an act must be capable of statement in general terms and must be such that it would apply to anybody without exception granted similar circumstances.

Kant's second formulation of the central moral imperative is 'act so as to treat humanity never only as a means but always also as an end'. We must note that he does not say that we should never treat a man as a means, which would be incompatible with our ever employing him to do work for our benefit, but that we shall never treat him only as a means, that is, we must never employ him under such conditions as involve a disregard of his well-being or human dignity. These words of Kant have had as much influence as perhaps any ever written by a philosopher; they serve indeed as a slogan for the whole liberal and democratic movement of recent times. But for their application we seem to need a fuller idea of the ends of man than Kant supplies together with more empirical content.

In the most important version of his third formulation Kant introduces the concept of a kingdom of ends all the members of whom treated each other as ends as well as means. Kant insists that we ought to act as if we were members of such a kingdom, though we know that not all our fellow-beings are such in their actions, for example, we ought not to cheat because others cheated us.

Kant emphasizes very strongly the 'autonomy' of ethics, by which he meant that moral principles must be derived from the nature of the rational will which refrains from acting on any principle that it could not consistently will to be universalized, and not from any idea of private advantage nor from some feeling nor from metaphysics nor theology. He is insisting on the unique status of ethics.

Immanuel Kant, *Groundwork of the Metaphysics of Morals*, tr. by H. J. Paton under the title of *The Moral Law*, 1948; *The Critique of Practical Reason*, tr. by L. W. Beck, 1949; H. J. Paton, *The Categorical Imperative*, 1947; W. D. Ross, *Kant's Ethical Theory*, 1954.

A. C. EWING

Kierkegaard, Søren Aabye

The whole thought of Kierkegaard (1813–1855) may justly be regarded as the effort to express the ethical as *the* Christian category. The prime difficulty in expounding his ethical views lies in the immensity, the intricacy, and the subtlety of this thought. Nor can any one part of his writings be specially adduced (e.g., the edifying discourses) or another part excluded (e.g., the pseudonymous writings); far less may the specifically 'Christian' writings (e.g., *Training in Christianity*, tr. by W. Lowrie, 1941) be dismissed as having to do with faith and not morality. Least of all may the evidence of the *Journals* be neglected.

Kierkegaard's basic concern is 'how to become a Christian'. In 1849 he wrote in his journal (*Papirer*, ed. by P. A. Heiberg and V. Kuhr, 1924):

There is an infinitely qualitative difference between God and man.

This means, or the expression for this is, that man is capable of nothing, it is God who gives everything, who gives man faith, and so on.

This is grace; and this is the primary thing in Christianity.

But in a *subdivisio* in this same entry, we read further:

Notwithstanding that there can be nothing, absolutely nothing, meritorious in any action whatsoever, just as little as believing can be meritorious . . . what matters is to dare to have a childlike relation with God.

If the *divisio* (i.e. the point in the first part of the entry) is everything, then God is so infinitely exalted that there is simply no real relation between God and the single man . . .' (X^I A 59).

The following year (1850), in the 'Moral' attached to Part I of *Training in Christianity* (1941, p. 71), we read:

And what does all this mean? It means that everyone for himself, in quiet inwardness before God, shall humble himself before what it means in the strictest sense to be a Christian, admit candidly before God how it stands with him, so that he might yet accept the grace which is offered to everyone who is imperfect, that is, to everyone. And then no further; then for the rest let him attend to his work, be glad in it, love his wife, be glad in her, bring up his children with joyfulness, love his fellow men, rejoice in life.

These two quotations represent the climax of Kierkegaard's views. Basic to his whole anthropology is the category of 'the single person' before God: in this situation man is called to decide. But the alternative before which a man is placed is not the choice between good and evil. But 'it is the choice by which one is willing or not willing to place oneself under the opposition of good and evil' (*Either/Or*, Anchor Books edn., II, 1959, p. 173, tr. by W. Lowrie with revisions by Howard Hong, translation altered, RGS). This is a matter of the will, of freedom, and of resolution. It is a demand upon man to choose what he is, in all its contingent and relative nature. 'This decision for himself is the expression of eternal consciousness' (J. Sløk, *Die Anthropologie Kierkegaards*, p. 87), for it is a decision in face of God. In this choice man is involved in the 'moment', and 'the concept, on which everything turns in Christianity, which makes everything new, is the fullness of time, and the fullness of time is the moment as eternal, and this eternal is also the future and the past' (*Samlede Vaerker*, IV, 1923, p. 397).

In this choice of the single person before God a highly dialectical situation arises. On the one hand there is no other reference but the reference to God as the absolute. On the other hand nothing in the world is excluded but is on the contrary restored. This is the point at which moralists in the Greek tradition falter. Is a teleological suspension of the ethical an ethical possibility? Was Abraham's obedience to God in being willing to sacrifice Isaac (cf. *Fear and Trembling*, 1941) not the abolition of ethics? Or, for that matter, was Kierkegaard's renunciation of Regine, his fiancée, which was accompanied by the effort to prove to her that he was a scoundrel, not strictly unethical? Kierkegaard's answer is that within the cultural, historical and philosophical situation of man there are nothing but relativities, arbitrary choices, and various kinds of 'immediacy'. None of these situations provides the absolute reference. It is only by the absolute relation to the absolute that all these relativities find their place, and are restored. Man becomes truly historical in relation to God, who himself concentrates the eternal in a relative and contingent reality, namely, in Christ the God-Man.

Kierkegaard's recognition of the primacy of the moral obligation comes up against the total situation of man's guilt; it is in the context of repentance, and of forgiveness 'in virtue of the absurd', that the limit of man's moral freedom is reached. From this point of forgiveness a return to the world of relative ends is possible. In the whole movement of Kierkegaard's thought the ethical demand is primary; but it is given such a turn, in face of God and his forgiveness, that now everything depends upon the *way*, the 'how', of man's existence before God.

Works and *Journals* of Kierkegaard, *passim*; T. Bohlin, *Die Dogmatische Anschauung Kierkegaards*, 1927; E. Geismar, *Kierkegaard*, 1926–8; H. A. Johnson and N. Thulstrup, eds., *A Kierkegarrd Critique*, 1962; J. Sløk, *Die Anthropologie Kierkegaards*, 1954; R. Gregor Smith, *Kierkegaard, The Last Years*, 1964; D. Swenson, *Something about Kierkegaard*, 1941; H. Thomas, *Subjectivity and Paradox*, 1957; R. Thomte, *Kierkegaard's Philosophy of Religion*, 1948.

R. GREGOR SMITH

Kingdom of Ends

This term was used by Kant for an ideal society in which the members treated each other never merely as means but always at the same time as ends. He insisted that we ought to act as if we were already members of such a society, even though others may not do likewise in their dealings with us. *See* **Kant and Kantian Ethics.**

A. C. EWING

Kingdom of God

According to Mark 1.15 Jesus began his ministry with a proclamation including the words '. . . the kingdom of God is at hand' (NEB 'the kingdom of God is upon you'). While comparatively infrequent in the rest of the NT the phrase 'kingdom of God [Heaven(s)]' occurs more than eighty times in the Synoptics and there are additional occurrences of 'thy kingdom', 'the kingdom', etc. It is clear that Jesus built his ministry around the proclamation of the Kingdom. The concept has been variously understood: Origen stated that Jesus was himself the Kingdom; some have taken it to refer to the proper spiritual relationship with God; some have identified it with the visible Church; others have equated it with a reformed social order; and still others have insisted that Jesus referred to an expected apocalyptic intervention by God.

Since Jesus nowhere defined the term, what were its various meanings in his own culture? 'Kingdom' meant 'reign' or 'sovereignty', and the phrase was used in at least three different contexts. It could mean, (1) the eternal and invisible reign of God which is independent of human response or knowledge, for example, Ps. 145.13; (2) the realization of God's reign in groups or individuals who accept his sovereignty, for example, a proselyte was said 'to have taken the yoke of the kingdom of heaven upon himself'; and (3) the eschatological kingdom at the end of history when all recognize the sovereignty of God, for example, the phrase in the Qaddish prayer 'May he establish his kingdom during your lifetime. . . .' The modern consensus is that – at least in his basic proclamation – Jesus referred to the Kingdom in a sense related to the third of these Jewish concepts, that is, he spoke of the coming of the eschatological phase of the Kingdom. But what was he saying about this phase of the Kingdom? Schweitzer ('consistent eschatology') argued that Jesus proclaimed the imminent arrival of the eschatological Kingdom and that his entire teaching was conditioned by this sense of imminence, cf. Mark 9.1; 13.30; Matt. 6.10; Luke 11.2. Dodd ('realized eschatology', or better 'inaugurated eschatology') contended that Jesus proclaimed the Kingdom to have arrived already in his own ministry, cf. Matt. 12.28; Luke 11.20; 10.23 f.; Matt. 13.16 f. A current tendency, for example, Kümmel, is to avoid a clear decision between these two views by arguing that while the eschatological Kingdom was still future it was effectively present in the ministry of Jesus.

While the tradition may reflect ambiguity concerning the time of the Kingdom's coming it is clear with respect to the way of life for those belonging to that Kingdom. The Kingdom comes through God's activity; but the NT stresses the distinctive characteristics of those who will receive or enter the Kingdom. *See* Mark 10.14 f., 17–31; 12.28–34; Matt. 5.3,10,20 (and probably the entire Sermon on the Mount, with Lucan parallels); 22.11–14; 25.31–46. The tension between the Kingdom as the gift of God's grace and as the response to the meeting of specific requirements is characteristic of the central paradox in Jesus' teaching: God welcomes the outcast sinner, God demands more than even the 'righteous' have done.

In a broad sense the Kingdom serves as a symbol for the will of God which may be carried out in particular situations through humble obedience, but which is never fully accomplished within the confines of history because of human limitations. Thus the Kingdom 'comes', but its final manifestation remains a future hope. And the Christian knows that the Kingdom came in a new sense in Christ, that it may come within his own life, but that it has never yet fully come. So he lives in the present world as an obedient citizen of that Kingdom while he prays in confident hope 'Thy kingdom come' and 'Maranatha, Our Lord, come'.

J. Bright, *The Kingdom of God*, 1953; C. H. Dodd, *The Parables of the Kingdom*, 1935; W. G. Kümmel, *Promise and Fulfilment*, German 1956, ET, 1957; N. Perrin, *The Kingdom of God in the Teaching of Jesus*, 1963; H.

Roberts, *Jesus and the Kingdom of God*, 1955;
R. Schnackenburg, *God's Rule and Kingdom*,
1963; A. Schweitzer, *The Mystery of the Kingdom of God*, German 1901, ET, 1954; E. F.
Scott, *The Kingdom of God in the New Testament*, 1931.

HARVEY H. MCARTHUR

Kingdom of Heaven.
see Kingdom of God.

Kingsley, Charles

Charles Kingsley (1819–1875), clergyman of
the Church of England, social reformer and
novelist, was a member of the group of Christian Socialists who came into prominence by
issuing a manifesto to the workmen of England
on the morrow of the failure of the great
Chartist demonstration in London in April
1848. Under the pseudonym 'Parson Lot' he
was the chief propagandist of the group and
contributed to the short-lived *Politics for the
People*, *Tracts on Christian Socialism* and *The
Christian Socialist*.

Kingsley, whose inspiration was derived
partly from S. T. Coleridge and T. Carlyle
and partly from F. D. Maurice, the theological
leader of the Christian Socialist group, also
contributed to the advancement of their cause
by his early novels *Yeast* (1848), originally published serially in *Fraser's Magazine*, and *Alton
Locke* (1850). Like the rest of the group he
looked rather to working-class education, co-
operative workshops and sanitary reform than
to political changes for the uplift of the masses,
and he wished to see the upper and middle
classes, including the clergy, taking the lead in
promoting such social reform.

Kingsley was an outstanding English clergyman of the 'muscular Christianity' type, with
an aversion to studied asceticism and a large-
hearted concern for the state of the labouring
classes both in town and country. Both of these
attitudes he encouraged by his writing.

R. B. Martin, *The Dust of Combat: A Life of
Charles Kingsley*, 1954; C. E. Raven, *Christian
Socialism 1848–54*, 1920.

STEWART MECHIE

Kirk, Kenneth Escott

Kenneth Kirk (1886–1954) was ordained priest
in the Church of England in 1913, and was
professor of moral and pastoral theology at the
University of Oxford from 1932 until his
appointment as Bishop of Oxford in 1937. He
is regarded as the greatest Anglican moral
theologian of recent times, and it is largely due
to his teaching and influence that there has
taken place a revival of interest in moral
theology in the Church of England. Kirk was
well versed in the moral theology of St Thomas
Aquinas (q.v.) and in the seventeenth-century

Anglican divines (*see* **Caroline Moral Theology**),
and he sought to combine this traditional
material with the new situation of modern
times, and with the demands of a free and enlightened conscience. In doing this, he believed
that he was carrying the spirit of Anglicanism,
with its peculiar combination of tradition and
freedom, into the moral sphere. He was a
prolific writer. Among his works may be mentioned: *Some Problems of Moral Theology*
(1920); *Conscience and its Problems* (1927);
The Vision of God (Bampton Lectures, 1931).

EDITOR

Koinonia.

Koinonia, a NT expression, may be translated
as 'fellowship', 'communion', 'participation' or
even 'community'. The basic idea is that of
sharing. The Christian life is a shared life,
shared with God through Christ, and with the
other members of the Body of Christ, the community of the Spirit. In ethics, the term is used
by those who hold that Christian action is
determined by the living context of the
community. *See* **Contextual Ethics**.

Labour Movement. *see* Industrial Relations; Industrial Revolution.

Laicity

Laicity is a term used (chiefly in France) to
mean the control of civil affairs by lay persons,
to the exclusion of clerical influence. The
principle is similar to that known in the USA
as 'separation of Church and State'. *See*
Church and State.

Laissez-faire

This phrase, first used by the French physio-
cratic writers of the eighteenth century, has
come to be used as a summary of the belief
that it is best to leave the working of the
economy to the free play of the self-interest of
producers and consumers, relying on the 'invisible hand' of competition in the market to
bring about the best interests of the community.

While Christian thought would emphasize
the importance of individuals being free to
exercise responsible judgment and choice, and
the dangers of excessive state power, yet
extreme laissez-faire has generally been condemned. It is incompatible with Christian
beliefs both about the fallibility of human
nature, which makes it impossible to rely on an
invisible hand to restrain the effects of greed
and exploitation, and about responsibility
for one's neighbours' welfare, which makes it
imperative to advocate collective action by the
community to correct the inevitable abuses of

individual self-interest. The Amsterdam Assembly of the World Council of Churches (1948), for instance, condemns laissez-faire capitalism as well as Communism, and the social encyclicals from *Rerum Novarum* onwards have also condemned it. V. A. Demant, in *Religion and the Decline of Capitalism* (1952) points out that the reliance of early nineteenth-century capitalism on the autonomy of the market was only possible because of the existence of a pre-capitalist community structure, from which society derived social cohesion and underlying values, but that market autonomy tended to destroy this and thus by its defects to lead to a reaction towards collectivism.

Most Christians would accept that fallible men need a blend of freedom for individual responsibility and control by the organs of the community. The exact proportions and form of these which are advocated will depend both on changing circumstances and on varying political beliefs.

JOHN F. SLEEMAN

Language. *see* Ethical Language.

Law

Law in its primary sense is a guide or directive of human actions. Specifically defined, law is a directive judgment of lawmakers regarding means necessary for the common welfare. This view of law, as essentially a directive, is part of the great tradition in human thinking. 'Teach me, O Lord, the way of thy statutes; and I will keep it to the end. Give me understanding, that I may keep thy law and observe it with my whole heart. Lead me in the path of thy commandments, for I delight in it. . . . Thy word is a lamp to my feet and a light to my path. . . . Therefore I direct my steps by all thy precepts.' (Ps. 119.33–5,105,128).

Sometimes law has been looked upon as an undesirable restriction on human freedom or as a necessary evil for remedying trouble-situations. Such a myopic outlook is usually the result of a foreshortened prelegal education that precludes viewing law in its true perspective. Law seen in its total sweep is, rather, like the guide marks on a map that restrict people only that they may more certainly reach a definite goal, even when this is the seeking of remedies.

Law is also used in a secondary sense that refers to a uniform order of sequence observable in nature. Such a usage is not uncommon in the physical sciences to denote the order perceived in natural phenomena or events. This use of the word 'law' was undoubtedly related originally to an interpretation of nature that saw in it the handiwork of a maker. When this maker was also seen in the formality of a lawmaker, the ordered sequences observable in nature were recognized as the expression of his directive judgments and the word 'law' was attributed to them. But such a use of the word 'law' is imprecise and equivocal, because law refers to the directive judgments of a lawmaker and not to the promulgation of these judgments. All the more so is the use of the word 'law' equivocal when it designates this uniform order in itself and unrelated to its intelligible rationale.

Similarly in the science of ethics, the word 'law' is used in such phrases as 'law of nature' or 'natural law' to denote either the basic drives that men observe operative in themselves, or the value judgments naturally made according to the demands of these drives and even the conclusions deduced therefrom by a reasoning process. Here likewise the use of the word 'law' is lax and equivocal. Men's drives at best, when seen related to a higher cause, are not law but the expression of a law. Nor are the basic value judgments that men make 'law', because they are not the directive judgments of a lawmaker who has the authority to direct all men to their common welfare.

In the perspective of God and man, there are two basic kinds of law: God-made, eternal law and man-made, temporal law. God-made law is known either through positive means such as the Decalogue or through natural means such as the elementary drives of men's nature. The positive promulgation of God-made law has been called by some 'divine law' and its natural promulgation has been termed 'natural law'. But, as already indicated, the use of the word 'law' to designate the publication of a law is incorrect and equivocal.

Man-made law is made for the most part by legislators. Judges, however, sometimes also make law. This is done interstitially when, in applying statutes, they have to fill up gaps left by the statute, or when they decide cases of 'first impression', or when as members of a highest court they render decisions by way of judicial review. Executives also may in certain circumstances make law by proclamation. Finally the people themselves, the political source of all lawmaking authority, make law by means of the customs they have established. Customs are ways of acting that are necessary for the common welfare, have been in use by the people over a long period of time and are recognized as such by legislators and judges. The lawmaking judgments of lawmakers out of office or long dead continue as law inasmuch as it is a matter of recorded fact that they did so directively judge and succeeding lawmakers are assumed to have made the judgments of their predecessors their own unless they give evidence of the opposite by attempting amendment or appeal.

The promulgation of man-made law to the people is, of course, a condition prerequisite for its effectiveness in directing the people to their common welfare. But the making known of a law does not constitute it as law. A law is fully fashioned before it is made known, somewhat like a road map is complete and finished before it is distributed as a guide. Custom-law has its own particular kind of promulgation. It is made known by the publicly repeated actions of the people which manifest their directive judgments regarding some practice as necessary for the common welfare.

The end of law, the common welfare, is a unique kind of good – the common good. This is not a total of goods proper to all individuals such as the sum of all producer and consumer goods. Nor is it a collective good such as the family fortune which diminishes as it is communicated to each member. The common good is, rather, the kind of good that is communicable to all and is not lessened by being so communicated. The peace, security and protection of law itself are prime examples. They are not lessened by the number of participants nor does this number cause each to have less. The effectuation of the common good is in proportion to the amount of co-operation put forward by the members of the society.

The content of law includes whatever is necessary for the common welfare – either absolutely necessary such as police protection or relatively necessary such as directional turning indicators on automobiles. Statutes that would purport to dictate, for instance, what people should believe or how they should worship would invade areas that pertain directly to the private welfare of individuals and not to the common welfare of the community. Such laws would be the embodiment of tyranny and dictatorship. On the basis of content, laws are either substantive or procedural depending on whether they are concerned with claims themselves or with methods of enforcing these claims. Laws are also private or public inasmuch as some laws regard the private claims of one citizen as against another and other laws are concerned with the public claims of all the citizens against one or many. Private law embraces torts, property, contracts, domestic relations, equity and the like. Public law is concerned with the constitution, administration, crimes and procedure.

The obligation of law derives from the necessity of the content of a law for the common welfare. For, obligation is the moral necessity of choosing a means that is necessary for a desired end. If I desire the safety of myself and others, I must choose to restrict my speed according to the limit set by the speed law. If I choose to exceed this limit, the safety of myself and others is in jeopardy.

In the long history of law, this objective, means-end foundation of obligation, has at times been lost sight of. Some have said that obligation had a subjective basis in the will of the lawmakers. A statute obliged me only if the lawmakers so desired. Otherwise, the law was merely indicative of what the lawmakers wanted

done but it was not obligatory. This type of philosopico-legal thinking gave rise to the theory of 'merely penal law'. This phrase was used to designate a law which supposedly did not oblige me to the execution of what was commanded (because the lawmakers did not so desire to oblige me) but merely to the payment of a penalty if I was apprehended violating the law (because this was what the lawmakers wished). Others, also considering men's will or practical reason to be autonomous and incapable of being put under any determination by an objective, means-end relationship, said that obligation derived from the interior reverence that I should have for law itself. The nobility of law itself, and not what it specifically stipulates, commands my respect. In this theory, obligation is for obligation's sake.

Still others, rejecting all models explaining obligation philosophically or morally, said that obligation was the same as sanction, that the obligation of a law was the same as its enforceability by power. Some who held this position did so not because they denied the validity of morals but because they wished to keep morals and legal obligation separate. Others who held this position did so because they believed that morals rested on an emotional basis and were consequently non-cognivist and non-scientific. Morals therefore, according to them, had no place in scientific thinking.

But time, the great practical tester of theories, has shown that once obligation is cut adrift from its means-end anchor, it loses all meaning. It becomes a will-o-the-wisp of either the lawmaker's will or of my own; or else it becomes synonymous with force and power, and this connotes might is right. Obligation is anchored in my desire for an end. There is one end which I cannot help but desire and this is my own complete self-actualization or happiness. It is the objective relation of a particular fact-situation to this end which gives substance to my obligation.

The sanction of law is of a different nature than obligation. Sanction refers to the rewards that are consequent upon the keeping of a law and to the punishments that follow the breaking of a law. Sanctions are either extrinsic to the law itself insofar as they are affixed to it, or they are intrinsic to the law insofar as they follow from the very content of the law. Examples of extrinsic sanction would be rewards offered by law for the apprehension of criminals, or punishments which consist in the deprivation of property by fine, of freedom by imprisonment, of physical well-being by flogging, or life itself by execution. Examples of intrinsic sanction would be the reward of safe driving conditions that result from observing traffic laws, or the punishment of dangerous driving conditions that ensue from violating the laws. Inasmuch as intrinsic sanction has to do with the accomplishment or non-accomplishment of the end of law and this same end is the anchor of my obligation to observe the law as explained, there is this relation between intrinsic sanction and obligation. The extrinsic sanction of force and physical punishment is undoubtedly needed to ensure the enforcement of law – the perverseness of men being what it is. But it is not of the essence of law itself and there can be valid laws without a stipulated, affixed punishment. The Constitutions of many nations are examples of this.

Law, then, is a directive for men regarding those things that are necessary for their common welfare, and obligation to observe law is based on this means-end relationship. This concept of law and obligation finds verification not only in the written laws of literate peoples but also in the unwritten, custom-laws of preliterate peoples. Recent and reliable research in anthropology and ethnology has shown that in many situations found among preliterate groups, regulations are observed and order preserved without the threatened sanction of physical force. Many times the threat of public ridicule, a much needed sanction in so-called civilized societies that so frenetically shun adverse publicity, is sufficient. Further, pre-literates' idea of why they are obliged to follow their regulations appears explainable only on the grounds of their implicit recognition that what is required by these regulations is in most instances something necessary for their own common welfare. *See also* **Law and Gospel; State.**

E. Bodenheimer, *Jurisprudence – The Philosophy and Method of the Law*, 1963; J. Dabin, 'General Theory of Law', in *The Legal Philosophies of Lask, Radbruch, and Dabin*, 1950, 225–470; T. Davitt, *The Elements of Law*, 1959; L. Fuller, *The Law in Quest of Itself*, 1940; F. Geny, *Science et Technique en Droit Privé Positif*, 1922; J. Hall, *Living Law in Democratic Society*, 1949.

THOMAS E. DAVITT, S.J.

Law and Gospel

The whole content of the word of God may be summarized in terms of 'law and gospel'. Martin Luther maintained that the ability to make the distinction and preserve the right relation was the most difficult of all theological tasks at which no one really succeeded.

Accordingly law is what God demands. It means a law-giver who coerces, rewards and punishes. Nothing less than unconditional and complete obedience can fulfil the demands of the law. The law, therefore, by definition, excludes mercy, grace, forgiveness. Under the law there can be no escape from its demands. Under the law a man gets what he deserves. The law is inviolable; it allows of no exceptions, or else it is not law. That is why an elaborate system of casuistry is necessary in order to apply the law in all fairness to specific cases.

The gospel, on the other hand, is what God gives. It runs counter to the law as the good news of God's grace and forgiveness, which does not deal with a man in accordance with his deserts, but accepts him as he is, in his unworthiness. It is love of the unworthy, of the enemy, it is 'justification by grace alone without the works of the law' (Rom. 1.16–17; Eph. 2.8–10). *See* **Justification by Faith.**

Defined in this way, the law and the gospel stand in direct opposition and are mutually exclusive. The gospel goes counter to the law and always accuses. The very meaning of the reconciling act of God in Christ is that it breaks through the order of justice. The fact that God is gracious can be defined in no other way. Otherwise the law loses all its meaning and power. If the law can be broken with impunity, all ordered living becomes impossible. Law has to be dependable or it is not law. Any game must be played strictly according to the rules with no forgiveness permissible, so then, *a fortiore*, with God's law and the game of life.

This alone makes meaningful the good news that God does not deal with us according to our iniquities. Forgiveness is not forgiveness, if it is based on conditions which must first be met and if the law must somehow first be kept, unless it breaks through the order of justice and goes counter to the law. Love is not *agape* except as love of the unworthy; it is most clearly manifest as love of the enemy and in vicarious suffering which is never just, but loving.

On this definition the law necessarily precedes the gospel. It presupposes man's fall. The fact that God must make demands is the sign of man's sinfulness, for if the relationship were right there would be only the indicative (I John 4.19). Thus the law serves to reveal man's sin and lead him to Christ (Rom. 3.20; 7.7; Gal. 3.24). This is the so-called proper, theological, pedagogical, or elenctical (judging) use of the law. The law is never itself salvatory, but it reveals man's bondage under God's wrath. It is, therefore, an essential part of Christian proclamation to awaken the terrors of conscience before the gospel can do its gracious work. True contrition of heart is worked by the preaching of both law and gospel, while trust and confidence are worked by the gospel alone.

In addition to leading to a sense of sin the law, however, also serves a second function, the so-called political use which prompts and coerces men to do God's will, even when they are not willing to do it freely. Since all men are sinful and the believers, too, continue to be sinful (simultaneously righteous and sinful), all men are at all times subject to this 'big-stick' use of the law. This is God's rule with his 'left hand' made necessary because of sin. It is

God's 'strange work' of coercion as opposed to his 'proper work' with the 'right hand' of grace. It applies not only to the laws of the State, but applies wherever men live, work and play together and cannot get along without rules to impose order upon them. Among sinful men it is unrealistic to dispense with law and to rely upon spontaneous obedience. As Luther said, the sheep would keep the peace, but they would not live long. Law and justice must be enforced as is so evident in the whole struggle for human rights and racial equality. The law must continue to function justly and with proper rigour in the home, the school, the State, and even in the Church as an institution. This is the meaning of the God-given power of the sword (Rom. 13).

Although some have advocated a third use of the law, the so-called didactic use, to serve as a guide to the Christian, this orientation would not allow such a third use. The law always functions *either* in its pedagogical use to convict *sinful* men of their sin or with its political use to keep sinful men in line. In so far as man is reborn as the new man he is free from the law and does the will of God spontaneously. Love is both the fulfilment and the end of the law (Matt. 22.37–40; Rom. 13.10; Gal. 5.14; I John 2.7–10). Love in obedience to law is not love. The one who acts in love is free to meet the needs of the neighbour creatively in the moment without being bound by principles or a code morality, even though, because he is still a sinner, he will submit also to the political use of the law out of love for the neighbour. The Christian is free to frame such laws as will meet the neighbour's needs (a contextual ethic).

This orientation does not deny the primacy of God's love, which is manifest in creation before it is manifest in redemption. God *is* love. Creation is a work of love by the same God who in Christ redeemed the fallen creation; it is creation through the Word and in the power of the Spirit; it is a work of the entire Trinity. God's love is manifest, therefore, also in the structures of creation, the lawful order of the world, which makes the world a fit theatre for the realization of God's purpose. Man is set down into the midst of interdependency; he is man-in-community, whose *human* life depends upon his observing the created order. The law of creation is love. Here, however, law does not mean the law which is connected with God's wrath and always accuses, but it means the dependable order which furthers man's well-being. On it are based and from it flow all man's potentials for conquering the earth and also for the development of a 'civil righteousness', that is, a righteousness before men, which, however, has no merit in the place of justification before God. All this (the family, the economic order, the State, education) is 'under the law', in the realm of creation and

not of redemption, not to be derived from the gospel in the sense of the redemptive work accomplished in Christ. (This is christocentricity as opposed to christomonism.) The 'new age' inaugurated in Christ does not change these given, created structures which remain under the law. It does, however, affect the men and women who enter into these given structures as new creatures, and through them the creative possibilities of those structures are opened up, without the law ever becoming redemptive in the sense in which only the gospel is redemptive. Though the whole creation is to share in the eventual fulfilment (Rom. 8; Eph. 1) in the *eschaton* when this age and history are over, it remains under the law as long as this present age endures. Only this positive emphasis upon the law enables one to claim the realm of culture for God. God claims all men in virtue of their creation and the fact that they have nothing which they have not received. There is 'good' in the world which is not derived from the reconciling act of Calvary but from the fact of creation. There is no profane realm but the whole creation is God's. The so-called 'secular', too, is holy in a 'sacred secularity' and man may take real delight in the law of God (Ps. 119).

If now the order is reversed this may be only to show that love is primary, that the choice of Israel (the covenant) antedated the giving of the law to Moses (Gal. 3.17), and that therefore the appeal for keeping the law is based on the prior fact of love's gracious act of deliverance. On that basis the law and the keeping of it within the covenant relation are not a burden but a delight. It is not the condemning voice of the accuser but the loving will of the gracious heavenly Father.

This, however, does not alter the fact that the law must first do its *judging* and *condemning* work before the gospel of the redemption in Christ can do its *gracious* work. Nor does it alter the fact that in so far as the Christian is still under the law he is so as sinner who is in need of coercion. When, therefore, the law is called 'the necessary form of the gospel' (Karl Barth), the terms are confused. Law is, to be sure, a manifestation of God's love in the sense defined above. In its political use it is the form which love takes under the circumstances of man's sinfulness. To refuse to enforce the law would not be loving. Also in its pedagogical use it is a manifestation of love by leading man to repentance. But the law which accuses and condemns can never be a form which the gospel, which accepts and forgives, takes on.

Moreover, if the law follows after the redemption, then the Christian life will again become a life under the law. With the best will in the world it cannot be prevented that the gospel becomes a new law and legalism, code-morality, and work righteousness take over as the history of Christian ethics clearly shows. The danger of antinomianism where the sequence is law and gospel is not as great as the danger of legalism and the loss of Christian freedom where the sequence is gospel and law (John 8.36).

The situation may be clarified if the NT distinction between the will of God (*thelema theou*) and the law of God (*nomos theou*) is observed (Paul Althaus). The will of God for man is always a will of love and the doing of it will be the delight of the redeemed. But the law of God is the tyrannous, coercive element which has no place in the new life in Christ. As a way of salvation in which man puts his trust it must be altogether rooted out.

The alternatives can thus be set in bold relief. On the one hand the law precedes the gospel and always accuses while only the gospel redeems. Moreover, the law continues to coerce the unwilling and thus preserves order. There is a 'sacred secularity' of the created world. And finally the new life under the gospel is one of creative freedom meeting the needs of the neighbour in love. On the other hand, when the gospel precedes the law, the law loses its power and the gospel becomes a new law. The created order loses its goodness under God and is turned over to the devil.

Paul Althaus, *Gebot und Gesetz, Zum Thema, 'Gesetz und Evangelium'*, 1952; Wilhelm Anderson, *Law and Gospel*, 1961; G. Aulen, *Church, Law and Society*, 1948; Karl Barth, *God, Grace and Gospel*, 1959; C. H. Dodd, *Gospel and Law; the Relation of Faith and Ethics in Early Christianity*, 1951; K. F. W. Walther, *Gesetz und Evangelium*, 1893; Gustav Wingren, *Creation and Law*, 1961.

MARTIN J. HEINECKEN

Legalism

Legalism is the type of ethic which seeks to prescribe rules for every conceivable occasion of moral choice; or for the type of mentality that follows what is supposed to be the rule in every situation. Some systems of ethics have in fact worked out extremely detailed rules of conduct, so that merely to remember them, let alone fulfil them, would be extremely burdensome. In practice, however, such systems have always allowed some flexibility, according to the demands of the situation. A legalistic mind is probably much more dangerous than a legalistic code of ethics. *See* Law; Law and Gospel.

Leisure. *see* Amusements;
Contemporary Society; Cybernetics.

Leo XIII, Pope

Leo XIII (1810–1903) held office during the major social, political and economic ferments of the late nineteenth century. For his teaching, *see* Pontifical Social Encyclicals.

Lesbianism

Lesbianism is female homosexualism of any kind. The word came from Lesbos, the home of the Greek poetess Sappho, who was said to have practised it. *See* Homosexuality and Homosexualism.

SHERWIN BAILEY

Liberalism

Liberalism is a term used in many different contexts, and is too vague to be easily pinned down. In ethics, the liberal could be contrasted with the legalist or the rigorist, in so far as he would allow more flexibility. In politics, liberalism stands for orderly change, the curbing of traditional privileges and the broadening of opportunities. Perhaps the heyday of liberal parties was the nineteenth century, when in many countries they successfully updated the social and political structures to meet the needs of industrial and urban conditions, without violent revolution. In theology, liberalism is contrasted with traditional rigid orthodoxies. Here too it had its heyday in the nineteenth and early twentieth centuries (Harnack is usually taken as the typical liberal) and broke the rigidity of the old systems while retaining and seeking to restate at least some of the central truths of the Christian faith. Political and theological liberalism have declined, but some of their insights remain valid, and some writers (e.g., Jaspers, Vidler) have suggested that the term 'liberality' might be used for those elements in the old-fashioned liberalism that have a continuing value. Openness to change, concern that change should be orderly, and perhaps above all respect for the freedom and worth of individual persons, are undying elements in the liberal tradition.

EDITOR

Liberality. *see* Liberalism.

Libertarianism. *see* Free Will and Determinism.

Liberty. *see* Freedom.

Liberty of Religion.
see Persecution and Toleration.

Life, Sacredness of

The Christian's belief in the sanctity of life is derived from his doctrine of God as Creator. God has made man in his image with power to reason and the capacity to choose. Each individual is infinitely precious to him and made for an eternal destiny. Thus the Christian attitude to human life can only be one of reverence – enjoined by the whole of the Decalogue (not only by the sixth Commandment) and confirmed by the incarnation – which is to be extended to every individual from the moment of his conception to extreme old age. Man's right to life, grounded in his divine origin, is the basis of all other human rights and the foundation of civilized society. Man's worth to God implies the duty of cherishing and preserving human life, and the taking of all moral means for the relief of suffering and the eradication of disease. It implies a proper regard for the human body itself and a refusal willingly to accept or deliberately to inflict any physical mutilation that is not necessary for the health of the whole organism. See **Sterilization**. Respect for both life and physical integrity set limits to the mode and extent of medical experimentation. See **Medical Ethics**. Because every man derives his right to life and his essential value from God, his value as a person is constant, whether he be rich or poor, strong or weak, handicapped or normal, socially 'useful' or 'useless'; therefore neither his life nor his well-being can rightly be sacrificed to the economic or political convenience of society: indeed, society itself is to be judged by its protection of and the solicitude it shows for its weaker members. Since a man has been given life that he might fulfil himself in the service of God and his fellow men, he may properly take actions which endanger his life, and even be ready to sacrifice it, in a weighty and righteous cause. But since God remains the absolute owner of all our lives it must always be a sin deliberately and directly to kill an innocent person, not simply for revenge but for any reason whatever. See **Homicide**. It is in the light of this conception of the sanctity of human life that the Christian must consider practices like abortion, infanticide, euthanasia, suicide, capital punishment, war (qq.v.). Because God is the Lord and Giver of all life, man has a duty to respect and act responsibly towards forms of sub-human life. God has given to man authority to exercise dominion over all other living things: he may kill them for food and harness them to his use, but he may not exploit them for his greed nor inflict unnecessary pain on them. See **Animals**.

THOMAS WOOD

Locke, John

John Locke (1631–1704) was the seventeenth-century English philosopher and liberal political theorist whose best-known works include his *Essay Concerning Human Understanding* (1690), his two *Treatises on Civil Government* (1690) and his *Letters Concerning Toleration* (1690).

Locke's *Essay* is one of the fundamental sources of the British empiricist tradition in the theory of knowledge, as it contains an early articulation of the doctrine that the mind is a *tabula rasa* and criticism of the rival thesis, found in different forms in the Cartesians and the Cambridge Platonists, of its power to advance knowledge out of its innate resources.

Locke certainly drew a clear distinction between our way of learning concerning, for example, our natural environment, and the sort of knowledge we could achieve in mathematics through rigorous deduction from premises known *a priori;* yet he classed with the latter our knowledge of the fundamental principles of ethics and politics and of the existence of God and the immortality of the soul. Moreover, where perception itself was concerned, he subscribed to a version of the causal theory, distinguishing the physical and the sensible properties of material objects. He also remained obstinately attached to what he (wrongly) believed to be the Aristotelian conception of substance, viz. a kind of clothes-horse draped with qualities, where his analysis of the nature of individual material things was concerned. In this respect, as well as with respect to his dualism of the sensible and the physical, he laid himself open to very subtle and searching criticism by Berkeley. Locke moved further, however, in an empiricist direction in his elaborate discussion of the relations between the nominal and the real essences of things. Yet he displays the actuality of his continued attachment to rationalism in his very acute discussion of the contribution made to human knowledge by the so-called 'association of ideas'. In later writers commonly said to belong to the British empiricist tradition, for example, David Hume, where one side of his epistemological thinking is concerned, and more particularly James Mill, this principle is cast for a quite fundamental role in discussion, for example, of the development of our knowledge of the external world. It is an example of Locke's insight that he queried the presuppositions of this enterprise in a brief chapter in his *Essay* before it had even been set in hand. Indeed the reader of his *Essay* is continually surprised and enlightened by individual discussions sometimes cutting across the flow of the argument as a whole. Another example of such insight is undoubtedly found in his very suggestive remarks concerning the significance of tactual as distinct from visual perception, even though his argument here is hardly integrated with the systematic presentation of his causal theory of perception. His well-known discussion of the question of degrees of belief deeply interested J. H. Newman (who, of all major nineteenth-century British religious thinkers, was the most subtly perceptive in his treatment of thinkers in the British empiricist tradition), and he devoted a not inconsiderable section of his *Essay in Aid of a Grammar of Assent* (1870) to its criticism.

Historically Locke's importance is, of course, much more as a political thinker than as a philosopher, even though the two sides of his work can hardly be separated; thus his conception of the mind as a *tabula rasa* was effectively invoked by those thinkers of the continental European Enlightenment who found themselves bound to criticize the doctrine of original sin, so frequently invoked by conservatives as a buttress of absolute monarchy; if the mind were indeed a *tabula rasa*, human beings might be said to 'start from scratch', innocent of the burden of the sin of Adam! Where his *Treatises on Civil Government* are concerned, the first is devoted to an elaborate criticism of the theory of divine right as found particularly in R. Filmer's *Patriarcha and other Political Works* edited by P. Laslett (1949). His *Second Treatise*, which Mr Peter Laslett has established as written during the period of the Exclusion Bill crisis in the reign of Charles the Second, is a classical source of liberal political theory, making use of the traditional liberal apparatus of inalienable, imprescriptible natural rights, pact of association, pact of government, etc. In his presentation of the theory of natural rights, Locke adheres rigidly to his view that the fundamental principles of ethics and politics are evident to a kind of rational intuition, able here to recognize what is essential to the status of man as man. But his *Second Treatise* includes much else; for instance, an account of property rights based upon a labour theory of value. Locke seems continually to oscillate between offering an *apologia* for the emancipation from public interference and direction of the property and enterprises of the rising Whig aristocracy with whom, through his attachment to Shaftesbury, he was intimately associated, and offering a defence of constitutional supremacy. His rejection of the theory of divine right, and indeed of the metaphysical image of the 'great chain of being' with which it was connected, issues from the application to the study of political principle of a highly personal amalgam of rationalist and empiricist conceptions seen to be characteristic of his theory of knowledge. But when he comes to criticize, e.g., the Hobbesian conception of unlimited sovereignty and to attribute to the legislative a supremacy that is less than the sovereignty later believed by A. V. Dicey to belong to the Queen in Parliament, he shows the influence of the 'judicious Mr Hooker'. In the unreconciled movement of his liberalism between constitutionalist and (to borrow Professor C. B. McPherson's useful phrase) 'possessive individualist' poles he reveals a classic contradiction in Anglo-Saxon liberal political thought, clearly discernible also in the writings of later liberal political theorists who abandoned the conception of natural right, and manifestly present also in the political institutions, history and thought of the U S A, so much in its beginnings in debt to Locke's ideas.

D. M. MACKINNON

Lottery. *see* **Gambling.**

Love

Few words so indispensable to discourse upon Christian ethics as well as Christian theology are so imprecise in their denotation as the word love. In common English usage love means a sentiment of strong attachment entertained towards a particular object or class of objects. A person may be said to love anything in which he takes special delight – the sea, flowers, birds, music, poetry. When the object of love is personal, it is usually individual rather than generic: we do not naturally speak of loving musicians or poets. In the Hebrew of the O T, the commonest word for love – *'ahebh* – generally has a personal object, though it can be used, for example, of savoury meat (Gen. 27.4) or cursing (Ps. 109.17). In Hebrew as in English, the word gets its most characteristic overtones from the fact that the strongest and most enduring form of personal love is that between man and woman. Neither language has a separate word for erotic love. The Septuagint translation of the O T generally renders *'ahebh* and its derivatives by the Greek *agapan* and its noun *agape*, even when as in the Song of Songs the natural word for the love described would be *eros*. In pre-biblical Greek *eros* is a passion, an ecstasy, a madness; while the verb *agapan* and the noun *agapesis* (the form *agape* seems not to occur earlier than its use in the Septuagint) denote the cooler and calmer love of rational preference, which chooses its object and holds to it freely. This is in accord with the most important feature of biblical usage, which is that the love of husband and wife includes the obligation of fidelity; and it is this element of loyalty in a covenanted relationship that is reflected when love, which as a spontaneous sentiment cannot be forced, is required in the Deuteronomic law (Deut. 6.5) as Israel's liege duty to the God who had entered into covenant with this people. The love of God is indeed often coupled with the keeping of his commandments (Deut. 11.1, etc.); but there is no need to evade an apparent paradox by arguing that the command to love God really means the requirement of obedience to God's law in all the actions of life. The command assumes that love in the natural meaning of the word is the natural response to the love so wonderfully bestowed by God himself upon the people whom he has chosen. To fail in this response would be to have forgotten the unique relationship in which Israel stands to Jehovah. Before the Deuteronomist, the prophet Hosea had already found in the figure of an adulterous wife the most speaking image for Israel's apostasy: Israel *ought* to be true in love to her divine husband. So Joshua demands that Israel shall 'cleave' to the Lord (Josh. 23.8), as the law of nature requires a man to 'cleave' to his wife (Gen. 2.24). In the same way, the command in the 'Holiness Code' of Leviticus

(19.18) – 'You shall love your neighbour as yourself' – is to be understood as a real command, based upon the natural bond of common membership in the elect nation.

It is possible that the combination of Deut. 6.5 with Lev. 19.18 had already been made in Rabbinic teaching before Jesus; for it appears in the *Testaments of the Twelve Patriarchs* (e.g., Issachar 5.2; 7.5). In any case, the scribe in Mark 12.28 ff. welcomes as 'said truly' Christ's summary of the law as love to God and love to neighbour; and both Jesus and his questioner must be taken to have understood the operative word in each of the two commandments so associated as having the same meaning: the second is really (as in Matt. 22.39) 'like' the first. There has been much discussion about the meaning of 'as yourself', and the nature of the 'self-love' which the saying appears to sanction. But the phrase will not bear the weight of any such far-reaching inferences; it simply describes a love as intense and compulsive as that of Jonathan who loved David as 'his own soul' (I Sam. 20.17) – so that the fortunes of the beloved are as important to the lover as his own. But it should be clear that to love one's neighbour as thus commanded does not *mean* to succour him in distress, any more than to love God *means* to keep his commandments. It is a separate question, in what kind of behaviour must the love of God or neighbour be exhibited and its genuineness verified?

In the teaching of Jesus, the pattern love is God's, which is displayed (1) in his indiscriminate goodness to all his creation, (2) in his free forgiveness for the repentant sinner, and (3) in his redeeming activity, going out 'to seek and to save'. So men are bidden to imitate the divine love (1) by doing good to all without distinction, (2) by forgiving as they have been forgiven, and (3) by ready response to every call of need. The love-ethic of the N T Epistles is true to that of the Gospels in the second and third of these characters; but the universalism implicit in Christ's extension of love to enemies is replaced by an emphasis on 'love of the brethren' which is hardly less marked in the Pauline than in the Johannine writings. For Paul, love is the greatest of the Spirit's gifts because it serves for the 'building up' of the Christian community. Love is the solvent of all divisive forces, all individualism which threatens the life of the one Body; it is the 'bond of wholeness' (Eph. 4.3; Col. 3.14). For John, the new commandment is that we love one another: this mutual love of Christians is to be the proof for all men that they are Christ's disciples, and by the love which unites them, as it unites Father and Son in the Godhead, the world will know that the Father has sent him (John 13.34 f.; 17.22 f.). Here certainly o t influence is at work. The Church is the true Israel, whose members are bound in the new covenant, sealed in Christ's blood, to be true in love to God and their brethren. It is the nature of love to be the supreme *unifying* power.

Apart from the summary of the law, there is not more than a single reference (Luke 11.42) in the Synoptic account of Jesus' teaching to man's love for God. In the rest of the N T the 'love of God' nearly but not quite always means God's love for men. In I John 5.3 love for God is expressly identified with the keeping of his commandments (cf. John 14.15,21); and Paul in Gal. 5.14 and Rom. 13.10 calls love of neighbour the *fulfilment* of the law. But these texts are insufficient justification for assuming an intentional reduction of the first great commandment to the second. Paul does speak of love for God without qualification, for example, in I Cor. 8.3; and we may be sure that it was not a love of neighbour but an answering love to the God whose own forgiving love he had known in Christ that took him to his death in Rome. For him as for the Rabbi Aquiba and many another persecuted Jew, martyrdom 'for the Name' was the ultimate fulfilment of the great commandment.

What is harder to find in the N T is any expression of love towards God which recalls the 'thirst' of the Psalmists (Pss. 42 and 63). And this is the sense of unsatisfied longing which dominated the minds and hearts of later Christians educated in the philosophic atmosphere of Platonism. The *eros* which in Plato was the desire for vision of the ideal beauty became for the Neoplatonist the desire for union with God; and union with God was not to be distinguished from the eternal life which was the promise of the Christian gospel. The famous words of Augustine in the Confessions (I.1), that our hearts are restless till they find their rest in God, would have been echoed by nearly everyone of his great predecessors, at least in the Greek-speaking Church, as voicing the essence of religion. And Augustine is the mainspring of the great tradition of Catholic mysticism which flourished throughout the Middle Ages. The tradition received its intellectual formulation from Thomas Aquinas. In the *Summa Theologica* all natural love is treated as a passion, stirred by some good to which the love is adapted; but the 'love of concupiscence', which is the desire of possession, is distinguished from the 'love of friendship', which seeks only the good of the friend. Charity as the super-natural gift of grace is a love of friendship, based on God's self-communication to man, in which God is loved 'for himself' and not for anything to be obtained from him.

The scholastic distinction, however, did not impress Anders Nygren, who in his influential study of the doctrine of love in Christian theology maintained that the '*eros*-motif' predominant in Catholicism is irreconcilable with the '*agape*-motif' of the N T because *eros* is always ego-centric as the pursuit of a good to be acquired for the self. The acquisitive nature of the desire is not affected by its transference from a 'lower' to a 'higher' good, from things earthly to things heavenly. *Agape* on the contrary is entirely unselfish, seeking only the good of others, and is therefore theo-centric because it is the reproduction of God's own outgoing love, a love 'uncaused' by any existing goodness in its object. In Nygren's view, Augustine (*see* **Augustine of Hippo, St**) attempted to achieve a synthesis of *eros* and *agape*, in which the restless longing for God in the human heart – a longing implanted by God himself – is met by the descent of the divine love in the incarnation, so that the union with God which is the object of desire is participation in the selfless love which is the very nature of God. But (so Nygren holds) the synthesis must be pronounced a failure, because it involves (contrary to Augustine's own principles) 'using' God for the satisfaction of a human need. The synthesis was shattered by Luther's 'Copernican revolution', in which the *eros*-inspired Catholic doctrine of love was seen to be the expression of 'works-religion', seeking fellowship with God on God's own 'level' by an ascent Godwards on the wings of spiritual desire; whereas the doctrine of justification by faith means that fellowship with God is only to be had 'on the level of sin', where God's love meets the sinner in Christ. *Eros* is always man's attempt to 'establish his own righteousness', to make himself fit for the vision of God; and it must therefore be ruthlessly extirpated to make room for the entry of *agape*. The logical conclusion, accepted by Nygren, is that since man may not love God in the sense of *eros*, and cannot love him in the sense of *agape* – the creature cannot 'seek the good' of the Creator – the love enjoined in the first great commandment is really indistinguishable from the faith which is man's only proper attitude to God; while the Christian love of neighbour is nothing less than God's own *agape* flowing through human hearts.

Nygren's confrontation of *eros* and *agape* may be compared with the position of Søren Kierkegaard in his *Works of Love* (1847). Kierkegaard contrasted Christian love not with the mystic's desire for union with God but with the love between man and woman or friend and friend, which is selective, concentrated upon a particular person or persons preferred to all others. Such love, depending as it does upon the presence of certain qualities in its object found lovable, is for Kierkegaard (as *eros* is for Nygren) only a disguised form of the love of self; and it is necessarily exposed to alteration and failure. Christian love, which does not choose its object but goes out to the neighbour who is everyman, is secure from change just because it is accepted as a duty, as obedience to a 'you shall'.

Karl Barth in his *Church Dogmatics* (IV, 2,68) agrees with Nygren that *eros* and *agape* are contraries; for *agape* conforms to the true nature of man as created for relationship to God and to his fellowmen, while *eros* opposes it. So, though in most if not all of us, both loves are present and active in varying degrees, they must always be in rivalry: the love which seeks self-fulfilment must be at issue with the love which is *Hingabe*, total surrender of the self. But Barth is too good a biblical theologian to approve the 'Puritanism' of Nygren's refusal to allow that man can have love towards God. Christ accepted the loving extravagance of Mary's offering, and rebuked the moralistic protests of his disciples. Without love to Jesus there can be no following of Jesus: without love to God there can be no obedience to God. Love is the *presupposition* of all else in the Christian life; and it is precisely the freedom to love both God and neighbour that is the gift of grace, the creation of God's own redeeming love in Christ. So Barth can see only an intolerable legalism in Kierkegaard's insistence that love must be made 'secure' by the obligation of obedience to a command. He holds equally firmly against Nygren (or Luther!) that the love of neighbour which springs from and is 'like' man's love for God must be a genuinely human activity; Christians are not mere 'channels' for God's love. But he maintains that because God's own love is not a disposition or a sentiment but an *act*, the same must be true of man's love for his fellowmen. The act in which it consists is essentially an act of witness to the gospel, to the accomplished fact of redemption; and accordingly Barth follows the Pauline and Johannine example in treating Christian love as in principle an act which is not indiscriminate in its reference, but has the 'brother' as its object – though it must always be ready to find a 'brother' in one who was not such before.

Differences in the understanding of Christian love arise to a large extent from the incurable ambivalence of a religious ethic. For secular morality there is an obvious distinction between the love which links persons to one another because of something peculiar to them as individuals or members of a class, and the love of humanity as such which expresses itself in the service of others not because of their characters but because of their situation. Kantian rigorism will allow moral quality only to the second of these loves. The 'problem of love' in Christian ethics is posed by its theological basis: What is the consequence for Christian behaviour of the belief that God is love? The image of divine fatherhood which was central to the teaching of Jesus does not suggest a love which is exhibited in pure altruism, regardless of any personal relationship to its recipients. The love of God of which the gospel speaks is more than a love of beneficence; it is a reconciling, in the strict meaning of the word an atoning love. We cannot suppose that the heavenly Father does not care whether his children love him or not. The labour of his love is to overcome the pride and covetousness which estrange men alike from God and from one another, and to bring them to that state of mutual attachment and mutual dependence which is proper to a family. Christian love therefore, cannot be perfected without the warmth of personal affection which is the cement of unity between parent and children, brothers and sisters. The grace of our Lord Jesus Christ is what gives that warmth to men's service of one another and to their loyal obedience to the law of God.

E. Brunner, *The Divine Imperative*, 1937; J. Burnaby, *Amor Dei*, 1938; M. J. D'Arcy, *The Mind and Heart of Love*, 1945; J. Guitton, *Essay on Human Love*, 1951; S. Kierkegaard, *Works of Love*, 1962; J. Moffatt, *Love in the New Testament*,1929; R. Niebuhr, *An Inter-, pretation of Christian Ethics*, 1936; A. Nygren, *Agape and Eros*: Part I, 1932; Part II, 1938; G. Quell and E. Stauffer, *Love*, Bible Key Words from Gerhard Kittel's *Theologisches Wörterbuch Zum Neuen Testament*, I, 1949.

JOHN BURNABY

Loyalty

Loyalty or faithfulness is a natural and widespread human virtue, without which the social life of man would be impossible. The loyal person is the one who can be relied upon to seek the good of those persons or causes to whom he has committed himself. The most common loyalties are, of course, directed to limited objects, such as the family, one's friends, one's country. There is always the danger that such limited loyalties may blind the person who has given himself to them to wider demands made upon him, and in extreme cases a loyalty may be in danger of passing over into fanaticism. Nevertheless, even a limited loyalty lifts the individual out of himself and expands the horizons of his being. Such limited loyalties, moreover, form as it were a kind of natural counterpart to the unreserved and universal loyalty to Christ and his kingdom, demanded of the Christian. In recent philosophy, the idea of loyalty has been chiefly developed by Josiah Royce (q.v.), who regarded 'loyalty to loyalty' as the fundamental ethical principle, and who believed that this principle found signal expression in the early Christian community. Royce's ideas have been much admired by Gabriel Marcel, whose notion of 'fidelity' is rather similar.

EDITOR

Lust

The word originally meant desire, so that one might talk of desires or lusts of the flesh. A Christian makes a distinction between lusts and sinful lusts (*see* Anglican Catechism). Sinful lusts may be described as lusts used only for their own sake – a sort of fleshly greed, or gluttony, for physical excitement as a good thing in itself. Nowadays 'lust' has always a bad meaning, that of uncontrolled sexual passion seen and understood only in terms of its physical expression. While the fact remains that sex in human beings can never be understood and expressed except in both physical and spiritual terms, men and women frequently try to separate the one from the other. Some use the physical act of sex as a drug that soothes or as a sensation which stimulates. Many look to sex experience as a distraction from the banality and monotony of so much modern city life. This indicates that lust cannot be considered as merely a physical happening but must be seen as the sign of a particular spiritual state.

R. E. C. BROWNE

Luther and Lutheran Ethics

For Luther (1483–1546), the biblical message of salvation is a tension-filled unity which can be viewed from the perspective of any one of its constitutive elements. He can speak of 'grace alone', 'Christ alone', 'Scripture alone' or 'faith alone' and mean thereby the same saving event in terms of either its eternal source, historical expression, apostolic witness or personal appropriation.

In fidelity to this Christ-centred faith, Luther roundly condemned the moral and rational work-righteousness inherent in the philosophical theology of Rome. Before God, reason must submit to Scripture and works must bow to faith. In an evangelical 'theory of the cross', men humbly confess that the righteous shall live by faith (Rom. 1.17).

With their salvation thus assured in the unmerited forgiveness of Christ, grateful and obedient Christians are free to redirect their reason and good works towards serving their neighbours' welfare. Luther grounds his ethic in the paradoxical nature of Christian freedom which accepts liberation from satanic bondage as the divine invitation for human service. All men act as their brother's keeper: willingly in faith, begrudgingly in rebellion. Since the Christian is at once righteous and sinful, his enforced service aids his self-discipline while his voluntary service meets his neighbours' needs. Against the presumption of Roman clericalism, Luther insists that all baptized Christians be permitted the beneficial exercise of their royal priesthood in loving service to their God-given neighbours.

In opposition to all unevangelical ethics of principles, 'blue laws', ideals, or rules and regulations, Luther portrays the biblical pattern of a life of 'faith working through love' (Gal. 5.6). A Christian ethic based on the 'divine indicative' of God's grace (rather than the 'divine imperative' of God's law) preserves the freedom of the believer under the guidance of the Holy Spirit through the Bible, the Church, and prayer, to discover anew in each concrete situation what the will of God permits or requires of him then and there.

For the biblical foundation of his Christian social ethic, Luther rooted his doctrine of the 'two realms' of creation and redemption in the Pauline eschatology of the 'two ages' (*aeons*) in Adam and Christ (Rom. 5). In the kingdom of God, the Redeemer rules all regenerate believers through Christ and the gospel in personal faith and love. In the kingdom of men, the Creator rules all sinful creatures through Caesar and the law in civil justice and obedience. As both Redeemer and Creator, God is at once the Lord of both kingdoms; as both righteous and sinful, the Christian is at once a subject of both kingdoms. Hence for an evangelical theology of society, the two kingdoms must always be properly distinguished, but never separated in secularism or equated in clericalism.

In this doctrine of the 'two realms' of creation and redemption, Luther reaffirmed the 'sacred secularity' of the ordinary tasks of the common life as those which best serve our neighbours' needs to God's glory. Whether empowered by Christ in faith-activated love (Christian righteousness) or compelled by Caesar in law-abiding reason (civil righteousness), the Christian saint-citizen lives not for himself but for the benefit of others.

Christian social action was a major concern in Luther's own life and thought. The profound effects of the Reformation in the area of religion is common knowledge to all. What is not so well known – or, at least, not so commonly acknowledged – is the impressive social reformation which Luther's theology envisaged and even partially brought about in the broad and inclusive expanse of the common life. Here again, Luther's contribution to a better world is incalculable.

This emancipation of the common life was not so popular a crusade as it might at first appear. Luther's understanding of the Christian ethical life compelled him to combat both extremes of clericalism and secularism as unevangelical. Against Anabaptists, he had to fight for the preservation of music, art and sculpture in the worship life of the Church (*Against the Heavenly Prophets*). Against Roman Catholics, he had to struggle for the opening of the monasteries and the freedom of all Christians to marry and to engage in secular pursuits without endangering their salvation (*On Monastic Vows*; *On Married Life*).

Against recalcitrant parents and lax public officials, he also fought for educational reforms and the establishment of community chests to replace the illiteracy and begging so prevalent in his day (*On Keeping Children in School*; *Preface to an Ordinance of a Common Chest*). Against irresponsible merchants, he attacked economic injustice and proposed government controls to halt unfair commercial and labour practices (*On Trading and Usury*). Against both the reckless mobs which confused their Christian freedom with their civil rights, and the arbitrary rulers who disregarded their responsibility under God for their subjects' economic and social welfare, Luther appealed constantly for both civil obedience and – less strangely! – for political justice in a community of law and order (*Admonition to Peace*; *Exposition of the Eighty-second Psalm*).

It is true, however, that Luther does not normally conceive of the Christian's social responsibility as transforming the existing structures of society. While persons can be transformed by the gospel in the Kingdom of God, institutions can only be reformed by the law in the kingdom of men. Men are to accept the social structures for what they are (the Creator's dykes against sin), and to try to act as responsible Christians within them (as the Redeemer's channels of serving love). When our secular occupations among men are faithfully acknowledged to be part of our religious vocation under God, then love provides law with its ethical content and law provides love with its social form.

For example, against those who would spiritualize marriage into a Christian sacrament, Luther protests that marriage belongs essentially to the realm of creation and not redemption. It is therefore ruled by God's law and not his gospel, and, as such, is one of God's temporal remedies against sin and not a sanctifying means of grace.

On the other hand, against those who would interpret this liberating message as justification for carnal lust and licence, Luther is equally insistent that marriage is rooted firmly in the creative will of God as one of his own divine ordinances. Although it is not a sacrament of the Church, there is nevertheless no higher social calling in which a Christian can exercise his faith in deeds of serving love for his family and neighbours. Hence, the ex-monk Luther eventually married himself as a public testimony of faith in witness to his restoration of the evangelical view of marriage and home life under God.

For Luther's social ethic, all offices and stations of life – ecclesiastical, domestic, economic, political, etc. – embodied in institutional form a particular command of God's law. They are all integrated within the earthly kingdom of men as the Creator's divinely-ordained bulwarks in his ongoing struggles against Satan. There is no particularly 'Christian' form of these 'orders'. Though corrupted by sin themselves, the 'orders' are the means by which the

Creator preserves his fallen world from even greater chaos, injustice and suffering.

This is why the Church can 'christianize' politicians and economists but not politics and economics. These 'orders' are ordained by God to remain secular, enjoying a relative autonomy of their own under the sovereign law of the Creator. Hence not faith and love but reason and justice are normative for the temporal realm of life. At the same time, however, faith can illumine reason and love can temper justice whenever Christian citizens meet their civil responsibilities as part of their religious discipleship.

It is obvious that the authority of Luther's theology cannot legitimately be used to endorse many of the unhealthy social and political developments which have since appeared in the Church bearing his name. To cite only the most notorious recent example, Luther could never have sanctioned a totalitarian regime ruling over a class-bound society in which a spiritually emasculated clergy could desist from prophetic criticism of the state in return for political and social favours. The vicious attempts to discredit Luther as 'Hitler's spiritual ancestor', for instance, must be denounced as theological and political fantasy – despite some deceptive wartime propaganda to the contrary (cf. Inge and Wiener).

Four articles may be cited from the Augsburg Confession, to show that Luther's restatement of the central thrust of Paul's ethic is afforded normative authority by the Lutheran Church.

On the personal level, Article 4 rejects all moral work-righteousness by grounding man's salvation solely in his being justified by God's grace for Christ's sake through faith alone. Then Article 6 militates against any ethical quietism by affirming that this Christian faith – 'a living, busy, active thing' – is bound to bring forth good fruits, and that it is also necessary for Christians to do those good works which are commanded by God for the neighbours' benefit.

On the social level, Article 16 guards against any secularism by insisting that Christians are not to espouse any rigorous dualism between the two kingdoms of creation and redemption but are rather to permeate all of society with personal love and social justice in the exercise of their Christian ethical responsibility. Finally, Article 28 complements this stress with a like rejection of all clericalism by sharply distinguishing the valid functions of the Church and the State in the two kingdoms. On the one side, the Church should not impose its will on the civil community by usurping the power of enforcement that rightly falls within the domain of government. On the other side, the State ought not interfere with the Church's prophetic role in holding public life accountable to the sovereign law of God.

Hence, in fidelity to the twofold rule of their Creator and Redeemer through his law and gospel, Lutheran Christians are to remain reverent to God's Word and relevant to God's world by exercising both their priestly 'yes' through faith active in love and their prophetic 'no' through love seeking social justice.

George Forell, *Faith Active in Love*, 1954; William H. Lazareth, *Luther on the Christian Home*, 1960; H. Richard Niebuhr, *Christ and Culture*, 1951.

WILLIAM H. LAZARETH

Lying

At John 8.44 Jesus is made to say that the devil is the father of lies. There is no doubt in general of the evil of lying. It destroys the basis of human association and in the end is stulifying. Christian thought, however, down the centuries has been much exercised whether it is ever right to tell a lie. The Fathers debated whether one was entitled to tell a lie to a pirate, and were much exercised about the lies in Scripture, for example, the Hebrew midwives of Ex. 1. In a controversy with St Jerome, St Augustine wrote two treatises against lies in any circumstances (*De Mendacio* and *Contra Mendacium*). Centuries later he was to be followed by the philosopher Kant, who wrote against the supposed right of telling lies from benevolent motives. Most theologians did not like to contradict St Augustine, but his conclusion did not seem sound. A way round it was found by not characterizing certain concealments of the truth as lies. An immense literature grew up on ambiguity, mental reservation and economy of the truth, which it is easy to caricature. It is clear that there may be circumstances in which it is right to tell a lie, but most people tell lies when they should not. The temptation comes swiftly and they succumb. Perhaps it is to get out of an awkward situation, or to practise some petty fraud or deception. The only way to have the sensitivity of spirit to know when a lie is called for in particular circumstances is to be habitually truthful. *See* **Truth and Truthfulness.**

RONALD PRESTON

Machiavelli, Niccolo

Machiavelli (1469–1527) ranks as one of the most important political philosophers of Europe. Like Thomas Hobbes in England, he has been largely misunderstood and misrepresented. His work has to be set and judged in the historical situation which called it forth. He was born in Florence, and held office there from 1498 to 1512, when he fell from favour. By 1520, his star was again in the ascendant, and he was commissioned to write the history of Florence. Out of his own immersion in the troubled politics of his time, his ideas were born. His most famous work, *The Prince* (*Il Principe*) dates from 1513. In this book, he states his case for freeing politics from morality. But he made this plea in a spirit of realism rather than of cynicism. In Bacon's words, he 'set forth honestly and sincerely what men are wont to do, and not what they ought to do'. The overriding need in Machiavelli's time was for a strong united government, and this in the long run would be beneficial to all. Machiavelli's studies of Roman history show, moreover, that he had no special liking for an autocracy as such. If the State might be united by the spirit of the people, as in the Roman republic, then this would be preferable to the dictatorship of an individual. But some strong authority there must be, prepared to pursue in single-minded fashion the good of the State.

H. Butterfield, *The Statecraft of Machiavelli*, 1955.

EDITOR

Magnanimity

The magnanimous man lives on the grand scale appropriate to one who is aware of the cosmic and eternal significance of what men do. Magnanimity is not the ability to make any occasion great but to recognize the greatness of particular occasions. The killing of the fatted calf, the breaking open of the box of precious ointment both have marks of magnanimity which are lacking in Herod's birthday party.

The magnanimous man praises good work no matter who does it and even if it is work he would like to do himself but cannot. At the same time, without losing patience or dignity, he attends to everyday routine.

There is no opposite to magnanimity; it springs from the doctrines of God and man which illuminate the quickly changing circumstances in which men must act. Magnanimity sometimes looks like extravagance, but extravagance is pseudo-magnanimity concerned with self-display or the desire to make some person, or institution, appear to be important. The magnanimous man is not obsessed with the possible results of what he is doing because he has a quality of sublime generosity more easily known and recognized than described.

Christians know that a person is magnified by his worship of God. The following quotations from the Magnificat (Luke 1.46–55) express this truth – 'My soul magnifies the Lord ... He who is mighty has done great things for me (hath magnified me).' The worship of God frees a man from imprisonment within himself or within a group. He does not worship for the sake of enlarging himself but in his behaviour magnanimity or its absence shows the quality and nature of his worship.

In church life magnanimity is seen in the forms in which praise is expressed and sinfulness acknowledged, as well as in the scope of intercessions and thanksgivings.

R. E. C. BROWNE

Maimonides, Moses

Moses Maimonides (1135–1204), Jewish philosopher, author of *Guide for the Perplexed. See* **Jewish Ethics; Mediaeval Ethics.**

Malice

Malice springs from hatred and is an active expression of ill-will. It is more characteristic of the small minded ungenerous person who sees his own failure in the success of others than of the strong man capable of sustaining deep hatred or deep love.

Christians are told not to bear malice. A man may pride himself in considering that he can check malicious words and deeds but the time comes when, in spite of his confidence, his secretly borne malice will express itself in word or deed. Christianity declares that though Christians are delivered from stultifying legalistic righteousness they must not let this deliverance blind them to their responsibility for keeping their hidden world of thoughts and wishes under such control as they are enabled to exert.

Malice is to be thought of not so much as acts but as one of the human states of being. Such states are complex and change quickly without pause. No state exactly repeats itself in its movements no matter how often it recurs. A malicious man is one whose characteristic state is malicious; his range of moods imprisons him in a narrow unhappiness. He does not rejoice with those who rejoice, he is angry with them because they have grounds for rejoicing. He does not weep with those who weep: if they are his enemies, he laughs at them. There is no quick remedy for malice but only the long way of repentance which entails the slow changing of the whole man.

R. E. C. BROWNE

Mammon

Mammon is an Aramaic word meaning 'wealth', 'gain' or 'possessions'. It was commonly used in Rabbinic literature without any pejorative meaning, for example, *M. Aboth* II, 12 'Let the property (*mammon*) of thy fellow be dear to thee as thy own'; but it was also used with negative connotations which were sometimes strengthened by the associated terms, for example, 'unrighteous mammon'. The word appears four times in the Greek NT: 'unrighteous mammon' in Luke 16.9,11; and 'You cannot serve God and mammon' in Luke 16.13 and Matt. 6.24. In this last and best-known passage wealth is personified as an idol standing over against the true God in the struggle for human allegiance. Through its

NT usage the term became part of the general Christian tradition. *See* Tertullian, *Against Marcion*, IV, 33; Augustine, *Sermon on the Mount*, II, 14; Chrysostom, *Homilies on Matthew*, XXI, 2 ('Tell me not of them that are rich, but of them that serve riches'); Thomas Aquinas, *Summa Theologica*, Part II, Second Section, q. 32, art. 7, obj. 1.

In the mediaeval period the personification of the term led to the mistaken impression that it was the name of a god or demon. *See* Nicholas of Lyra or the commentary attributed to Thomas Aquinas, on Matt. 6.24. This view was further popularized by Milton's *Paradise Lost*, I, 678, etc. 'Mammon' continues to be used as a symbol for wealth or earthly possessions. The term connotes the capacity of these material objects to fascinate man so as to lead first to his devotion and then to his enslavement.

D. M. Beck, 'Mammon', *The Interpreter's Dictionary of the Bible*, III, 1962, pp. 234 f.; J. Hastings, ed., *Encyclopedia of Religion and Ethics*, VIII, 1916, pp. 374 f; *TWNT*, IV, pp. 390–2.

HARVEY K. MCARTHUR

Man, Doctrine of

The Christian doctrine of man is founded on the Hebraic viewpoint as stated in Gen. 1–3. It affirms that God formed man out of the dust of the ground, and breathed into him the breath of life. That he created man in his own image: 'in the image of God created he him' (Gen. 1.27). Thus man is understood in terms of this unique relationship to God. Moreover, man is given dominion over the rest of creation, as signified by the commission to cultivate the garden and to name the animals and birds. And he is endowed with freedom of choice, as symbolized by the divine prohibition.

Biblical thought maintains that man repudiated his creatureliness by attempting to be like God. It therefore regards pride as the essence of sin. And it sees the consequences of man's pride in the distortion of existence at every level and in total range.

Christianity locates the truth of the stories of creation and the fall not in their historical character, but in their religious insights. It finds in them a vivid expression of man's original goodness, his dignity and freedom, his responsibility and guilt, and the consequent alienation between himself and God. This tragic condition is the common presupposition of human existence – individual and social (this is the meaning of 'original sin').

Sinful mankind stands under divine judgment. His rebellion escalates and issues in ever more destructive manifestations and consequences. This is indicated in Gen. 4–11 by the progressive nature of evil and its punishment from wanton violence resulting in the alienation of Cain, to total apostasy resulting in mass discord and confusion (Babel).

Christian teaching accepts the call of Abraham ('in whom all the families of the earth shall be blessed') as the initial chapter in the 'history of salvation'. It sees the fulfilment of this history and the perfect embodiment of manhood in Jesus the Christ. In him the estrangement between God and man is overcome, and the goal of human existence is realized. He is the 'new man', the 'second Adam'.

Those who find in Christ the healing, regenerative activity of God, already know something of the wholeness which is man's true nature and destiny. They discover possibilities for the realization of essential manhood. They see some of the cleavages of human life overcome, the sense of worthlessness and despair conquered, and the tendencies towards violence and injustice brought under control (this is expressed in the traditional doctrines of justification and sanctification).

Now Christianity does not claim that human perfection is attainable within the present life. Not all of the capacities and consequences of sin are overcome. Man remains a sinner – albeit a *forgiven* sinner. The ultimate perfection of the individual and society is not a historical possibility. This total salvation is represented for the individual by 'the resurrection of the body', in which the whole man – flesh and spirit – attains fulfilment. And for society by 'the Kingdom of God' in which mankind together with the entire created order achieves its goal.

It is the task of Christian theology to relate its doctrine to all that can be learned from the scientific study of man. Theology does not prescribe either the methods or the conclusions of these studies. It seeks rather to co-operate with them in the analysis and description of human nature. It profits from their insights and gives perspective to their findings. An example is the increasing collaboration of psychosomatic medicine, social psychology, and theology.

The Christian concept may be brought into sharper focus by comparison with one of its major alternatives – the Marxist concept. The Marxist view takes as its starting point the position of man within society. It sees the human essence not in some metaphysical abstraction, but in the totality of man's social relationships. It does not recognize any ideal or normative concept which is not derived from concrete, historical mankind. Thus Marx quarrelled with Feuerbach's anthropology.

In the Marxist view, man is distinguished from non-human nature by the intelligent, conscious development and reproduction of himself in the historical process. His independence and freedom are based on his self-creation. Man is free, in Marx's words, only '. . . if he affirms his individuality as a total man in each of his relations to the world, seeing, hearing, smelling, tasting, feeling, thinking, willing, loving – in short, if he affirms and expresses all organs of his individuality. . . .'

Marx presupposes a primal state of human solidarity, a kind of primitive communistic order. The appearance of social cleavage through class structures disrupts this original harmony and threatens man's existence. It marks the beginning of human history as well as self-estrangement. Estrangement (or alienation) is for Marx the experience of nature, others, and oneself as passive, receptive, as a subject separated from an object.

The individual cannot disengage himself from the ills which afflict society. Yet he is always tempted to conceal them by creating ideologies. According to Marx, ideologies (such as Christianity) are merely devices for disguising the exploitation and dehumanization of private property under capitalistic conditions.

Marxism proclaims the conquest – partial in the present, total in the future – of social conflict and the establishment of a classless society. It recognizes that the nearer its goal is approached, the more intense will be the conflict. The conquest is first realized not by society as a whole, but by the proletariat. This group, though divided within itself between the more and less active, advances the cause with the utmost zeal. It overcomes alienation and dehumanization in principle and in fact by the abolition of private property as well as by discovering new methods of co-operation and new forms of productivity. The extent to which, under existing circumstances, a complete victory will be achieved short of a revolutionary catastrophe is doubtful. But the Marxist goal remains the restoration of social relatedness in conformity with man's true nature. This final goal is often described as perfect freedom.

The similarities between the Christian and the Marxist concepts of man are obvious. However, these are not similarities in ideas, but in thought-structure. And, as many have observed, it is the fundamental structure of 'prophetic Judeo-Christian anthropology' which is common to both.

The basic difference in ideas lies in the theistic foundation of Christianity as opposed to the humanistic foundation of Marxism. In the former, man is understood in relationship to God. In the latter, he is defined in relation to society. This distinction is manifest at a number of points. The one sees creation as divine; the other as man producing himself. The one views man as made in God's image; the other sees God as made in man's image. The one regards sin as individual rebellion against God; the other as class revolt against social co-operation. According to one, the consequences of sin are universal; according to the other, they affect only a certain period of existence. One finds the solution to mankind's

problem in divine grace; the other in human endeavours. And finally, one looks for the fulfilment of human nature beyond temporal history; the other seeks its goal within temporal existence. Accordingly, for one hope, transcends death; for the other, hope – for the individual, at least – is terminated by death.

This may serve to show how the differences in ideas between the Christian and Marxist views of man revolve around an opposition between theistic and humanistic standpoints. And it may also serve to illustrate the uniquely Christian doctrine. *See also* **Communism, Ethics of Marxist.**

Martin Buber, *The Knowledge of Man*, 1965; Abraham J. Heschel, *Who is Man?* 1965; Reinhold Niebuhr, *The Nature and Destiny of Man*, 2 vols., 1941–43; Ronald Gregor Smith, *The New Man*, 1956; P. Teihard de Chardin, *The Phenomenon of Man*, 1959.

WILLIAM B. GREEN

Mandates. *see* Orders.

Manichaeism

Manichaeism is a religious system founded by the Persian teacher Mani in the third century. St Augustine was an adherent for a time in his youth. Manichaeism is strongly dualistic, and the expression 'Manichaean' is sometimes used in a derogatory sense for anyone who represents a moral problem in extremes of black and white. The mythology of Manichaeism and its ethics were very similar to those of the gnostic sects. *See* **Gnosticism.**

Marcus Aurelius

Marcus Aurelius (121–180), Roman emperor, author of the famous *Meditations*. *See* **Stoicism.**

Maritain, Jacques

Jacques Maritain (1882–   ) is one of the most prominent writers on Thomist ethics. Born in Paris, he studied at the University of Paris (under Henri Bergson) and did research in biology under Hans Driesch at Heidelberg. With his wife, Raissa, he became a Catholic in 1906. After devoting several years to the private study of St Thomas Aquinas, Maritain began his long career as a teacher and writer, first in France and, from 1940 onward, in the USA. His publications are numerous and they treat of most of the problems that occur in traditional philosophy (*see* D. and I. Gallagher, eds. *The Achievement of J. Maritain – a Bibliography, 1906–1960*, 1963).

Maritain insists that ethics, as a purely philosophical discipline, is a mere abstraction and does not provide adequate guidance for a good life. A fully-developed ethics would have to be a 'Christian ethics', borrowing certain starting-points from faith, or from moral theology. This is the theme of 'philosophizing in the faith' which he introduced in 1935, in the book later translated as *Science and Wisdom*, 1940. Man, in his present condition, is subject to the deficiencies stemming from the fall of Adam; original sin cannot be known through philosophy but it is a fact which must be acknowledged by any ethician who attempts to treat the moral agent in his existential status. Similarly, the view that man's nature is directed towards union with God in the beatific vision, after death, is essential to Christian ethics but only knowable through religious belief.

Many details in Maritain's ethics have been worked out in terms of the theory of natural law (q.v.). He maintains that every human being is equipped by nature with the conscious ability to intuit certain general rules of good behaviour (e.g., 'Do no injury to others') and to apply such naturally known moral laws to the judgment of concrete moral problems. Such practical applied judgment is moral conscience. Natural law is especially significant in interpersonal dealings, in social and political ethics (*see The Rights of Man and Natural Law*, 1943). Maritain's political philosophy stresses democracy, liberalism and the rights of the individual person; he favoured the Loyalist cause in the Spanish civil war.

In more recent books (*Neuf Lecons sur la philosophie morale*, 1951, and *Moral Philosophy*, 1964) Maritain has emphasized 'connatural knowledge' as a source of moral convictions. This is a theory of pre-conceptual, affective, somewhat instinctive awareness of what is right and good. It bears some resemblance to his parallel theory of esthetic intuition.

J. W. Evans and L. R. Ward, eds., *The Social and Political Philosophy of J. Maritain*, 1955; G. B. Phelan, *Jacques Maritain*, 1937; *The Maritain Volume of the Thomist*, 1943.

VERNON J. BOURKE

Marriage

Marriage regulates relations between the sexes in all known forms of society and governs the status and education of children within the community. It also extends its influence to the wider group of those related to one another by marriage or consanguinity. In the OT the institution of marriage went through a number of developments which by the time of Christ had resulted in general monogamy. The Jews considered marriage to be the duty of every man so as to perpetuate his family name. The family (q.v.), of which marriage is the basis, played a part of great importance in Jewish life.

The NT took the essential teaching of the OT and deepened it, but did not introduce any radically new concepts in the place of what was already there. The passages in the NT which deal with marriage put the emphasis on the inner content of married life. Divorce is a failure of the marriage relationship and is therefore to be shunned. Whether Jesus was intending to legislate for the future or not, it is clear that he regarded divorce and remarriage as essentially to be deplored. *See* **Divorce.** Jesus himself refers to marriage in the following passages – Matt. 5.31; 19.3–12; 22.23–30; Mark 10.2–12; 12.19–25; Luke 16.18; 20.27–35. Other NT passages are Rom. 7.1–4; I Cor. 6.16–18; 7; Eph. 5.22–33; Col. 3.18–19; I Tim. 5.9–16; Heb. 13.4; I Peter 3.1–8.

The Christian concept of marriage was affected by the high place which women filled in the NT. The position of the wife still appears in St Paul's writings as subordinate to that of the husband, yet his use of the metaphor of the mystical union between Christ and the Church as applying to marriage had a beneficial effect on Christian ideas about it.

In the traditional teaching of western Christendom marriage has three purposes: first, the procreation and nurture of children; second, mutual help and comfort; third, a remedy against sin. These three ends are to be found plainly stated in the 1662 Book of Common Prayer and in Roman Catholic canon law. The teaching of the Roman Church regards marriage as a contract in which each of the partners gives the other an exclusive and permanent right to his or her body for proper sexual purposes. The properties of a Christian marriage are unity and indissolubility in which the good of the offspring, of the faith, and of the sacrament, are safeguarded.

The traditional teaching of the Church has been that the ministers of the sacrament of marriage are the parties themselves and that the priest is present to accord to them the blessing of the Church. The presence of the priest is therefore not strictly necessary for the performance of a Christian marriage, which requires only that the necessary promises be taken before witnesses. On this basis a civil marriage is just as much a Christian marriage as one celebrated in a church. But in recent times the Roman Catholic Church has ruled that for the validity of a marriage in which one or both of the partners are Roman Catholics it must take place in the presence of a priest. This makes invalid (from the Roman Catholic point of view) most mixed marriages between a Roman Catholic and another Christian which take place elsewhere than in a Roman Catholic church, while it does not call in question the validity of marriages between Christians who are not Roman Catholics. This regulation has caused frequent bad blood between the Roman Catholic Church and other Christians.

The Roman Catholic Church also opposes civil marriages and commonly teaches that compulsory civil ceremonies are offensive both to religion and to the natural law, since it regards a civil marriage as not a real marriage.

The question of the indissolubility of Christian marriage is a disputed point, but it seems to be clearly the teaching of the Anglican and Roman Catholic Churches. It is sometimes maintained that marriage in the Christian sense is not only a contract between the parties, but also a status made by God ('into which holy estate'). The Eastern Orthodox Church would also seem to hold to this teaching in theory, but, by introducing into broken marriages the notion of 'moral death', it in fact allows divorce and remarriage for many reasons. Anglican churches commonly refuse to marry in church any person whose previous divorced partner is still living, though remarried persons may be admitted to the sacrament of holy communion with due safeguards concerning their sincerity.

In recent decades the attitudes of Christians towards the sexual aspect of the married life has considerably changed, and more and more it is recognized that the sexual activities of marriage are a positive element within marriage and not merely a means of procreation, still less a 'remedy against sin'. Christian history has been plagued by an attitude to sex which was negative and forbidding. Other attitudes can also be found in the Christian past, but for the most part they were overborne. The change in modern times has come about in part from the deeper understanding of human character and emotions which modern psychological study has brought. The new positive attitude towards sex in marriage has caused Christians first to accept and then to welcome contraceptive methods which permit full sexual intercourse. *See* **Procreation.**

Marriage within the so-called prohibited degrees has made such marriage invalid, but the prohibitions have in fact varied from time to time. In England in modern times marriage with a deceased wife's sister or a deceased husband's brother has been made legal and has been accepted by the Church as permissible.

In Roman Catholic canon law a diriment impediment makes a marriage invalid, whether the parties contracting the marriage know of it or not. Such impediments may originate from infractions of natural law, positive law, ecclesiastical law, or civil law. But all Christians accept certain diriment impediments as making marriages invalid. Among them are an error of identity or a trick, which affects the necessary free consent; abduction or terrorization; consanguinity or affinity within the prohibited degrees (whatever these may be); physical incapacity for marriage, such as impotence; or one of the parties under the age of puberty. Roman Catholic canon law speaks of a marriage as 'putative' in the case of an invalid marriage which has been contracted in good faith, so far as at least one of the parties is concerned. So long as both parties are not aware of its invalidity it remains putative and

the children born of it are considered to be legitimate. *See* **Legitimacy.**

Serious questions of conscience arise in cases where people are converted to the Christian faith in a society which commonly practises polygamy. Church regulations in such cases differ in different regions and churches. Problems of duty arise in the case of a man who has more than one wife and whose support is necessary for the well-being of the wives in question and perhaps for their status in the community. To insist that all the wives but one should be cast out may in fact be a cause of serious injustice and public scandal. On the other hand monogamy is an essential feature of Christian marriage, not only for traditional but also for theological reasons.

The question of civil marriage ceremonies causes difficulties in a number of countries. In spite of the dislike of certain Roman Catholic teachers there seems to be a good case for urging compulsory civil marriage for all and for returning to the earlier Christian teaching that in the case of two Christians being married in such a civil ceremony, the sacrament of Christian marriage is in fact celebrated, the two parties being the ministers of the sacrament. Christians could then resort to church to receive the blessing of the Church on their union, and by doing so they would be publicly acknowledging the teaching and discipline of the Church for their marriage. It is no longer either possible or desirable to have the laws of the Church enforced by the State, and those who wish to make their marriages fully Christian can only do so by their own willing consent to the spiritual authority of the Church.

But one should note that according to the Confession of Peter Mogila (1638) accepted by Orthodox Christians the priestly blessing and the prayer for the Holy Spirit are essentials of a valid marriage. Nevertheless even with this view, there seems to be no insuperable obstacle to having two ceremonies, one civil and one ecclesiastical.

The Church and the Law of Nullity of Marriage, Report of the Commission Appointed by the Archbishops of Canterbury and York, 1955; *The Family in Contemporary Society*, Report of the Group Convened at the Behest of the Archbishop of Canterbury, 1958; *Putting Asunder*, Report of Group Appointed by the Archbishop of Canterbury, 1966; Helmut Thielicke, *The Ethics of Sex*, 1964.

HERBERT WADDAMS

Martineau, James

Types of Ethical Theory (1885) of Martineau (1805–1900), the fruit of his long teaching in a Unitarian theological college, was one of the outstanding English ethical treatises of the century. Its classification and examination of the types of theory, preceding the exposition of his own, make it still valuable as a textbook. Although originally trained in civil engineering, he found any purely naturalistic approach unhelpful, and therefore ranged himself against the utilitarians, positivists and evolutionists. He followed Butler and Kant in finding the root of morality in a sense of duty and an intuitive perception of particular duties. We are in fact so built that when two incompatible impulses spring up we have a spontaneous tendency to choose not by felt intensity or by pleasure-bringing probabilities (merely subjective features) but by the idea of an intrinsically higher and lower. For thus locating moral value in motives Martineau was criticized for undervaluing the moral importance of the predictable consequences of actions, to which he replied that a motive bears within itself a reference to some sort of consequence; for example, benevolence as more than an emotion is a desire for someone else's good. His emphasis on a higher and a lower committed him to consider a *scale* of values or motives, but his moral practicality prevented him from taking the scale as absolute, that is, from regarding what is higher in it as in all circumstances preferable to what is lower – there are situations in which a lowly task is required. He substituted a scale so understood for the traditional positing of a single supreme good to which every virtuous motive is subservient: for him there is a plurality of virtues or right motives, but just because they are ordered in a scale they are not a mere plurality, a heap. One of his strongest contentions was the objectivity of moral distinctions: 'The rule of right, the symmetries of character, the requirements of perfection, are no provincialisms of this planet: they are known among the stars.' Hence they are valid for and binding on the atheist; but the only way of grounding them metaphysically is by reference to God.

T. E. JESSOP

Marx, Karl

Karl Marx (1818–1883), founder of modern Communism. *See* **Communism, Ethics of Marxist.**

Mater et Magistra.

see Pontificial Social Encyclicals.

Maurice, Frederick Denison

Many would agree that of all nineteenth century churchmen F. D. Maurice (1805–1872) was 'incomparably the greatest, alike in life, in vision and in achievement' (Raven). His independent and original mind provoked the hostility of all ecclesiastical parties. For his rejection of the literalist view of endless future punishment in hell (*Theological Essays*, 1853) he lost his chair at King's College, London. For his association with the underprivileged

many conventional churchmen thought him eccentric. He was a theologian first and last, a reformer because he was a theologian, and a leader despite himself. Like Coleridge whom he admired he preferred to dig rather than build. Of his numerous books (many of them lectures on biblical subjects) perhaps none was more important than *The Kingdom of Christ* (1838). With its exposition of the 'theocratic principle' it contained all his future social teaching in embryo. True reform was not attainable by refashioning society according to the best human ideas. God had acted before man and for man. Through creation and redemption his Kingdom, the universal community of Christ our head, was already 'the great practical existing reality which is to renew the earth'. His loving will must therefore be regulative not in 'religion' only but in all human affairs. Here lay the significance of Christian Socialism (q.v.): for Maurice it meant 'the assertion of God's order'. In 1866 he became Knightbridge Professor at Cambridge, revived the old title of the chair (Casuistry and Moral Theology) and quoted Jeremy Taylor (q.v.) extensively in his lectures on *The Conscience* (1868). *See also* **Christian Social Movement.**

W. Merlin Davies, *An Introduction to F. D. Maurice's Theology*, 1964; C. Jenkins, *F. D. Maurice and the New Reformation*, 1938; F. Maurice, *Life and Letters of F. D. Maurice*, 2 vols., 1884; A. M. Ramsey, *F. D. Maurice and the Conflict of Modern Theology*, 1951; A. R. Vidler, *The Theology of F. D. Maurice*, 1948 (In the USA *Witness to the Light*, 1947).

THOMAS WOOD

Mean, Doctrine of the

Doctrine of the mean is part of Aristotle's definition of the moral virtues. Having shown that virtue is not an occasional or fitful quality but an established or habitual disposition, and not the mere having of certain feelings or desires but a choice or decision, he proceeds to specify as the mean the kind of object to be chosen. The idea of moderation involved in this was already traditional among the Greeks: Aristotle sharpens it by using the mathematical term 'mean' with its sense of what lies between two extremes. As a biologist, he notes that both too much food or exercise and too little spoil health, and as a writer on aesthetics, that a perfect work of art is one to which nothing can be added and from which nothing can be taken away. The point for ethics is that each virtue is opposed to *two* vices, one of excess and one of deficiency; for example, courage is the mean between foolhardy rashness and cowardice (he illustrates also from thirteen other virtues). He explicitly denies, however, that the precise mathematical sense of *equal* distance from two extremes is applicable to moral choice. He speaks of 'the mean relative to us', that is, to the individual's status, his given particular situation, and his strong points and weak ones, on the last making the observation that if we have a proneness to one of the extremes we should lean towards the opposite extreme. In respect of emotions, pleasures and pains the mean is the feeling that is not only of the right quantity but 'at the right time, towards the right objects, towards the right people, for the right reason, and in the right manner'. In short, the mean is what the experienced and sagacious man would detect to be such in each case. Almost at the beginning of his *Ethics* Aristotle had said emphatically that in moral matters general prescriptions are true only 'on the whole', because we are here thinking of what is contingent and individual. St Thomas took over from him the notion of the mean, but did not make it the guiding one of his system of the natural moral virtues, returning instead to the pre-Aristotelian conception of four cardinal virtues.

T. E. JESSOP

Mediaeval Ethics

The term 'ethics' is first used in the Middle Ages in the title of Abelard's *Ethica seu Scito Teipsum* (Greek commentaries on Aristotle's *Ethics* excepted) but under the name *moralia* or *philosophia moralis*, or equivalents in the other languages of the mediaeval scholarship, some ethical writing is found throughout the period. In general, mediaeval ethics is much influenced by Plato, Plotinus and the Stoics, up to the first decades of the thirteenth century, at which point the *Nicomachean Ethics* of Aristotle becomes central and remains so until the Renaissance. Most mediaeval ethics concentrates on the ideal of the 'happy life' for man, in continuity with Greek eudaimonism. The approach is nearly always teleological. The basic ethical question is: what is the ultimate good, or end, towards which man's free actions should be directed so that he may live well? Almost all mediaeval ethicians are theists and they are in general agreement that the only satisfactory final goal of human striving is the perfect good, God. Diversity is found, however, on the manner of attaining to God, or on the subjective character of man's ultimate happiness. This problem is discussed by Augustine (*City of God*, Bk. XIX), by Boethius (*Consolation of Philosophy*, Bk. III), by Aquinas (*Summa contra Gentiles*, Bk. III), and in many other treatises. Some thinkers identify ultimate happiness with volitional activity (love), while others think that it must be essentially cognitive (contemplation). Even within the area of cognition, the distinction between the speculative use of the mind (concerned with knowing only) and the practical use (concerned with knowing how to act, with *praxis*) is generally recognized. Another broad characteristic of this period is the use of a natural law (q.v.) approach to ethical

problems. The theory of four principal, or cardinal, virtues (wisdom-prudence, temperance, fortitude and justice) was widely held. Finally, the early Middle Ages (and even the later mystics, such as Meister Eckhardt) pictured the successful and good human life as a return (*reditus*) of the soul to its origin, to its first cause, in God the Creator. Some sort of immortality was granted to man in practically all schools of thought; hence mediaeval ethics looked to a future life for man, in which good men would be rewarded and evil punished.

Anselm of Canterbury (1079–1142) is typical of the early Christian theologians who wrote no special ethical treatise but did influence later thinking in the field. For Anselm moral rectitude is a matter of the disposition of the human will (*affectio voluntatis*). After the fall of Adam man's will retained a disposition towards what is useful (*affectio commodi*) but divine grace is required to restore the higher disposition to justice (*affectio justitiae*) which is a gift of God (*De voluntate*, PL 158, 487). Anselm defines justice as 'rightness (*rectitudo*) of will, which rightness is preserved because of itself' (*De veritate*, c. 12; ET in R. McKeon, *Selections from Medieval Philosophers*, 1929, I, 173–9. *See also:* J. R. Sheets, 'Justice in the Moral Thought of St Anselm', *Modern Schoolman*, XXV, 1948, 132–9).

In the next century, Peter Abelard (q.v.) continued the emphasis on the interior, psychological action as contrasted to the exterior, bodily 'deed'. The opening chapters of his *Ethics* stress what he calls the *intentio* (the agent's will-act of consent) as the key factor in morality. That is to say, the goodness or evil of what a man is doing lie not so much in the objective nature of his complete action as in what he thinks he is doing. However, Abelard proceeds to ask whether such an intended act must be in accord with the law of God, in order to be good and meritorious, and he answers that it must. So, Abelard's ethics is far from being merely subjective (*Abailard's Ethics*, tr., J. R. McCallum, 1935, pp. 19–33).

Christian ethics before the thirteenth century is generally a theological approbative theory in which God's wisdom, or will, or law, is the highest and ultimate norm of morality. Human actions are good and right, when they conform to this eternal law; bad and wrong, when they are in discord with it. God's will or law is known in two ways: (1) through faith in what has been specially revealed by God, for instance the Decalogue and the NT precepts of love of God and neighbour; (2) through reasoning on the basis of what is deemed fitting to man's nature acting in the concrete context of human life. Efforts to develop this second mode of knowledge led to the growth of natural law doctrines.

With the translation of the *Nicomachean Ethics* (the entire work only became available in the 1240s, through the efforts of Robert Grosseteste), mediaeval Christian ethics grew more complicated and more philosophical. Aristotelian analyses of the moral powers of man, the theory of habituation and the formation of virtues and vices, the whole doctrine of voluntariness, and the great emphasis on right reasoning (*recta ratio*) – all these come to the fore (V. J. Bourke, *St Thomas and the Greek Moralists*, 1947). In the main, moralists in the Dominican school (Albertus Magnus and Thomas Aquinas) stress the intellectual origins of moral obligation and view moral conscience as a practical judgment of man's intellect (M. Wittmann, *Die Ethik des hl. Thomas V. Aquin*, 1933; A. D. Sertillanges, *La philosophie morale de s. Thomas d'Aquin*, 1946; I. T. Eschmann, 'St Thomas's Approach to Moral Philosophy', *PACPA*, XXXI (1957), 25–36). On the other hand, thirteenth-century Franciscans (Roger Bacon, Bonaventure, Peter John Olivi) put more emphasis on the role of will in moral activity and in the acceptance of moral principles and law. Where Aquinas regarded the final beatitude of man in heaven as an act of intellectual contemplation, Bonaventure (and Duns Scotus later) situated man's ultimate felicity in the volitional act of loving God. (Z. Alszeghy, *Grundformen der Liebe. Der Theorie der Gottesliebe bei dem hl. Bonaventura*, 1946; R. Prentice, *The Psychology of Love according to St Bonaventure*, 1951).

In the fourteenth century, Duns Scotus and William Ockham are outstanding for their ethical influence; they both continue the Franciscan tradition. Scotus endeavours to balance the claims of appetition and intellection but Ockham is more evidently a voluntarist. Late mediaeval ethics tends to identify eternal law with a fiat of an omnipotent divine will, to locate man's initial awareness of moral duty in some sort of volitional experience of rightness, and to focus upon obligation as the central feature of ethics. Thus the ethical thinking that characterized the fourteenth and fifteenth centuries, and which was reacted to by early modern philosophers and religious reformers, was not Thomism but a blend of Scotism and Ockhamism (P. Vignaux, *Justification et prédestination au XIVe siecle*, 1934; F. Schwendiger, 'Metaphysik des Sittlichen nach J. D. Scotus', *Wissenschaft u. Weisheit*, I (1934), 180–210; II (1935), 18–25, 112–35; III (1936), 93–119, 161–90; A. Garvens, 'Die Grundlagen der Ethik Wilhelms von Ockham', *Franziskanischen Studien*, XXI (1934), 243–73, 360–408).

Non-Christian ethical thought in the Middle Ages is allied with the religious moralities of the o T and Jewish comment thereon, or with the Koran and its interpretations. The twelfth-century *Duties of the Heart*, by Bahya ibn Pakuda (ed. and tr., Moses Hyamson, 5 vols., 1925–47) is an example of a religio-moral treatise in the tradition of mediaeval Judaism. Moses Maimonides (ben Maimun, 1135–1204) makes the most important contributions to ethics. His *Guide for the Perplexed* (tr., S. Pines, 1963) shows the influence of Aristotle and Averroes but is basically a Jewish treatise. Its theory of mental reservation in relation to truth-telling becomes influential in Latin moral treatises in the ensuing centuries (J. I. Gorfinkle, *The Eight Chapters of Maimonides on Ethics*, 1912; I. I. Efros, *Ancient Jewish Philosophy: A Study in Metaphysics and Ethics*, 1964; M. Kadushin, *Worship and Ethics*, 1964.)

Muslim ethics (q.v.) was influenced by both Plato and Aristotle. The tenth-century Alfarabi (Abu Nasr Muhammad ibn Muhammad ibn Uzlag al-Farabi) made a compendium of Plato's *Laws* (ed. and tr. into Latin, F. Gabrieli, 1952) which popularized Greek theories of social ethics. Avicenna (Ibn Sina, 980–1037) is the great eastern sage. He used Aristotelian psychology and ethical notions to develop a theory of moral and mystical perfection culminating in a union (ittisal) of man's soul with the Agent Intelligence (for three selections from Avicenna, illustrating his views on human happiness and social order, *see* R. Lerner and M. Mahdi, eds., *Medieval Political Philosophy*, 1963, pp. 95–121). The greatest Spanish Moslem ethician is Averroes (Abu al-Walid Muhammad ibn Ahmed ibn Rushd, 1126–98). Whether he accepted the personal immortality of the individual human soul is not clear but he did teach that ultimate happiness consists in speculative contemplation of the highest truth, in a presentation that is reminiscent of the *Eudemian Ethics* of the school of Aristotle (S. Gomez-Nogaliz, 'El destino del hombre a la luz de la noetica de Averroes', *L'Homme et son destin*, 1960, pp. 285–304).

Of histories of mediaeval philosophy, ethics is best covered in: F. Copleston, *A History of Philosophy*, II, parts 1 and 2, 1950; O. Dittrich, *Geschichte der Ethik*, Bd. III: *Mittelalter bis zur Kirchenreformation*, 1926; O. Lottin, *Psychologie et morale aux XIIe et XIIIe siècles*, 6 vols., 1942–60.

VERNON J. BOURKE

Medical Ethics

The term 'medical ethics' is used two ways to mean (1) the code of manners and conduct expected of physicians as matters of convention, social grace and guild discipline, and (2) problems of right and wrong or good and evil which arise in the medical care of patients and pose issues for patients as well as physicians. What follows has the second and broader sense in mind. The subject of medical ethics is largely ignored in the curricula of medical schools and in the ethics of Protestantism; only the Roman Catholic moral theologians and their schools and hospitals treat it with

descriptive and analytical care and thoroughness.

The *Principles of Medical Ethics* of the
American Medical Association, and their
counterpart in the British Medical Association,
are quite brief and focused on the fraternity or
guild obligations of the profession. The AMA's
Judicial Council rarely deals with a non-pro-
fessional problem of conscience. The first major
ethical code for English physicians was drawn
up by Thomas Percival in 1803; the first in
America was one formulated for the AMA by
Isaac Hughes of Philadelphia in 1847. It has
served as the model for state and county
societies too. These codes have never been
detailed or explicitly religious in sanction, as is
the *Charakha* of India (100 AD). They always
include a full assumption of responsibility by
the physician, which is increasingly impossible
under the interdependence of modern specialization. Doctors may serve whom they choose
but are required by code to respond to emergencies. And they are required to forswear
every exclusive (medical) dogma or sectarian
system, as well as public advertising and the
sale of drugs.

In pre-scientific cultures the medicine man
had a priestly and charismatic role. Medicine
and religion were always closely associated
until in modern times. In Europe they were
effectively divorced at the end of the Middle
Ages when the Church forbade clerics to
practise medicine or surgery except by special
indult (harder to get for surgery). Scientific
medicine has completely separated medicine
and religious ministry, except for the 'encounter' of pastors and doctors in treatment situations. The 'personalism' of modern philosophy
and psychology, putting human values at the
centre of attention, may tend to create greater
interest in ethics than the problem-centred or
research-centred approach to the care of
patients. For some but not all doctors and
nurses the *ethics* in medicine is expressed in
Kant's second maxim, to treat men as men and
not as means. As Tillich puts it, 'person' is a
moral concept.

One of the pervasive issues in medical care
is freedom – the question whether men have
a moral right to take their health in their own
hands as the medical sciences and arts increase
our human control over life and death. The
issue arises often in the ethics of reproduction,
around fertility control, or with respect to
donations of vital organs such as kidneys for
transplant to others. Is this 'interference with
nature' and what kind of theodicy or doctrine
of creation and providence is entailed? To what
extent have men the stewardship of life and of
health? Have they any initiative, or must they
abide by 'nature's' decree in cases of sterility
or loss of vital function or the depersonalization of senility? (Medicine obviously 'inter-
feres' with nature by using nature when it suits

human purposes, otherwise outwitting it.) To
this question there are various answers proposed in theological ethics. Until recent years
the Catholic view tended to be naturalistic, but
of late some personalistic theologians have
appeared in their ranks.

The greater interest and concern of Catholic
theologians in medical ethics is manifest. They
have effective medical guilds (e.g., the Federation of Catholic Physicians' Guilds) and journals dealing with the ethics of medicine (e.g.,
the *Linacre Quarterly*). Protestants have no
equivalents, although they turn out magazines
and journals which deal with pastoral counselling in general and care of the sick in particular.
If Catholic moralists are challenged at any
point it is usually with respect to their major
premisses in somewhat syllogistic arguments,
since their careful and thorough knowledge of
the medical data and their careful logic are
usually beyond reproach.

The story of medical progress traces battle
after battle with theological ethics, over
human rather than animal anatomical research,
allowing the heterodox to practise medicine,
ectopic excision, craniotomy, artificial insemination, contra-respiration of monsters at delivery,
sterilization, therapeutic abortion, anesthesia,
contraception, male obstetricians and many
such matters. Notions such as that 'only God
gives life', that the body is a 'temple' (I Cor. 6),
that 'nature's way' is God's will, that suffering
is redemptive, that nature has 'intentions' and
purposes (the pathetic fallacy), that vital organs
are divine functions, that human mastery over
life and living becomes demonic – these are
elements in classical theological ethics which
have caused much friction with medical science
and practice.

Most of the ethical problems of medical care
arise around advances in knowledge and skill.
They are *success* problems. For example,
artificial insemination in some cases of childlessness represents a new remedy for barren
marriages but it also raises questions (as adoption does) about the nature of parenthood and
relationship. So with contraception, especially
the pill and the ring. The problem of anti-
dysthanasia, whether and when to let the
patient die, is posed by medical success in pro-
longing life for most people to senescent age
levels. In addition to the issues mentioned are
such questions as the ethics of experimentation,
truth-telling in diagnosis, non-therapeutic
abortion, euthanasia, organic transplants,
artificial functions (e.g., electronic cardiac
machines), temporary and permanent sterilization, the obligation of doctors to testify
adversely in malpractice suits when justified,
the integrity of professional confidences in
group medical practice, the requirement of the
patient's consent for various treatment procedures. Here are a baker's dozen of such
ethical issues. There are many more.

Ethical problems are raised not only by scientific and technical gains; they are posed also by the new structures of medical care. The traditional privacy of relationship is disappearing as medical care becomes more a multiple service by several specialists who exchange information freely. The transfer of the patient from his home to a hospital, from a single general practitioner's care to a staff's; the fact that patients tend now to go to the doctor rather than he to them: such things change relationships and values. The enormous cost of modern medicine with its expensive technology and equipment, and of the professionalized paramedical personnel (occupational therapists, social workers, hospital staff), creates issues of social ethics over 'socialization' and welfare legislation and insurance investment.

The image of the 'doctor' is changing as he leaves the intimacy of general practice for the less personal form of special services. At the same time his income, especially in America, has increased to nearly the top level for professional people. In plain fact no competent physician can any longer practise medicine, either in diagnosis or treatment, out of a little black bag! The equipment now is beyond individual practitioners' capital and competence. All of this 'mass effect', as seen in the hospital which is a medical collective, poses new ethical and social questions for which the profession is not prepared in training or sensitivity. There are no courses in the ethics of medicine, as distinguished from professional code rules, in any medical school in America or Europe, except for those under Roman Catholic auspices.

Representative studies of medical problems in theological ethics are: for Protestant works, Joseph Fletcher, *Morals and Medicine*, 1954; for Roman Catholic works, E. F. Healy, S.J., *Medical Ethics*, 1960; Gerald Kelly, S.J., *Medico-Moral Problems*, 1958; for Jewish works, Immanuel Jacobowitz, *Jewish Medical Ethics*, 1959.

JOSEPH FLETCHER

Meekness

Meekness is not the refusal to take power but the acceptance and use of it. Every individual has power by his birth, every relationship increases this power. Every office bearer in an institution is to exercise the power he has because of his office. A great many men long for power and at the same time are reluctant to use the power they already have. Without power the coherent movements of living and loving would not be possible. Power has a corruptive potentiality but it is difficult to imagine any act more seriously wrong than the refusal to use the powers committed to one on the grounds of meekness. The Church is given

power in society and it is meekness on the part of its members to accept this fact and discipline themselves to understand the nature and use of power.

Meekness is neither self-depreciation nor making little of the work one is doing. Meekness, strictly speaking, has no opposite. The quest for importance which might appear to be an opposite belongs to such a completely different way of life that meekness and the desire for importance are, as it were, on different planes. Meekness is not a longing to be unimportant; it is not timidity or insipidity. It is a quality of living characteristic of a man who knows he is participating in the creative activity of God, not as a pauper but as a son.

The meek man works reliably at his immediate task. He is not disdainful if the task is small or boastful if it is large. He does not heed the criticism made by others unless it shows him how to improve his work. He must often criticize the work of others but he makes this criticism impersonally because to the meek the work matters more than both the doer and the critic.

In the Sermon on the Mount our Lord said 'Blessed are the meek for they shall inherit the earth' (Matt. 5.5). The meek are those who are not broken by flattery, by monotony or by longing for recognition and recognizable results of their work. They are the people who inherit all the best things in earth – that is, they are participating in the ceaseless creative activity of God.

R. E. C. BROWNE

Meliorism

Usually credited to William James, meliorism stands midway between optimism and pessimism on the grounds that they misread the facts about man, history and ultimate reality. Holding that existence is neither predominately evil nor incontrovertibly good, meliorism says that man is able to make it *better*. It is one form of the American challenge to responsible action. Man, William James held, is able, by the use of his creative intelligence and through education to improve his physical, mental, social and moral condition.

Meliorism regards history as a record of man's tortuous emancipation from magic and superstitious beliefs and his employment of the scientific method for understanding and controlling himself and his environment.

Finally, in regard to ultimate reality meliorism holds that even God's very being may be said to draw sustenance from man's effort to improve life – a metaphysical and ethical line of thought appearing in Whitehead and others.

CHARLES W. KEGLEY

Mental Health

Mental health means literally wholeness of mind. It is a relatively new term, having originated in the nineteenth century as a result of the change in the basic conception of mental and emotional disturbances from possession and perversity to that of illness. In current usage it has two distinct though related meanings: (1) Mental health is used by many psychiatrists to mean the absence of clinically detectable mental or emotional illness which would require treatment. Though this meaning is applied only to the absence of disturbances which have known organic bases by a few psychiatrists it is used more generally to apply to the absence of all mental disturbances, whether organically based, or purely functional disturbances which have no known organic lesions associated with them. These latter include most disturbances called neurotic and schizophrenic. (2) The second widespread use of the term mental health is in the sense of positive characteristics of wholeness. Though many criteria have been proposed for mental health in this sense, none has gained universal acceptance. Marie Jahoda in her *Current Concepts of Positive Mental Health* (1958), has brought together the following six widely used concepts: self-acceptance, long range motivation (or self-actualization), integration, autonomy, distortion, free perception of reality, and environmental mastery. These concepts have obvious value connotations, and have tended to acquire the status of ethical norms for some persons. For this reason, and because the concept of health seems almost meaningless to some clinicians when stretched this far, there has been a recent trend towards either the restriction of the use of the term to the absence of illness, or towards limiting its use in the positive sense by employing more descriptive and less value laden criteria than some of those mentioned by Jahoda. Further, as Jahoda recognized, some of these ideal concepts are potentially conflicting in some circumstances.

In the current trend towards more restricted use of the term the concept of adaptation, understood both as changing the environment when possible to meet one's needs, and changing one's behaviour pattern to meet environmental demands, seems destined to play a leading role. It is a positive, though minimal concept, which is capable of adjusting to changing clinical approaches and new knowledge. While it is not entirely value free (the value connotation of all positive behavioural criteria is now widely recognized by clinicians), it can provide a bridge to ethics without determining specific norms.

For descriptions of various forms of mental disturbance, *see* A. H. Maslow and B. Mittelmann, *Principles of Abnormal Psychology*, 1951; For a practical treatment of mental health in relation to religion *see* Richard V. McCann, *The Churches and Mental Health*, 1963.

JAMES N. LAPSLEY

Mercy

Christians pray that God may treat them in mercy and not with justice. To ask for justice would be a plea to be treated as his equals. God's love and power are most clearly seen in his mercy and primarily seen in his care for beings he could crush. Because we are made in his image our strength is most clearly seen in deeds of mercy. It is a sign of weakness whenever mercy becomes sentimental or ostentatious.

Our Lord said: 'Blessed are the merciful, for they shall obtain mercy' (Matt. 5.7). This is not the offering of a reward but the statement of a fact. To be merciful is to lead a particular style of life which makes both being merciful and receiving mercy possible. To speak of this being and receiving is one of the many ways of talking about God's love of men and men's love for him. In short, it is a way of saying that one of the expressions of love is the care the strong are to have for the weak in every situation.

In the OT and in the NT in Jewish thought and in Christian thought, a government is judged by its attitude towards the weak as seen in legislation and in administration of justice. All legislation is hard on at least one section of the community; change of legislation can only deal with this burden by transferring it to another section of the community. No legislation can avoid this inequality and churchmen must always be ill at ease over the ways of government and justice. They are not to be self-righteous but to have in mind the difficulties in the governing of any country at any point in human history.

Churchmen are to be merciful to their fellow-members as well as to all other men. Within the Church there are the strong and the weak; those who are strong are not to conserve their strength but to expend it in mercy on their weaker fellow-members.

Our Lord says: 'Be merciful, even as your Father is merciful' (Luke 6.36). Being merciful is an eloquent proclamation of the nature of God.

R. E. C. BROWNE

Merit

Merit is the worth or esteem which someone acquires as a result of his good actions or his special abilities; or again, it is the deservingness of recognition or reward on the part of such a person. The use of the concept of merit in Christian moral theology has been the subject of fierce controversy. The Protestant reformers were vehement in their denunciations of the mediaeval penitential system, and stressed the utter worthlessness of all human achievements in the sight of God. We may well agree that no man could be meritorious before God, and that his salvation must be by divine grace. In this regard, the Reformers' insistence on justification by faith through grace alone (*see* **Justification by Faith**) was correct. But we must not allow this valid insight to be exaggerated into a doctrine of total depravity (q.v.) which levels all human action down to the undifferentiated worthlessness where 'everything proceeding from the corrupt nature of man is damnable' (Calvin). This rules out all the relativities of conduct, whereby one course of action may be reckoned more meritorious than another, even if no human life is free from sin or can claim merit before God. The Christian acknowledges that in the last resort, true merit belongs to Christ alone. The Christian has no merit of his own, but in the life of the body of Christ, and especially its sacramental life, he participates in the merit of Christ.

EDITOR

Mill, John Stuart

J. S. Mill (1806–1873) was the most influential British philosopher of the nineteenth century whose contributions to social, political and ethical thought are key works of the movement known as 'philosophical radicalism'. In James Mill's *Analysis of the Phenomena of Human Mind* (2 vols., 1829) we have the clearest exposition of the associationist psychology which the radicals claimed enabled them to fulfil the task of doing for mental philosophy and science what Newton had done by his inverse square law (better known as 'the law of gravity') for the physical world. By this law, whereby the worlds of astronomy and dynamics were unified, the behaviour of all physical bodies, both microscopic and macroscopic alike, was rendered perspicuous. The associationists thought that in the laws of association of ideas (whereby mental particles were presented as gravitating towards one another in accordance with ascertainable laws) they had found the analogue of gravity, where the cognitive, conative and affective lives of human beings were concerned. The significance of this supposed discovery was as much practical as theoretical, enabling a system of incentives and deterrents to be devised and operated in place of the traditional systems of laws, moral rules, conventions, etc., aimed at achieving the maximum in human satisfaction.

As his *Autobiography* (1873) reveals, it was in the straitest sect of this school that John Stuart Mill received his earliest formation; and one of the causes which give to his work its perennial fascination is to be found in the way in which in early manhood he realized he could no longer accept the unyielding dogma in whose profession he had been educated relentlessly. His own record of this crisis is to be found in the *Autobiography*; but the kind of evaluation of the conflicting tendencies of his age that made it possible for him later to achieve is to be found in his essays on Bentham

and Coleridge, whom he regarded as the competing master-spirits of its intellectual traditions.

The long tale of his published writings bear witness at once to the range of his interests and to his sensitivity to the main intellectual currents of his age. His relations, for instance, with men as different as Thomas Carlyle and Auguste Comte are alike revealing in the light they throw on the conflict of ideas in the nineteenth century. His *Essay on Liberty*, acutely criticized at the time of its appearance by Fitz James Stephen, remains a classical presentation of the liberal *mystique* (in Péguy's sense) of freedom and acquires a curiously searching significance if today read as an *apologia* for the unique import of the creative individual. In it Mill seems to have moved a long way from Bentham. Indeed it might be thought to belong to the same world as Matthew Arnold's *Culture and Anarchy* (1869), even of Dostoyevsky's 'Grand Inquisitor'! In the pamphlet *Utilitarianism*, written a few years later, he attempts a more sophisticated presentation of Benthamite ideas freed of their underlying philistinism and strengthened by the recognition of the significance of moral tradition. Similarly, where political and social theories are concerned, Mill moved a considerable way from the insistence on an economy independent of any sort of public regulation characteristic of his father, towards the moderate *dirigisme* commended by another nineteenth-century liberal, T. H. Green, with the aid of Rousseau's, and in a very diluted form Hegel's, ideas in his posthumously published *Principles of Political Obligation* (1879–80), and practised by him as a member of the Oxford City Council, as well as a Fellow of Balliol. But the complexity of Mill's social and political thought demands that the reader attend also to his *Principles of Political Economy* (1848) and to his work on *Representative Government* (1861). If in his essay *On Liberty* (1859) he seems to have moved far from the Benthamism in which he was bred and indeed to suggest sometimes Dostoyevsky rather than Coleridge, it is characteristic of the restlessness of his thinking that a few years later in *Utilitarianism* (1863) he had in a measure returned to the faith of his father.

Where pure philosophy is concerned, Mill's best known work is his *Logic*; but in his *Examination of Sir William Hamilton's Philosophy* (1865) he developed a doctrine of physical objects as sets of permanent possibilities of sensation, which remains an important landmark in the development of phenomenalist conceptions of the external world of the sort made fashionable by twentieth-century radical empiricist writers on problems of perception. Mill's *Logic* is a long and complex work and it is easy (and misleading) to ignore what he says, for example, about deduction; but it is with induction that he is principally concerned, seeking at once to extend its scope and to systematize its methods, which he identified with those of the exact and observational sciences. Of Mill's *Logic* one can truthfully say that it remains a landmark in the history of the subject, and whether one thinks of the idealist logic of F. H. Bradley, of the work concerning the foundations and nature of mathematics undertaken by Frege and Russell, or of the criticism of the assignment of the key role to induction in the logic of scientific method associated with the influence of Sir Karl Popper, one thinks at the same time of these various writers' criticisms of aspects of Mill's work. Little, if any, of the important work done in the philosophy of logic since he wrote has been able to bypass discussion of his views. If he is very often, even usually, wrong, it could be claimed, as a matter of historical fact, that it was necessary for the development of the philosophy of logic that someone should make just these mistakes!

Mill left posthumous essays on religion, which include a very sharp criticism of the thesis that a study of the actual processes of nature, which he saw as arbitrary, cruel and destructive, could provide men with any significant moral insights. In the third essay, which deals explicitly with theism, Mill argues tentatively in favour of the existence of a limited deity, finding the actuality of physical evil so emphasized in the essay on nature conclusive against attributing to him sovereign creative power. There is a quality of honesty in these discussions often lacking in the theological reflections of those whose piety is stronger, but whose human sensibility is weaker than that of John Stuart Mill.

No account of his life and work, however brief, would be in the least adequate which did not take account of his relations with Harriet Taylor, to whom he was for long years devoted and whom he eventually married. It is clear that she helped in a measure to free him from a tendency to a humourless over-seriousness which was among his worst faults. Yet whatever criticism may be levelled against Mill personally or intellectually, it remains true that in the disentanglement of the contradictions of his thought the intelligent reader is made most effectively aware of the stresses and strains characteristic of nineteenth-century liberal thinking. If Mill was often wrong and even more often inconsistent with himself, it could be claimed for him that he tested a set of received ideas to destruction and by a strange mixture of nearly Benthamite consistency, critical insight and sheer self-contradiction, revealed more clearly than any before him the limitations of empiricism in the field of logic, of ethics and of political theory. If Butler is justified in rejecting Utilitarianism on the grounds of its *simplisme*, it was left to John Stuart Mill to reveal by the manner of his adherence to its tradition, the places where in theory and prac-

tice its consistent profession is revealed as sheerly impossible. Although it may seem paradoxical to say so, in conclusion it remains true that no writer raises the problem of ethical intuition more sharply than Mill, the avowed champion of the universal authority of induction.

D. M. MACKINNON

Mixed Motives

Motives are said to be mixed when an action is performed from a principal motive while a subsidiary motive is also at work. A wealthy man may endow a charitable trust from the motive of benevolence, but may also be somewhat swayed by the prospect of receiving a public honour; the motive of vanity is mixed with that of benevolence. Morally indifferent acts also can have mixed motives, for example, taking exercise to keep fit and to please a companion.

The question of mixed motives in morals is almost exclusively the result of that 'interiorization' of morality which Christianity brought about, distinguishing the good or the bad of an outward action from the movements 'of the heart' which prompt it. Augustine emphasized the force and value of these inner motives in his exposition of the Psalms. Aquinas held that the outward act (the object) and the motive (which he designated 'the end') each has its own moral quality (*Summa Theologica*, Part II, First Section, qq. 18, 19).

Later moralists differ on the relation between the two objects of moral judgment, the act and the motive; and this variation affects the treatment of mixed motives. Bishop Butler held that acts of benevolence are not morally invalidated by mixture with self-love. (*Sermons*, 1897 edn., Preface and Sermon 11.) Others have appealed to the Beatitudes of Christ for biblical confirmation that the desire for rewards is not necessarily incompatible with hungering and thirsting after righteousness, in other words that fulfilment of some desires can go along with a sense of duty or love to God.

The view that a perfectly pure motive is absolutely necessary for a morally good action would condemn nearly all human behaviour, though this appears to be the view of Kant, (*Groundwork of the Metaphysics of Morals*, 1785, pp. 8–13). To this Rashdall replies: 'It does not follow that the desire to do one's duty must always be the sole and exclusive motive of right conduct, or that conduct not consciously inspired by respect for the moral law as such must possess no moral value at all' (*The Theory of Good and Evil*, I, 2nd edn., 1924, p. 119). Many moralists hold that a right act is often done, perhaps always so far as we can tell, from mixed motives; further, that if we are constantly concerned with the purity of our motives only we shall be neglecting the most obvious duties. J. S. Mill maintained that motive has nothing to do with the morality of actions, but much with the worth of the agent. 'He who saves a fellow creature from drowning does what is morally right, whether his motive be duty or the hope of being paid for his trouble' (*Utilitarianism*, 1910, rep. 1954, p. 17). And according to James Martineau, to know that our motives are not simple or pure does not cancel the moral value of good acts (*Types of Ethical Theory*, II, 1885, pp. 218 ff., 'How to Estimate Mixed Incentives'). A fuller discussion is to be found in N. H. G. Robinson, *The Claim of Morality*, 1952, Chap. 9, 'Act and Motive'. *See* **Motives and Motivation**.

V. A. DEMANT

Monasticism

Monk, *monachus* (from the Greek *monos*, alone) is originally the general term for a Christian ascetic who separates himself from the common life of the world. The word is commonly used, however, for one who lives with others in a monastic community – in Greek the *coenobites* (man of the common life) as distinct from the individual anchorite (from *anachoreo*, to withdraw) or hermit (from *heremos*, man of the desert). Beginning in the late third century, traditionally with some who fled to the desert from the persecution of Decius (250–51), monasticism became the outstanding form of intense Christian piety in the fourth. Egypt was the classic centre of the monastic movement, but Syria was not far behind, and it soon spread to Asia Minor and the Latin West. The numerous hermits of northern Egypt inevitably came together in informal communities, such as the crowds of disciples who gathered around St Antony (*c.* 260–343); in upper Egypt the organized common life was developed under the leadership of Pachomius (died 356). Monastic communities became widespread, though the East has continued to admire the apparently more heroic life of the hermit. However, Basil of Caesarea (d. 379), the great legislator of Greek monasticism (*Longer* and *Shorter Rules*), definitely preferred the common life as the normal sphere for the exercise of Christian virtues. Eastern monasticism has not gone through the varied developments of western, but is not without history. In the early Byzantine period monks were numerous near the great centres of church life, and so were often involved in ecclesiastical and even secular politics; since the tenth century Mount Athos, the 'holy mountain', has been the outstanding centre of Greek monasticism. The stricter Greek monasteries are coenobitic; in others, called idiorhythmic, the monks lead more separate lives, assembling only for certain meals and services. Eastern monasteries have not developed the active ministries of western monasticism, but have been important as centres of devotion and art, and as places of pilgrimage. Their ancient tradition of spiritual guidance flourished again in the monastic Elders (*startsi*) of nineteenth-century Russia.

The early history of western monasticism is reflected in the writings of such Fathers as Augustine and Jerome, and later in a series of Rules drawn up by various leaders for monks or nuns. A remarkable development was the monasticism of the Celtic Church, which combined the austerity of monastic Egypt with the enthusiasm of the Celtic spirit. In the absence of cities, monasteries were the chief centres of church life – and Celtic monks became missionaries and explorers, more it seems out of a zealous desire to be strangers and pilgrims on earth than for the sake of the results achieved. The germs of this tradition can be seen in St Patrick. Its greatest figures are St Columba (died 596), whose monastery of Iona was for two centuries the centre of the Scottish Church, and his younger contemporary St Columban. Meanwhile in Italy two centuries' experience of monasticism was brilliantly codified in the *Rule* of St Benedict (*c.* 540), which combines ascetic piety with the classic spirit of moderation and the Roman feeling for law and order. By the time of Charlemagne (died 814) the Benedictine Rule had replaced all others in the Western Church, except for some lingering Celtic survivals. But in the feudal age Benedict's pattern of work, study and worship was distorted by the abandonment of physical labour. For those not occupied in business or intellectual pursuits this left a gap which was only partially filled by the increase of devotional exercises. The result was to give mediaeval Benedictinism a certain ponderosity which even its great reforms did not escape, such as those associated with the great centre of Cluny (founded 910), or the revival of the monastic life in England inspired by St Dunstan (after 940).

New forms of the monastic life developed as mediaeval life became more complex and sophisticated. The *Rule* of St Augustine (derived from two of his letters) was revived after the tenth century. Having the advantage of simplicity and flexibility, it was found useful by those who wished to combine the monastic life with active work for the Church – missionary, educational, pastoral, even military. On the other hand, longings for a return to ancient austerity led to the appearance of settlements of hermits. Out of these grew several Orders which combined the common and the solitary life – the most significant are the Carthusians (founded by St Bruno, but organized by their third prior, Guigo, after 1110). Among Benedictines the Cistercians (after 1098) aimed at a return to the primitive life of the *Rule*, while avoiding the dangers of isolation by a federal organization of their numerous monasteries. A new inspiration entered the ascetic tradition with the vocation of St Francis of Assisi (q.v.) to follow 'the naked Christ' in poverty and joy. In 1209

Pope Innocent III recognized his followers as the Order of Lesser Brothers (Friars Minor), and meanwhile St Dominic had organized the Order of Preachers, to fight the spiritual battle of the Church by preaching and teaching. The two groups influenced each other and were imitated by others, so the active and centralized Order became the typical form of the monastic movement (for which the term friar, as distinct from monk, should be used).

In the later Middle Ages there was more official regulation of the monastic life than before. In 1215 the Fourth Lateran Council ordered Benedictines and Augustinians to federate, and forbade any new monastic Rules; in 1274 the Second Council of Lyons recognized four Orders of Friars (those mentioned above, Carmelites and Augustinians). There were few new developments in the following centuries. Catholic reformers combated in various ways the trend to secularism which was aggravated by the decline in numbers after the Black Death of the mid-fourteenth century. The more mystical and personal piety of the age found its home in several new groups, such as the Order of the Saviour founded by St Bridget of Sweden (died 1373) and the Brothers of the Common Life, who derived from the work of Gerard de Groot in Holland. The latter was an informal association, but had a monastic wing, the Augustinian Congregation of Windesheim, from which comes the best-known classic of monastic spirituality, the *Imitation of Christ* of Thomas a Kempis.

In the sixteenth century most of the Reformers attacked the idea of a special ascetic vocation, and monasticism was weakened even in Catholic countries. But the Counter-Reformation led to revival and reform in many of the older Orders (through such movements as the Capuchins in the Franciscans, and the Carmelite reform, after 1562, famous for its missionaries and mystics) and produced a new type, the 'Regular Clerks', whose emphasis is less on renunciation of the world than on work for the Church. The Society of Jesus (recognized 1540) is one of the first, and the most conspicuous, of these. Active Sisterhoods devoted to education followed, and in the seventeenth century St Vincent de Paul (died 1660) succeeded in the radical step of bringing his Sisters of Charity out from the cloister into active work in the world. In modern Catholicism all forms of monasticism, from the strictly contemplative to the primarily active, play an important role. Though challenged by the eighteenth-century Enlightenment, and in many countries suppressed after 1789, the monastic life revived with the nineteenth-century Catholic revival, and has grown steadily since 1830. In recent years efforts have been made to integrate the ascetic vocation with the common life of mankind – as in the Little Brothers and Sisters of Jesus, inspired by the example of Charles de

Foucauld, the soldier-hermit of the Sahara – and a new type of society recognized in canon law since 1947 as the Secular Institute.

Most remarkable has been the revival of monasticism in areas where it had been either condemned in principle or abandoned in practice. There has always been some aspiration in the Church of England towards the monastic life, suppressed under Henry VIII. Under the influence of the Oxford Movement the first modern Sisterhood was founded in 1845, followed by active Orders for men and women, and later by the more traditional forms of the monastic life as well. In definitely Protestant circles eighteenth-century Pietism included several attempts at monasticism, and the Lutheran deaconess societies (since about 1830) have many aspects of active Sisterhoods. Much as ancient monasticism flourished amid the crises of the late Roman world, Protestant monasticism has become conspicuous since the second World War. Its best-known centre is the Community at Taizé in Burgundy; and mention should also be made of such disciplined though not strictly monastic societies as the Iona Community in Scotland (comparable to which is the Zoë Brotherhood in the Greek Orthodox Church, which works in the world in a way that the traditional Eastern monk does not).

History seems to show that the special monastic response to the call to leave all and take up the Cross is, in one form or another, a permanent feature of the Christian life. *See* **Asceticism**. In the words of a modern Benedictine scholar: 'The true monk, in whatever century he is found, looks not to the changing ways around him or to his own mean condition, but to the unchanging everlasting God, and his trust is in the everlasting arms that hold him' (David Knowles, *The Religious Orders in England*, III, 1959, p. 468).

For general surveys: Paul B. Bull, *The Revival of the Religious Life*, 1914; David Knowles, *The Monastic Order in England*, 2nd edn., 1963; Herbert Workman, *The Evolution of the Monastic Ideal*, 1913. On recent developments: Francois Biot, *The Rise of Protestant Monasticism*, 1963; Olive Wyon, *Living Springs: New Religious Movements in Western Europe*, 1962.

E. R. HARDY

Monergism. see Synergism.

Monogamy

Monogamy is the lifelong union of one husband to one wife. See **Marriage**.

Moral Argument

One of the arguments for the truth of theism proceeds from the facts of the moral life to the alleged need for their completion or supplementation in the life of religion. *See* **Religion and Morality, Relations of.**

Moral Philosophy

Moral philosophy is the old-fashioned name for ethics (q.v.).

Moral Theology

Moral theology is the discussion of the principles which govern, or should govern, the behaviour of a Christian man, and of their application to particular circumstances or classes of cases. Its sources are Scripture, reason inspired by faith, the teaching of the Church and in particular of certain pre-eminent Fathers and Doctors – for example, St Augustine and St Thomas Aquinas.

Moral theology judges and advises on the morality of actions and of agents in the light of man's true end, the vision of God. It judges everything by one simple standard and principle – does it conduce to the attainment of man's last end; does it conform to what is known of the will of the Creator; does it obey the laws which the Creator has laid down for attaining man's last end, as those laws are revealed in Scripture or perceived by enlightened reason or apprehended in the teaching and tradition of the Church, where faith illumines and guides reason?

Text books of moral theory, accordingly, all start with a section on Man's last end. But because moral theology is the study of human behaviour, they continue with sections which analyze the nature of a human act, the necessity for it to be the result of a free act of will accompanied by adequate knowledge and intention of the end or purpose of the act. Having established the essential ingredients of a human act, moral theology goes on to consider the morality of actions, the grounds on which an action is to be judged as right or wrong; the considerations which are to be taken into account; the interaction of the immediate and inevitable consequences of an act and the intention of the agent and the circumstances in which the act was performed. Of obvious importance in this connection is a judgment whether the act does or does not conform with law. And so there follows a section on the different kinds of law under which man lives – the eternal law, natural law, positive divine law, and human law both civil and ecclesiastical – and the obligations which they impose and how and when those obligations cease or are altered.

Next the distinction must be drawn between the objective morality of the act and the subjective morality of the agent. For the act may be wrong but the agent have thought it right. And so there follows the important section on conscience, with the distinctions between a true and an erroneous conscience, lax and scrupulous, clear, doubtful and perplexed. In this discussion is included a description of the so-called systems of moral theology, which are different ways of enabling a man whose conscience is in doubt to arrive at a state of certainty as to what he ought to do. The systems are: tutiorism, probabiliorism, equiprobabilism and compensationism (qq.v.).

All this may be regarded as prolegomena to moral theoloy. The main business of moral theology is the consideration of the general norms or principles with which Christian behaviour should conform and their application. The usual scheme adopted for this purpose is to treat them either under the heading of the Decalogue or of the Seven Virtues. Each of the Commandments in order is analyzed into the actions which it commands, explicitly or implicitly, and the actions which it prohibits. Or the virtues are examined and the kind of conduct to which each prompts is discussed and the vice or vices opposed to the virtue are similarly dealt with. For example, in the case of prudence, first comes a definition, then an analysis of its different parts, then the opposed vices of imprudence and anxiety.

Though the moral theologian is primarily concerned with describing and analyzing that conduct which is in closest agreement with the will of God for man, and in expounding and commending those virtues which all men should seek to acquire and those types of action through which the virtues find expression, yet he cannot avoid dealing with difficult cases when two or more virtues seem to conflict and to impose irreconcilably opposite duties. Then the moral theologian has to try to determine which is the least of the evils and to advise its choice. Nor can the moral theologian altogether avoid answering questions which are couched in the form 'May I do this or that?' 'Is such-and-such permissible?' For the moral theologian has the duty of advising and helping the pastor in his task of leading the errant and sometimes unwilling sheep gently up 'the steep ascent to Heaven'. Sometimes to recommend the heroic or the highest course of action does more harm than good, and it is important, if not more important, to know what is the lowest course of action to fall below which would be gravely sinful. It is, no doubt, from this part of the moral theologian's work that casuistry has acquired its sinister reputation. Yet casuistry, in the best sense, is expert moral and spiritual guidance in solving difficult problems of conscience, in resolving an agony of doubt and indecision. The method is to introduce a number of parallel and analogous situations and by comparing them to bring to light the essentially relevant considerations and pin-point the precise area of difficulty or obscurity.

But there is, also, the other side of casuistry, the delineation of minimum standards of conduct. Here the moral theologian overlaps the canonist. Every Christian community has to lay down some minimum standard of external conduct below which it cannot allow its members to fall. This is demanded by the duty of the community to bear faithful witness to the ethical teaching of the Christian religion. It is also demanded by the duty of the community to protect Christ's little ones. Some standard must be publicly maintained so that 'the little ones' are not made to stumble by an apparent condonation or even approval of conduct which is obviously and scandalously contrary to the demands of the Christian life. In consequence every Christian community must lay down certain minima in the form of laws. It then becomes the business of the moral theologian and the canonist to interpret these laws and to determine precisely what they do and do not require. In other words, to answer the question 'Is this or that permissible?'

It is usual to devote the second half of a text-book of moral theology to a treatment of the sacraments. Books on moral theology have tended to be written more as guides and helps for the clergy than aimed directly at the laity. A great deal of the work and thought of the clergy is taken up with the administration of the sacraments and with instructing and preparing the laity to receive them. This, perhaps, is one reason why the sacraments occupy such a large place in the moral theology text-books. Then again, advance in holiness and the living of the good life depends so much on a reverent use of the sacraments, since holiness cannot be attained without grace, that it is, perhaps, natural to follow the exposition of the good life by a treatise on the sacraments which are so important a means for attaining it. And thirdly, canon law prescribes the conditions necessary for the valid administration of the sacraments, and the dispositions required for their lawful and worthy reception. The clergy need expert help in the interpretation of these canons, especially in the case of the sacraments of marriage and penance. A great mass of law attaches to these two sacraments and it requires expert handling to explain its application and its purpose.

In the Roman Catholic Church moral theology has been the subject of continuous study. The most famous Roman Catholic moral theologian is the eighteenth-century St Alphonsus Liguori. The nineteenth and twentieth centuries have produced Lehmkuhl and Prümmer respectively. In the Church of England the seventeenth century produced a number of eminent moral theologians notably Jeremy Taylor, R. Sanderson and J. Hall. *See* **Caroline Moral Theology**. From the eighteenth century to the twentieth the subject was little studied. An attempt to revive interest was made by K. E. Kirk between the wars, but it has met with limited success. The Protestant churches have always mistrusted moral theology because of its alleged tendency to fall into legalism and formalism. Protestant writers have tended, therefore, to concentrate on 'Christian ethics', that is, a treatment of general principles and ideals rather than get involved in the details and qualifications which the moral theologians can scarcely avoid.

For a selection from the extensive Roman Catholic literature, *see under* **Roman Catholic Moral Theology**. Anglican writings include: Lindsay Dewar, *Moral Theology in the Modern World*, 1964; K. E. Kirk, *Some Principles of Moral Theology*, 1920; *Conscience and Its Problems*, 1927; *The Vision of God*, 1931; R. C. Mortimer, *The Elements of Moral Theology*, 1947; Herbert Waddams, *A New Introduction to Moral Theology*, 1964.

R. C. MORTIMER

Morality and Religion. *see* Religion and Morality, Relations of.

Mortification

Mortification as a term in ascetic theology derives from the Pauline injunction to 'put to death' (Latin *mortificate*) selfish desires (Col. 3.5). It expresses strikingly the character of the life of the Christian as one who is crucified with Christ (Gal. 2.20; 5.24), and who can say with Ignatius of Antioch 'my desire (*eros*) is crucified' (Rom. 7.2), or with John Wesley 'Nail my affections to the Cross' ('O thou to whose all-searching sight', 1738, based on a hymn by N. von Zinzendorf). The term is commonly used in a lesser sense for acts of self-denial (q.v.) going beyond the common rules of prayer and fasting. For instance ancient ascetics would deprive themselves of comfortable sleep and normal food or clothing (cf. the practice of Origen in his youth, Eusebius, *Church History*, VI, 3,9–12) – recite the Psalter daily, perhaps standing in cold water (a practice of Celtic hermits), or renounce baths, considered in ancient times as a luxury. St Benedict suggests more mildly that his monks could give up during Lent some of the allowance of food, drink, sleep or conversation usually permitted (*Rule*, Chap. 49). In the Middle Ages painful mortifications were often undertaken as a challenge to worldliness, in the cloister or outside it – the hair shirt of Thomas Becket is a famous example. For the Reformers discipline and self-denial should characterize the whole Christian life rather than being a special part of it (*see Augsburg Confession*, Part II, 5). In modern Catholicism the more spectacular mortifications are unusual, though not unknown. But the etiquette of pious houses and convents still offers opportunities for refusing slight indulgences otherwise permitted – and many Episcopalians preserve the custom of 'giving up' this or that for Lent. Serious discussion of the subject often takes the line that 'voluntary mortifications' are less useful than involuntary, that is the acceptance of the stresses and frustrations which life itself and our particular vocation impose upon us. And as writers as different as Thomas a Kempis and Martin Luther have emphasized, we must still come to the Kingdom by the bearing of the cross (*Imitation of Christ*, II, 12; *Ninety-Five Theses*, no. 95).

For a classic treatment of the subject *see* Augustine Baker, *Holy Wisdom*, 1657 (reprinted 1874 and 1949), Second Treatise. For some mediaeval and later examples, *see* Louis Gougaud, *Devotional and Ascetic Practices in the Middle Ages*, 1927; Alfred O'Rahilly, *Father William Doyle, S.J.*, 1920.

E. R. HARDY

Moses

Moses, perhaps thirteenth century B C, led the Israelites out of their captivity in Egypt and taught them the law which he received from Yahweh. *See* **Decalogue; Jewish Ethics; Old Testament Ethics.**

Motives and Motivation

Motives and motivation in the broad sense means why men behave as they do, one of the classic themes of psychology. More narrowly, motivation refers to the internal factors which produce human behaviour, rather than to external stimuli, though these are partly comprehended in some theories of motivation; nor does it refer to the efforts of other persons to influence behaviour through incentive, a common non-technical usage. Motive has sometimes meant the conscious factors in behaviour, but now is virtually synonymous with motivation.

As is the case with many of the larger themes of the discipline, psychologists are divided in their approach to motivation. Most agree that the paramount questions are what needs are being met in behaviour – that is, what deficiencies are felt, and what goals are being sought to meet these needs. Goals are either intrinsic or extrinsic (learned). Beyond this psychologists are divided in their methods of assessing the processes of motivation, whether motivation should be understood as a molecular or a molar phenomenon, whether it can completely be comprehended in terms of tension reduction, and whether it is primarily conscious or unconscious, to name four significant issues, which, though not exhaustive of the differences, represent the spectrum of issues.

Many classifications of motivation theories have been proposed. The one used here is based on aspects of mental functioning: drives, emotions or affects, and cognition, and the issues will be related to them. The basic point is that theories of motivation tend to give pre-eminence to one of these aspects as motivational factors, not that they hold them to be the exclusive root of motivation. It is generally recognized that motivation is not related solely to one kind of behaviour or function, but is pervasive of the personality. Nevertheless, some aspects are regarded as more basic than others.

The first group of theorists emphasize the drive character of motivation. Though such drives as hunger, sex and thirst are innate, or instinctual (*see* **Instincts or Drives**), they can be greatly modified and directed towards differential goals with the aid of the affective and cognitive functions. One group of drive theorists is represented by Sigmund Freud, the founder of psychoanalysis. Freud held that the drives and especially the sexual drive, broadly conceived, determined much apparently unrelated behaviour. He later modified his view to include a second basic drive, that of aggression (*see* his *Introductory Lectures on Psychoanalysis* 1922, 2nd edn., 1929, and *New Introductory Lectures on Psychoanalysis* 1933, 2nd edn., 1937); *see also* **Psychoanalysis**. Freud and his followers use indirect means of assessment of motives – inferences from clinical material; they were and are molar in their approach to motivation; they emphasize unconscious motives, and hold that motivation is tension reducing exclusively. They are not 'pure' drive theorists, having long emphasized the role of anxiety and guilt in behaviour, and also recognize cognitive regulating factors.

A second group of drive theorists, in origin at least, are the behaviourists. Although the concept of drive is regarded as formally unnecessary by many of this group because of its inferred character, the stimulus-response model employed by them requires a drive component as the need factor in the model, as is recognized by James Olds, for instance (*see The Growth and Structure of Motives*, 1956). B. F. Skinner is perhaps the outstanding contemporary representative (*see* his *Science and Human Behaviour*, 1953). Behaviourists employ direct, laboratory methods of assessing motivation; they take a very molecular approach (although some, like Olds, Dollard and Miller, have attempted to relate their thought to more molar approaches), they regard most motivation as tension reducing or reinforcing (excepting curiosity), and they are generally unconcerned with the question of consciousness versus unconsciousness.

A third group of theorists, at present small but growing, are those who emphasize the role of emotions. While they recognize the underlying motivational position of the drives, they stress the amplifying and modulating function of the affect system. S. S. Tomkins, whose four-volume *Affect-Imagery-Consciousness* began to appear in 1963, is perhaps the leading exponent. P. T. Young's later work also emphasizes this factor (*see* his *Motivation and Emotion*, 1961). Tomkins uses both direct and indirect methods of assessment, both molar and molecular approaches to understanding (though perhaps stressing the latter), stresses both conscious and unconscious factors, and employs a tension reducing (though not necessarily drive reducing) model.

The fourth group, those who stress the controlling and regulating functions of cognition, may be divided into two camps. The first sees motivation primarily in cognitive conflict (*see* Leon Festinger, *A Theory of Cognitive Dissonance*, 1957), and stresses tension reduction. The second group stresses the integrating, adaptive and creative functions of cognition, which they conceive to have a considerable degree of autonomy from the drives and the affects. Gordon Allport (*Pattern and Growth in Personality*, 1961) is a leading exponent. A. H. Maslow had contributed provocative and suggestive ideas (*Motivation and Personality*, 1954). These theorists stress the possibility of tension increasing motives, use indirect means of assessment, are molar in their approach, and emphasize conscious factors.

Some theories of motivation defy classification into one of these types, such as Henry Murray's need-press theory, in which motivation is seen as the outcome of internal and external factors which cut across all levels of personality (*Explorations in Personality*, 1938). Theories of self-actualization as the sole or prime motive of personality also involve all levels of functioning, though they stress a molar approach and conscious factor (*see*, e.g., Carl R. Rogers, *Client-Centered Therapy*, 1951).

The principal implication of studies of motives and motivation for ethics is perhaps that the complexity of all motivation is being increasingly recognized, so that no simplicistic determinacy or indeterminacy is adequate in assessing behaviour.

In spite of the seeming power of 'motivation research' in the advertising industry, most theorists continue to stress the fragmentary nature of present knowledge of motivation. Relationships between 'molar' and 'molecular' motivational patterns are still not well understood, and until they are, it may be premature for any approach to human behaviour to settle on one kind of model to the exclusion of others. K. B. Madsen's *Theories of Motivation* (1963) presents concise summaries of many positions.

JAMES N. LAPSLEY

Muslim Ethics

Muslim ethics are based on the Qur'ān, therefore, on divine revelation, which, though it only covers a limited sphere, sets the tone. This was supplemented and enormously expanded by *hadīths* or traditions based on the sayings and acts of the Prophet Muhammad (their reliability which has often been questioned does not affect their contribution to Islamic ethics). At the same time *hadīth* provided the basis for the developing *corpus* of Islamic law. The law reduced the ethical material in the sources to a system of rules and regulations. It is from the law that the Muslim learns what he must or must not do.

Islam, therefore, possesses a legal morality of universal application whose sanction is God and that means in practice the books of the law. It tolerates (in theory) no authority other than its law in the government of individual and social life. Legalistic morality, as conduct or duty, is essentially social; but also, with its doctrine of reward and punishment, it is personal. The individual can obtain salvation apart from the group and punishments also fall on the individual (cf. Qur'ān, liii. 39, xxxi. 32). Certain pre-Islamic ideas of communal morality which might be regarded as out of line with this conception (e.g., the principle of retaliation for homicide, Qur'ān, ii. 273) were retained.

As with other aspects of Islam, alongside the regulated standards of morality there were parallel elements drawn from other traditions. Elements of the ethical outlook of peoples of the Near East other than the Arabs, felt to be essential for the social life of the Muslims of that region, were embraced in the books of *adab* (originally 'custom', then 'civility', Latin *urbanitas*, which term also acquired the intellectual meaning of profane learning), especially the collections of anecdotes. Thus there came into existence a body of approved (since supported by *hadīths*) adab or secular ethics. Customary law ('*āda*) also plays an important part in regulating the life of Muslims in the various regions and consequently contributes towards the ethical outlook. Yet the whole, both the retained and the new, coalesced into something which could be regarded as clearly Islamic.

The growth of ethical legalism, the view that moral conduct can be embraced within a body of law, has meant that orthodox Muslim thought has paid little attention to the principles upon which conduct is based. This is natural, for it is obvious that it should be sufficient to the believer to be told that God wills this or that. Sin is rebellion against God's will.

Yet although the direction that ethics took cannot be questioned because of the doctrine of *ijmā'* or consensus ('My people cannot err' – the infallibility of the doctors of law), it would be quite incorrect to say that Islamic ethics are purely legalistic. Although it is possible to fulfil one's ethical requirements through fulfilment of the letter of the Law, many Muslims were concerned too about the spirit of the regulations, and stressed that the 'intent' (*niyya*) counts for more than the actual observance (*see* al-Ghazālī on *niyya* in *Ihyā'*, iii. pp. 330 ff.). Further, the whole ethical outlook was tempered by the development of ascetical and mystical tendencies within Islam which, through the Sufi orders, mediated practical ethics to the ordinary man.

Not only the mystics found little assurance (practical morality) in the observance of legalistic precepts, but philosophers also sought to discern by rational thought the reason for and purpose of obedience to moral laws (intellectual morality). Although ethics never became an Islamic science in its own right, a 'science of ethics' ('*ilm al-akhlāq*) was developed by the philosophers who derived it originally from the Greeks through Syriac writers and in method of presentation from the *adab* books. This was based on the Aristotelian method of the mean – a system of inter-related virtues and vices. One of the first philosophers to write on ethics was al-Fārābī (died 950), but the fundamental work on systematic moral philosophy is *Tahdhīb al-akhlāq* of Ibn Miskawaih (died 1030) from which all later books derive (*see* the analysis given in D. M. Donaldson, *Studies in Muslim Ethics*, 1953, pp. 121–33). Such thought was limited to a small (and suspect) circle and remained outside the mainstream of Islamic thought. Yet al-Ghazālī accepted such philosophical developments in his considerable writings on moral conduct (his system of ethics is presented in the third part of his *Ihyā' 'ulum ad-dīn*) and in consequence many elements of ethical theory became incorporated (even if not integrally) in the orthodox system. Although he did not differ essentially from other Muslim theologians in regarding the law as sufficient in itself as a guide for moral conduct, his work led to a truer conception of ethics than the dominant legalism.

Five main trends of ethical thought, therefore, existed parallel to each other: the legalistic, the customary or empirical, the humanistic (*adab*), the mystical and the philosophical. The first dominated Islamic life, modified in practice by elements from the others, but the whole amalgamated as the ethics of the Muslim community.

The orthodox attitude towards '*ilm al-akhlāq* is shown by Hājjī Khalifa (*Kashf az-Zunnun*, ed. Fluegel, i.200) who regards it as an intellectual exercise of no practical importance: 'the utility of this science can only be effective if character can be changed . . . , whereas the contrary is obvious', a conclusion he supports by *hadīths*. At the present day, although there is no basic change in the outlook of the orthodox leaders, 'laymen' have been feeling after new types of ethical theory which will open the way for a reformulation of Islamic ethical conceptions based on the foundations of Qur'ān and *hadīth*.

J. S. TRIMINGHAM

Mysticism and Ethics

Discussion of the relation between mysticism and ethics has, in traditional Protestantism, rested upon the assumption that mysticism is homogeneous, going back in one way or another to the kind of Neoplatonism made influential in Christian history by the work of pseudo-Dionysius (fifth century). The basis of this mysticism is the assumption that that which is most spiritual is most removed from the bodily and material. Hence there is a tendency to 'angelism' in its anthropology and to an asceticism based on metaphysical dualism. Matter as such is unredeemable; history and time are unrealities from which the spiritual man will seek to be detached, 'sin' is combination of ignorance and imperfection, redemption from which is a process of enlightenment. By spiritual exercises a mystic can achieve the proper destiny of man which is absorption into deity.

If this is how mysticism is understood, it is not difficult to see what the charges to be brought against it in the field of ethics are: (1) First there is the suspicion that ethical rights and duties are being rooted not in a divine act of redemption and seen as the fruit of the tree but are being radically re-interpreted so as to be identical with a new experience of heightened awareness which the mystic seeks to cultivate and retain by his system of discipline. The 'ethics' of mysticism are derived from this particular experience and hence have no necessary relation to the historical incarnation and atonement of Christian belief. (2) Mysticism is held to involve an attitude towards asceticism which is incompatible with Christianity. In the latter, asceticism is eschatologically and not metaphysically conditioned, that is, it is based on the inevitable tension of a life lived in two ages simultaneously, and not on the notion that matter itself is inherently evil. Hence it is commonly assumed that mysticism is bound to lead to a self-centred asceticism where the practitioner is absorbed in his own self-culture. Mysticism is understood as unreservedly and unconditionally 'world-renouncing' in a way which is incompatible with the Christian doctrines of creation and redemption. (3) Closely associated with this stricture is the criticism that mysticism is noticeably feeble in its social ethic. A tendency to treat evil as unreal means an absence of indignation or protest, and an emphasis on contemplation and ecstatic experience which dulls social awareness. The 'ethics' of mysticism are believed to be inevitably aristocratic in temper and content. It has 'no message for the toilers' (John Oman) and is 'unavailable for the burden-bearers of the world' (Reinhold Niebuhr). Fundamentally mysticism is a self-centred cult of a particular experience. The fundamental theological objection to mysticism is accordingly that it is thought to be inevitably a form of 'salvation by works', and so the Protestant emphasis on divine grace and justification by faith strikes 'a fatal blow at mysticism' (E. Brunner).

It would not be difficult to point to passages in the writings of the Christian mystics, even of those suspected of tendencies towards Neoplatonism, which necessitate the qualifying of such outright indictments. On (1) for instance, no one could be more explicit about the prior necessity for a divine act of redemption than Henry Suso or Julian of Norwich. Certainly, in regard to (2) there is a tendency for some mystics to turn asceticism into a technique for attaining states of higher awareness, but in classical Christian mystics like Teresa or John of the Cross this is guarded against by an insistence on the necessary context of grace. The charge in (3) could not be brought against, for example, Catherine of Siena or Francis of Assisi or Ignatius Loyola or Teresa or even Eckhart ('It is better to feed the hungry than to see even such visions as St Paul saw'). The teaching of main-stream Christian mysticism has been that mystical awareness is potential in all men and that what the mystics are speaking about is the life of prayer in which all may engage. Even in Buddhist mysticism the emphasis is on the duty of *helping others* towards such awareness.

Recent studies have suggested that there is in the Christian tradition a type of mysticism to which the usual strictures against the Dionysian variety do not apply. This is the Christian patristic concept of 'mysticism as mystery'. The early Fathers use 'mystical' either of Scripture as containing more than meets the literalist's eye and pointing typologically or allegorically to Christ, or of the sacraments as again signifying more than meets physical sight. Mysticism in this sense is a compelling awareness mediated through the 'mystery' which is some revelatory object or situation, what Tillich calls the 'sign-event'. This is a mysticism which is extroverted and maintains the closest contact with the 'mystery', the concrete historical 'sign'. Hence the incarnation is here not peripheral but central, and sacraments are seen as the normal and essential means of mystical apprehension. Post-Dionysian mysticism detached what Tillich calls 'ecstasy' (a uniquely coercive insight) from the 'sign-event' and equated mysticism with the experience of elation which accompanies this kind of perception. The tendency then was to attempt to cultivate the conditions thought to be conducive to the experience, simply for the sake of experience. Against mysticism of this kind the strictures against its ethical insensitivities are often justified. But there is an authentic mysticism of the Christian variety which plays an important role in preventing religion from being reduced to a moralism.

J. Dalby, *Christian Mysticism and the Natural World*, 1950; F. von Hügel, *The Mystical Element of Religion*, 1927; T. Hywel Hughes, *The Philosophic Basis of Mysticism*, 1937; A. Plé and others, *Mystery and Mysticism* (a symposium), 1956; W. T. Stace, *Mysticism and Philosophy*, 1961.

E. J. TINSLEY

Nationalism

Nationalism, or the deep devotion of citizens to the interests of their nation, is an ideology with strong emotional support. It is based on whatever unifies the nation – language, territory, culture, race, common history, or other interests. It is cultivated through various devices of education, propaganda, myths, slogans and symbols. It has frequently become a supreme devotion involving unquestioning allegiance and the subordination of other loyalties.

As a unifying factor in the growth of the nation state, nationalism has been a progressive force. It helped enlarge effective community by pulling together smaller political units. It frequently contributed to liberty by stimulating independence movements against foreign domination. Nationalism may continue to play such a constructive role in new nations emerging from colonialism.

Nationalism has also become a divisive allegiance between nation states. Expressed in isolationism, it refuses to accept responsibility for other peoples. As imperialism, it seeks national domination over other peoples. One of its important manifestations is in economic nationalism, or the pursuit of policies supporting the selfish economic interests of a country. In either its political or economic forms, this attitude of preferential support has intensified conflict between nations and remains one of the important causes of war.

The nationalist spirit has supported the widespread conviction that national interest is a sufficient basis for defining the goals of foreign policy. Even though outstanding specialists in international affairs defend that proposition, it is nevertheless challenged by the concern of love for a circle of neighbours more inclusive than the nationals of any country. As a counterpart to Adam Smith's 'invisible hand' in economics, it is often assumed that the political defence of national interest will contribute to the wider welfare of the world. The Christian perspective, however, gives priority to the needs of neighbours. In general, one's own highest welfare is seen as resulting as an unsought byproduct from service in the welfare of others.

Nationalism was once a unifying factor. Now, unless checked, it may become a disintegrating element in the larger society. A tempered form may still make a contribution, however, within a generous enthusiasm for the legitimate interests of all nations. Since religion was one of the ties holding early nations together, it contributed to the growth of nationalism. May religion now contribute to a new manifestation by enlarging the circumference of men's loyalties at the same time that it stresses responsible support for a unified nation? *See* **Patriotism; Internationalism.**

HARVEY SEIFERT

Natural Law

The view that there are certain precepts or norms of good and right conduct, discoverable by all men is the broadest signification of natural law. Actually, the term has been used for a variety of positions in ethics and jurisprudence. Sometimes natural law means that part of God's eternal law which governs the free actions of men; in another usage, natural law designates those rules of justice which may be found written in the hearts or consciences of men; and thirdly, it describes a set of ethical judgments obtained by reflecting on man's ordinary experience, as contrasted with the divine laws that may be supernaturally revealed.

In Greek ethics, Socrates, Plato and Aristotle (qq.v.) seem to agree that there is a natural justice, or a right thing to do (*dikaion*), and that most men can recognize it. Thus Aristotle remarks: 'Of political justice part is natural, part legal – natural, that which everywhere has the same force and does not exist by thinking this or that; legal, that which is originally indifferent, but when it has been laid down is not indifferent' (*The Nicomachean Ethics*, Bk. V, Chap. 7). Sophocles had earlier given literary expression to the same view that there is a 'higher law' to which one may appeal in exceptional moral cases (*Antigone*, lines 450–60). This is part of the ancient and classical conviction that there is a reason or law (*logos* or *nomos*) which runs through all change and underlies all existence. As Cicero sums up the Stoic position, 'there is present to every man reason, which presides over and gives laws to all; which, by improving itself and making advances, becomes perfect virtue' (*Tusculan Disputations*, ii, 21). In other writings (*For T. A. Milo* and *The Republic*, iii, 22) Cicero explicitly speaks of natural law as 'universal, unchanging and everlasting', and as superior to all man-made laws.

Through the Fathers of the Church (Ambrose, Augustine, Isidore of Seville and John Damascene) and through the legal tradition of the late Roman Empire the theory of natural right or law (*ius naturale*) was transmitted to Christian moralists of the Middle Ages (*see*: Grabmann, Rommen and Lottin). The theory is not unknown to Mohammedan and Jewish philosophers of the period (Alfarabi, Averroes, Maimonides). One of the clearest formulations of the mediaeval Christian view is found in Thomas Aquinas. 'Now among all others, the rational creature is subject to divine providence in a more excellent way, in so far as he himself partakes of a share in providence, by being provident both for self and for others. Therefore he participates in eternal reason, through which he possesses a natural inclination to a fitting act and end. Such participation on the part of a rational creature in the eternal law is called natural law.' (*Summa Theologica*, Part II, First Section, q. 91, art. 2; for more on natural inclinations and moral law, see q. 92, art. 4.) Aquinas never attempted to give a list of precepts of natural law, each man is to discover these for himself; nor did he claim that all such rules are immutable. He admitted that the more specific judgments of natural law must contain facts and conditions that are open to change. What he insisted on was the stability of the general and primary principles of natural rightness, for example, 'no harm should be done voluntarily to any person'. Thomistic approaches to natural law stress its dependence on right reasoning (*recta ratio*), on practical experience, and situate this function in the intellect. Later Scholastics (Duns Scotus, William Ockham, Francis Suarez) tend to shift the law-making function into the area of willing (both in the case of God as Lawmaker and of human legislators), so that legal command (*imperium*), or obligation, is more and more viewed as a volitional act rather than an order or judgment of intellect.

This growth of legal voluntarism influenced the course of natural law thinking in modern philosophy. By the sixteenth century, most theorists are convinced that any law must be imposed on its subjects by a volitional fiat. The earlier (Thomistic) claim that moral laws may be discovered by intellectual reflection on natural experience is no longer even discussed (*see* Oakley). On the continent of Europe, Grotius (1583–1645) and Pufendorf (1632–94) produced influential treatises on natural law jurisprudence but in the voluntarist tradition. The same is true of the classical British moralists: they see natural law as a set of commands imposed on man by the will of God, commands which need have no connection with the nature of man or of the universe. Thomas Hobbes writes: 'the laws of nature . . . are not in propriety of speech laws, as they proceed from nature. Yet, as they are delivered by God in holy Scriptures, as we shall see in the chapter following, they are most properly called by the name of laws. For the sacred Scripture is the speech of God commanding over all things by greatest right' (*Philosophical Rudiments*, Chap. 3, Section 33). This version of natural law is valid only for those who believe in the Bible.

Contemporary ethics, if we except Thomism and a few realists, generally rejects or ignores natural law theories. Such is not the case in legal philosophy and jurisprudence. Several European countries (notably West Germany and Italy), as well as Japan, have made much use of natural law principles as a foundation for post-war legislation and the establishment of new political institutions. The same is true of the efforts of many of the emerging nations of Africa to find some legal bases for their legislatures and courts (*see* studies by G. Dietz, F. von der Heydte, G. Fasso, H. Rommen, E. von Hippel, Seiichi Anan, D. V. Cowen and M. Gluckman in issues of *Natural Law Forum*, from 1956 to 1964). There has even been a growth of interest in natural law thinking in the courses in jurisprudence in many USA law schools. *See also* **Law**.

A. P. D'Entrèves, *Natural Law: An Introduction to Legal Philosophy*, 1951; M. Grabmann, *Das Naturrecht der Scholastiker von Gratian bis Thomas von Aquin*, 1922–3; O. Lottin, *Le droit naturel chez s. Thomas et ses prédécesseurs*, 1931; F. Oakley, 'Medieval Theories of Law: William of Ockham and the Significance of the Voluntarist Tradition', *Natural Law Forum*, VI (1961), 65–83; H. Rommen, *The Natural Law*, 1948; J. Wild, *Plato's Modern Enemies and the Theory of Natural Law*, 1953.

VERNON J. BOURKE

Natural Rights

A right is an entitlement, a due liberty and power to do or not to do certain things; 'natural' means what is neither of human devising (by law or by agreement) nor conferred by a special command of God. Natural rights are thus entitlements belonging to human nature as such, in virtue of its superanimal sensibilities and capacities, and therefore to every human being. Something like the notion lies in the Stoic doctrine of the metaphysical kinship of all men, and in the thence derived Roman and mediaeval juristic idea of a natural law as a test of state-law; but that it can be traced back continuously to them has been disputed, for the shift of emphasis from law to a prior right was in practice momentous. The notion of entitlements arising out of the character of human nature itself (whether created by God or no) came out forthrightly only in the eighteenth century, to commend and vindicate a radical political programme, first in the American Declaration of Rights (1776) and next in the French Declaration of Human Rights (1789), which proclaim that the securing of natural rights is the primary and overriding function of political government. The language of the second is 'the natural and imprescriptible rights of man', of the first that 'all men are created equal, that they are endowed by their Creator with certain inalienable rights, that among these are life, liberty and the pursuit of happiness'. In both cases the notion is put forward as self-evident to reason, not as a complex interpretation or as an affirmation of religious faith; and therefore as valid universally, cutting across all the usual human distinctions – in America pulling and holding together men of vehemently diverse convictions, in France inspiring a campaign across the frontier for the military liberation of neighbouring peoples. It has been objected that logically the notion is not axiomatic, and anyhow that specific rights cannot be *deduced* from it; juristically, that the allegation of a right valid independently of the will of the ruling body is incompatible with the idea of sovereignty as the fount of law and therefore of enforceable rights; and practically, that if rights are to have good social consequences they must be relative to the mental and moral level of a people. The postulation of natural rights is but one way, perhaps theoretically too simple, of expressing the conviction of the intrinsic worth of every human individual. The denial of this would involve the denial of other hard-won moral beliefs, for morality is a system. The question for Christian ethics is whether the worth of man (1) rests on his created nature, and is heightened, and the motive to respect it powerfully reinforced, by the dispensation of grace, or (2) has been so obliterated by sin that it now rests only on this dispensation. If the latter, we should have to ask whether the Christ-conferred value could be given legal or other political expression in a non-Christian (of another religion, or secular) state or in one of mixed religions.

T. E. JESSOP

Naturalistic Ethics

This may be defined as covering any theory which seeks to reduce all ethical concepts to concepts of a natural science, usually psychology, but sometimes biology or sociology. If 'good' be taken as the fundamental concept of ethics and be defined as meaning, for example, 'desired' or 'satisfying', or 'right' be taken as the fundamental concept and defined as, for example, 'generally approved', ethics becomes on principle a branch of psychology; if either is defined as 'in accordance with the line of evolutionary development' or as 'conducive to social stability', it becomes respectively a branch of biology or sociology. The term, naturalism, in this sense is derived from G. E. Moore, who in *Principia Ethica* (1903) maintained that any naturalist definition of good was on principle impossible. By 'definition' is here meant 'analysis in terms of something other than itself', and not the naming of a property which merely accompanies the property defined. It might be possible to mention properties which are always present when anything is good and *vice versa* without analyzing goodness; to take an analogous example, the scientist can give a definition of yellow in terms of the accompanying wave-lengths, but the colour yellow as seen still cannot be analyzed in terms of something else in such a way that a man who had not experienced it could know what it was like. To say that ethical concepts cannot be reduced to non-ethical is by no means an unplausible statement, and if it is true it must be impossible to give a naturalist definition of them all. It would be a mistake to suppose that what was indefinable could not be known, because it might be known by direct apprehension of what it was like, that is, yellow. It must further be borne in mind that Moore's theory was applied only to one of the senses of 'good', that one in which it signified good in itself. A person who held Moore's view on this might well accept a naturalistic definition of some other sense of 'good', for example, instrumentally good.

Moore held that we could see directly (by 'intuition') that what had certain empirical qualities must also have the quality of goodness (or badness), but he called the quality itself 'non-natural' so as sharply to differentiate it from qualities which were themselves empirical. 'Ought' might similarly be regarded as signifying a non-natural relation. Opposed to this is any view which regards ethical terms as standing for a quality observable in introspection or a causal property. Moore called the confusion of good with any such property the 'naturalistic fallacy'. No doubt there have been many writers in whom it was a fallacy, since they implicitly assumed or committed themselves to such a definition of good without being clear what they were doing, but since Moore's work the doctrine of naturalism has been deliberately reasserted by people who were well aware of Moore's position, and this conscious assertion of naturalism, even if held mistaken, should not be described as just a confusion or fallacy.

The advantages of a naturalist theory are that it provides an empirical basis for ethics and assimilates it to the natural science which represents the modern ideal of knowledge and that it avoids the need of appealing to intuition in ethics. It has also been widely felt that it is extremely doubtful whether we can detect in ourselves any awareness of the alleged indefinable quality of goodness, but it would be easier to claim that we had such an awareness of the distinctive notion signified by 'ought' and a theory which took ought as fundamental could be non-naturalistic as well as a theory which thus took good.

The main general objections to naturalism in ethics are as follows: (1) If naturalism be true, ethics should be an empirical science and its conclusions should then be capable of establishment by simple observation or empirical generalization, but this is not at all the method one follows in order to arrive at ethical conclusions. (2) In regard to any particular naturalist definition offered of right or good, it seems plain that it would not be self-contradictory to assert that something was right or good and yet deny that it conformed to the definition, so the definition cannot give what is meant by 'right' or 'good'. (3) 'Ought' is essentially different from 'is' (though perhaps inferable from what is), but naturalism would reduce all ought-propositions to propositions about what is, that is, propositions about the actual attitudes of people or about the kinds of empirical things which are good. The only alternative to naturalism is not Moore's; many thinkers would say that both sides have a false assumption in common, namely that the function of what we call moral judgments is not to give us information about the properties (natural or non-natural) of the real but to do something quite different, namely express a practical attitude (emotive theory). The chief difficulty about such a theory is to reconcile it with the degree of objectivity we have to admit in ethics and the fact that we do not merely express an attitude in moral judgments but claim to have good reason for it, but very many philosophers are seeking a middle ground between these rival theories.

R. B. Perry, *General Theory of Value*, 1926, and the earlier philosopher David Hume, *An Enquiry Concerning the Principles of Morals*, 1751, are among the best examples of a naturalistic ethics. For criticisms of naturalism, *see* A. C. Ewing, *Definition of Good*, 1947, Chap. 2; R. Hare, *The Language of Morals*, 1952, Chap. 5; G. E. Moore, *Principia Ethica*, 1903, Chap. I, B. For a criticism of Moore's attack on naturalism, *see* G. C. Field, *Moral Theory*, 1921, Chap. 5.

A. C. EWING

Negligence

There are various ways in which a person may act without thinking what he is doing; he may be tactless, inconsiderate or absent-minded. One such lack of thought is carelessness. 'Negligence', which is more commonly used in legal than in ordinary language, is usually defined by lawyers as legally culpable carelessness. Carelessness, or negligence, is a failure to give thought or to pay attention to the risks inherent in one's actions and to take the appropriate precautions against these risks. This failure of attention may appear either in the manner in which one does something, as when someone shows carelessness, or negligence, in his driving, or in the very commission or omission of the deed itself, as when through carelessness someone drives too near the middle of the road or omits to sound his horn on a corner. But an instance of carelessness, for example, failing to sound the horn, is not an effect of carelessness, for example, killing a pedestrian. One's carelessness might, fortunately, have no effects; but it could not be without an instance.

Each kind of task has its peculiar mistakes,

blobs, muffs, errors, accidents, dangers and pitfalls. Because attention to these risks in what one does may be necessary to insure the successful doing of it, carelessness, or negligence, is something one ought not to show; it is something necessarily blame-worthy. Yet because lack of care is not intentional, neither commonsense nor the law blames the careless, or negligent, offender as harshly as the intentional offender.

What is done from carelessness need not be done from ignorance either of what one is doing or of its nature; I know that I did not sound my horn on rounding the bend and I know that not to sound my horn in such circumstances is dangerous. But I am negligent in so far as my failure to sound my horn was a failure to give my attention to the risks involved in my driving and to take the proper precautions against them.

As well as the lack of care that may be displayed in the commission of particular illegalities, modern law takes account of what is known as an independent tort of negligence. In such a tort it is immaterial whether what is done was due to lack of thought or to ignorance, incompetence, mistake or even deliberate intent. What matters is that the offender has neglected a definite duty of care, for example, to use his side-lights when driving at night or to fence in dangerous machinery.

ALAN R. WHITE

Neighbour

Neighbour is an important concept in Christian ethics. In earlier ethical thinking, the neighbour was the person of the same land or nation, as distinguished from the stranger. But in Christian thought, as is shown especially in the story of the Good Samaritan, the neighbour is the person whom one meets here and now. The concept therefore specially stresses the concreteness of the ethical task. All men are *brothers* and entitled to love and respect; but in any concrete situation, one of these brothers has become the *neighbour*, for whom brotherly love must assume a concrete form.

Neoplatonism

The name 'Neoplatonism' is attached to a philosophical movement which originated in the teaching of the third-century thinker Plotinus. This movement is the culmination of the first and second century revival of Platonism which, in the earlier 'Middle Platonism' of such writers as Albinus and Plutarch, had created an eclectic philosophy in which varying elements of Stoic and Aristotelian thought were grafted onto the Platonic stem. The genius of Plotinus, working on the problems engendered within this tradition, gave birth to a new synthesis of classical thought which was at once an integrated philosophical view of the world, and an analysis of human ethical and religious experience writ large.

Plotinus' teaching attracted a group of disciples and created what was to become the dominant school of philosophical thought in the later Roman Empire. He had taught in the West, at Rome; and his *Enneads*, rendered into Latin by Marius Victorinus, were a significant influence not only upon pagan thinkers, but also upon such Christians as St Augustine and Boethius. In the East, Neoplatonism dominated the philosophical schools at Athens, Alexandria and Antioch. Its exponents were prolific in the production not only of philosophical treatises, but also of learned commentaries on the works of Plato and Aristotle. When in 529 the Emperor Justinian closed the last school of pagan philosophy at Athens, a number of teachers migrated to the Persian Empire; and it was through these men, as well as through Syrian Christian translators and commentators, that the Islamic culture of the Middle Ages became an heir of the classical Greek philosophy. A developed Neoplatonism was thus the form in which the intellectual heritage of Greece was passed on to the successors of the Roman Empire in West and East alike.

The followers of Plotinus did not preserve inviolate either the spirit or the content of his thought. Beginning with the Syrian Iamblichus (died *c*. 330) and culminating in the work of Proclus (410–485), a revision of the Plotinian system took place. This was in part motivated by a desire to clarify, rationalize and supplement the thought of the *Enneads*. But partly too it was the fruit of a desire to make of Neoplatonism the systematic theology of a paganism now fighting for its life within the Christian Empire. In this process much of the simplicity and nobility of Plotinus' teaching were lost. Plotinus' mysticism had emphasized the access of the morally purified soul to the contemplative life of pure Intelligence, and even to ecstatic apprehension of the transcendent Good. For this emphasis later Neoplatonism substituted an interest in the magical and theurgic practices associated with the rites of pagan religion. At the same time, by a systematic multiplication of intermediary spiritual beings in the Plotinian hierarchy, later Neoplatonism found an apparent intellectual justification for practical polytheism – as well as a means of clarifying and articulating the Plotinian picture of the world.

In spite of these variations, however, Neoplatonism conserved certain characteristic ideas which mark it as an identifiable outlook. One of these is its essential monism, which sees the world as an eternal, hierarchically ordered derivation from a single transcendent Principle. Another, corollary, theme is its analysis of evil, not as materiality (which would imply the sort of gnostic dualism which Plotinus had strongly repudiated), but as deficiency in being, the inevitable product of the progressive derivation of Unity into multiplicity. A third, most prominent perhaps in Plotinus himself, is its correlation of the levels of being beneath the transcendent One with the hierarchy of the activities of the soul – from intuitive intelligence, through discursive reason, to the essentially vital and biological functions of soul as embodied.

These themes provide the essential foundations of the Neoplatonic ethic, whose basic imperative demands the soul's full realization of its highest nature as contemplative intelligence. Obedience to this imperative requires an inward conversion of the soul from material things, not because they are evil as material, but because for the soul they represent only an inferior good. The virtuous man therefore purifies himself of attachment to worldly affairs and fleshly pleasures, in order to move inwardly at the highest level of life of which he is capable: that of the impassive contemplation of intelligible reality in its integrated wholeness.

At its best and at its worst Neoplatonism was a pagan philosophy. Many of its prominent exponents (and notably Plotinus' disciple Porphyry) were openly hostile to Christianity. Conversely, most Christian thinkers after the beginning of the fourth century were explicitly conscious of the conflict between certain Neoplatonic teachings and the teaching of Scripture. Nevertheless, this philosophy supplied, for Christian as well as pagan, the general intellectual framework in terms of which life and belief were ordered and understood. Thus not only in Augustine (for whom Neoplatonism was the intellectual means of conversion to Christianity), but also, signally, in the Cappadocian Fathers in the East, one finds a Christianity whose theological structure is at every point influenced by Neoplatonic modes of thought. This influence is evident not merely in their doctrines of God and of man, but also in their conception of the shape of the Christian life: in their emphasis on mystical vision as the goal of the believer's pilgrimage; in their understanding of Christian discipline as purification from passion and detachment from worldly interests; in their understanding of freedom as self-realization. Neoplatonism did not replace Christianity; but Christians inevitably learned to interpret their belief in terms of the prevalent intellectual outlook of their times.

A. H. Armstrong, *An Introduction to Ancient Philosophy*, 1947; E. Bréhier, *The Philosophy of Plotinus*, 1958; Plotinus, *The Enneads*, 2nd edn., tr. by S. MacKenna, rev. by B. S. Page, n.d.; Proclus, *The Elements of Theology*, ed. and tr. by E. R. Dodds, 1933; T. Whittaker, *The Neoplatonists*, 1918; R. E. Witt, *Albinus and the History of Middle Platonism*, 1937.

R. A. NORRIS, JR

New England Transcendentalism

New England Transcendentalism was a liberal religious, philosophical, ethical and literary movement which arose in reaction to the limitations of Unitarian Christianity in the 1830s. Ralph Waldo Emerson (1803–82) was the central figure in the movement, but with him were associated a number of other young Unitarian ministers, including George Ripley, Frederic Henry Hedge, James Freeman Clarke and William Henry Channing. Theodore Parker was also related to Transcendentalism, though his position blended certain Enlightenment and transcendentalist views. All of these men had studied at Harvard College and Divinity School; Orestes A. Brownson, who lacked the advantage of much formal education, belonged to the movement while in the Unitarian phase of his spiritual pilgrimage which later led him to Roman Catholicism. A number of others who were to make their mark in the world of literature were members of the Transcendental Club, which customarily met in Emerson's study in Concord, chiefly Margaret Fuller, Bronson Alcott and Henry David Thoreau.

Unitarian thought was strongly rooted in the Enlightenment tradition and in Lockean philosophy. To Emerson and the others, that position was too cold, too rational, too negative. Influenced by various strands of idealism – Platonic, Neoplatonic, and German classical or essentialist philosophy as mediated by Carlyle and Coleridge – the transcendentalists rejected authoritarian patterns in thought and religion to stress the intuitive approach to truth. Their name came from the fact that they believed in an order of truths which transcends the sphere of the external senses. Some of the ministers resigned their posts, as had Emerson in 1832, but others, including Clarke, Hedge and Parker, remained in the ministry. Emerson, after travels abroad in which he met Carlyle and other leaders of thought, became a lecturer and author, reaching a wide public through his tours and writings. In his book *Nature* (1836) the main outlines of transcendental philosophy are clearly set forth; some of his best-known essays, such as 'Self-Reliance' and 'The Over-Soul', popularized the transcendentalist gospel.

A central belief of the transcendentalists was in the immanence of God, the nearness of the divine. This view underlay their sharp differences with Unitarianism at several points, for they denied a sharp antithesis between the natural and the supernatural, between natural and revealed religion, and between Christianity and non-Christian religions. The transcendentalists also presented a more optimistic doctrine of man than was then current, for they stressed man's native capacity directly to apprehend spiritual truth by intuition. The more extreme among them, especially Emerson and Parker, denied that Jesus had any final authority; he was to be seen as a remarkable man but not divine in any other sense than all men could be. When Emerson stated his views in the famous 'Divinity School Address' of 1838, he was accused of infidelity by the unitarian leaders. Some of the more conservative transcendentalists, like Clarke and Hedge, had a more positive assessment of historic Christianity, yet rejected classical christological views and traditional doctrines of the atonement.

The social ethics of the transcendentalists were predicated on their belief that every man had the divine reason within him and were radical in their day, resolutely devoted to democracy and freedom. Transcendentalists were reformers in church and society; they were active in many of the social crusades of their time, such as those against war, alcohol, economic injustice and slavery. Brownson was especially forthright in his social views; in his *Boston Quarterly Review* (1838–41) he expressed the radical reformist side of the movement. More moderate was Brook Farm, a communitarian experiment under transcendental auspices which was hopefully to provide an example to the nation of a social utopia. Ripley resigned his parish in 1841 to guide the experiment, but by 1845 it became a Fourieristic Phalanx before dissolving.

Transcendentalist influence spread into Unitarianism despite resistance to it, contributing to the theological leftward drift of that denomination. Emersonian ideas were also appropriated by leaders of 'new thought' and 'divine science' movements in the later nineteenth and early twentieth centuries.

William R, Hutchison, *The Transcendentalist Ministers: Church Reform in the New England Renaissance*, 1959; Perry Miller, *The Transcendentalists: An Anthology*, 1950; Ralph L. Rusk, *The Life of Ralph Waldo Emerson*, 1949.

ROBERT T. HANDY

New Testament Ethics

Just as the ethics of Judaism presupposes the faith of the O T, so the ethics of the N T is incomprehensible apart from the faith which underlies the latter. Taken as a whole, biblical morality is so closely related to the worship of one sovereign and righteous God that the biblical writers seldom distinguish clearly between ethics and faith or between ethics and religion. Throughout the Scriptures morality is rooted in religious faith, and the latter is always understood as including a moral demand because God is apprehended as righteous will.

The characteristic features of N T ethics, then, can be adequately understood only in the context of the basic convictions of Christian faith as the latter finds expression in the various writings of the N T. The attempt has frequently been made to extract certain of the ethical maxims of the Gospels from their religious setting and to assume that they have a universal applicability, but it is evident that the ethical teachings are altered in the process, for they are inevitably abstracted from the underlying religious faith which both determines the distinctive content which they have in the Gospels and also provides the distinctively religious motivation for fulfilling them. N T ethics does have points of contact with non-religious ethics, but the former cannot be reduced to the latter. Jesus was not primarily a teacher of morality, but his prophetic perception of moral possibilities and moral claims was inseparable from his apprehension of God's nature and will. That which is distinctive in the ethic of Jesus is determined by the particular quality of his faith in God and his convictions about God's relationship to man and the world. Moreover, the ethic of Jesus cannot be adequately understood either as an ethic of duty or as an ethic of aspiration after certain goods or values, although it contains elements both of duty and of aspiration. Rather, the ethic of Jesus and the ethics of the N T as a whole are best understood as an ethic of man's *response* to the divine action and will with which faith perceives the self always to be ultimately confronted.

The central theme of Jesus' message was the announcement that 'the Kingdom of God is at hand' (Mark 1.15), and this proclamation of the nearness of the Kingdom was accompanied by the summons to repentance and obedience to the divine will. In his teachings concerning the will of God Jesus reaffirmed the ethical teachings of the O T, including both the law and the prophets, but he went beyond these in that he intensified, radicalized, and universalized the ethical demands of Judaism. His ethic differed from that of the O T and of Judaism, moreover, both in the close relationship which he saw between love for God and love for one's neighbour and also in the absolute priority which he gave to love in relationship to all other virtues.

Jesus' ethic may be characterized as an 'ethic of the Kingdom of God' in the sense that it describes the absolute will of God which will prevail when his Kingdom is fully established. But this ethic is not intended only for life in the future age when evil has been completely overthrown and presumably there will be no more occasion to turn the other cheek or go a second mile after one has been forced to go the first mile. Neither is it merely an 'interim ethic' (Schweitzer) intended only for a short interval between the proclamation of the coming of the Kingdom and the imminent advent of the latter, for it points to the perfect will of God, and its content is essentially unaffected by the nearness of the end. Rather, the ethic of the Sermon on the Mount represents the absolute will of God who is even now acting to establish his Kingdom and through Jesus' own ministry summons men to repent, to put their trust in him, and to obey his will in the present age. The ethic of Jesus, including the Sermon on the Mount, is an ethic of grace, and the moral demands which Jesus makes are both demands and possibilities which arise out of his understanding of God's grace which is manifest in the giving of the Kingdom. The radical nature of the divine grace and love impose upon those who would enter the Kingdom the demand for whole-hearted trust in God, unlimited forgiveness, and unselfish concern for the neighbour in need.

While the moral teachings of Jesus are frequently cast in the form of law, it is evident from the Gospels that Jesus did not undertake to prescribe answers to the ethical issues which men face in the fixed rigid way in which the Pharisees did. Indeed, he rejected the legalism of the Pharisees because of its inevitable tendency to issue in spiritual pride and also because it placed greater importance upon the letter of the law than upon human need. Jesus fulfilled the law, but he did so by being faithful to the intent of the law rather than to its precise wording. On the whole, instead of speaking in terms of generalized ethical maxims and laws he characteristically illustrated the kind of action which was required in terms of parables and specific demands which were laid upon particular individuals and especially upon his disciples in view of the crisis created by the coming of the Kingdom and his own peculiar relationship to it.

While Jesus' ethic represented the fulfilment of the law in the sense noted above, it was not legalistic. Jesus demanded 'radical obedience' (Bultmann) to God, and this meant openness to a fresh disclosure of the divine will that could not be formulated in terms of a law or a tradition; yet this 'radical obedience' was not without content, for it included the law and the prophets insofar as these represented the will of God, and it also included his own ethical teachings. The God whom Jesus summoned men to obey was the God of Abraham, Isaac and Jacob; he was the God who had made himself known in a concrete way in the history of Israel through the law and the prophets. It was this God who even now was acting to establish his Kingdom and whose will is to be done 'on earth as it is in heaven' (Matt. 6.10). The specific content of the divine will must be freshly apprehended in each new moment of decision in the light of the neighbour's need, but the ethical teachings of Jesus, as well as the law and the prophets, are indispensable guides and directives for the Christian, pointing him to the will of God which transcends any formulation of that will in terms of an unexceptional law other than the law of love.

The ethic of Jesus also differed from many other types of ethics in the sanctions to which he appealed. While it is true that he sometimes appealed to eschatological sanctions of rewards and punishments, this was not the fundamental sanction for his ethic. As Wilder points out, the eschatological sanction was a formal and secondary appeal; moreover, it was basically a mythological representation of the consequences of moral choices in a universe which is under the sovereignty of a righteous God. The essential sanction for Jesus' ethic, on the other hand, was the religious-prophetic appeal to gratitude, to obedience, to the desire to be children of the heavenly Father. His ethic is an ethic of trustful, joyful acceptance of the divine grace and love and a humble, grateful and wholehearted commitment to the will of the 'Lord of heaven and earth' (Matt. 11.25) whom he taught men to call upon him as their Father. Participation in the divine grace is its own reward. The acceptance of forgiveness, the overcoming of man's estrangement and alienation from God, and the joy of perfect fellowship with the Father in the Kingdom – these are the true rewards of faith and obedience.

When we turn from a consideration of the ethic of Jesus as it is portrayed in the Gospels to an analysis of the ethic of the early Church as it is reflected in the remainder of the NT, we find that the latter is also fundamentally an ethic of *response* to the divine action, the final meaning of which is now seen to have been disclosed in the cross and the resurrection. Through these events the first Christians saw the depths of the divine love most fully disclosed, and it was this good news about God which called forth in their hearts the response of love for the neighbour for whom Christ had died: 'Beloved, if God so loved us, we also ought to love one another' (I John 4.11). The gift of God's love to men even while they 'were yet sinners' (Rom. 5.8) constituted a claim upon believers to love their fellowmen even as God in Christ had loved them. Indeed, so close was the relationship between a living faith in God and love for the neighbour that the former spontaneously expressed itself in the latter (I Cor. 13; Gal. 5.6; cf. I John 4.20).

As the early Christians sought to be obedient to Christ, they were faced with the necessity of interpreting his teachings and applying them to a variety of new situations. Some attempted to turn his teachings into a new legalism; others tended to reject all forms of discipline and moral rules in the name of their new-found freedom. In opposition to such tendencies the writers of the NT on the whole recognize the authority of Jesus' ethical teachings without turning them into a system of casuistry. This is true of the Gospels generally with the possible exception of Matthew, who portrays Jesus as the giver of a new law in his account of the

Sermon on the Mount; for the Gospels make it clear that Jesus rejected the legalism of the Pharisees and summarized the entire duty of man in the twofold commandment of love for God and the neighbour. While the other writings in the NT do not purport to preserve Jesus' ethical sayings themselves to the same extent as the Synoptic Gospels, the words of Jesus are frequently reflected in their moral exhortations. This is particularly evident, for example, in the letters of Paul and in Acts. It is apparent, moreover, that the early Church continued to recognize the validity and the authority of Jesus' ethical teachings after the hope of an immediate end of the present historical order had waned. His moral demands were seen to be essentially independent of his own eschatological expectations. Not only did the writers of the NT appeal to Jesus' ethical sayings, however, in their own moral exhortations, but they also appealed to his personal example. Christians were summoned to be imitators of the life, death and resurrection of Christ. Thus, they were encouraged to be faithful even to martyrdom. Since they were now already made new creatures through God's reconciling action in Christ (symbolized, for example, by baptism), they were exhorted to live as the new persons which they in actuality already were – forgiven, reconciled, set free, made new. Moreover, the appeal to believers to be imitators of Christ was not limited to the exhortation to imitate in their own lives the redemptive action of God in Christ; it included also a call to imitate the virtues of Jesus, not just his remembered words, in the daily round of living (I Cor. 11.1; I Thess. 1.6; I Peter 2.21–23). Paul's letters, for example, are filled with exhortations to imitate Jesus' love, meekness, gentleness, humility, patience, forbearance, generosity and mercy as well as the generally self-giving quality of his life.

While both the words and the pattern of Jesus' own life remained normative for the early Christians, it became increasingly difficult to rely exclusively on these for ethical guidance in the NT Church. Indeed, they could not be made a blueprint for Christian conduct without violating the very spirit of Jesus' teaching and his openness to the divine will and the neighbour's need. Gradually, as the result of a long struggle within the Church between the Judaizers on the one hand and such defenders of liberty from the law as Stephen, Paul, and even to a certain extent Peter, the NT Church recognized that obedience to Christ was dependent upon the gift and guidance of the Holy Spirit. The Spirit was given, not to isolated individuals, but to the Church as the body of Christ at Pentecost. Moreover, the Spirit is represented in the NT as having a strongly ethical quality and not primarily as an ecstatic power. Thus Paul gives a catalogue of virtues which he calls 'the fruit

of the Spirit' (Gal. 5. 22–23) and makes love the criterion of the Spirit's presence and activity (I Cor. 13). In a word, the ethic of the NT Church may be described as a *koinonia* ethic – that is, as the ethic of a community which had been called into being by the action of God in Christ and which looked finally to the Spirit rather than to law or tradition for moral guidance.

Finally, it remains to be pointed out that neither in the ethic of Jesus as this appears in the Gospels nor in the ethic of the NT Church is there any explicit concern with the role of Christians in the transformation of society at large. In part, this is due to the expectation that God would soon intervene in history to overthrow evil and establish his Kingdom; hence, there was little time remaining for the reformation of society by human action and indeed the latter seemed unnecessary. In part, the absence of concern with social reform generally was also due to the cultural situation in which the early Christians found themselves; they constituted an extremely small portion of the population, and they lived in an authoritarian society in which they had no effective political or economic power. On the whole the early Church counselled Christians to be obedient to the secular authorities as deriving their power from God.

Yet, despite the fact that the NT is not directly concerned with social ethics in the sense of participating in the struggle for social justice, a strong basis for such a concern is implicit in the NT understanding of God's sovereignty, his righteous will, his grace, and the commandment of neighbour-love. As Christians have come to exercise a greater responsibility in the life of culture and as their understanding of the extent to which man's capacities and needs are socially determined has increased, these elements of their faith have caused them to join in the struggle for social justice out of love for the neighbour and as an act of obedience to God who is the Creator and the Judge even while he is the Redeemer of men. *See* **Jesus, Ethical Teaching of; Paul, Ethical Teaching of St.**

Rudolf Bultmann, *Jesus and the Word*, 1934; Martin Dibelius, *The Sermon on the Mount*, 1940; C. H. Dodd, *Gospel and Law*, 1951; 'The Ethics of the New Testament', in Ruth Nanda Ashen, ed., *Moral Principles of Action*, 1952; William Lillie, *Studies in New Testament Ethics*, 1961; T. W. Manson, *Ethics and the Gospel*, 1960; L. H. Marshall, *The Challenge of New Testament Ethics*, 1947; E. F. Scott, *The Ethical Teachings of Jesus*, 1924; A. N. Wilder, *Eschatology and Ethics in the Teaching of Jesus*, rev. edn., 1950; 'Kerygma, Eschatology and Social Ethics', in W. D. Davies and D. Daube, eds., *The Background of the New Testament and Its Eschatology*, 1956; Hans Windisch,

The Meaning of the Sermon on the Mount,
1951.
                                    E. CLINTON GARDNER

Niebuhr, Reinhold

Reinhold Niebuhr (1892–   ) is one of the
major American theologians of the twentieth
century and the most decisive influence in the
development of Protestant social ethics. Of his
many writings *The Nature and Destiny of Man*
(I, 1941 and II, 1943) is the most representative.
These volumes which contain his Gifford Lectures develop his theological ethics with discussions of their presuppositions in relation to
major theological themes concerning man and
his salvation. His *Moral Man and Immoral
Society* (1932), an essay in political ethics informed by his developing Christian realism as
a theologian, was the sharpest contribution to
the debates of the 1930s concerning the limitations of the liberal theology and of idealistic
hopes and strategies in the midst of political
conflicts. He was for several decades best
known to the churches and to the public as the
polemical opponent of the prevailing optimistic
rationalism with its belief in secure progress.
Always he has been theologian and preacher
whose insights as a very free exponent of the
theology of the Reformation illumined his
social ethics and his political judgments. Also
he has great influence as an acute critic of
events and as a leader on behalf of political
causes. In the 1930s he was to the left of the
Roosevelt New Deal and in the 1940s and 50s
he was a spokesman for the more 'liberal' wing
of the supporters of national Democratic
administrations and candidates. He is Vice-
Chairman of the Liberal Party in New York
State. Beginning as a socialist his thought
moved away from all doctrinaire approaches
to public issues to an acceptance of a mixed
economy with great emphasis on the responsibility of the federal government for social welfare. He was one of the founders of 'Americans
for Democratic Action'. He was the leader for
many years of the 'Fellowship of Socialist
Christians' which, with his changing attitude
towards socialism came to be called 'The
Frontier Fellowship' and he edited its journal
which was called *Radical Religion* and later
Christianity and Society. He was also chief
founder and editor of *Christianity and Crisis*.
He became the best known abroad of all
American theologians both because of the original way in which his thought illumined
traditional problems and because of its relevance to events.

His influence on both the theorists and practitioners of foreign policy has been especially
notable. Often he is regarded as the father of
American political realists because of his
emphasis on American responsibility as a
super-power and the limits of moral choice in
the international sphere. However, he has
always emphasized the religious and moral
checks on national pride and his distinctively
Christian ethic has always qualified his realism.
His volume, *The Structure of Nations and
Empires* (1959), provides his most mature
thought on the world of nations.

Niebuhr was born in Wright City, Missouri,
the son of Gustav Niebuhr, a minister of what
was then the Evangelical Synod (later to be a
part of the Evangelical and Reformed denomination which joined with the Congregationalists
to form the United Church of Christ). He was
graduated from Elmhurst College and Yale
University. Thirteen years in a pastorate in
Detroit of which he gives a vivid account in
Leaves from the Notebook of a Tamed Cynic
were followed by a remarkable career as Professor and Vice President at Union Theological
Seminary from which he retired in 1960. His
wife, Professor Ursula Niebuhr of Barnard
College, a theologian in her own right, has
always been a close collaborator in the
development of his thought.

Niebuhr has never developed a system of
theology. He has written about the issues which
seemed important for an understanding of
history especially as it was unfolding before
him and has never elaborated, for example, the
christological themes. In rejecting the optimism
of the liberalism which had influenced his early
thought he emphasized the fall of man as a
mythical expression of the deep sources of
pride and self-centredness on every level of
cultural and moral and religious advance. He
did much to change the climate of thought in
the churches and he also had wide influence in
some sophisticated secular circles. He has been
best known for his emphasis on sin but he also
has a strong doctrine of the *imago dei* and he
has always stressed the availability of divine
grace as forgiveness. He sees in the cross of
Christ the supreme disclosure of this grace and
also the revelation of sacrificial love which for
him is the pinnacle of ethics. He has avoided
all exclusivistic or authoritarian Christian
approaches and, while he has regarded the
Church as a community of grace and of
worship, he has rejected doctrines which seemed
to him to support ecclesiastical pretensions.

His thought has been hammered out in continuous debate with all forms of thought which
seemed to him to encourage perfectionist or
absolutistic claims, including Christian pacifism,
uncritical Marxists especially when they
followed the Stalinist line, Catholic claims for
the Church or for formulations of doctrine or
of natural law, Protestant individualism and
every orthodox version of the very biblical or
traditional ideas in which he has found most
illumination. The key to his ethics is the dialectical relation between love and justice. Justice
embodies but never completely fulfills the
requirements of love. Love widens the idea of
and application of justice, but it can not be

substituted for the institutions of justice. The method of his thinking is best seen in an essay entitled 'Coherence, Incoherence and the Christian Faith' published in *Christian Realism and Political Problems* (1953). Niebuhr's critics include those whose thought he has criticized so radically but also those who, while sympathetic with his main purpose, see a neglect in his thought of any basis for confidence in the continuing effects of grace or of the Holy Spirit. They often feel that his fear of ecclesiastical pretensions has prevented him from developing an adequate doctrine of the Church. His response to such criticisms in recent years has been to admit limitations of his own thought at these points. An invaluable guide to Niebuhr's thought with a full bibliography is the symposium edited by C. W. Kegley and R. W. Bretall: *Reinhold Niebuhr – His Religious, Social and Political Thought* (1956). On the personal and biographical side June Bingham's *Courage to Change* (1962) is the best reference.

JOHN C. BENNETT

Nietzsche, Friedrich

A classical scholar and a brilliant stylist, Nietzsche (1844–1900) proclaimed a 'philosophy' of life that condemned his day as mean and summoned it to greatness. From his classical studies he caught an admiration for the Homeric heroic age, from Schopenhauer the idea of will as the primary reality, and from Darwin the theory of evolution as the survival of the fittest. Taking these as ideals he surveyed the main strands of western civilization. The noblest expression of the Greek mind was not Apollo, the god of order, but Dionysus, the god of enthusiasm and prodigal vigour. Christianity, spreading (he claimed) first among slaves, imposed on Europe a servile morality – submission, gentleness and care for the weak and ungifted. Later intellectualists extolled the pale virtues of the study, and the growth of industrialism has produced an inordinate love of material conveniences and playthings. Against all these he preached will as the assertion of life, that is, bodily vigour and mental daring, without petty scruples. Those in whom will is strong and presses on to greatness of mind and deed are 'supermen'. It is these who make history, and it is for them that society exists. They alone are entitled to privilege, to dominance in every sphere, to freedom from subordination, morality as usually understood, and religion, which is false anyway and which they do not need. Other men exist for them, as tools. These, weak in will, try to get what they want by cringing or cunning, or by combination for collective strength, democracy being simply a device of the little to hold down the big, other devices being such religious and moral pretensions as that all men are equal and that we should be kind to one another – all which is contrary to the plain intention of the evo-lutionary process. Nietzsche's famous phrases 'the revaluation of all values' and 'beyond good and evil' mean not the rejection of morality but the supersession of one form of it by another – a democratic by an aristocratic, a rationalist or sentimental by one of will, a religious by a naturalist one. Strictly the supersession is for supermen only: for them a 'master-morality' involving no obligation to the servile rest, for these a 'slave-morality' of obedience and hard work and a religion which they alone need to keep them to their proper natural lot. Instead of arguing Nietzsche flung out his ideas in aphorisms, a reasoned philosophy being among the things he despised as anaemic.

T. E. JESSOP

Nihilism

What the term suggests philosophically fits only the dictum attributed to Gorgias, an Athenian teacher of rhetoric of the fifth century BC: Nothing exists, and if it did it could not be known. In fact the term is used (very little in English) as a condemnatory label for a theory supposed by the critic to imply the undermining of certainty or truth (e.g., scepticism), the impossibility of metaphysics (e.g., phenomenalism), or the denial of either objective moral standards or of generally accepted moral convictions. The only writer who used it of his own theory seems to have been Nietzsche, to indicate his need to destroy traditional moral notions in order to set up radically new ones. In the latter part of the nineteenth century it was a name for the political reformism of a mixed lot of Russian radicals, and popularly for the violent ideas and practices of a minority of these.

T. E. JESSOP

Nonconformist Conscience

The term originated in the last years of the nineteenth century and first appeared in print in the correspondence columns of *The Times* in connection with Captain O'Shea's divorce of his wife (November 17, 1890) on the ground of her adultery with the Irish political leader, Charles Stewart Parnell. On the Sunday following the court finding, Hugh Price Hughes, Methodist preacher and Christian philanthropist, speaking in the name of English Nonconformists publicly denounced Parnell's immorality and called for his resignation. The result was that the Irish politician was deposed by his party and disappeared from political life.

The force, of which Hughes was the mouthpiece, had been at work many years before this public scandal. It was rooted in Puritanism and revealed itself in the positive aims of nonconformity which were heard in the repeated calls for liberty of conscience, the right to worship without State interference and equal opportunities for all.

In the Industrial Revolution the Nonconformist conscience was the moving spirit behind the constant pleas for integrity, justice and compassion. Proof of this is seen in the number of journals that commenced publication at this period – *The Nonconformist, The Christian Weekly*. The Unitarian editor of the *Manchester Guardian* was also an advocate of the same opinions. In the social life of England the best practical example of the Nonconformist Conscience was the founding of the Salvation Army and the same influence was also at work in the beginnings of the British Labour Party in 1893.

The present century, however, has seen a waning of its power except for the champions of Sunday observance, total abstinence and anti-gambling campaigns. Its last advocate was probably the Baptist preacher John Clifford who led the movement for 'passive resistance' to the Education Act of 1902 because of its supposed injustice to nonconformists. It was largely due to his influence that the unionists lost the 1906 election. However, the continuing British preference for democracy, liberty of speech and equal rights for all are in no small measure the outcome of the once vigorous Nonconformist Conscience.

H. L. Cocks, *The Nonconformist Conscience*, 1943.

S. J. KNOX

Nullity

A declaration of nullity in regard to a marriage establishes that there has never been a true marriage, whatever may have appeared to be the case, and however long the parties may have lived together. Various reasons, such as defective consent or other impediments, may make a supposed marriage null. Nullity must be clearly distinguished from the Roman Catholic act of annulment, in which the pope dissolves the marriage bond in certain cases.

HERBERT WADDAMS

Oaths

Many Christian bodies have interpreted Matt. 5.33-37 as a total prohibition of all oaths and have forbidden their members ever to take an oath in any circumstances. The Roman Catholic and more general interpretation of the passage is that it forbids unnecessary, promiscuous and frivolous swearing. The Church of England in Article 39 interprets it this way and expressly authorizes the taking of an oath before a magistrate.

An oath may be either a solemn affirmation of the truth or a solemn declaration of an intention to do this or that. To say what one knows to be untrue under oath is to commit the grave sin of perjury. It is a grave sin, to swear to do something without the intention of doing it or without in fact doing it. The binding nature of an oath is roughly the same as that of a vow (q.v.) and is terminated in the same ways and for the same reasons.

R. C. MORTIMER

Obedience. *see* Counsels; Monasticism.

Obligation. *see* Duty.

Oedipus Complex

Oedipus complex is the term coined by Sigmund Freud to denote the situation in which sexual identity first begins to emerge in the third and final stage of the psycho-sexual developmental process in childhood, characterized by feelings of marked ambivalence towards the parents, and particularly the parent of the same sex. Freud argued that male children choose their own mother as their first external object of sexual desire and that this brings them into a situation of conflict in which the continuing affection felt for the father becomes complicated by hostility directed against him as a sexual rival and by fear of his superior strength. The analogous situation for a female child was formerly called the Electra complex but this term has fallen into disuse.

Freud regarded the reaction to the Oedipus complex as fundamental to all later personality adjustment and to the establishment of later moral standards. In the normal process of healthy development, other and more suitable love objects are subsequently chosen and all memory of the negative feelings, the stresses, and the guilt (q.v.) of the original oedipal situation are repressed into the unconscious (q.v.). Where the resolution of the complex is incomplete, however, the seeds are sown for later neurosis. *See* S. Freud, *A General Introduction to Psychoanalysis*, rev. edn., 1920, *and* **Superego**.

The name derives from the legend dramatized in Sophocles' *Oedipus Rex* in which Oedipus unwittingly slew his father and married his mother. Freud regarded the play as a dramatic representation of a universal wish. The oedipal wish is sometimes manifested in contemporary life in dreams of the death of the father.

In *Totem and Taboo* (1919) and *Moses and Monotheism* (1939), Freud suggested that religion, and other moral and social institutions, derive from a prehistorical oedipal situation in which the rebellious sons killed the primal father to gain access to his wives. Psychoanalysts today do not necessarily concur in this.

The Oedipus complex was responsible for much of the early opposition to psychoanalysis (q.v.) and is still rejected in its strict Freudian form by many psychologists. Many 'neo-Freudians' have taken exception to the claim for universality and to the exclusively sexual basis posited by Freud. *See* Karen Horney, *The Neurotic Personality of Our Time*, 1937. There is no general agreement as to an acceptable alternative explanation for the actual phenomena Freud documented. A widely held view among dynamically oriented psychologists is that all societies will make use of some mechanisms to assist in the establishment of sexual identity and in the working through of deep ambivalences, but that the Oedipus complex is only one form that such mechanisms may take.

GRAEME M. GRIFFIN

Old Age

Old age, the period before death, during which an average person's physical powers are failing, is becoming more important as medical skill increases. There have, of course, always been a number of old people in every community, and some of these have attained great ages, but before the industrial revolution they were a small element in the population. Among primitive peoples the old were sometimes killed when they became burdensome on the group, but among the Hebrews, in classical times, and in all other communities that we call civilized, the old have been held in respect. The manorial system, serfdom and even slavery were capable of absorbing the old and giving them some security. Agricultural communities were able to offer work at different degrees of intensity and where 'extended' families existed side by side with a low expectation of life the burden of looking after the old could be widely shared.

The freeing of workers from manorial ties and their proletarianization changed the situation. The family tended in time to become the two generational family, work was geared to the timing of larger production units, and the concept of a free market in labour weakened the bargaining position of the frail. With the reduction of mortality rates the period of senescence has increased and brought with it very considerable increases in the number of people of sixty-five and over, who in modern England now constitute 12 per cent of the total population, a figure which it is estimated will increase to 13.7 in 1982.

The old need these things: (1) economic security; (2) varying degrees of personal attention; (3) varying degrees of medical attention; (4) in many cases specialized housing; and (5) companionship. Most countries had, by the beginning of the twentieth century, a system of relief which would provide a minimum income to old people in need. Denmark had established a definite old age pension as early as 1891; England did not produce a pension till 1908. Germany grafted a pension into their social insurance scheme as early as 1889, but slowly as countries developed systems of social insurance the pensions schemes were

embodied in them, thus killing the concept of 'charity' and the stigma of relief. It should, however, be remembered that social insurance schemes for pensions, are not insurance schemes in the commercial sense of the term, for their reserves are never fully funded, and most experts consider it impractical to do so. They are forms of transfer payment, based on taxation.

As old people grow feebler they require more and more aid in the form of personal care. At first very little is needed but it can increase until in extreme cases it may need full time attention from one person, or even hospitalization. This is much more difficult to provide for; it is a burden which quite clearly first falls on the family, and in its extreme form on the community. It is a field in which neighbours can help and in which voluntary organizations can play a great part.

The study of aging, geriatrics, is now a medical specialism and its practitioners can help the aged to make the best use of failing powers. But the old must have ready access to medical aid for they tend to suffer, not only from senescence but from many other ailments too, and may, in fact, be in progressive stages of a fatal disease.

The modern tendency is to keep old people active for as long as possible and many old age pension schemes provide for a considerable increase in the basic pension if people remain at work longer. Many national schemes also aim at keeping old people in the ordinary community for as long as possible and provide social services to aid those who are looking after them. This is called 'community care'. These services include old peoples clubs, restaurants and meals, 'day' hospitals and domiciliary nursing aid. Some schemes – recognizing the enormous strain that old people can impose on relatives for very long periods of time – provide for the hospitalization of old people for short periods in order to give respite to those who care for them.

We can assume that the problem presented by the aging is likely to increase in intensity for though extrapolation of birth statistics is dangerous, being based on an unknown, that is, the number of children parents will have, a similar extrapolation of statistics concerning the old is based on an existing population.

Mary Penelope Hall, *The Social Service of Modern England*, 1952; David Owen, *English Philanthropy, 1660–1960*, 1965; Kathleen M. Slack, *Over Seventy*, 1954; Peter Townsend, *The Family Life of Old People: an Inquiry in East London*, 1961.

BRIAN RODGERS

Old Testament Ethics

The OT contains no ethical system or body of ethical principles. Its ethic is derivative from literary contexts of many different forms and types. It is influenced by the social structures and cultural *milieux* of different times. It emerges out of many historical situations throughout the course of more than a thousand years. One should not, therefore, expect to find any uniformity or homogeneity in its formulations. Biblical ethics is inextricably related to religion. What God wills is right, and it is right because it is God who wills it. Ethics is conformity of human activity to the will of God. To the question, 'What ought I to do?', the answer is 'Obey God'. Already in very early traditions man is summoned to obedience. He is confronted with the demand for decision, and the issue of the decision is fateful (Gen. 2.4b–3.24).

Despite the vast diversity of the traditions, the religion and ethics of the OT rest upon three great historical foundations: (1) the deed of liberation from slavery in the Exodus from Egypt; (2) the commitment of the people in the covenant at Mount Sinai; and (3) the stipulations which determine the nature of the bond between the people and God in the giving of the law. The three events are the best remembered of all the events of Israel's history, and they belong together. When one is isolated from the other, the way is opened to misunderstanding and corruption; the laws, for example, are only to be understood in the context of Exodus and covenant.

The Exodus is the divine initiative in history. It marks the beginning of Israel as a people. In this event Yahweh was demonstrating not only his power to defy the imperial power of Pharaoh, or to effectuate a historical action, but also his purpose for this people. It is constantly interpreted, therefore, as a summons to responsible life in history. More than any other single event, the Exodus determines the nature of Israel's self-awareness and self-consciousness as it reveals the nature of the God who gives a particular history to this people. The reality and the meaning of the event extends throughout the whole of Israel's history from first to last, and it becomes contemporary and alive on each new occasion when the event is celebrated and rehearsed, as is superbly illustrated in the Passover *haggada*. The deed of liberation happened in the thirteenth century BC, but it happens again each time the words are spoken, above all in period of crisis and threat of destruction (Hosea, Jeremiah, Ezekiel). Yahweh is the source of Israel's freedom. Commitment to him liberates her from every historical servitude (e.g., Isa. 40–55) or bondage of the human heart (Psalms). But the Exodus is also understood as the election of Israel. This choice of a people was no act of privilege or favouritism, but rather a call to obedience and service (Amos 3.2). Israel is chosen, not because of any inherent superiority to other peoples or because of any religious or moral

qualifications, but solely because of the unmotivated love of her God (Deut. 4.37; 7.6–8; 9.4–5). The Exodus elicits praise and thanksgiving (Ex. 15.21; Pss. 77.16–20; 78.12–16; 80; 81; 95; 105; 106; 114; etc.) and thus supplies the motivation for obedience (Ex. 20.2; Lev. 11.45; 19.36; 22.33; etc.). Every person who belongs to Israel shares a common historical memory and a common historical destiny. It is not surprising, therefore, that the event should be re-formulated as the new Exodus in eschatological time (Isa. 40–55).

In the covenant at Sinai a relationship is established between a God and a people, a relationship which rescued Israel from the perils of the fear which haunted the minds of other Near Eastern peoples and from an ultimate isolation. The classical formula, 'You shall be my people, and I will be your God', undergirds the whole of the OT. Thus the people is aware that it belongs to God, that it is Yahweh's possession, and that it is accountable to him for its life. The covenant is not to be defined in terms of a natural relation. It demanded decision on the part of Israel. The people must decide for or against this particular God of history, and the choice has no element of coercion in it, but is contingent upon obedience: 'Now, therefore, if you will obey (listen to) my voice and keep my covenant, you shall be my own possession among all peoples . . . and you shall be to me a kingdom of priests and a holy nation (Ex. 19.5). These conditionals continue throughout all the covenant contexts of the OT (Josh. 24.15,16; I Kings 18.21; Deut. 8.11–20; 11.13–15,22–25,26–28; 28.1–6,15–19; Pss. 81; 89.3–37; Jer. 4.12; 7.1–15; etc.). The prophets never weary of placing Israel before the realities of choice and decision, and they do so precisely because at the source of its life decision was required. Israel's commitment to the God of history meant that there was a demand upon her that was transcendent to any and every historical relativity. Neither the State, nor the king, nor the economic order, nor any institution could ever require absolute obedience, for there was always a higher court before which men and nations are judged. The more confusing and perplexing the political or international situation, the clearer is the word sounded by the prophets. The prophet can stand over against the king, as Nathan did before David (II Sam. 12.1–15a), or Elijah before Ahab (I Kings 18.16b; 21.17–25) or Amos before Jeroboam in his words to Amaziah (Amos 7.16–17) or Jeremiah before Zedekiah (Jer. 32.1–5). The covenant is the bond which unites Israel into a single community; in allegiance to this one God, Yahweh, Israel is one people. This is the norm and standard of Israelite ethics. This unity of Israel receives its classical expression in the words of the *Shema* (Deut. 6.4–9). The great keywords of the covenant are *hesed*, steadfast or covenant love; *mishpat*, justice; *rahmim*, mercy or compassion; *emunah*, faithfulness; *da'ath elohim*, knowledge of God, but they are never employed as ethical abstractions. We are always told what the words mean in concrete situations.

A scrutiny of the laws of Israel and of the prophetic interpretations of the divine requirements makes it clear that the relation between Yahweh and Israel is not merely legal. Juristic categories do not exhaust the meaning of the bond. Yahweh does not meet his people with a *do ut des*. He is the protector of the community against all the destructive forces that threaten its life. The ancient legal codes of the Near East are predominantly class legislation, but in Israel already in early times all men are equal (Ex. 20.22–23.33). All the people, with the exception of the slave, live under the same law and are equal before it. But even the slave has his rights as a person. The poor and the weak, the widow and the orphan and the resident alien are Yahweh's special concern, and the Israelite is commanded not to show partiality to anyone because of his prestige or social position. Again and again in the Book of Deuteronomy Israel is reminded that it is a family, and that all who belong to Israel are brothers. Even the resident alien must receive justice. As Yahweh has shown his love for his people by what he has done for them in the course of his history, so Israel must be guided by the imperatives of love in all its dealings with others. The demands of justice are rooted in love, and the whole range of Israel's social life is set forth in detail to make it clear what the requirements of love are in individual stituations. In the Holiness Code (Lev. 17–26) the holiness of God is implemented in the loving relationships of Israel to the members of the community: 'You shall love your neighbour as yourself' (Lev. 19.18). It is noteworthy that many of the laws are expanded by motivations; the people are told *why* they should obey the law and, indeed, why they should wish to obey it (Ex. 23.8; Deut. 5.12–15; 24.6; 25.3,15–16; 30.11–14; etc.), and among these motivations the most prominent is the liberation from slavery. Moreover there are numerous passionate appeals and exhortations to obedience. The Deuteronomists are very confident that man can do what he ought to do (Deut. 30.11–14).

The prophets of Israel address themselves to every area of Israel's communal life. They are the politicians of the covenant who keep reminding the people of the politics of God. Thus Elijah enters into the social and political conflicts of the Omri dynasty, Amos denounces the exploitation of the poor by the rich and exposes the social enormities of the privileged, and Isaiah pronounces the divine judgment upon the whole civilization of his time (Isa. 2.6–19). The prophets recite and elaborate the ancient laws and interpret their contemporary relevance, they castigate their countrymen, both men and women, for their moral delinquencies, they appeal to them to turn to the ancient ways of convenant loyalty and obedience, they identify themselves with the underprivileged and disinherited, they assert the categorical imperatives of 'You shall not' over and over again, and never weary of placing the people before the bar of the divine judgment.

In many ways the Wisdom literature of ancient Israel forms an exception to the foregoing discussion. While the laws have influenced many of the formulations of the wise, nothing is said of the Exodus and the covenant. The sages have been profoundly influenced by the Wisdom literatures of other Near Eastern peoples. But like the prophets and lawgivers they range over the whole of life and society, and like them they are always definite and concrete. They give a clear answer to the question of what goodness means. They are the teachers of Israel, and they instruct Israel in the way it ought to walk. They are the champions of justice and righteousness, and they exhort their disciples to live a life of charity, integrity, prudence and discipline.

JAMES MUILENBURG

Omission, Sins of. *see* Sins of Omission.

Optimism

Optimism is a way of thinking and living which affirms on the one hand the capacity of man to improve himself and the whole human condition, and on the other hand, claims that ultimate reality, being under the control of good rather than evil, supports, if not guarantees, this improvement. There are various degrees of optimism, various grounds on which it is affirmed, and several different philosophical and theological frameworks of which it is an integral part.

An extreme version of optimism is expressed in Browning's phrase, 'God's in his heaven, all's right with the world'. A second extreme version is exemplified in Leibnitz's philosophy that because God is the all good, all wise and all powerful he has created this 'the best of all possible worlds'. Both of these fit with the derivation of the word – *bonus, melior, optimus* – that is, belief that the best is in control. More moderate versions of optimistic philosophy, directly related to belief in progress, are illustrated in the Spenserian evolutionary naturalist and Hegelian Marxist beliefs in the inevitability of progress, and in the Deweyian affirmation that man has and can, by the use of intelligence, that is, applied scientific knowledge, achieve the enrichment of all human life.

The *grounds* for optimism may be said to centre chiefly on judgments about the nature of man, history and ultimate reality. As a philosophy of life it involves sometimes a belief in the basic goodness of man, at other times a more cautious affirmation that man is capable of improvement and of increasingly achieving human well-being and happiness. In both the Roman Catholic and evangelical Protestant theologies there have been surprisingly optimistic estimates concerning man's achievement of goodness, always, it must be noted, as a result of God's guidance and grace. In the former, man's capacity both to perform good works by his own effort and with God's help to achieve saintliness are affirmed; among the latter, one encounters John Wesley's counsel to Christian perfectionism, and the Social Gospel movement, which was certainly optimistic in talking about building the Kingdom of God in the future.

Historical grounds for optimism usually involve teleological assumptions, that is, not merely that history has discernible meaning and purpose, but that it is moving towards a particular end. The Hegelian and Marxist view is of a patterned historical process moving towards a rational and good end. In contrast with dialectical materialism, one Christian version holds that God acts and guides within history in such a way that it is moving towards the Kingdom of God and/or towards an eschatological end.

Optimism has related the above beliefs about man and history to metaphysical assertions. Central among these is the claim expressed by William James as the essence of all religion that 'the eternal is good'. Still more contemporary instances are modern theologians such as Paul Tillich who, in agreement with classical theology, emphasizes that the ontological ground of being is good. Optimism has appeared within such differing and even conflicting frameworks as that of Herbert Spencer's biologically grounded belief in the inevitability of progress, the transcendentalist poets, and the Christian theologies as indicated above. *See also* **Progress, Belief in.**

All varieties of optimism have been criticized and its extreme versions ridiculed on the following grounds: (1) on general grounds of personal experience, namely, that events in the lives of individuals are at best a frightening mixture of good and very real evil, issuing into despair as well as hope; (2) religious, that man's original sin, though it may be forgiven, leaves him always a sinner, capable of incredible cruelty and destructiveness; (3) historical, that is, that the disasters of two World Wars and man's seeming capacity and readiness to threaten total destruction renders the outlook of optimism unwarranted at best, absurd at worst.

Is a Christian necessarily optimistic? Those who say 'yes' usually emphasize St Paul's statement: 'In everything God works for good with those who love him' (Rom. 8.28). Jowett coined the phrase 'apostolic optimism', a view which is temporarily pessimistic, that is, about the actual condition of man, but ultimately optimistic, holding that God is the Lord of history. Finally, Jesus' statement, 'Be of good cheer, I *have overcome* the world' (John 16.33), is often used as a basis for the qualified affirmation that Christ has already won the victory of good over evil and so furnishes the ground for Christian hope and joy.

CHARLES W. KEGLEY

Orders

In his doctrine of the 'two realms' of creation and redemption, Luther reaffirmed the 'sacred secularity' of the ordinary tasks of the common life as those which best meet our neighbours' needs in the service of Christ. He further refined this doctrine with his view of the three 'orders' or 'estates' of society which provide men with divinely-ordained bulwarks against sin in the fallen realm of creation. He wrote (*WA* 26, pp. 504 f.):

> The holy ordinances and foundations instituted by God are these three: the ministry, marriage, and civil authority. . . . Service in them constitutes true holiness and pious living before God. This is because these three ordinances are grounded in God's Word and command (Gen. 1.28), and are thereby sanctified as holy things by God's own holy Word.
>
> Above and beyond these three foundations and ordinances is the general order of Christian love which constrains us even beyond the boundaries of the three ordinances to serve the needs of our neighbours by feeding the hungry, giving drink to the thirsty, forgiving our enemies, praying for all men on earth, suffering all kinds of evil on their behalf, etc. These are good, holy works.

This means for Luther's social ethic that the earthly kingdom in the 'old age' of Adam must be ruled primarily by God's law through human reason. Since most of God's creatures are not numbered among his saints, and because sin persists even in the life of the redeemed, the 'fruits of the Spirit' can play only an auxiliary role in governing the world of temporal affairs. 'Faith working through love' (Gal. 5.6) can nourish a sinful and unjust world only indirectly through the social action of Christians. The Church can never directly 'christianize' the secular 'orders' of politics, economics, education, etc., even though it is essential for loving Christian politicians, economists and educators to hold society and the State accountable to God's sovereign law by making justice as humane as possible.

Luther's dialectical teaching on the relative autonomy of the 'orders' (free from Church-rule yet bound to God-rule) belies those ethical dualists, like the Nazified *Deutsche Christen*, who have tried to give a 'Lutheran' sanction to the 'orders of creation' (*Schöpfungsordnungen*) which would permit the 'orders' (especially the State) to become absolutely autonomous unto themselves (*Eigengesetzlichkeit*).

To stress both sides of these theonomous but historical 'orders' – that they are divinely-ordained but also subject to God's law, dykes against sin but also corrupted by sin themselves – many Protestant theologians now prefer to speak of the Creator's 'orders of preservation' (*Erhaltungsordnungen*) or 'emergency orders' (*Notordnungen*) or even 'mandates of God' (*Mandaten Gottes*).

WILLIAM H. LAZARETH

Organism-Field Theory

The terms 'organism' and 'field-theory', when taken together, denote a certain point of view and a model in personality theory which attempts to place emphasis on both the integrated goal-seeking of the individual and upon his complex exchanges and relationships with the environment. More specifically, the term organism denotes the individual's flexibility in goal-seeking or self-actualization (termed by some theoretical biologists 'equivinality' – as contrasted with the rigidity implied in mechanical models) and the open system character of the human being as a biosocial being engaged in constant chemical and social interaction with the environment, including other persons. *See* **Development**. The term 'field-theory', derived from physics, stresses the inter-relationships and mutually determinative character of the field of forces constituted by both individual and environment, as opposed to a 'billiard ball' model which envisions individual substances existing in space and exerting unilateral or lateral effects upon one another.

This approach is designed to overcome the difficulties posed by mechanical models which envision the individual simply as reacting to the environment, such as those employed by some reductive behaviourists, and by substantive models which envision the individual as either not related to the environment in a fundamental way, or else as basically master of it, as in some forms of personalism.

Earlier theorists who made basic contributions to the development of this point of view include Kurt Goldstein (b. 1878) and Ludwig von Bertalanffy (b. 1901) who pioneered in organismic theory, and Kurt Lewin (1890–1947), who developed the field-theory concept out of early association with *Gestalt* psychology, from which the field-theory emphasis on the determinative character of the whole, as contrasted with parts, was derived. Gardner Murphy is perhaps the leading contemporary exponent. *See* G. Murphy, *Personality: A Biosocial Approach to Origin and Structure*, new edn., 1967. For a psychiatric development of this

theme *see* Karl A. Menninger, et al., *The Vital Balance*, 1964.

The organism-field theory approach offers a basic model of personality to ethics which, while grounded in biological relationships, nevertheless is compatible with an emphasis upon purposiveness. It appears to be adaptable to a wide range of positions, excluding perhaps those which radically disjoin man in his essence from his physical environment.

JAMES N. LAPSLEY

Origen

Origen (*c.* 186–252), exegete, apologist and speculative theologian of the Alexandrian Church was also head of the Catechetical School at Alexandria from the age of eighteen, and taught during the last two decades of his life in Palestinian Caesarea, where he died after a period of imprisonment for his faith. Criticized, revised, repudiated, and often misrepresented by his intellectual heirs, Origen laid the foundation for much of later Greek theology and exegesis, and his teaching established, as it exemplified, the formal principle that Christian wisdom consists in the understanding and interpretation of the inspired text of the OT and NT.

The ethic which Origen's allegorical method of exegesis discovers in Scripture is based upon a Platonistic view of the world and of man. Depreciating, though not condemning, the material frame of human existence, Origen sees man's salvation to consist in the restoration of the rational soul to that contemplative knowledge and enjoyment of God which is its normal state and from which it had fallen prior to the creation of the visible world. This restoration is made possible by the activity of the external Word and Wisdom of God, whose revelatory and saving work culminates in his historical incarnation. Origen sees in Christ at once the victor over the demonic powers which bind man to the life of the present world-order, and the one in and through whom man may come to a spiritual apprehension of the divine reality.

Origen's ethic has at least three basic presuppositions. First (contrary to some Stoic and earlier, more naive Christian conceptions), he assumes that the restoration of man to his destined beatitude is a gradual process, a progressive growth from mere *faith* to spiritual *knowledge*. Second, he sees this growth as conditioned at every point upon the saving action of the divine Word, who not only frees man for growth, but is himself man's Teacher, the one in whom the soul comes to know God. Finally, against the gnostics, Origen insists that this salvation is open to all. Its achievement depends not upon innate endowments or dispositions, but the free exercise of the soul's capacity for self-determination.

The initial stage and constant presupposition of the soul's restoration is its ethical purification: the continuing process by which the soul frees itself from the passions which enslave it to the visible world, cultivates the moral virtues, and thus fits itself for the contemplative life in which its moral purity is perfected. Restored in this way to itself, the soul is awakened to the transience and relative un-reality of the material order and its values, and in this awareness begins to grasp and to love the higher reality of the intelligible order. From there it progresses – and the principal means of this progress is for Origen the study of Scrip-ture in its spiritual meaning – to knowledge of the mysteries of the divine Wisdom, until it is united in knowledge and love with the Word himself. Origen's ethic is thus essentially an ascetic doctrine, which provides the basis, though not the full substance, of later Greek-Christian mystical teaching, and much of the theological basis of later monasticism.

R. A. NORRIS, JR

Original Sin

Biblical authority for this doctrine has been found in Ps. 51.5 and Rom. 5.12 ff. The latter passage states a causal connection between Adam's sin and our sin and this connection was defined more closely and linked with the sexual act by Augustine. His argument goes as follows: The Church is baptizing infants. Baptism cleanses from sin. Infants have not sinned themselves (Rom. 9.11). Therefore they must have inherited sin. They do this because conceived in the act of sexual intercourse. 'That alone was not sinful flesh which was not born of such concubinage' (*On Marriage and Con-cupiscence*, I, 13). What Augustine professes to find wrong in sexual intercourse is that in it the sexual organs are not under the direct control of the will (the same is true of the secretion of the gastric juices when eating). Augustine finds this a consequence of the Fall. Because Adam rebelled against God, his body rebelled against him. That is at any rate true of his sexual organs. It is because they are not like, for example, the arm, in direct control of the will that man finds shame in connection with them. This rebellion is transmitted through the act of sexual intercourse and as a result unbaptized infants are excluded from heaven (presumably a test tube baby would not be). Calvin refused to accept Augustine's exclusion of unbaptized infants from heaven. But the latter's influence on the doctrine of original sin remains as one main, and by no means academic, problem for the Church. The Church today is to distinguish between the good and the not so good in Augustine's teaching. Over against his clear view of the universality of sin and the need for divine grace must be set his unbalanced view of sex. It must at least be considered whether any sound Christian view of marriage can be framed today without some break with Augustine.

It would, however, be unfortunate if the idiosyncrasies of Augustine's view of sex or the lack of historicity of Gen. 3 were to blind men to the importance and necessity of the Christian doctrine of original sin. It is an attempt to provide a solution to the problem that sin (q.v.) though universal is not necessary. Even more important, it expresses the conviction that evil is something which cannot be eradi-cated from human life by social and political measures, valuable though these may be. The evil in life is something like the dent in a burst ball, something which can be got rid of in one place only to reappear in another.

IAN HENDERSON

Orphans

Orphans are children who have lost or have been deserted by *both* parents. The Bible mentions full orphans only once, the fatherless a great deal and the motherless not at all. From this one can assume that the Hebrews were able to absorb orphans and motherless children into the extended family system, but that the lot of the fatherless child was tied up with that of the widow.

The numbers of true orphans have always been small and within extended families pro-vision for them was comparatively easily made. The mediaeval Church took a considerable responsibility for the care of orphans and as early as the sixth century the diocese of Trèves accepted all children placed in the church porch. The Council of Nicea (787 A D) extended the practice and the first true Foundlings Home was started in Milan in the same year. Most countries have since then set up a variety of hostels of different kinds for the care of parentless children. In England the Foundling Hospital started by Captain Coram in 1739, was the first of the large institutions. It must be remembered of course that the development of systems of public assistance in most countries gave such authorities responsibility for orphans, and in England the Elizabethan Act setting up the Poor Law made specific mention of orphans and charged those responsible for the Poor Law with their especial care. Though this responsibility was not always exercised as humanely as one would have liked it is arguable that since 1601 more orphan children in England have been cared for by public authorities than by private charity. In the mid-nineteenth century Dr Barnardo, who was distressed by the large number of homeless children in London, started a Home of Refuge in 1867, financing it from voluntary funds. This started a great national movement for the provision of homes for children; the Nonconformist 'National Children's Homes' in 1869 and the Church of England 'Waifs and Strays Society' (now the Church of England Children's Society) in 1881. In the USA the Infants Hospital was started in New York in 1868, the Sisters of Charity

Foundling Asylum in 1869 and the Infant Asylum in 1871. In spite of the fact that under the Children Act of 1948 the basic responsibility for the provision of Children's Homes in England (unlike the USA) is now a local authority function, a very large number of children are now being cared for by voluntary societies. In the past, large numbers of children in the care of the big English Children's Societies were sent to Canada, Australia and New Zealand as emigrants, when they grew up.

The ideal solution to the sad problem of the orphan is, of course, adoption (q.v.). This was made possible in England by an Act of 1926. Adoption is not, however, suitable for all children and must be rigorously controlled if exploitation is to be avoided. Public provision for orphans now include children's homes, preferably very small homes which are like ordinary houses in ordinary districts, and the boarding out of children with recognized foster parents. *See* **Children**.

Mary Penelope Hall, *The Social Services of Modern England*, 1952; Jean S. Heywood, *Children in Care*, 1959; Mary Hopkirk, *Nobody Wanted Sam*, 1949; David Owen, *English Philanthropy, 1660–1960*, 1965.

BRIAN RODGERS

Orthodox Church, Ethics of the Eastern

1. *Introduction.* An essay on the modern view of the ethics of the Eastern Orthodox Church must start with the statement that no other Christian group has been so deeply affected by the contemporary world as has been the case with the Eastern Orthodox Church. The contemporary social revolution has nowhere left its imprint of violent change as markedly as it has among the peoples who belong to the Orthodox Church. This is due to the fact that this revolution has been captured, motivated and fully exploited by the communists, under whom the majority of Orthodox now live.

Contemporary Eastern Orthodox ethical concerns are directed chiefly to the problems of the modern world which are raised by Communism, especially those where the atheistic world-view of Communism has the greatest destructive consequences. The most important of these is in the sphere of human personality, for Communism completely disregards man as a person, that is, a self-motivating agent seeking through his free creativeness to realize himself as a being whose inherent value and justification for his existence lie within himself. Communism conceives man exclusively as an instrument of an ideology engaged in the creation of a social system for whose sake alone man exists.

2. *Orthodox Ethics of Personalism.* For Orthodox Christianity, to be a man means to know oneself as a being deeply inter-related to other human beings and to the world around him. This inter-relationship implies a responsibility which is primarily neither social nor psychological, although these elements are very much present. Rather, it is spiritual and religious in character, for its depths are transcendent, their source being God. To an Orthodox Christian the human and cosmic world are deeply theocentric, for they proceed from God and are understood only when approached with the spiritual response of love. Because of this, it is a world whose nature is communal and which demands from man the response of communion as a basic attitude to life. It is a supremely personalistic world, for in it each one is known as a being for the other and both for God. It is a world of deep engagement, participation and commitment. The meaning of the inner tension and struggle arising in it is the search for mutual fulfilment and reconciliation in God, in whom and for whom all being exists and he for it. This is the only principle from which Orthodox ethics can be rightly approached. In it extremes of individualism, collectivism and cosmism are excluded. Rather, it is personalism, a mutual and sacrificial response of each for all and all for each particular being. This principle has been described by the Russian word *sobornost*, catholicity, all-togetherness.

Ernst Benz sees in this principle a safeguard from that bane of all ethics, an overemphasis of polarities. Thus he wrote:

> The Orthodox doctrine of *sobornost* achieves a nice balance. It avoids the West's occasional overemphasis on the claim of individuality which may end by alienating the person from the mystical body of Christ. On the other hand, it also avoids an overvaluation of a collective that kills all individuality, such as has emerged from the Bolshevik social doctrine.

For the creation of the personalistic world the Orthodox ethics calls for the response to the other by three elements of man's spirituality, *agape, creative suffering* and *kenosis.* All these elements derive from the NT and are totally christocentric in character. They all point to the fact that the natural world is resistent and very often hostile to its theocentric origin and is alienated from it. This calls for a creative redemptive effort on the part of a Christian to restore the world to God and to overcome its alienation from him. The idea of *agape* or love in the Christian sense of the word, as a task of personalistic ethics, has been superbly stated by Dostoyevsky, chiefly in his novel, *The Brothers Karamazov*. Dostoyevsky's exponent of this doctrine is an Orthodox *staretz*, a saintly monk, Zosima, through whom Dostoyevsky expounds the Orthodox concept of *agape*. Its dictum is 'love men even in their sins, for that is a symbol of divine love, and the highest love on earth'.

The idea of *creative suffering* was briefly but profoundly stated by Julia de Beausobre in her little book, *Creative Suffering*, which expounds the Orthodox teaching, which she illustrated by her own experience as a victim of Communist persecution. She describes how the spirit of man, illumined by the grace of God, refuses to separate itself from other men, even under the extreme suffering inflicted by the other, even when he is not only a torturer but also a professed enemy of God. Rather, it seeks his redemption by taking upon itself the suffering for the other and thus maintaining communion with him.

The idea of *kenosis* as the love which seeks the other at the depth of alienation of the other, inspired by the Pauline teaching of Phil. 2.7 and profoundly experienced by Eastern Christianity as the form of personalistic ethics, has been meaningfully described in some of its aspects in the book *The Humiliated Christ in Modern Russian Thought* by Nadejda Gorodetzky. The nature of *kenosis* has been developed by many Orthodox, especially the Russian Orthodox, religious thinkers. One of these is M. M. Tareev, whose view Gorodetzky summarizes thus:

> A Christian through Christ is in the centre of creation. God works through him and he himself if he truly follows the Master sees his vocation in his disposition to be sacrificed for all.

3. *Eastern Orthodox Ethics and the Problem of the State.* The problem of the State is one with which Eastern Orthodox Christianity is deeply concerned. This springs from the community-orientated outlook of Eastern Orthodox Christianity. The manifold needs of the community cannot be taken care of by the Church, for her apostolic mission is first and foremost to mediate to men the message of the Kingdom of God. This is her primary concern. But as men live in the world and depend so much on it for their economic, social and educational needs and for other forms of welfare, the State is necessary to men and the Orthodox Church looks upon it as a sort of divinely ordained diaconate. From the time of Constantine to our own day, Eastern Orthodox Christianity has tried to foster this positive attitude to the State and to respect and safeguard its religious character as a diaconate. In her concern not to destroy the character of the State as a diaconate, the Eastern Orthodox Church has gone so far as to speak about the apostolate of the Church and the diaconate of the State as mutually interdependent partners. The classical doctrine in regard to the State-Church relationship developed by the Eastern Orthodox Church is known as symphony – or harmony – the harmony of each assisting the other in its respective task. Needless to say, this principle has been more often an ideal than a reality, and the State has tried to exercise the more dominant role in this relationship and has finally, in the Communist state, exemplified by the Soviet Union, subjected the Church to complete dependence and subservience and, it hopes, to eventual extinction.

Modern Eastern Orthodox ethics is deeply exercised by this principle of the demonic image of the State as the Absolute Power without any regard to its nature as the divinely ordained diaconate. The reaction to this image of the State has varied from the call to resistance and excommunication of the Communists, as was the case of the Russian Patriarch Tikhon in 1917, to an attitude of willing suffering of the State's absolutism and oppression. However, it would be a mistake to think that this acceptance of the absolutist power of the State and the atheistic ideology which underlies it is acquiescence in and spiritual surrender to it. The Eastern Orthodox Church deeply believes in the promise of Christ that the Church is so established that the gates of hell cannot prevail against it and because of its deep commitment to this belief it is not ontologically threatened by the State and its hostility. Rather, faithful to the personalistic principle of its ethics, it tries to convert the State to its character as a diaconate, rather than to destroy it. There are many who deem the Eastern Orthodox Church too idealistic in regard to this possibility, but this idea is deeply entrenched in the Eastern Orthodox consciousness and it dominates the approach of the Orthodox Church to the State.

The novel thing in the modern Eastern Orthodox approach to the problem of the State is that it has ceased to look upon any particular form of government as the one to which the Church should be committed. The Eastern Orthodox believe that any form of government could receive the charisma of the diaconate, so far as the Church is concerned, provided the State divest itself of the myth of itself as an absolute idea bearing absolute power. This is a new development in Eastern Orthodox ethics of the State. The Orthodox Church has been associated traditionally with monarchy and has believed it to be the most suitable form by which the relationship of the Church and the State as a symphony could be maintained and the idea of the State as a diaconate perpetuated. The reason for this change is that, due to its long experience, the Eastern Orthodox Church has come to know that 'demonic elements' may be present in any form of government, traditional monarchy included, and the idea of the divine diaconate could be manifested in any State where the idea of God as the final reality to which all 'principalities and powers' are subject is known and accepted.

4. *Social Action and Orthodox Ethics*. One of the yardsticks by which we measure any particular religious ethics is what it has to say on the problems of man's social life, both in theory and in practice. Judged by its theoretical aspect, Eastern Orthodox ethics falls short of the achievement of some other Christian groups in this field. This has led many to assert that the Eastern Orthodox Church is other-worldly and insensitive to the plight of man's social life. The Orthodox, on the other hand, answer that social problems need a sensitivity and spontaneity of response and must be met practically rather than theoretically. O. Fielding Clarke in his book, *For Christ's Sake* (2nd edn., 1963), tells how a group of young English Christians discussed the problems of social witness with a group of Russian Orthodox Christians. When they were asked about their attitude to social problems, the Orthodox were puzzled as to what was meant by the question. When they finally understood it, they replied: 'Oh, we simply get on with the job.' Anyone who has witnessed the tremendous activity of the Eastern Orthodox Church among refugees since the Russian revolution, through the last War and to this day, would realize that her care is that of a mother who bears all the afflictions of her children and who has a deep concern for all the problems which those in her pastoral care face. Ernst Benz and others have written in glowing terms of the Apostoliki Diakonia of the Orthodox Church in Greece, stating that 'The social activities of the Greek Church are probably the strongest historical evidence to counter the vague charges of Orthodox failures in the realm of social ethics.'

Orthodox social consciousness is too deeply permeated by the spirit of St Basil the Great not to care for man in his social distress. Nevertheless, insufficiency of theoretical consideration of social problems is a great handicap to the Orthodox ethics in dealing successfully with them.

5. *General Aspects of Orthodox Ethics*. Scholars of Orthodox Christianity generally agree that the subject of Orthodox ethics needs far more research. The existing literature on it is fragmentary and scattered.

One of the main characteristics of the Orthodox ethics which Orthodox and other writers point out is a certain world detachment. Various explanations are given for this. Nicholas Zernov ascribes it to the fact that the ancient pessimism of the Greco-Roman world crept into Eastern Orthodox Christianity and influenced it. Others, the present writer included, think that this detachment is the legacy of the ancient Church, in which the world was viewed eschatologically. Whichever of these may be true, they account for a very serious attitude of the Orthodox to the world. This in turn explains what S. Bulgakov calls the 'maximalist inflexibility' of Orthodox ethics.

Some writers see a weakness in the Orthodox ethics in the fact that in it the heart rather than the will is stressed. On the other hand, it is denied by others that this is a negative characteristic, for this kind of ethics penetrates the world and heals it from within, rather than acting externally and in a disciplinarian manner.

Finally, Eastern Orthodox ethics is exclusively based on the biblical revelation and knows of no concept of natural law. This gives to Orthodox ethics the inspirational character epitomized by the Ten Commandments and the Beatitudes. In this lies its religious dynamism, but also its weakness because it is not conducive to being expressed in the form of a scholastic system. But then, this ethic is not a philosophical system, but a religious concern for the world.

Julia de Beausobre, *Creative Suffering*, 1940; Ernst Benz, *The Orthodox Church*, 1963; Sergius Bulgakov, *The Orthodox Church*, 1935; William C. Fletcher, *A Study in Survival: the Church in Russia, 1927–1943*, 1965; Nadejda Gorodetzky, *The Humiliated Christ in Modern Russian Thought*, 1938; Ruth Korper, *The Candlelight Kingdom*, 1955; John Meyendorff, *The Orthodox Church*, 1962; A. J. Philippou, ed., *The Orthodox Ethos*, 1964; Alexander Schmemann, *The Historical Road of Eastern Orthodoxy*, 1963; K. Timothy Ware, *The Orthodox Church*, 1963; Stefan Zankov, *The Eastern Orthodox Church*, 1929; Nicolas Zernov, *Eastern Christendom: The Church of the Eastern Christians*, 1961.

CHARLES B. ASHANIN

Other-Worldiness

While the Christian life contains an element of world-renunciation, this is a dialectical element that must be held along with world-affirmation. Nowadays the expression 'other-worldiness' is generally used in a somewhat pejorative sense for an undialectical withdrawal from the world and an excessive preoccupation with the world to come. *See* **Eschatology; Secularism; Worldiness.**

Pacem in Terris. *see* Pontifical Social Encyclicals.

Pacifism. *see* Peace and War.

Paederasty

Strictly, this term denotes homosexualism between a man and a boy (from the Greek *paiderastes*, a boy-lover), but it is loosely used as synonymous with sodomy (q.v.). A propensity to paederasty does not imply that the subject is homosexual; it may be evidence of some quite different form of personality disorder. *See* **Homosexuality and Homosexualism.**

SHERWIN BAILEY

Pain. *see* Suffering.

Pardon. *see* Absolution; Forgiveness.

Parenthood. *see* Family; Procreation.

Patriotism

In general usage this term is often used synonymously with 'nationalism'. 'Patriotism' may, however, be used to refer to the individual's attitude of love and loyalty directed towards his own country. 'Nationalism' may then be used to connote the spirit of citizens as a group shaping policy which is directed also towards other nations.

From the standpoint of Christian ethics one's own group does exercise a claim. Every man should demonstrate loyalty to fellow workers, family members, or other members of his church. No one should neglect proper devotion to the legitimate interests of his country. Each Christian has a mission in his situation. He is called to express high regard for those near at hand as well as for those at a distance. Cooperative effort is impossible unless individual members can be counted on by the group. Fellowship involves reciprocal service.

Conscientious disobedience may on occasion be consistent with patriotism. It may be in the best interests of one's country that seriously detrimental policies be not supported. Facing a demand for compliance in evil, the citizen must weigh the injustice of conformity against the perils of social disorder involved in disobedience. On matters of major importance 'my country, right or wrong' remains true in the sense of uninterrupted love, but not in the sense of participation in pernicious policies.

For the Christian, patriotism is always to be defined in terms of a hierarchy of loyalties. His first allegiance is always to God alone. Among human groupings loyalty to the national state is to be tempered by consideration for other nationalities. The thoughtful man is loyal to his class and to his college, but even more to the whole community of learning.

So also the spot on which a man lives is located in a nation. Simultaneously it is located in a smaller unit like a neighbourhood or town, and in a larger grouping like a hemisphere or the world. The emotional connotations of 'homeland' might also be associated with 'village' or with 'world'. The claims of these various groupings may normally not conflict. Whenever they do, the Christian faith stresses the inclusive nature of *agape* and finds a more ultimate concern in a more comprehensive devotion. Loyalty to nation is to be regarded as good, so long as it is consistent with and subordinate to God's calling to love every man on earth. *See* **Internationalism; Nationalism.**

HARVEY SEIFERT

Patristic Ethics

For Christian Ethics, the Patristic era – roughly the period from the beginning of the second to the middle of the fifth century – is a time of change and development. During this era, the pattern of the Church's relation to the world around it underwent critical and far-reaching alterations. The effective establishment of Christianity in the Roman Empire after the conversion of Constantine (312) not only marks a radical change in the Church's relation to the power-structure of the imperial society, but also records the success with which Christian teaching had become acclimatized to the thought-forms of hellenistic-Roman culture: and both of these developments are important for the growth of the Church's moral ideal.

Such early documents as *I Clement, The Epistle of Barnabas, The Didache* and *The Shepherd of Hermas* formulate an ethic which is, in content and manner, reminiscent of the ethical catechesis of the NT. Whether descriptively or prescriptively, these documents portray in fairly concrete terms the form of the new life which the Christian is meant to lead – a life which rejects the vicious excesses of the pagan world, and which is marked by love, patience, chastity and simplicity. Except perhaps by the sort of implication which it is dangerous to draw, these documents exhibit no ethical theory. Rather, they depict in quasi-legal and no doubt idealized terms the way of life of a community which had rejected the hopes and standards of the Roman world and chosen to live by standards consistent with its hope in the coming Kingdom of God. They are informed therefore by an attitude of moral hostility to Roman society, as well as by a spirit of perfectionism and even rigorism.

In the West, at least until the time of Ambrose and Augustine, this early moral tradition was interpreted primarily in a moralistic and legal way which owed not a little to Roman and Roman-Stoic influences. Especially under the guidance of Tertullian, the Christian way was understood as a *law*, an historically revealed and transmitted way of salvation which comprised canons of belief as well as of action. Conformity to this law was the means by which the baptized recipient of divine grace made satisfaction for his sin and gained merit in the eyes of the divine Lawgiver and Judge. At the same time such conformity was the essential mark of the Church as an historically identifiable community with an historical mission. Both the Church and the individual were thus called to exhibit a strict holiness of life which consisted in separation from the world through self-denying obedience to the will of God – the reward for which was salvation in the day of judgment.

Not unnaturally, this understanding of the Christian life tended towards legalism, and it inevitably raised in an acute form the question what to make of groups or individuals within the Church who seemed to fall away from the minimal standards of the ethical tradition. It was this question which stimulated, or provided occasion for, the rigorist schisms which beset the Western Church from the time of Tertullian and Pope Calixtus; just as it was this question which compelled the Western Church to concentrate attention on the doctrine of forgiveness, and to work out that theology of baptism and penance whose stable outlines become finally clear in the writings of Gregory the Great.

In the East the course of development was somewhat different. From the time of Clement of Alexandria and Origen, Christian thinkers (with the notable exception of at least some representatives of the Antiochene School) tended to interpret the primitive ethical catachesis of the Church in terms of an outlook which was not so much legal and moralistic as it was mystical and ascetic. The end of the Christian life was explicitly taken to be the knowledge or vision of God, achieved by a process of purification and illumination by which the soul was re-formed after the divine image. The traditional prescriptions of the Christian ethic therefore tended to be understood not merely as the way of life appropriate to the man reborn in Christ, but also as a definition of the path to be followed in the soul's pilgrimage from absorption in the finite, visible world to absorption in the knowledge and love of God. This ascetic ethic was concretely embodied in the ideal of monasticism, whose high valuation of poverty and virginity expressed the prevalent sense of the inconsistency between love for God and involvement in the distractions and passions of ordinary worldly life. The Neoplatonism which in part shaped this interpretation of Christian life was embodied in the Western Church's ethic by the work of Ambrose and Augustine as well as by the westward spread of monasticism, and in this way became a part of the common heritage of the Christian community.

Throughout the era of the Fathers, in the Eastern and Western Churches alike, it was understood that Christian vocation involved a rejection of the world and its ways. This attitude implied not only the separateness of the Christian community from the society in which it was set, but also a negative judgment on the individual, social and political aims of the Roman imperial world. The virtual establishment of Christianity after Constantine, which made of the Church an accepted part of the structure of Roman society, therefore created serious practical and theoretical problems, as the Church itself became worldly and certain Christian thinkers (e.g., Eusebius of Caesarea) sought to baptize the social and political ideals of the Constantinian Empire. One answer to this problem was the asceticism which in the East and West alike came to be identified with the Christian way at its highest, and which sought to recapture the essential separateness of the Church from the world. Another form of answer is provided by the Ambrosian-Augustinian analysis of the relation of the Church to natural and sinful human society. Both of these answers retained as an element in their solution the traditional Christian pessimism about the character and potentialities of the secular order; the latter, however, envisaged a relative transformation of the structures of a formally Christian society.

E. V. Arnold, *Roman Stoicism*, 1958; C. J. Cadoux, *The Early Church and the World*, 1955; H. Chadwick, *The Sentences of Sextus*, 1959; J. Daniélou, *Platonisme et Théologie Mystique*, 1944; T. C. Hall, *History of Ethics within Organised Christianity*, 1910; A. von Harnack, *The Mission and Expansion of Christianity*, 2 vols., 1904–5; J. N. D. Kelly, *Early Christian Doctrines*, 1958; K. E. Kirk, *The Vision of God*, 1950; W. Telfer, *The Forgiveness of Sins*, 1960; E. Troeltsch, *The Social Teaching of the Christian Churches*, I, 1931.

R. A. NORRIS, JR

Paul, Ethical Teaching of St

1. *Sources.* Of the thirteen NT letters that purport to have been written by Paul the three Pastorals (I, II Tim., Titus) are widely regarded as deutero-Pauline and will be considered in a final section. Eph., Col. and II Thess. have also had their authenticity questioned by numerous critics and will be named when used as sources for Paul's ethics.

2. *Background.* At least three elements may be distinguished in Paul's background. He was a Jew and, according to his own claim, 'as to the law a Pharisee' (Phil. 3.5). This is reflected in his identification of theology and ethics, in his respect for the Mosaic Law (despite his rejection of it as a means of salvation), and in details of his ethical thought, for example, his attitude towards sexual morality, or his views on litigation between Christians (I Cor. 5–6). Presumably Paul's hellenistic contacts began in his home town of Tarsus (Acts 22.3; cf. 9.30; Gal. 1.21). Probably he had no formal education in this tradition, but the street preachers and the common talk of an intellectual centre such as Tarsus must have provided him with concepts foreign to his Jewish world. This background may explain his use of something resembling 'natural revelation' and 'natural law' in Rom. 1–2, or his adoption of

the term 'conscience' (Rom. 2.15; 9.1; 13.5; etc.). Yet it must be remembered that hellenistic Judaism, in all its forms, represented an amalgam of these two traditions, and it cannot be assumed that Paul must always have borrowed directly either from Palestinian Judaism or Hellenism. The third element in Paul's background was the Christian tradition, that is, the stories about Jesus, the life of the early Church, and his own Christian experience. It has been argued with increasing cogency that in the Christian community there was an established ethical or parenetic tradition which is reflected indpendently in Paul's letters, I Peter, James and Hebrews (Hunter, Carrington, Selwyn). Thus some of his parenetic material may not have been aimed at the special needs of his readers but may, instead, have expressed general, Christian, ethical teaching.

3. *Theological Framework*. It was central to Paul's thought that ethical behaviour is a consequence rather than the cause of a right relationship with God (Rom. 3–6; Gal. 2–3). This perspective is reflected in the pattern which dominated a number of his letters, namely, first a theological section and then parenesis (*see* the ethical sections in Rom. 12–15; Gal. 5–6; Eph. 4–6; Col. 3–4; less clearly I Thess. 4–5; II Thess. 3). While this pattern may have been part of the style of the hellenistic-Jewish homily it was peculiarly suited to Paul's theology. Yet it must be stressed that ethical behaviour, while second in the Pauline pattern, was not secondary. The way of faith was not intended to 'overthrow the law' but rather it was the true way to 'uphold the law' (Rom. 3.31). As much as the most orthodox Jew he insisted that each person will be required to give an account for his deeds (Rom. 2.6; 14.10–12; II Cor. 5.10; Gal. 6.5,7; Eph. 6.8; Col. 3.25); the purpose of God for believers is their sanctification (I Thess. 4.3; cf. II Cor. 7.1; Eph. 5.25–27; II Thess. 2.13) and immorality bars one from the kingdom (I Cor. 6.9 f.; Gal. 5.19–21; Eph. 5.3–6; Col. 3.5 f.; I Thess. 2.12); Paul continues to discipline himself lest, despite his faith, he should be disqualified (I Cor. 9.27); the suggestion that believers are free to 'continue in sin' fills Paul with horror (Rom. 6–7); Christians are saved not 'because of works' but nevertheless 'for good works, which God prepared beforehand, that we should walk in them' (Eph. 2.8–10).

4. *General Norms*. Since Paul was not a systematic theologian there is no single way in which he describes the norm or pattern by which the Christian life is to be lived. It is to be lived according to the will of God, or well pleasing to God (Rom. 12.1 f.; 14.17 f.; Eph. 4.24; 5.10,17; 6.6; Col. 1.10; 4.12; I Thess. 2.12; 4.1–3); it consists of walking in the Spirit or in obedience to the Spirit (Rom. 8.1–14;

I Cor. 3.1 ff.; Gal. 5.16–26; 6.7 f.; Eph. 4.30); Paul exhorts his readers to imitate him (I Cor. 4.16; Phil. 3.17; I Thess. 1.6; II Thess. 3.7–9), but this presumably means 'Be imitators of me, as I am of Christ' (I Cor. 11.1); the Christian life means to live 'in Christ', or in conformity with his way (Rom. 6.1–14; 13.14; I Cor. 11.1; II Cor. 10.1–6; Gal. 2.20 f.; 3.27; 6.2; Eph. 2.4–10; Phil. 1.10 f.; Col. 2.6); it demands behaviour which edifies and assists the community of believers (Rom. 14.13 ff.; 15.1 ff.; I Cor. 8.1 ff.; 10.25 ff.; 14.3 ff.; 14.12, 17,26; II Cor. 13.10; Gal. 5.13; 6.2; Eph. 4.25; Phil. 2.4; Col. 3.12 f.); finally, paralleling the teaching of Jesus, Paul declares 'love' to be the norm for Christian conduct and he understands this to be the fulfilling of the law (Rom. 13.8–10; 14.15; I Cor. 13; 16.14; Gal. 5.6; 13–15; Eph. 4.15 f.; 5.2; Col. 3.14; cf. I Cor. 8.1; 9.19; II Cor. 8.24; Phil. 2.1 f.; I Thess. 3.12; 4.9 f.).

5. *Specific Applications and Details*. Stated in general terms these norms are too abstract to give a clear picture of the Christian ethical life, except perhaps in the case of the 'love' norm. These norms, however, were given content and concreteness by the contexts in which they were set, by accompanying statements, or by lists of vices and virtues. Thus I Thess. 4.1 ff. defines being pleasing to God as including the abstaining from immorality, while in Col. 3.20 it is indicated that the obedience of children to parents is pleasing to the Lord (Christ?). In Gal. 5.16–26 walking 'by the Spirit' is explained as involving 'love, joy, peace, patience, kindness, goodness, faithfulness, gentleness, self-control' and as the opposite of 'immorality, impurity, licentiousness, idolatry, sorcery, enmity, strife, jealousy, anger, selfishness, dissension, party spirit, envy, drunkenness, carousing, and the like'. (For other lists *see* Phil. 4.8; Col. 3.12–15; Rom. 1.29–31; I Cor. 5.11; 6.9 f.; II Cor. 12.20; Eph. 4.31 f.; 5.3 f.; Col. 3.5–8.) *See also* **Household Codes.** In Phil. 2.5 ff. the example of Christ is used to support the demand for humility and service. The genius of Paul lay in his ability to see beyond the details of a petty squabble to the ultimate issues of God, Christ, the Spirit, the good of the community and the commands of love. This is especially clear in his handling of the problems considered in I Cor., his only predominantly pastoral letter (*see* on church divisions, I Cor. 1–4; food taboos, I Cor. 8–10; differences over spiritual gifts, I Cor. 12–14).

With respect to social institutions such as marriage and the family, slavery, or the State, Paul took an essentially conventional or perhaps conservative attitude, although he attempted to lift the obligations involved up into the religious sphere. He displayed little interest in the reform of the outward structures of these institutions. This may have been due to his instinctive conservatism, to his eschatological expectations (cf. on marriage in I Cor. 7.29–31, 'the form of this world is passing away'), or to his conviction that institutions should be transformed from the inside. Thus he accepted the traditional subordination of women to men (I Cor. 11.2–16) but digressed to affirm their mutual interdependence 'in the Lord' (I Cor. 11.11 f.). Similarly he took slavery for granted (Philemon; I Cor. 7.20–23; Col. 3.22–4.1; Eph. 6.5–9) but affirmed that this legal relationship was transcended in the Christian community so that Onesimus, though still presumably a slave, was also 'more than a slave', yes, 'a beloved brother' (Philemon 16; cf. Eph. 6.9). Despite the aberrations of Caligula (37–41 AD) Paul took a positive attitude towards the Roman State and advocated respect for duly constituted authority 'for the sake of conscience' (Rom. 13.1–7). Probably he retained this view in spite of the Neronian excesses, but certainly in any conflict of interest he would have shared the apostolic view, 'We must obey God rather than men' (Acts 5.29).

Though gifted with the ability to examine local problems in the light of the gospel he could not always escape the limits of his cultural conditioning. This appears in his argument that women should keep their heads covered when worshipping (I Cor. 11.2–16) and that they should not take an active part in church services (I Cor. 14.33b–36). Some, particularly Protestants, would add to this list his rather negative attitude towards marriage (I Cor. 7). Yet it must be remembered that in all these instances he was legislating for a specific situation and he might have been the first to agree that different situations called for different regulations. His great achievement was the relating of the command to love to the immensely confusing problems of the emerging, religious community. He had little to say about ethics for the outside world 'For what have I to do with judging outsiders? . . . God judges those outside' (I Cor. 5.12 f.).

Questions: 'How can we who died to sin still live in it?' Paul never clearly answered this question but, recognizing that new converts sometimes lived old lives, he turned immediately to imperatives and exhortations (Rom. 6–7). *Again:* it is understandable that when Paul found Christians living unworthily he brought the law back as a guide desiring 'that the just requirement of the law might be fulfilled in us' (Rom. 8.4). But it is striking that the law which Paul brought back was not the entire Mosaic Law, including its ceremonial regulations, but only its ethical aspect. It is curious that he did not feel obliged to discuss the difference between the status assigned to the ceremonial and that given to the ethical aspect of the Law. *Third:* how is this ethic to be applied by one who is not only a member of the Christian community but also a responsible citizen of a larger society which has more permanence than Paul expected? It may not be enough to live 'Christianly' within the inherited structures; these themselves may need to be changed. But how much change is feasible and how is it best brought about?

6. *The Pastorals.* It is a mistake to denigrate the Pastorals as 'mere manuals of bourgeois piety and static orthodoxy' but the contrast with the other letters ascribed to Paul remains clear. In the other letters one observes the emergence of a new religious community; in the Pastorals the community has 'arrived' and is concerned to maintain its conformity with the inherited tradition and its respectability before the surrounding non-Christian culture. The considerable ethical material reads like Household Codes which have been expanded to include bishops (I Tim. 3.1 ff.; Titus 1.7 ff.), deacons (I Tim. 3.8 ff.), deaconnesses (? I Tim. 3.11), widows (I Tim. 5.3 ff.) and elders (I Tim. 5.17 ff.; Titus 1.5 f.) as well as slaves (I Tim. 6.1 ff.; Titus 2.9 f.), older men and women (Titus 2.1 ff.), younger men (Titus 2.6 ff.) and Christian men and women generally (I Tim. 2.1–15). The characteristic note is struck in I Tim. 2.1 f. which urges that homage be paid to the authorities 'that we may lead a quiet and peaceable life, godly and respectful in every way'. Yet the command to love is still sounded strongly (I Tim. 1.5; 4.12; 6.11; II Tim. 1.7; 2.22; Titus 2.2); and the reader has the impression of small conventicles of Christians living humbly and industriously in the larger world, bound together by a genuine concern for one another and for those of their number in distress.

In addition to the relevant volumes listed under **Jesus, Ethical Teachings of** and **Household Codes** see the commentaries and general studies on Paul. *See also* M. E. Andrews, *The Ethical Teaching of Paul*, 1934; W. A. Beardslee, *Human Achievement and Divine Vocation in the Message of Paul*, 1961; P. Carrington, *A Primitive Christian Catechism*, 1940; O. Cullmann, *The State in the New Testament*, 1956; W. D. Davies, *Paul and Rabbinic Judaism*, rev. edn., 1955; M. S. Enslin, *The Ethics of Paul*, 1930; A. M. Hunter, *Paul and his Predecessors*, rev. edn., 1961; E. G. Selwyn, *The First Epistle of St Peter*, rev. edn., 1947.

HARVEY K. MCARTHUR

Peace and War

In its broadest dimension peace has economic and political, as well as military, meanings. Peace may be thought of as including also political stability, international economic cooperation and national security. In the vision of Micah (4.3–4) absence of fear and the prosperity of owning one's own fig tree are associated with beating swords into ploughshares.

In a narrower sense, peace is the absence of military hostilities between nations. Such avoidance of violence may be imposed by the coercive strength of great powers. More desirably it rests on a sufficient degree of general security, order and justice, so that no nation is dissatisfied enough to incur the costs of war. Peace, on the other hand, becomes a precondition for maximum economic and political development. This benign spiral in which international peace and domestic social values each strengthen the other is both a biblical and a secular dream, an important manifestation of the spirit of love in human affairs.

Our expectations for early permanent peace are the more modest as we are impressed with the depth of egoism in individual man and with the cultural differences and complex relationships of social groups. Our hopes for avoiding serious wars can be the higher, however, because we have made social inventions which now allow us to handle the problem of organization on a world scale, and because the stakes are so much higher that we should be more actively motivated. Peacetime possibilities have now become more apparent as they have come to include technological possibilities for abolishing poverty or for world wide communication, education and cultural development. At the same time the threat of war is vastly greater.

Modern warfare has taken on characteristics which make it demonically dangerous. The first atomic explosion, in the words of Henry Nelson Wieman, 'cut history in two like a knife'. The revolution in weaponry scarcely leaves the word 'war' adequate to describe the carnage now possible. By nuclear, chemical and bacteriological means it has become possible to exterminate populations, or by continuing genetic damage to alter the quality of human life.

Outcomes of wars involving such weaponry may be decided with a new rapidity. In the past, devastation struck one or a few places at a time, and partial recovery was possible before the next blow. Now decisions may need to be made instantly and secretly. The gravest of consequences may then be suffered by men without any involvement by them in decision-making, thus reversing the trend of the centuries towards greater political freedom.

Under centralized direction whole populations tend to be involved in preparation and support for modern wars. Entire economies may be mobilized, and the distinction between military and civilian increasingly breaks down. Under crisis conditions government controls become more detailed and propaganda more manipulative.

In important respects massive modern war has become more impersonal and mechanical. Missiles operate at long range. Intricate electronic circuits replace direct individual release of firing mechanisms. At the same time that men are morally responsible for more, they may feel personally responsible for less. They can claim to be helpless, subordinate parts of a vast machine.

In addition to weapons of mass destruction, other novel forms of modern warfare raise distinctive ethical problems. Guerilla warfare, for example, involves forms of deceit and cruelty which can be quite personal and vastly different from old canons of civilized warfare. So-called 'brainwashing' techniques open possibilities for human exploitation and control unknown to previous generations.

Even in times of peace we now live with a greater burden of anxiety. The grave uncertainties associated with the threat of war place a serious strain on social customs and moral standards. With no guarantee of a tolerable future, many seize the immediate pleasures of the day. A sense of helplessness before seemingly unassailable concentrations of power tempts some to the kind of aggression against society found in weird individualism or in delinquency. Sex standards and family life face even in peacetime the kinds of strains which have formerly been experienced in wartime. Even more serious for morality, entire populations may learn to live with the possibility that at any moment they may become the destroyers of entire nations or civilizations. This necessitates either a mammoth load of guilt or a serious erosion of moral sensitivity.

Modern war confronts the Christian faith with basic contradictions. Out of the prophetic tradition of the OT and the love ethic of the NT peace emerges as an important social goal. The resources of God, intended for the welfare of man, are misdirected when used for massive destruction. Man finds his highest calling in relationships of creative harmony rather than in competition to develop the devices of death.

Yet the Christian is committed to other social goals in addition to peace. He is also concerned about justice, security and freedom. In some situations the protection of peace may bring with it the continuation of exploitation, aggression or domination. This being the case, a nation is confronted with a choice between two sets of values. Peace has not always then seemed the most important value. War, with all of its contradictions of moral values and religious faith, has under such circumstances been given widespread public support.

At least three considerations now complicate this popular resolution of the ethical problem. One is the increased destructiveness of war which makes it more difficult to choose as an alternative to other evils. Another factor is growing evidence of the dysfunctional nature of modern war. Major nuclear war would probably result in such a collapse of social organization and of the economic base for life as to contribute not to the defence of freedom and security, but rather to the spread of totalitarianism and want. A third novel consideration is the growing availability of other methods than war for defending desirable values. New developments in diplomacy, international organization, and non-violent resistance require reassessment of the ethics of war and peace.

Any sophisticated analysis must take into account possible distinctions between different types of war. For example, would it be possible so to restrict hostilities, with respect to weapons used, number of participants or geographical areas affected, that such a limited war would become an acceptable alternative? Such limitation might be secured by multilateral partial disarmament before the war or by self-restraint by the belligerents during the war. Limited wars might be ethically more tolerable, but unfortunately the moral dilemma is not appreciably relieved. An agonizing weighing of values still remains, since small-scale wars can at best secure only minor ends. If matters basically vital to national interest were at issue, nations under present circumstances could be expected to escalate the war rather than to accept a major loss.

A second kind of limitation has also been presented as a possible solution to the ethical problem. Might preparation for war, perhaps including production of even the most devastating weapons, become a substitute for war? Some who consider modern war immoral are nevertheless willing to stockpile even nuclear weapons and to threaten retaliation in order to deter other nations from attack. Whether deterrence is a permanently dependable policy, especially with atomic arsenals, is highly questionable. In addition, this alternative involves the ethics of the bluff. Should morally sensitive persons be willing to threaten massive retaliation when at the same time they could not support the actual use of such weapons?

Modern war presents such desperate dilemmas that every stance with respect to it involves serious moral ambiguities. The one clear goal for responsible action is the building of such foundations for peace as will make possible the elimination of major wars. To the strengthening of such political and economic alternatives for war the people of God need much more devotedly to turn. *See* **International Order; Just War.**

Roland H. Bainton, *Christian Attitudes toward War and Peace*, 1960; Robert C. Batchelder, *The Irreversible Decision, 1939–1950*, 1961; John C. Bennett, ed., *Nuclear Weapons and the Conflict of Conscience*, 1962; Herbert Butterfield, *International Conflict in the Twentieth Century – A Christian View*, 1960; Donald Keys, ed., *God and the H-Bomb*, 1961; William R. Miller, *Nonviolence: A Christian Interpretation*, 1964; William J. Nagle, ed., *Morality and Modern Warfare*, 1960; Paul Ramsey, *War and the Christian Conscience*, 1961; Harvey Seifert, *Conquest by Suffering: The Process and Prospects of Nonviolent Resistance*, 1965; Charles S. Thompson, ed., *Morals and Missils*, 1951; Papal Encyclical, *Pacem in Terris*, 1963.

HARVEY SEIFERT

Pelagianism. *see* Grace.

Penance

A sacrament of the Church, penance may, like baptism and the eucharist, claim NT evidence for its dominical institution (John 20.23). It was developed to take care of sins committed after baptism. The penitent makes sincere confession of his sins, declares his genuine sorrow for them, and his purpose of amending his life and making restitution to those whom he has wronged. The priest, on his part, gives counsel, penance and absolution. *See* **Absolution; Confession; Restitution.**

Penitence. *see* Repentance.

Penology. *see* Capital Punishment; Corporal Punishment; Prison Reform; Rewards and Punishments.

Perfectionism

In Christian ethics it may mean (1) taking the 'evangelical counsels of perfection' as binding duties; or (2) John Wesley's doctrine of 'perfect love' (also called 'scriptural holiness'), in his sense, a state of regeneration in which attitude and motive are sinless, even though conduct may be objectively faulty because of creaturely limitations of knowledge, etc. The term is sometimes applied to an ecclesiastical view that church-membership should be restricted rigidly to those who are wholly committed and show the moral fruits of such religious sincerity. In philosophical ethics the original Latin sense of *perfectio*, completeness, persists: it indicates the full development of one's distinctively human capacities, cognitive, aesthetic, moral, religious. In this wide sense the notion comes from the Greeks, who included health or bodily perfection. It rose to a philosophical doctrine in Plato and Aristotle. In the nineteenth century a new metaphysical turn was given to it in Hegel's doctrine of completeness as wholeness: the individual mind is an organ of the world-spirit, which latter presses on from potentiality to actualization and from individuality or separateness to union with the Whole. Hegel held that in its moral aspect the process is achievable not in the individual but only in the social whole. T. H. Green (q.v.), though largely Hegelian in metaphysics, conceived perfection as self-realization, and spelled this out into the Greek and Christian virtues, insisting on its social reference but preserving individuality.

T. E. JESSOP

Persecution and Toleration

Persecution, or discrimination which amounts to a measure of persecution, inflicts disabilities upon those who differ from ideas or practices strongly held. Although the power to persecute exists in the general community, the act and the term are usually associated with public authority which treats differences as public offences. In this article there is special concern with religious differences as objects of persecution and with religious beliefs, sentiments or pretexts, as motivating or justifying persecution, even though public authority is usually the force at work to compel. Intolerance is the attitude that impels towards persecution, a will to demand conformity either to an existing or to an ideal pattern of thought and behaviour. Intolerance exhibits such characteristics as these: (1) rigid assurance of the rightness, even the necessity, of the pattern held; (2) fear of the damage ascribed to rejection of the pattern; (3) detestation of the deviant ideas and practices; and (4) hatred of those who reject the pattern.

Presupposed in all the foregoing is the experience in community of the apparent benefits of unity, solidarity, in tribe and in State, often corrupted by the advantages to rulers accruing from effectual obedience. The basic fact and value of solidarity had its ethico-religious aspects, fostering all bonds through ritual directed to common deities and mighty ancestors – and, by extension, to quasi-divine rulers – who were the sanctions of traditional beliefs and morals. It is against this background that we must understand the persecution of the deviant as a peril to religion and also a traitor to the institutions and values of society. Familiar instances are Socrates, the Christians of the second and third centuries, the Quakers in early Massachusetts, the Moors in old Spain. Needless to say, the merits of solidarity should not be pressed to the point of stifling creative thought and action, or ever-needed reform. Here is one of the basic arguments for tolerance, as over against conformity and at some risk to order.

It is regrettable that Christians, who in their faith have deep potentialities for tolerance, have played their full part in persecution, often mingling socio-political concerns with religious factors. Conviction that man's eternal salvation depended upon his acceptance of the Christian truth as held by those with authority, has fostered stern inferences therefrom. Let St Augustine's Letter 100 represent them at a high level, when he pleads with an official not to harm the cause of the Church by inflicting the supreme penalty upon Donatists: 'It is not their death, but their deliverance from error, that we seek to accomplish by the help of the terror of judges and laws, whereby they may be preserved from falling under the penalty of eternal judgment.' Christians who today insist, and rightly, that tolerance and liberty for all are Christian virtues rooted in love, and who hold them in the face of coercion by states, ideologies and other religions, must humbly admit the long centuries of chastening and learning experience, the contribution of political pragmatism and of secular opposition to religious claims, which have put away now the dangerous text beloved for a millennium and more – 'Compel them to come in'. At the same time, critics of Christianity and breast-beaters within the Church do well to remember that in the political, the social and economic, the racial, the intellectual and the educational arenas, there have been and still are other subjects and other objects of persecution, and of toleration, than religion.

In the western tradition, with partial analogies elsewhere, the transition from a tribal to a territorial society, considered both factually and conceptually, plus urbanization and the complexities of imperial expansion, challenged in some measure the reality and validity of traditional solidarity. The rulers of the wider community might, grudgingly or of course, recognize that each sub-community had its own deities and internal bonds; but they distrusted this peculiarity, and super-imposed, often against continuing resistance, their own religious or political system. Few territorial states have in fact been homogeneous. Moreover, developing societies and broadening states have tended to differentiate in some degree the religious function and the political function, the religious community and the political community. On the religious side, Christianity and some other faiths have stressed in certain aspects the relation of the individual to God, and in other aspects the universalism of a God of all men. These two emphases are co-ordinate in their revision of the tribal or one-State character of religion. Again, every extensive religion has experienced with itself deviation, reform movements, schism.

A good deal of human experience, therefore, has comprised the interaction of a predominant and often persecuting authority, in the name of more or less unitive doctrine, with a historic or a developing pluralism which raises the question of tolerance. In the West, despite the complications of Christian empires, divine-right monarchies, and ecclesiastical states, the Church or churches as effective communities have tended to work towards differentiation. Moreover, in the last century the religious factor in public life has been much less prominent than of old, while the secular concerns of states have multiplied. They rely on law, administration, education, propaganda, to maintain the common life and common mind. Patriotism has replaced religion as national faith. The churches, on their part, tend to rely upon and to cherish voluntary activities and often to fear state control even when accompanied by state aid. This 'voluntaryism' in a pluralism of religious bodies, with states completely or essentially secular, is characteristic of the later phases of the western-type societies usually called constitutional or democratic, liberal or 'welfare'.

In the past thirty years or more, the long-time decline in frequency of gross persecution has suffered shock and reversals. Communist action against the religions of Russia and then of other peoples in Europe and Asia, Nazi action against the churches but above all against the Jews, are extreme but extensive instances of intolerant ideologies inspiring and implementing totalitarian regimes which in varying manners have demanded unity and conformity at great cost to hundreds of millions. Here intolerance approaches a zenith in the assertion of power and truth through the immense organizational and technological resources of the modern state in vastly expanded functions. Work, food, housing, education, opportunity depend directly upon such a state and are used by it for complete control. Nationalism, cultural pride, a political ideology which emotionally displaces religion, have been skilfully employed by a managerial elite of the totalitarian states. Variants, often as arbitrary but less effective, are found on the five major continents, sometimes reasserting certain elements of traditional religion – Muslim, Hindu, Buddhist, animist – as stones and cement in new national structures.

A corollary of ethnic religion is a certain inter-ethnic tolerance: let each people have its own gods and practices. Parallel is religion by inheritance: let each man remain undisturbed in the religion of his fathers, and let him not betray it by transfer to another religion. Each of these positions assumes global polytheism and avoids any issue of absolute, perhaps even of central truth. The great complex of beliefs and practices known as Hinduism has extraordinary comprehensive and absorptive power; but its philosophic eye is a monism that declares each sub-religion within Hinduism and each non-Hindu religion also, to be simply one more manifestation of the Absolute, in principle welcome if it accepts this Hindu perspective and sheds all separate claims and organization. Thus the Hindu Absolute, while condemning exclusiveness and proselytizing on the part of other religions, requires that they submit to its own version of relativism. Another phenomenon of tolerance has been conspicuous in historic China and Japan, namely, that many individuals simultaneously hold to beliefs and practices of more than one religious system. Indeed, the sole and jealous God of the Judaic-Christian faith, even though loving and merciful, and Mohammed's stark deity, are not easy for ordinary men to worship in exclusive rigour. Nor have Christians and Muslims developed an adequate theological understanding for their own claims of distinctive truth which is at the same time universal, for the mutual relation of their faiths and communities with the Hindu, the Buddhist, the animist.

Tolerance, emphasizing attitudes and voluntary relationships, is sometimes used in the ethical and theological realms for the friendly outlook of one religion and religious community toward others, as the Christian to the Buddhist. In general, syncretism is neither approved by committed and thoughtful believers, nor convincingly successful in practice. But mutual knowledge, appreciation of truth, love and faithfulness in the believer and in his differing religion, tend to grow. Part of the change is due to the shrinkage of the world which makes it easier to sense a global community requiring peace and common action for well-being, righteousness and culture, as over against conflict, social evils, materialism, ignorance, wherever they are found; and a realization by the believer that his counterpart in another religion may be not only a competitor but also an ally, however inadequate, against the dangers that threaten all the higher values. At this point we note the more general consideration that complete tolerance includes not merely the other but also the enemy, who is part of the same humanity, likewise a child of God; not merely a rival faith but a devouring ideology or movement. Can intolerance be tolerated, the destroyer of liberty be allowed freedom to do his work at the infinite cost of many? The Communist and the Nazi enterprises have raised the old question in desperate poignancy, now deepened in the international realm by unthinkable weapons of mass destruction. The stammering answer of this decade is carried in the current term for perilous tolerance on the level of crude survival: coexistence, but with horrifying defence against horrifying aggression. For some, we have already left the ground of ethics and religion. For others, here is the supreme call upon ethics and religion.

The connections between the religious order and the political order, as they are concerned with tolerance, demand further comment. Western Christians, particularly Roman Catholics, are accustomed to distinguish between dogmatic tolerance, usually equated with religious indifference and disregard of truth, and worthy of attention only in its opposite, dogmatic intolerance as required by faith; and civil toleration, which is permissible for the sake of peace in the political community and which is now increasingly approved by papal authority and advocated by reformists. In actuality, neither the Roman Catholics nor the diverse Protestant bodies have found it easy in contemporary discussion or practice to state their faith with clarity and to seek definite commitment of believers, while fostering internal cohesion, and to do it all with appropriate concern for Christian freedom and the working of the Spirit. The question of tolerance within a religious body is widely open. Even in the elaborate and hierarchical system of Rome it is considered in a new mood.

Toleration is sometimes distinguished, as revocable at the will of the authority that tolerates, by grant or by inaction, from the recognition of right or liberty assured by constitutional or other stable limitation of the ruling power in question. Indeed, many who today are most deeply concerned for the values of tolerance do not use the word, nor any cognate of it. They promote and protect the rights of man, civil liberties, human rights, believing that the most substantial guarantees of tolerance for the religious interests of all are to be found in legal measures for freedom of opinion, speech, press, association, beneficial to the widest possible range of persons and interests in the community. The best indicator of the mid-twentieth century position, at once attainment and ideal, significant even while massively ignored and despised, is the Universal Declaration of Human Rights (1948), which may be illustrated by its Article 18:

> Everyone has the right to freedom of thought, conscience and religion; this right includes freedom to change his religion or belief, and freedom, either alone or in community with others and in public or private, to manifest his religion or belief in teaching, practice, worship and observance.

There is no treatise which comprehensively considers persecution and toleration, either historically or conceptually. The student of this field can find certain plots cleared for him, such as: the persecutions of the early Christian centuries, of the manifold Inquisitions, of Japan from the seventeenth century and Indo-China from the eighteenth; of the Jews over far too long a span and critically in the Hitler period; of Buddhists in Chinese history and of various peoples under Muslim violence or pressure. The issues of toleration have been carefully studied in relation to major Christian thinkers such as Augustine, Aquinas, Luther, Calvin and some of the secular writers of the Enlightenment and their successors; the Roman and the Reform positions in the sixteenth and seventeenth centuries, and the Roman in the nineteenth and early twentieth; the wide-ranging discussion in England in the seventeenth century; the pluralist development in the USA. With political, ethical and religious concern, the Nazi power and the vastly more important system of the Communists have been examined. Human rights and freedoms, various rubrics of 'liberty', pluralism, discrimination, respectively have their relevant literatures. Seldom are the regions of the non-Christian cultures integrated with study and writing about the European tradition and its extensions; though the literatures on the Near East, on Christian missions, on imperialism and recent national resurgence, offer some beginnings.

M. Searle Bates, *Religious Liberty: an Inquiry*, 1945; A. F. Carrillo de Albornoz, *The Basis of Religious Liberty*, 1963; Wilbur K. Jordan, *The Development of Religious Toleration in England*, 4 vols. covering sixteenth and seventeenth centuries, 1932–40; Walter Kolarz, *Religion in the Soviet Union*, 1962; Joseph Lecler, *Toleration and the Reformation*, 1960; Gustav Mensching, *Toleranz und Wahrheit in der Religion*, 1955; Anson Phelps Stokes, *Church and State in the United States*, 3 vols., 1950; Luigi Sturzo, *Church and State*, 1939.

M. SEARLE BATES

Personality, Psychological Views of

The term 'personality' is in common but imprecise and ambiguous use. According to Gordon Allport, hundreds of definitions are available, and he has listed almost fifty in his now classical *Personality: A Psychological Interpretation* (1937). Probably no single definition will ever satisfy all the interested parties; indeed the word is a battleground on which many of the issues of modern psychology have been contested. It is generally agreed by those who use the term that it is comprehensive in basic meaning, designating whatever is regarded as total and significant about psychic life and activity (although it is used by some in the restricted sense of temperament and motivation measured by 'personality tests', thus excluding the cognitive dimension). Beyond this there is little consensus.

There are two basic ways of viewing personality within psychology, with several additional issues tending to be decided according to the choice made at this basic level.

The first of these may be designated as 'external effect'. This way of understanding personality corresponds to the root meaning of the term *persona* in classical Latin – that of the mask worn by a player in a drama, that of appearance. The stress here is on the effect that the individual has upon other persons, and has both a popular and a scientific usage. In ordinary language personality means the impact that one has socially, so that some persons are said to have a strong personality, others a weak one, while still others are said to have 'good' or 'poor' personalities, according to whether or not they are pleasing to those about them. Many psychologists with a behavioural bent share this basic idea in more sophisticated and non-evaluative language. For instance, the following is the definition proposed by David McClelland: 'the most adequate conceptualization of a person's behaviour in all its detail that the scientist can give at a moment of time' (*Personality*, 1931, p. 69). In both the popular and the behaviourally oriented views, personality can only be known in the social situation, and is not a relevant construct in other situations. The behaviourists point out that the external effect is all that can be known of the individual, and suggest that to go further is to indulge in the metaphysics of the mind-body problem, which they wish to avoid as meaningless. As a rule, though not uniformly, behaviourally oriented psychologists also regard personality as an aggregate, rather than an organized system. Some extreme behaviourists and positivists following John B. Watson do not use the concept of 'personality' at all.

The second basic way of viewing personality is as an internal structure, controlling and organizing behaviour. G. W. Allport, a leading proponent of this view, offers the following definition: 'Personality is the dynamic organization within the individual of those psycho-physical systems that determine his characteristic behaviour and thought' (*Pattern and Growth in Personality*, 1961). This definition is typical of the internal structurist position, and also emphasizes the unity of personality and its organizing function. Most psychologists until the present time, including Freud and all those who followed him, held this position. Though it is close to some philosophic meanings which suggest a substance or entity, such as the 'essence' or 'soul' of the person, it may be differentiated from these by recognizing that psychologically it is possible for one individual to have more than one personality, as in the case of 'Doris' reported by Morton Prince, which is presumably not possible from the essentialist philosophical point of view. Here the organizing aspect of personality is accentuated, in that Doris had three organizing systems relating her 'mind' to the environment in three different ways.

Perhaps the most successful attempt to mediate between the internal and the external positions is Gardner Murphy's biosocial approach, which emphasizes the organism's dynamic relation to the field of forces about it, and of which it is a part, though maintaining the organizing function of personality. *See* G. Murphy, *Personality: a Biosocial Approach to Origins and Structure*, 1947.

Personality is generally differentiated from character by its connotation of totality of behaviour, and/or the structure which produces it, as opposed to the defensive quality of character. Personality includes adaptive and sometimes creative behaviour, as well as primarily defensive aspects. *See* **Character.** Character is frequently used as a synonym for personality by European writers.

From the standpoint of ethics, the conceptions of personality used in psychology present more problems than they solve, since, as in philosophy and theology, it is a global term which each writer fills with content that pleases him. More analytical constructs in psychology may be of more use, though in some contexts there is no suitable substitute.

The standard survey of personality theories is *Theories of Personality*, by Calvin S. Hall and Gardner Lindzey (1957), which also contains an excellent discussion of the issues treated here briefly. A newer book, *Concepts of Personality* (1963), edited by J. M. Wepman and R. W. Heine, offers articles written by proponents of various views. *See also* **Persons and Personality.**

JAMES N. LAPSLEY

Persons and Personality

The notions of person and personality are of central importance in the study of general and Christian ethics. Ethics might almost be defined as the study of what it means to be a person. The inquiry is particularly urgent in the contemporary world because a number of factors are converging to cast doubt upon the ultimate existence and significance of the individual human being. The existence of the human soul as well as the existence of God are in doubt. For instance, the sheer vastness of the universe in time and space have increased the difficulty of believing that the individual seriously matters and that it is reasonable to expect that he will in some sense survive his death. And the social pressures of totalitarian states, whether polite or brutal, have made it appear that the individual has no rights or powers other than those which he has received from the State and which can be withdrawn by the State. The facts of brainwashing and of some conversion techniques have reduced our confidence in the capacity of the isolated individual to remain invincible against all external pressure. When attention is concentrated upon the evolutionary process, the suggestion is easily made and accepted that the individual organism has no essential function to fulfil other than that of playing its part in ensuring the continuity of the species. This affects the attitudes which are taken towards old age and death. Popular awareness of the influence of heredity jumps too easily to the conclusion that the individual is completely formed by his antecedents. Beyond the factors which are known and recognized as depreciating the importance of the individual, there is a fear of factors operating without being known and recognized. When they are defined as unknown, they necessarily remain elusive. The cumulative effect of these and other factors is tending to deny the reality and effectiveness of the individual person.

It would be misleading to suggest that there has been a simple evolution of the notion of persons and personality in the history of human thought. Though there must have been a general awareness of personal being from the earliest periods of human history, the attempts to understand it have been curiously spasmodic. Both practical and theoretical interests have prompted deeper inquiries. Broadly speaking, these investigations have taken place in the fields of law, morality, theology, metaphysics and the empirical sciences. Advancing social life inevitably raised questions about the rights of person and property. Communal life raised issues about the respective rights of society and the individual. Questions of justice raised questions about human rights. Courts of law faced the problem of legal and moral responsibility. Deepening acquaintance with the practical and theoretical problems of individual and social morality raised all the questions about the nature of the moral agent; his knowledge of a moral law; and his power to obey it. The Jewish-Christian theological tradition was intimately concerned with the nature of personal being. There was an increasing concern for the importance and uniqueness of the individual man or woman and views of the personal nature of man were associated with the belief that God was personal. The study of personality in this theological tradition was of God and man as personal. The notion of being a person or personal was a perennial issue in christological and trinitarian controversy. Metaphysical studies have always been profoundly influenced by the historical situation in which they have been pursued. No analysis of the actual world either in its methods or conclusions is entirely insulated against the actual state of the world when the analysis takes place.

But these metaphysical inquiries may be distinguished into those which finally explain personality away and those which acknowledge personal being as ultimately irreducible to anything which is not personal. Boethius defined a person as 'individual substance of a rational nature' and Kant defined personality as 'the freedom of a rational being under moral laws'. Personalism and impersonalism remain the metaphysical alternatives, though there are innumerable types and varieties of each. The influence of these major metaphysical theories upon popular estimates of the importance and significance of the individual is usually somewhat delayed, but it is nevertheless salutary for moralists to study the contemporary metaphysical movements which are likely to be influential later at the level of moral practice and theory. We happen to be living in a metaphysically diffident age which is liable to produce moral bewilderment. Metaphysically more confident ages are liable to produce moral stability with the danger of some loss of originality in moral living and thinking. At present we are somewhat hypnotized by the success of the empirical

sciences but it is being realized that the various forms of naturalism somehow fail to do justice to what we know to be true about personal being. It is probable that the existentialists who claim in one way or another that man has no essence but is free to create his own existence and his own standards are making a protest against all reductionist theories of personality.

The notion of personal being has not yet attained any agreed finality. It still includes a series of unresolved contradictions. Perhaps, the only progress which has been made is to recognize the inadequacy of those solutions which give an appearance of accounting for the facts by overlooking those which are inconvenient. The series of contradictions represent a number of ways in which the mysterious ambiguity of personal being presents itself to our observation. Persons as we know them are embodied persons. The relations of the body and the mind remain obscure but they are not clarified by the simple expedients of reducing mind to body, or body to mind, or both to a neutral somewhat which is neither. Personal being is also curiously unique and yet universal in the variety of ways in which these difficult words may be used. Human thinking seems to be essentially individual but good thinking is subject to the universal laws of logic. Each person is a baffling combination of unity and diversity. His personal life can be analyzed into many types of atomic unity but this analysis does not explain how all the parts come to be genuinely parts of a single human life. An enumeration of the parts does not disclose the whole truth about the unity of the whole. Moreover, the continuity of personal life which is commonly accepted as a fact of experience is curiously broken by various kinds of discontinuities. Sleep and the process of forgetting are not yet fully understood. There is the standing unsolved problem of human freedom. The life of a person can be read both in terms of freedom and determinism but it is hard to think that both can be true. Distinctions are drawn between personal normality and abnormality, and these distinctions have practical value and importance, but it is not really plain how we make or justify this distinction. Personality is somehow composed of what is conscious and what is unconscious but the nature and mechanics of the relation between them is still under examination. A distinction is recognized between authentic and unauthentic living where a person expresses his real self or simply reflects the mood of the crowd but the nature of this real self remains obscure. In personality there is much which is plainly transitory but in some ways there are intimations of immortality. Personal relationships seem to call both for justice and love and these sometimes appear to conflict. In brief, all the fundamental problems are present in the problem of persons and personality but it may well be that their solution is also somehow present within the same situation.

John Laird, *Problems of the Self*, 1917; John Oman, *Grace and Personality*, 1917; Gilbert Ryle, *The Concept of Mind*, 1949; Max Scheler, *On the Eternal in Man*, 1960; F. R. Tennant, *Philosophical Theology*, I: *The Soul and its Faculties*, 1928; C. C. J. Webb, *God and Personality*, 1918.

G. F. WOODS

Pessimism

Pessimism may be understood as a reflective attitude, asserting as a philosophy that reality is evil, either predominantly or essentially and totally. The pessimist puts the least favourable construction on actions and events, and views life as basically futile. Both as a set of beliefs and outlook on life, it says that man's nature is weak and evil, and his capacity for improvement small or non-existent. For example, those Christian estimates of man which emphasize not only man's original sin, but also his continuous state as a sinner even when forgiven, are matched by other less theologically informed interpretations which hold that man is basically stupid and indolent. And on a deeper level, the latter dwells upon psychological and sociological research which now seems to show that man is controlled by non- and irrational forces to a far greater degree than had hitherto been imagined.

Pessimism also involves historical evaluations. Thus, it characteristically judges history to be, if not meaningless, then at least without any discernible meaning. Its attitude is basically one of gloom and despair. Russell, while not a pessimistic philosopher, sums up this view when he compared life to a bird which flies from the darkness and coldness through the momentary light and warmth of a castle and thence out again into the endless night. Hindu philosophies of life, dwelling upon the doctrine of Karma, are alleged to produce a pessimistic resignation in face of an endless cycle of changes in which no improvement may be expected. Christian thought, especially that of NT times and of the period of monasticism, expresses a deeply pessimistic outlook at least about the present world.

In addition, pessimism embodies central metaphysical assertions, some of them directly related to one's philosophy of history. Thus, one school of thought claims that not only the total amount of evil exceeds that of the good, but that things are going from bad to worse. Another point of view has its best known embodiment in Schopenhauer's *The World as Will and Idea*, in which he claims that life expresses blind will. Life is intrinsically self-defeating, because in seeking to fulfil its desires mankind is doomed to alternate between the pain of want and the boredom of satiety.

Finally, pessimism, whether on grounds of its doctrine of man, history, metaphysics, or all three, has usually led to the following attitudes: (1) belligerent resentment by man of his nature and condition, for example, 'the angry young man', beatnik; (2) resignation, for example, the conservatives (religious and secular) who reject progress and yearn for a past age; and (3) despair and anxiety, as analyzed by depth-psychologists and by theologians (Tillich).

Is the Christian pessimistic? A distinction must be made between the object and grounds of the estimate; that is, man is said to be a sinner in a sinful world, nonetheless man is capable of response to and rapport with God's love, and history may be seen as the drama under his guidance. Concerning the ultimate ontological status of good and evil, Christianity has consistently rejected Manichaean dualism, that is, the belief that good and evil are equally ultimate forces in reality.

CHARLES W. KEGLEY

Phenomenology

Phenomenology may in general be defined as the study of the appearance of things as perceptual wholes rather than as an attempt to analyze things in order to understand their origin and significance.

In a more restricted sense phenomenology denotes a movement in psychology and philosophy begun by Edmund Husserl and others at the beginning of the twentieth century. Philosophical phenomenology is a complex position, of which the following features are perhaps most salient: (1) It is non-empirical in the strict sense of approaching objects through an intuitive grasp of appearances, rather than as objective sense data to be described and interpreted. (2) Though in one sense it is a descriptive approach, as opposed to an analytical or normative one, it describes objects which are in the mind in their concrete 'essence'. The physical world is held to be real, but abstract from experience. (3) It follows that many conventional common sense and philosophical dichotomies are held to be false – notably the subject-object split. (4) Phenomenologists hold that their approach, despite its pre-occupation with immediate appearance, can nevertheless reveal the essence of things, for, it is held, there is no other approach to the truth in its concreteness. This last point has also become a starting point of modern existentialism, with its insistence that existence comes before essence. *See* **Existentialist Ethics.**

Maurice Merleau-Ponty continued the more narrowly defined phenomenological programme of Husserl in his *Phenomenology of Perception* (1962) and other works. Both phenomenology and existentialism have made considerable impact on European psychiatry. For a sympathetic account in English, *see* Rollo May, ed.,

Existence: A New Dimension in Psychiatry and Psychology, 1958.

The influence of phenomenology on American psychology and psychiatry has been indirect but important. The work of Donald Snygg and Arthur W. Combs (*Individual Behaviour*, 1949) reflected the basic phenomenological position, in that it presented an approach to understanding individual differences by viewing behaviour as an expression of a relatively idiosyncratic self-concept which can only be known as revealed by communication from the person regarding how he 'appears' to himself. They denied that persons could be understood in their concrete uniqueness either by behaviouristic or psychodynamic approaches. Carl R. Rogers based his very influential psychotherapeutic programme on these principles, though he was not directly indebted to Snygg and Combs. Rogers held that only by attempting to convey acceptance and understanding of the person as he presented himself could therapeutic change take place. *See* Carl Rogers, *Client-Centred Therapy*, 1951.

This point of view also became influential in pastoral counselling through the work of Carroll A. Wise, Seward Hiltner and others. These men were not exclusively phenomenological in their approach, but they did stress the necessity of taking the parishioner's communications seriously and of refraining from premature analyses of motives and behaviour.

Phenomenology, as an emphasis, though not necessarily as a complete approach, serves as a reminder to ethics to take the uniqueness of the individual with utmost seriousness, and to respect the value of concrete, immediate experience in its theoretical formulations.

JAMES N. LAPSLEY

Philanthropy

In the broadest sense philanthropy means 'love of mankind' and the word is occasionally used in that sense. In common usage, however, it refers to the act of making economic provision for the less fortunate members of society. This is seen more clearly in the word 'philanthropist', which refers almost exclusively to a rich person who gives substantially to others. Philanthopy is sometimes used synonymously with 'charity'.

In the past many churches, hospitals, almshouses, schools and university colleges have been endowed by philanthropists who have provided capital – usually land – the income of which maintained the institution or the beneficiary concerned. The Church of England, even today, relies for a major portion of its income on endowments of this type. Naturally England possesses many very ancient endowments, and some of these have had their terms of reference altered because these were unjust or did not apply to a new situation. These charities were first controlled by an Act of Queen Elizabeth, but the modern Charity Commission was established in 1853 as the result of a survey extending over many years, and an Act of 1960 has made it compulsory for all charities to be registered.

Philanthropy takes the form of small contributions as well as large, and in the USA, Canada and Great Britain the amount contributed to social services in small sums is still very large, but the latter nineteenth century and the twentieth century have seen the growth of the giant philanthropic trusts. These have been created by extremely wealthy men, starting from Carnegie, and have set up staffs of experts who have now developed large organizations and a considerable expertize in giving away astronomical sums of money. These large Trusts have been, in fact, encouraged by legislation, for the setting up of a trust usually results in the avoidance of a large measure of estate duties and income tax. Many of these Trusts are now financed permanently by the industrial enterprise in which the founder made his fortune; the Carlsberg Glyptotek in Copenhagen, for example, is financed by profits of the famous Carlsberg brewery. Many of these foundations show remarkable imagination in the disposal of their incomes and some have even initiated philanthropic ventures; on the other hand some have shown a preference for the making of large grants to big organizations.

In England most local authorities have powers and resources to give some aid to philanthropic ventures apart from their statutory power to give grant-aid to special services.

In the USA there is less of this kind of grant-aid, but very considerable sums are raised still by voluntary collections in the form of community chest.

Lord Beveridge, *Voluntary Action: A Report on Methods of Social Advance*, 1948; Kirkman Gray, *History of English Philanthropy*, 1905; David Owen, *English Philanthropy, 1660–1960*, 1965.

BRIAN RODGERS

Pietism

Pietism in Germany originated towards the end of the seventeenth century as a reaction, on the one hand, to Protestant orthodoxy with its one-sided emphasis upon intellectual assent to correct doctrine, which, however, represented a departure from the Reformation emphasis upon the right proclamation of the gospel as alone leading to faith and renewal of life in Christ. On the other hand, it was also a reaction to the legalistic attempts which were being made to bring order and discipline into the disrupted church life, particularly after the ravages of the Thirty Years' War. Instead, the Pietists advocated a deepening of the inner 'spiritual' life.

Its chief proponents in Germany were Philip

Jacob Spener (1635–1705) and August Herman Francke (1663–1717) who gave a great impetus to the work of social as well as foreign missions. Count Nicholas Zinzendorf (1700–1760) developed a community of Brethren who cultivated a religion of the heart and an intimate personal relation to the Saviour. Pietism is particularly in evidence today in Württemberg. *Via* Schleiermacher it has influenced modern theology with its attention focused on inner religious experience. It has again and again manifested itself whenever the Church has become formal and institutionalized and too much 'conformed to this world' (as in England, e.g., at the time of the Wesleyan revival).

In general it may be said that Pietism insists upon a conscious conversion experience and a living faith relation to Jesus as personal Saviour from sin, resulting in a changed life and in outward evidence of this change. Right *belief* is set over against *right* belief with the former receiving the major emphasis. Reliance upon sacramental ministrations is regarded as a mechanical *ex opere operato* not requiring personal response. The objectivity of the means of grace is thus set in opposition to the subjective reception of God's grace, distorting the unity of the divine-human encounter in which revelation and faith are always corollary with God as the author of both. Hence faith in one's own faith tends to replace reliance upon God's promise.

Likewise, with insistence upon outward evidence of inner conversion, the emphasis falls upon externalities of conduct under man's control. The Sermon on the Mount is taken as a set of principles rather than as paradigms of the new life of love. It is forgotten that it is the *hidden* life of love which is known by its fruits.

Moreover, the continued presence of the old sinful self along with the 'new man' is obscured, leading to false 'perfectionism'. The complexity of the human situation is underestimated along with the ambiguity of moral choices. It is forgotten that the will of God is always particular, at a time and place, affecting a unique individual within given structures. The gospel tends to become a new law while the law loses its coercive power.

Nevertheless, Pietism has been and continues to be a valid protest against sterile orthodoxism and false sacramentalism and constitutes a proper plea for a genuine break with the old sinful self and an unregenerate 'world'. In its best manifestations it has resulted in active concern for the needs of men. The danger lies in a self-righteous separation from the world instead of a free and joyous living 'in and for the world' in the servant-form. It destroys the 'hiddenness' of the one, holy, Christian, apostolic Church.

R. N. Flew, *The Idea of Perfection in Christian Theology: An Historical Study*, 1934; Arthur

W. Nagler, *Pietism and Methodism*, 1918; Koppel S. Pinson, *Pietism as a Factor in the Rise of German Nationalism*, 1934.

MARTIN J. HEINECKEN

Pius XI, Pope. *see* **Pontifical Social Encyclicals.**

Plato and Aristotle, Platonism and Aristotelianism

The ethical teaching of Plato may be approached chronologically through a study of the attempts in the earlier so-called Socratic dialogues to establish definitions of the various virtues, for example, courage, piety. The inquiry regularly takes the shape of an attempt, frequently by no means successful, to establish what, for instance, all acts which we would naturally class together as courageous have in common, thus justifying our so classifying them. With the *Gorgias* (and to some extent the *Protagoras*) a new note is struck; the former dialogue is largely concerned with a critical discussion of the sort of moral outlook which markedly disfigured Athenian behaviour in the bitter years of the Peloponnesian War, illustrated by her attitude to Mytilene and to Melos but also reflected in the speeches set by Thucydides in the mouth of Pericles himself. These ideas Plato attributed, perhaps unfairly, to the influence of the sophists, itinerant teachers who claimed to be able, for a sum of money, to equip men with the rhetorical skill which they required for public life.

The questions discussed in the *Gorgias*, together with his reflections on the implications of the condemnation of Socrates, of whose trial he offered an account in the *Apology* and of whose last hours an account in the *Phaedo*, stimulated Plato to attempt a systematic examination of the metaphysical foundations of morality. This begins to take shape in the *Meno*, a dialogue largely devoted to discussion of the question how men may learn to be good. But it is in the *Republic* that we have his most extended treatment of this question. The value of his discussion is obscured for many readers by its close involvement with the exposition of a political theory which advocates as a remedy for cultural, social and political decline, the concentration of seemingly limitless executive and legislative power in the hands of a carefully selected and elaborately educated cultural elite. But woven together with this totally unacceptable doctrine is an extremely searching investigation of, in fact, the ontological import of the life of the saint typified for Plato in the historical Socrates. So regarded, the whole work may be seen, from the beginning of Book II, as an elaborate essay in *fides quaerens intellectum* aimed at indicating how men may reach a place from which their sense that the perfectly good man, however ineffective on the plane of action in the world, has the root of the matter in him where what finally can be seen to be the case is concerned. It is in this context that the exposition of the 'theory of forms', of which we also have accounts in the *Phaedo* and the *Symposium*, belongs in the *Republic*, and one may claim that it is only in this context that the theory as there expounded begins to be intelligible. The student of the *Republic* would do well continually to contrast its moral ideas with those implicit in, for instance, the speeches of Pericles and other leaders in Thucydides' *History of the Peloponnesian War*; he will also learn more clearly what Plato is trying to do if he contrasts Plato's conception of the sort of insight which will establish beyond reach of doubt men's elementary appraisal of the significance of goodness with the kind of insight into the human scene mediated, for example, by the tragic drama of Sophocles. It was, for Plato, the tragedians' error to confuse an enlargement of the horizons of sympathy with a discipline of the imagination by concentration in the direction of the vision alone capable of establishing our moral beliefs.

In the dialogues of his later period Plato included one, the *Philebus*, which embodied a lengthy discussion of pleasure and in its method and style adumbrated certain characteristics of the approach to ethical problems associated with the name of Aristotle. We have also in the *Laws* his last words on political theory.

The student of Aristotle's *Nicomachean Ethics* is only likely to appreciate the full implications of his method if he sees in it a deliberate and critically informed departure from the emphases of Plato. Thus early in the first book he includes an extremely valuable and most searching criticism of the central Platonic doctrine of the 'Idea of the Good'. In the very dense and many-sided argument of this passage he in fact reviews what we have suggested above to be the heart of the Platonic approach to ethical problems, namely the belief that there is one central problem, (viz. the metaphysical problem of the ontological significance of moral excellence, and the reconstruction upon the assumption that such excellence is supremely revealing of the nature of what is, of for example, our commonsense understanding of knowledge and belief), which we must devote all our energies to solve but whose solution will bring with it a complete mastery of all the issues that face us on the plane of practical behaviour. It is from this pivotal rejection of Plato's method that we must trace the somewhat disjointed, if amazingly comprehensive, range of Aristotle's ethical discussions. In his *Politics* he accuses Plato's aristocratic political theory of sacrificing to the cause of unity a proper appreciation of the complexity of the human material with which the statesman must deal. Similarly in the *Ethics* we find a series of discussions of the individual virtues, treated by Aristotle as means between extremes. Thus courage is regarded as a mean between foolhardiness and cowardice. For Aristotle these virtues are *hexeis* or dispositions and just as Plato paid in his ethical writings close attention to the form of the true *paideia*, so Aristotle is closely concerned with the *ethismos* or training by which these virtues take root in the individual. In the fifth book, Aristotle includes his treatment of justice (*dikaiosunē*); while Plato in the *Republic* virtually identifies justice with the whole of virtue, Aristotle, while acknowledging the legitimacy of this use of the term, proceeds by a minute analysis, for example, of the nature and relations of commutative and retributive justice. There is much valuable discussion in the *Ethics* on questions of moral psychology, including an account of incontinence or moral failure which suggests the depth of Aristotle's as distinct from Plato's attraction towards the identification of such failure with a breakdown of attention to the nature of the circumstances to which a man's action is a response. Yet Aristotle's account of the practical syllogism remains a landmark in discussion of the practical efficacy of reason.

The work includes a long exposition of the nature of friendship and its role in human life. The two mutually conflicting, extremely intricate, but continually illuminating discussions of the nature of pleasure in the sense of enjoyment remain at once masterpieces of conceptual analysis and sources of continual enlightenment to those who in moral practice seek a middle way between the conflicting errors of hedonism and Puritanism. Finally a defence is offered of the superiority of the contemplative life which involves some reference to Aristotle's metaphysical theology; the contemplative life is judged the highest because it is the most akin to God's activity which in *Metaphysics*, Book XII, Aristotle seems to characterize as *noēsis noēseōs*, the reflexive contemplation of his own contemplation. It is noteworthy that there is nothing in Aristotle to correspond to the burden laid upon Plato's philosopher kings in his allegory of the 'Cave' in *Republic*, Book VII, to return from the vision of all things in the light of the Idea of the Good to the re-ordering of the false life which by their deliverance they have been compelled to lead. The 'Cave' is no doubt in one sense an allegory of political redemption; but it is also certainly Plato's intention that we should find in it a presentation by way of a complex image, of the unity of theoretical and practical in the life of the man in whom moral excellence has been enabled to find confirmation by way of the enlargement and transformation of his understanding. Whereas in Aristotle the contemplative life is allowed to fall apart from the practical, in Plato both are woven together.

Professor Basil Willey, in the recently

published version of his Cambridge lectures on various representative moralists for students reading the English Tripos, remarks on the extreme dullness of Aristotle's *Ethics* (*The English Moralists*, 1964). Whereas Plato's appeal is obvious to specialists and non-specialists alike, Aristotle is a 'philosopher's philosopher'.

If the account given of his *Ethics* seems too much of the nature of an inventory, at least this advertises the extent to which his permanent importance as a moralist (as well indeed as a descriptive and speculative metaphysician) lies in his concentrated attention to individual issues in contradistinction from Plato's too exclusive involvement in a supposedly all-embracing ultimate question. Something of the same quality is manifested in his *Politics*. Whereas Plato found the origin of human society in the field of economic relations, Aristotle found its source in human sexuality. The *Politics* as we have the work begins by offering an account of the emergence of the city-state, regarded by the author as the norm of properly human association, which involves the application to the emergence of political institutions of the conception of growth presented in his treatises on nature. But it is followed by an extraordinarily diffuse and frequently very illuminating appraisal, for example, of the different sorts of constitution with which he was familiar in the world of his day. He committed himself to the thesis that some men are by nature slaves, a thesis which the Stoics (cf., e.g., Seneca) riddled with criticism before the end of the ancient world. But in spite of this his *Politics* reveals the same virtues as his *Ethics*, providing those who wish to study issues in detail with continual illumination. Indeed Aristotle's greatness resides in part in his continual awareness of the vulnerability of the sort of systematic construction to which one side of his nature enticed him and in his readiness to provide throughout his writings detailed analyses of individual concepts of extraordinary subtlety and penetration.

It should be noted that a proper appreciation of the ultimate divergences between Plato and Aristotle must not only take stock of the manners in which their ways divided in metaphysics, philosophy of nature and ontology, but also attend to the vastly different appreciation of the significance of tragic drama contained in the *Poetics* contrasted with Plato's allusions to the same theme in the *Republic*.

D. M. MACKINNON

Pleasure

The study of this topic is best approached initially along the lines of Aristotle for whom it sometimes represented the unimpeded exercise of an activity (whether eating, swimming, doing mathematics or philosophy) and sometimes the crown, which, as it were, perfected the manner of a man's presence to the successive phases of his life, supervening on those phases as its bloom upon the spring of the year. For Aristotle pleasure is not something abstractible from the states of affairs to which it belongs. We cannot separate the pleasure of swimming from swimming nor that of doing mathematics from mathematical work. Yet we know that sometimes we enjoy ourselves in these activities and sometimes we do not. On this view pleasure is identified with enjoyment and enjoyment is intimately bound up with the activity or the state enjoyed. In consequence when we ask what various pleasures have in common, or on what principle they are grouped together as pleasures, we have to recognize that they cannot be regarded as possessing a generic or specific identity; rather they must be judged properly grouped together as pleasures by analogy, viz. in the same way in which Aristotle grouped together in the last chapter of his *Categories* various forms of having, whereby a man may be said to have a wife, an overdraft, a Siamese cat, a copy of the Archbishop of Canterbury's sermons, a hole in his trouser pocket, etc. It is Aristotle's view (often denied on abstract, dogmatic grounds by earnest Christian apostles of self-sacrifice, and by their modern existentialist successors, but very often true, for all that) that men do best what they most enjoy doing and that therefore in certain cases a man's relish for a given form of activity is evidence that he is morally wise in adopting it.

For the thorough-going hedonistic utilitarian, for whom pleasures were ultimately homogeneous and measurable, pleasure is identified with satisfaction and assumes in the end the status of a technical term in his system. The utilitarian denies the viability of any critique of satisfactions, and urges moral tolerance as well, of course, as religious, within a framework capable of either providing for men an increasing over-all product of satisfaction or else guaranteeing their private and individual pursuit of happiness against interference by those who, from selfish motives or from dogmatic conviction, menace the kind of life which most fulfils their needs. *See* **Utilitarianism.**

In the history of the theory of pleasure we must distinguish Aristotle's logical analysis of the concept of enjoyment from the utilitarian so-called 'psychological hedonism' which is less an empirical generalization (if it is so, it is certainly false), than a programme for abandoning any attempt at a critique of satisfactions in the name of an empirically based tolerance where questions of value are concerned, coupled with a determination to gear moral principles, customs, laws, etc., to the fulfilment of actual human needs.

D. M. MACKINNON

Plotinus

Plotinus (205–270), founder of the school of philosophy called Neoplatonism, was a Greek-speaking Egyptian who relatively late in life began the study of philosophy at Alexandria under Ammonius Saccas (of whose teaching historians know little or nothing). After an attempt to reach Persia and India with the ill-fated expedition of the Emperor Gordian, Plotinus set up a school in Rome, where he taught until his death. A mystic as well as a speculative thinker, he was an exemplary type of the hellenistic philosopher for whom philosophy was a religious and ethical way of life as well as an intellectual discipline. During the ten years prior to his death, Plotinus composed a number of unsystematic essays on philosophical problems, which were assembled after 270 by his disciple Porphyry in six books under topical headings. These books, the *Enneads* (so-called because each book contains nine essays), are the source of our knowledge of Plotinus' thought.

In his own view, Plotinus is a school-philosopher: an expositor of Plato. But to his understanding of Plato he brings a close knowledge of Aristotle and a mind partly shaped by the teachings of the later Stoics. His philosophy therefore, while undoubtedly Platonic in its general spirit and outlook, is also a subtle and profound synthesis of Greek thought. Though his system is unfinished and not always coherent in detail, it represents a new and creative departure in the history of western thought.

Plotinus is a monist. The world as he sees it is an eternal and living movement of derivation from, and return to, a single, transcendent First Principle which Plotinus calls 'the One' or 'the Good'. In its simplicity and perfection this Principle is beyond the natural grasp even of intuitive reason. By a process of 'emanation' in which the Source is never diminished, this Unity overflows into multiplicity at a series of descending levels of reality. The highest level is that of intuitive Intelligence, in which idea and apprehension are logically distinct without being really separate. The lowest level is that of the visible, material world, which, since it is distended in space as well as time, represents the limit of multiplicity beyond which reality disintegrates into non-being. Between the immaterial, timeless Intelligence and the visible world of space and time lies the median level of Soul, which is at one with Intelligence in its highest phase, and in its lower phases informs and governs the material order.

Soul is thus an amphibian: naturally embodied, yet naturally aspiring to the higher unity of contemplative Intelligence; forever moving out from the One, yet forever returning towards it. In this tension lies the problem of the Plotinian ethic. Man is essentially (embodied) soul. His highest good, therefore, consists in an interior ascent to, and realization of his union with, Intelligence. The means of this ascent is purification from passion: detachment from the seductive distractions of the material

order which threaten the soul with loss of its integrity. Its ultimate end is the act of self-transcendence (ecstasy) by which the soul as intelligence is mystically united with the One. The Plotinian ethic is therefore in essence an ascetic practice which enables contemplation. Plotinus, we are told, lived 'like a man ashamed of being in the body'. *See* **Neoplatonism.**

R. A. NORRIS, JR

Politics. *see* International Order; State.

Polygamy

Polygamy is the condition of having more than one spouse. *See* **Marriage.**

Pontifical Social Encyclicals

This article presents a summary of the major Catholic Pontifical Social Encyclicals of recent times.

Rerum Novarum, written by Pope Leo XIII in 1891, concerns itself principally in searching for a true and just remedy 'for the misery and wretchedness which press so heavily at this moment on the large majority of the very poor', which included at that time the entire working class, a situation in which 'a small number of very rich men have been able to lay upon the masses of the poor a yoke little better than slavery itself'. Leo first rejects as an illusory solution the type of Socialism based on a denial of God and all religion, on a rejection of all private property, and on an intense bitter class hatred. The basic right to the possession and use of private property is demanded by the needs of the human person and society in the concrete historical order in which man lives. Without this right as a reward for his labours and industry, man suffering from the tendency to selfishness and laziness would frequently not undergo the exertion and sacrifice needed to develop and expand the riches of the earth as the basis of a growing economy. Without this growth the poor could never improve their condition.

But the Christian solution which he offers is not based simply on a blind and absolute right of private property, rather on the more fundamental and absolute purpose of material goods, namely, that God created all things ultimately for the assistance and happiness of all men. Hence, the proper distribution and use of material goods and wealth as resulting from the right of private property must be governed by their more fundamental social nature and purpose.

The Christian vision of the socio-economic order will be formed not only by principles of natural justice, but by the realization in faith of the dimensions of Christian love. No Christian truly aware of the mystery of God's personal love for man as revealed in Christ Jesus and the vocation of every man to be a member of Christ's Body on earth can remain passive and indifferent towards a malfunctioning socio-economic order which forces vast numbers to live in conditions utterly unworthy of their dignity as human persons and as members of Christ's Body. Leo XIII then enunciates the principle that the civil society has an obligation to foster socio-economic growth, to safeguard the proper and adequate distribution of wealth, to protect especially the lowly and needy. Finally, he expounds the principle of a just living wage, he attacks poor working conditions especially of child labour, and he defends the right of workers to organize into associations and unions.

Quadragesimo Anno was written by Pius XI in 1931 on the fortieth anniversary of *Rerum Novarum* to reaffirm the Christian social teachings enunciated by Leo XIII, to develop them more fully, and to expose more clearly the roots of modern social disorders. He admits that capitalism is not an intrinsically evil system, but he insists that any theory of extreme individualism, uncontrolled economic determinism or absolute free competition and despotic economic domination is not compatible with a Christian view of man and of the world. The State again is called upon for necessary intervention in fostering and harmonizing the socio-economic common good. But this intervention must be based on the principle of subsidiarity, namely, that no larger or higher organization should arrogate to itself functions which can be performed efficiently by smaller and lower bodies. Again, for the Christian the ultimate solution for the social evils is not only commutative justice, necessary though this be, but also Christian charity which motivates the Christian in seeking to reconstruct and improve the social order for the true benefit of all men as children of God.

Divini Redemptoris, on atheistic Communism, was written by Pius XI in 1937 to expose the conflict between bolshevistic, atheistic Communism and our Christian civilization. The fundamental evils of Communism are its basis in atheism and its espousal of dialectical materialism by which all reality, even the human person, is viewed only as a phenomenon of matter. Communistic social philosophy, insofar as it is deeply rooted in such theories of atheism and materialism, cannot in the long run truly solve the social ills afflicting man since the human person, even the poor, would ultimately in this philosophy have no basis for human dignity and rights, but would be subordinated to dialectical materialism and the tyranny of the State. On the positive side, Pius XI laments the social injustices and evils which cause so many of the poor to fall so easily for the illusions of Communism. He reiterates the Christian social teachings of *Rerum Novarum*

and *Quadragesimo Anno* by which Christians are obliged in the sincerity of Christian love to strive earnestly for the Christian reconstruction of the socio-economic order. Specifically, he develops the notion of social justice, as distinct from commutative justice, by which individuals as members of society are obliged to remedy by united social action those social ills which cannot be solved adequately by individuals alone.

The Christian view of the State as opposed to that of Communism is that the State arises by necessity from the social nature of man, hence, from God as the author of man, and that the authority of the State necessary for achieving its legitimate end is rooted in God. On the other hand, the State is not an end in itself, but exists for the common good of its citizens. Hence, the State cannot defraud the human person of his God-given rights or become absolute in itself.

In *Mater et Magistra*, on Christianity and social progress, written in May, 1961, John XXIII first states that although the Church was instituted by Christ primarily as a means of saving and sanctifying souls, she is also concerned with conditions and problems of the temporal order since these are not unrelated to man's participation in supernatural goods. Reaffirming and applying the social teachings of Leo XIII and Pius XI to modern conditions, he emphasizes again that in economic affairs first place should be given to private initiative. At the same time, the general welfare requires that public authorities foster economic growth and social progress. This is especially true today because of increasing complexity of modern life and advances in science and technology. As a result, common social organizations and action, both private and public, are often demanded and beneficial today in numerous areas of the socio-economic order. But care must be taken that such action does not excessively diminish the freedom and initiative of individuals. In large areas of the world there are still great numbers of impoverished workers, especially in countries not yet sufficiently industrialized. Such conditions are harmful not only to the common good of the individual nations, but even of the world community of nations. He treats specifically the depressed state of agriculture and calls for renewed efforts for rural development and a more just distribution of its benefits to rural citizens. A most pressing problem of our day concerns the relationship between economically advanced countries and those in process of development. The plight of these underdeveloped countries is the concern of all and Catholics especially should recognize their responsibilities in this regard. Scientific, technical and financial co-operation on the part of the international community of nations is needed to remove underlying causes of poverty and hunger. Technical aid and capital investment should be fostered as well as student and professional exchange.

The encyclical *Pacem in Terris*, 'Peace on Earth', written by John XXIII in April, 1963, seeks to establish universal peace in truth, justice, charity and liberty. Peace on earth can be firmly established only if the order between men and nations laid down by God and rooted in the nature and dignity of the human person is observed. A foremost principle of this order – the foundation of every human society – is the fact that each human being is a person possessed of certain universal, inviolable and inalienable rights and duties. From Christian revelation we know further that all men are redeemed by the blood of Christ and are called to be the children and friends of God.

Every man has the right to life, to bodily integrity, to things requisite for a human manner of existence. Each has the right to respect for his person and reputation, the right to freedom in seeking truth, in communicating ideas, and the right to be informed truthfully about public events. Man has the right to a share in the benefits of culture and to basic education and even the opportunity where possible for advanced study according to merit and ability. Every person has the right to honour God according to the dictates of his conscience, and hence to worship him publicly and privately. Human beings have a natural right to free initiative in the economic field, the right to work and to human working conditions. There is also the right to assembly and association, and with it the right to act with initiative and responsibility within the societies established. Human persons have the right to freedom of movement and residence within their countries, to participate in public affairs, to juridical protection of their rights in an efficacious, impartial and just manner. All men are equal because of their dignity as human persons. Hence, racial discrimination can in no way be justified.

But these rights of the human person correspond to duties of the same human person. A man who claims his rights on one hand and neglects to carry out corresponding duties or to respect the rights of others defeats his own purpose. Because man is social by nature, he should live and work with others for their mutual welfare.

Political society is based on truth and will be well-ordered and beneficial if its citizens are guided by justice, if they respect the rights of others and recognize their own duties. The authority of the State has God alone as its ultimate source and derives its obligatory force from the moral order. Inasmuch as realization of the common good is the reason for civil authority, the latter must provide the necessary laws and further this good in its essential elements. Foremost among the ways of promoting the common good is to guarantee and protect the personal rights and duties of individuals. The government should foster social and economic progress among its citizens, but not to the extent of excessive intervention. The proper aim is to protect freedom and initiative, and to expand the area of freedom, combined with responsibility, to the extent possible.

The same moral law which governs relations between individual human beings serves also to regulate the relations of political communities one with another. Their relationships must be harmonized in truth, in justice, in a working solidarity, and in liberty. But truth requires the elimination of racism and a consequent recognition that all states are by nature equal in dignity. Each has a right to existence, to self-development, to the means necessary to its attainment, and to the one primarily responsible for self-development. Although nations have reached varying levels of culture, civilization or economic development, this does not give one nation a right to take unjust advantage of another. When disagreement arises between states, it should be settled in a mature and reasonable manner rather than by force, deceit or trickery. The common good of individual states cannot be divorced from the common good of all men and nations. Hence, there is need for mutual collaboration and exchange to offset the inequalities existing among nations in population, land and capital. The arms race entails vast outlays of intellectual and economic resources needed for constructive purposes in less developed countries. Nor should the possibility of world conflagration and the possible harm from continual nuclear testing be forgotten. Justice, right reason and humanity demand that the arms race cease, and that work go forward on disarmament, with effective controls assured. Disarmament must be the outcome of inner conviction. For peace depends on mutual trust rather than on equality of arms. In assisting developing countries the wealthier states should respect the liberty, self-initiative, moral values and ethnic characteristics of the people they are aiding. In this way a contribution will be made to the formation of a world community wherein each nation works towards the universal common good, while remaining fully conscious of its own rights and duties.

In view of the interdependence of nations, no political community today successfully pursues its interests in isolation. Since the universal common good poses problems of world-wide dimensions, there is need for a public authority formed by common consent which can operate effectively on a world-wide basis, coping with situations beyond the capacity of individual countries or regions. But such an authority is not intended to limit the sphere of action of the public authorities of individual political communities. Rather, it is to create a situation in which the public authorities as well as individuals may better fulfil their duties and exercise their rights with greater security. The establishment of the UN represents an important advance in co-operation, as do the various inter-governmental agencies associated with the UN. It is strongly desired that the UN, in its structure and its means, become ever more equal to the tasks before it.

John XXIII concludes with pastoral exhortations, calling upon all men of good will to take a more active role in public life, both on the national and international level. All institutions need the co-operation of all sincere men, and especially of those acting in the light of faith and with the strength of love. These ideas are repeated and expanded in Vatican Council II's *Constitution on the Church in the Modern World* and in Paul VI's Encyclical *Populorum Progressio* – on the development of peoples. *See also* **Roman Catholic Moral Theology (Contemporary)**.

JAMES P. SCULL, S.J.

Poor, Care of the

See the second of the two articles on **Poverty**.

Population Policy

While a few countries, like France, still try to encourage a higher birth rate by pro-natalist social policies, the question of population policy today arises mainly in the less developed countries of Asia, Africa and Latin America. A number of the low-income countries, particularly in Asia, confronted by rapid declines in mortality under the impact of successful public health programmes, are taking or studying measures to encourage the extension of family planning in the interest of new demographic balance. Issues for the churches arise in countries undertaking or contemplating population policies, and in the more affluent societies in regard to international assistance. Also the question of birth control in publicly supported hospitals and clinics arises in a religiously mixed society like the USA.

Since most of the programmes involve methods of family planning regarded in Roman Catholic teaching as illicit, opposition from some Catholic governments and religious groups has been strong. In the latest years, however, there have been many signs of greater accommodation in regard to public policies, which reflect differing religious and ethical points of view.

During the past decade the rapid growth in the Protestant consensus for responsible parenthood has helped to secure in some of the western countries more objective consideration of population problems and of policies to deal with them or to help countries seeking help. The United States National Council of Churches in 1961 urged favourable consideration for 'governmental and inter-governmental

aid for family planning', when such aid was requested. Also in 1961, the Committee of the World Council Assembly dealing with international affairs stated:

> While some developing countries have taken steps to promote responsible family planning, more energetic and comprehensive steps are needed even in such countries. The more developed countries should provide technical knowledge and assistance when so requested by developing countries.

The 1964 Consultation of the East Asia Christian Conference strongly supported both points.

The types of inter-governmental assistance which are shaping up are largely those not too immediately related to family planning: help in the statistical field, medical research and training, support for public health and education services. Stress on such forms of indirect aid reduces the dangers of international misunderstanding and also helps to reduce the area of religious controversy.

RICHARD M. FAGLEY

Poverty

There are two articles on this subject. The first considers poverty as a voluntary condition accepted by Christians who have a vocation to the religious life; the second considers poverty as a social problem.

Poverty · I

Poverty is in the OT an object of sympathy (cf. Ps. 41.1), especially when suffered by the righteous, but not considered in itself desirable. The praise of poverty as bringing freedom from the burdens and temptations of wealth can be found in Hinduism – where traditionally the householder, having discharged family obligations, should end his life as a wandering ascetic – and among some Greek philosophers, of whom Diogenes in his tub is the most famous example. In the NT poverty is commended by the example and precept of Jesus (cf. Luke 9.58; 6.20) and by the call addressed, at least to some disciples, to abandon property in order to follow him more closely (cf. Luke 5.11; 12.33; 18.22; etc.). St Paul gave a further example of 'apostolic poverty' in labouring for his support and refusing to live by the gospel (I Cor. 9.18; II Thess. 3.8; Acts 18.3). And the voluntary generosity of the Christians of Jerusalem (Acts 2.44–45) provided a precedent for later monastic communities. But about 190 Clement of Alexandria (*Who is the Rich Man who is Being Saved?*) suggested the milder interpretation that the essence of true poverty is freedom from the desire of wealth, which may be consistent with its actual possession.

However, the early Church generally admired and often practised the 'philosophic life' of poverty and simplicity (Eusebius used the term of Origen's asceticism, *Church History*, VI, 3,13). The more ascetic hermits carried this to the greatest possible extreme, yet even they had to possess some means of subsistence. A different interpretation was developed in coenobitic monasticism, and finally codified by St Benedict. He wished his monks to have no personal property whatever, but to find their needs provided for by the community adequately though not luxuriously. But in a well-administered and perhaps hard-working community individual poverty may be combined with corporate wealth; this experience was repeated more than once in monastic movements which began with a return to apostolic simplicity – for instance, the Cistercians often became prosperous agriculturists and graziers. St Francis of Assisi (q.v.) attacked this danger by committing his followers to corporate as well as personal poverty, living by work or alms (as long as not received in money); his ideal was adopted, though less rigorously, by the Dominicans and other active Orders. But the effort to turn the Franciscan challenge into a law led to difficulties – the Conventual Franciscans accepted adjustments which became evasions, while the 'Spirituals' fell into a rigoristic legalism. Nevertheless a return to the freedom of poverty was the mark of later Franciscan revivals, such as the Observants in the fifteenth century and the Capuchins in the sixteenth. The Franciscan call, with its basis in the Gospels (cf. Matt. 10.9–10) remains as a challenge to easy acceptance of any property system, whether feudal, capitalist or socialist.

Protestantism has generally thought in terms of stewardship of wealth, with an awareness of its dangers (cf. Luke 12.21), rather than of renunciation, except in the case of a special missionary or evangelistic vocation, for example, the quasi-Franciscan discipline imposed on its officers by the Salvation Army. As with mediaeval monks, movements dedicated to simplicity and work have sometimes found themselves facing the problems of prosperity – for instance, the English Quakers in the eighteenth century, and somewhat later the Methodists. In a world aware of the problems of poverty we need witnesses to the balancing truth that property also can be a spiritual danger. Modern religious communities, Catholic and Protestant, and others who voluntarily adopt the life of the poor bring the challenge of Francis or the milder witness of Benedict to our time. In the words of the *Rule of Taizé* (1961, p. 57), which may be considered as presenting an existential interpretation of holy poverty, 'the spirit of poverty is to live in the gladness of today'.

Cuthbert Butler, *Benedictine Monachism*, 2nd edn., 1924, Chap. 10; Joseph F. Fletcher, ed., *Christianity and Property*, 1947; David Knowles, *The Religious Orders in England*, I, 1948;

M. D. Lambert, *Franciscan Poverty*, 1961; *Poverty*, Religious Life, IV, tr. by Lancelot C. Sheppard, 1954.

E. R. HARDY

Poverty · II

Poverty refers to the absence of qualities, attributes or resources, but particularly to the absence of material and economic resources. In this sense the concept is usually a relative one, in that it does not refer to the absence of economic resources in all mankind but to their absence in certain nations, groups or individuals. In other words, poverty means that some people are suffering from the lack of resources which other people do not lack. It follows from this that poverty is a term which is never absolute but which changes with the level of economic development in a given group; and many people who are regarded as living in poverty in the highly industrialized countries in the 1960s would not have been so regarded a hundred years ago.

Attempts to define poverty are apt to be defeated by this relative element. The only really successful attempt to create an absolute level of poverty – a 'poverty line' – was made by B. Seebohm Rowntree in 1900, when he defined poverty as the possession of an income 'insufficient to maintain merely physical efficiency'. Rowntree gave to this the name of 'primary' poverty and created the category of 'secondary' poverty to describe those whose incomes were higher than this but who were clearly still living in poverty. He later created another level – the human needs standard – which laid down the level below which – he argued – the community should not allow people to fall.

In the Hebraic and Christian traditions the relief of poverty has always been regarded as a virtue, a virtue verging on a duty, though poverty itself was sometimes thought of as virtuous (*see* the first article on this subject). Many religious institutions have played an important part in giving aid to the poor. As nations have grown richer and social classes have become more differentiated most states were forced to provide a statutory system of poor relief. In England this was established after a number of false starts by the Poor Law Act of 1601, which placed the onus for the relief of poverty on each civil parish. This system grew and developed many anomalies but was not reformed until the Poor Law Amendment Act of 1834. This reform introduced the famous concept of 'less eligibility' and was based largely on the philosophical premise that few need really be poor and that poverty was the result of individual moral failure. The relief of poverty must therefore be dominated by near-penal methods.

Little, however, was known of the incidence of poverty until Charles Booth published the results of a survey of London in 1889 and demonstrated that 30% of the population of London were living in poverty, a result that was largely confirmed by Rowntree's survey of York some years later. Thereafter much was learnt about poverty and its causes. These were now found to be: (1) death, disability or disappearance of chief wage earner; (2) lack of employment for many different reasons, but the chief of which was economic depression; (3) old age; (4) large families.

Greater knowledge, greater social sensitivity, the experience of legislators who had been poor, the growth of new social theories and other factors all combined in the early twentieth century to create a new attitude towards the poor. Older philanthropic attitudes tended to give way to new ideas which emphasized the importance of giving in a way which did not undermine the self-respect of the recipient, and which emphasized the community's duty to share the benefits of greater industrial out-put with its weaker members. This led to the twin concepts that the poor had a 'right' to be aided, and that poverty was in large measure removable by social action.

The introduction of social insurance into England in 1911 did much to stimulate this new attitude, and the mass unemployment of the inter-war years killed ideas of moral causation of poverty. The Beveridge report of 1942 crystallized the newer thinking and the post-war legislation in Great Britain clearly regarded poverty as a major evil to be removed by social measures.

The methods by which poverty is relieved in Great Britain are: (1) a system of social insurance covering the whole population; (2) a system of national assistance and supplementary benefits for those who have escaped insurance or for whom National Insurance is insufficient; (3) family allowances; (4) a Health Service which is very nearly free has virtually eliminated ill health as a major cause of poverty. Underlying all these is the government's undertaking to maintain full employment. There is also a small, though by no means negligible, distribution of private charity.

During the industrial depression in the USA, President Franklin D. Roosevelt's 'New Deal' policies established a measure of social security, including unemployment insurance and pensions for the aged. Suspicion of 'socialized medicine' and reluctance to extend governmental control have meant a much more restricted movement towards the 'welfare state' concept than in Great Britain. Surveys in the 1960s showed that even in the affluent USA, many people are still living in poverty, and an anti-poverty drive became a major element in President L. B. Johnson's policies, with schemes for self-help and job-training.

Mary Penelope Hall, *The Social Services of Modern England*, 1952; B. Seebohm Rowntree, *Poverty and Progress*, 1941; B. Seebohm Rowntree and G. R. Lavers, *Poverty and the Welfare State*, 1951.

BRIAN RODGERS

Power

Power is the capacity to effect intended results. According to the Bible all power belongs to God who is himself Power (Matt. 6.13; 26.64). God shares his power with man and with the created order. He gives man the freedom to choose how he will exercise that power, in the service of his neighbour and the care of the earth, or for prideful self-deification. Man's choice to exercise power irresponsibly results in his becoming the slave of the forces he was created to command. God's purpose for man is to restore him to a responsible and loving exercise of power. God discloses this purpose in history, centrally in Jesus Christ in whom the power of love is lived out to the death and by whom dehumanizing and destructive forms of power are dethroned and harnessed, not annihilated. Thus the gospel calls man to share in and exercise power (*dominium terrae*), and man's abdication of his responsibility as God's steward is the sin of sloth (*acedia*).

Christian theological ethics has often made the mistake of assuming that any exercise of power was sinful, but sin has more to do with how power is exercised. Although Lord Acton claimed that power corrupts, it is also true that the unwillingness or inability to exercise power also corrupts. By using power man orders his common life, specifies the goals of society and distributes its goods. Not to share in power means not to share in the life of the community. Since sharing in the community is an indispensable ingredient of human life, misusing or being deprived of power reduces man to something less than manhood.

The problem of civil power has long been a central issue for theological ethics. State sovereignty is the way in which civil power is organized and legitimated. There is no single biblical view of State power. Luke-Acts accepts the legitimacy of the Roman empire almost uncritically. The Book of Revelation views it very negatively. For many years the passage in Rom. 13 respecting 'the powers that be' was interpreted as a sacral legitimation of state power and sometimes even as a Christian metaphysic of the State. This frequently led to an ultra-conservative view of the State. Some Christians see the State as an 'order of creation'. More recent exegesis, however, generally agrees the Rom. 13 contains no theology or metaphysics of state power. In it the Apostle Paul merely answers a specific question of the Church in Rome, using the understanding of state power available to him at the time. Current theological ethics tends to view the State, like other institutions for exercising power, as strictly instrumental to hnman justice and devoid of metaphysical substance or super-natural grounding in divine creation. This allows for a much more pragmatic view of institutions and suggests the possibility of altering them when they no longer serve a humanizing purpose.

A more recent issue in theological ethics is the problem of revolution, the seizure of power through extra-legal means. Although Thomas Munzer raised this question in the early six-teenth century in connection with the German Peasants Revolt, Christian theology has usually denied the legitimacy of the revolutionary exercise of power. Calvin taught that when the sovereign is unjust, the lesser magistrates should assume responsibility for replacing him. Luther rejected the right of revolution insisting that even an unjust ruler does preserve that order without which political life is impossible. Dur-ing the Puritan period in England, the revolu-tionary reorganization of the State according to the demands of God was seen to be the duty of Christian men. Thus the use of power to alter political institutions to serve moral purposes became not just a right but an obligation.

In recent years the ideal of the 'responsible society' has been used to suggest that power should be utilized in response to the legitimate needs of those governed. Though the term 'responsible society' is now used less frequently, the idea that men should control and participate in the institutions that exert power over them continues to find wide support. Power is not always responsible. It is exercised in various ways and with varying degrees of legitimacy. It can take the form of (1) coercion, in which people are forced by extrinsic means to act contrary to their will; (2) authority, in which power is exercised by agencies in some way answerable to those ruled; (3) manipulation, by which people are made to act against their will without realizing it. Only when power is controlled and exercised by legitimate authority can it be called responsible.

The subject of power occupies a central place in the sociological study of communities and therefore is crucial to social ethics. Some sociologists speak of a 'power elite', that is, a relatively closed circle of influential decision makers only peripherally responsive to those outside. Others see power distributed much more widely and diffusely, with 'decision-making centres' emerging and disappearing from issue to issue. All agree that the sources of power in a community include wealth, property, holding elective or appointive office, reputation, control of information and media, and organizational skill.

Recent studies have emphasized the increas-ing importance of technical skills and scientific knowledge as sources of power in advanced industrial societies whose dependence on technology steadily grows. Some have even compared the role of scientific technologists today with the role of bourgeois capitalists at the close of the age of feudalism. Both were used at first by the predominant groups of their time with little recognition of how this might effect the distribution of power. Both began to exercise their power to change the structure of the society itself, the capitalists demanding mercantilist measures that eventually subverted feudal economies, the scientists requiring a type of planning and resource allocation that will eventually undermine capitalism. If the values of scientific technologists influence the coming society as much as those of the capitalists have influenced the present one, then respect for empirical verification, unlimited research, free exchange of information and the thrust towards quantification may become more pervasive as the power of science grows.

In international relations, power is organized in nation states limited only marginally by international organizations and world opinion. Before the first World War, the concept of the 'balance of power', that is, not concentrating too much power in any single nation or group of nations as opposed to any other, was relied on to maintain peace. After the first World War the balance of power theory fell into dis-favour, with such diverse figures as Woodrow Wilson and Nicolai Lenin opposing it. The idea of collective security organized through the League of Nations was introduced as a substitute. America's decision not to join the League and the failure of the League to prevent aggression resulted, after the second World War, both in a strengthening of the idea of collective security in the UN and the return of a de facto balance of power between the USA and its allies on one side and the USSR and its allies on the other. The introduction of nuclear weapons and the theory of deterrence in inter-national affairs led some to refer to the new situation as a 'balance of terror'. Recent years have seen this new balance of power disrupted both by the weakening of the two coalitions, mainly through the independency of France vis à vis the USA and China vis à vis the USSR, and the emergence of the 'third world' of Africa and Asia, determinedly uncommitted in the power struggle between the USA and the USSR. The most recent dilemma for the large powers has been posed by so-called 'wars of national liberation' in formerly colonial areas. Strategies of massive deterrence built on nuclear weaponry seem unable to quell guerilla uprisings in territory where the insurgency has widespread popular support, forcing a serious redefinition of the nature and limits of military power.

Future theological research on power will have to clarify how Christ's defeat of the dehumanizing powers and the gospel's call to man to subdue the earth and exercise respon-sible stewardship can illuminate such obdurate ethical problems as the legitimacy of revolution, the alienation of large segments of the population in industrial countries from effective participation in governing, the growing influence of technology and the awful hazards of nuclear deterrence as a method of securing peace.

HARVEY G. COX

Practical Reason

By this is understood usually reason as controlling action. The term is specially associated with Kant who contrasted it very sharply with theoretical reason. The latter tells us what is in fact the case and is limited to the realm of experience (or the world of appearances), but practical reason which lays down moral laws is conceived by him as *a priori*, and therefore it can serve as the ground of arguments in metaphysics for God, freedom and immortality which quite transcend experience. *See* **Kant and Kantian Ethics.**

A. C. EWING

Pragmatism

Pragmatism, a movement considered by many to be America's most important contribution to philosophy, made its greatest impact in the first four decades of the twentieth century. It arose in reaction to idealist philosophies, drew heavily on empirical, scientific and evolutionary thought, and tended not to build philosophical systems but to address specific problems of philosophy and life. It has had considerable general influence in many areas, including education, ethics and religion. As a philosophical movement, Pragmatism was dominated by two brilliant and prolific thinkers, William James and John Dewey.

William James (1842–1910) was educated at Harvard, where he studied first at the Lawrence Scientific School and then at the Medical School (M.D., 1869). Three years later he began his lifetime of teaching at Harvard, serving successively in the fields of physiology, psychology and philosophy. In his definitional work, *Pragmatism* (1907), James indicated that the general background for the movement was British Empiricism associated with such names as Locke, Hume and Mill; appropriately James subtitled the book *a new name for some old ways of thinking* and dedicated it to the memory of John Stuart Mill. The work of Charles Sanders Peirce (1839–1914) provided the specific point of departure for Pragmatism. Peirce also had divided his time between science and philosophy, and was devoted to the mood and method of the laboratory. His seminal article, 'How to Make Our Ideas Clear', was popularized by James twenty years after its first appearance in 1878. Peirce affirmed that beliefs are really rules for action which establish habits. Different beliefs are to be distinguished by the different modes of action to which they give rise. To develop a

thought's meaning, then, we need only to determine what conduct it is fitted to produce; to attain clearness in our thoughts of an object, we need to consider what practical effects the objects may involve.

James developed this principle of Pragmatism in his own way, especially applying it as a test of truth. In *Pragmatism*, he declared that '*True ideas are those that we can assimilate, validate, corroborate and verify. False ideas are those that we can not*'. The truth of an idea is not some stagnant property inherent in it, he insisted, but rather: 'Truth *happens* to an idea. It *becomes* true, is *made* true by events.' The meaning and value of all our conceptions and terms must be evaluated in a radically empirical way by attention to their practical consequences in use. James rejected any fixed or static interpretations of the universe to insist on the changing and evolutionary character of reality, especially in *A Pluralistic Universe* (1909). All theories, including metaphysical and theological theories, were to be considered as instruments to be tested in their working.

James made much of the distinction between the 'tender-minded' (who tend to be rationalistic, idealistic, religious, monistic), and the 'tough-minded' (empiricist, materialistic, irreligious, pluralistic). He classified himself among the latter, yet he continued to be fascinated by the religious question. He found that religion is always a live hypothesis, and that the choice for or against it is momentous and cannot really be evaded, for evasion is itself a denial in practice. In *The Will to Believe* (1897), James showed the part played by inner or emotional evidence in determining one's world-view, and justified the appeal to purpose and will as an unavoidable element in the process. In his famous Gifford Lectures, published in 1902 as *The Varieties of Religious Experience*, James affirmed that there is a certain empirical justification for religious experience in the way that it enriches life and shapes conduct. He demonstrated a willingness to be open to all kinds of experience in the search for new truth. His understanding of religion was open and searching but certainly not traditional; the study of experience led him to suggest a finite God in the pluralistic universe.

James was deeply concerned with the moral life. Though he never developed his ethical views systematically, he discussed them often. For him, ethics admits no trans-empirical basis, rejects all intellectualistic demands that it be based on reasoning only (for the emotions and the will must be consulted and respected) and denies that any one individual or group has the final word in ethical questions. Ethics is, however, more than mere description of man's actual concrete behaviour; it does provide standards of conduct. But they are those which have grown up within the experiences of men; they are to be verified pragmatically by seeing if they help men to deal successfully with their practical problems. On pragmatic considerations, James frankly based ethics on the will to believe those concepts which answer human cravings for moral order and which direct men fruitfully in organizing their experiences. Though not unaware of the importance of social factors in individual moral choice, James stressed the importance of the individual's decision and of his freedom to make it. Once made, however, a decision is open to revision as it is tested by results.

John Dewey (1859–1952) drew much from James, but in a long and fruitful career gave Pragmatism an interpretation often called 'Instrumentalism' or 'Experimentalism', and became the acknowledged leader of the later Pragmatists. Educated at the University of Vermont and at Johns Hopkins (Ph.D., 1884), he taught at the Universities of Michigan, Minnesota and Chicago before coming to Columbia in 1904, where he taught until retirement a quarter century later. A man of broad interests, he wrote in the fields of philosophy, logic, ethics, education, religion, art and politics. Much of his philosophical work centred on the epistemological problem, and of the relationship of thinking to conduct. As he put it in an important work of 1903, *Studies in Logical Theory*: 'Thinking is adaptation *to* an end *through* the adjustment of particular objective contents.' Mind is thus a tool of the organism to guide action; the function of mind is to redirect activities by an anticipation of their consequences. Dewey later defined instrumentalism as 'an attempt to constitute a precise logical theory of concepts, of judgments and inferences through their various forms, by considering primarily how thought functions in the experimental determinations of future consequences'. His development of Pragmatism was along more naturalistic and less individualistic lines than James'; he devoted much more attention to the social dimensions of personality. In his Chicago years, Dewey was associated with George Herbert Mead (1863–1931), a Pragmatist who did much of his work on the social nature of the self. In *Experience and Nature* (1925), Dewey explained that all acts are of both the organism and its environment, natural and social. The world cannot be called a whole or given a meaning as a whole; meanings, purposes, ideas, and minds are being generated continually. Experience is not seen as subjective, but as a process of undergoing, of doing and suffering, as a relationship between various types of objects. Thus the human and the mental are seen to be in continuity with natural processes – all of them subject to modification. 'Ideas are worthless,' wrote Dewey in *The Quest for Certainty* (1929), 'except as they pass into actions which rearrange and reconstruct in some way, be it little or large, the world in which we live.'

Dewey was more critical of traditional religion than James. He rejected any association of ideas about value with Antecedent Being, arguing that they should be associated always with practical activity. He himself espoused a position of religious humanism, signing the 'Humanist Manifesto' of 1933 and the next year publishing *A Common Faith*, in which he urged the separation of religious values from organized religion, in order that the values might be focused on the actual possibilities of life.

Concern for ethics marked Dewey's entire career. One of his very early books, *Outlines of a Critical Theory of Ethics* (1891), was based on dynamic idealism, but as his pragmatism developed his ethical approach was largely recast. The new approach shows in many of his later books, as for example, *Ethics*, written jointly with James H. Tufts in 1908. Ethics became for him an examination of the norms which actual conditions continually generate for the adaptation of habitual conduct to new circumstance. In *Human Nature and Conduct* (1922), Dewey affirmed that 'morals is the most humane of all subjects. It is that which is closest to human nature; it is ineradicably empirical, not theological nor metaphysical nor mathematical'. All conduct is interaction between elements of human nature and the total environment. Hence behaviour is controllable through the modification of the physical and social setting. Ethics always looks ahead, not back; punishments are not ends in themselves but are instruments for the development of responsibility in persons. Ethics for Dewey involves a never-ending search for actual interests and values; through the making public of various and often hidden factors a truly open, democratic society in which continuous reform is possible can be maintained. Thus ethics is not normative or merely descriptive, but always prospective, studying the total range of individual and social behaviour in the quest for ways of living that lead to more enriching, satisfying and freeing relationships of persons to others and to the world about them.

The impact of Pragmatism on Protestant theological and ethical thought and practice was strong, especially on Liberalism. Centring at the University of Chicago, efforts were made to reinterpret Christian faith in terms of pragmatic and empirical philosophy. The religious education movement, immensely influential in American Protestantism in the earlier decades of the century, drew heavily on progressive and pragmatically-based educational theories and practices. Ethical thought of conspicuously different orientation from Pragmatism nevertheless had to take account of the emphases of Pragmatism. With the rise of realistic and neo-orthodox trends in Protestant theology and ethics in the 1930s, the influence of Pragmatism began to wane.

Bernard P. Brennan, *The Ethics of William James*, 1961; Irwin Edman, ed., *John Dewey, His Contribution to the American Tradition*, 1955; Ralph Barton Perry, *The Thought and Character of William James*, 2 vols., 1935; Herbert W. Schneider, *A History of American Philosophy*, 1946.

ROBERT T. HANDY

Prescriptivism

Prescriptivism is a name commonly given to views which hold that moral judgments are in some strong and special sense action-guiding, and that this forms part of their meaning, in addition to any descriptive meaning which they may have (thesis (1) of **Ethics**). It is to be distinguished from emotivism, relativism, subjectivism (qq.v.).

R. M. HARE

Pride

The proud in the OT are those who rely upon themselves or their chosen means instead of upon the Lord. Christ, by example and precept, rebukes those who assume their salvation on account of ancestry (Luke 3.8), social position (Matt. 22.16), or moral achievement (Luke 18.11). St Paul warns against self-congratulation and insists that all that men possess they owe to Christ (I Cor. 4.6; II Cor. 12.9; Phil. 3.9).

In the Christian moral tradition pride is sinful. As such it is distinguished from states of mind which look like it but have no moral disqualification and are often commended, such as pride in one's job, self-respect, commendable 'self-value' (Hume) or reasonable self-love (Butler). It was valid pride which sent the Prodigal Son home (Luke 15.17). Pride as sinful arises when a man's attention is fixed on himself as the doer of a good action or as the possessor of an admirable quality, rather than upon the worth of the act or the quality. A work may be good in science, art, literature, building, statesmanship and so on, but the doer of that good work is not thereby good. Many a bad man has produced good works, and worldly prelates have promoted holy men. Pride argues: my work is good, therefore I am good.

Self-congratulation when the work is not good or satisfaction over qualities one does not possess is relatively harmless; they exhibit conceit which is an error. And the inordinate sensitiveness which is always wondering what others are thinking of one is the weakness of vanity or vainglory and therefore a misfortune. But to be puffed up because of what one can do or really is, that is pride as sinful. It is relatively innocent to be pleased with one's ancestors, one's country or one's inheritance because one has done nothing to have them; they are like Lord Melbourne's garter decoration: 'There's no damned merit in it!' But it is sinful to be proud of making money, of being intellectually distinguished and, most disastrous of all, of achieved moral goodness. 'The man who is proud of what is really creditable to him is the Pharisee, the man whom Christ himself could not forbear to strike' (G. K. Chesterton, *Heretics*, 1905). 'The Pharisee is that extremely admirable man who subordinates his entire life to his knowledge of good and evil and is as severe a judge of himself as of his neighbour to the honour of God, whom he humbly thanks for this knowledge' (D. Bonhoeffer, *Ethics*, 1955, p. 151).

Making of the self instead of what it does into an object of value becomes the meat of sinful pride. The object of pride is self (D. Hume, *Treatise*, 277), but pride in ourselves is excited only when something not ourselves 'turns our view' to ourselves (278). For the theologian pride is one of the seven capital sin (miscalled deadly), that is, the root of others, for example, arrogance, anger, despising others and taking pleasure in their humiliation. Pride and sensuality have been considered as the two primary human sins; pride presuming upon the human spirit's power and freedom (the image of God), denying its creaturehood; sensuality when the spirit immerses itself in matter and vital processes, denying its dignity and freedom. R. Niebuhr describes pride and sensuality as twin fruits of anxiety which fails to trust in God (*The Nature and Destiny of Man*, I, 1939, Chaps. 7 and 8). In this he follows Augustine's doctrine that weakness of the flesh is a consequence of the evil will of the spirit, and that pride begins with the rebellion of Satan. The disobedience of Adam 'would never have been done, had not an evil will preceded it' (*De Civ. Dei*, Bk. XIV, Chap. 13) and 'Of all these evils pride is the origin and head, and it rules in the devil though he has no flesh' (Bk. XIV, Chap. 3).

In the *Commedia* of Dante pride makes other vices worse. When the mark of pride, the first P (*peccatum*), is erased from his forehead a heavy burden is lifted and he climbs more easily, receiving the promise that the ascent will be easier still when all the seven Ps have been wiped off (*Purgatorio*, canto XII, 127–34). Pride also corrupts the virtues; even its apparent opposite, humility, can conceal it. Self-abasement or parade of inferiority is often pride seeking to escape from demands in which one may fail: 'I'm such a poor creature, no one can expect much of me!' Conversely, the 'inferiority complex', identified by Alfred Adler, is compensated for by a striving for recognition, power and superiority (*Understanding Human Nature*, Chap. 5). To be proud of appearing humble has often been detected, for example, Socrates declares: 'Through the holes in your cloak, Cleanthes, your vanity peeps out.' Pascal's realism declares: 'Discourses on humility are a source of pride to the vain, and of humility to the humble; few speak of humility humbly' (*Pensées*, 377).

Pride is frequently divided into pride of power, of knowledge and of righteousness. The spiritual writers define it as concupiscence of the mind. The cure for it is twofold: reform of the judgment by knowing oneself, and this means knowing oneself as God knows one (Rom. 12.3), and reform of the will by submission of the human spirit to the Holy Spirit (cf. I Cor. 2.14,15) knowing its need of grace (John 15.5). The most subtle of all forms of pride is that of those who aspire to or claim sanctity. Authorities on the spiritual life have much to say about this, for example, St John of the Cross, *The Dark Night* (Bk. I, Chap. 2) and St Theresa, *The Mansions* (Bk. I, Chap. 2). They also teach that pride as sinful is quite different from proper knowledge of human value, for example, St Bernard, 'Knowledge also will be double, when we know that this same dignity, or any other good in us, both dwells in us and is not from ourselves' (*De Diligendo Deo*, Chap. 2).

Thomas Aquinas, *Summa Theologica*, Part II, Second Section, ff. 161–2; St Bernard, *The Twelve Degrees of Humility and Pride*, tr. by B. R. V. Mills, 1929; John Calvin, *Institutes*, Bk. I, Chap. 4; Albert Farges, *The Ordinary Ways of the Spiritual Life*, 1927, Chap. 3; Dorothy L. Sayers, *The Six Other Deadly Sins*, 'Pride', 1943.

V. A. DEMANT

Primitive Ethics

All peoples distinguish in various ways between good and bad behaviour, and have ways of transmitting these values to their growing children. The content of this morality, its goals and ideals, the personality characteristics selected for approval or disapproval, the rules and expectations, sanctions and justifications, however, all differ widely among 'primitive' peoples.

The study of the ethics of pre-literate groups is not very advanced. Few anthropologists have been primarily interested in this phase of the culture of the groups they were studying, and few philosophers have entered the complex field of the cross-cultural study of cultures. Ethical values, of course, are a part of many aspects of the life of groups, and most of the information about primitive ethics is thus buried in other contexts in anthropological descriptions.

The psychological undergirding of morality varies widely in primitive groups. Guilt is not widespread. Shame at being caught, at the ridicule of members of the community is more nearly universal. Pride sustains many peoples in their support of the moral code, as the Plains Indian undergoes torture rather than betray his community. Fear of illness, of spirits, of mana, of ancestors are often very powerful forces.

Morality in primitive societies may be taught or expressed in a variety of ways. There are injunctions to children, moralism, proverbs; the fear, horror or revulsion of relatives is transmitted to the child, as when he learns to feel disgust and revulsion over the idea of sexual contact with his mother's sister's child but not his father's sister's child in a society where cross-cousin marriage but not parallel cousin marriage is permitted. Laughter, approval, scolding, punishment, threats, are many of the devices of society to instil its moral values in the young learning member.

Some pre-literate societies have developed highly specialized sanctions for the enforcement of proper behaviour. Among some Plains Indian groups the infant learns not to cry by having water poured down its nostrils every time it starts. The gods periodically come in the form of masked men to Hopi children, whipping them for their misdeeds. Some kinship systems have a 'joking' relationship, allowing considerable sexual licence and the right to tease and ridicule the joking relative with impunity. The whole community shares in the laughter and keeps the deviant in line. In the Eskimo drum contest one man challenges someone who has wronged him to a rhyming contest, and the community, through its laughter and ridicule, supports the cleverer verse-maker of the two, regardless of who is at fault. The skill shown in reciting appropriate proverbs will often win an African legal case rather than the evidence shown in court. Armed force, ambushes and raids may be a principal institution for retribution.

Variety in the content of morality is also very wide. The Pueblo Indian must not be competitive. It is shameful to seek to do better than his neighbours. The neighbouring Plains Indian is highly competitive and aggressive in war and trade, seeking an individual vision from the gods to set him apart from his fellows. In some groups an individual has the rights to the fruits of a tree he inherited no matter how long ago his ancestors sold the land to someone else. In others no crop is private. All produce is communal property. For a man to eat a deer may be the most shameful of acts, causing him to become ill and die, whereas his wife may eat it with impunity. He belongs to the Deer clan and she does not.

As wide as the variety of good and bad behaviour may be, some kinds of action are universally condemned. Incest is one such well-known universal prohibition. Relations with mother or sister are almost always included within the incest restriction, but beyond that cultures differ widely in the size and scope of the incest group. It may include all the mother's relatives, in an extended family comprising scores of people who would not be counted in our kinship system, or a multitude of other relationships, large and small. It may be ritually broken on special highly-charged emotional occasions for religious purposes. But whatever the variety, the incest prohibition is there.

In-group aggressions are limited or controlled in all societies to some degree. The degree of limitation may be the Zuni extreme of eliminating all competition, or it may allow a large amount of friction, tension, fighting and ill-will, but there are always limits. Some kind of reciprocity in the group, some requirement of telling the truth, at least under certain circumstances, is universally required.

The size of the world of a primitive group is smaller than that of industrialized society. The world to which ethical behaviour is required may also be much smaller. The outsider, the stranger, may often and without compunction be treated far differently from 'people' as the primitive often calls his own group in distinction to others. The rights of humanity in the abstract are not likely to be a part of the morality, but interpersonal relationships in the community or family may be sharply defined.

Real behaviour and ideal behaviour often differ. The very fact of ideal behaviour among a people, however, is evidence of moral values. This ideal behaviour among primitives is not formally coded. When people have it called to their attention it is justified in the terms that 'our fathers did so formerly', 'the gods have commanded it', 'the ancestors would be displeased if it were not done', or 'the consequences of infringement would be terrible'. In the actual structure of the society, however, ideal behaviour is tied in with the rest of the culture in its prevalent themes and value system, its economics, its social structure and religion, deriving its strength from its functional relationship to them.

Richard B. Brandt, *Hopi Ethics*, 1945; May and Abraham Edel, *Anthropology and Ethics*, 1959; John Ladd, *The Structure of a Moral Code*, 1957.

WILLIAM A. SMALLEY

Prison Reform

Prison reform cannot be entirely separated from penal reform. The earliest prison reformers, however, were not dealing with prisons as places of punishment but with prisons as places of detention for persons awaiting trial, for persons failing to pay their fines or their debts, as well as for persons facing execution or transportation overseas. Jailers, being unpaid, charged fees and sold liquor. Sanitation was lacking, and the prisoners were herded together without distinction of criminality, age or sex. Supervision, nominally in the hands of local magistrates, was generally neglected.

The pioneer in a comprehensive and detailed investigation into the facts was John Howard (1726–1790) whose book, *The State of the Prisons in England and Wales, with Preliminary Observations, and an Account of Some Foreign Prisons*, published in 1777, may be regarded as the beginning of the prison reform movement. Howard, who became High Sheriff of Bedfordshire, took seriously his responsibility for the county's prisoners, and his first visit of inspection at Bedford started him on his life work. Before his book was published he had visited every prison and bridewell in the country and had inspected numerous prisons on the Continent as well. His suggestions for improvement included the provision of adequate food, water, bedding and air; separate cells by night but work in association by day; separation of men and women, debtors and felons, old and young offenders; regular inspection; the abolition of fees and liquor selling with the consequent provision of a salary for the jailer. Some of Howard's proposals were embodied in Acts of Parliament, but no effective provision was made for their enforcement and Howard died just before Europe was plunged into a generation of war and reaction, leaving the situation little better than he had found it. A generation later Elizabeth Fry (1780–1845) was stirred by the deplorable state of the women in Newgate prison and devoted herself to their welfare with conspicuous success.

Improvement in prisons generally began with Sir Robert Peel's Gaol Act of 1823 which set up a code of rules for prisons. Jailers were to become servants of the justices and the latter were to exercise supervision and make reports to the Home Secretary. Meantime steps had been taken in the USA which affected the prison systems of the old world. For instance, under Quaker influence Pennsylvania introduced cells for solitary confinement and in time the provision of separate cells became standard practice in Britain and Europe.

The importance of prisons was enhanced by the disuse of the old methods of disposing of convicted persons. Transportation to the USA ceased with the revolt of the American colonies and transportation to Australia which replaced it ceased in 1857. By that time capital punishment had been abandoned except for a few serious crimes. The necessary result of these penal changes was the establishment in Britain of numerous new convict prisons alongside the old local jails which were taken over by the State in 1877. At this period the point of view embodied in the Pennsylvania system was influential and convicts spent the first part of their sentences in solitude before being transferred to establishments like dockyards where they could be employed on works of public utility. The new prisons therefore were built with the cellular system in view and, apart from the recent 'open prisons', these are the buildings still in use, though workshops, educational facilities and moderate spaces for exercise have had with some difficulty to be added. It was long believed that the deterrent aspect of prisons involved not only solitary confinement but also hard monotonous labour such as the treadmill. Not till 1895 was work of this kind condemned officially by the Gladstone Committee, as a result of whose report the Prison Act of 1898 gave power to the Secretary of State to make regulations and thus allowed the introduction of new ideas into prison administration without the necessity for new legislation.

An American counterpart to John Howard appeared in Enoch C. Wines (1806–1879), secretary of the Prison Association of New York. His report on the prisons of the USA and Canada (1867) stimulated efforts towards reform and encouraged experimenters like Zebulon R. Brockway (1827–1920) who, aiming at reformation rather than punishment, successfully advocated the 'indeterminate sentence' and acted as superintendent of Elmira Reformatory for the last quarter of the century. Wines visited Europe to study prison methods and largely as a result of his efforts twenty-two countries were represented at the first International Penitentiary Congress in London (1872).

By that time prison reform had everywhere become dependent on penal reform, for progressive officials cannot do much to improve prison methods without the support of public opinion enlightened by the Howard League in Britain and similar bodies elsewhere.

For John Howard see DNB, XXVIII, pp. 44–48; Howards' The State of the Prisons is in Everyman's Library No. 385. For Elizabeth Fry see DNB, xx, pp. 294–6 and John Kent, Elizabeth Fry, 1962. For Enoch C. Wines see DAB, xx, p. 385. For Zebulon R. Brockway see DAB, III, pp. 60 f.

STEWART MECHIE

Probabiliorism

Probabiliorism is the system in moral theology which holds that when in doubt it is lawful to follow the opinion favouring liberty only when it is more probable than the opinion favouring the law. The system was developed in opposition to probabilism (q.v.) and for a time was the dominant system. It has now largely been discarded, chiefly because in practice it is of little use. The accurate weighing and balancing of the relative probability of two contrary opinions requires more time and skill than are usually available to a man in doubt. Consequently the system, in practice, tends towards Tutiorism (q.v.).

R. C. MORTIMER

Probabilism

Probabilism is the system of moral theology, used to resolve problems of doubt or perplexity as to the right or lawful course of conduct in any given set of circumstances. It is based on the principle 'A doubtful law does not oblige' and allows an action to be lawful if there is any doubt, however slight, about its unlawfulness. In other words, Probabilism in its extreme form holds that it is lawful to follow a probable opinion that an action is lawful, even though it is more probable, even much more probable that the action is unlawful. This extreme form flourished in the sixteenth and seventeenth centuries, was associated with the Jesuits and was the prime object of Pascal's attacks.

Because of its tendency to laxism, probabilism came increasingly under attack, and probabiliorism (q.v.) grew in popularity. A reaction started with St Alphonsus Liguori. This great moral theologian abandoned probabiliorism as too rigid and adopted a modified probabilism. His great authority and prestige together with the influence of the restored Society of Jesus ensured that from the nineteenth century onwards probabilism has become the predominant system in the Roman Catholic Church. But it is probabilism in a modified form with strong safeguards to prevent it from degenerating into laxism. The most important safeguards are (1) that the probable opinion must be a 'solidly' probable opinion and (2) probabilism may not be adopted where the doubt concerns the validity of a sacrament or a vital interest whether of the agent himself or of somebody else.

R. C. MORTIMER

Procreation

Parental duties in regard to procreation are dealt with mainly by implication in the teachings of the NT. The OT image of an abundant society of teeming families and teeming flocks is swallowed up in a preoccupation with the imminent coming of the Kingdom. The focus of concern is the spiritual transformation of life rather than its natural continuation. The claims of the Kingdom transcend those of marriage and family life: 'He who loves son or daughter more than me is not worthy of me' (Matt. 10.37). Even the direct references to child-bearing in I Tim. are concerned with other matters: the salvation of a woman of exemplary life (2.15), and the avoidance of scandal by the younger widows (5.3 f.). It should be added that some scholars, for example, Weymouth, Moffatt, Phillips, give a different sense to the first reference, translating the phrase to mean that a good and faithful woman will come 'safely through childbirth'.

Despite the ascetic elements in the Gospels and Epistles, there are significant positive factors in relation to marriage and family life, beginning with the family setting of the incarnation. The high view of marriage as a union of two persons, the concept of the 'two become one' found in Genesis, is preserved and deepened. Jesus taught that God himself is the author of true marriage (Mark 10.9), and Paul found in such marriage a profound symbol of the union of Christ and the Church (Eph. 5.31) and a calling in holiness (I Thess. 4.3 ff.). At other points, Paul takes a lower view of marriage as a remedy for concupiscence (I Cor. 7.2 ff.; Rom. 7.3). But he also urges the Christian member of a mixed marriage to avoid divorce to consecrate the spouse and to assure the holiness of the children (I Cor. 7.14). Paul does not reveal the great love of children evidenced by Jesus, yet he adjures fathers to bring up their children in 'the discipline and instruction of the Lord' (Eph. 6.4; cf. Col. 3.20–21).

The early Church required a more specific position on the question of procreation than it found in the NT teaching. A particular need stemmed from the gnostic heresy, which condemned procreation as the imprisonment of good souls in evil bodies. The Fathers turned to the 'increase and multiply' verses of Genesis to affirm the essential goodness of procreation in the Christian view. Any whole-hearted affirmation of the Judaic ethos, however, was precluded by the increasing asceticism of the early Church, with growing stress on celibacy as a higher form of religious vocation, and corresponding fear of lusts of the flesh. The positive attitude towards procreation, as found in the *First Epistle of Clement*, became gradually diluted until Tertullian could argue that the 'command to continence' (I Cor. 7.29) had 'abolished that "grow and multiply",' which was an indulgence granted 'until the world should be replenished'.

The more typical patristic view was that procreation offers justification for marital relations, provided that the lusts of the flesh are kept within bounds. Whereas Paul had advised against prolonged marital abstinence (I Cor. 7.5), the ante-Nicene literature abounds with references to the need for temperance and self-restraint within marriage. Athenagoras even asserted that 'the procreation of children is the measure of our indulgence in appetite'.

The generally austere treatment of the husband-wife relationship, in the patristic writings, reflects, of course, the Pauline concept of 'flesh' (*sarx*) as representing the sinful element in human nature and the enemy of the spiritual life. The Greco-Roman view of marriage as a utilitarian contract for the begetting of legitimate issue helped to focus attention on the procreational purpose of marital intercourse, to the exclusion of relational values. Similarly, the common error that the male contribution to conception was seed in the full sense increased the tendency to condemn any non-procreative use of sex. Further, persistent pagan charges that Christians engaged in sexual orgies led the Fathers to give a particularly austere character to their descriptions of Christian marital relations.

The question of any limitation of procreation, save by marital abstinence, hardly arises in the early patristic literature. The practice of abortion and infanticide in the pagan world is strongly condemned. The *Revelation of Peter* pictures a special section of hell for 'the accursed who conceived and caused abortion'. 'Christians,' says the *Epistle to Diognetus*, 'marry, as do all; they beget children; but they do not destroy their offspring' – literally, 'cast away foetuses.' Indeed, the question of family limitation did not become a pressing one in the early Church; none of the early ecumenical councils felt it necessary to deal with the matter.

The thought and teaching of Eastern Orthodoxy, in regard to procreation, is still strongly informed and shaped by the patristic traditions. Mutual sanctification is seen to be the primary purpose of marriage in one of its dimensions and the passage in Ephesians forms a central element in the Orthodox marriage service. Other statements speak of procreation as the primary end of marriage, and condemn any non-procreative use of sex. Recent pronouncements of the Orthodox bishops indicate a sanction for marital abstinence, in cases where it is necessary to avoid having additional progeny, but condemn any methods, including periodic continence, which involve contraceptive intent. This hostility appears to be rooted in the patristic condemnation of abortion and infanticide.

It should be added, however, that since the seven ecumenical councils did not pronounce on questions of family planning, much less the modern refinements of such questions, there is no official Orthodox position on the regulation of fertility. The ethos of Orthodoxy is less legalistic than that of the Western Church, and this places a correspondingly greater weight on the conscientious decisions of husbands and wives. In practice, it is clear that many married priests and lay people take a less rigorous attitude towards marital companionship apart from procreation, and towards family limitation, than that reflected in some of the utterances of the monastic clergy. It is easier, in the Eastern tradition, to modify the practical application of doctrines, than it is to clarify or develop the doctrines themselves.

In the Western Church, Augustine, whose conversion took the form of a revulsion against sexual indulgence, cast a long shadow on the approach to marriage and procreation. His threefold definition of the blessings of matrimony – 'offspring, conjugal faith, and the sacrament' – shaped the framework of the Roman position. Augustine insisted on a nexus between marital intercourse and procreation, to relieve the sinful malady of concupiscence. He argued that the sin of Onan lay, not in refusing his levirate duty, but in preventing conception. He was equally hostile towards contraception ('evil appliance') and periodic continence as means to this end.

In his great summation, Aquinas combined the teaching of Augustine and Aristotle's concept of natural law. In the process, he modified the rigours of the Augustinian position by giving marriage and family life more positive and humane content. But he strengthened the primacy of procreation as the first purpose of marriage and of the marital act by identifying it with the inherent 'nature' of both. The primary end of marriage was gradually broadened into a double objective, the 'procreation and education of children'; the biological end of the marital act has remained dominant in Roman Catholic teaching.

Only abstinence, whether complete or periodic, has been given Vatican sanction as a means for deferring procreation, and then only when serious reasons exist for not having a child. Abortion is most strongly condemned as murder of an innocent child. Sterilization, whether permanent or temporary, is condemned as a means of birth control, but is acceptable as a secondary effect, if the sterilizing procedure is necessary for the good of the body as a whole. Contraception is condemned as destroying the integrity and denying the procreative nature of the marital act.

The chief modern formulation of the Roman position was that of Pius XI in his 1930 encyclical, *Casti Connubii*. This reiterated the modified Thomistic position, and described the parents of large families as 'generous'. It strongly condemned 'any use whatsoever of matrimony exercised in such a way that the act is deliberately frustrated in its natural power to generate life'. But it also gave greater expression to the 'secondary' ends of marriage, such as mutual love. Further, it was interpreted as leaving room for periodic continence as a means for the spacing and limitation of pregnancies when sound reasons therefor obtain. This modification of the traditional position had been initiated by a cautious decision of the Sacred Penitentiary in 1853. Finally, the encyclical opened up a potential new vista, by describing the 'mutual inward moulding of husband and wife, this determined effort to perfect each other' as offering a broader view of the chief reason and purpose of matrimony than the traditional preoccupation with procreation and education.

While efforts to emphasize the relational values of marriage on the basis of this paragraph brought a reaction under Pius XII, the latter in 1951 also spoke more clearly of the eugenic, medical, economic and social indications which could justify a resort to periodic continence, and expressed the hope that 'science will succeed in providing this licit method with a sufficiently secure basis. . . .' This gave added sanction for the rhythm method, even though the position implies acceptance of contraceptive intent for valid reasons, so that the 'nature' of the act is maintained only by its procreative manner.

The practical difficulties of finding a 'sufficiently secure basis' for this method has led to widespread lay sentiment for a further evolution of the Roman position. Some clerical and lay writers argue for acceptance of the 'pill', in that it only defers ovulation and does not cause a mutilation which is the traditional basis for a condemnation of sterilization. Others call for a more radical review of the Thomistic categories and the preoccupation with the biological function of marriage and the marital act. The Second Vatican Council in the chapter on Marriage and the Family of the Pastoral Constitution, *Gaudium et Spes*, provided the framework for a far-reaching renovation of the traditional Roman Catholic teaching. It stressed the essential goodness of the marital act within the bond of marriage; held the relational end to be not of less account, *non posthabitis*, than the procreational-educational end; elevated the concept of responsible parenthood, and the conscientious decision of the couple; and indirectly warned of dangers in methods which interrupt the full intimacy of married life. While Pope Paul has reserved to himself a determination on the morality of methods, the bishops have offered a framework for *aggiornamento*, which would bring the main branches of Christianity closer together on this basic concern.

While the Reformers gave a new dignity and status to marriage, they did not re-examine the traditional teachings on parenthood. Perhaps the under-populated character of Northern Europe at the time was a factor. Luther regarded procreation as more of a blessing conferred by God, despite the sinfulness of man, than as a command; but he did not challenge the primacy of the biological purpose. Calvin thought that companionship was the key biblical insight on the man-woman relationship (cf. Gen. 2.18); but he applied this mainly to the non-sexual side of marriage, and did not question that the 'increase and multiply' verses were normative for the sexual side. For most of its history to date, the Protestant ethos, with its view of marriage as a religious vocation, has helped to sustain high levels of fertility.

The change in the official teachings of the Anglican and Protestant churches began with the Lambeth Conference of 1930. Pronouncements by church assemblies, however, were preceded by a full half century of change in lay opinion, as husbands and wives, with little relevant guidance from their churches, attempted to adjust the size of their families to falling death rates and the demands of an increasingly complex and costly education. The succession of church statements on responsible parenthood since 1930, moreover, came first under the goad of the Great Depression and then under the impact of the massive and unprecedented population pressures in Asia, Africa and Latin America.

The influence of the non-theological factors has clearly been strong in this process. But if the main impetus came from the social situation, it has been followed by increasingly significant theological and ethical analysis, which has deepened as well as broadened the Protestant consensus. It is noteworthy that as this growing consensus has renewed its roots in the biblical teaching, it has grown beyond the confines of the communions which formally co-operate in the ecumenical movement. Within a few short years recognition has come of the large and widening area of agreement among Evangelical leaders in a field long neglected. The more important recent statements include the Lambeth Report on 'The Family in Contemporary Society' (1958), the Mansfield Report of an ecumenical study group, entitled 'Responsible Parenthood and the Population Problem' (1959); the Statement on 'Responsible Parenthood' of the United States National Council of Churches (1961); and the Report on 'The Asian Churches and Responsible Parenthood' of a consultation called by the East Asia Christian Conference (1964).

The heart of the emerging consensus lies in a deeper understanding of the meaning of marriage, based on the central biblical concept of the 'two become one'. True marriage is a union of two persons – body, mind and spirit – joined together by God; it is also a covenant to be fulfilled by husband and wife. Both as new creation and as covenant, as being and becoming, marriage is fundamentally spiritual in character, which lifts the man-woman relationship above the realm of nature, without wholly escaping it, into the realm of the spirit, the realm of freedom and responsibility. At its deepest level, the purpose of the 'two become one' is to serve and worship God, and to provide mutual aid in spiritual growth.

This high view of marriage as a union of two persons, reflecting the fullness of human nature, gives quite a different perspective on the claims of procreation from that provided by a one-dimensional focus on biological function. Procreation is one of the valid purposes of marriage as are marital companionship and vocation. One or another of these separable ends can serve, in relation to a given time and circumstance, as a primary means by which husband and wife care for and express their 'one-flesh' union. The couple, in God's design, have an inherent freedom and corresponding duty to choose between the proximate ends of marriage. The new knowledge, which can facilitate or prevent conception, is seen as reinforcing this freedom.

Parenthood, through which most couples are privileged to co-operate in God's continuing creative work, retains its high evaluation in the Protestant ethos; the totality of parental duties are seen to place increasing stress on the quality, as over against the quantity, of family life. Marital intercourse apart from procreation is now understood to have an inherent goodness as a means to nourish the 'one-flesh' union; this reverses the ancient view that sexual companionship is sinful unless made pardonable by procreative intent. Vocation, the calling of the couple in society, normally finds major expression in the family; but this calling can exert a conflicting claim.

Holding that the purpose of the marital act is to serve the 'one-flesh' union, the Protestant consensus rejects any bondage to the biological function. Husbands and wives are free to use the gifts of science to promote or to defer conception, provided the means are mutually acceptable, injurious to neither spouse nor to new life, and sufficiently effective to meet the needs of the couple. The Mansfield Report found no inherent moral distinction between periodic continence, contraception or drugs to defer ovulation if free from injurious side effects. Abortion is strongly condemned as a method of family planning though it may be justified by therapeutic or related reasons. Warnings against sterilization, because of its generally permanent character, have been common, though some recent statements have shown a more permissive attitude; it is pointed out that one ethical decision is not necessarily less responsible than a series of decisions, particularly if reasonable alternatives are lacking.

The concept of responsible parenthood, however, has typically been thought of in terms of day-to-day decisions by a couple in relation to the changing circumstances of their marriage. The considerations to be weighed include the claims of existing children and the right of each child to love and nurture in the full sense, the mental and physical health of the mother and the prospects for health of a future child, the claims presented by the witness of the couple in society, and, some would add, the needs of the social order of which the family forms a part. Faith is another prime ingredient. As the United States National Council statement put it:

> Parents need to remember that having children is a venture in faith, requiring a measure of courage and confidence in God's goodness. Too cautious a reckoning of the costs may be as great an error as failure to lift the God-given power of procreation to the level of ethical decision.

The weakness of the present Protestant consensus is that it is still too limited to the leadership of the churches. It has not sufficiently permeated the taboos surrounding this area to reach the mass of church people and become a matter of shared conviction and witness.

This is particularly true of the theological groundwork which sustains the ethical insights. The task of Christian education in this field looms large.

D. Sherwin Bailey, *The Mystery of Love and Marriage*, 1953; William G. Cole, *Sex in Christianity and Psychoanalysis*, 1955; Stanislas de Lestapis, S.J., *Family Planning and Modern Problems*, 1961; Richard M. Fagley, *The Population Explosion and Christian Responsibility*, 1960; Athenagoras Kokkinakis, *Parents and Priests as Servants of Redemption*, 1958; E. C. Messenger, *Two in One Flesh*, 1948; Otto A. Piper, *The Christian Interpretation of Sex*, 1941; Helmut Thielicke, *The Ethics of Sex*, 1964; M. A. C. Warren, et al., *The Family in Contemporary Society*, 1958.

RICHARD M. FAGLEY

Professional Ethics

A profession is not only a way of making a living; it is the carrying out of an occupation to which standards of competence and responsibility are attached. Professor Robert K. Merton has named the social values which make up the concept of a profession as 'first, the value placed upon systematic knowledge and the intellect: knowing. Second, the value placed upon technical skill and capacity: doing. And third, the value placed upon putting this conjoint knowledge and skill to work in the service of others: helping'. A profession normally stands higher in public esteem than other types of remunerative work or trade; this is not only a matter of social class, but is consequent on the belief that a professional person is committed to maintaining standards. These are partly standards of competence; he will normally have been expected to have secured recognized qualifications for entry to the profession. They will also be standards of 'professional integrity'. Professional ethics concern the particular kinds of conduct recognized as necessary to this integrity in the profession in question. In some cases, notably the medical profession, professional ethics form an explicit code, disregard of which can be a matter for disciplinary action on the part of the profesional association. In other cases, notably certain forms of social work, the matter of professional ethics is undergoing keen discussion among practitioners, but no recognized formal expression has been given it. The earliest known instance of a 'professional code' is the Hippocratic Oath (q.v.), probably of fourth century BC:

I will look upon him who shall have taught me this Art even as one of my parents. I will share my substance with him, and I will supply his necessities if he be in need. I will regard his offspring even as my own brethren, and I will teach them this Art, if they would learn it, without fee or covenant. I will impart this Art by precept, by lecture and by every mode of teaching, not only to my own sons, but to the sons of him who hath taught me, and to disciples bound by covenant and oath according to the Law of Medicine. The regimen I adopt shall be for the benefit of my patients according to my ability and judgment, and not for their hurt or for any wrong. I will give no deadly drug to any, though it be asked of me, nor will I counsel such, and especially I will not aid a woman to procure abortion. Whatsoever house I enter, there I will go for the benefit of the sick, refraining from all wrong doing or corruption, and especially from any act of seduction, of male or female, bond or free. Whatsoever things I see or hear concerning the life of men, in my attendance on the sick, or even apart therefrom, which ought not to be noised abroad, I will keep silence thereon, counting such things to be sacred secrets.

This oath is still read to medical students, when they receive instruction in medical ethics in the course of their training. This code emphasizes the need to maintain a relationship of confidence between doctor and patient; the patient must be sure that the doctor will respect information given him in the course of his professional service. This is analogous to the 'seal of the confessional' between a priest and his penitents, whereby a priest is bound not to divulge what he hears in confession. (In this case there are sacramental as well as ethical reasons, since the priest is looked on as instrumental in the relation between the penitent and God.) In some countries these communications are 'privileged', that is, the recipient is not bound to disclose them in a court of law under threat of contempt of court if he refuses. Communications between lawyers and their clients are privileged. The reasons for this were given by L. J. Knight-Bruce, in *Pearse v. Pearse* (1846), De Gex and Sm. 28.29:

Truth, like all other good things, may be loved unwisely – may be pursued too keenly – may cost too much. And surely the meanness and the mischief of prying into a man's confidential consultations with his legal adviser, the general evil of infusing evil and dissimulation, uneasiness, suspicion and fear into those communications which must take place, and which, unless in a condition of perfect security, must take place uselessly or worse, are too great a price to pay for truth itself.

This pronouncement throws light on the general character of professional ethics. Professional ethics do not concern the general obligations of human beings to other human beings as such, but canalize certain of these obligations in relation to the functional requirements of carrying out a particular kind of service. They formulate the sort of conduct needed if the relation between the professional person and his client is to be such that the work in which they are both interested can be done. The relation between the professional person and his client is, however, only one of the role relationships in which he is professionally concerned. There are also his relationships to his colleagues, and his relations as a professional person to the lay public. Thus, though a barrister is under an obligation not to divulge communications between himself and his client, he also has a duty to the court and to the cause of justice. While his duty is to put the best interpretation he can on the evidence in the interest of his client, he must not deceive the court by making a statement he knows to be false. Professional ethics as between colleagues are intended as means of maintaining mutual trust and collaboration within the profession. They normally prescribe that a professional person shall not advertise his services, shall not entice clients from another practitioner, shall be ready to help a colleague in case of need. Some of these matters are questions of 'professional etiquette'; the borderline between etiquette and ethics is, however, not easy to draw, as for instance in the practice of a barrister only seeing a client in the presence of his solicitor and only accepting a brief through a solicitor.

An important part of professional ethics is concerned with the maintenance of what Talcott Parsons called 'affective neutrality'. Some personal relations are such that affections and emotion enter into them in a particular and intimate way. The relation between husband and wife is an outstanding case in point. Professional relationships are best served where the professional person can achieve a certain emotional detachment while at the same time being genuinely concerned to help his client. This does not mean he need be a 'cold fish'; it means he must avoid the kind of emotional involvement which could cloud his judgment; and while he may not be able to avoid liking some of his clients better than others, he must not let this be a reason for giving them preferential treatment. A sexual relationship between a doctor and patient can be a matter for disciplinary action and for striking the doctor's name off the register. Psychoanalysts in particular have had to give careful thought to the ethical restraints necessary in the 'transference' situation, where an emotional attitude on the patient's part has to be allowed temporarily for therapeutic reasons.

A professional code can therefore be presented as a form of functional role morality, designed to promote the kind of relationships within which a required service can best be carried out. Beyond this, the behaviour so enjoined also becomes valued on its own account as a matter of professional integrity,

and adds to the respect with which professional persons are regarded in the community. Professional ethics are therefore not only concerned with relations with patients, colleagues and members of the public, but also with maintaining the public image of the profession. In the case of the established professions in particular, professional ethics are pre-eminently conservative in the non-party sense of conserving the moral and intellectual traditions of the profession, and also in the sense of being administered by what tends to be a conservative hierarchy not always sensitive to new social conditions. Nevertheless, they can represent a tradition of careful thought and experience concerning certain specific problems which a practitioner is likely to meet in the course of his work. They thus protect him against certain kinds of pressure – for instance the pressure to use professional influence in a 'nepotist' way to secure jobs for relations and friends whose qualifications may not be equal to those of other candidates; and above all against the pressure to divulge confidential information. The work of a professional person, especially perhaps that of a doctor, gives rise to a large number of often very difficult problems for moral decisions. That the lines for guidance on some of the more typically recurrent of these has been laid down in his professional ethics is not likely to mean that his own powers of moral judgment need go unexercised, or that he need not acquire skill and sensitivity in personal relationships. *See* **Business Ethics; Medical Ethics.**

W. W. Boulton, *A Guide to Conduct and Etiquette at the Bar of England and Wales*, 1953; A. M. Carr-Saunders and P. A. Wilson, *The Professions*, 1933; R. K. Merton, *Some Thoughts on the Professions in American Society*, 1960; Talcott Parsons, *Essays on Sociological Theory*, 1949, Chap. VIII, 'The Professions and Social Structure'; *The Social System*, 1952, Chap. X, 'Social Structure and Dynamic Process: the Case of Modern Medical Practice'; Willard L. Sperry, *The Ethical Basis of Medical Practice*, 1952.

DOROTHY EMMET

Progress, Belief in

Progress – the view that both the ends of natural and human life and the means to those ends are improving and that desirable goals are being achieved – is a characteristically modern notion. Belief in progress was almost non-existent in the Greek, Roman and even Far Eastern world views, particularly as long as the dominating notion was that of fate. Even early Christian thought, holding that the end of the world was soon to come, looked forward to a better condition only in the next life and then only for those who are saved.

Belief in progress is based on the conjunction

of two modern notions: (1) the view that *change* characterizes all existence, that this is a growing universe from the microscopic to the macroscopic levels; (2) the doctrine of *evolution* – the view that all existence is growing in complexity and longevity. Joining these two basic notions with certain historical considerations, nineteenth-century thought (Spencer) held that progress is not only possible, but inevitable. In various theories of progress there are diversities of views concerning the *rate* and the *pattern*, for example, that it proceeds in a straight line, that it is cyclical and embodies periods of regression, etc.

Believers in progress, along with believers in democracy, usually emphasize the increasing domination of matter by mind (Peirce) and the guidance of the mind by ever higher ends. As a consequence, there is little if any debate about what is usually called 'outward progress' – control over environment, communication, relief of pain and growth in health. Argument exists chiefly, if not solely, about the fact and degree of so-called 'inward progress' – that is, man's capacity to become a free and responsible person in a world of free and responsible nations. Thus, from Will Durant to Bury, contemporary man, while placing serious strictures on evolutionary naturalism's belief in the inevitability of progress, soundly reaffirms belief in the idea of progress, either from the naturalistic and humanistic context or within the framework of Christian theology. The latter emphasizes the possibilities of man's personal and collective growth when under the guidance of God. Indeed, there is a contemporary reassessment of the whole doctrine of nature and grace which, employing both philosophical and biblical insights, stresses, though cautiously and critically, the redemptive and therefore improving character of all life under God.

John Baillie, *The Belief in Progress*, 1951; Carl L. Becker, *Progress and Power*, 1960; J. C. Bury, *The Idea of Progress*, 1932; Kurt W. Marek, *Yestermorrow: Notes on Man's Progress*, 1961.

CHARLES W. KEGLEY

Propaganda

It is embarrassing for the modern Christian to remember that as a matter of semantic history 'propaganda' has been used synonymously with 'evangelism'. When the Congregation for the Propagation of the Faith was instituted in 1633 or the Society for the Propagation of the Gospel in Foreign Parts (1701) 'propaganda' was clearly assumed to be a suitable word for evangelism or the mission of the Church. Propaganda was appropriate when it meant persuading men to become Christians. The embarrassment for the modern Christian is that 'propaganda' has now come to mean contriving conditions where men's critical resistances are so weakened and their freedom of choice so severely reduced that acquiescence follows. This kind of acquiescence is incompatible with the free responsible response of faith.

The biblical material and Christian practice suggest the necessity for clarifying the distinctions between education, propaganda and evangelism. In Christian history 'religious education' has frequently amounted to propaganda, in the same way that in Marxian thought communist propaganda is equated with education. The object of education however is to increase the understanding of knowledge and the ability to handle it with humility, patience and a critical appreciation. It seeks to enlarge the range of experience and to nurture independence of judgment. In propaganda, on the other hand, there is a systematic attempt to influence people by reducing the amount of information and discussion available and encouraging them to act on impulse. Those to be persuaded are led to believe that only one line of action in a particular situation is possible.

Christian evangelism may be defined as a way of handling the gospel in a manner which is appropriate to the manner of Christ. This manner is that of the 'sign' which is at the same time a *skandalon*. Jesus did not engage in propaganda about himself, or about God. He spoke and acted in a 'signful' parabolic way which suggests that he believed that not he, but the Father, would do the revealing. His vocation was not to preach himself or explain himself, but to do the task the Father had given him. This explains what Kierkegaard called the necessarily 'indirect' manner of communication of Jesus, and it has as a corollary a certain indirectness in the manner of Christian evangelism. This is necessary to safeguard the freedom and autonomy of the decision of faith and to eschew the kind of language which assumes, for instance, that the divinity of Christ is logically demonstrable and that faith is simply another word for ability to follow an argument.

In what ways, then, would propaganda as presented above be inappropriate for the activity of Christian evangelism? Propaganda would violate the 'signful' character of communication which the NT shows to be normative for Christians. Christ's method of parable, allegory and irony needs to be reflected in the manner of those who seek to act and speak in his name. In the words of C. S. Lewis: 'Christian evangelism should by its very means convey the gospel which heals the wound of individuality without undermining the privilege of it' (*An Experiment in Criticism*, 1961, p. 140). Propaganda is as inimical to Christianity as it is to art and for the same reason: it destroys the economy, which is the feature of both modes of communication, by saying too much and leaving too little margin for the free response of the person addressed.

E. J. TINSLEY

Property, Ethics of

The attitude of Christian thinking towards property has always been an ambivalent one. The ownership of property in some form has normally been accepted as essential for the full expression of personality under the conditions of this life, and therefore as one of the basic personal rights. Voluntary communism, as practised by the church in Jerusalem in its early days, or by monastic orders and other communities, has been regarded as exceptional. Most men need to own things, even if it is only clothes, tools, or a house. But the rights of property have always been regarded as conditional, not absolute, for all things come from God and are to be held in trust, as under stewardship.

While there is general agreement as regards personal property, there would be less unanimity about property rights in the means of production, which give employers power over the lives and earnings of their employees. There is a tradition of Christian socialism which would accept that as an ideal such property should be collectively owned. A more generally accepted view would be that there is nothing inherently right or wrong in private ownership of businesses or factories or land or houses for letting and similar productive enterprises. Private ownership may provide a stimulus to greater enterprise, but it may also open the way to the abuse of economic power over others. It must be justified by its achievements, as an effective means of meeting the community's wants, and in so far as it leads to abuse, the community has the right and the duty to intervene.

In the modern world corporate ownership is increasingly replacing individual ownership of the means of production. The large-scale company may not be very different in its ethos from the public board or the government department or local authority. The ordinary shareholders of a company are a constantly shifting body with little knowledge or experience of the company's operation, and provided reasonable dividends are forthcoming, the directors need take little notice of them. Yet they are the legal owners, and the Board is obliged by law to consider their interests, whereas it has no obligation to consider those of employees or customers or the general public, while the benefit of any appreciation in the value of the company's assets accrues to them alone, through the rise in the price of their shares. As against this, they bear the ultimate financial risks, and they are still necessary as a source of risk capital.

In the face of such changes, different strands of Christian thinking have taken different attitudes. The traditional Roman Catholic view has always stressed the right to property as a natural right (cf. *Rerum Novarum*, 1891, paras. 5–12). Hence Roman Catholics have tended to advocate the wider ownership of property, including acquisition by employees of shareholdings in the companies which employ them. They tend also to stress co-operative ownership as an ideal, including the favouring of social security provision by contributions by the insured and their employers to semi-autonomous funds, based on industry or local area, rather than through nation-wide schemes with an element of exchequer finance on the British model. But Roman Catholic thought also insists that the right to property is a social right as well as an individual one, a means by which goods destined for the whole human race may more truly serve their purpose (cf. *Quadragesimo Anno*, paras. 45–52). Hence the community has the right to regulate its use.

In non-Roman thinking of recent years, there has probably been less stress on the dispersal of property ownership as desirable in itself and more ready acceptance of public ownership as well as public regulation, in those cases where it seems desirable. D. Jenkins in *Equality and Excellence* maintains that property which involves the livelihood of others and the well-being of the community is affected with a public interest which justifies public control and sometimes public ownership. In Britain the Liberal Party advocates co-ownership and co-partnership, but many others would place more emphasis on the duty of the State to regulate the conditions under which the private sector of the economy shall operate.

There has long been concern about the ownership of property as a source of inequality of income, opportunity and power, since incomes from property tend to be much more unequally distributed than those from work. In particular, the right of inheritance, in spite of death duties, still raises the question how far the desire of parents to provide for their children should be allowed to justify their being enabled to give them an unduly favourable start in life.

Private ownership of house property also causes problems. With the rise in housing standards and building costs, the ownership of houses for renting has ceased to be a remunerative form of investment, except in the case of luxury flats. This has led to an encouragement of owner-occupancy, helped by facilities for the easy raising of mortgages, but rising house prices mean that such ownership is not available to those with lower incomes. In Britain the gap has been partially bridged by widespread building of houses at subsidized rents by local authorities, but, especially in more rapidly growing areas such as London, scarcity of land and hence very high building costs, together with a rapid influx of population and the deterioration of older properties under rent control, have led to serious abuses and widespread public concern, though as yet to no agreed solution.

D. T. Jenkins, *Equality and Excellence*, 1961;
D. L. Munby, *Christianity and Economic
Problems*, 1956; *God and the Rich Society*,
1961; Papal Encyclicals, *Mater et Magistra*,
1961; *Quadragesimo Anno*, 1931; *Rerum Novarum*, 1891.

JOHN F. SLEEMAN

Prophets

The prophets of Israel have a unique place in
the history of theological ethics as pioneers in
stressing the ethical dimension of religion, in
criticizing cults that had no moral value, and
in demanding personal and social righteousness.
See **Jewish Ethics; Old Testament Ethics;** and
articles on individual prophets.

Prostitution

Prostitution in its common sexual sense is the
offering of one's body for sexual purposes in
return for money or other favours. It usually
refers to the practice of women offering
themselves to men for sexual intercourse in
return for money, though it need not be confined to that practice. Male prostitution exists
in which a man does the same thing to satisfy
the physical desires of another male homosexual. These are the two most common forms
of prostitution though for a man to offer himself for a woman's sexual satisfaction or a
woman to a woman homosexual for payment
would also be forms of prostitution.

The practice of prostitution is widespread in
India and carries no social or moral stigma.
It was also frankly accepted by the Greeks, and
historically it has played a part in a number of
religious rites. Since the beginning of the Christian Church prostitution has been theoretically
condemned, but there have been periods during
which it has received different degrees of
toleration.

In its most common form there have been
moralists who have held the view that prostitution could be tolerated because it was necessary
to avoid a greater evil. St Thomas Aquinas was
among those who took this view (*De Regimine
Principium*, 1,c.14). It was thought that unless
women were allowed to practise prostitution
there would be an increase in adultery, rape,
and homosexual practices. Controlled prostitution was considered to be one means of keeping
within limits an evil which could not be altogether removed. This attitude was generally
adopted during the Middle Ages, and it has
continued in some countries until modern
times.

Recently there have been tendencies to
stiffen laws against prostitution in the West, but
the cause seems to have little to do with the
moral considerations, but more to do with
questions of hygiene. The widespread practice
of prostitution carries with it dangers of infec-
tion from venereal diseases, and the consequent

spreading of these diseases. This increasing
awareness of health hazards has been accompanied by some lessening of demand for professional prostitutes owing to the increasing
availability of contraceptives and the consequent
greater freedom of sexual intercourse between
ordinary people.

From a Christian point of view prostitution
is altogether to be condemned as a misuse of
one of the most sacred human attributes, that
of sex. The sacramental reality of human nature
makes prostitution a misuse of the human
person. It involves 'using' another person for
one's personal physical relief without consideration for the personality of the person used. Both
these principles, which are fundamental to
Christian ethics, must be conclusive for Christian moral judgment. The NT condemns such
practices, and the sacramental aspect of human
nature is strongly stressed by St Paul in writing
that the body is the temple of the Holy Spirit
(I Cor. 3.16).

HERBERT WADDAMS

Prudence

Prudence is the practical expression of wisdom,
wisdom being the poise and habitual disposition
of the wise man which enables him to see the
connections between happenings more clearly
than can the man blinded by fear or his own
opinions. Prudence is not to be mistaken for
caution, which indicates the man who takes
care of his property, his money and his
reputation.

The prudent man's reaction to a situation is
quick because he is alert and aware of what is
happening. He does not deal with persons and
occasions by well tested techniques. He acts in
the light of his knowledge of the various relationships which compose the situation in which
he is acting, for example, he will not try to be
the father of an orphan who needs affection
– he will be to him only what he can be.

Six characteristic activities of prudence are:
(1) the hidden work of being clear in mind as
to the obligations consequent upon one's
several relationships; (2) reflection on the
possible kinds of action which might express
the truth that human behaviour is more than
concern for the obvious immediate needs of
people in one short-lived situation; (3) acting
in awareness that each short-lived situation
moves into another situation without pause;
(4) knowing that in some cases it is difficult to
see the difference between courage and foolhardiness; (5) rebuking, encouraging and teaching without humiliating, flattering or patronizing others; and (6) being loyal to institutions
mindful of their deficiencies and evils.

In the mediaeval table of virtues prudence,
the first of the cardinal virtues, immediately
follows the three foundation virtues of faith,
hope and love. Perhaps this is so because faith,
hope and love cannot be translated directly

into human behaviour. If this is so, then prudence is the activity of seeing and attempting to do what is appropriate to the quickly altering environment of human behaviour.

In the life of the Church prudence has to do with the ordering of public worship; the relationship of church members with one another; the preaching of the Word; the appreciation of what is happening in the world; and all that is to be done in the way of evangelization. In specific instances prudence must dissuade man from looking for martyrdom, while at another time church members must be prepared to be martyred. At all times prudence watches in case the Church's zeal to transform the world ends in its being conformed to the world.

The prudent are known by their promptness, courage and patience. The judgment of prudence requires the subtlety of an artist, the precision of a scientist, the clarity of a philosopher, the firmness of a lawyer, the mercy that only the strong can show, the love of a saint and the humility that no man can make for himself.

R. E. C. BROWNE

Psychoanalysis

Psychoanalysis means three things originated by Sigmund Freud: (1) a particular method of psychological therapy; (2) an organized movement of persons qualified to practice such therapy; and (3) a basic theory of personality, and of psychological illness and aberration, originally derived from therapeutic experience.

In psychoanalytic therapy the patient lies on a couch, with analyst seated unseen behind his head, and relates not only events and conscious feelings but also dreams and the mental associations their elements evoke in him upon reflection. As the patient recovers long-forgotten events and feelings, and comes to feel their meaning in a new way, he is permitted to 'transfer' feelings he once had towards real people in his life to the analyst. But the latter, unlike the original person, aids him to analyze and understand the meaning of that feeling in its original relationship. This therapy usually requires at least an hour a day five days a week for not less than two or three years, and sometimes much longer, depending upon the severity of the original condition. Such therapy has been rightly compared with certain delicate forms of surgery. It is therapeutically helpful only to some people. One who is relatively well does not need it; and many mental sufferers are too sick to profit from it. Increasing study is being made to predict those persons who may best profit from it.

The psychoanalytic movement organizes practitioners in two ways: in societies for professional fellowship, and in institutes for the education of new practitioners. The number of qualified practitioners is small, not much above a thousand in the USA. But education of practitioners is lively, with nearly as many

candidates in training as there are qualified analysts. Ordinarily today, the candidates are persons who have attended medical school, taken a medical internship, and served residency in psychiatry. Their education in psychoanalysis consists of two principal parts: instruction in theory and supervision of therapeutic practice. Since most candidates are over thirty on beginning their psychoanalytic training, they work as psychiatrists during the day and have their analytic instruction at night. In the USA the current average age at which they become fully qualified as psychoanalysts is just under forty. Most psychoanalytic institutes are organizationally unrelated to other institutions; but recently a few have affiliated with medical and psychiatric institutions. A few small groups of practitioners split off from the main body of psychoanalysis, organized other societies, and some of them continue to use the term 'psychoanalysis'. But ordinary usage reserves the term to the 'orthodox' groups.

By far the greatest influence of psychoanalysis has been as a theory. It was the original 'dynamic' or 'conflict' theory of personality. Under the term 'unconscious mind', it demonstrated that there are forces within the person of which he is unaware but which vitally affect his thinking, feeling and behaving. At first this theory stressed the previously neglected aspects of psychic life. More recently, it has given new attention to the ego, the partly conscious and integrating and creative dimensions of personality. Some of the terms coined by this theory are defined elsewhere in this dictionary, such as id, ego, superego, Oedipus complex and repression. Especially in the USA this theory is regarded as growing and changing, although its relationship to Freud's ideas is still clear. In Europe the theory tends to be more sectarian, and its practitioners more isolated from other physicians. Far more sufferers are now helped with insights and methods derived from analytic theory than from the application of analytic techniques.

Although early charges against Freud and psychoanalysis for over-emphasizing sexual factors, for muckraking in the slime of psychic life and for reducing everything to the biological level can no longer be sustained by intelligent investigators, it is true that the Freudian revelation of the influence of the unconscious has given ethics a new dimension of life that must be considered seriously. Freud held that man is both more moral and more immoral than he realizes.

There is no better introduction to psychoanalysis than Freud's early lectures to laymen, *A General Introduction to Psychoanalysis* (rev. edn., 1920, paperbacks available). Freud's complete works are available in a standard edition. Several books by Freud are now available in paperback. There are several heavy journals devoted entirely to psychoanalysis.

Freud's principal work dealing with morals and ethics was *Totem and Taboo* (1912). The most thorough consideration of psychoanalysis in relation to ethics is J. C. Flugel, *Man, Morals, and Society* (1945). *Man for Himself* (1947), by Erich Fromm, is comparable in scope, but is regarded by 'orthodox' analysts as coming from a 'deviant school'.

SEWARD HILTNER

Psychology and Ethics

Nearly all forms of psychology today are regarded by psychologists as either descriptive or clinical disciplines. In the latter, such as psychiatry, there is effort to help and heal as well as to understand. But the goals of change are limited to a health criterion. Psychologies, then, by general agreement, are not normative disciplines in the sense of ethics. If particular psychologists set forth normative ethical views, therefore, their colleagues regard them as having moved beyond the self-limitations of psychology itself. To discover the significance of psychology for ethics, the inquirer should look first at something other than the ethical opinions of psychologists.

Modern psychology makes available to ethics two broad lines of relevant data. The first reveals the kinds of factors and their relative strength, that tend to determine or greatly affect the values of a person or group. Developmental psychology, for instance, provides new and sometimes unexpected information about attitudes towards values as influenced by one's stage in the developmental pilgrimage. Social psychology reveals such knowledge as the weighty influence of social class rearing or aspirations upon choices. Experimental psychology sheds light on such value-predisposing factors as open-mindedness or closed-mindedness. It seems to have identified a so-called 'authoritarian personality', such that if the psychologist knows the person's attitudes towards minority groups he may confidently predict also his attitudes towards who is boss in the family. The above are only samples of the increasing amounts of useful understanding being made available to ethics by psychology as a group of descriptive sciences.

The clinical branches of psychology also make contributions to the same points already noted, and in addition demonstrate the processes by which values may be reinforced or unified, or how they may be changed in one direction or the other. For example, some of the researches done under the direction of Carl R. Rogers that include both clinical and experimental methods, suggest that psychotherapy tends to make real changes in the valuing of one's self or of other people but little change in the ideal conceptions of value. A related finding from many clinicians is that when good therapy is done with a person who is emotionally constricted, he becomes able in a new way to experience joy on proper occasions, and at the same time to experience sadness when the situation is appropriate. An early, and still important, contribution from the clinical area was the demonstration that declared values, especially when held tightly or rigidly, are often more precarious within the person than they appear.

Psychologists concede that the 'brain-washing' in Communist countries makes use of the same processes for changing values that are activated in therapeutic work, but for quite different ends, thus underscoring the importance of an ethics for the clinician. Views differ on the evaluation of advertising especially 'hidden persuaders', political and economic propaganda, and other means of persuasion, as being threats to personal integrity in view of their ability to shape and mould some human values without the person's being aware of what is taking place. As psychological knowledge makes possible an increasing, although still very limited, amount of prediction about certain kinds of value choices and behaviour, some observers have viewed this with alarm as 'control'. Others point to increasing power to predict and control as humanly beneficent, for example, eventually decreasing the number of fetal conceptions that will be born with severe mental or physical deficiencies. But no one denies that the increasing knowledge of how to affect and change values is a two-edged sword.

When Christian ethics is understood not merely as law or commandment or behaviour by itself, nor as a prideful search for the good as ideal, but as involving gospel and freedom in the sense of Paul and thus stemming from thankful awareness of relationship with Jesus Christ, then the psychological data probably have even more to contribute than to a legalistic, idealistic, behaviouristic or aspirational understanding of ethics. Recent competent works in Christian ethics have barely begun to acknowledge their indebtedness to psychology, and few have pursued the connection articulately or systematically. So far, such authorities have made better use of the findings from sociology and cultural anthropology and economics. There is still no competent general work on the significance of psychological findings for Christian ethics. Several specific areas of ethical concern have been dealt with effectively, such as Gordon W. Allport's work on prejudice, or that of William Graham Cole on sex.

SEWARD HILTNER

Public Media

Technical advances have made possible communication with mass audiences through newspapers and magazines, radio and television on an increasingly extensive scale. Sociological observers are in no doubt that these media already, in varying degrees, influence the formation of values, standards and beliefs. The major question of social ethics posed by this development is therefore whether the media are to be regarded as public services accountable to the people through Parliament (by means of debates on annual reports from such bodies as the Press Council, an Advertising Council, etc.) or whether they are to be managed by private enterprise. The problem is that the latter, especially when dependent upon revenue from advertising, is bound to be concerned with what will attract and keep the largest possible audiences and readership and is therefore ready to allow public media to approximate themselves more and more to the entertainment industry. Large circulation newspapers in Great Britain, controlled by a shrinking number of owners, illustrate this tendency. This has a restrictive influence on the amount and range of material considered suitable for a mass-audience; minority features and programmes are squeezed out. Further, if the chief aim is to hold mass-audiences, there will be little serious and sustained attempt to challenge or change public opinion on major contentious issues, although occasionally some 'pseudo-event' will be created and treated contentiously for sensational purposes. There is therefore an inevitable tendency for the public media to develop propagandist habits unless adequate safeguards are maintained. *See* **Propaganda.**

The major Christian point of reference in a consideration of the public media will be the doctrine of man (q.v.) especially man as made in the image of God (and therefore pro-creator), as 'fallen', and as re-created in Christ. A Christian anthropology, firmly based on belief in an authentic incarnation and in its realistic implications, should provide resources for detecting the debilitating kind of fantasy which poses as the real (Richard Hoggart's 'candy-floss world'). The public media, by their very nature, are likely to exhibit the distortion of human life and experience which Roy Campbell has called 'elephantiasis of the soul' and Fr William Lynch 'the grandiose imagination': 'that kind of work in literature and art which leaps too quickly to the splendid, the spectacular, the dream, the magnificent, skipping in the process all those intermediate realities of man and nature which might give some support to our leaping'. Thoroughly analyzed, this treatment of man, with its easy acceptance of the glib and shallow generalization, its appeal to easily aroused emotions and avoidance of the thorny controversial issues, implies a 'gnostic' inability or unwillingness to live genuinely near the full range of the realities of human life and experience.

A significant feature of the public media, because of its influence in the long run on the formation of values, is the development of persuasive advertising where powerful and

ingenious attempts are made, based on extensive and expensive market research in 'motivation', to 'sell' more than the article itself. This kind of advertising with its commendation of ambition, constant appeal to snobberies and desire for 'status', and the insistent suggestion that there is a magical short-cut to the satisfaction of the basic human needs for security, love and significance, presents a popular alternative to the NT concept of the good life, and elevates to the level of virtues the 'deadly' sins of, for example, avarice and envy in traditional systems of Christian moral theology.

The immediate need is for some kind of public control of the media which is compatible with basic human rights and freedom. It would have to risk the charge of 'paternalism', but it is hard to see how the serious and courageous exercise of responsibility in this field could avoid that. The long-term need is for the development of high standards of literary and visual appreciation, especially ability to detect attempts made to blur judgment by the use of 'emotive' language (I. A. Richards's 'mnemonic irrelevancies') or sentimentality. A Christian humanism, informed by the corollaries of belief in the incarnation and the atonement, and with a fully articulated theology of the relation between the creation of God and the creativity of man in terms of man as 'pro-creator', is one of the safeguards necessary to sustain the 'humanizing' of modern culture.

Stuart Hall and Paddy Whannel, *The Popular Arts*, 1964; Richard Hoggart, *The Uses of Literacy*, 1957; William F. Lynch, *The Image Industries*, 1959; *Report of the Committee on Broadcasting*, 1960 (The Pilkington Report) especially Chap. III; National Union of Teachers, *Popular Culture and Personal Responsibility*, 1961; Nicholas Tucker, *Understanding the Mass Media*, 1966.

E. J. TINSLEY

Public Opinion

The precise meaning of the term 'public opinion' is difficult to determine. It does not necessarily imply a general consensus because public opinion can contain both majority and minority elements. Again it is not to be equated with public taste since it is a socially significant attitude capable of influencing national policy. It can exist without being articulated; some particular major issue will have to arise before it achieves public expression.

Serious interest in and study of public opinion is a comparatively recent phenomenon. Greek and Roman writers generally express contempt for the opinion of the public and this attitude was common until the eighteenth century when it came to be assumed that public opinion is formed according to rational processes, and that public opinion is sufficient as a sanction for moral codes (cf. D. Hume's *An Enquiry*

Concerning the Principles of Morals, 1751): *vox populi, vox Dei*. The twentieth century has seen a sharp decline of confidence in the idea that the formation of public opinion follows the laws of human reasoning. This is due to increased awareness, especially as the result of researches in psychology and social investigation, of the part played by subconscious and irrational fears and prejudices. This is particularly the case where changes are proposed in the laws relating to contentious issues, for example, homosexuality, race relations or capital punishment. On these issues it cannot be argued that public opinion is inevitably in the right. It may be the case that an enlightened minority will succeed in moving a government to legislate on such matters long before the majority of the people would themselves have wished to take action. But while changes may thus be brought about which are in advance of public opinion they stand very little chance of success if they are too far ahead of it.

E. J. TINSLEY

Public Ownership. *see* Socialism.

Punishment. *see* Capital Punishment; Corporal Punishment; Rewards and Punishments.

Puritanism

Puritanism arose in the sixteenth century as the English expression of Calvinism. From the negative angle its aim was to purge the established Church of the 'dregs of Popery', but positively its purpose was to reconstruct that church on Genevan lines. It was therefore a movement within the English Church and in origin had no association with Separatists like the Brownites and Barrowites. According to Thomas Fuller (*Church History of Britain*, Bk. IX, para. 66) the term 'Puritans' was not used until 1564 when it was applied by the English bishops to those clergy who refused to subscribe to the liturgy, ceremonies and discipline of the established Church.

The Puritan movement was initiated by those Protestant exiles who on the accession of Elizabeth I returned to England from Geneva, where they had resided during Mary's reign. Two leaders eventually became prominent, Thomas Cartwright, the Cambridge professor, and Walter Travers, whose *Ecclesiasticae Disciplinae . . . explicatio* (1574) became a second textbook for the Puritans. Their first was the Bible in which they found not only 'right' doctrine but also the 'right' form of church government intended by Christ, namely government by elders (presbyters). Thus the first English Puritanism had two emphases, a doctrinal and an ecclesiastical. The Queen was prepared to accept the first but not the second

since the established Church served her political aims better. Consequently by the end of the sixteenth century Elizabeth, assisted by her bishops, had brought the movement's ecclesiastical attempts to an end. But she was unable to annihilate Puritanism as a doctrinal and ethical force because it had already permeated the whole of English church life.

In the seventeenth century, after the Hampton Court conference when King James uttered the historic words 'no bishop, no king', all attempts at reforming the established Church were abandoned and the Puritans joined the Separatists. In 1620 the Pilgrim Fathers carried the Puritan way of life to New England and thereby gave to the New World those moral principles in state and society which are the foundations of American life at its best.

In England after the Restoration Puritanism as a distinct movement was no longer recognizable, but its influence continued as is evidenced in the writings of Milton, Baxter and Bunyan. The evangelical revival in the next century owed much of its power to Puritanism but towards the end of the nineteenth century its influence declined.

Although Puritanism began as an intellectual movement, its greatest impact was not on thought but on action. The Bible was the primary textbook, but the interpretation was purely literal and while Christ was held to be God's supreme self-revelation, there tended to be a preference for the teaching of the OT. This gave rise to the impression that the Puritans stressed law rather than grace, though they believed that salvation was by faith alone. The OT emphasis meant that they were strict sabbatarians. Since the Puritans held to the doctrine of original sin, they regarded all of life as a struggle, first against the evil in one's own heart, and secondly against the work of the devil in society. Great stress was laid on man's individual moral responsibility to a righteous God whose glory it was man's primary duty to promote.

Although they aimed at purity of character and daily living, the Puritans could never be accused of Pharisaism, for their tremendous awe of God inculcated a sense of humility and human self-abasement. They were a people that deeply believed in personal discipline, the purpose of which was to make them more efficient in the service of their Maker.

Their serious regard for work led them to believe that the accumulation of wealth was the sign of God's favour and hence the Puritans had a definite influence upon industry and productivity. All time and talents were to be used to the fullest and not to use them was a sin.

With regard to the relationship of Church and State, believing that all things must serve God, the Puritans saw the State as God's instrument for the working out of his purpose, but since the Church is God's primary instrument, the State must never be allowed to interfere with the Church. In a Christian society the State should be the Church's handmaid. Because every individual was of worth in the sight of God, the Puritans held by the democratic form of government as that which was most likely to give the greatest scope to human freedom. While Church and State were to be kept separate, they taught that the State should be prepared to punish those who broke the laws of God. The State's function was to promote good and also to discourage evil.

In the sphere of education the Puritans played a notable part in every country where they were found. Men should be trained to love God with their minds as well as with their hearts. Yet in one aspect of education the Puritans have been grossly misjudged. They have been criticized on the ground that they were opposed to the arts and that they blatantly destroyed works of beauty as well as discouraging all forms of entertainment. The truth is that they discouraged only those arts that were impure or valueless in promoting the good life. They were not opposed to art as such nor did they disapprove of either drama or fiction as is evidence in the works of their greatest writers like Milton, Bunyan and Defoe. Because the Puritans desired what was plain and simple, it meant that at times they had to dissociate themselves from what was merely aesthetic but wanting in positive moral content.

It can be justly claimed that in the English-speaking world the Puritan tradition has been among the most important factors in moulding the character of its peoples, for it imparted to them those great qualities of will-power, personal responsibility and complete dedication. If the Puritans sometimes failed to manifest to others the Christian characteristic of joy, they undoubtedly possessed the inner joy found in total consecration to the service of the Most High. Their God was their glory.

W. Haller, *The Rise of Puritanism*, 1938; S. J. Knox, *Walter Travers; Paragon of Elizabethan Puritanism*, 1962; J. Marlowe, *The Puritan Tradition in English Life*, 1956; A. F. S. Pearson, *Church and State*, 1928; R. B. Perry, *Puritanism and Democracy*, 1944; A. Simpson, *Puritanism in Old and New England*, 1955.

S. J. KNOX

Quadragesimo Anno.
see Pontifical Social Ecyclicals.

Quietism
Quietism is the attitude of passivity and receptivity before God, as opposed to activism. *See* Contemplation; Mysticism and Ethics.

Race Relations
Man as a social, historical being finds his identity (at least to a significant degree) in human groups, in which he participates in shared experiences. The individual is never simply a sample of humanity; he is a particular man in his time and place, part of a people with a distinctive history. This particularity belongs to the finitude and variety of mankind, not to sin. In the Christian understanding of man, God is the creator of all persons and exercises his providence over all peoples.

If the particularity of man's social identity is not due to sin, the effect of sin is to introduce suspicion, fear, and hostility between groups. The ancient record of the tower of Babel is an imaginative account of the divisive power of sin, which makes groups of men unable to understand each other.

The grace of God overcomes human divisions, reuniting mankind. 'There is neither Jew nor Greek, there is neither slave nor free, there is neither male nor female; for you are all one in Christ Jesus' (Gal. 3.28). At Pentecost the Holy Spirit reversed the history of Babel, enabling men of diverse tongues and nations to understand one another. The Jewish disciples soon baptized an Ethiopian and a Roman, for Christ had come to save all.

The word *race* has no precise meaning in the NT. The Greek word *genos* is translated as family, relatives, nation, people, countrymen. It may refer to Christians themselves as a 'chosen race' (I Peter 2.9), for their unity in faith is stronger than any ties formed by ancestry or political history.

In modern anthropology the concept of race is almost as imprecise as in the Bible. A race may be defined as any group of people with identifiable traits that are biologically inherited. Working with such definitions scientists may distinguish as few as three races of mankind (Caucasian, Mongoloid, Negroid) or as many as 200. Racial inheritance is determined by certain genes, which are few in man's total genetic constitution but which govern such highly visible traits as skin pigmentation.

It is necessary to talk of race relations because human beings often meet each other not simply as persons but as members of races. Race relations offer a highly significant case study in human behaviour, which may be studied both sociologically and theologically.

Sociologically, the issue hinges upon the difference between an in-group and out-groups. Men characteristically organize themselves in in-groups. The phenomenon may be in part a healthy one. Within the in-group the person has an identity; he is recognized as one of the group, who need not constantly justify himself and his habits. He enjoys the experience of belonging.

But one of the gratifications of belonging to

an in-group is the recognition that not every-body can belong. The in-group contrasts itself with out-groups, whom it distrusts or rejects. The power and universality of rejection of the out-group has been described by a modern anthropologist, Ruth Benedict, in her *Patterns of Culture* (1946, pp. 6–7), as follows:

All primitive tribes agree in recognizing this category of the outsider, those who are not only outside the provisions of the moral code which holds within the limits of one's own people, but who are summarily denied a place anywhere in the human scheme. . . . We are not likely to clear ourselves easily of so fundamental a human trait, but we can at least learn to recognize its history and its hydra manifestations.

Theologically race relations display a pheno-menology of sin, as described by Reinhold Niebuhr in *The Nature and Destiny of Man* (2 vols., 1941–3). The human group (like the individual) lives in an anxiety that is native to a creature who is finite, yet enjoys enough trans-cendence to recognize his finitude and inse-curity. Other groups appear as threats to him. Instead of meeting such threats with a faith and love that could heal anxiety, the group answers with the proud attempt to dominate the out-groups or with a false subservience that seeks to placate. Hence race relations frequently exhibit the pattern of fear, which turns to estrangement, hostility and will-to-power. Races fight each other, enslave each other, deny each other elemental human rights and the respect of fellow creatures made in the image of God.

Racial *prejudice* is the categorizing of a racial group in such a way that the prejudiced indivi-dual cannot meet others as persons but must confront them as members of a race which he approaches with hatred, condescension or envy. Racial prejudice is *per se* not morally better or worse than the many other forms of prejudice that are characteristic of a sinful man-kind. But it has more devastating consequences than most forms of prejudice. Because the marks of race are visually recognizable and are permanently stamped upon persons by biologi-cal heredity, racial prejudice can easily be institutionalized and transmitted among people. The rejected group can become the victim of enforced discrimination. A society can develop laws and customs that work to persecute a race, denying its members the most elemental rights and opportunities. People living in such a society and schooled by it from infancy are likely to share in its prejudice, even though they reject the prejudice on moral and rational grounds.

The theological understanding of prejudice, as a concrete manifestation of human sin, in-volving a sickness in human nature, has been attacked by two popular views, sharply opposed

to each other. The one doctrine insists that racial prejudice is innate and instinctual, inde-pendent of man's will and irremovable. This doctrine has been advanced by racialists who want to preserve discrimination and excuse their own prejudice. It has been refuted by widespread evidence of people living together without racial prejudice, in particular by children who often are innocent of the racial prejudices of their society.

The opposing view insists that prejudice is not natural to humanity but is learned by each generation from the bad example or deliberate instruction of its elders. This doctrine, often taught by liberal rationalists, has been used in efforts to overcome prejudice. But even when used in good causes, the argument is inade-quate. By attributing each generation's pre-judice to its forerunners, it pushes the origin of hostility backward to some unknown time, when an unhappy accident inflicted a malady on society, which society somehow has not shaken off. It does not account for the fact that, while specific prejudices undoubtedly are learned, human beings have an unusual apti-tude for this kind of learning. And it neglects the fact that children, even when they do not share the prejudices of their parents, often develop their own antagonism between in-group and out-group.

A Christian understanding of prejudice sees it as neither innate nor innocently learned. It belongs to 'the mystery of iniquity', which is not the work of an inevitable fate but is also not a deliberate choice. It belongs to man's freedom in exactly that area where freedom may be vitiated by the bondage of the will. The prejudiced group has usually not *decided* to be prejudiced; its prejudice emerges from its history yet not without the wilful participation of the group.

Such a theological interpretation of prejudice encourages also the investigation of many specific causes of particular prejudices. Religi-ous causes have led to fanatical persecution of persons who are categorized as infidels and heretics. Economic causes have produced many rationalizations designed to protect special privilege or to justify enslavement and exploita-tion of other races. Sexual causes, arising out of the peculiar attractions and fears that operate between races, have led to vast mythologies and networks of custom that shape race relations. Ignorance has encouraged unscientific notions of race and misconceptions of racial and ethnic groups, thus supplying false reasons to defend prejudicial conduct.

The last of these causes, ignorance, offers a specially revealing insight into the nature of man and his prejudices. Idealists, noting the frequent coincidence between ignorance and prejudice, have often thought that rational enlightenment, by removing ignorance, would overcome prejudice. Usually the method has disappointing results because of the nature of the ignorance involved. It is not an ignorance due merely to lack of information. It is a functional ignorance; that is, it serves the purpose of helping the prejudiced group maintain its prejudice. The ignorance is as much the result of prejudice as the prejudice is the result of ignorance. Prejudiced people usually resent correction of their misconceptions. In terms of traditional Christian theology, both intellect and will are corrupted by sin. Contemporary social psychology takes account of the same phenomena in its frequent finding that prejudice affects the cognitive faculties, making some kinds of learning difficult or impossible.

The Christian Church, insofar as it is faithful to its reconciling ministry, overcomes the alienation between races. As a community of faith, it enjoys a unity that transcends racial differences. As a missionary community, it seeks to do a work of divine reconciliation among all races.

As a community of fallible and sinful men, the Church distorts the gospel it proclaims and corrupts the mission it undertakes. To the extent that the Church shares in the sin of mankind, its guilt in race relations is not surprising. This guilt belongs to its corruption, not its fidelity. It is an occasion for repentance and renewal, not for complacency. But it is hardly an occasion for surprise in a community that knows itself to be constituted of sinners.

However, the Church cannot apologize for its failure in race relations on the grounds that it has simply failed to purge itself of human sin. The actual record shows that the Church, rather than modifying racial antagonism, has frequently intensified it. The two chief evidences, prejudice of white gentiles against Jews and against coloured peoples, are proofs of the ability of man to use even his religion as an instrument not of redemption but of pride.

In the case of prejudice against the Jews, religion has been a primary cause. Throughout the centuries Christians have blamed the Jews for rejecting Christ and have justified hatred and discrimination on this ground. The Jewish people are more accurately regarded as an ethnic than as a racial group, since their racial inheritance is highly diversified. But, practically speaking, prejudice against the Jews shows most of the characteristics of racial prejudice. *See* **Anti-Semitism**.

In the case of prejudice against coloured peoples, religion has been less a cause than a rationalization. In the period of European exploration and colonialization, from the fifteenth to the twentieth centuries, white men carried their religion, along with their commercial and military interests, into many parts of the world. Some Christian missionaries did an authentic work of evangelizing and educating. Others unconsciously took paternalistic attitudes with them. And many governmental and business agents used the Christian religion to justify exploitation of the colonized areas. The worst fruit of this racism was Negro slavery, which persisted in the USA until 1863. The legacy of slavery has been continuing racial bitterness and exploitation through the century following emancipation. Often Christians have given biblical and theological justifications, first of slavery, then of segregation.

The answer to unjust and unloving race relations, as seen by Christian ethics, involves two similtaneous activities: (1) institutional and legal changes, which eliminate enforced discrimination and segregation, and which make the opportunity for races to meet in ways that encourage understanding; and (2) the healing of the anxieties and insecurities that give rise to racial animosity.

By the mid-twentieth century the leadership of world Christendom – including the Vatican, the World Council of Churches, and the official voices of most major denominations – has taken unequivocal stands in favour of racial equality and inter-racial understanding. Many local Christian groups have shown considerable courage in combating prejudice. And the forces of hostility within the churches, although still powerful, are clearly on the defensive.

Gordon Allport, *The Nature of Prejudice*, 1954; Kyle Haselden, *The Racial Problem in Christian Perspective*, 1959; Visser 't Hooft, *The Ecumenical Movement and the Racial Problem*, 1945; Gunnar Myrdal, *An American Dilemma*, 1944.

ROGER L. SHINN

Racism

Racism is the belief that certain racial groups are, by nature and heredity, superior to the rest of mankind and therefore justified in dominating and discriminating against inferior groups. While prejudice may be merely an attitude (conscious or unconscious), racism is a dogma, deliberately cultivated and transmitted. It purports to describe factual or even metaphysical differences within mankind. It consigns some human races to an inherent inferiority at the core of their being.

Elements of racist thought are evident from ancient times, for example, in the distinction between Greeks and barbarians, in the caste system of India, or in the claims of various peoples to a special destiny denied to others. In later times Shinto combined nationalism and racism in Japanese religion. It remained, however, for the modern West to develop philosophical expressions of racism in systematic form.

Starting with Count Joseph Arthur de Gobineau's *Essay on the Inequality of Human Races* (1853–5), a series of books asserted the superiority of the 'Nordic' race. These books, published over the next century, included: Houston Stewart Chamberlain, *Foundations of the Nineteenth Century* (2 vols., 1910); Madison Grant, *The Passing of the Great Race* (1917); T. Lothrop Stoddard, *The Rising Tide of Colour against White World-Supremacy* (1920); Adolf Hitler, *Mein Kampf* (2 vols., 1925-7). These writings express hostility variously against 'the yellow peril', the coloured peoples, and the Jews. They are filled with historical absurdities and can make no claim to scientific standing.

The doctrine of white supremacy, often found in modern racism, has met some counter-doctrines. The Black Muslims have asserted the racial superiority of dark-skinned peoples, and the nationalist movements of Asia and Africa have sometimes sounded racist overtones. In a time when racism has met the strongest possible rejection on both scientific and ethical grounds, it has become an increasingly portentous menace. The historian Arnold J. Toynbee has suggested that mankind's greatest conflicts may shift from nationalistic rivalries of the past to racial rivalries of the future.

Although the Christian Church has often been afflicted by racism, the Christian ethic rejects radically any doctrine of racial superiority or any breach of human fellowship on racial lines. The NT teaches that God can from stones 'raise up children to Abraham' (Matt. 3.9) and that in Christ 'there is neither Jew nor Greek' (Gal. 3.28). To Christian faith racism is heresy and idolatry.

George D. Kelsey, *Racism and the Christian Understanding of Man*, 1965; Ashley Montagu, *Man's Most Dangerous Myth; The Fallacy of Race*, 1945; Edmund D. Soper, *Racism: A World Issue*, 1947.

ROGER L. SHINN

Rauschenbusch, Walter

Walter Rauschenbusch (1861-1918), leading prophet and theologian of the Social Gospel (q.v.) in America, was born in Rochester, New York. The son of a German-born minister, he was educated in both the USA and in Germany. He graduated from the University of Rochester in 1884, and from the Rochester Theological Seminary in 1886. He was called as pastor of the Second German Baptist Church in New York City, on the edge of the depressed 'Hell's Kitchen' area. The young minister, raised in an individualistic pietist tradition, was greatly disturbed by the evil social conditions he saw; he began to participate in social reform movements and to study progressive and socialist literature.

The central theme of his life was the effort to relate his profound and evangelical Christian faith with his passion for social reform. During a leave from his parish in 1891 he studied social movements in England and the NT in Germany, and returned with a vision of the Kingdom of God which for him brought together the two main concerns of his life. Accepting a liberal

theological orientation in the Ritschl-Harnack tradition, Rauschenbusch kept with it a firm christocentrism and a bright hope in the coming of the Kingdom of God on earth as an historical possibility. As the central figure in the Brotherhood of the Kingdom, founded in 1892, he worked with others to spread Kingdom theology. In 1897, he was called to teach at Rochester Theological Seminary, where he later became professor of church history. In 1907, he published *Christianity and the Social Crisis*, which catapulted him into fame. Until his death from cancer, he was in the forefront of the American Social Gospel, then at its peak of influence.

His social ethics combined motifs from his early Pietism, from the sectarian tendencies of his German Baptist background with its affinities for Anabaptist thought, from his evangelical Liberalism, and from a Neo-Calvinist 'transformationism' which stressed the possibility of the christianization of society. His concept of God owed much to the prophetic tradition, combined with an emphasis on divine immanence, characteristic of Liberalism. He believed in the 'immense latent perfectibility in human nature', and felt that Christ's law of love really put to work in individual and social life would lead to the dawn of the Kingdom. In spelling out the specific details of his social ethic of love, Rauschenbusch drew heavily on the progressive, mildly radical, socialistic thought of his time. In *Christianising the Social Order* (1912) he argued that four of the five major areas of life (family, church, education, politics) had already undergone certain constitutional changes so that they could serve to some degree as part of the organism through which the spirit of Christ could do its work in humanity, but that the one remaining area – business – was the unregenerate section of the social order. Social justice could be established by such things as the abolition of special privilege, the unionization of labour, the democratization of the economic order and the extention of consumer co-operatives. He called himself a Christian socialist, but his was an evolutionary, non-doctinaire, really non-political form of socialism. His climactic work, *A Theology for the Social Gospel* (1917), written in the shadow of the first World War, expressed his profound awareness of the way evil was transmitted corporately, and sought to provide theological roots for the movement in which he played so central a role.

D. R. Sharpe, *Walter Rauschenbusch*, 1942; Donovan E. Smucker, 'The Origins of Walter Rauschenbusch's Social Ethics', unpublished doctoral dissertation, University of Chicago, 1957.

ROBERT T. HANDY

Recreation. *see* Amusements.

Red Cross

Red Cross is the name of a national and inter-national organization primarily for the care of the sick and wounded in war, whose emblem is a white flag bearing a red cross. It took its origin from the publication in 1862 by Henri Dunant, a Swiss banker, of a booklet *Un Souvenir de Solférino*. Shocked by the sufferings of the wounded on the battlefield of Solferino, Dunant urged the necessity of constituting societies in different countries for the relief of the wounded in war. His appeal evoked a response in Switzerland where he found himself associated with General Guillaume Dufour, commander-in-chief of the Swiss army, in a body later known as the Comité International de la Croix-Rouge. Founded in 1863, this com-mittee, while international in respect of the scope of its work, consists of twenty-five Swiss citizens so as to secure in every country the protection of the traditional Swiss neutrality. In 1864 representatives of twenty-six govern-ments framed the Geneva convention which enunciated certain principles: respect for the wounded, neutrality of military hospitals, pro-tection for the personnel and material of the medical services.

The world-wide Red Cross movement now comprises the national Red Cross societies, the League of Red Cross societies and the Inter-national Committee. It is part of the work of that committee to encourage the formation of national societies and to promote the observ-ance and development of humanitarian con-ventions by the governments of the world. In time of war the Red Cross has also sought to disseminate information about prisoners of war and to improve their material and moral condition. Since the first World War the move-ment has in practice extended its interest and help to include the relief of suffering caused by calamities other than war, such as earthquake and flood, while the American and British societies provide a wide range of welfare ser-vices for the citizens generally. Thus the Red Cross is tending towards more comprehensive efforts for the prevention and relief of suffering of many kinds.

Ellen Hart, *Man Born to Live: Life and Work of Henry Dunant, Founder of the Red Cross*, 1953; James Avery Joyce, *Red Cross Inter-national*, 1959.

STEWART MECHIE

Relativism

Relativism is the view that the morality of actions, etc., depends upon the attitudes taken to them by particular societies or individuals. It is to be distinguished from emotivism, prescriptivism, subjectivism. *See also* **Relativism in Ethics.**

R. M. HARE

Relativism in Ethics

Relativism in ethics can take a number of forms. As a popular doctrine, it is the thesis that what is right or wrong, good or bad, for a person varies in relation to the cultural group to which he belongs. This may be called 'cultural relativism'. It involves the denial that there is a standard or objective morality in principle applicable to all men; and it rests on the empirical premise that in fact men's values and mores differ as between one culture and time and another. This premise may be called 'descriptive relativism'. It is not so much a thesis in ethics as in comparative anthropology (its truth has been, in a qualified way, ques-tioned by one or two anthropologists, notably Ralph Linton). Cultural relativism, as a moral doctrine, holds not merely that what is believed to be right differs, but that what actually *is* right differs, even though relevant circumstances are similar. Thus polygamy can be right for the people of one culture; monogamy for those of another.

The term 'relativism' can also be used to signify a theory about ethical concepts, namely that they are relational. This theory may be called 'analytic relativism'. Thus 'X is right' is interpreted in some such way as this: 'X is approved by —' ('valued', 'commended', etc.), the blank being capable of being filled up in various ways. Since feelings and emotions seem to play an important role in morality, such relativism commonly takes the form of a sub-jectivist theory. Since relativism in this sense raises problems about the justification of moral judgments, relativism is also used in a wider way to mean the theory that there is no rational or objective way of justifying basic ethical judgments, so that different basic ethical judgments can be equally valid ('meta-ethical relativism').

The thesis that ethical terms are relational does not by itself entail a recognition of equally valid moral systems or judgments, since the analysis of 'right' as 'commanded by God' would, given faith in God as described in a certain way, uniquely determine a single moral-ity as the only valid one. However, one ground for a relational analysis of moral terms is the fact of moral disagreement, and thus analytic relativism is usually stated in such a way that it has pluralistic consequences.

The plausibility of cultural relativism rests not merely on the fact of moral disagreements and variations between culture, but also on two aspects of moral thinking. First it is generally held that a man should obey his conscience and that he should not be blamed for ignorance (normally). If a man acts according to his lights, what he does is in a sense right, or at least not wrong, even if 'objectively' his act conflicts with what we believe to be the true morality. From this point of view, what is right for a polygamous Muslim differs from what is right for a monogamous humanist. Second, a person's duty depends on circumstances; it can be thought that cultural differences themselves constitute relevantly different circumstances, so that a man has a duty A in culture I, but a duty B in culture II.

Neither of these points (about intentionality and about the situational aspect of morality) in fact entails cultural relativism, and once they have been understood they are seen to constitute all that is confusedly valuable in the thesis of cultural relativism. First, the fact that a man should act according to his conscience does not entail that all consciences are equally valuable. Integrity, etc., are relevant to judgments about a person's character, but are only indirectly relevant to the worth of the morality he professes or acts upon. It remains important to know what moral rules are best for society. Of course, cultural *milieu* can be important when it comes to trying to apply the best rules. It may be that imposing monogamy on a polygamous society may have side-effects much more disastrous than the institution of polygamy itself. This is a problem in social engineering, rather than about moral ends as such. Second, the situational aspect of morality only entails that where circumstances are different in morally relevant ways do duties differ. It is quite another thing to hold, as cultural relativism implies, that there can be different moral duties in relevantly similar circumstances. It may of course be held that as a matter of contingent fact circumstances are never relevantly similar as between one person and another. This would be compatible with holding that *if* they were, then the same duty would apply. It would be a puzzling belief, however, as it would fail to explain how general terms in morality ('lying', 'stealing', etc.) have come to be used.

Analytic relativism, in its subjectivist form, encounters the difficulty that moral arguments ought to evaporate. For if 'A is wrong' means 'A is disapproved of by Henry'; and if George disagrees, so that 'A is not wrong' means 'A is not disapproved of by George', there is no incompatibility between 'A is wrong' and 'A is not wrong'. There is no incompatibility between the propositions that Henry disapproves of A and that George does not. Thus analytic relativism is not a good reflection of the way moral concepts actually work, since people take moral disagreements to be genuine disagreements. Further, Henry's disapproval of A is a biographical fact, not a moral assertion, and analytic relativism, even in its non-pluralistic forms, does not take account of the gap between 'is' and 'ought' (that is, it commits the so-called naturalistic fallacy). Emotivism, or an expressive analysis of moral terms, does not fall under this objection, since on this analysis, when Henry says 'A is wrong', he is expressing his emotions, attitude, etc., and not (strictly)

making a statement. However, emotivism seems to imply meta-ethical relativism. The latter, however, remains quite unproven, since it is not clear that differences in supposedly basic ethical judgments do not themselves depend on differences of belief about empirical facts (for example, western and Indian attitudes to animals differ, but so do western and Indian beliefs about the nature of animals). Nor is it clear that there is no unique set of moral reactions to other people without which a person would not be capable of using moral concepts.

The chief value of relativism is that, by drawing attention to cultural diversity, it has brought philosophers to distinguish between moral rules, etc., and laws of nature, and has encouraged a critical appraisal of the grounds offered for divergent moral judgments.

William K. Frankena, *Ethics*, 1963, Chap. 6; A. Macbeath, *Experiments in Living*, 1952; Charles L. Stevenson, *Facts and Values*, 1963, Chap. 5; Edward Westermarck, *Ethical Relativity*, 1932.

NINIAN SMART

Religion and Morality, Relations of

Historically, morality and religion have been thought to be related to each other in four different ways. The first view, which was the earliest, was that morality is so closely related to religion as in practice, if not in theory, to be indistinguishable from it. Morality thus not only depends upon religion, it is an aspect of it. This view was exemplified not only in such a major western religion as early Judaism, but also in Confucianism and even in some forms of Buddhism. The second view is that morality is independent of religion. This position, seen in embryo in the words of Plato and Aristotle, in fact is a distinctly modern one. Kant is usually considered its first and powerful advocate. Although asserting the autonomy of morality, Kant, with most eighteenth- and nineteenth-century philosophers, thought that it sustained a special relation to religion, expressed in his famous phrase that to be moral is 'to consider ethical imperatives as divine commands'. Continuing this tendency to exalt the role of morality at the expense of religion, a third view sees religion as a mere aspect of morality. The classical expression of this is Matthew Arnold's statement that religion is 'morality touched with emotion'. Curiously, even the theologian, Ritschl, taught that the essence of religion is to live 'from the power of the highest good over one's inner life'. The fourth and latest view is that morality not only is autonomous and can and should conduct its work in independence of religion, but even stronger, it holds that ethics can perform the functions formerly assigned to religion. In theory and in practice, for technical ethicists as for many educated people today, ethics replaces religion. John Dewey while hedging on the autonomy of ethics as regards its dependence on psychology and sociology, was emphatic in advocating that the noun 'religion' should be replaced by the adjective 'religious', and he defined 'religious' in ethical terms. This position has recently grown in influence and enjoys increasing support from psychological, psychoanalytic and sociological scholars, as, of course, from philosophers.

In light of the historical development above mentioned, and in spite of the powerful trend on the part of morality not merely to declare its autonomy, but even to replace religion, there is today a vigorous reassertion on the part not only of theologians, but also of many scientists and political theorists, that ethics does depend on religion and/or metaphysics. Because these claims are expressed in varying and conflicting ways, the following issues constitute the growing points of thought today.

The general claim of religious ethics is by no means clear, but there are at least two main schools of thought. The more extreme religious ethicists claim that there is no true and valid morality in separation from theology and theological beliefs. The milder version neither denies the existence of a secular ethics nor its relatively important contributions, thought of chiefly in terms of clarification and factual information. What it does claim is that secular ethics is inadequate and misleading as compared with an ethics inspired and informed by theological commitments (P. Lehmann). Often associated with this is the claim that any adequate ethical theory must be conceived within the framework of the existentialist terminology of traditional Judaic-Christian theology. Both the nature and the grounds of this latter claim are ambiguous and dubious. For example, with some the claim seems to mean that no adequate ethics is possible without the traditional theological virtues of 'faith', 'hope', and 'love'. It is further implied, if not asserted that these 'supernatural' values or virtues are, in turn, dependent on the existence and grace of God and of a life of communion with God (Richard Niebuhr, Ramsey, Herberg). Often, however, the claim takes a different form, asserting that religious ethics, particularly Judaic-Christian, is inextricably bound to a metaphysical framework of the supernatural variety. Others who claim equally to be Christian (Tillich, Wiemann) are as vigorous in repudiating the claim that religious ethics involves supernaturalism. In fact, they, with Bultmann and others, regard this as a falsification of the Judaic-Christian standpoint.

A specific consideration of the various claims made by theological or religious ethics must be prefaced by taking into account an important division between problems of ethics. Generally,

it is between (1) *descriptive* ethics, which is an historical or scientific study carried on jointly by ethicists, anthropologists, psychologists, sociologists and historians, and whose aim is to describe and explain ethical experience; (2) *normative* ethics, which, from Socrates on, tries to inquire into the nature of 'good', 'right', 'obligation', et al. and to examine various principles or standards of ethical judgment; (3) *meta-ethics*, which is concerned solely with the analysis of the meaning and nature of ethical judgments and with the logic or rationale of their justification. *See* **Ethics.**

It is the last area of study, meta-ethics, which not only dominates creative ethical discussion today, but further, it is this area which is of crucial concern in the present day for all discussion of morality *vis-à-vis* religion, as will appear in what follows. Contemporary meta-ethical writing, regardless of peculiarities of the nation or school of thought within which it operates, highlights more than anything else the fact that theologians customarily are lacking in the intellectual vigour and clarity of their philosophical counterparts. The latter, on the other hand, while embodying these qualities, usually ignore or give dubious and somewhat inaccurate accounts of the better theological interpretations of Judaic-Christian ethics. There are a few notable exceptions among the philosophers, for example, Frankena.

Illustrative of this dominance of meta-ethical problems are precisely the main claims to justification by religious or theological ethicists. Thus, to take one major instance, *the* characteristic claim is made that truth and validity, if not indeed all ethics, depend on theological beliefs and/or metaphysical doctrines. It is rarely made clear, however, in what way(s) this justification is to be accomplished. The justification is usually made on logical, ontological, and/or psychological grounds, and furthermore, unexamined epistemological assumptions, that is, knowledge-claims, infect all three.

The first claim for justification is the strongest. It says that, in contrast with purely empirical, scientific or rational justification, religious ethical judgments may be *deduced from* what is 'commanded by God', what is in obedience with God's nature (love) or with his will (goodness), or, as with William Sorley, that moral values are no less objective than our knowledge of natural facts. One may omit, but only for the moment, the question as to *how* this ethical content and these values are known, that is, by intuition, authority, revelation, etc. In this context, Reinhold Niebuhr's statement that religious ideas are the ultimate sources of moral standards and that Christian faith is the foundation and roof of an adequate morality is often echoed. The ethics of Jesus, accordingly, is held to proceed *logically* from the central beliefs of biblical religion. With reference to this, Frankena, Brandt, Hospers and other philosophical ethicists point out: (1) that this claim contains a hidden premise, namely, that we ought to imitate or obey God, or 'love what we are at one with'; (2) that *this* suppressed premise is not derived from religious presuppositions; (3) further, that the premise itself is infected with fatal epistemological objections.

Those holding to the dependence of morality on religion may, secondly, put the stress on ontological rather than on logical dependence. This was illustrated in the nineteenth-century idealists, the Cairds, T. H. Green, and today in Tillich, Wild and many Neo-Thomists, all of whom emphasize the fact (as do Protestant theologians generally) that freedom and obligation are grounded in a personal God who is the source and standard of goodness. According to this way of thinking, both love and justice – central ethical values without doubt – are held to be rooted in 'the nature of things', and ethical questions are answered from the standpoint of a doctrine of *being*. This usually involves the assumption that ontology verifies ethics, and that ethics verifies ontology. This, in turn, involves one version of natural law theory, namely, that the law given by God is in 'man's essential nature'. This, it is widely agreed today, validates no, at least no specific, moral judgment, and further, it is a position which self-realizationalists and naturalists (Garnett, Wild) hold equally with religious ethicists. The point is that it does not really base ethical on religious principles, but rather on empirical grounds, that is, what human nature requires.

More appealing to many religious ethicists, and certainly more clear and frequently stressed, in contrast with both the above, is the alleged *psychological* dependence of ethics on religion (Tillich, Lehmann, Ramsey). This claim, the nature of which is at least clear to most secular ethicists, is that any adequate and effective morality must 'go beyond mere ethics' and afford the sense of an 'absolute imperative', which alone is capable of motivating man to the good life. The nature of this motivation varies, for example, as obedience to divine command (Thomists, Neo-Orthodoxy) or as expressions of love and gratitude to a redeemer-God. All (A. C. Garnett, E. Vivas), including religious existentialists and dialectical theologians (Kierkegaard, Barth, Brunner, Buber), unite in asserting that basic ethical judgments and their expressions in 'right action' depend *psychologically* on commitment to a God of love and justice. In passing, it must be recorded that this claim – that without belief in and commitment to God people will not be good – is widely repudiated because, it is held, some evidence supports, whereas other contradicts it. For example, not only is the professedly religious person and/or group often flagrantly immoral, but, on the contrary, many of the most compelling moral

advances – anti-slavery, tolerance, world-peace and even democracy – are largely the achievements of persons who are avowedly non-theistic and certainly indifferent or hostile to institutionalized religion.

In considering the clarification and justification of the above-mentioned claims, the problem of knowledge becomes a central issue. What is involved are questions about the sources, nature and tests of any claim to knowledge. For both philosophical and theological ethics, the answer is varied and often contradictory. For the former, it divides today into the schools of intuitionism (Moore) and empiricism, both naturalism (Dewey, Hook) and pragmatism (James), and cognitivism or metaphysical ethics. All agree, however, on the ultimate criteria of reason and experience. For the latter, the religious ethicists, major answers are the following: (1) Some – even Thomists (Ryan) and existentialists – are intuitionists, claiming as they do that in fact man has a direct and unmediated awareness of the good qua God's command, the law of nature, etc. (2) Others say that revelation is the source of religious ethics. These divide into the traditionalists, who espouse a biblical literalism and legalism (Protestant and Roman Catholic fundamentalism and Orthodox Judaism), and the contemporary biblical theologians, whose views (Buber, Brunner, Bultmann) of 'dynamic revelation' holds that the 'divine imperative' is known through a personal encounter with God's *Word* and Truth. (3) Still others candidly base the ethical claims on grounds of authority – pointing to an institution, a set of writings, an infallible voice, etc. Concerning the former, the customary criticism is that if the revelatory experience is said to be *self*-authenticating, no neutral criterion exists for 'testing the spirits', whether they be of God or of the latest quack. As for authority, more must be said later, but here J. S. Mill's judgment should be quoted: 'There is a very real evil consequent on ascribing a supernatural origin to the received maxims of morality. That origin consecrates the whole of them and protects them from being discussed or criticized' (*Three Essays on Religion*, 1874, p. 99). So each of the bases on which the knowledge-claim is made – intuition, self-evidence, revelation, authority – is considered open to serious objections.

Still more fundamental, as it appears in much contemporary literature, is the case of ethical theism, that is, for the existence of God. For, it is widely held, if there is no God there can be no ethical imperative and inspiration. Further, standard apologetics, Evangelical-Protestant, Catholic, and Orthodoxy until recently based its defence of the faith and so of ethical theism on the traditional proofs for the existence of God. One of the several unprecedented shifts in present-day thinking is seen in the fact that these arguments, save two, have simply ceased to play any major role. It is often said that (1) they were never intended as demonstrations or 'proofs', and (2) even if taken as proofs, the criticisms of them – at least in their traditional expression – have destroyed their utility. Two still are employed, the moral and the ontological. The former (following Kant) claims that there *is* a moral world order, that there is purpose and value in nature and history (and so in man's experience of good and evil) and hence (C. E. M. Joad) God exists and is the ground and guaranteer of justice and goodness. The latter, argued, curiously, chiefly by philosophers (C. Hartshorne, N. Malcolm) dwells on the second form of the Anselmic argument. Some (J. Hick) even propose an eschatological kind of verification of belief in God and a life of love, that is, in eventual membership in the Kingdom of God.

Ethical theism so far as it claims to give an empirical ground for the principle of benevolence and justice remains a serious contender in the ethical field. It is generally agreed, however, that its claim to afford a *logical* ground for the dependence of ethical on religious principles is to be denied. In short, an approach appealing to the principle of 'faith working-by-love' and willing to be judged by the fruits of an ethic of love is expressive of the modern mood.

Any account of morality as related to religion must, in conclusion, review the following special issues. One puzzling and unresolved development in contemporary ethics relates two otherwise hostile types, existentialists (Kierkegaardians) and other theists, and philosophical analysts who are agnostics if not atheists (A. J. Ayer). The common base is the contemporary stress on 'act' and on 'decision' as contrasted with principle and rule. Rejecting the older principle-style ethics – benevolence, justice, and even love – as misguided, 'act-deontology ethics' (E. F. Garrett, H. A. Prichard) takes as its thesis H. Aiken's phrase 'decision is king'. The claim is that we must decide in each particular situation – the existentialists add 'with difficulty and anxiety' – what is the right thing to do. The result is that many religious ethicists of the act type and some atheistic positivists join in saying that value judgments are, to be sure, in a special sense arbitrary decisions which represent highly personal commitments, and which may be pronounced right decisions even though they are flatly contradictory, that is, as expressed by two persons facing the same ethical situation. Observers of this development ask whether the consequence is not pure, though unacknowledged, relativism combined with a dangerous irrationalism.

Related to the above is a growing tension between the two extremes of absolutism and relativism in ethics at the expense of consideration of other more responsible alternatives.

Absolutism has had a resurgence among widely diverse religious moralists, on the one hand – Roman Catholic, fundamentalistic Protestant – and has its roots both in the religiously motivated ethicists (Henry Davis, S.J.) and in political theorists. Absorbed with the conviction that there are ethical absolutes or there is no effective ethics at all, religious and secular absolutists insist on propositions, that is, statements about goods and rights, which they claim hold everywhere and always. That there are obvious exceptions, even to such basic and timeworn propositions as 'killing is wrong', or 'promise-keeping is right', appears not to disturb the absolutist mentality in what John Dewey called the naive 'quest for certainty', and what other ethicists designate the impressiveness of tautologies.

Revolting against absolutism, and encouraged by psychological, sociological and related scientific studies, is the modern drive towards relativism. This takes the form of (1) descriptive relativism, which, often exaggeratedly, points to differing evaluative judgments as between both individuals and societies; (2) semantic relativism, which holds that in the absence of any objective, empirical way of justifying ethical judgments, it is irrelevant to argue about their truth or falsity; and (3) normative relativism, which asserts that what is good for one individual or society may not be so for another, even though the situations are, for all purposes, identical. The descriptive form, because of its tendency to overstatement and failure to see that the differences often are not about ends, but rather about means, is declining in influence. Semantic and normative relativism, because they seem to violate the criteria of consistency and of the universalization of ethical judgments, have lost their early attractiveness.

What seems to be the next step for both philosophical and theological ethics is an advance beyond absolutism and relativism in the direction of a critical undertaking of meta-ethical problems. Among those of theistic persuasion morality and religion would appear to join in some version of the biblical doctrine of *agape*.

William K. Frankena, *Ethics*, 1963; John Hospers, *Human Conduct*, 1961; Ian T. Ramsey, *Christian Ethics and Contemporary Philosophy*, 1967; Paul Ramsey, *Deeds and Rules in Christian Ethics*, 1965; Paul Tillich, *Beyond Morality*, 1964.

CHARLES W. KEGLEY

Remorse

Remorse is sometimes confused with repentance. It can be a movement towards repentance but it has its own distinct nature. Remorse may come to a man when he sees the enormity of what he is doing and the irreparable harm he has already done to others and to himself. He cannot forgive himself and he cannot imagine men or God forgiving him.

Remorse can be temporary, recurring or permanent but in all cases Christian doctrine holds that it is made bearable through repentance and pardon.

R. E. C. BROWNE

Renaissance, The

While it produced nothing new in philosophical ethics, it introduced a change of general perspective that helps to explain the differences of method and criteria between the mediaeval and the modern views about morality. The recoil from the mediaeval outlook and way of living had undoubtedly a variety of causes (e.g., natural reaction, mental maturing, commercial advance and political events), but the usual reference to the recovery of the knowledge of the ancient Greeks and Romans has still to be stressed. The broad effect of that recovery was an excited recognition of the width and height of the achievements of the classical age. These smote astonished minds with the force of a revelation; and the vision of the past became an apocalypse of the future, for what two western peoples had done might be done again. The ancient philosophy and science showed that the structure of the physical world and the laws of its processes could be investigated; the ancient literature showed that it could be admired, honoured and loved; and the ancient ways of living showed that the human lot could be handsomely alleviated by hygiene, self-respect and gracefulness (there were Renaissance manuals of good manners). The contrast with the mediaeval outlook, temper and manner of life was immense. Men, it now seemed, were not merely sinners, in need of little but a post-mortem salvation. Their present life was not just a testing for the next, a testing in which the material and temporal were to be despised as corruptible and corrupting. It had much value of its own, human nature being instinct with high and versatile possibilities that could and should be realized here. The classical world was indeed being pictured too rosily; nevertheless what the Renaissance scholars saw in it really was in it. They caught the force and fragrance of forgotten ideals, and revived them in letters, conversation and to some extent in conduct. They became a new aristocracy, and some of the ruling aristocrats welcomed them, the most remarkable instance being the close association of the Medici dukes with the Florentine Academy, the noble first-fruit of the Renaissance.

The changed attitude was called in a later period 'humanism', intended as a term of praise. In its very recent disparaging use it would not be applicable generally. True, the attitude could, and here and there did, contract into a purely this-worldly one. Its original basis was certainly the sense, evoked by the intellectual and artistic greatness of the Greeks and the moral heroism and political magnanimity of the best Romans, of the wrongness of a low view of human nature. A low view had been propagated by the Church's doctrine of original sin; but a high view could be grounded on other Church doctrines, or in the Platonic theory of the supremacy of the Good, or in the Stoic conviction that every man is a part of the divine Reason. Although, then, in some persons and groups humanism took a very earthy form (for a while even in papal circles), largely under the ideal of 'virtù' (virility as proved by powerful action, sometimes splendid, sometimes merely gross), it was not in general anti-religious. On the whole it had in the writers a high tone, varying from aesthetic idealism and cosmic emotion to Platonism pure or christianized, or to a Christianity inwardly liberalized. It gave us, among other things, the NT in Greek and the Greek Fathers.

So far as philosophy was concerned, one feature was an exchange of ecclesiastical authority for the authority of the ancient pagan thinkers, whose systems were revived rather than rethought, one consequence being that Plato's *Republic*, Aristotle's *Ethics*, Cicero's *On Duties*, and Epictetus's *Manual* came to be the favourite ethical books of the seventeenth and eighteenth centuries. In another respect philosophizing came to mean an escape from the mediaeval kind that served the Church to the Greek kind that stood on its own rational and empirical feet. The very few relatively independent philosophers let themselves go, unclassically, in riotously imaginative speculation about nature as a whole. For them the problem of man's place and rightful life does not seem to have been central. Rather than being interested in men as particular living beings with problems of conduct daily facing them, they were thrilled at the discovery of how much (and how well) man was able to think and feel about; that is, their attention was directed more on the universe than on themselves. This objective interest ran also into the groove that led to modern astronomical physics, that is, to Galileo and Newton, but before it reached these the largely mediaeval priest Copernicus (d. 1543) had pushed the earth from the centre of the solar system, and the unmediaeval monk Bruno (d. 1600), a pantheist of passion and genius, had announced entranced an infinity of worlds beyond the solar system. This reduction of man's abode by the former to a peripheral and by the latter to a minute status in the physical universe embarrassed orthodox Christians and delighted sophisticated libertines, but hardly became formative of an anti-religious and wholly this-worldly morality until the new science had proceeded to something like proof, and even then the effect was ambiguous, for a vaster and more marvellous universe was seen by many as resounding to the greater glory of God, and the spatial pettiness of the earth as leaving untouched either the humanist's conviction of man's spiritual greatness or the Christian conviction of man's responsibility, immortality and privilege under God.

The few works of moral reflection that are remembered from this period do not support the common view that the Renaissance was wholly a wave of individualism, for they are about social and political morality. Macchiavelli's *The Prince* belongs to political science, and More's *Utopia* to serious imaginative literature rather than to ethics. Campanella's *City of the Sun* is an adaptation of Plato's *Republic*. The one weighty ethical treatise was late, Grotius's *On the Law of War and Peace* (1625) in which the Stoic and Roman concept, familiar to the mediaevals, of natural law as the rational (though God-given) criterion of right human laws was applied to the changed situation of emerged and emerging nation-states. This work virtually created international law as a subject of modern technical juristic study. It is more than an addendum to note the controversy (1524–7) between Erasmus, prince of Renaissance scholars, and Luther, on the subject of moral responsibility. The former argued for it with restraint, acknowledging the mystery of God's sovereignty; the latter could think only of sin and unmerited grace. The issue was that of Pelagius and Augustine again (to be renewed a century later by Arminius). The clash is a reminder that the Reformation was contemporary with the Renaissance. The relation between these two reactions against ecclesiastical authority was neither simple nor constant: felt affinity and felt hostility varied with the personalities involved. The one was intellectual and aesthetic, the other a practical passion for religious and moral righteousness; yet both were liberating, and both, in shifts of harmony and conflict, shaped the modern era – with the difference that the Reformation reached much more quickly the common people.

J. Burckhardt, *Civilisation of the Renaissance in Italy* (ET, 3rd edn. rev., 1951), still invaluable as a general survey, though confined to the first home; on the philosophical and scientific ideas, see H. Höffding, *History of Modern Philosophy*, 1924, Books 1 and 2.

T. E. JESSOP

Repentance

Christian thought about sin and repentance can be represented by the figure of a man with his back turned to God and moving away from him; the figure stops still and then turns to face God and begins to move towards him. This, of course, is no literal or allegorical description of sin and repentance but an indication of the way to think about such happenings. Sin can be talked about in countless ways; two are

suggested here: (1) the refusal to control what can be controlled; and (2) the attempt to control what cannot be controlled. In either case the sinner experiences what some call a godforsakeness – a state in which all zest and meaning seems to be drained out of life and nothing left but fear of the consequences of actions and the hopelessness of living without power to act significantly.

Christians sometimes talk as if leaving and returning to God were two specific acts capable of exact definition. There are countless descriptions of what is meant by 'leaving God'. One of them is to consider leaving God as persistently restricting the attention to immediate manageable thoughts and actions so that one is seemingly confined within a narrow world of one's own making. 'Returning to God' can be described as beginning in a readiness to look for connections between happenings and people so as to recognize the extent of one's responsibility for things and people in God.

Repentance seen as turning to face God is typified by the behaviour of the apostles in the passion of our Lord. On Maundy Thursday night at the first sign of danger they all forsook him and fled. Their remorse and sorrow is unimaginable; but they came back to one another and stayed with one another as if this were the first step to make life possible again. Their return in fear and shame ended in the power and peace of forgiveness. From this incident we see that repentance is more than a private matter between the individual sinner and God. Full repentance entails re-taking one's place in the Body of Christ.

A man's deeds are personal in the sense that he is responsible for them but public because they affect all men in varying degrees. A man's sins are public in the sense that others, knowingly or unknowingly, strengthen the source of his temptation and are capable of feeling responsible and guilty for what he has done. An act of repentance is personal in the sense that through it a person is made whole again, but this act is public because all men benefit by it, specially those of the household of faith.

R. E. C. BROWNE

Repression

Repression is the term introduced by psychoanalysis (q.v.) and later adopted by other forms of dynamic psychology to express the exclusion from consciousness of impulses, ideas, wishes, attitudes, feelings, etc., which would result in intolerable threat or pain if openly acknowledged. Repression is regarded as the most important of all the defence mechanisms (q.v.) and is carried out in such a manner that the person concerned remains unaware either of the continued presence of the threatening material or of the steps taken to prevent its intrusion into consciousness.

The felt necessity for repression arises in the developing child's experience of conflict between his own instinctual impulses and the restrictions placed upon him by parents or other figures in the outside world. The child may come to feel that not only is he liable to punishment if he expresses his impulses without regard to the standards and values of parents or society, but also that he is in danger if he so much as acknowledges to himself that he even thinks such thoughts. If the threat involved is sufficiently great, the impulses and thoughts may be 'pushed down' into the unconscious (q.v.). Repression may arise as a result of specific traumatic incidents or from a series of distorted perceptions of the social restraining forces. The term *suppression* is sometimes used to distinguish conscious rejection of ideas and impulses from this unconscious mechanism of repression. *See* Sigmund Freud, *A General Introduction to Psychoanalysis*, rev. edn., 1920, or Anna Freud, *The Ego and the Mechanisms of Defence*, 1937, for detailed discussion.

Repression can be effective against even the most powerful instinctual impulses but since it involves a refusal to recognize and accept whole tracts of psychic life, it can also result in the destruction of the integrity of the personality. Even when not pathological in degree, repression can rob a person of much richness in life. If, for any reason, the repression ceases to be effective, the consequences can be explosively disruptive. The aim of much psychotherapy, however, is precisely to bring repressed material into the light but in such a manner that it can be freshly examined by the person concerned and robbed of its destructive power. Mental health would seem to require the ability to recognize and accept a wide range of one's personal feelings, attitudes, wishes, etc., together with discrimination and discipline in their translation into actual behaviours.

GRAEME M. GRIFFIN

Rerum Novarum. see Pontifical Social Encyclicals.

Resistance to Tyranny

The organized State has a certain claim to obedience. Existing authorities 'have been instituted by God' in the sense that government as a general institution is essential to human welfare. The maintenance of justice and order among men always requires a political administration. No man should resist his rulers without first weighing the cost in terms of social disorder. Having done this, however, he may also be led to resist any particular government as a religious duty. Losses due to disobedience may be far outweighed by the losses which would result from obedience. Changes in an existing government may be essential if the general function of government is to be well performed.

God is a higher authority than any chief of state. 'We must obey God rather than men' (Acts 5.29) is a better general guide than 'let every person be subject to the governing authorities' (Rom. 13.1).

The unacceptability of tyranny may be due to its insistence on mistaken policies or to its restrictive methods for adopting policy. Death camps for Jews are to be resisted regardless of the form of government. The fact that fundamental freedoms have been seriously restricted in the formulation of any edict is additional reason for opposing the regime.

This does not mean that only one narrowly defined constitutional pattern is acceptable. Several somewhat differing forms may still allow essential freedoms. Educationally immature populations in less developed nations may constitute an exceptional case in which even highly centralized governments might temporarily provide the greatest possible freedom. Wherever more democratic forms could function, tyranny is to be opposed.

The form of resistance adopted is also ethically important. The modern technology of terror makes the choice of means peculiarly difficult, as many Christians in totalitarian lands can testify. Possible methods range from violent revolution at one extreme to mild attempts at persuasion on the other. A characteristic method of the Church has been some form of non-violent resistance, involving the courageous action of faith and the acceptance of consequent martyrdom. The problem of responsible resistance is the problem of all moral choice, adopting the strategy of love which is appropriate within the limitations of each concrete situation.

HARVEY SEIFERT

Responsibility

Responsibility means literally answerability. It is used basically in two senses: (1) Retrospective, in the sense of accountability and/or culpability, is the primary legal use and refers usually to the mental status of a person. If he is thought to 'know right from wrong' he is judged to be sane and hence accountable. The theological traditions of western Christendom have also made much use of the concept of responsibility in the sense of accountability for sin; it was a key issue in the Augustinian-Pelagian and Calvinist-Arminian debates. (2) Prospective, in the sense of being able to take responsibility, or being able to answer for what one will do, is used primarily in ethics, and implies a degree of freedom as moral agent. A derived restricted use is reliability or trustworthiness.

The impact of the behavioural sciences in general and dynamic psychology in particular upon responsibility in the *retrospective* sense has been to reduce the scope of its applicability, since these sciences are concerned with antecedent factors and environmental determinants. For instance, a California case of what appeared to be first degree murder, involving 'premeditation' and 'malice aforethought' was recently adjudged to be second degree murder in which 'malice aforethought' played no part, on the basis of a psychiatrist's testimony that powerful unconscious motives governed the action. The defendant in this case was not adjudged 'insane'. Also developmental psychology has shown that general responsibility cannot be imputed all at once at a certain age, as was held, for instance, in mediaeval canon law. Rather moral capacities develop gradually at different paces, and pass through stages of external conformity and expediency before being fully developed as internal value systems.

Clinical psychology and psychiatry, on the other hand, have had the effect, through psychotherapy, of increasing prospective responsibility, in that, when relatively successful, it gives the individual better knowledge and control of himself, thus increasing his answerability for his actions. This does not mean that psychotherapy automatically leads to more moral behaviour, but that it may make this possible. Psychotherapy sometimes leads to less conformist behaviour which some ethicists would also judge less moral. But in all cases responsibility is increased.

Experimental and social psychology, while contributing to increased prospective responsibility by illuminating determinative factors in the past, may also lead to more control and manipulation of man by man, and hence to a decrease in responsibility, as in 'brain-washing' techniques.

The principal treatment of the general question of morals from the psycho-dynamic standpoint is J. C. Flugel's *Man, Morals, and Society* (1945). *See also* **Psychology and Ethics.**

JAMES N. LAPSLEY

Restitution

Genuine sorrow for a sin implies not only the desire for future amendment of life but the desire to repair or minimize the injuries inflicted by the sin or sins already committed and now repented of. Restitution is the making good of whatever injury has been inflicted. Of course, it may sometimes be impossible to make restitution. Wherever possible, however, an act of restitution or the sincere intention of performing such an act must be regarded as a necessary part of repentance, and as a condition for receiving absolution.

Retribution. *see* Rewards and Punishments.

Rewards and Punishments

The modern approach to the problem of rewards and punishments must be governed by an understanding of its roots in history. Rewards represent the workers' hire, the exchange received for goods, and the fair price paid in normal conditions. Honour, wealth and a long life are a sign of divine favour. Punishments, however, belong to the abnormal sphere of offences. The Judaic-Christian tradition reflects the long process of taming the instinct of vengeance for wrongs suffered. The law decrees that justice be administered impartially and that punishments are inflicted on evil-doers for the protection of the good life, that is, of life and property. The principle of the *lex talionis* is to restrict the destructive effect of penal consequences and to secure a measure of restitution proportionate to the victim's loss. Punishment is not meant to be reformatory and there is no system of imprisonment to deprive the offender of his liberty. The purpose of retribution is to secure, as far as is possible, a state of normality by eliminating the consequence of the offence. The conditional laws of the Torah and of subsequent legislations, Jewish and Christian, determine in advance the steps to be taken to establish the equilibrium of society.

Owing to the peculiar development of Jewish apocalyptic this legal tradition became enshrined in a far wider setting of distinctly otherworldly proportions, so that both rewards and punishments were seen to be appropriate to an eternal existence. The martyrs' struggle against fearful odds postulated a moral necessity that heroic endurance be rewarded with compensations which this life cannot afford. The apocalyptic writers developed a veritable dialectic of such compensations, making the poor rich, the weak victorious, etc. Above all, those who resist to the point of giving their own lives are rewarded with eternal life, while those who betray the fight are 'rewarded' with everlasting shame. The Christian dialectic mirrors this conviction in the NT and early Christian writings, where Christian mortifications and sacrifices are not considered abnormal but the normal way of life. Thus the poor own the Kingdom of Heaven, the mourners are consoled, the meek inherit the earth; the martyrs for truth, mercy, and righteousness receive their stake back a hundredfold in the regeneration of the world. The eschatological future is thus called in as the turning point when at the point of judgment the 'sheep and goats' receive their 'due reward'. No one is exempt from the eternal tribunal and there is no sentence except life or death. Moreover, the mythological setting of the Last Judgment surrounds heavenly rewards and punishments with a supernatural setting, in which good and evil angels minister to fulfil the will of God and in which Christ consummates his work as the Judge.

The power of the ecclesiastical institutions had the effect of imparting to the apocalyptic portrayal of rewards and punishments a forensic rigidity which extended not only to heroes and renegades but to all ordinary Christians and non-Christians. Assuming the existence of a Book of Life, as evidence produced in the divine Court, the doctors of the Church taught that salvation and condemnation were the alternate destinies awaiting men. The unbaptized as well as the wicked could only qualify for the eternal torment, and the pessimism of the Dark Ages made it appear probable that even the just stood in need of mercy. The popular doctrine of rewards and punishments can best be appreciated by a study of the typical Judgment scene over mediaeval Cathedral porches: the blessed mount to pleasures which are heightened by the spectacle of the miseries of the damned. This symmetrical representation knows of no qualifications, except that the doctrine of purgatory and good works (Masses, intercessions, alms) provided some mitigation of the severity of the system of retribution. Similarly the postulate of degrees of hell and heaven acknowledges a differentiation in the stages of individual destinies. But the essential and hard core of the retributive character of man's final state remained unaltered even when the political life of Europe required perhaps a less drastic eschatology and when the Reformation shifted the general interest away from a primary concern with death and the fate of the departed. Indeed, the doctrine of predestination only accentuated the moral problem, for how can a just and loving God predestine men to any reward except a good one?

The tension inherent in the whole complex of retribution, which must be accentuated by the fears of the community, has never failed to evoke protests, most of which converge upon the teaching of Origen. This third-century scholar and martyr propounded a doctrine of universal restoration in which even the hardest punishments were interpreted as remedial. Origen also held that 'we punish ourselves' and that our conscience is our own executioner. In all similar schemes rewards and punishments are no more final than death itself. Or, if death be considered final, immortality itself is considered conditional and thus a loop-hole for liberal feeling remains open, in as much as immortality itself is the reward for a good life, and death the natural punishment of life abused.

Although the execration of Origen and his followers on the part of othodox Christianity will find no approval among modern moralists and a liberal view of punishment is apt to prevail among most theologians – leaving the judgment to God – the fundamental thesis that the life on earth causes incontrovertible consequences after death is not so easily disposed of. Even if punishment be considered essentially immoral if it has an element of vindictiveness in it, and admitting that human beings cannot

simply be divided into sheep and goats, the respect for human personality and the high regard for freedom and responsibility suggest that the future of man in eternity cannot be separated from belief and conduct on earth. A sentimental attitude can only lead to indifferentism, that is, a very low estimate of man and a type of disinterested religion which is incapable of making passionate and rational discriminations between good and evil. The sin of indifference, branded as infernal by Dante, is hardly a commendable prop for the doctrine of the love of God which underlies the postulates of future rewards.

The problem is indeed not as new as some moderns allege. St Thomas Aquinas, for example, discusses at length the proposition whether the pangs of conscience cannot be equated with eternal punishment or whether evil-doers may not escape the dire consequences of their misdeeds by death. It is difficult to see how his moral logic can be faulted when he points out that the identity of personality demands strict continuity of existence and that the very perversion of evil states the moral need for objective judgment. It is of the nature of the demonic criminal that he deems himself in the right and that he would change the whole moral structure of the universe in order to be found in the right. Moreover, for the wicked eternal life would mean on their own terms the free indulgence of immeasurable evil. Therefore, argues St Thomas, their privation of freedom is punishment, for they can no longer do as they would.

The correctness of this view needs to be qualified, however, with the tentative insight that all men share the demonic nature. Hence a psychological light may be thrown upon the moral calculus of crime and punishment by our insisting upon the reality of self-exposure as a necessary and ultimately healing form of punishment. But this therapeutic estimate cannot operate beyond certain limits, for healing is not apposite in cases of resistance. The freedom of personality is such that it can decree its own dissolution into the nothing of a God-less existence.

Since God is the end of all life, and the source from which rewards and punishments flow, we must be prepared for an ineffable mystery which transcends all earthly conceptions of recompense. As in all Christian discourse, the earthly analogies prepare us for the 'how much more' of the heavenly reality. A purely legal framework which results in convictions and acquittals can hardly do justice to the God-centred eschatology of Christian love. Rewards do not ultimately come to the ingodded souls by way of privilege and position – which they despised on earth – but by the mystical union with God in which love itself is the reward and seeks for none other. Similarly the final punishment of the devils is not to be found in fire and decomposition, valid though the pictures may be, but in the separation from God and eternal loss. If the latter, however, be deemed to be a mitigation of torment – 'the wicked suffer *only* separation from God' – such a view, though perhaps satisfying to those who are sensible of the impossibility of eternal punishment, suffers from an inadequate conception of God.

A religious ethic, such as the Christian, is bound to decline in vigour as it forsakes its original mainspring. The Christian doctrine of judgment, involving the difficulties of rewards and punishments, is unthinkable without eternal incentives and warnings which provide the spur to Christian behaviour. The dismissal of these final realities would undermine the Christian ethic for most ordinary people. At the same time it is equally intolerable for so transcendent a theme to be contained in the narrow confines of the weighing up of merits on the one hand, and sins on the other. The reality of God and the infinite complexity of the whole universe in all its vastness must never fail to impinge upon and interpret our belief in retribution.

J. A. Beet, *The Last Things*, 1897; T. D. Kendrick, *The Lisbon Earthquake*, 1956; H. Quistrop, *Calvin's Doctrine of the Last Things*, 1955; U. E. Simon, *The End is Not Yet*, 1964; Thomas Aquinas, *Compendium Theologiae*, ET, 1952, Chaps. 149–84, 241–5.

ULRICH SIMON

Right and Wrong

It has been common in ethical writing to distinguish between moralities expressed in terms of the words 'right' and 'wrong' and those expressed in terms of 'good' and 'bad'. Both sets of terms, however, share certain characteristics: they seem to have some sort of 'action-guiding' or 'prescriptive' function, and are applied to acts, etc., in virtue of something about the act in question which is the reason for applying the word. *See* **Ethics**.

The following differences between the 'right' group of words and the 'good' group are to be noted, among others. (1) 'Good' has a comparative, 'right' normally has not. (2) An act can be neither good nor bad; but it cannot be neither right (in the sense of 'all right') nor wrong. (3) There is, however, another sense of 'right', normally only in the phrase 'the right . . .', in which an act can be neither wrong nor yet 'the right act' (in the circumstances). On the other hand, we cannot normally speak of 'the good act'; we say, rather, 'the best act'. (4) It is sometimes said that an act is called right solely in virtue of its own qualities and the circumstances in which it is done, whereas an act is called good in virtue of being the sort of act that a good man would do in these circumstances – that is, 'good' carries, and 'right' does

not, some allusion to the character of agents. (5) Except for the use mentioned in (3) above, the word 'wrong' rather than 'right' (to use the late J. L. Austin's expression) 'wears the trousers'. That is to say, we normally, in deciding whether an act is right, ask first whether there is anything to make it wrong, and if not call it right. This procedure will not work with 'good' and 'bad', for reasons connected with (2) above.

These logical features of the words account for the above-mentioned difference between the characters of moralities expressed in terms of them. A morality of right and wrong is likely to have a clear-cut character; there will be definite prohibitions against certain types of action, and actions not so prohibited will be all equally permitted. Such a morality can be very strict or very lax, depending on how many kinds of acts are prohibited. A morality of good and bad, on the other hand, will set out certain positive ideals which we are to try to realize; there will be infinite gradations between complete success and complete failure, both humanly impossible.

Christian morality has at various times and in various societies combined elements of both types – as must any satisfactory morality. There are, however, logical difficulties and dangers in seeking to combine them. An example of these is the problem of giving an adequate account of 'works of supererogation'. Perhaps the simplest account of these is that they are acts which are good but whose omission would not be wrong; that is, they are approaches to the ideal set forth by one type of morality, but are not specifically required by the other.

This account of the matter, however, is ruled out if we take the command 'Be ye therefore perfect' as implying that it is always wrong to fail to do what the best of men would do; this interpretation of the command implies that there are no works of supererogation but only a comprehensive series of duties, in which we all fail; that is, the 'right-wrong' morality is screwed up to the limit, so as to enjoin the complete fulfilment of the ideals of the 'good-bad' morality. This is done at the cost of making all men sinners, not to be saved except by redemption.

The latter view is no doubt more typical of Christians than the former. Nevertheless, the word 'wrong' is not, like 'sinful', tied specifically to religious moralities; and therefore Christians must expect to find atheists – and indeed their fellow-Christians at times – using it in the former, less exacting way.

R. M. HARE

Righteousness

There is no one specific act, or series of acts, which can be called righteousness in the sense that anyone who performs the one specific act, or series of acts, would be righteous. A righteous man expresses his righteousness in every act, even his sins are different from the sins of the unrighteous. It is easier to perceive righteousness than describe it, but some attempt at description must be made in every generation lest Christian behaviour become a shapeless mass of vague goodwill and sentimentality or be withdrawn from significant action in the world. With this description the criteria by which righteousness can be judged must also be given and intelligibly explained. The criteria are preserved in the liturgy, Scriptures and preachings of the Church and made intelligible by the knowledge given to the Church through its love of the world God loves.

The NT writers describe two types of righteousness – the legalistic and the creative, that is, the righteousness of the Pharisees and that of the Sermon on the Mount. Legalistic righteousness implies that: (1) Acts are more important than attitudes or motives. (2) All significant human behaviour emerges from obedience to a code. (3) There is usually time to deliberate before acting. (4) Every human situation can be literally interpreted and dealt with by taking action as the law provides for the occasion. (5) Legally unclassifiable acts, if there are such acts, are of no importance. (6) The law reveals both the nature of God and of man. (7) The law is hard and demanding but it offers the reward of righteousness to those who keep it.

The creative righteousness of the Sermon on the Mount (q.v.), among much else, teaches that: (1) Each individual is of measureless value. (2) No human situation is repeated. (3) Of necessity, the most significant human acts are spontaneous, in fact the bulk of human behaviour is extemporaneous. (4) Men are to preserve their freedom because without it there can be no creative action. (5) Human life cannot be completely explained in terms of morals or personal relationships – yet neither of them should be neglected.

The Sermon on the Mount is no code of law which men can obey by an act of will. It describes the disposition a disciple is to develop and maintain. This development and maintenance is part of his creative activity which begins in God. This activity is not a matter of suppressing thoughts and wishes or forcing them to move in carefully chosen directions but of letting them follow in the wake of the attention given to events in the ceaseless divine-human creative activity. A legalist could say 'I have kept the law'. But creative righteousness has no like finality to offer; rather it has an air of uncompleted adventures such as known by explorers, inventors, artists and mystics. This freedom, this readiness to meet the new, make thinking and acting dangerous, but creative righteousness is more concerned with truth and love than with the safe behaviour which is neither fully truthful nor completely loving.

The Sermon on the Mount says 'Blessed are those who hunger and thirst for righteousness, for they shall be satisfied' (Matt. 5.6). The activities of thought, word and deed symbolized by this hungering and thirsting are countless and varied. Their common nature is found in considering all that a man does to increase his knowledge of himself, things and men in order to glorify God and enable his fellows to live more truly. They that hunger and thirst after righteousness shall not be filled with righteousness; they are given its fruits and the raw materials out of which it is made. The fruits are the acts which express it in human situations: 'every sound tree bears good fruit' (Matt. 7.17 ff.). The raw materials include faith, hope, love, watchfulness, patience, courage, imagination, intelligence.

The call to be righteous is a call to live creatively. The Fourth Gospel supplements what the Sermon on the Mount says about creative living – for example, in our Lord's words as given in Chapter 15 – 'I am the true vine and my Father is the vinedresser. . . . every branch that does bear fruit he prunes that it may bear more fruit. . . . By this my Father is glorified, that you bear much fruit, and so prove to be my disciples' (vv. 1–8). This Gospel (in Chapter 17) represents our Lord as praying that the disciples should not be taken out of the world but that they should resist the world's temptations. That is, they should not be unrighteous (uncreative) but righteous (creative) with all the attendant risks. There is no neutral zone in living; men are either making or destroying; they are either righteous or unrighteous, but none is righteous in every act and none is unrighteous in every act.

N. Berdyaev, The Destiny of Man, 1937, specially Part II; D. Bonhoeffer, Letters and Papers from Prison, 3rd edn., revised and enlarged, 1967; C. Gore, The Sermon on the Mount, 1925; F. J. A. Hort, The Way the Truth the Life, 1893, specially Lecture I; L. Lavelle, The Meaning of Holiness, 1954; G. Marcel, The Mystery of Being, 1950; A. Miller, The Renewal of Man, 1952.

R. E. C. BROWNE

Rights

Rights can be characterized as powers reserved to the individual such that he can demand of others that they not be interfered with or taken away. Rights involve a mutual acknowledgment on the part of each individual of the claims or rights of others; rights are thus correlative with duties. Rights have frequently been divided into two classes, political rights and civil rights. The former have to do with the voice the individual has in determining the form and operation of the government under which he lives, while the latter have to do with the extent of the individual's freedom in conducting his personal affairs within the body politic. Among civil rights are generally listed such rights as the right of property, the right to work, to marry, to be secure from arbitrary arrest, etc.

Both forms of rights are rooted in some theory of the status of right as such; such a theory is at the foundation of political life in all its forms. Among the major theories of rights we may mention the theory of divine or natural right according to which every individual is endowed by either God or nature with certain rights that should never be violated; secondly, there are various forms of the contract theory according to which the State is based on a contract in which the individual retains such rights as he could not conceivably contract away; thirdly, there are utilitarian theories according to which individual rights are made to depend on the general welfare; fourthly, there are the *prima facie* theories of rights; and finally, there are the totalitarian theories according to which the individual has no rights save those granted to him by the civil power which is the sole source of rights.

One of the most perplexing questions in the theory of rights concerns the extent to which it is possible to maintain absolutely universal rights for all individuals. The fact that every right for an individual must be correlative with a duty or obligation on the part of all the other individuals seems to make any guarantee of absolutely universal rights virtually impossible to maintain. Sometimes the problem has been approached by interpreting universal rights in a purely formal way as when we say, for example, that every individual has an absolute right to equal treatment or consideration under all circumstances. Some philosophers and political theorists have held that the right to self-realization or to at least a minimum development of one's own capacities and potentialities is the one universal and absolute right and indeed the liberal democracies of the West have made this right absolutely basic.

In the sphere of political rights the continuing debate is between forms of government based on 'consent' and operating through representative persons and offices, and states governed by an imposed dictatorial power where there is little or no machinery through which the individual can be represented or the governmental power criticized in the light of the diverse interests existing in the state.

The rapid development of communication and of transportation in recent decades has brought the nations of the world into closer connection with each other. Moreover, common problems introduced by the threat of nuclear war have raised questions about international law and the rights of states *vis-à-vis* each other. The existence of such organizations as the UN testifies to the concern for endowing the acknowledgment of human rights with an international sanction.

G. H. Sabine, *A History of Political Theory in the West*, 1938; John Wild, *Plato's Modern Enemies and the Theory of Natural Law*, 1953.

JOHN E. SMITH

Rigorism. *see* Tutiorism.

Ritschl and Ritschlianism

Albrecht Ritschl (1822–1889), born in Berlin, was one of the most influential Protestant theologians of the nineteenth century. He was professor at Bonn from 1853 till 1864, and at Göttingen from 1864 until his death. Though he began his career under the influence of the Tübingen school and of the Hegelian metaphysic, he broke away from these positions, and his mature thought was shaped by the ideas of Kant and Lotze. In particular, he accepted the Kantian rejection of metaphysics. This does not mean that he became a positivist. He accepted that there is a God who reveals himself in Christ, but that we cannot reach him through speculation; and that there are mysteries in the Christian faith, but that we cannot analyze these in metaphysical concepts. The propositions of theology, as Ritschl understood them, are not objectifying statements, like the propositions of science, but are rather value-judgments. To say that Christ is God is not to make a metaphysical affirmation about his person (though something of the sort may be implicit) but to acknowledge his uniquely supreme status. Whatever the difficulties in such a theological orientation, it is clear that it lays special stress on the ethical and practical aspects of Christianity, rather than on the intellectual and speculative. In Ritschlian theology generally, the organizing concept is the Kingdom of God, ethically conceived, rather than the Logos of classical theology. However, Ritschl did not allow the element of subjectivism in his theology to drive him into individualism. He gives a special place to the Church, as the community where reconciliation is taking place. It is in this community that freedom and love become possible, and advance is made towards the realization of the Kingdom. Other prominent members of the Ritschlian school were Theodor Haering, author of a substantial work on ethics; Wilhelm Herrmann, teacher of both Barth and Bultmann; and Adolf Harnack, usually regarded as the typical representative of liberal theology. With him, the dogmatic and theological element in Christianity is reduced to a minimum. Christ becomes, in his teaching and example, the hero of the human race. The Christian life consists in following this teaching and example, and in realizing the kingdom of brotherhood and love under the benign aegis of a somewhat shadowy Father in heaven. Ritschlianism, through such writers as W. Rauschenbusch (q.v.) and H. C. King, exerted a powerful influence in the USA, especially in the rise of the Social Gospel (q.v.). The presuppositions of the Ritschlian movement were subjected to devastating criticism by Loisy, Schweitzer and others, but its ethical and social concern remains as a permanent contribution.

A. E. Garvie, *The Ritschlian Theology*, 1899; J. K. Mozley, *Ritschlianism*, 1909.

EDITOR

Roman Catholic Moral Theology (Contemporary)

1. *General Moral Theology*. There is perhaps no area within contemporary Catholic life and theology undergoing renewal and reform to a greater degree than Catholic moral theology. One of the most characteristic trends of the renewed contemporary moral theology is the emphasis given to a profound integration of the Christian life with its inner source, God's word to us in Christ as found in Scripture and the faith of the Christian community, the living Church. The primary emphasis tends to be less on the external, practical, moralistic side of the Christian life, but more on the living reality of the inner dynamism of God personally coming to us and being one with us in his forgiving love through and in his Son.

Another fundamental characteristic is the re-emphasis that all religious morality, instead of being a mere observance of impersonal regulations or imperatives, is fundamentally centred in a personal dialogue between God and the individual and in one's personal response to God and his love as one perceives what he is asking of one in the concrete historical moment. Sin then is one's failure in freedom and knowledge to make this religious response to God's love. This personal emphasis has restored the integrity of one's personal conscience to its traditional place in Christian teachings. It is in his personal conscience that the individual ultimately must in sincerity face the personal responsibility of deciding what God is asking of him here and now. On the other hand, the personal dimensions of morality will all the more strongly demand of the sincere individual in his personal dialogue with his God to do his reasonable best to discover what God actually wants of him, in other words, to form his conscience according to the objective Christian truth as opposed to mere moral relativism or subjectivism. For the Christian the same one God will be speaking to him in a diversity of ways. As the God who is the author and creator of man as a human person in the image of God himself, he will be speaking to the individual through the needs and demands of the dignity of the human person, that is, through the law of nature. As the God of salvation, he will be speaking to the

individual through the message and teachings of Christ present in the Scriptures and the living divine faith and teachings of the Christian community, the Church, as she authentically fulfils the teaching mission of Christ in the world. Finally, as the God who through the Spirit guides and works in love with each unique individual, he speaks through the personal guidance and movements of the Holy Spirit in the depths of each person as he faces the concrete unique moments and situations of his life which also come from God as the Lord of history. Thus, the universal demands and needs of the human person and the universal truths of Christian revelation as authentically interpreted and taught by the Church remain valid, but it also remains the personal responsibility of the individual person in the sincerity of his conscience to apply these truths through the personal guidance of the Holy Spirit to the unique historical concrete personal moments of his own life.

The Christian Pauline dimension and understanding of law, so scripturally and dynamically expressed by St Augustine and St Thomas Aquinas, but later often lost sight of at least in practice, is restored to its position of primacy in contemporary moral theology. The New Law of Christ is primarily internal, not external. It is the inner mystery of God personally one with us in his self-giving love through Christ. The impulse and force of God's personal love as communicated to us through Christ tends of itself to express and manifest itself in love, love of God and of our fellow-men. Thus, every external law in the Christian order has primarily an internal function, namely, to guide and assist the expression of the divine love within us. To the extent that one is under the influence of grace and divine love one will experience a truly valid and necessary external law as a guide directing one towards that to which one's inner life of grace and love almost spontaneously tends. But to the extent the Christian experiences himself to be under the sway and influence of egoism and concupiscence, he will experience external laws in their secondary role and function, namely, as restrictive and external, because the valid demands of the law are painfully experienced as contrary to what the inner impulse and movement of egoism and concupiscence desire. It is at such moments that even for the Christian the law will be the occasion of temptation, sin and death.

All the various types of true and valid laws as universal norms or rules are rooted ultimately in God and the truth of his being and they are in their own limited way an expression of God himself to man. This positive appreciation of the inner value and meaning of all law demands from the Christian, therefore, more than just a mere external observance of the letter of the law, but rather a true sincere inner desire of the whole man to achieve the full truth and good which the spirit of the law should intend.

In addition to the eternal law, which is simply the eternal truth and goodness of God himself, there is the law of nature or the natural law. Put very succinctly, the natural law is nothing else than the demands which flow from the dignity and needs of what one is as a human person and hence from God as the author and creator of the human person in the divine image. Divine positive law springs forth from a free decree of God over and beyond the reality of creation. This law which has God as its immediate author is made known to man only through divine revelation. The basic example is the whole mystery of Christ and the economy of Christian revelation. Human positive law is made by a free act of a human legislator with legitimate divine authority. The first principal type is ecclesiastical or church law which has for its immediate author not God or Christ himself, but the human legislative power in the Church with authority given to her by Christ. Examples of this type of law are the obligation of participating in the divinely instituted liturgical eucharistic celebration of the Mass precisely on Sunday, the laws of fast and abstinence from meat, liturgical rites and ceremonies, the celibacy of the clergy. In the light of the understanding of the New Law of Christ as opposed to the Old Law, these human laws of the Church should not in the spirit of the Christian mystery be made an end in themselves, or multiplied needlessly in a way to stifle the freedom and inner movement of Christian love and grace or to deflect from the supreme guide and manifestation of God to us, Christ Jesus, but rather they should exist insofar as they are judged to be necessary or highly useful in the light of historical changes either in further determining the more universal laws and teachings of Christ or in giving necessary assistance to man in his weakness. Human positive civil law is the true and just law which has the civil legislator as its immediate author with the divine authority that comes necessarily to the civil society as an institution flowing by necessity from man's social nature and hence from God as the author of human nature.

But all laws, insofar as they are universal expressions of and guides to the true and good, cannot precisely in their universality express and exhaust in themselves the totality of the uniqueness of the particular concrete historical situation. For this reason there is always the need for the particular concrete historical application and realization of the universal law here and now which can be achieved in its perfection only by the unique individual involved in the sincerity of his conscience as guided by the Holy Spirit. Consequently, this calls for the principle of sincere *epikeia*, especially in the case of human laws, by which one sincerely judges in his own conscience that under certain unique particular circumstances the human legislator could not reasonably intend the letter of the law to apply, for example, either because the hardship involved would be out of proportion to the purpose of the law, or because the good intended by the law would not be achieved but rather frustrated, or because there is an unforeseen conflict with a higher and more necessary good. This principle is naturally subject to abuse, but it is also in line with the positive appreciation of the inner value and meaning of all law as a communication and expression to us of God himself in his love through Christ, calling for the inner personal response in love of the whole man for the achievement of the good proposed by the law.

2. *Special Moral Theology.* The fundamental free personal religious response of the Christian is the response of personal faith in Christ. Upon this response and growth of personal living faith animated with love as directed by the inner movement of grace, the entire Christian moral life as basically religious and personal depends. From this primary reality of the inner dynamism of the Christian life according to its maturity will flow all the other fundamental and even secondary relationships between the individual and Christ in the Christian community, the Church, in her active mission and role in the world. From it will result the realization of the fundamental need and meaning of prayer in and through the living Christ, the meaningful participation through faith and love in the divine sacramental liturgy of the living Christ in his people, the Church. From it will come one's response of inner faith and love for the Church and her divine mission and authority as the continuing living mystery of Christ ever present visibly and authoritatively on the earth. This will result in the sincere inner obedience to the Church as to Christ himself, but with the realization at the same time that the Church by the necessity of her human element will exercise her teaching mission and authority, although always authentically, nevertheless according to various degrees of direct and certain relationship with divine revelation and hence according to various degrees of certitude.

For the individual who has encountered through faith the mystery of divine love for him and all men through Christ, there will mature within him the divine power and virtue of hope in the unlimited power of God and his personal love for him and all men through Christ. This divine hope and trust in Christ together with one's faith and love is what the Christian with the assistance of divine grace must primarily cultivate as the basic foundation and inner dynamism of his whole Christian life.

As is most clear from Scripture and the living tradition of Christian faith, the basic inner reality of God personally with us through Christ in his self-giving healing love will tend primarily and basically to express itself through true sincere Christian love of one's fellow-men. The mystery of the Church in her deepest meaning is the continued visible earthly presence of Christ in his people united one with another in love through and in Christ, by which the mystery of the good news of God's self-giving and healing love continues visibly active in the world. So too the life of the individual Christian is his participation in this divine-human mystery through his union with Christ in his people in expressing visibly and actively through his own person God's self-giving love in service for all men in Christ.

This Christian love is the guiding force not only in the personal individual life of the Christian, but also in his social life as a member of society. In other words true Christian love for his fellow-men obliges the Christian, first of all, to form for himself and others an authentic Christian social conscience and, secondly, to strive according to his position and influence in society to bring about the united social action necessary to alleviate and remedy the social ills, injustices and sufferings resulting from a malfunctioning social order.

Roman Catholic social doctrine, although always present implicitly in the Christian message and tradition, was first synthesized and integrated into an organized unity by Pope Leo XIII in the latter part of the nineteenth century, especially in his famous *Rerum Novarum*, on the condition of the working classes and the socio-economic revolution of that time, and has been further developed according to historical needs by Pius XI in his *Quadragesimo Anno*, on reconstructing the social order, and *Divinis Redemptoris*, on atheistic Communism, by Pius XII in numerous social messages and documents by John XXIII in his *Mater et Magistra*, on Christianity and social progress, and *Pacem in Terris*, on peace in all its dimensions, in the Constitution of Vatican Council II *On the Church in the Modern World*, and by Paul VI in *Populorum Progressio*, on the development of peoples.

In brief, Roman Catholic social doctrine teaches that God created material goods for the use of all men, but that at least in the present fallen order of sin the right and use of private property is demanded by man's nature and hence by God in order that man might properly and fully develop and cultivate the material world. But this right of private property is not an absolute right, but relative to the absolute social nature and purpose of material goods. Hence, a sincere Christian love for his fellow-men and a desire to fulfil and accomplish God's plan of creation require of the Christian to strive to correct a social or economic order which forces great numbers to be subject to conditions and circumstances contrary to justice and the dignity of the human person and

a child of God. At the same time, true enlightened Christian love will prevent one from turning to false utopian social solutions such as Communism with its basic denial of private property and its class hatred, in the realization that they cannot fulfil the true needs of man and the human person.

The State is a society demanded by man's social nature and its authority comes from God as the author of man's social nature. But the State exists not as an absolute power, but only to achieve the true common good of its citizens. And as the civil society is nothing else than a civil union of men striving together for the common good, it as well as its individual citizens is under God and his laws. Although there has long been the traditional Roman Catholic doctrine about the just war (q.v.), there has been growing dissatisfaction and disillusionment among many Roman Catholic theologians about the ease with which this doctrine has been so often used by so-called Christian peoples and nations during the many past generations to justify war after war. In this age of thermonuclear war there is much deep soul-searching, study and disagreement in the search for the Christian answer. This very complicated question has not yet found a unanimous or official Catholic solution. John XXIII in his famous *Pacem in Terris* comes out strongly against nuclear war and the nuclear arms race and makes it abundantly clear that the primary image of the Christian message should always be above all else a sincere and earnest quest for peace. But one cannot necessarily use this to justify unilateral disarmament which could in reality turn out to be the greatest threat to peace under present circumstances. But Roman Catholic social doctrine, from the time of Leo XIII and especially under John XXIII and Paul VI in the face of the modern dilemmas in regard to world peace, demands that Christians sincerely strive for the development and perfection of an international world organization as a necessary means for achieving world peace. Finally Roman Catholic social doctrine, especially as clarified by recent popes and bishops, cannot in any way be reconciled with any form of racism (q.v.). True Christian love for Christ in his fellow-men, especially the lowly and suffering, demands that the Christian both as an individual and as united with others strive sincerely and effectively to alleviate and remedy racial injustices and sufferings.

In the area especially of human sexuality and marriage many theologians in the Church today are attempting to clarify and express more forcibly the inner relationship and enlightened contribution of the dimensions of human Christian love. Human sexuality has no meaning apart from true human love and it is the human Christian ability to love as a human person which is the fundamental basis enabling one to integrate his sexuality into his total mature human Christian personality. Erotic, sexual or conjugal love of its very nature implies first of all true human love, but an unique exclusive love that has developed in intensity between a man and a woman, leading them to the final decision of an exclusive personal commitment and self-giving surrender in love of the one to the other forever. The concomitant sexual union is by its very nature physically, psychologically and spiritually the unique human Christian symbolic expression of this final decision of total self-giving of oneself and total acceptance of the other in love. But this conjugal love is so unique and rich that it is creative and productive of human life in the overflow of love. It is, therefore, from the very nature of this conjugal love, as an exclusive love forever between a man and a woman and as productive of human life, that there arises the permanent union of human and Christian marriage. The complete nature of conjugal love is, therefore, the basis of all human and Christian morality in regard to human sexuality and marriage.

It is precisely this human conjugal love in all its rich dimensions as the foundation of the human family which, according to Roman Catholic faith, Christ has made sacramental, that is, he has taken this human love and its expression as a symbolic expression of the ever-enduring intimacy and union in self-giving love of God with us in Christ Jesus, so that in and through this sacramental symbol of human conjugal love he is especially present, giving himself to and sanctifying the human couple precisely in their conjugal love for one another and in their expression of this love.

In regard to the problem of contraception, the Church has taught that the intrinsic relationship between conjugal love and the generation of children cannot be positively frustrated or excluded. But full insight into what this relationship precisely consists in is another question and it is now through the aid of new knowledge provided by science in union with theology and philosophy that the Church is seeking a deeper understanding of this relationship and hence of possible legitimate means of birth-regulation. The Church is fully aware that conjugal love and marriage are related not only to the generation of children, but also to their development and education as human persons and Christians, and that in the concrete practical order many serious and complex problems in this area face both many married couples and society as a whole.

Although there are many additional specific areas and problems which could be well treated in this article on contemporary Roman Catholic moral theology, because of the limitations of space it has been thought more beneficial and enlightening to present some of the fundamental principles and an understanding of the Christian life as expressed by the contemporary renewed Roman Catholic moral theology and its application only to certain general areas of major importance in the Christian life today. *See also* **Natural Law; Pontifical Social Encyclicals; Thomas Aquinas.**

For a more thorough and detailed study of the renewed contemporary moral theology, consult the following works and their bibliography: Bordeaux, F. and Danet A., *Introduction to the Law of Christ*, Alba House, Staten Island, N.Y., 1966; Häring, B., *The Law of Christ*, 3 vols., The Newman Press, Westminster, Maryland, 1963; Monden, L., *Sin, Liberty and Law*, Sheed and Ward, New York, 1965.

JAMES P. SCULL, S.J.

Romanticism

Romanticism is a term used so vaguely that its usefulness has been much questioned. In its original use it was a name for a mood and movement excitedly and powerfully operative round about 1800, which may be characterized generally as an assertion of high sentiment and intuition against cool and standardized rules in all the main spheres of culture, and a reaching out towards the Infinite: for example, in poetry, a rebellion against the constrictions of perfect form, and a claim that aesthetic sensibility can give insight into moral and religious truth, to which intellect should not claim a monopoly; in theology, a return to the immediacies of religious experience, to which abstract constructions should be evidently related; in philosophy, a revolt led by Fichte, Schelling, and Hegel against the old tight logic of a persisting scholasticism, against the empiricism, commonsense reasonableness and utilitarian temper of the Enlightenment (*see* **Enlightenment**), and against Kant's agnosticism. In ethics, Schiller's ideal of the 'lovely soul' was an aesthetic protest against Kant's moral rigorism of the 'good will' (from which Fichte did not break loose). A demand arose for an ideal that would engage man's entire nature: so, for example, Hegel, but more attractively in Schleiermacher (qq.v.), in the special form that the possibilities of the spiritual factor in the universe are so vast and many-sided that they can be realized and brought together only through the use by each of us of his individual gifts. The Romantic movement was not predominantly individualistic: it was standing for a social solidarity that cannot be contrived by rationalist planners but has to grow through community of interest and spiritual affinity in an expanding tradition. One expression of this respect for tradition was a love of things mediaeval, another a gathering up for the first time of Germanic and Indian lore and an admiring use of them in literature and philosophy. European culture was at last breaking its local bounds.

T. E. JESSOP

Rousseau, Jean-Jacques

Rousseau (1712–1778), was a moralizer with a literary genius, not a systematic thinker; his great influence lay in his one-sided insights and in the magic of his moods, images and words. His moral ideas have to be collected from all his works and torn out of their bewitching contexts. Negatively he was recoiling from the doctrine of original sin, the oppressions of political despotism, and the materialism, artificialities and trivialities of current social life. Positively he depicted a 'natural man', as he comes from God, who could not have made him evil. Man was born good, free and happy, his actual wickedness, servitude and misery being due to society. Not that he is morally good: he breaks no rules only because there are none in him and none over him. He is innocent, naively satisfying his few needs, the inequalities among natural men not being such as to prevent each from doing so. He is not selfish, for selfishness is a reflective and deliberate affair; nor is he altruistic, this too being reflective, but he has a spontaneous pity at seen cases of misfortune and helps others when he is free from care. It is in these senses that he has happiness, freedom and goodness. It is society that robs him of these and perverts him; for social inequality, chiefly through property, means privilege, wealth, leisure, satisfaction without leisure, for the few, and for the rest toil on behalf of those, with poverty and pain. Society is not, however, intrinsically wrong; it has merely taken the wrong turn. There is no need to return to wild simplicity; it is better to be intelligent, cultured, consciously humane. What is required is a higher form of happiness, freedom and goodness, to be attained by different social means. In one work he outlines the kind of State in which they are to be guaranteed: every individual surrenders his primordial freedom to the whole community, but does not really lose it because his obedience is to a control which he has helped to found. In another work he narrates the upbringing of a fictitious boy, Emile, by a perpetually present tutor who arranges every detail to ensure his 'natural' development. In yet another work, a romance, he portrays a new and different Héloïse, in genuine love with one man but married to another to whom she remains faithful, the moral of which seems to be that marriage and family have a natural sanctity which neither love nor the absence of it is to break. On the whole it may be said that he trusted unspoiled feeling instead of reason, and balanced the current stress on well-doing by emphasizing personal qualities (e.g., simplicity and purity), lauding inner rightness rather than its expression in conduct, beauty of character rather than moral utilities.

T. E. JESSOP

Royce, Josiah

Josiah Royce (1855–1916), idealist philosopher especially remembered for his *Philosophy of Loyalty*, graduated from the University of California in 1875, studied in Germany, and then took a doctorate at Johns Hopkins in 1878. After teaching in his native California for a few years, he was called to Harvard, where he taught (1882–1916) for the rest of his brilliant career. He was widely influential in his time, but the diminishing importance of Philosophical Idealism restricted his continuing impact. Fully conversant with the trends in the scientific and philosophical thought of his time, as with the rise of Pragmatism (q.v.), his defence of Absolute Idealism was careful and ingenious.

In his first philosophical book, *The Religious Aspect of Philosophy* (1885), Royce presented an original argument for the existence of the Absolute. He contended that the conditions which determine the logical possibility of error must themselves be absolute truth; the fact that there can be error implies such truth. Already foreshadowed in this book was the theory of the community of interpretation, later developed in many works, including his Gifford lectures, *The World and the Individual* (2 vols., 1900–01), *The Philosophy of Loyalty* (1908), and *The Problem of Christianity* (2 vols., 1913). Royce elaborated the idea that the Infinite is actual as community of interpretation. Interpretation he defined as a mode of cognition more adequate than perception or conception; it has a triadic form, for there is something to be interpreted, an interpreter, and him to whom the interpretation is given. The result of the interpretation demands further interpretation, and so the process goes on endlessly. The goal of interpretation is the practical one of creating community where none existed before; it can lead to that synthesis of individual wills that produces social integration.

Royce devoted much attention to religion, which for him has to do with the ultimate meaning of life and the final destiny of the individual as related to God. He maintained that the essence of Christianity is the 'beloved community', the rock on which the Church is based. In *The Problem of Christianity* he defended metaphysically the ultimate reality of the actual Infinite, God, and of his redeeming power effective in the beloved community.

Royce also devoted much attention to ethics, understood as that which concerns the relations between persons in society. His key idea was that of loyalty, which, when properly defined, he saw as the fulfilment of the whole moral law. Loyalty is the willing and practical and thoroughgoing devotion of a person to a cause. It is the cohesive principle which forms the bridge between the free individual and social claims. He held loyalty to be not only good but the good; his ultimate principle was 'loyalty to loyalty'. He was anxious to reduce the barriers of prejudice between man, but saw the value of a 'wholesome provincialism' in civilization – matters he discussed in *Race Questions, Provincialism, and Other American Problems* (1908). In the last years of his life, Royce faced the problems of war. The social movements which lead to war have a dyadic character, but a community of interpretation requires three members. The principle of insurance does have the necessary triadic character and so is suitable to large-scale development in the interests of a great, international community; these ideas were elaborated in *War and Insurance* (1914) and *The Hope of the Great Community* (1916).

Stuart G. Brown, *The Social Philosophy of Josiah Royce*, 1950; John E. Smith, *Royce's Social Infinite: The Community of Interpretation*, 1950.

ROBERT T. HANDY

Rule of St Benedict.
see Benedict, St.

Sabbatarianism. *see* Sunday Observance.

Saintliness

In the NT the word saint was used as the word Christian is used now; for example, St Paul wrote: 'All the saints greet you, especially those of Caesar's household' (Phil. 4.22). Later, 'saint' and 'saintliness' were used only with reference to outstanding Christians. In what follows here 'saintliness' is taken to mean the state of holiness to which all Christians are called. Saintliness is not sinlessness; no man can acquire it any more than he can acquire genius or charm. Saintliness can best be looked on as a gift from God. The offering and receiving of this gift is not an automatic giving-taking operation completed in a single movement or series of movements. The receiving consists in a lifetime's use of thoughts, words and deeds to make the gift our own. Here are descriptions of some of the modes of reception: (1) rejoicing in being freed from the bondage of sin, fear, death and time; (2) regarding every act of God's creation as also an act of his revelation; (3) interpreting human life through frequent meditation on the birth, life, death and resurrection of the Lord of glory; (4) being penitent with the dignity of one who has been led to think of himself as a son and not as a slave; (5) expecting to see God in all things and all things in him; (6) loving others not only as separate individuals but as those who are caught up with us in the complex movements

of the whole of humanity; (7) appreciating the discoveries of contemporary scientists, artists, philosophers and theologians; (8) remembering that, despite all seeming evidence to the contrary, God is more clearly known in the mind and works of men than in the mysteries of the whole physical universe; that is, poetry, science and philosophy disclose more of the nature of God than the remote mountain tops and the movement of the four seasons; and (9) reverencing God through reverencing all his creatures, animate and inanimate.

There is a great difference between thinking about saintliness and being saintly. Being saintly does not mean waiting to feel blessed; it is thinking as a saint would think; talking, praying, repenting as he would; it is acting in love of all men with a particular responsibility for church members.

The Church primarily exists to worship God and to love the world he loves. The quality of this worship and this love is largely dependent on the degree of the saintliness of church members. The saintliness of one member affects the life of the whole Body of Christ and the saintliness of one cannot be apart from fellowship with the other members. Saintliness empowers and enlightens both the Church and the world.

R. E. C. BROWNE

Sanctification

The place of sanctification in the Christian life has occasioned much theological debate and confessional differences. The biblical sense of the term is in general that of a status of holiness. St Paul's frequent use of it, often in alignment with justification (I Cor. 6.11), is the ground from which varying interpretations arise. Is sanctification entirely conferred by divine grace, or also achieved? If conferred is it entirely imputed or also imparted? If achieved, how much depends upon the unmerited favour of God and how much on the Christian man's endeavour? These questions have divided Christendom about the scope of divine grace and the meaning of reconciliation between God and man. The main contention is whether God reconciles the sinner by a justification which forgives a sinfulness he cannot overcome, or whether he is also offered the possibility of achieving a holiness which is not only done for him but also in him. (See Reinhold Niebuhr, *The Nature and Destiny of Man*, II, 1943, Chap. 4.)

As a generalization sanctification is the ethical working out of justification, imparted because first imputed. Reformation theology tends to make sanctification one with justification. Roman Catholic doctrine sets much store upon a real holiness of life as the result of 'sanctifying grace'. The Anglican Caroline divines, like Jeremy Taylor in *Holy Living* (1650), were upholders of the need of sanctification, as were also the later Tractarians. See H. R. McAdoo, *The Structure of Caroline Moral Theology*, 1949, Chap. 6. Methodism also preserved the idea of sanctification as a state of perfection expected of the believer. See Vincent Taylor, *Forgiveness and Reconciliation*, Chap. 5. The Eastern Church, though not using the Western term, has a powerful doctrine of sanctification under the name of deification or *theosis* for which appeal can be made to II Peter 1.4. *See also* **Holiness; Perfection.**

Sanctification as the supremely Christian way of life has a large literature, mainly under the heading of perfection. For Anglican treatment *see* F. P. Harton, *Elements of the Spiritual Life*, 1932; K. E. Kirk, *The Vision of God*, 1931; for Catholic works *see* Walter Hylton, *The Scale of Perfection*, ed. by E. Underhill, 1923; J. de Guibert, S.J., *The Theology of the Spiritual Life*, 1954; St Teresa of Avila, *The Way of Perfection*, 1567; for Free Church works *see* R. N. Flew, *The Idea of Perfection in Christian Theology*, 1934; P. T. Forsyth, *Christian Perfection*, 1899.

V. A. DEMANT

Sanderson, Robert

Robert Sanderson (1587–1663) was one of the greatest of the English moral theologians of the seventeenth century. 'I carry my ears to hear other preachers, but I carry my conscience to hear Mr Sanderson' (Charles I). 'The best casuist of our nation and may be of any nation else' (Bishop Barlow). A few of his replies to the many who sought his guidance were published posthumously (e.g., *Nine Cases of Conscience Occasionally Determined*, 1678). They exhibit the extraordinary precision, acute analysis and tendency towards rigorism characteristic of all Sanderson's writings. In 1642 he became Regius Professor of Divinity at Oxford, and in 1646 delivered his seven lectures *De Juramenti Promissorii Obligatione* (published, 1647; ET, 1655). He made his finest contribution to the century's casuistical divinity in the ten lectures *De Obligatione Conscientiae* (1647) which discuss the meaning and authority of conscience and treat of the problems that arise from the varied obligations imposed by human laws. They were published in 1660, the first English translation appearing in the same year. In 1851 W. Whewell edited the Latin text; and in 1877 a revised English version, *Bishop Sanderson's Lectures on Conscience and Law*, was provided by Bishop Christopher Wordsworth as a set-book for ordination candidates in the Lincoln diocese. Sanderson was hardly less famous for his sermons, many of which were lengthy discourses (only preached in part) interpretative of Christian moral teaching in the social, political, and economic contexts of his time. He became bishop of Lincoln in 1660,

attended the Savoy Conference of 1661, and drafted the Preface to the 1662 Book of Common Prayer. *See also* **Caroline Moral Theology.**

W. Jacobson, *The Works of Robert Sanderson*, 6 vols., 1854; G. Lewis, *Robert Sanderson*, 1924; I. Walton, *The Life of Dr Sanderson*, 1678; Thomas Wood, 'A Great English Casuist', *CQR*, cxlvii (1948), pp. 29–45.

THOMAS WOOD

Scandal

Scandal arises when a member of the Christian community, by his action or opinions, goes against the commonly accepted standards of the community and causes distress to his brethren, perhaps even bringing the whole community into disrepute. From the earliest times, the Church has had to exercise discipline (q.v.) in order to deal with erring members and to maintain its standards. The really difficult case, however, is the one in which the person who gives rise to the scandal is acting not from carelessness or rebellion against the Church, but from conscience, sincerely believing that he has a right or a duty to declare the opinion or perform the actions which are scandalizing his brethren. In such cases we should remember the advice given by St Paul in I Cor. 10. Things which are lawful may not be expedient, and even where the individual is passionately convinced of the rightness of his act or opinion, he ought to act with charity towards his brethren. It may become a very difficult matter to decide between the prompting of the individual conscience and the distress caused to the community. Conscience cannot be coerced, but before causing scandal by some unilateral act, a member of the community should consider very carefully whether he is acting with charity to his brethren, and whether he really is impelled by conscience or by less worthy motives, such as pride and the desire for notoriety.

EDITOR

Sceptics

Like all the hellenistic philosophers the Sceptics sought for *ataraxia*, serenity, the untroubled mind. They found it in 'a state of mental rest in which we neither deny nor affirm anything' (Sextus Empiricus, *Outlines of Pyrrhonism*, i.10).

The Sceptic held that there is absolutely nothing which is certain. A tower may look one shape from one angle, and another from another. A thing will taste sweet or bitter according to what you have eaten immediately before it. To every argument there is an equal and opposite argument (Sextus Empiricus, *Outlines*, i.12,202). Peace will come when a man realizes this and when he .completely suspends judgment, and is content not to know.

It is, of course, true that the Sceptic held even this undogmatically, for quite clearly on this view it is not even certain that nothing is certain. The Sceptic found his peace in consenting not to know.

So the Sceptic had a series of catch phrases: 'Not this more than that'; 'Perhaps and perhaps not'; 'Possibly, possibly not'; 'Maybe and maybe not'. This uncertainty issues in suspension of judgment (*epochē*) which in turn issues in *arrepsia*, equipoise, which in turn issues in *aphasia*, non-assertion. 'I determine nothing', said the Sceptic (Sextus Empiricus, *Outlines*, i.188–200).

This obviously paralyses action because the mind is never made up. To solve this Arcesilaus held that the Sceptic acts on what is reasonable in the light of wisdom (Sextus Empiricus, *Against the Logicians*, i.158). Carneades worked out the degrees of probability which anything may have (Sextus Empiricus, *Outlines*, i.227), and formed a theory of graduated probability.

All this seems to abolish all standards and to abolish all possibility of ethics. Carneades in a notorious speech in 156 BC argued that there is no such thing as natural right, that law and justice are merely expedient agreements for mutual protection, and that self-interest is the real end of life. An intelligent man, he said, despises justice (Lactantius, *Institutes*, v.15,16; Cicero, *De Repub.*, iii.iv.8–12; Quintilian, *Instit.* xii.i.35). But in point of fact the Sceptic did recognize a fourfold standard in life (Sextus Empiricus, *Outlines*, i.24). There is the guidance of nature, which makes us capable of sensation and thought. There is the tradition of custom and laws, whereby we regard piety as good and impiety as evil. There is the constraint of the appetites, which makes us eat and drink. There is the instruction of the arts. The real ethic of the Sceptic was simply convention. He lived 'in accordance with the rules of life', but 'quite undogmatically' (Sextus Empiricus, *Outlines*, i.21). The Sceptic practised conventional virtue because it seemed to him that in all probability there was no other way to be happy.

We may add one more odd idea of the Sceptics. They held that God cannot possess virtue, because virtue presupposes a fault to be overcome. He alone is continent who could be incontinent. And further, virtue is something *above* its possessor, and there can be nothing above God (Sextus Empiricus, *Against the Physicists*, i.152–75).

In the end Scepticism perished because a man cannot always remain suspended in mental space. Scepticism broke down before 'the exigencies of life . . . before the fact that man is not only a spectator of reality, but a maker of it' (E. R. Bevan, *Stoics and Sceptics*, 1931, p. 141).

WILLIAM BARCLAY

Schleiermacher, Friedrich Ernst Daniel

The chief influence of Schleiermacher (1768–1834) lay in theology, in which he is a landmark: he broke the sway of dry and imperious Protestant dogmatics, shifting the starting-point from creeds and other official formularies to the nature of religious experience as present in individuals nourished by the common life of a church. In resting his thinking on something felt, he was the chief theological mouthpiece of Romanticism, to the first flush of which his *Addresses on Religion* (1799) belongs. He proceeded later to more and more intellectualization, but kept this tied to the task of clarifying and explaining the religious sentiment in general and the Christian sentiment in particular. Romanticism in its larger aspect of width of sweep and height (not merely warmth) of aspiration is evident in his philosophical writings, on which the impress of Plato and Spinoza was strong. Within philosophy he gave considerable attention to ethics. He defined morality as 'reason' acting on 'nature', meaning the realization of spiritual ideals in the cause-effect network of mental and bodily behaviour (in his metaphysics he maintained that the natural realm is destined to be the pliable tool of spirit). Such control has various aspects – a harmonization of spirit and flesh in the attainment of good ends, actions that in accordance with moral laws (conceived as causal, not as imperative) are means to such ends, and an exertion of spiritual power of which the specific forms are the virtues (Schleiermacher could not forget that etymologically 'virtue' means potency). He therefore developed a doctrine of 'goods', duties, and virtues. He then considered the several spheres in which moral action works, bringing them under four heads – social organization as effected by law in the State, communally good attitudes and behaviour in our free relations with one another, thought or belief as disciplined and shared in educational institutions, and 'feeling' or 'revelation' as found in the distinctive fellowship of a church. In thus including political, intellectual, aesthetic and even religious concerns as well as what is usually regarded as moral concern he was stretching ethics extremely to cover man's total function and excellence, the integrated flowering of all his higher capacities. His examination elsewhere of Christian ethics, though strewn with insights, is less thorough intellectually, and is not the part of his work that made him influential. His general monism (which has been well called, paradoxically, a theistic pantheism) prevented him from distinguishing sharply the natural and the theological virtues: he contended that moral intelligence and will are always, even when unwittingly, a response to the divine ordering in the universe, but that they rise to a higher level when that ordering is experienced feelingfully in the deep sentiment of our utter dependence on the one eternal Power in and behind it. This sense of dependence, for Schleiermacher the very essence of religion, becomes articulate as the awareness, in many degrees of imperfection, of God, and in its Christian form takes shape in the life of the Church, in whose common consciousness the Holy Spirit operates, imparting to us, according to the measure of our response, the perfect awareness of God that was possessed by Jesus, so that it is under this stimulus that our virtues acquire the Christian quality, range and power. On sin Schleiermacher's strong moral sense led him to take an almost Pelagian view. While retaining the notion of original sin he rejected as unthinkable the dogma that such sin is culpable; it stands for the ubiquitous fact of a deeply seated (1) obscuration of the awareness of God, and (2) conflict of flesh and spirit, and what it testifies to is the universal need not for forgiveness but for redemption. It is our racial solidarity in sin, which each age bequeaths to its successor, infecting institutions and temper and so providing inevitable provocations to actual sins by individuals, for which alone we are culpable. Schleiermacher's emphasis on feeling led him not to anything like individualism but to a reduction of the weight of theological dogma and to regard this, when so reduced, not as final propositional truth but as the best explanation we can find of the massive fact of Christian experience individual and collective.

R. R. Niebuhr, *Schleiermacher on Christ and Religion*, 1965; W. B. Selbie, *Schleiermacher*, 1913.

T. E. JESSOP

Schopenhauer, Arthur

Arthur Schopenhauer (1788–1860) was the philosopher of pessimism, and a fine stylist. Always a melancholic (moping over the miseries of the world at seventeen), pessimism was his starting-point as well as his conclusion, to which he reasoned his way by taking his theory of knowledge from Kant though rejecting the latter's agnosticism, and borrowing much from the ancient philosophy of India. His system, expressed in *The World as Will and Idea* (1819, much enlarged 1844) was a reaction against the rationalism and optimism of the then dominant Hegelianism. Reality is indeed, he granted, one cosmic mind, rising to consciousness in individual human minds. It is not, however, reason but will, a blind force in us as in nature, with no goal and therefore with no gain. In its guise of desire it is insatiable, finding its very satisfactions distasteful and thus painful. This is the worst of all possible worlds. The moral problem (as in Buddhism) is how to lessen the inevitable misery. Suicide is no

escape, for it destroys only the body (which is but an idea), the cosmic will in us being unquenchable. The radical step is to get rid of the illusion of an individual self: we are all orifices of the one will. Out of this recognition that we are one, all in the same plight, will spring sympathy for the sufferings of others and (another Buddhist idea) of animals. This sympathy, the only moral way out of the vain hunt for our own satisfaction, gives rise to the two basic virtues, the negative one of not hurting others, the positive one of helping them. Further, although we cannot extinguish desire we can diminish it by seeing its futility and by cultivating those forms of contemplation in which desire is not aroused, namely the apprehension of pure truth and of beauty in the arts, among which music gives the greatest release. Here is our closest approach to the Nirvana of non-individuality.

T. E. JESSOP

Schweitzer, Albert

Schweitzer (1875–1965), Christian theologian and philanthropist, was born in Alsace, then part of Germany. He taught at the University of Strasbourg from 1902, but resolved to give up his academic career and to found a medical mission in Africa. He set up his famous hospital at Lambarene in 1913, and this remained the centre of his labours until his death. Theologically, Schweitzer's name is associated with his criticism of Ritschlianism and the nineteenth-century quest for the historical Jesus. The humanitarian Jesus and the ethical kingdom of heaven that the Ritschlians had pictured to themselves were, Schweitzer maintained, fabrications of the modern mind and far removed from the historical realities behind the NT. Jesus' teaching had in fact been dominated by eschatological expectations concerning the end of the age; the Kingdom of Heaven was not an ethical but an eschatological and supernatural conception, to be realized by the intervention of God alone; the ethical teaching of Jesus was not meant to have relevance to ordinary conditions of life, but was an 'interim ethic' for the brief period that remained before the end of the age. Schweitzer claimed that the teaching of Paul was similarly dominated by eschatology. The effect of Schweitzer's ideas seems at first to make the whole NT teaching, including its ethic, quite irrelevant to modern times, and to relegate it to an age dominated by apocalyptic superstitions. But Schweitzer believed that the essential core of the gospel, a 'religion of love' as he called it, could be disengaged from its eschatological setting, much as Bultmann, at a later time, sought to 'demythologize' the gospel. Schweitzer's own career is an adequate testimony to this enduring truth that he found in the NT. His ideas were developed in terms of a philosophy based on 'reverence for life', where 'life' does not mean just biological life, but is a more metaphysical conception, something like that of Bergson. The reinterpreted eschatology of the NT does not lead to other-worldliness, but to a dialectical process which goes through world-negation to world-affirmation. It is through resignation and submission to the life-process that man attains an inward freedom, which in turn leads him to an affirmative ethic of love. He was a prolific writer. His most important theological work was *The Quest of the Historical Jesus: from Reimarus to Wrede* (1910), while the development of his ideas and their relation to his work may be studied in *My Life and Thought* (1933).

EDITOR

Science and Ethics

The word 'science' covers a wide range of meanings: (1) a system of knowledge, split up into distinct 'sciences', for example, physics and sociology; (2) a method of investigation tending to create a characteristic attitude towards experience – 'the scientific attitude'; (3) applied science (technology) – the ability to manipulate the natural world successfully. 'Science' in all these senses is of concern to ethics, and thus the relation between the two is complex. It will be considered under four main heads.

1. *Science as a Source of Factual Information.* To judge a moral issue rightly we need to know the facts of the case and the probable consequences of our actions. Science likewise is concerned with facts and with making predictions in the light of what is known. Our general scientific understanding of the world is therefore an important part of the background to our moral choices; for example, a general knowledge of the physiology, psychology and sociology of sex is essential to any informed discussion of sexual moral problems, just as the general findings of biologists about animal sensitivity are relevant to the ethics of hunting. There are also particular scientific discoveries which relate to particular moral choices, for example, the link between cigarette smoking and cancer of the lung, or the dependence of health upon hygiene; the ethics of selling dirty milk are transformed by a knowledge of bacteriology. Psychology is a fruitful source of relevant facts, both about our own motives and dispositions and about the probable effects of our actions on other people. Information derived from sociological surveys is becoming of increasing importance and most of the best discussions of social problems now make extensive use of statistical data, for example, on contraception and population growth. Surveys of behaviour are still treated with suspicion by some moralists, on the grounds that no amount of knowledge about how people actually behave can settle the question of how

they ought to behave; the Kinsey reports on sexual behaviour have had an unfortunate side-effect in hardening such suspicions. There are others, however, who will not admit sharp distinctions between actual and permitted behaviour, since clearly in the long run social custom and morality are intimately connected.

There are also less direct ways in which scientific information has influenced ethical thinking. First, anthropology has weakened the appeal of authoritarian ethical systems by its disclosure of the enormous variety of social patterns and of the ways in which morality is socially conditioned. Secondly, the general spread of the scientific attitude has led to a greater emphasis on the factual element in moral decisions, even though the relevant facts themselves may not be, strictly speaking, scientific ones. Thirdly, the moral sense itself has become an object of scientific study. Work on the social behaviour of animals, developmental psychology, and the psychological origins of guilt and conscience, may lead to a drastic change in our understanding of the nature of moral judgments, and may suggest new criteria of moral health. This point is considered further under the next heading.

2. *Science as a Source of Values.* Ever since G. E. Moore described the 'Naturalistic Fallacy' (q.v.) it has been customary to hold that statements of value cannot be derived exclusively from statements of fact; in other words, science by itself cannot tell us what is right and wrong. Undeterred by this denial, some scientists have tried to base ethical systems on scientific considerations alone. Most famous among them are the systems of Evolutionary Ethics (q.v.), especially those of Julian Huxley, C. H. Waddington and (with a strong Christian bias) P. Teilhard de Chardin. Less well-known, but in some ways more subtle, are systems based upon psychological definitions of maturity, for example, Erich Fromm's ethic of 'productive love'. Anthropological research seems to suggest that the quest for some universally valid criterion of psychological maturity is a hopeless one, but when the quest is set within an evolutionary context, it is possible that some universal goal will emerge. Meanwhile it remains to be seen how far increasing contact between East and West will change the structure of psychology. A weakness in all such systems is that they only appear to carry conviction when they affirm values already held on other grounds; this suggests that they contain an element of rationalization.

A more modest way in which science by itself may contribute to the solution of some ethical problems is by causing them to disappear; for example, recent work on the psychology of punishment in animals and man strongly suggests that rewards are far more effective than punishments in changing behaviour patterns, and that punishments may defeat their own ends. If these findings are generally accepted, the ethics of punishment may cease to be a relevant issue.

3. *The Ethical Presuppositions of Science.* Scientists form a community with its own professional code concerned with such matters as honesty in reporting facts, the publication of unfavourable as well as favourable evidence, the acknowledgment of sources and the safeguarding of original discoveries, co-operation with colleagues irrespective of nationality, etc. In addition the successful scientist requires personal moral qualities such as open-mindedness, a readiness to accept criticism, patience, persistence, love of the truth for its own sake, even an element of passion. Some have described science as an adventure of faith. Scientific progress would not be possible unless scientists could trust one another, and there are occasional reminders (such as the Lysenko affair in Russia and the Piltdown skull forgery in Britain) that such trust is sometimes misplaced. In its beginnings modern science depended on the moral and philosophical assumptions of Christian Europe. Nowadays, in view of its achievements, science has become a self-authenticating activity, and is not so dependent as it was on prior moral conditioning. Misplaced trust is eventually exposed, and the overwhelming weight of scientific opinion acts to reinforce the values of the scientific community. In fact so widely accepted are these values, that some have turned the original relationship between ethics and science upside-down, and have made scientific success the criterion of value: what promotes the scientific attitude is good; what denies or stultifies it is bad.

4. *Science as a Source of New Ethical Problems.* Applied science has given men increasing power to control and adapt their environment, and this power is gradually being extended to include human life and society. Totally new powers always create ethical problems of peculiar difficulty, since there are no precedents to act as guides. Nevertheless certain general principles do apply. Broadly speaking, answers to such problems reflect differing views about man's place in nature. At one extreme there are those who stress the 'givenness' of the natural world and the dangers of upsetting the existing order of things. *See* **Natural Law.** At the other extreme are those who doubt whether 'givenness' means much in an evolving universe, and who see every new advance as increasing the range of human choice, and hence the possibilities of human freedom and personal fulfilment. Both extremes are found among Christians, some emphasizing

human creatureliness, and others the command of God to 'subdue the earth'; the weight of Christian opinion has generally been on the side of conservatism, and in particular there is a long history of Christian opposition to new medical techniques. *See* **Medical Ethics.**

Technical power is often morally ambiguous, and the art of using it lies in accepting the freedom which it brings without becoming enslaved to some other aspect of it. Atomic energy provides a clear example of such ambiguity. The motor-car is another; a machine which enormously increases the range of human experience has become a dominating influence in our civilization, and is rapidly destroying many existing amenities. The widespread use of insecticides threatens many forms of wild life, and possibly human health as well, and raises the same general questions about how far it is both safe and desirable to produce radical changes in our environment.

Advances in the biological sciences closely affecting human life itself have scarcely yet begun to make their impact. Techniques like artificial insemination are likely to be extended and refined, and in the fairly near future it may be possible to choose the sex of children, or even to interfere chemically with human heredity. The possibilities of biological warfare, already considerable, may become a source of even more acute moral problems than thermonuclear warfare, especially if biological weapons are developed which can be used without fear of detection.

In addition to the general issues involved, there are particular moral problems for scientists engaged in such projects, and there is no agreement about whether some research may itself be immoral, quite apart from the uses to which it is put. The subsequent reflections of those who worked on the first atomic bomb suggest that scientists cannot avoid all moral responsibility in connection with their discoveries; often it is only they who are in a position to realize the full implications of what they are doing.

Psychology and the social sciences create a wide variety of ethical problems, both theoretical and practical. Psychology puts a question mark against many habitual moral judgments and crude ideas about moral responsibility, whereas the social sciences reveal the extent to which moral attitudes are socially conditioned. Both increase the possibilities of changing human habits or manipulating human beings, and thus they share the moral ambiguity of the rest of science. Brain-washing is the most obvious practical example of the abuse of psychological insights, but it can be argued in its favour that it is only an extension of the techniques of education and evangelism. When more is known about the dynamics of social change there will be a strong temptation to indulge in even more subtle and widespread forms of social engineering. *See also* **Evolutionary Ethics; Naturalistic Ethics.**

E. Fromm, *Man for Himself*, 1949; A. V. Hill, *The Ethical Dilemma of Science*, 1960; J. S. and T. H. Huxley, *Evolution and Ethics*, 1947; Otto Klineberg, *Social Psychology*, 1954; J. E. Meade and A. S. Parkes, eds., *Biological Aspects of Social Problems*, 1965; M. Polanyi, *Personal Knowledge*, 1958; A. M. Quinton, 'Ethics and the Theory of Evolution' in *Biology and Personality*, ed. by Ian Ramsey, 1965; P. Teilhard de Chardin, *The Future of Man*, 1964; W. H. Thorpe, *Science, Man and Morals*, 1965; C. H. Waddington, *The Ethical Animal*, 1960.

J. S. HABGOOD

Scrupulosity

Scrupulosity is a term used in Catholic moral theology to denote the over-use of the confessional for the confession of trivial and diminutive sins. Though absolution is eagerly sought, it is never fully satisfying to the scrupulous person in this sense of 'over-scrupulous', who fears he may have forgotten something, and who will soon return to confess many of the same offences.

From the standpoint of psychology, scrupulosity is closely related to an obsessive-compulsive neurotic pattern of behaviour. Persons afflicted with this disorder are obsessed with certain ideas which they can only put out of their minds by repeating certain actions, such as a hand-washing compulsion, which is associated with the need to assuage guilt feelings. In such cases the thing for which guilt is consciously felt (dirty hands) is a disguised representation of unconscious guilt too painful to bear in conscious awareness. This is the reason that the confessions of scrupulous persons deal with such trivial matters. The trivia cloak unconscious guilt feelings which usually relate to childhood experiences with parents and the fantasies about these, such as the wish to kill the father, though they often have associations with adult life as well.

Though Protestants who do not have formal confession do not use the term, the phenomenon is present in the over-zealous church worker who seemingly cannot find enough to do in the church, and also frequently seeks the pastor out to pour out his troubles and get his advice, which is seldom taken. In such cases psychiatric help may be indicated, though such help may be unwanted, since the symptoms are partly intended to keep the person unaware of his disturbing unconscious guilt feelings as well as providing a degree of release from them. *See also* **Guilt; Defence Mechanisms.**

JAMES N. LAPSLEY

Secularism

The recent shift in the meaning of secularism is one of the most significant developments in contemporary religious thought. Traditionally the word 'secular' has been the antonym of 'religious'. It has been taken to mean a way of life pursued without reference to religious realities. Where the functions of religious institutions are taken over by the State, secularization is said to have occurred, as in programmes of education and social amelioration. Understandings of life without reference to the idea of God and his alleged intervention in the process of the world are called secular views.

The inception of secularism in western culture is usually dated at the Renaissance and ascribed to the afflatus of human pride. Man at that epoch put himself at the centre of reality and arrogated to himself authority over life and responsibility for it. Christendom since the Renaissance has been hard pressed to justify its theocentric universe and its traditional confessions to a God who is all powerful, to man who is abased and weakened by finitude and sin, and to a system of things which is contingent upon the sustaining power of God as expressed in miraculous interventions in history and nature.

Friedrich Schleiermacher was the first theologian to attempt to express the Christian faith in terms of the new understandings of the modern world which the Renaissance introduced. Protestant theology following the first World War made Schleiermacher its primary target. The situation after the second World War is quite different, even though the experiential grounds for man's despair over his secular adequacy have seemed even more obvious than after the first World War. Now it is being seen that secularism, far from being the enemy of the Church, as theology in the mediaeval and orthodox Protestant orientation has tended to hold, is the product of the Christian faith. The Protestant Reformation is held to be the only major attempt since the Apostolic Age to reintroduce the meaning of the Christian movement as the secularizing of the world.

In contemporary Christianity two theologians, mainly, have contended for this view. Dietrich Bonhoeffer, in fragmentary suggestions through his prison correspondence prior to his death, conceded that modern man had 'come of age'. That is to say, he is capable of handling his affairs without invoking a god. That is secularism. Bonhoeffer was probably unique in the conclusions he drew for this description of modern life, a description already patent in the Renaissance period. His conclusion for Christianity was that the Church ought not force this modern, mature man to become weak in the world in order to convert him to faith. It might rather call him to discipleship at the point of his strength. For Bonhoeffer this was no simple compromise with modern man. It was the nub of the Christian revelation. The meaning of the faith is that God has allowed himself to be edged out of the world onto the cross. Because of the cross, therefore, man can know that the world is now left to him as his responsibility.

Friedrich Gogarten has given this theme its most systematic and comprehensive treatment. The major text for Gogarten's explication is Gal. 4.1–7. The significance of Jesus of Nazareth is that in him God has called the world to obedience. The call to obedience is given in the context of God's gift of the world to man as his responsibility. In Jesus of Nazareth mankind is delivered from the time of its childhood and slavery where the world had become the vehicle by which man was required to justify his life before God. In the cross, it is God who justifies men. Men no longer need to justify themselves. That means that the world no longer needs to be exploited for religious purposes. To say it positively, that means God has given man the world as his responsibility, as a father gives his heritage to his son.

Nietzsche and Kierkegaard had both addressed themselves to the situation of secularism in the modern world. Both saw that secularism was a Christian outcome. Kierkegaard regarded the outcome as bad, and believed it was his responsibility to reintroduce a purer Christianity into the secularized Christendom. Nietzsche regarded it as good, but doubted that Christianity was an adequate basis for supporting the secularism it had inaugurated. Gogarten, on the other hand, believes Christianity is indispensable to the conservation of secularism. His reasoning is as follows: God has turned the world over to man as that for which man is responsible. If man does not continually receive the world from God as the one *to* whom he is responsible, he may make the world itself his new object of responsibility, as Judaism and Hellenism did before the time of Jesus, worshipping the creature rather than the creator and thus converting law and wisdom into demonic powers which thereby lost their status as instruments of responsibility. If man becomes responsible *to* the world, he will lose his capacity to be responsible *for* it. In the Christian proclamation through which man learns to receive the world from God, responsibility *to* God is kept alive, and with it, responsibility *for* the world, which is the condition we know in the modern world as secularism.

Dietrich Bonhoeffer, *Letters and Papers from Prison*, 3rd edn., revised and enlarged, 1967; Friedrich Gogarten, *The Reality of Faith*, 1959; *Verhängnis und Hoffnung der Neuzeit*, 2nd edn., 1958.

CARL MICHALSON

Segregation

Segregation is the exclusion of a group (usually a racial group but sometimes a sexual, religious or occupational group) from the right and opportunity to participate in social institutions and the common life. Segregation may be systematically enforced throughout a society by governmental action; or it may be practised on a smaller scale by employers, trade unions, schools, stores, hotels, churches and clubs.

Segregation usually accompanies a claim to superiority by the dominant group, who feel themselves tainted or annoyed by association with inferiors. It is most effectively practised against a group who are readily distinguished by appearance, especially by colour, so that segregation is easily enforceable. Colour segregation has been practised often in history; for example, the Hindu caste segregation is believed to have originated in colour distinctions, which led to occupational distinctions.

In the modern world segregation has been most noticeable in three areas: (1) in regions where white colonial powers have excluded coloured natives from social institutions; (2) in South Africa where a white minority has sought to segregate the Bantu and Indian peoples; (3) in the USA, where as an aftermath of slavery 'Jim Crow laws' and customs have enforced segregation against the former slaves and their descendants.

In the USA, although the Fourteenth Amendment to the Constitution (1868) guaranteed full rights to all citizens, legal segregation continued under the terms of a Supreme Court decision authorizing 'separate but equal' treatment (1896). Democratic and religious groups increasingly made a moral protest against segregation, as did Negroes themselves. In 1946 the National Council of Churches took its formal stand for 'a non-segregated church and a non-segregated society'. In 1954 the Supreme Court, in effect reversing the decision of 1896, determined that compulsory segregation was itself a denial of equality in education. Later rulings have extended the principle to include public accommodations. *See* **Race Relations.**

ROGER L. SHINN

Self and Selfhood. *see* Personality, Psychological view of; Persons and Personality.

Self-denial

Self-denial is likely to be the term used by Protestants where Catholics would speak of mortification (q.v.), but its meaning should not be reduced to particular acts of discipline or renunciation. As Gregory the Great observed, it is easier to give up what one has than to renounce what one is (*Homilies on the Gospels*, 32, on Luke 9.24). But it is to this renunciation that Jesus calls us – cf. Luke 14.26; and St Paul adds, when urging a particular form of self-denial, that even Christ did not please himself

(Rom. 15.3). We are here confronted with the paradox of Christian ethics, that the gospel presents us with an ethic of fulfilment (cf. John 10.10 – 'life more abundantly') as well as of sacrifice, indeed with an ethic of fulfilment in and by sacrifice (cf. Mark 8.35 and parallels – 'whoever loses his life for my sake and the gospel's will save it'). One modern writer like Kierkegaard may find in the teaching of Jesus a call to utter renunciation; another may comment with equal truth, though not as the whole story, that 'the Gospel is a message of joyous eudaemonism' (Paul Elmer More, *The Christ of the New Testament*, 1924, p. 121). As St Augustine observes in commenting on John 12.25, to love one's life 'in this world' is in fact to lose it, and to lose one's life is in fact to save it. We are not indeed called on to renounce desire for our own true welfare, but to find it in self-sacrificing love – and the NT does after all accept the OT precept to love one's neighbour 'as oneself' (Mark 12.31 and parallels, from Lev. 19.18; cf. Rom. 13.9). This is presumably the answer to the doctrine of 'pure love' maintained by Fénelon against Bossuet in a famous seventeenth-century controversy – or the idea popularized by Nygren's *Agape and Eros* (3 vols., 1932–9) that Christian love is wholly free from self-regarding aspects. Yet it remains that in an ethic of love selfishness disappears; as St Augustine points out, two cities are formed by two loves, the earthly by love of self even to contempt of God, the heavenly by love of God even to contempt of self. (*City of God*, XIV, 28).

E. R. HARDY

Self-examination

Self-examination is critical reflection upon one's own conduct and character, in relation to the standards that one has accepted. While indeed there is the danger of falling into a morbid introspective brooding or into scrupulosity (q.v.), conscience will scarcely develop unless there are honest attempts at self-assessment. The examination may be given a systematic framework by basing it, for example, on the Ten Commandments. St Paul enjoins self-examination, especially before receiving the Holy Communion (I Cor. 11.28). In the same connection, the BCP urges that we should 'examine our lives and conversations by the rule of God's commandments', seeking God's forgiveness and making restitution to any persons wronged; and it adds that if any 'cannot quiet his own conscience' by these means, he should resort to the sacrament of penance.

EDITOR

Self-love

The OT (Lev. 19.18) injunction to love one's neighbour as oneself is reiterated in the NT in Matt. 19.19; 22.39; Rom. 13.9; Gal. 5.14; James 2.8. Taken by itself the injunction can be read as a vindication as well as a limitation of self-love. There seems little merit simply in making oneself miserable and some, though not all, asceticism would probably now be ascribed by psychiatrists to the pathology of the self rather than to Christian living. In an age where psychological categories are widely known, it is as well to make it clear that masochism is a counterfeit of Christian discipleship, even if at times it has succeeded in passing itself off as the real thing.

On the other hand, Luke 14.26, 'if any one ... does not hate ... his own life', set as it is in the midst of references to martyrdom is a reminder of the sterner side of Christianity. Martyrdom is a possibility of the Christian life and the path of the martyr from Stephen to Bonhoeffer is not that of those who put self love unduly high in their scheme of things.

In view of this dialectical attitude to self-love, it is not surprising that the references of theologians to it have sometimes appeared ambiguous. Augustine, for instance, sometimes speaks of self-love as a good and sometimes as an evil. But in the former case he is probably simply referring to the fact that all our desires are conditioned by the structure of the self, which has in turn been created by God. In the latter he is referring to the fact that sometimes the soul puts itself before God.

Of all theologians, perhaps Butler has given the clearest and most rational defence of self-love, pointing out its superiority as a principle of action to the particular passions (such as hunger and sex). Surrender to any one of the latter at a particular time may be as imprudent as it is wrong and thus self-love is established as a principle second only to conscience.

Butler, however, though a great theologian, was a figure of the eighteenth century with all its distrust of enthusiasm, and one wonders if his enthusiasm for cool self-love is compatible with the kind of reckless behaviour which is sometimes praised in the Bible. The three valiant men (II Sam. 23.13–17) who fetched the water of Bethlehem for King David were obviously little concerned for their expectation of life. Nor was the widow (Mark 12.42–44) who put her last coin into the collection plate paying much heed to her calory intake.

IAN HENDERSON

Self-realization. *see* Idealist Ethics.

Sermon on the Mount

The Sermon on the Mount, Matt. 5–7, is the best-known section in the NT. In the early Church Matt. 5 was more frequently quoted than any other chapter in the Bible, and the same is probably true for the modern period. St Augustine described the Sermon as 'the perfect standard of the Christian life' and many outside the Church have regarded it as the most precious possession of the Christian tradition. Yet, curiously, the Christian community continues to be uncertain as to the precise place of the Sermon in the total tradition. Does it express the very essence of Christianity or is it only one aspect of the Christian faith? Tolstoi and many others have supported the former view, but T. W. Manson asserted that 'for the primitive Church the central thing is the Cross on the Hill rather than the Sermon on the Mount. . . .' And Jeremias insists strongly that if we are to understand the Sermon we must recognize that 'it was preceded by something else. It was preceded by the proclamation of the Gospel.' Perhaps this is the central question in connection with the Sermon and it is this question which is part of the continuing tension in life and thought between Law and Gospel, between God's demand and his grace. (For other questions raised by the Sermon *see* **Jesus, Ethical Teaching of**.)

The present arrangement of Matt. 5–7 is the work of the Evangelist, as Calvin recognized in the sixteenth century. But a comparison with Luke 6.20–49 indicates that there was a still earlier version of the Sermon which both Gospels appropriated. Matthew enriched this earlier version with materials borrowed chiefly from 'Q' and 'M'. In its present position it is the first, the longest, and the most impressive of five major discourses presented by the Evangelist, each of which concludes with the formula 'Now when Jesus had completed these sayings (commands, parables) . . .' (Matt. 7.28; 11.1; 13.53; 19.1; 26.1). For the Evangelist each of these discourses presented some basic facet of the Christian life. The Sermon proclaimed to those who listened to Jesus, or the Christian community, the righteousness characteristic of 'The New (True) Way'. While any outline must be imposed somewhat arbitrarily on the materials, the following approximates the Evangelist's pattern.

5.3–16 INTRODUCTION: A Sketch of the New (True) Way

  5.3–12 Portrait of Its Representatives: Beatitudes

  5.13–16 Their Relation to the World: Salt, Light

5.17–6.34 THE NEW (TRUE) WAY AND THE OLD (FALSE)

  5.17–20 The Basic Principle: The Old Fulfilled and Transcended

  5.21–48 Six Illustrations of Ethics: Antitheses (Anger, Lust, Divorce, Oaths, Retaliation, Enemies)

  6.1–18 Three Illustrations of Religious Piety (Almsgiving, Prayer and Lord's Prayer, Fasting)

  6.19–34 The New (True) Way and Possessions

7.1–12 MISCELLANEOUS INJUNCTIONS (V. 12 the Golden Rule)

7.13–27 CONCLUSION: Four Exhortations to Obedience

The Sermon illustrates the two central principles of the ethical teaching of Jesus, namely the demand for radical obedience to God and the demand for radical concern for the neighbour. The Matthean version of the Sermon and its subsequent textual history reflect the tendency for the absolute demands of Jesus to be qualified when they were adopted as legislation for the actual life of the Christian community (*see* the 'escape clause' in Matt. 5.32, the prohibition of divorce, and the phrase 'without cause' introduced into the text of Matt. 5.22). Even with such qualifications the document remains a unique instrument to trouble the conscience of mankind and to exalt the absoluteness of the divine claim on every sphere of human life.

In addition to commentaries on Matt. 5–7 *see*: Augustine, *The Sermon on the Mount*, c. 400; G. Bornkamm, 'The History of the Exposition of the Sermon on the Mount' in *Jesus of Nazareth*, 1960, pp. 221–5; R. W. Bowman and R. W. Tapp, *The Gospel from the Mount*, 1957; J. Calvin, *Commentary on a Harmony of the Evangelists*, c. 1558; Chrysostom, *Homilies on St Matthew*, c. 400; W. D. Davies, *The Setting of the Sermon on the Mount*, 1964; M. Dibelius, *The Sermon on the Mount*, 1940; A. M. Hunter, *Design for Life*, 1953; J. Jeremias, *The Sermon on the Mount*, 1961; M. Luther, *The Sermon on the Mount*, c. 1528; T. W. Manson, *The Sayings of Jesus*, 1954; H. K. McArthur, *Understanding the Sermon on the Mount*, 1960; E. Thorneysen, *The Sermon on the Mount*, 1964; H. Windisch, *The Meaning of the Sermon on the Mount*, 1941.

HARVEY K. MCARTHUR

Seven Deadly Sins

They are pride, covetousness, lust, envy, gluttony, anger, sloth. *See* the articles on each of them.

Seven Gifts of the Holy Ghost

These are the gifts enumerated in the LXX version of Isa. 11.2. They are: wisdom, understanding, counsel, fortitude, knowledge, piety, and the fear of the Lord (godly fear). St Augustine considers them in reverse order as 'seven steps' in the development of the Christian life.

Sex

'Sex', according to the *Oxford English Dictionary*, denotes 'either of the two divisions of organic beings distinguished as male and female respectively'. Its original purpose was evolutionary no less than reproductive. Binary fission, the earliest and simplest form of reproduction, served only to propagate more or less identical organisms; but sexual specialization made possible an infinite range of variation through the co-operation of dissimilar yet complementary individuals whose characteristics were transmitted to, and combined in, their offspring. Thus sex made possible the progressive development of ever higher and more complex forms of life, and the establishment and elaboration of distinct species. Within the several species it also led to an increasingly marked differentiation between male and female. With the emergence of human beings a new factor, personality, sharpened and deepened this differentiation, creating a profound metaphysical antithesis or polarity between man and woman over and above the biological distinction between them.

In humanity the metaphysical, personal significance of sex is uniquely important. Nevertheless, western conceptions of sexuality have been coloured chiefly by the biological and physical (venereal) associations of sex. This tendency has culminated in a virtual restriction of the word 'sex' to generative and venereal contexts. 'Sex' has also acquired limiting or distorting overtones and emotional content; it conveys a subtle hint of sensuality or salacity – it can disturb or offend, it can excite disgust or prurient interest. Often it is used simply of coition, a common synonym for which is 'sex'. Thus the important metaphysical and personal dimensions of human sexuality have become obscured and neglected, with far-reaching consequences in many areas of social and personal life.

Man cannot be considered apart from his sexuality – that is, his existence as male and female; and to define sex is, in part, to define Man. The biblical accounts of Man's creation afford convenient and suggestive starting-points for an elucidation of sex. The earlier (J) myth (Gen. 2) is simple and primitive. It describes how God makes an 'adam' ('ādhām, i.e. Man in the generic sense) or 'human prototype', conceived by the myth as being in male form, from which he takes a rib and fashions it into a woman – so resolving, as it were, the original being or 'adam' into its sexual components and endowing them with separate personal existence as man and woman. Brought together, they recognize their common origin, and cleaving together as husband and wife they become 'one flesh', thus in some sense restoring the original unity of Man. The later (P) narrative assumes this basic unity; Man is created in the image of God as male and female (Gen. 1.27), and God expressly calls their name 'Adam' (Gen. 5.1).

The Rabbis tried to reconcile and explain these narratives by supposing that the 'adam' was androgynous (a notion possibly borrowed from Plato); but this hypothesis is scientifically and theologically objectionable, and a more satisfactory interpretation is suggested by the idea of Man as an image of God. It is impossible to say what precisely this expression meant to the writer, but it is clear that he regarded the 'adam' as in some significant way a reflection of the divine nature. In the past, theologians have sought this 'image' chiefly in Man's possession of spirit, freedom, reason or moral consciousness, but recently attention has been directed to its relational implication. Christianity conceives God as a coinherence of three divine Entities or 'Persons', and Man, the finite image of God, reflects the structure of the Godhead; he is a 'being-in-relation', but one in whose constitution the basic element is a personal sexual polarity – that of man and woman.

Thus sex in Man is not simply and solely a reproductive device. Man was created as a 'dual being', comprising two distinct, correlative personal components, man and woman, each individually, fully and independently human, yet both naturally orientated towards one another, and existing in a mutual belongingness which they are continually impelled to realize in manifold kinds of relation. In Man the reproductive aspect of sex is only one element in a total factor of great complexity which divides humanity radically into two opposite yet complementary parts, and permeates the individual's being to its depths, conditioning every facet of his or her life and personality. Human sex is nothing less than the personalization of an ontological distinction in Man. Creation in the image of God means that from the moment of his emergence out of the pre-human condition Man was something new and unique – a 'two-fold being', a sexual duality having man and woman as its individual and personal poles.

Man's sexual structure creates certain obligations for men and women in their personal lives and relationships. First, they must preserve their sexual integrity by repudiating false and debased conceptions of sex, and by seeking to conform to true patterns of manliness and womanliness. This entails a critical appraisal of cultural stereotypes of sexual roles and characteristics. Manliness and womanliness are relative and not absolute qualities, and consist not in conformity with contemporary sexual stereotypes but in being true to the principles implied in the creation of Man as a sexual duality. Man has no intuitive comprehension of the meaning of manhood and womanhood, for awareness of the fact of sexual distinction conveys no metaphysical understanding of sex; that can only be learnt through relation itself. This is the significance of the deep sleep into which, according to the J creation myth, God cast the 'adam' when he created sex; the man and woman are aware of the fact of sex when they awake, but not of its inner meaning. Hence God's further act is bringing them together; true sexual knowledge is always empirical and relational.

Sexual relation of every kind, on every level of intimacy, means moving into a new dimension of experience in which, through personal encounter, sex becomes meaningful in personal terms. To be truly manly or womanly means to lose all false or artificial sex-consciousness (of the kind stimulated by many influences in our culture) in relations of sincerity and integrity with the complementary half of humanity. In such relations, of whatever kind, manhood and womanhood are discerned to be more than maleness and femaleness – which are simply impersonal sex. The significance of sex consists, not in what one is oneself, but in what one is for another – *this* particular person, encountered in *this* particular relation.

Secondly, there is the duty of sexual partnership. The two sexes are naturally orientated towards one another; being complementary and mutually dependent, they need each other for everything in life, and not merely for procreation and domesticity. Sexual partnership means the free, equal and responsible association of man and woman in all the multifarious interests and enterprises of social, political and ecclesiastical life, thus liberating the creative dynamic of sex for the furtherance of the common good and the enrichment and elevation of human life.

Unfortunately there are obstacles to partnership. Our cultural obsession with the venereal element in sex creates a barrier between men and women, and gives an unwholesome twist to what should be a natural and normal feature of human life. The persistence, often in subtle forms, of androcentric theories of sexual status and function inhibits creative co-operation between the sexes and buttresses false stereotypes of their social roles and standing. There are no evolutionary, scientific or empirical grounds for holding that woman is in some sense subordinate to man. But it is difficult to conceive more positively of sexual order for, like sex itself, it is essentially mysterious – something of which we have no *a priori* or intuitive knowledge. As with manhood and womanhood, its meaning can only be discovered in and through responsible and sincere relation – the experience of man and woman as they live and work together in real partnership. It cannot be defined, for it is as variable as sexual relation itself, but this at least can be affirmed: sexual order is always basically one of complementation. Headship and subordination are irrelevant issues; each sex must complement the other by playing the role appropriate in the particular relation of the moment.

It will be evident that Man's sexual structure and the obligations which proceed from it have profound and far-reaching ethical implications which range well beyond the limits to which discussion of the ethics of sex is usually confined.

D. S. Bailey, *Common Sense about Sexual Ethics*, 1962; *The Man-Woman Relation in Christian Thought* (in USA: *Sexual Relation in Christian Thought*), 1959.

SHERWIN BAILEY

Sick, Care of the. *see* Medical Ethics; Social Service of the Church.

Simony

Simony is the practice of buying or selling ecclesiastical preferment.

Sin

Sin for us today is essentially a religious term. The word would hardly be used seriously by someone who did not believe in God. Whether, however, Brunner (*Dogmatics*, II) is justified in defining sin in the biblical sense not in moral terms but as the condition requiring redemption, is more doubtful. In such important OT accounts of sin as Job 31 and Ps. 15 the field where sin is committed is clearly the set of relations between man and man. Matt. 25.44, 'When did we see thee hungry . . . ?', and I John 4.20, 'If any one says, "I love God", and hates his brother, he is a liar . . .' bring together two possible fields of sinful action and consequently also the theological and the moral connotations of sin. Our neighbour is, as it were, the mask behind which God hides, and to fail in human relations is to fail God.

Sin is an irrationality, something akin to a surd in mathematics, and that is perhaps why the theological treatment of sin is full of problems which are easier to formulate than to solve. The first of these is why sin should arise in a world which had been created by God and which was, we are told, very good (Gen. 1.31). To find a reason for this we naturally turn to Gen. 3, but that passage, while giving a penetrating description of innocence (q.v.) and temptation (q.v.) and setting forth the reason for a number of other factors in life such as why the ground throws up weeds and why women suffer pain in childbirth, fails to give a similar aetiological account of sin, for the account presupposes the existence of sin in the person of the serpent.

It is true that St Paul (Rom. 5.19), in the course of going off at surely one of the most fateful tangents in any theological argument, found a causal connection to exist between Adam's sin and our sin. This passage provides one main support to later theological exponents of the doctrine of original sin (q.v.). But, of course, it threw no light on the cause of sin and indeed, as Kierkegaard pointed out, later theology of original sin, both Catholic and Protestant, tended to highlight the difference between our caused and Adam's uncaused sin. Kierkegaard, whose *Concept of Dread* (1844) is one of the most profound contributions to this difficult subject, was much too wise to try himself to explain sin. For to explain sin is to show that it is necessary and that is to explain it away, for anything that is necessary, for example, the seizure that an epileptic patient can't help having, is not sin.

The non-necessary character of sin contributes to another of the problems which have dominated the theological treatment of the subject. This one arises from the fact that Christianity has generally felt itself constrained to assert the universality of sin. This position is not too easy to maintain, for who are we to call the roll of all mankind of every age from China to Peru and find each one wanting? But for it there is good biblical support. It is true that at times in the OT characters appear who seem to be pretty nearly perfect. Of Noah it is said that he was a just man and perfect (Gen. 6.9). The writer of Ps. 18.23 says 'I was blameless before him (God) and I kept myself from guilt', and that of Job 33.9 'I am clean, without transgression, I am pure, and there is no iniquity in me'. But over against such occasional exceptions the OT in the main puts the emphasis on the other side, cf. 'the imagination of man's heart is evil from his youth' (Gen. 8.21). 'The heart is deceitful above all things and desperately corrupt' (Jer. 17.9). The writer of Ps. 90.8 would have reminded his more complacent brethren that even if they were satisfied with themselves, there were secret sins. In the NT this is brought home in the parable of the Pharisee and the publican addressed to 'some who trusted in themselves that they were righteous' (Luke 18.9). It is clear that Jesus considered that the complacent were dangerously mistaken about themselves, cf. Luke 13.3 'unless you repent you will all likewise perish'. That St Paul's opinion was similar seems to follow from Rom. 3.23 and Gal. 3.22.

Another reason (apart from the biblical grounds) for holding the universality of sin is that the very people who would seem to be exceptions to it are those who would refuse to be treated as such. It is the greatest saints who have had the most profound consciousness of sin. Yet another reason – and one which has a great deal to do with Christians holding on to the position – is that to say that there are some men who have not sinned seems tantamount to saying that there are some men who do not need Christ.

We seem therefore entitled to accept the truth of the proposition 'all men are sinners'. The trouble is that normally universality implies necessity. Thus 'all isosceles triangles have their base angles equal' is equivalent to 'the base angles of an isosceles triangle are necessarily equal'. But while you can say 'all men are sinners' you cannot say 'a man must necessarily sin'. For what a man does of necessity is something for which he is not responsible. But sin, if it is anything, is something for which a man is responsible.

All theories of original sin (q.v.), artificial though some of them are, are attempts to solve this real difficulty. That is why Adam plays in them a central role that he does not play in the biblical teaching about sin. (Jesus and the prophets who speak profoundly about sin do not mention Adam once.) But in theological treatment of original sin Adam inevitably plays a leading part. For he, their common ancestor, is one thing all men have in common. If in some sense it can be shown they have a share in – and, though this is more difficult – a responsibility for his sin, then the problem seems well on the way to solution. In Adam's act all men sinned and yet since Adam's act was voluntary, there is no necessity about the matter.

We have seen that St Paul in Rom. 5.19 asserted a causal connection between Adam's sin and our sin. St Paul does not define this connection more closely. The later theology of original sin can be seen as a series of attempts to do so. Is it that we were all present in Adam's loins and so had a share in his sin? Possibly, but if so, it is not an easy conception, for most of us do not feel responsible for the sins of our more remote ancestors. Is it that Adam acted as the representative of mankind and that we are responsible for his actions as some (though by no means all) Germans felt themselves responsible for the actions of Hitler? That again is a possible meaning of St Paul, who sometimes indulged in this type of group thinking. But again it is a difficult conception, for while it might be argued that the Germans could have done something about Hitler – though plenty will point out that they could not – it is hard to see what we could have done about Adam. Or does it mean that we have inherited Adam's sinfulness? May be, but if so, are we responsible for our inheritance as distinct from the use we make of it (cf. the example of people who inherit a tendency to alcoholism)? Or does it just mean that since Adam sinned, everybody has been born into an evil environment and in the end environment gets us all down? Again may be, and yet all human sin cannot be attributed to environment. One of the earliest and most creditable motives for monasticism was the desire to get away from an evil environment. Yet even in the desert and the cloister men met with temptation.

All these interpretations of the causal connection between Adam's sin and our sin have their obvious difficulties. But they are attempts to find a solution to the real problem arising out of the fact that sin while universal is not necessary.

Of modern writers on sin among the most significant are T. R. Malthus, whose *Essay on the Principles of Population* (1798) while not directly concerned with the subject makes the salutary point that evil is something that cannot be eradicated by social and political revolution. Then there is F. R. Tennant, whose *The Sources of the Doctrine of the Fall and Original Sin* (1903); *The Origin and Propagation of Sin* (1902) and *The Concept of Sin* (1912) were written at a time when sin was an unfashionable topic. Tennant made a sustained effort to correlate the traditional teaching with the fact that man has evolved and that moral standards change so that what is sinful action to one generation is not so to a later one. Written earlier but influential later is Kierkegaard's *Concept of Dread* (1844), one of whose insights has been the recognition that the sins of the flesh and the sins of the spirit are basically the same flight from the *Angst* which is a feature even of the state of innocence. Finally in *Moral Man and Immoral Society* (1933) the young Reinhold Niebuhr faced courageously up to the fact that religion by absolutizing the relativities of man's struggle for power, has sometimes, though not always, served to intensify rather than to ameliorate sin.

IAN HENDERSON

Sins of Omission

This subject has a meagre theological literature, though it has a large place in Christian devotion, especially in forms of self-examination and in guidance for Catholics making a confession 'that I have sinned in thought, word, deed, and omission', and in general confessions, for example, 'we have left undone those things which we ought to have done'. Those who complain that commandments and moral codes are mostly in negative terms, enumerating sins to avoid, do not realize that any list of positive duties would be endless. Therefore the sins of omission cannot comprehensively be generalized and specified; they can only be identified in terms of the actual situation of a person or group acting as a moral agent. Duties neglected are much more in the field of the agent's opportunities, promises, vocation and walk of life, than of violation of specific rules common to all who adhere to a standard of morality (cf. F. H. Bradley, 'My Station and its Duties' in *Ethical Studies*, 2nd rev. edn., 1927).

Sins of omission are not to be equated with failures due to weakness of will, ignorance or inadvertence. They are as positive as sins of commission, requiring, in order to fall under the definition, that the agent wills to omit the fulfilment of a duty or decides to do something he knows to be incompatible with it, whether that duty is keeping one of the recognized moral precepts of a general kind, or maintaining a standard of conduct in personal or social life one has accepted out of a special vocation (cf. Aquinas, *Summa Theologica*, Part II, First Section, q. 72, art. 6).

The NT gives two dominical judgments which fit these two kinds of moral omission. The scribes and Pharisees are rebuked by Christ for having left undone 'the weightier matters of the law, justice and mercy and faith' (Matt. 23.23). The parable of the Sheep and the Goats condemns those who do not minister to him in the least of his brethren (Matt. 25.45). Thus, a modern French layman can say that the words '. . . and by omission' gabbled in a night prayer seem to mean nothing at all, 'but we have the authority of our Lord Jesus Christ that it is quite simply the substance of the Last Judgment (Jacques Debout, *My Sins of Omission,* 1930, translated from '*Et par Omission*').

V. A. DEMANT

Situation, Situation Ethic

A situation ethic seeks to do justice to the concreteness and to the personal character of the moral life by claiming that the rightness of an action is to be judged in relation to the situation in which it takes place, rather than with reference to laws or universally binding rules. It should be noted of course that even legalistic systems of ethics have always had some regard to the situation; for instance, if an ox or ass fell into a pit on the sabbath, it was to be pulled out in spite of the law against sabbath work (Luke 14.5). An extreme situation ethic, as found among some existentialist thinkers, rejects all laws and rules; action is to be decided only on the basis of what will realize one's authentic being in the particular situation. Some Christian writers, who believe that traditional ethics has been too much dominated by laws and rules, have come forward as advocates of a Christian situation ethic, but it is doubtful whether any of them go the length of a thoroughgoing antinomianism. The new stress on the situation may well help to redress the balance by insisting on the spontaneity and supremacy of love and charity in the Christian ethic, and the danger that these distinctive marks may be stifled by impersonal laws and abstract generalizations. But where the notion of a situation ethic is taken to extreme lengths, serious errors ensue. Action gets broken up into a series of unrelated acts (almost in the manner of David Hume) and it is hard to see how this can be reconciled with the unity of personal being, and still more with the solidarity of a community. Furthermore, it seems to be assumed that somehow one intuits what is right in a situation from the situation itself. Even if some people have this remarkable gift of insight, there are stages on the way to moral maturity and a great many persons need the guidance of those rules and generalizations which the community has built up from its experience. Finally, it must be asked whether, from a Christian point of view, a situation ethic takes sufficient account of the sinful tendencies at work in all men, including Christians. To take a realistic view of the matter, one has to acknowledge that as often as not it is the restraint of a law rather than a spontaneous pursuit of the good that determines action in a situation. The situationists are right in stressing the concrete and personal character of the moral life, and it may freely be conceded that laws are sometimes harsh and even distorting in their incidence. But some of their own slogans, such as 'people before principles', are just as empty and abstract as any rules. The situation can be reckoned as only one element in the very difficult and complex matter of deciding what is the right thing to do on any particular occasion. The reader should be careful to distinguish situation ethics from contextual ethics (q.v.).

Joseph Fletcher, *Situation Ethics*, 1966.

EDITOR

Slander

Slander is one of the sins of speech. It is not interested in speaking the truth but in damaging someone's reputation in the most efficient way possible. To slander is bad but the state of envy, hatred and malice which prompts it is much worse. Hurtful though it is to be slandered, the slanderer does more harm to himself than to his victims. It is not easy to say which is more reprehensible – the slander coldly and deliberately spread to calculated advantage, or the one hastily made on the spur of the moment, for it can be spiritually as dangerous to sin without realizing it as to sin with knowledge of what you are doing. All who listen to slander or encourage it share the slanderer's guilt. A person needs self-control to accept that he has been slandered without matching slander with slander.

In every generation, masters of the religious life stress the dangers of immoderate talking; they believe that in talking too much men are apt to lose control and say things they should not say. A dull silence is a more true expression of love than hastily used hurtful words.

R. E. C. BROWNE

Slavery

Slavery is a form of involuntary human servitude in which persons become the property of others. As property, slaves can be bought and sold, commanded and used; and they have few legal rights or protections. The function of slavery has been to serve the economic advantage, the vanity, and the sexual lust of slave owners.

Slavery was practised in most ancient societies, including those of the Bible. The biblical records include many allusions to slavery and many laws governing it. Masters had few legal responsibilities towards their slaves and could punish them severely. In some respects the slave was considered more as property than as a person. Yet he was part of the master's household, sharing in the Sabbath rest (Ex. 20.10; 23.12) and in the religious feasts (e.g. Deut. 12.12). If his master abused him to the extent of destroying an eye or a tooth, the slave was entitled to freedom (Ex. 21.26–7).

The impersonal property system might be mitigated in fact by affection between master and slave. A slave could become the heir of his master or on occasion marry the master's daughter. Sometimes a high sense of justice and moral responsibility entered into the system (e.g. Job 31.13 ff.).

The NT begins with the proclamation of the Kingdom of God, which throws judgment upon all human institutions. God's kingdom is a blessing upon the poor; it means that the meek shall inherit the earth. Jesus brings the good news of release for captives and liberty for the oppressed (Luke 4.18). Thus he offers a fundamental theological criticism of slavery and of the whole social order in which man is alienated from man. But Jesus in heralding the Kingdom of God does not prescribe new social institutions for the age that is passing.

For Paul the whole inherited meaning of slavery has been shattered by Christ. In Christ there is no distinction between bond and free (Gal. 3.28). Slave and master become brothers in Christ (Philemon). But in the expectancy of the new age, there is no effort to modify the institutions of the old age.

As the Church developed within the Roman Empire, it took for granted the persistence of slavery. But a slave might become a leader, even a bishop, within the Church; his legal and economic status did not modify his value as a Christian.

In its early centuries the Church was powerless to change the institutions of the empire. When the Church became established, it transferred its revolutionary impulses to otherworldly expectations and sought to ameliorate rather than upset prevailing social institutions. The Church itself, inheriting pagan properties, became a slave-holder. St Augustine declared that slavery was a consequence of sin. This doctrine clearly encompassed a more profound moral insight than Aristotle's teaching that some men were born to be slaves; but it had the effect of conditioning Christians to expect the persistence of slavery until the distant consummation of the Kingdom of God.

In European history slavery gradually gave way to serfdom in the feudal order. But the exploration of Africa and the discovery of America produced a huge slave trade. Increasingly the humanitarian spirit, both in Christianity and the Enlightenment, became critical of slavery; and the Congress of Vienna brought an end to the slave trade among the European powers. Slavery itself then declined.

In the USA, where slavery remained economically profitable in the South, a struggle of conscience ensued. Christians used the Bible both to attack and defend slavery. The Civil War ended slavery (Emancipation Proclamation, 1863; Thirteenth Amendment, 1865), but the USA still suffers its bitter legacy.

In the following years slavery ended throughout most of the world. But in parts of Africa and Asia it has persisted well into the twentieth century.

Both moral and economic impulses have contributed to the doom of slavery. Morally the idea of liberty has undermined the traditional ideologies of slavery. Economically the drudgery, once performed by men, is increasingly the work of machines, which have become the slaves of the present and the foreseeable future.

Isaac Mendelsohn, *Slavery in the Ancient Near East*, 1949; U. B. Phillips, *American Negro Slavery*, 1918; Ernst Troeltsch, *The Social Teaching of the Christian Churches*, 1931 (original German edition, 1911).

ROGER L. SHINN

Sloth

Sloth, in modern speech laziness, is the constant desire for bodily rest and sleep. The lazy man avoids all physical exertion as far as he can. His state is that of one who disbelieves in both God and the significance of human activity.

There is also a state which could be considered as mental sloth; that is, a condition wherein a man is physically energetic, but reduces his conscious mental processes to a minimum. He banishes or refuses to pay attention to facts that disturb him. In many cases mental sloth is seen in one who spends a large amount of time in giving himself over to television, radio, newspaper headlines and conversations which are largely an exchange of gossip.

Mental sloth in Christians is seen in a desire to find a way to get necessary understanding of all things without effort, or to discover a code, a set of doctrines, or some simple formula which can be directly and literally used in every circumstance of life.

Fear is often an element in sloth. The slothful man in some cases is afraid of action because every act leads him into unfamiliar territory from which there is no return.

Sloth in scholars, philosophers, poets, theologians (pastoral or academic) is seen in a reluctance to check references and an unwillingness to write and rewrite.

Accidie (q.v.) and sloth are much alike, but whereas the slothful man can often be amusing company, the man suffering *accidie* is usually morose and irritable.

R. E. C. BROWNE

Social Class

Social class is a slippery concept. Almost everyone uses the term freely, and thinks he knows what it means. Yet any group of persons is likely to discover after a few minutes of conversation that each has a slightly different understanding of the concept.

The principal indices of social stratification are occupation, income, style of life, prestige (status), and pattern of social interaction. Confusion results from the fact that different analysts emphasize different indices, sometimes emphasizing only one to the virtual exclusion of others. For Marx, class meant economic position, and it was an objective condition which would be clearly recognized by everyone except for the ideological masking projected by the ruling classes in order to perpetuate their superior power over the oppressed masses. For W. Lloyd Warner, whose postulation of six social classes has been accepted as *the* theory of social classes in popular thought in the USA, the prestige index is all-important, and placement on the social scale is subjective, in that it depends upon the opinion about an individual's placement voiced by other individuals in a community. Warner's scheme not only minimizes the power element; it has been accused of bearing a bourgeois ideological taint, because of the following remark in Warner's *Social Class in America*:

It is the hope of the author that this book will provide a corrective instrument which will permit men and women better to evaluate their social situations and thereby better adapt themselves to social reality and fit their dreams and aspirations to what is possible.

Some of Warner's critics are quite willing to confine the term 'social class' to the prestige and interaction dimension of social stratification, so long as it is remembered that stratification is a much broader and more complex phenomenon than class: Bendix and Lipset define social classes as 'strata of society composed of individuals who accept each other as status equals, and are hence qualified for intimate association'.

As the above paragraph indicates, confusion also arises from the fact that the different indices by means of which social classes are measured are dimensions of social placement which are relatively autonomous and sometimes even contradictory. One may change occupations without changing either income or prestige – but income may increase without a corresponding rise in status, or status may rise even though income does not. People with the same income do not always have the same style of life, yet the anticipatory socialization involved in adopting a style of life beyond one's present means and in interacting with members of the reference group with which one desires to be identified may become a self-fulfilling prophecy: the young lawyer who goes in debt while hobnobbing with the country club set may, because he lives as they do and mingles with them, soon be accepted as 'one of that crowd', and he may soon get enough wealthy clients to establish himself as a secure member of the group which was originally beyond him. Power may be held by individuals whose prestige and income are low, and those with all the right connections and the money to go with them may nevertheless be surprisingly powerless. Both power and prestige are usually limited, furthermore, to specific areas of interest and competence: the 'cosmopolitan', an influential who is oriented to values and reference groups outside the local communities, may have (or exercise) very little power at home, and may actually be little known or lightly regarded by homefolks. People of equal status who share a similar style of life do not necessarily interact – although it may be shown (through an analysis of voting or consumption patterns, for example) that such persons 'interact' psychologically in the sense that their choices of candidates and products reflect similar values, and that their power is exercised lor similar ends in the communities where they five. The comprehensive correlation between power, prestige and style of life assumed in the stratification theory of community power (notably in the 'Middletown', 'Yankee City', 'Elmtown-Jonesville' and 'Regional City' studies) has been challenged by writers (notably Robert Dahl and Nelson Polsby) who have found in other cities a multiplicity of power structures in which individuals of widely different occupation, income, prestige and style of life have decisive influence in determining policy on different issues.

The concept of social class should be seen, then, as an intellectual device, a kind of mental shorthand, which enables one to speak of a large group of persons who have certain characteristics in common. The fact that few individuals in a given class will possess all of the attributes contained in the ideal type description of that class is not surprising, and is not important so long as they are members of the class in terms of the index being emphasized by the person applying to them the label of a particular class. The important thing is that writers should be explicit about the indices they have in mind when they talk about 'middle-class people', or that readers should seek to discern what these indices are before they accept or reject what is being asserted about the people in question.

We might think of social class in terms of the following diagram:

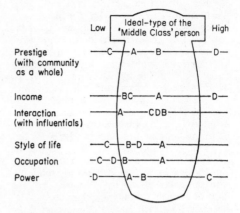

A An apolitical lawyer who deals mainly with lower-class clients.
B Son of a highly respected long-term resident who founded a small business that is now declining.
C Labour leader.
D Entertainer.

A class would be composed of the individuals (indicated by letters) who fall within the circle on most of the lines crossed by the borders of the circle. It can certainly be shown that many persons *do* fall within the range encompassed by the circle on each continuum, and therefore it can be maintained that there is such a thing as class; that is, that it is useful to refer to the individuals sharing these characteristics under one rubric. All that is necessary is that the range included in the definition on each continuum should be specified, and that individuals who do not fall within the circle on certain continua should be noted as deviant in this or that respect. So long as the meaning of the ideal-type is clearly explained, it can be asserted that individuals A and B are middle class. It would be very misleading to speak of individuals C and D as middle class, except 'in regard to . . .'

The ideal of a classless society has wide currency not only in Marxist social theory, but also in the American myth of freedom and equal opportunity. Unless one assumes that human nature as well as the ubiquitous structures and processes of social interaction can be radically altered, examination of the causes of social stratification give little grounds for hope that this ideal can be realized. In advanced societies, where an exceedingly complex division of labour exists and where specialized scientific and administrative skills are of such crucial importance, the individuals who occupy positions in which decisions determine the smooth co-ordination of work contributions, and who possess the skills necessary for the advancement as well as the smooth functioning of the societal machinery, will inevitably have enormous power. Whatever their style of life or their interaction pattern, their prestige is apt to be commensurate with their power in a society where mass communications make awareness of power and skill far more widespread than in previous societies; furthermore, as Veblen wisely observed, they will probably adopt a style of life and an interaction pattern unattainable by others, and use their wealth and power in such a way as to enhance their prestige. (The new practice of public relations is merely a subtle refinement of the will-to-power appropriate in a society where one can be more privileged than others so long as he does not flaunt his privileges too outrageously, and so long as he demonstrates his solidarity with the lower orders by occasional gifts of time or money to the proper causes.) And since the increased size of the society's pie depends upon the presence of adequate incentives to various elites to attain requisite skills and exercise essential responsibilities, it is not in the interest of the lower orders to protest that their slices of the society's pie are smaller. Thus social stratification will probably continue – only those on the bottom won't mind so much, and those on top will have to enjoy their privileged position more discreetly than in the past.

Bernard Barber, *Social Stratification: A Comparative Analysis of Structure and Process*, 1957; Reinhard Bendix and Seymour M. Lipset, eds., *Class, Status and Power*, 1953; August B. Hollingshead and Frederick C. Redlich, *Social Class and Mental Illness*, 1958; Joseph A. Kahl, *The American Class Structure*, 1957; Seymour M. Lipset and Reinhard Bendix, *Social Mobility in Industrial Society*, 1959; W. Lloyd Warner and Paul S. Lunt, *The Social Life of a Modern Community*, 1941; *The Status System of a Modern Community*, 1942.

HENRY B. CLARK

Social Contract

This has been a recurring conception in the history of philosophy, to account for the origins of society and for the fundamental nature of obligation. The theory of a social contract has taken many forms. All of them begin from the idea of an original individualism, in which each human being lived for himself, though whereas some writers (Rousseau) thought of this primitive state as a happy one, others (Hobbes) regarded the primaeval anarchy as a miserable existence. In any case, the individuals agreed to surrender some of their 'natural rights', and thus society and social obligation were born. Like the story of the fall of man, one should not press the question of historicity too much here, for the story is a parable rather than an historical account. It is open to various objections. Can one properly speak of 'natural rights' (q.v.) or of any kind of rights without corresponding duties? But if

rights and duties are correlative, there is no pre-social condition of man, either chronologically or logically. This points to the main weakness of the theory, namely, that it thinks of man as 'naturally' individualistic. A modern version of something like the social contract theory was put forward by Freud (q.v.) to account for the origins of religion and morality.

EDITOR

Social Ethics

There is a sense in which one may say that all ethics are social ethics, for ethics has to do with the problem of right conduct, and no conduct is purely self-regarding. It is not true, for instance, that there are vices or indulgences that affect only the person engaging in them, for, if continued in, they diminish his effectiveness in the community. There can be no genuine personhood in isolation from other persons. These points are all specially recognized in the Christian ethic, with its stress on love and communion, and the notion that we are all members one of another.

For convenience, however, one may distinguish between those ethical matters which have to do chiefly with the individual and those which concern groups of people. Even so, the borderline may be somewhat blurred. We might think of sexual conduct as belonging to the ethical life of individuals, and of chastity as an example of a personal or individual virtue; yet sexual conduct can also give rise to social problems, such as prostitution, which flourishes where there is a large number of promiscuous individuals. On the other hand, changing social conditions exert influence on conduct even in the most intimate and private areas of life. But although the border is a fluid one, a rough distinction can be made between those ethical concerns that belong to personal integrity and those which affect larger social groupings; and between those ethical tasks and duties that belong to individuals, and those that can be laid only upon a group or association, and that are too big to be undertaken by individual agents, though these may indeed (and frequently do) arouse the conscience of the Church or nation or community to its responsibilities.

While it was said that the Christian ethic does not visualize the individual agent in isolation, it must frankly be admitted that there is very little in the way of a social ethic in the NT – at least, explicitly. There are a few scattered remarks about the State, about race, about slavery, and some other matters, but these do not add up to anything like a burning concern to change the structures of human society. This may well have been due to the eschatological background of the NT teaching. Since this world and all that it contained was supposed to be passing away, there would be little point in trying to ameliorate it. It was enough that individuals should hear the summons to obedience before the end. Certainly the Kingdom of God (q.v.), whatever modern visionaries may have made of the conception, had originally nothing to do with the notion of a super welfare state. Even when it became clear that the *eschaton* was not going to happen in the immediate future, no social ethic emerged. This may have been because the tiny persecuted Christian minority had apparently no hope of influencing a hostile or indifferent society. But when Christianity became a permitted religion, we do find some of the Christian writers (e.g., St Athanasius) commenting on the cleansing of society that was taking place through the decline of paganism and the wider acceptance of Christian standards.

However, it is in modern times that Christian social ethics have become really important. With the industrial revolution, the concentration of people in conurbations, and the abolition of distance, all human life is more and more dominated by large-scale social structures. Christians have learned that even if a social ethic is not explicitly taught in the NT, it is implicit, and that even if the NT ethic found expression in terms of rural and familial patterns of life, its truths can be reinterpreted and applied to the contemporary situation. But this means also a reawakening of Christians to the meaning of the gospel. Perhaps they have too often been content to pursue personal integrity, and have been too little aware of social evils. There are in our cities many fine churches gifted by pious nineteenth-century manufacturers, who sweated the money for them out of their workers, and these churches may be regarded as ironic reminders of how Christians may be given to all kinds of good works and yet remain blind to social evils.

Today, the great ethical problems and also the great threats and evils have a social character, or even an international one. War is the greatest of all these threats; race rivalry comes not far behind it; poverty is still another. Also, to an ever-increasing extent, life is shaped by large social bodies, in which it is much harder to fix responsibility than it is in the case of the actions of individuals, and which tend to be much more impersonal and even immoral in their acts than individuals. National governments and departments, international organizations, commercial corporations, trade unions, the bodies which control the public media – these all shape life, and their influences are felt even in the most intimate personal and family affairs.

Faced with this situation, the need for developing a Christian social ethic is more and more widely recognized in the churches. The tendency is helped by an increasing willingness to recognize that (in Bonhoeffer's language) the Christian must concern himself with the 'next to last things' even if he is finally concerned with the 'last things'.

Yet there are grave dangers in all of this. The most serious is that Christianity may come to misunderstand itself as merely another programme for social improvement, as has indeed happened from time to time among enthusiasts for the 'Social Gospel'. There is also the risk that Christians will rush in with pronouncements on difficult technical matters which they do not understand, and this too has often happened when ecclesiastical committees have given fatuous advice on economics or politics. Sometimes, of course, this kind of risk may have to be taken. But the risk can be reduced if more responsibility is given to Christian laymen who are conversant with the complexities of the different areas of modern life. The professional moral theologian can no longer have sufficient knowledge of all these complex areas of modern life to be able to give guidance throughout them all, but must share his knowledge of the basic principles of Christian ethics with the technical knowledge of politicians, economists, medical men or others in the various areas.

Readers are referred to the articles dealing with specific themes in social ethics, for example, **Contemporary Society; Industrial Relations; Power; Property, Ethics of; Race Relations;** etc.

EDITOR

Social Gospel

Nineteenth-century Protestant ethics were deeply influenced by the theories and practices of individualism which often made it difficult for the churches to come to terms with the social consequences of the industrial revolution. As some of the unfortunate human consequences of the concentration of economic power, of the unequal distribution of wealth and of the growth of vast cities became clearer, certain Christians challenged the widely-accepted identification of Christian faith with individualistic philosophies. In the late nineteenth and early twentieth centuries social Christian movements which based their approach on the message of the prophets and the teachings of Jesus and which also drew on the insights of the developing historical and social sciences appeared in most western countries. In the USA, the social Christian movement developed conservative, progressive and radical forms. Of these, the progressive, mildly reformist, moderate, generally middle-class strand was by far the most significant in its time, and to this movement the term Social Gospel is generally given. Shaped in the closing decades of the nineteenth century by men of evangelical liberal theological premises who had accepted biblical criticism and the theory of evolution, and who were informed religiously by Ritschlian 'Kingdom of God' theology and socially by the progressive movement, the Social Gospel had wide influence in American Protestantism from about 1890 to the 1940s.

The 'father of the Social Gospel' was Washington Gladden, for over thirty years liberal Congregational pastor in Columbus, Ohio, and author of many books on liberal and social themes. The leading prophet of the Social Gospel was Walter Rauschenbusch (q.v.), who first confronted the social question in an unforgettable way as pastor of a German Baptist Church on the edge of New York's 'Hell's Kitchen'. The Social Gospel grew strong in Congregational, Baptist, Methodist, Episcopal and Presbyterian churches of the north, and was conspicuous in the movement for co-operative Christianity, as seen especially in the formation of the Federal Council of the Churches of Christ in America in 1908.

Certain key ideas, rooted in liberal theology, were characteristic of the Social Gospel. For their authority, Social Gospel leaders looked to the 'real' Jesus, as they believed he could be known by historical scholarship. The principles of Jesus were put forward as reliable guides for personal and social life in any age. Preachers of the Social Gospel explained that at the very centre of Jesus' message was the doctrine of the Kingdom of God, which they understood to be an historical possibility soon to come on earth in some fullness, to bring with it social harmony and the elimination of gross injustices. Though some proclaimers of the coming Kingdom were more cautious than others, the high sense of expectancy in the early arrival of a more ideal social order gave the Social Gospel movement an utopian cast. There was also great stress on the immanence of God, on his nearness, though his transcendence was not denied. He was seen to be at work in the regular processes of nature and history, progressively working out his purposes. Thus the Social Gospel believed heartily in *progress* – but did not usually refer to it as inevitable or automatic, for it was seen as conditional upon man's response to divine leading. The Social Gospel estimate of man and his potentialities was high, however; in most cases, it was affirmed, man could be educated to make the right choices and so contribute to the ushering in of the Kingdom.

Social Gospel's 'ethics of the Kingdom of God' put great emphasis on the law of love. God who is Love works in and through man towards the Kingdom of Love, a co-operative commonwealth in which socialized and enlightened men will work for the good of all. Sin was considered to be primarily selfishness, but men can be educated to prefer social good to private advantage. The Social Gospel was sensitive to the facts of the corporate transmission of sin through human institutions, yet believed that social salvation would come as institutions as well as individuals come under the law of love. Through determined moral effort, men can hasten the day of the Kingdom's coming; through self-sacrifice the Christian can become a hero of the coming dawn.

The practical ethical concerns of the Social Gospel focused around economic issues, especially on the relations between capital and labour. The right of labour to organize in the struggle for recognition and justice was forthrightly upheld, but as democracy was extended into the industrial order it was affirmed that co-operation would replace competition and strife. The 'Social Creed of the Churches', as endorsed by the Federal Council of Churches in 1912, declared that the churches must stand for the principles of conciliation and arbitration in industrial dissensions, for the abolition of child labour, for the reduction of hours of labour, for a living wage as a minimum standard in every industry, for the most equitable division of the products of industry as can ultimately be devised, and for the abatement of poverty.

Much Social Gospel thought was pacifistic, especially in its later phases between the two World Wars. In the 1930s and 40s the movement was sharply criticized by Reinhold Niebuhr (q.v.) and others, who challenged its view of man as over-optimistic and its strategy of preaching and pronouncement as naive. The Social Gospel era passed, but a deeper awareness of social realities and a lasting concern for social justice remain in Protestant life.

Robert T. Handy, ed., *The Social Gospel in America, 1870–1920*, 1966; C. Howard Hopkinds, *The Rise of the Social Gospel in American Protestantism, 1865–1915*, 1940; Henry F. May, *Protestant Churches and Industrial America*, 1949; Robert Moats Miller, *American Protestantism and Social Issues, 1919–1939*, 1958.

ROBERT T. HANDY

Social Service of the Church

In principle the Christian accepts his Saviour's law of love and becomes the channel of that divine love which, shed abroad in the heart by the Holy Spirit, flows forth in generous service to others. Even in the early centuries of the Church's history, observers noted the impact of Christian philanthropy upon society. Moreover, in ages when Church and nation were practically synonymous, the Church might be the agent of the State in matters of social welfare. In Scotland, for instance, the Church had statutory concern with the care of the poor and with education until well into the nineteenth century. At a time when everyone in the country stood in some relationship to the Church there could hardly be social service by the Church in the modern sense. Before that could emerge two important changes had to be initiated. One was the spread of secularism involving the withdrawal by large numbers of the population of their allegiance to all the churches. The second and more significant was the industrial revolution which involved a rapid increase in population, a transfer of population from country villages to industrial towns and cities, and the emergence of new forms of misery and degradation. The result of these changes was that the Church was now set over against society in a fashion without parallel since the early centuries, and that Christian compassion began to prompt action, individual action and then church action, in respect of masses of the population in evident material and moral as well as spiritual need.

If the social action of Jean Frederic Oberlin (1740–1826) in his mountain parish of Wald-bach is regarded as an outstanding example of what a pastor can do for and with his people, while the social action led by Thomas Chalmers (1780–1847) in St John's parish, Glasgow, is held to fall under the social service of the Church, the difference is not in the Christian motive of the two men but in the fact that in the latter case industrialization, by divorcing the people from organized Christianity and pro-ducing conditions of life hostile to morality and religion, had issued a challenge which only corporate Christian action could hope to meet. Again, if such notable instances of social service as are rendered by the YMCA and the Salvation Army are passed over, it is not because of any doubt of their Christian inspiration, but because their organization is independent of the churches.

The Roman Catholic Church with its religious orders and congregations has long made a vast contribution to social service. Suffice it here to name as one example out of many hundreds the Sisters of Charity of St Vincent de Paul founded in 1633 as the first female congregation without enclosure and with a wide sphere of service in the care of the sick and the poor irrespective of race and creed. Since 1800 new congregations, particu-larly of women, have been established in large numbers. They may be regarded as an adapta-tion of monasticism to modern conditions and they are organized for very varied work: orphanages, hospitals, homes for diverse categories of deprived and afflicted folk.

In Germany the Inner Mission can be traced to the action of Johann Hinrich Wichern (1808–1881), who in 1833 began a work of reclamation among the neglected children in the slums of Hamburg. The impact of the revolutionary year 1848 stirred the Protestant churches to concern for the masses, and soon a vast amount of religious, charitable and social work was co-ordinated under the Inner Mission. Its national organization with local units carries on a variety of agencies, including training institutions for its agents. Wichern perceived the responsibility of the layman, as the representative of the Church in the world, to manifest his solidarity with the world and work among sections of the population with which the official Church finds it difficult to

make contact. A contemporary pastor, Theodor Fliedner (1800–1864), saw the need and the possibility of women's work and founded in 1836 at Kaiserswerth a training institution for deaconesses devoted to the care of the sick and the education of neglected children.

In England the earliest social service of the church took place in the sphere of elementary education. In the early eighteenth century the Charity School movement and after 1780 the Sunday School movement were both under Christian inspiration, but after the turn of the century it was apparent that much more was required and the churches made their contribu-tion through two societies. The earlier, founded in 1808 and known from 1814 as the British and Foreign School Society, proceeded on un-denominational lines. Its moving spirit was Joseph Lancaster, a Quaker, who when teach-ing poor children at Southwark hit upon the idea of 'monitors', older children set to control and teach the younger. The Anglican counter-part was the National Society for Promoting the Education of the Poor in the principles of the established church, founded in 1811 by Dr Andrew Bell, a clergyman of that church who also used the monitor method. These two societies were principal agents in furthering popular education in England and Wales before the national system was introduced by the Act of 1870. The Anglican sisterhoods which began to be founded in the 1840s under the stimulus of the Tractarian movement with-drew from the world under strict rules for the purpose of serving the world in many practical ways including education, industrial schools and rescue homes.

The Church of Scotland, already holding a statutory connection with education through the parish schools, took a further step in 1824 when the General Assembly appointed a Com-mittee on Education which began to establish what were known as assembly schools in distinction from sessional schools supported by kirk-sessions.

Examples of social service in Britain in more recent times may be briefly mentioned. Wilson Carlile (1847–1942), an Anglican clergyman, formed in 1882 the Church Army on the model of the Salvation Army. The Church of Scotland established the Deaconess Hospital in Edin-burgh in 1894 and in 1904 the General Assembly appointed a committee on social work, now known as the Department of Social and Moral Welfare which runs eventide homes and agencies for deprived young people of different types.

In the USA the Indians and the Negroes at first took the place of industrialized masses as objects of Christian compassion and service, and the social service of the Church may be said to have begun in efforts to christianize and educate these special groups. As regards the Indians, missionaries for a time bore the main burden of their education, while the contribution of the Church to the emancipation of the Negroes and to their education, both elementary and in institutions of higher learning, has been immense. Before and after the turn of the present century the 'Social Gospel' emphasis led to the establishment of social settlements in needy districts, and this type of service is continuing in such experiments as the East Harlem Protestant Parish in New York.

S. L. Greenslade, *The Church and the Social Order*, 1948; F. H. Stead, *The Story of Social Christianity*, II, 1924.

STEWART MECHIE

Socialism

One difficulty in discussing the ethics of socialism is the wide range of different meanings of the word. Traditionally it has been taken to imply public, or at least collective, ownership of the means of production, but recent British writers on the right wing of the Labour Party have tended to see the essence of it as being not so much public ownership as public control, planning of the economy and equality of opportunity. Marxists, on the other hand, use it in a precise sense as meaning a state in which capitalism has been superseded, but abundance has not yet been achieved. H. Smith, however, sees the essence of socialism as a state where there is no longer conflict, since basic needs are satisfied and people are content not to strive to satisfy ever more wants. In this sense, he doubts whether it can be achieved in the West.

The ideal of the social control of the means of production to ensure their use for the benefit of all receives general agreement in Christian thought, but on the narrower issues of public ownership there has been marked difference of opinion. The primitive communism of the early church in Jerusalem, together with later experiments at voluntary pooling of possessions by small communities, is generally regarded as exceptional. It expresses an ideal suitable for a small group who feel called to contract out of the wider economic order, but it is not relevant as a model by which to judge the working of a large-scale economic system.

Socialism, in the Marxist secularized form associated with Continental Social Democratic parties, was condemned by Pope Leo XIII in the encyclical *Rerum Novarum* (1891) as being contrary to the natural right of private property and therefore not conducive to welfare. Forty years later, even though the views on class warfare and private property had become much modified, it was still condemned by Pius XI in *Quadragesimo Anno* on the ground that it conceived human society as instituted merely for the sake of material well-being, and sacrificed freedom to the greater economic efficiency of collectivism. Since then, Christian Democrats and Social Democrats in western Europe have been brought together by common experience

of resistance to Fascism and Communism, and have come to understand one another's respective values better, so that socialists now appreciate the value of personal liberty and Christian democrats the need for more extensive State control.

In non-Roman circles attitudes to socialism are more varied. Demant, in *Religion and the Decline of Capitalism*, while recognizing it as a reaction from the liberal belief in the autonomous free market, holds that regulation by the market and regulation by the State both equally fail to meet men's deeper needs for the security of a life rooted in community and having a significance which transcends this present world. On the other hand, in Britain and countries of British influence, the Labour movement was Christian in inspiration rather than Marxist, and many Christians of the Left have conceived of socialism as embodying Christian ideals of social justice and a responsible community, with public ownership as a means towards securing them.

Although some Christians have gone a long way with the Marxists, and most would recognize in Marxism valuable insights which are an essential corrective to a too other-worldly and idealistic interpretation of history, most non-Roman opinion also would endorse the belief that Marxism in its dogmatic form, as preached by the Communist Party, is incompatible with the Christian faith. In addition to its avowed atheism, it has an inadequate view of human nature, which does not take account of the radical perversion of sin, and hence maintains that a perfect society can be achieved, provided private ownership of the means of production is eliminated. Its moral relativism, which justified any means that further the cause of the Party, must also be condemned. Yet many Christians would be sympathetic to socialism, at least on some definitions.

J. C. Bennett, *Christianity and Communism*, 1948; J. M. Cameron, *Scrutiny of Marxism*, 1948; V. A. Demant, *Religion and the Decline of Capitalism*, 1952; M. P. Fogarty, *Christian Democracy in Western Europe*, 1957; A. C. MacIntyre, *Marxism – An Interpretation*, 1953; D. L. Munby, *Christianity and Economic Problems*, 1955; *God and the Rich Society*, 1961; J. F. Sleeman, *Basic Economic Problems, A Christian Approach*, 1953; H. Smith, *The Economics of Socialism Reconsidered*, 1962; Papal Encyclicals, *Mater et Magistra*, 1961; *Quadragesimo Anno*, 1931; *Rerum Novarum*, 1891.

JOHN F. SLEEMAN

Society, Sociology. *see* Culture, Society and Community.

Socrates

The question of the historical Socrates is only

a little more complex than that of the historical Jesus. And even if we refuse (against the views of the late Professors Burnett and Taylor) to allow that the 'theory of ideas' developed in Plato's middle dialogues is part of Socrates' teaching, we have still to face the issue of the contradiction between the likeness of Socrates discernible in Plato's earlier dialogues, including the *Apology*, and that presented by Xenophon in his *Memorabilia*. In the latter work Socrates is represented as virtually identifying the good with the useful, and although we must not underestimate the utilitarian element in Plato's earlier dialogues, it is hard to reconcile such a presentation of Socrates' central emphasis with, for instance, the figure in the *Apology* who, at his trial, defends himself against the suggestion that he is a Sophist by insisting that while the Sophists taught rhetoric for money, he engaged in dialogue with his fellow citizens under a religious imperative. It was Apollo whose oracle at Delphi had declared Socrates to the wisest man in Greece, and it was because he found the deliverance incredible that Socrates had felt it necessary, out of respect for the god, to put it to the test, learning in consequence that in this alone he was superior to his fellows, that he knew his own ignorance.

It is in the *Charmides* that Socrates distinguishes his conception of self-knowledge from that of the Sophists, with whom he indeed was frequently confused (compare also Aristophanes' savage caricature in the *Clouds*). The reader is also advised to compare Socrates' attitude to self-knowledge with that displayed in the tragic treatment of the theme by Sophocles in the *Oedipus Tyrannos*. For Socrates the ultimate evil was the 'unexamined life' and by his interrogations, often conducted with a playful irony, illuminating to compare with that of the tragedians and of the Fourth Evangelist, he forced upon men recognition of their own ignorance. It woud seem that there was in his temper as Plato portrays it, a combination of the profoundly reverent with the profoundly sceptical. The eminent Platonic scholar, the late M. Léon Robin, conjectures an element of attachment to the Orphic tradition in his mentioning, in particular, his reliance in moments of crisis upon the guidance of his *daimonion*. Yet among his intimates his example encouraged a scepticism far more searching than that of the Sophists. In the supreme crisis of the Peloponnesian War, when the survival of the whole Athenian culture and civilization was at issue in a power-struggle with another Greek society, whose military strength on land was at least as great as Athens' maritime resources, and whose social and political system morally revolted Pericles by its prodigal wastage of excellent human material in the perpetuating of a fantastic order of conquest and subordination, Socrates'

views seemed inevitably to encourage *apragmosunē*, a scrupulosity destructive of human energy. Again there was the figure of Alcibiades, who loved Socrates but whose profligacy and radical instability played its part in the disasters that led to Aegospotami, even as his impiety was attested by his suspected involvement in the mutilation of the Hermae on the eve of the Athenian fleet's departure for Sicily. 'Do men gather grapes of thorns or figs of thistles?' If the Socratic *elenchus* was irrefutable, the Socratic *paideia* seemed to result in distintegration; so Socrates' history issued inevitably in condemnation and death with his refusal to flee or to see in his drinking the hemlock anything other than a duty owed in part to the community which nurtured him, a last manifestation of his surprising spirit.

For Plato he is the type of the 'perfectly just man' in *Republic* II, portrayed with subtle admission of the justification of his reputation for injustice, even as it is arguable that the lineaments of the 'perfectly unjust man' are suggested by Pericles. It is the Socratic *elenchus* that Plato may have had in mind when he described the forceful conversion of the prisoners in their cave to the light, when bewildered they would fain return to the familiar environment they have hitherto known in their place of radical *apaideusia*. It is with the ontological validation of the Socratic way that Plato is obsessively concerned in the ethical and metaphysical sections of the *Republic* and it is one of the most illuminating ironies of the history of philosophy that the enterprise involved suggesting as a metaphysically final form of human association a closed non-hereditary aristocratic paternalism in which the rigorous and disciplined loyalty of its civil service and police woud have crushed at birth the slighest manifestation of the quizzical Socratic temper.

In the work of Kierkegaard a valuable contribution to christology has been achieved through comparison of the work of Socrates with that of Christ. According to Plato, Socrates described himself as a midwife, bringing to consciousness what men already innately (viz. dispositionally) knew; a *locus classicus* here is the *entretien* with the slave-boy in the *Meno*. But as Kierkegaard saw, Christ faced the task of communicating himself and therefore required an indirection quite other than that caught in those of the Platonic dialogues which would seem to echo most faithfully Plato's recollection of the words and methods of his master.

D. M. MACKINNON

Sodomy

Strictly sodomy (from Sodom) denotes coition, either homosexual or heterosexual, by anal penetration, but it is loosely used for male homosexualism in general. *See* **Homosexuality and Homosexualism.**

SHERWIN BAILEY

Sophists

The title – Sophists – is given to the itinerant teachers in fifth-century Greece, who offered, for a fee, to instruct young men on the threshold of public life in the skills of rhetoric. As they were itinerant they were familiar with the variety of moral and political traditions to be met with in Hellas, and became in consequence sympathetic with relativistic as distinct from absolutist conceptions of morality. In recent appraisals of their work there has been sharp reaction against supposing them fairly presented in Plato's vivid but damning portrayals of Callicles in the *Gorgias* and Thrasymachus in the first book of the *Republic*. Thus the teaching of Protagoras that man is the measure of all things has been construed as the principle of a genuine humanism, and the role played by the Sophists' work in dissolving the power of traditional ties of blood and family in the Athens of Cleisthenes, Ephialtes and Pericles, and substituting more rationally conceived bonds of human association, has been stressed. We find examples of their influence in Euripides' handling of the ancient myths in his tragedies, and we cannot, for instance, withhold our admiration for the way in which, in his *Electra*, he displays Orestes and his implacably dedicated sister as alike devastated in the climax of the play by experiencing at first hand the actuality of matricide. If the killing of Clytaemnestra can, in primitive penal theory, be justified as an action of retributive justice, its execution reveals itself as a human outrage, involving its perpetrators in a sense of guilt that no traditional casuistry can expel. A question-mark is here set against an appalling moral convention, and we must admire the men whose teaching made it possible.

If Plato is always the relentless critic of the Sophists, quick to bring out the extent to which their relativism encouraged *in the end* an indifference to the distinction between what is and what is not the case, and if, further, a study of the political commentary embodied in the speeches of Thucydides' *History* and in such sections of his text as the discussion of civil war following the account of its outbreak in Corcyra, the Mytilenean debate and the Melian dialogue must to some extent confirm his unfavourable view of their influence, we must acknowledge that he is also himself the heir of their sharp diremption between the natural and the customary, between *phusis* and *nomos*. His presentation of the democratic state in *Republic* VIII identifies democracy with a morally permissive society, the democratic man with the one whose moral tolerance is indistinguishable from a complete indifferentism. Yet the presentation shows the depth of his attachment to Athens, for all his tendency sometimes to romanticize Sparta. At some level of his being he realized that it was only in the context of an Athens wherein Periclean political institutions and the cultural style partly represented by the Sophists combined to make radical questions concerning the foundations of human life possible, that Socrates' and his own work could have been done.

D. M. MACKINNON

Sovereignty, National

National political sovereignty can be defined as the claim of the State to supreme coercive power. In our present national state system each nation asserts authority over all within it and autonomy from any political control outside itself. In such a framework of legal non-accountability nations recognize only those obligations to which they have given consent.

Political sovereignty must reside somewhere if disorder is to be minimized and conflicting interests balanced in a rough approximation of justice. A hierarchy of authority can be defended as a necessity in a complex society with many inter-related groups. The question is where ultimate social power ought to reside. The claim of the State to sovereignty is to be evaluated in the light of four relationships.

The first of these is defined in the statement of the 1937 Oxford Conference that the State is 'under the ultimate governance of God'. On political matters also, God alone is final authority over all men. The State ought never to assert a claim to absolute sovereignty in a metaphysical or moral sense. It is, of course, possible to claim sovereignty only with respect to human political groupings. Citizens and rulers may accept the higher authority of God. Even this introduces an important moral qualification into the political definition of sovereignty.

In relationship to its own citizens Hegel was clearly wrong in considering the State 'an absolute unmoved end', with 'supreme right against the individual, whose supreme duty is to be a member of the State'. Such a claim involves both idolatry and tyranny. Rather the State is to act as agent, while final human authority resides in the sovereign people.

Neither is the State autonomous with respect to other peoples. States are made for man. The Christian is concerned about man universally. In an interdependent world, those whose welfare is affected by a decision have a right to participate in its making. While such participation continues to lie in the future, national sovereignty ought now to be used as though it resided in the peoples of the world.

National sovereignty becomes a divisive factor in relationship to other nations. Without a superior authority, persisting disputes between states can finally be settled only by a contest of power. Disorder and domination are consequences of an anarchy of sovereignties in which all nations act without external restraint. An unsolved problem is finding more adequate definitions and limitations to national sovereignty. *See* **World Government.**

HARVEY SEIFERT

Spencer, Herbert

Herbert Spencer (1820–1903) was a leading English agnostic philosopher, and an exponent of the scientific ideas of the nineteenth century. Religion, in his view, had to deal with the unknowable; science deals with the knowable. Ethics is to be withdrawn from the tutelage of religion, and based upon the data of science. Important among these, for Spencer, was the doctrine of evolution and the belief in progress (q.v.) which was erected upon it. He attempted to construct a complete system of philosophy on scientific principles. The component works of his system were: *First Principles* (1862); *Principles of Biology* (1867); *Principles of Psychology* (1872); *Principles of Sociology* (1877); *Principles of Ethics* (1893).

EDITOR

Spinoza, Baruch de

One of the metaphysical principles of Spinoza (1632–1677) is that everything has in it a tendency to maintain and expand itself. In man this shows itself first in impulse and desire, which so far as they succeed or fail bring pleasure or pain, these being at this level the entire meaning of good and evil. We are here simply reacting to the impact of things and events outside us, both impact and reaction being determined in accordance with fixed laws of nature. This is the level of the 'bondage of the emotions'. The only escape is through another part of our being, namely knowing. By this instead of merely feeling emotions we can turn them into objects coolly contemplated, so draining them of their force. In such contemplation we come to recognize the causal necessity of all external events, and therefore the folly of being vexed by adverse ones and of seeking happiness in pleasing ones (a Stoic note), and the pettiness too of calling the universe good or bad simply by its effects on us. That is virtually all that Spinoza has to say within his system on the morality of the ordinary man. In a small minority knowing moves by inherent impulsion beyond sense, even beyond science, which conceives the universe as a system of particular things bound together causally, to an intuition that sees the bond as logical and therefore timeless, and the parts as losing their separateness in an infinite and perfect unity. Here knowing fulfils its function of self-expansion. Because it does so without external interference it is a free activity; because it is successful it carries within itself a unique kind of joy; and because the unitary whole it contemplates is God, Spinoza calls this final experience the 'intellectual love of God'. This is the supreme virtue, needing no reward outside itself. He who attains it can die physically, but in mind only so far as this has been determined physically, for the knowing of what is eternal is itself timeless. Spinoza's rationalist pantheism springs from his deeply Jewish moral and monotheistic sensibility, from his shrinking from anthropomorphism, and from his intellectual rejection of the current Calvinist theology and Cartesian philosophy, which alike make everything depend on God's inscrutable *will*, a view that, he believed, would make reason useless because there would be nothing intelligible for either thought or conduct.

T. E. JESSOP

Spiritual Direction. *see* Direction, Spiritual.

State

The State is the institution in which the ultimate social authority and power are located, authority and power which are necessary to maintain order and to give conscious direction to the life of a society. In the modern world we think of the State as being an essential structure of the nation, as being the expression of its sovereignty and the source of its government. The modern nation has given to the State a much clearer form than was the case with ancient empires or the fluid feudal order of the Middle Ages. Christian thinking about the State developed in response to those earlier conditions of political life. It was coloured by the descriptions in the OT of the political kingdoms of Israel and Judah and these were seen against the background of a theocratic ideal which in principle limited the authority and power of kings (*see* stories of Nathan and David, and Elijah and Ahab).

The passages in the NT which refer to government (especially Rom. 13.1–7; I Peter 2.13–17 and Rev. 13) naturally refer to the authorities of the Roman Empire. It is not possible to derive from these passages adequate guidance for Christian ethics in relation to the State as the political structure of a nation in which Christians have the rights and responsibilities of citizens. The first two passages assume a positive attitude toward the political authorities as God-given instruments of order in society. The passage in Revelation recognizes that the Roman Empire had become an idolatrous power, for its demand for worship of the emperor exceeded its authority and therefore Christians were bound to resist it by suffering. No form of political resistance could have been considered at the time. *See* Oscar Cullmann, *The State in the New Testament*, 1956.

The NT teaching about the State sets the outside limits within which Christian political ethics has moved. It warns at the same time against anarchism and against the unlimited state. The great words of Peter in Acts, 'We must obey God rather than men' (Acts 5.29) have had great force in Christian history but in relation to the State there has been a tendency for them to be nullified by the words in Rom. 13.1: 'Let every person be subject to the governing authorities.' It has often seemed possible to harmonize these two passages even in the face of the most difficult historical circumstances by assuming that in spite of appearances God was expressing his will through the governing authorities of the moment. Since the recognition of the Church by the Roman Empire at the time of Constantine this readiness to harmonize these two principles has usually dominated Christendom. There has, however, been a contrary tendency which was present especially in the Protestant sects and on Calvinistic soil in spite of the main tendency in Calvin's thought. In Roman Catholic thought there have been resources for the independence of the Church and even for the sanctioning of political resistance against the State – the proclamation of natural law as being above the State and the authority of the Pope over against that of emperor or king – but there has also been a strong presumption in favour of political authorities with some claim to legitimacy. This latter tendency was especially prominent in the nineteenth century when the Church was controlled by fear of the influences from the French Revolution. The modern experience of totalitarianism on the part of both Catholics and Protestants has brought about a shift of emphasis, and theological sanction for political resistance to tyranny in extreme cases is now more widely held among Christians than ever before.

One pervasive contrast in Christian attitudes toward the State is the difference between those who think of the State as having chiefly the negative function of providing a dyke against sin and those who see the State as a natural consequence of the social nature of man. The Roman Catholic teaching about the State which has been influenced by Aristotle's positive attitude toward the political order of the city is the clearest case of the view of the State as the expression of man's social nature, as belonging to creation rather than to the fall. See H. Rommen, The State in Catholic Thought, 1947. The negative view of the State is most characteristic of Luther and of important strains in Lutheranism. Calvinism is closer to the positive view of the State in spite of its dark view of sin. There are some confusions in this continual debate. One confusion has to do with the extent to which the State is distinguished from other aspects of society. If the State is limited to the coercive aspect of society the

negative doctrine of the State is more plausible than is the case when the State is understood to include a wider range of the activities of the society. The theory of the essentially negative function of the State is still held in some countries which have seen an extensive development of the welfare state. This theory hardly seems to fit these conditions but there is another form of the negative view of the State that has been encouraged by the experience of totalitarianism. The State, especially when its power is swollen by great military establishments, can be seen as an especially destructive embodiment of sin. Even its welfare activities, especially its control over education, become instruments of its demonic power. Democratic states have often been dominated by popular frenzy in time of war. See Herbert Butterfield, Christianity, Diplomacy and War, 1953. Experience of a great variety of states should prevent the crystallization of a one-sided theological theory about the State.

The problem of limiting the State will always be present but Christian ethics does have to balance the danger that the State may become unlimited and even demonic over against the danger that the State may be too weak to deal with the problems of modern society. Sometimes the primary issue is the preservation of social order where society is vulnerable to tribal or economic or political conflict. Sometimes there is a tendency towards stalemate as between management and labour in industrial societies and the State must be strong enough to bring about a decision. In a complicated technological society the State inevitably acquires many economic functions. It alone has the authority or the resources to deal with many national problems that require large scale action. There is no one Christian pattern that is relevant to the needs of all societies for the relating of the function of the State to that of private bodies of all kinds. But there is a Christian emphasis on the needs of the people who are neglected or exploited, of the poor who have no private economic power. This emphasis does often call for united action by the society working through government to direct the use of the resources of the society for the sake of all the people, especially the weak and neglected ones. Christian ethics offers no sanction to a consistent capitalism or a consistent socialism but it should encourage openness to the most varied combination of public and private action for the sake of justice and welfare. The teachings of the encyclicals of the Popes since Leo XIII, most recently Mater et Magistra of John XXIII, and the dominant social teachings of the World Council of Churches, for examples, reports of Amsterdam (1948) and Evanston (1954) Assemblies of the World Council, are quite similar in the way in which doctrinaire solutions of these complex problems are transcended.

Just as there is no one Christian pattern for the relating of government to economic institutions, so there is no one Christian form of government. The Church has had to live with many forms of government but this does not mean that all are of equal merit. There is a conflict between Christian ethics and totalitarian regimes and also between Christian ethics and any form of despotism that leaves very little opportunity for freedom of expression for persons or groups. Indeed Christian ethics is favourable to the trend associated with political democracy so long as it includes both lawful limits on the power of government and the sovereignty of the people as a whole with political channels for the expression of the popular will. See **Democracy**.

The role of the national state in the international sphere raises another dimension. All that has ever been said by theologians about the State as the providential instrument for preserving order applies to the need for an instrument to preserve order amidst the anarchy of nations. No national state should regard itself as ultimate. The serving of the welfare of humanity as a whole, the breaking down of barriers between peoples, the prevention of fratricidal war, even of mutual annihilation in the nuclear age, call for the development of the institutions of world order which will limit the power of national states. Christian teaching always points beyond the national state to God's love for all mankind and the Church by its very nature is the structure of a community that transcends all nations and is under the authority of no national state. See also **Church and State**.

JOHN C. BENNETT

Sterilization

The Council of Nicea in 325 pronounced against castration and this has been traditionally linked with the broader question of bodily mutilation, which is condemned, unless required for the health of the body as a whole. Pope Sixtus V in 1587 placed a ban on marriages by eunuchs, on the ground that 'no true utility' arises from such unions, which rather 'occasion both temptations and incentives to lust'. During the period of Nazi sterilization practices, the Holy Office, asked 'whether the direct sterilization of man or woman, either perpetual or temporary, is licit', replied in February, 1940 that 'it is forbidden by the law of nature'.

This extension of the ban on mutilation to cover a temporary impairment of function was later applied to the use of oral contraceptives. In September, 1958, Pius XII stated that a direct and therefore illicit sterilization is provoked when medicines are used 'to prevent conception by preventing ovulation'. Some Catholic scholars, like Canon Louis Janssens of Louvain, argue a distinction between

sterilization and a deferment of ovulation since the ovum is not destroyed by the use of steroid pills. This is one of the matters under current Vatican review.

Protestant statements during the past generation have generally warned against the possible consequences of surgical sterilization, because of its normally permanent character and the dangers of foreclosing an unknown future. In recent years, however, a more permissive attitude has become evident in Protestant pronouncements, particularly in regard to situations where acceptable alternatives to limit the size of the family may be lacking. It has been argued that one decision, if thoroughly and prayerfully considered, is not necessarily less responsible than a series of decisions required by less drastic means of birth control. As for temporary sterilization, such as oral contraceptives (the 'pill'), recent Protestant statements find no inherent moral difference between these and the older contraceptives, provided the new drugs are free from serious side effects.

It seems probable that the introduction of new intra-uterine devices will have practical impact on the incidence of sterilization particularly in low-income societies. This inexpensive and reversible means of regulating fertility is already reducing the number of surgical sterilizations in some countries. While it is still unknown whether the IUD impedes a union of sperm and ovum or impedes implantation of the fertilized ovum, the growing availability of an alternative long-range means of birth control may well have some impact on Protestant attitudes towards sterilization. See also **Procreation**.

RICHARD M. FAGLEY

Stewardship

Stewardship is one of the root concepts in Christian ethics, based on the recognition that all gifts come from God and must be used to his glory, and applying equally to all types of gifts, whether of money, time or talents.

In practice, however, stewardship has tended often to be conceived in too narrow a way. It is thought of purely individually, in terms of what a man should do with his own income or leisure time, rather than corporately, in the sense of thinking out the duties and responsibilities of the profession or occupation to which he belongs, in the light of their effects on the whole working of the economy and the whole life of society. In recent years the so-called Stewardship Movement has led to more active thinking about its implications, but even here there has been the danger of too great a concentration on more efficient fund-raising by church congregations.

Roman Catholic thought has perhaps gone furthest in working out its wider implications, on the basis of the teaching of the mediaeval

Church. The concepts of the Just Price and the Just Wage are themselves applications of stewardship. The duty of almsgiving has been accepted teaching from the earliest days. St Thomas Aquinas' doctrine that once a man has enough for his own needs and those of his household, so as to keep up becomingly his condition of life, it then becomes a duty to contribute to the needs of the indigent, is reaffirmed in the encyclical *Rerum Novarum* (1891, cf. para. 19). On the basis of this the French research centre 'Economie et Humanisme' worked out a theory of consumption in which it was suggested that once basic goods, necessary for a satisfactory life, were assured, the emphasis should be on developing the supply of spiritual goods, which help men to develop their higher capacities, rather than on luxury goods, which represent only material comfort.

The emphasis in Roman Catholic social thinking on the responsibility of corporate groups based on professions and industries is also an attempt to work out the wider implications of stewardship, as is Pope John XXIII's detailed concern for justice in industrial relationships, as seen in his encyclical *Mater et Magistra* (1961).

In a less organized form there is plenty of non-Roman thinking on similar lines. We may compare the work of Bowen on the theory of the *Social Responsibility of Businessmen*, which traces the development of a body of professional ethics by which business decisions can be taken with full and responsible understanding of their implications for consumers, employees, competitors and the community in general. Writers such as Munby, who have tried to assess critically the working of the economy in Christian terms, are also helping to make possible a more effective exercise of stewardship.

H. R. Bowen, *Social Responsibilities of the Businessman*, 1953; M. P. Fogarty, *Christian Democracy in Western Europe*, 1957; D. L. Munby, *Christianity and Economic Problems*, 1956; *God in the Rich Society*, 1961; Papal Encyclicals, *Mater et Magistra*, 1961; *Rerum Novarum*, 1891.

JOHN F. SLEEMAN

Stoicism

For the Greek, philosophy was divided into three parts, logic, physics and ethics (Cicero, *De Finibus* iv.ii.4), but for the Stoic the other departments of learning existed solely for the sake of ethics. If the Stoic speculated, it was in order to live (Diogenes Laertius 7.84; Epictetus, *Discourses* iii.2).

Basic to the Stoic idea of ethics is the Stoic idea of God. God is everywhere and in every man 'God is near you, with you, within you. I say it, Lucilius, a holy spirit sits within us,

spectator of our evil and our good, our guardian' (Seneca, *Letters* xli.,12). But not only is God everywhere present. Everything is settled and arranged by God. Thus the Stoic has two allied conceptions. There is the conception of *heimarmenē*, which is fate. This in itself might be detached and mechanical. But to it there is joined the conception of *pronoia*, which is providence. The control of God is carried out in care for all living things (Cicero, *De Natura Deorum* ii.liii.132; ii.lvi.164). Fate and providence are one, and literally nothing happens but by the will of God.

An obvious question emerges. If everything is settled and arranged, how does man come into it at all? How can there be such a thing as ethics? To man there is left one thing, and it is all important – the power of assent.

This then gives us the key to Stoic ethics. Goodness is willingly to accept the will of God, or, to put it in another way, to live according to Nature. If everything is the will of God, then the secret is to learn to want what we have (Epictetus, *Manual* 8). Seneca says: 'To obey God is liberty' (*De Vita Beata* xv.7). 'He does not will it,' says Epictetus, 'I do not wish it' (*Discourses* iv.i.89). Man can either accept the will of God willingly, or he can struggle against it. Accept it he must. This has certain consequences. (1) Virtue is a thing of the mind. It comes by putting one's mind to it, and, like walking in a child, it comes by practice. (2) Virtue may therefore be learned, and in the end virtue is knowledge and vice is ignorance. (3) Virtue itself is all sufficient; nothing else matters. Everything else is *adiaphoros*, indifferent. But if everything is indifferent, then action is paralysed. So the things which are indiffererent are divided into things to be sought, like health and beauty and honour and good birth, and things which are to be rejected. (4) The Stoic draws a distinction between things which are in our power and things which are not in our power. Only one thing is in our power – the assent of the will. Here we come to the most characteristic aspect of Stoicism. If the will is everything, then the supreme evil is emotion. To have emotion is to be diseased (Cicero, *Tusc. Disput.* iii.x.23). The wise man must become *apathēs*, not apathetic, but cleansed of all emotion, so that he can endure the greatest pain, and see even the death of his nearest and dearest, and say only that this is the will of God (Epictetus, *Discourses* i.iv.111,112).

Stoic ethics consist of the remembrance that life is lived in the presence of God, that man is a sacred thing and the resting-place of the Divine (Seneca, *Letters* xcii.13; cxx.14), and that goodness means the total acceptance of the will of God, which is expressed in events.

WILLIAM BARCLAY

Strikes. *see* Industrial Relations.

Subjectivism, Ethical

Ethical subjectivism is the view that moral judgments are equivalent to statements about the psychological states or attitudes of those who utter them. It is to be distinguished from emotivism, relativism, prescriptivism (qq.v.).

R. M. HARE

Suffering

The widespread idea that suffering befalls a person as a judgment for his sins and wrong-doing is already denied in the OT drama of Job and is explicitly rejected by Jesus. It is true that some kinds of sin, especially sins of indulgence, may bring suffering upon the sinner; and that all sins bring suffering upon someone. But there is certainly no mechanical connection between sin and suffering. On the other hand, suffering may contribute to the development of moral character. This would certainly be true in the Christian life, for in so far as this is a conformation to Christ, it is a conformation to the crucified One. It is hard to imagine how there could be much depth of sympathy and love in a person who had not known suffering. But while some suffering would seem to have this morally educative character, there is much more in which it would be difficult to find any value whatsoever. The apparently pointless sufferings of human beings and the vast suffering that goes on in nature belong to the mystery of evil (q.v.).

EDITOR

Suicide

Discussions on the morality of suicide are often confused by a failure to distinguish between the willing surrender of one's life and the deliberate taking of it. Traditional Christian teaching affirms that in certain circumstances a man may innocently relinquish his life. They are occasions which call for self-sacrifice – for example, in the performance of his duty while on military service, in the defence of a friend unjustly attacked, in ministering to the infectious sick, in witnessing to his faith in time of persecution. In every instance of this kind the person concerned does not primarily or directly will his own death, but he is prepared to accept it as the unavoidable consequence of his performing some act of charity, justice, mercy or piety, to which he believes that God has called him. If the same acts could be performed without his death he would not choose to die. But the act which can properly be called suicide, namely, the direct and deliberate taking of one's life (with or without another's assistance) for any self-regarding motive, is another matter. In antiquity and in modern times it has been defended as permissible or even virtuous, on the grounds that a man's life is his own and that in the last resort he must therefore be allowed to terminate it at his discretion. A very small minority of Christians have attempted to justify it in cases of extreme senility or painful and wasting incurable disease. See Euthanasia. But (notwithstanding those instances of suicide in the Bible which are not expressly condemned) the overwhelming weight of traditional Christian opinion has held suicide (as defined above) to be a grave sin. A man is not the author of his own life nor its absolute owner. It is entrusted to him by God, to be used in the service of God and his fellow men in this world, and it is not for him to decide for how long it shall be so used. Directly and deliberately to destroy one's own life is therefore (1) a sin against God its creator and redeemer, a rejection of his love and a denial of his sovereignty; (2) an offence against the proper love of one's own person made in God's image to share his glory, a violation of the sixth Commandment, an act of despair which precludes repentance; and (3) an offence against mankind in that it both deprives one's family and society of a member prematurely, and also denies them any opportunity of ministering to one's needs. It is in accord with this teaching that some codes of criminal law have imposed penalties for suicide and attempted suicide, and that ecclesiastical law has withheld Christian burial from one who has 'laid violent hands' on himself. It has always been recognized, however, that acts of suicide may vary from the coldly premeditated to the utterly compulsive, and that in any particular case the degree of culpability depends upon the state of mind in which it is done. In the present century increasing attention has been paid to the psychopathology of suicide, and it seems clear that suicide is far more often a less voluntary act than was hitherto assumed. Thus, without conceding either that one has the right to take one's own life or that all who make the attempt must be presumed insane, a growing number of Christians support the view that neither suicide nor attempted suicide should be regarded as crimes since medical and sociological studies have already shown the irrelevance of the criminal law to the solution of the problem.

Church Assembly Board for Social Responsibility, *Ought Suicide to be a Crime?*, 1961; N. St John-Stevas, *Life, Death and the Law*, 1961; S. E. Sprott, *The English Debate on Suicide*, 1961.

THOMAS WOOD

Summum Bonum. *see* Goodness.

Sumptuary Laws

Sumptuary laws are laws passed to restrain extravagant expenditure and to prevent the spread of habits of luxury. Such laws were being passed as long ago as the days of ancient Rome, and they may be compared with the 'credit squeezes' of modern times.

Sunday Observance

The weekly day of rest was probably familiar to the Babylonians and the Egyptians, and was certainly known in the Gentile world before Christ. Under the Roman Empire it came to be associated with the worship of the sun. When therefore Martin Luther stated that while in principle one day is as holy as another yet human nature requires a regular day of rest, he was recognizing the same custom as that acknowledged in Roman Catholic and indeed in non-Christian countries. The economic importance of periodic rest was dramatically illustrated by the drop in production which occurred as a result of Sunday work during the early years of the first World War. In democratic countries public opinion has often reinforced the demand for a day of rest though with emphases differing according to circumstance and country. At the present time, the mechanization of industry has made possible a second free day, while it is possible that the coming of automation will still further increase opportunities for leisure. This means that the coincidence of natural needs and Christian observance may no longer occur, and it is therefore urgently necessary for Christians to think out afresh the grounds of Sunday observance.

The Jews believed the sabbath day of rest was divinely sanctioned and indeed commanded. By the time of Christ, the regulations for its observance had become very detailed and oppressive. Hence our Lord laid down the principle that 'the sabbath was made for man and not man for the sabbath' (Mark 2.27). Gentile Christians, though emancipated by Paul from the strictures of the Jewish sabbath, came early to recognize the first day of the week as the Lord's day, the opportunity for celebrating the mighty acts of God in history, and in particular the resurrection of Christ.

As ordered worship developed, and with the continued recognition of the OT, some fusion between the Christian observance and the sabbath idea became inevitable; but in the early centuries the statements of the Fathers of the Church show conclusively that joy was the main characteristic. The recovery of this element is the chief need of the Church's Sunday observance today. *See* Joy Davidman, *Smoke on the Mountain*, 2nd edn., 1963, Chap. 4.

After the official recognition of the Lord's Day (called Sunday in the northern territories) legislation from Constantine onwards restricted Sunday work and in spite of frequent relaxations in favour of 'necessary' labour and the permission to shop-keepers to sell foodstuffs, medical supplies, etc., even in England, workers generally have appreciated until recently the need on social grounds to preserve Sunday rest. Free Saturdays and 'double time' for Sunday work have now led to serious confusion, however, on the relation between the first day and the other days of the week.

Recreation was generally allowed after Church attendance (often compulsory) until Protestants began to fashion Sunday along the lines of the Jewish sabbath. The 1625 Sunday Observance Act in England on the profanation of the Lord's day has been modified in a number of respects by subsequent Acts. However, the Crathorne Committee set up by the British Government recommended in 1964 that restrictions on a wide variety of entertainments should be removed, and the legislation governing Sunday games relaxed provided that participants were not paid. The report assumes that it is not healthy for a society to rest the use of Sunday on archaic legislation.

In modern industrial society, the quiet Sunday appears to have had less justification for the 'working' class than for the 'middle' class and people living in the countryside, for Sunday travel gives an opportunity to escape from the built-up area. Public opinion is not now inclined to accept a Puritan Sunday, though there seems general agreement that the right of Christians (a minority in most countries) should be safeguarded.

Contrary to the general view, the Roman Catholic Church and the major Protestant denominations are agreed upon the principles which should guide the use of Sunday, namely, freedom to worship without noise or hindrance, and freedom to witness to the community at large. Such witness is assumed to include the reality of forgiving friendship within the Christian fellowship, the emphasis upon family life on a day when parents and children can be together, the aspiration after culture and re-creation of the mind and spirit, dialogue between Christians and non-Christians (cf. Papal Encyclical, *Mater et Magistra*, 1961; and British Council of Churches' statement on 'The Use of Sunday', Appendices on Trade and Entertainment, which brings together statements of major Protestant denominations).

Legislation is bound to be prohibitive in its provisions, but can be positive in purpose, that is, designed to secure a framework within which people of differing views can agree upon a compromise and how best to safeguard one another's rights and responsibilities on Sunday. Christians generally hold the view that while friendly games and entertainment are allowable after times for worship have been safeguarded, the gathering of large crowds for public games at commercial prices would tend to destroy what is best in Sunday customs which have grown up over the centuries.

Joy Davidman, *Smoke on the Mountain*, 2nd edn., 1963; W. Hodgkins, *Sunday: Christian and Social Significance*, 1960; M. Glazebrook, 'Sunday', *HERE*, XII, pp. 103–11.

C. H. CLEAL

Superego

Superego is the term introduced by Sigmund Freud in his later topographical model of the human mind. Although often equated with conscience the superego is both a broader and a narrower concept than conscience. It includes the self-observation which is a necessary preliminary to the judging dimensions of conscience but there are many aspects of the mature adult conscience which are not represented in the superego concept.

Freud believed that the superego developed between three and five years of age as a result of the resolution of the Oedipus complex (q.v.) and reflects the child's understanding of what his parents approve and disapprove and hence of what they are likely to reward or punish. These judgments, which may be inaccurate, then become part of the child's own psychic structure and are capable of bringing considerable pressure to bear on the ego (q.v.) to inhibit or prevent ideas or actions of which the superego disapproves. Associated with the superego is the *ego-ideal*, a conception of an ideal or perfect self modelled on the parental standards. It is as if there is a faculty in the ego which stands off and constantly watches, criticizes, and compares the actual performances of the ego against this ideal. *See* S. Freud, *The Ego and the Id*, 1927. Some later workers have emphasized the importance in the early development of the superego of the infant's projection on to its parents of its own impulses and of its fears of retaliation for having such impulses. *See* Melanie Klein, *Psychoanalysis of Children*, 3rd edn., 1959. This point of view is controversial among workers in the field.

The adaptive function of the superego seems to be to effect moral self-regulation in the child and thus to promote his welfare within the boundaries prescribed by society. But his superego can also be too severe and make excessive demands upon the ego, limiting freedom of action – particularly for the adult who must live in a world of much greater complexity than that of childhood. Sustained conflict between ego and superego can produce deep psychic distress and guilt (q.v.). It is generally agreed that the course of mental health should involve increased control by the ego and decreased control by the superego.

The superego is regarded by some as the psychic structure responsible for acceptance of and adherence to religious beliefs. Inasmuch as religion is an unreflective take-over of parental views or dependent upon experiences with the earthly parents, this would seem to be acceptable. But this is certainly not the whole truth of the Christian understanding of God and even some psychologists, such as Carl Jung, see the more profound religious experiences mediated elsewhere in the human mind. *See* **Conscience**.

GRAEME M. GRIFFIN

Supererogation, Works of

In the traditional moral theology, these were deeds going beyond what could be regarded as of strict obligation. For instance, to obey the counsels of perfection (q.v.) was to go beyond what is demanded by duty. Protestants have tended to reject the whole notion of works of supererogation, and of course it is surely the case that nothing that a man can do could be more than he owes to God. Yet it is equally true that one can distinguish between acts that are obligatory on all and acts which arise from a distinterested and wholehearted pursuit of the good. To give a concrete illustration, one could hardly say that it was Schweitzer's *duty* to give up his career and train as a doctor. It may well be that he himself saw it as a duty, once he had pondered it; but no one would have dreamed of blaming him had he continued his earlier activities. Perhaps we could say that in such cases there is unusual sensitivity to what constitutes one's duty. But judged by the common level of human and even Christian conduct, one might well call such extraordinary acts 'works of supererogation'.

EDITOR

Synderesis, Synteresis

Synderesis, synteresis, is a term used by mediaeval theologians for our knowledge of the first principles of moral action. The word is generally supposed to be a corruption of the Greek *suneidesis* 'conscience' (q.v.).

Synergism

Synergism was the expression used by Melancthon to express the idea that the human will 'works with' the divine grace, though he maintained that priority belongs to the latter. The opposing point of view is monergism.

Taboo

Taboo refers to prohibition such that supernaturally caused danger will result from infringement of the prohibition. By extension it also refers to anything forbidden by general cultural sanctions or *mores* (rather than legal ones).

The term 'taboo' came into the English language from Polynesian languages. The concept is most fully developed and explicitly elaborated in the cultures of the Pacific region. In this area it is always associated very closely with the concept of *mana*, non-personal extraordinary power. Whatever has powerful mana is taboo to the person who is not protected from that mana, or whose mana is not itself stronger. Thus mana at work in a man's garden makes it taboo to another man who therefore cannot steal from the garden because of the danger of calamity resulting from contact with mana from which he has no protection. Unusual mana which by definition goes with high status in Polynesian society made it impossible for a king and a commoner to come in physical contact because of the danger to the commoner, thus forcing the most powerful of kings into lonely, isolated lives.

In less elaborately defined fashion taboo can be seen on all levels of ancient and modern life. The Ark of the Covenant and the Holy of Holies were taboo to the ancient Israelites. Here danger stemmed partly from inherent mana and partly from the wrath of God, depending perhaps on the sophistication of the observer. The caste system of India is an extraordinary complex of taboos, as are the attitudes of many racists for whom calamity runs in the form of the degeneration of the 'pure' race in some undefined but deeply feared manner.

Incest is taboo for all societies, although not all societies define incestual relationships in the same way, and some provide occasional ritualized rites for breaking the incest taboo with impunity. These are emotionally highly charged religious occasions.

Where taboos are strong they support the ethical system peculiar to the culture because of their built-in sanctions. Like any other custom a taboo may eventually lose its force, be broken with impunity, or become a perfunctory relic to which lip service only is given. Shortly before the arrival of missionaries in Hawaii, the people, led by the king and an important priest, suddenly gave up an extremely complex taboo system. The king publicly broke the taboos by way of demonstration, and much of the population followed. The system had become so onerous that its repudiation was a great relief. More typically, however, taboos disintegrate under the impact of culture contact, urbanization, education, scepticism, etc., because people gradually cease to believe in some of the forms of danger and calamity ascribed to them.

WILLIAM A. SMALLEY

Taylor, Jeremy

Jeremy Taylor (1613–1667) is known for his eloquent preaching as 'The English Chrysostom', and unrivalled among Anglican pastors of his day for his experience as a spiritual guide. His Oxford sermon on *The Anniversary of the Gunpowder Treason* (1638) revealed his potential powers as a moral theologian which reached maturity during his chaplaincy to the Carbery family at Golden Grove in Carmarthenshire. Here he produced an impressive series of works of practical divinity. They include *The Great Exemplar* (1649), *The Golden Grove* (1655), and the two for which he is best known, *The Rule and Exercises of Holy Living* (1650) and of *Holy Dying* (1655). In his own mind these, together with *Unum Necessarium, or The Doctrine and Practice of Repentance* (1655) were by way of preparation for *Ductor Dubitantium* (1660), dedicated to Charles II. All the classical problems are raised somewhere or other in its four books which treat of the nature and authority of conscience; the nature, authority and interpretation of laws natural, revealed, civil, ecclesiastical; and the factors which determine the morality of human actions. A prospective reader might be deterred by its inordinate length. Its presentation is also marred by numerous digressions and an excess of illustrative material. But it remains the greatest single treatise on moral theology ever produced by an English churchman. As bishop of Down and Connor (consecrated 1661) Taylor published in two parts *A Dissuasive from Popery* (1664, 1667), both of which include discussions of certain points of moral theology which were and continue to be controversial. *See also* **Caroline Moral Theology.**

Jeremy Taylor, *The Whole Works*, ed. by R. Heber, 1822; revised and corrected by C. P. Eden and A. Taylor, 10 vols. 1850–59; H. Trevor Hughes, *The Piety of Jeremy Taylor*, 1960; C. J. Stranks, *The Life and Writings of Jeremy Taylor*, 1952; Thomas Wood, 'The Tercentenary of Ductor Dubitantium', *Theology*, LXIII, 1960, pp. 369–74.

THOMAS WOOD

Technology. *see* Contemporary Society; Science and Ethics.

Temperance

A man is to be temperate in all things – even in the practice of the virtues and specially in the practice of temperance. Temperance does not lie in not doing too much of anything, but in a general sobriety of living in which a person is controlling what can be controlled and does not attempt to control what cannot be controlled.

Intemperance is evident in one who thinks too much, too quickly about too many subjects. Temperance is quietness of mind in which concentration makes for profound lucid thinking. The intemperate talk too much to too many people, taking too many into their confidence. Temperance is a readiness to pay attention to what others have to say and only talking about subjects appropriate to the occasion and relationship. The intemperate are too grateful, too sympathetic, too prone to give advice. Temperance is grateful and sympathetic in proportion to the occasion for gratitude or sympathy. To be intemperate is to have too much travelling on account of too many appointments, committees, obligations, commitments and responsibilities. The temperate man knows that a man's life, and usefulness, does not consist in the abundance of his activities; he knows also that the attempt to do too many pieces of work, at the same time, has almost the same result as if no such attempt were made. Temperance entails a ruthless selection of activities on the part of artists, scientists, philosophers, social workers, pastors and all other serious people.

Some take to talking and work in the way others take to alcohol and other drugs as a means of dulling the edges of their fears and keeping themselves from becoming too aware of what is happening to them, within them and through them. All forms of intemperance contain a neurotic element and arise from causes best described as spiritual.

Institutions, societies and the Church itself, through officials, need to be watchful in case the over-willing (the intemperate) be given more work than they can do. In particular the Church is to preserve temperance through maintaining the balance of urgency and tranquillity in all authentic Christian living. In the table of the seven virtues, temperance is placed before fortitude – perhaps to suggest that only the temperate can be brave and that temperance requires bravery. Christian Scripture says: 'Let your moderation be known unto all men'. That is, let your temperance be known because the truth can only be spoken and done by temperate men. *See also* **Temperance and Temperance Movements**.

R. E. C. BROWNE

Temperance and Temperance Movements

Temperance is a quality of personal fitness achieved by self-control (I Cor. 9.25), based on the conviction that the discipline of Christian love preserves the free enjoyment of God's gifts, while self-indulgence destroys it. When organizations have restricted it to adherence to a single cause, then judgmental attitudes have obscured the principle of Christian freedom thus arousing controversy.

Initially the 'cause' was that Christians should abstain from meat offered as disinfected from demons through sacrifice to a food idol (I Cor. 8.4). Since the early nineteenth century the demon has been strong drink. Rigorous advocates insist on 'teetotalism' and promote organizations, religious and secular, for the abolition of all intoxicating beverages as invariably injurious and 'unclean'. Since indulgence is held to be morally wrong, teetotalism is a condition of membership in such organizations. In answer to the objection that teetotalism must either distort or deprecate our Lord's example, teetotallers argue that the Bible contains teachings of such seminal power that they produce a progressive development of

insight and faith extending beyond its laws and producing new rules essential to new social conditions. The abolition of slavery is seen as a precedent. Teetotalism was politically successful in the USA and prohibition demonstrated that a decrease in liquor outlets diminished drunkenness and alcoholism. It provoked social discontents and disorders which led to its defeat, since no substitute for alcohol was offered at the secular social level to give the sense of relief from anxiety, acceptance of self and others, which drinking serves to promote.

Less rigorous is the 'total abstainer' who regards abstinence not as morally imperative upon all men but only upon himself as a privilege of religious witness in a particular relationship; it is generally incumbent upon all Mohammedans. St Paul teaches that abstinence may promote fellowship with the scrupulous or provide an example for the weak (I Cor. 8.10–13). It may be expedient on occasion to use our own judgment in foregoing Christian liberty for the sake of others (I Cor. 8.9; Rom. 14.21) but Christ has set us free from the rule of inflexible law (Gal. 5.1,13). Since only God may judge personal motives we must not judge each other (Rom. 14.3). There would be a denial of Christian liberty and a fragmentation of fellowship and evangelism if all Christians had to give way to all minority scruples (I Cor. 10.29–32). All things may be used to further the love which enables Christians to become all things to all men according to their need in every individual context (I Cor. 9.22). Our Lord did not become a total abstainer for the sake of the 'weaker brother'.

St Paul fought for the revelation that man holds to the full the perilous freedom of personal choice and so, as he courageously casts off legalistic reductions of personal responsibility, he comes into position to accept the Holy Spirit's gift of self-control in things which, while permissible in moderation, may be dangerous in excess. Thus he is enabled to assess each human situation in its own right and opportunity for creative action. The teetotaller proclaims obedience to his inflexible law as strength, but, in Pauline teaching, he is in fact the 'weaker brother' himself because he thus 'quenches the Spirit'. So St Peter's visit to Cornelius (Acts 10) illustrates how the Holy Spirit's guidance to share 'unclean' foods and relationships created a new fellowship between Jew and Gentile. The more things that a Christian dares to use in loving identity with others according to their needs rather than preconceived moral requirements, the more will his temperance be creative in its utility. Its proper *milieu* is not the moralistic institution but the fellowship of personal freedom and mutual tolerance in which it becomes possible to make such friends of the 'mammon of unrighteousness' (so designated by the institution) that they can welcome us into 'everlasting habitations'. The 'authority' of Jesus lay in a temperance far above the moralistic distortions which prevented the Pharisees from seeing human situations objectively, so that he could truly enjoy a feast with 'sinners' (Luke 5.29–32) and form redemptive fellowships outside their law.

Teetotalism still illustrates the illogicality of inflexibility in its interpretation of the restrictive demands made by the weak upon the strong, for it alleges that the self-control of the moderate drinker creates the modern drink evil by attracting the weak into immoderation; yet how can Christians share their strength by remaining outside those situations where others may succumb? Obvious abstention for the alcoholic's sake exacerbates his morbid guilt in not only being unable to enjoy his own drinking but in compelling others to be denied their enjoyment too, so he avoids their help. The temperate life is free to explore the full range of human experience and yet is so fortified that no single desire or activity disturbs the balance of the others or the equanimity of the whole. In these conditions wine may still be a gift of God which gladdens man's heart (Ps. 104.15) by relieving his misery (Prov. 31.7).

The writer believes that a valid distinction may be drawn between the use of liquors naturally fermented, where an alcohol content of 13% arrests the action of the yeast, and those scientifically distilled or fortified to an artificially high content; so, while naturally fermented drinks may be acceptable as beverages, the alarming increase in habituation and addiction since distilled liquors became common suggests that they should be controlled like other narcotics. Frequently 'short drinks' are taken with other drugs to quicken their effect. These now include new synthetic drugs and are broadly divided into stimulants ('pep-pills') which cause feelings of energy and alertness, sedatives which quieten nervous agitation, and tranquillizers which are widely used for this 'age of anxiety'. Stimulants can produce unpleasant side-effects and disastrous personality deterioration, and sedatives can undermine health, effort and behaviour; while alleviating psychological problems, they can produce addictions which result in mental breakdowns. Tranquillizers can produce a pitiful habituation and these drugs should never be taken except under medical prescription. Treatment requires teams of highly trained people and new medicines can now allay the distress of drug withdrawal. In all cases of rehabilitation the most important factor is the community attitude. If the community to which the patient returns subjects him to social censure or ostracism, relapse will follow the renewal of his uncertainties about his ability to become a normal member of society.

The controlled use of drugs now presents the new possibility of a scientifically induced 'temperance' – a balancing of the personality by habituation to the appropriate drugs rather than by habits of self-control; some persons have envisaged a chemically promoted heaven on earth where all are content and peaceful through the official issue of 'happiness pills'. It is recognized, however, that such drugs limit the range of creative forms, restrict the quality of human relationships and deny depth and freedom to human fellowship.

Opposing denominational convictions about drink are proving a problem in re-union conversations. Methodist Standing Orders prescribe unfermented communion 'wine' while the Anglican Revised Canon now specifies the fermented juice of the grape. This revision, while clarifying dialogue with the Roman Catholic Church, is a stumbling-block to the Nonconformist Conscience. Dr John Robinson points out in *Liturgy Come to Life* (1964) that the Lord's Supper should begin with the 'Liturgy of the People' when families in the congregation present bread and wine from their own tables to the Minister. Whether the wine is fermented or unfermented depends upon the particular view of each family, so, when the united congregation is able to honour every family's freedom of choice by fully sharing what they have brought for the blessing of God (Rom. 14.3), then this contentious issue will be resolved according to the Christian privileges of freedom and tolerance.

Rigid convictions tend to maintain strong distinctions between 'sacred' and 'secular'. Creative temperance breaks down false antitheses, promoting 'holy-worldliness' rather than 'other-worldliness', fully using all things which promote fellowship. By sacramentalizing them, it corrects situations in which they may become vulnerable to abuse because they are stigmatized as 'secular'. Alcoholic excess has traditionally been used to lift sexual taboos and has tragically contributed to sexual licence. The sacramental use of intoxicating wine has a beneficial significance in relation to its association in excess with so many abuses. The Jewish communities provide ample evidence that the abuse of strong drink is best precluded by sacramentalizing rather than forbidding it. Orthodox Jews bless and use wine on nearly two hundred family occasions each year, yet their incidence of drunkenness and alcoholism is insignificant compared with other ethnic groups and delinquency is particularly low. So the temperate do not refuse any good gift of God but 'drink it new in his Kingdom'.

Temperance movements multiplied from the early nineteenth century. Originally they held in common prohibition from spirits which were then a social curse, but they became more controversial as they advocated teetotalism. The US Temperance Union was formed in

1834, its earliest society dating from 1826, and movements rapidly arose in Ireland, Britain and continental Europe. The Independent Order of Good Templars, founded in New York in 1851, promoting teetotalism and general prohibition, led to the International Order in 1852. In Ireland, from 1838, Father Theobald Mathew's campaign promoted the Roman Catholic Total Abstinence Leagues in Britain and the USA. In Britain the Band of Hope movement, specializing in juvenile education, arose in 1847 while a major political association, the United Kingdom Alliance, was formed in 1852 to promote an electoral will for prohibition. The other European countries were also producing temperance and anti-alcohol societies, including branches of the Swiss Blue Cross movement and of the Women's Christian Temperance Union which, starting from the USA in 1872, spread as far as Australasia. Here temperance organizations first spread from Tasmania in 1832. In the 1860s various denominational committees for temperance began to appear in Britain. The Church of England Temperance Society started as a total abstinence movement in 1862 but was reconstituted to include moderate drinkers as members in 1873 and began to pioneer the treatment of alcoholism as a disease, while the Salvation Army specialized in rescuing the 'skid-row' drunkard. These Church of England, Free Church, Salvation Army and Roman Catholic organizations formed the Temperance Council of the Christian Churches in 1915 using the Church of England Temperance Society's 'dual basis' for membership. Some movements developed as working-men's Benefit and Friendly Societies, such as the Independent Order of Rechabites (Jer. 35) in Manchester in 1835 and the Order of Sons of Temperance in New York in 1842, which grew internationally. There are also associated building, life and car insurance societies which offer special terms to abstainers.

Arnold B. Come, *Temperance – A Christian Approach*, 1964; Herman Levy, *Drink – An Economic and Social Study*, 1951; R. G. McCarthy and E. M. Douglass, *Alcohol and Social Responsibility*, 1949; A. E. Morris, *The Christian Use of Alcoholic Beverages*, 1961.

J. B. HARRISON

Temple, William

William Temple (1881–1944), one of the most outstanding Anglican scholars and churchmen of modern times, was also keenly interested in ethical and social problems. He was Bishop of the industrial diocese of Manchester, 1921–29, then Archbishop of York, 1929–42, and was appointed Archbishop of Canterbury in 1942. His death two years later deprived the Church of a great leader. His theology was in the authentic Anglican tradition, that is to say, on the one side it stressed the incarnational and sacramental teaching of Christianity, while on the other it respected reason, conscience, natural theology and the achievements of science and philosophy. Temple had begun in the idealist philosophical tradition that prevailed in England around 1900, but he eventually developed a 'dialectical realism' which, he believed, gave more adequate recognition to Christianity's recognition of the value of the natural and the material. This philosophy found its fullest statement in his Gifford Lectures, *Nature, Man and God* (1934). What Temple altogether rejected was the division of the world into two spheres, the spiritual and the material: and so he equally rejected both a false spirituality that undervalues the secular, and a short-sighted materialism that is locked up in the immediate concerns of everyday existence. It seemed to him that the incarnational and sacramental principles of the Christian faith invested the material with worth and overcame the separation between spirit and matter. So the Christian must be concerned in realizing his faith in the daily life of the world, its economics and its politics. 'It is in the sacramental view of the universe, both of its material and of its spiritual elements, that there is given hope of making human both politics and economics and of making effectual both faith and love.' Among his specifically ethical writings are *Christianity and the State* (1928), and *Christianity and Social Order* (1942).

Robert Craig, *Social Concern in the Thought of William Temple*, 1963; Joseph F. Fletcher, *William Temple, Twentieth-century Christian*, 1963; F. A. Iremonger, *William Temple, Archbishop of Canterbury*, 1948.

EDITOR

Temptation

The situation where we are attracted to a course of action incompatible with our proper relation to God is well known to the Bible. From Gen. 3, which describes man's first temptation, to Rev. 3.10, which hints at a great final trial at the end of time, the theme of temptation, coming in its varied forms to a Jacob, a David and a Peter, is worked out in detail. And it is clear not only from the temptation narratives but from Luke 22.28 and Heb. 2.18 that the life of Jesus was not exempt from temptation. Indeed the first lesson to be drawn from the Bible on the subject is that almost anything, the ambition of a Jacob, the sexual desire of a David, the cowardice of a Peter, the sufferings of the writer of Ps. 42, the prosperity of the rich fool of the parable (Luke 12.18), the rectitude of the Pharisees and the sense of divine mission of Jesus himself can provide material for temptation.

Gen. 3 contains a penetrating study of temptation. By giving the woman the chance to put him right (Gen. 3.1) the serpent induces in her that state of complacency which is so often a prelude to wrong action. By assuring the couple that they will be as gods (3.5) he appeals to the urge to escape from the limitations of finite existence which is a feature even of innocence (q.v.) and which we have learned, since Kierkegaard, to call dread or *Angst*. By stressing that to be as God is the primal temptation, the Bible makes it clear that sin (q.v.) is not as the evolutionists thought, a relic of the brute. For to be as God is not a temptation primarily of those most at the mercy of their animal passions (though they may seek in surrender to these a temporary release from the uncertainties of human existence). It is rather a temptation of the competent and the well disciplined, the follower of a good cause and the ecclesiastic.

If the Bible is unambiguous about the prevalence and diverse character of temptation, it is less so about its origin. In the OT in particular there is found the thought that temptation is really trial and comes ultimately from God (cf. Deut. 13.3). Abraham and Job are outstanding examples of those whose temptations are interpreted in this way and trial of this kind can even be sought after in Ps. 139.23–24. It should be noted that to the writer of Gen. 3 the serpent was simply the serpent and not the devil of popular theology, a much later conception. Even in the Book of Job Satan is not a proper name, but the name of a functionary, the Satan, who has his proper place in the heavenly court.

In the NT the thought is rather that God does not himself bring about temptation (James 1.13). His part consists in not letting the temptation go too far (I Cor. 10.13). The temptation, if not from the person himself (James 1.14) or from others (I Cor. 15.33), proceeds from Satan, conceived now as an evil personal superhuman being (Mark 1.13; Luke 22.31). This raises the question whether the Christian view of temptation implies belief in a more than human tempter. Such a figure appears in the teaching of Jesus and belief in him plays a leading part in the religious life, for example, of Luther, though by the eighteenth century he is no longer taken so seriously (Burns, in his *Address to the Deil*, thinks of him not without humour and compassion). It is interesting that the twentieth century which in its third and fourth decades saw something like an apocalypse of evil, shows little sign of revived belief in a personal devil. This is perhaps in some measure due to realization that in the history of the Church belief in evil spirits has played an unhappy part in witchcraft hunts and in the cruel and improper treatment of mental illness. The rise of modern psychiatry coincides with abandonment of belief in demonic possession. This does not mean that the concept of a devil is devoid of content. On the contrary, it is, so to speak, a limiting concept, bringing out the fact that man needs to be tempted before he sins, whereas the mythological figure of the devil is that of a being who, as it were, sins spontaneously.

The only account we have of Jesus being tempted is the scene in the wilderness and perhaps also that laid in the garden of Gethsemane. But Luke 22.28 speaks of temptation as a continuing feature in his life and Heb. 2.18 links it with his sufferings. As McLeod Campbell reminds us, not the least of these sufferings must have sprung from the fact that loving both God and man with a perfect love, he found the two estranged from each other. To love two parties at variance with one another inevitably involves suffering in proportion to the purity of the love. Did the temptation then lie for Jesus in reducing the suffering by loving God or man with a love less perfect? It may not be irreverent to find in the two words from the cross, 'Father into thy hands I commit my spirit' (Luke 23.46) and 'Father, forgive them; for they know not what they do' (Luke 23.34), the triumphal outcome of the supreme trial of Jesus' love of God and man.

IAN HENDERSON

Temptation of Jesus

The temptation narrative is found only in Matt. 4.1–11 and Luke 4.1–13 although Mark 1.12–13 also refers briefly to a period of testing following Jesus' baptism. Except for a reversal in the order of the second and third temptations, variations between the Matthean and Lucan accounts are minor.

While the details of the story represent the work of early Christians, it seems probable that the narrative had its origin in Jesus' own account of an inward, spiritual struggle which he faced shortly after his baptism and reflects in dramatic and symbolic language his wrestling with the implications of his vocation. Whatever his own conception of his vocation may have been at the beginning of his ministry, the early Church acclaimed Jesus as the Messiah, and it interpreted his decision about his vocation as essentially a decision concerning the manner in which he should fulfil the messianic role.

The first temptation, according to both Matthew and Luke, took place while Jesus was in a state of intense hunger, resulting from a long period of fasting. Under such circumstances the devil urged him to use his miraculous power to turn stones into bread, thus enabling him to satisfy his own immediate need and also to gain a popular following by giving the hungry masses bread. Jesus rejected this prompting of the devil as a temptation to use his power selfishly and also to confuse man's true good with the satisfaction of physical hunger alone.

According to Matthew, the second temptation consisted of the subtle suggestion that Jesus demand a sign that he was indeed the Son of God by casting himself down from the pinnacle of the Temple, thus compelling God to intervene with a miracle in his behalf. As proof that God would not permit the Messiah to be harmed the devil cited the LXX text of Ps. 91.11–12, interpreting the latter as a messianic prediction. Not only would such a dramatic rescue remove any lurking doubt which Jesus might have concerning his own mission, but it would likewise cause the crowds to accept him as the Messiah. But Jesus answered Satan with the reply that man does not have the right to put God's will and promises to such a test; man is summoned to trust God unconditionally and to obey him without first demanding proof of God's power and providence.

Finally, again following the order in Matthew, Jesus was tempted in the third place to be a political Messiah. The devil, who was believed in rabbinic and early Christian circles to have the kingdoms of this earth in his power, promised to deliver them to Jesus if the latter would only bow down and worship him. If Jesus would use his power and divine favour as the Messiah to overthrow the Roman rule and restore Israel to national independence and glory, he would quickly gain a popular following. But Jesus rejected this temptation to seek an easy, popular way to fulfil his messiahship as a form of self-will and idolatry. In his reply to Satan he singled out the central requirement of Judaism, namely, that man shall worship and serve the God of Israel and him alone.

E. CLINTON GARDNER

Ten Commandments.
see Decalogue.

Tertullian

The first writer of Christian theology in Latin, Tertullian (Q. Septimius Florens Tertullianus, *c.* 160–*c.* 220) was a lawyer by profession, a pagan by birth, and a Christian by a relatively late (*c.* 195) conversion. His Christian life was spent in Carthage, the place of his education, where he may have become a presbyter, and where he composed a notable series of apologetic, dogmatic and moral tracts whose influence on western Christian thought has been deep and lasting. His later works (after *c.* 202) reflect his conversion to the tenets of the Montanist sect, whose moral strictness he found attractive.

Tertullian the moralist is indebted, as were most of his Christian contemporaries, to the ethical teaching of the Stoics. This fact is clear not merely from the ethical terminology which he frequently employs, but also from his insistence upon 'nature' and 'reason' as sources for ethical norms. Nevertheless it is always to Scripture that he turns for definitive formulations of moral law, and it is the personal will of God as legislator which he sees reflected in the

dictates of nature and reason. In the last resort, the good, for Tertullian, is simply what God commands; and the commandment of God is sufficiently revealed in that 'discipline', that way of belief and life, which Christ taught to his Apostles and the Apostles in turn handed on to the churches. The vocation of the man who has received the grace of forgiveness in baptism is to keep this discipline in separation from the world, and thus to maintain himself in the favour of God against the impending day of doom and judgment.

The keynote of Tertullian's moral teaching, even before the time of his conversion to Montanism, is thus a puritan rigorism in which there seems to be almost no admixture of the mystical interest which informed the ethic of his younger contemporary Origen. The Christian believer has been rescued from the dominion of Satan and his angels, and through the mercy of God in Christ has been received into a community where the true will of God is known and may be served. But continuance in this state depends upon entire dedication to observing the precepts of the Lord. Hence the believer must understand himself as one set apart from, and hostile to, the world around him. He is called to abstain not merely from the world's pleasures, idolatries, and frivolities, but from much of its ordinary business as well – even though this policy should entail serious economic or social inconvenience. His life is to be one of penance, self-discipline and unending watchfulness, governed by the acknowledgment that nothing is 'indifferent': whatever is not of God is Satan's.

Tertullian realizes that lapses from righteousness are inevitable; and for minor lapses the believer may make acceptable satisfaction to God by fasting and other acts of penitence. But in the case of major sins, which require public confession, penance and formal reconciliation to the Church, Tertullian acknowledges the possibility of only one opportunity of forgiveness after baptism; and in his Montanist period he withdrew even this concession to weakness. Tertullian's moralism and perfectionism influenced later North African movements based on the ideal of a 'pure' church.

R. A. NORRIS, JR

Theft. *see* Property, Ethics of.

Theocracy

Theocracy is domination of the civil power by the ecclesiastical. *See* **Church and State.**

Theological Virtues

The three theological virtues are faith, hope and love (or charity). These three are, of course, mentioned by St Paul in I Cor. 13.13. Strictly speaking, they are not virtues in the narrower sense, but may be thought of as introducing a new dimension into the moral life with its natural virtues – the dimension of grace, based on God's action on human life. *See* **Cardinal Virtues; Faith; Hope; Love; Virtue.**

Thomas Aquinas, Ethics of St

This is the most widely taught type of moral philosophy in Roman Catholic colleges and centres of advanced studies. St Thomas (1224–1274) was a south Italian who studied liberal arts at the Imperial University of Naples, entered the Order of Preachers (Dominicans) about 1243, and took the degree of Master in Theology at the University of Paris in 1256. As professor of theology at the Universities of Paris and Naples, he made abundant use of the then newly-available Latin translations of Aristotle's philosophic works, including the *Nicomachean Ethics.* Perhaps the only purely ethical work produced by Aquinas is his lengthy commentary on this Aristotelian treatise; it is a Latin exposition (written in the 1260s) in which there is very little effort on the part of the commentator to introduce Christian views. Theological treatises in the moral field include: *Scriptum in Libros IV Sententiarum* (Bks. II and III), *Summa contra Gentiles* (Bk. III), *Quaestiones Disputatae de Malo* and *de Virtutibus,* and the *Summa Theologiae* (Part II).

If we distinguish ethics from moral theology (as most Thomists do), saying that ethics uses naturally known facts and conclusions about man's moral life while moral theology adds items of religious faith from divine revelation, then the ethics of Aquinas will obviously be something less than his complete picture of moral science. St Thomas would say that philosophical ethics should be acceptable to all men irrespective of their religious commitments, whereas moral theology would vary from one sect to another. In general, Aquinas' ethics may be viewed as a self-realization theory with emphasis on the unified teleology of human activity. The moral agent is considered capable of performing certain actions that are voluntary (at least partly known and controlled by the agent himself) and so he is responsible for them. Such voluntary activities are judged good when they accord with 'right reason', that is, when they are appraised as in keeping with his own nature as a man in the concrete circumstances of activity. When voluntary actions are judged unfitting, or unreasonable, they are morally evil. Repeated good action develops good moral habits (virtues) and perfects the agent, bringing him closer to the knowledge and love of the Perfect Good (God), which is the final goal of his moral life. (In his moral theology, St Thomas describes this ultimate end in terms of the beatific vision of God in heaven.) Conversely, immoral actions tend to deter man from the attainment of his ultimate end. Judgments as to the moral good or evil of universal types of activity (for example, almsgiving, controlling one's temper, telling lies, harming other persons) constitute the conclusions of Thomistic ethics. 'Almsgiving is of itself a good kind of action' is such an ethical judgment. Obviously, this cannot mean that every act of giving alms is morally approvable: the concrete circumstances of an action (including the agent's purpose, the time, place and manner in which the act is performed) modify the moral quality of the generic action. Unreasonable circumstances may make a typically good act to be concretely immoral but appropriate circumstances cannot make a generically bad action to be good; they can render it less evil, however.

Moral judgment on one's own concrete action (not a universal but a singular judgment) is identified as moral conscience. Such conscience is the agent's immediate guide to good moral action. Provided one has such a conscience, that is, provided a person is able to judge that this act is now to be done (or not), then one is assured of good activity by acting in accord with conscience. This is equivalent to saying that everyone should do what he honestly thinks to be best on any given occasion. If he does not know what to think, then he has no conscience in the matter and is not able to direct his actions rationally. Thomistic ethics does not make conscience a special power or moral sense; nor is conscience the source of general rules of living; it is the individual application of previously known rules to one's own moral problem.

God's wisdom, or eternal law, is viewed by Aquinas as the ultimate source of the distinction between moral good and evil. In some imperfect way, man comes to know part of that eternal law when he reasons to appropriate conclusions in ethics. This partial understanding of God's law is 'natural'; it is available to anyone, whatever his religious beliefs or unbelief may be. This quite ordinary participation in eternal law by mankind is called natural moral law. There is nothing mysterious about the Thomistic theory of natural law: men are able to make certain universal judgments concerning morality, on the basis of their regular experience and intelligence. The principle of synderesis (moral insight): 'Do good and avoid evil' is a primary rule of moral reasoning but many present-day Thomists interpret it formally, insisting that more specific and practical rules must be derived from personal experience and the data of various sciences. The imperative, 'Do no injury to others', is an example of a naturally known moral law. While all men are thought to have sufficient quasi-instinctive knowledge of morality to make their own personal decisions, expertness in ethical reasoning would be a skill developed by a few people after long study.

Four areas of ethical problematics are distinguished: (1) problems of achieving rightness in interpersonal relations (the field of justice); (2) problems of moderating sense desires (temperance); (3) problems of strengthening emotional responses to physical dangers and emergencies (fortitude); and (4) problems of practical reasoning (prudence). In moral theology, there are the additional areas of faith, hope and charity. This division of the material content of morality under the virtues is typical of Aquinas' own thought; some modern Thomists use other divisions, such as the Suarezian three duties: to God, to other men, and to self.

In addition to general ethical theory, there is a second part of Thomistic ethics, usually called applied or special ethics. Here more specific and definite judgments concerning typical problems are attempted. While the broad character of these moral views will be found basically similar to those of other Christian ethicians (condemnation of murder, theft, sexual promiscuity, jealousy, uncharitable feelings and actions – approval of respect for the divinity and parents, assistance to other persons, brotherly love, etc.), there are certain judgments made by Thomists that are distinctive. Certain kinds of human activity are regarded as evil in themselves: telling lies is probably the most notorious instance. Lying is not defined as a deception of other persons but as an unreasonable use of significant expression in conflict with one's inner conviction (*locutio contra mentem*). This voluntary abuse of the capacity to communicate thought is considered evil, quite apart from its influence on others. Similarly, various sexual irregularities are condemned, primarily as forms of intemperance and only secondarily as offences under justice. Thomistic thinking on some of these questions may appear somewhat rigid but two points mitigate this apparent dogmatism. First, these judgments apply to species of actions and are still in the form of somewhat universal rules: concrete actions are not judged by ethics but by conscience. Second, the Thomist tries to define lying, or sexual immorality, or other such things, in a very exact way – thereby hoping to exclude borderline cases (white lies, non-voluntary sexual aberrations, etc.) which other schools of ethics may include under these categories. Disapproval of artificial contraception (the use of drugs or physical devices which permit sexual union but prevent conception) and of perfect divorce (breaking of the matrimonial bond with permission to remarry) falls partly into this same pattern. Both contraception and divorce seem to the Thomist to run counter to the basic purpose of procreative action and marriage. On the other hand, there are Thomistic views on other special problems (gambling, the use of intoxicants) which may appear quite permissive.

Contemporary Thomism is by no means a monolithic discipline. Recent controversies have been conducted concerning: whether man's ultimate end is naturally knowable or not (O'Connor, Pegis, Brisebois); whether ethics should be subalternated to moral theology (Maritain, Von Hildebrand, Ramirez, Gauthier); whether obligation is central in ethics (MacGuigan, Stevens); whether the common or the personal good is most important (Eschmann, de Koninck); and whether value theory is adaptable to Thomistic ethics (Ward, de Finance, Fagothey, Gilson).

While there is no complete critical edition of the Latin works, reliable printings of most can be obtained from Casa Editrice Marietti, Turin, Italy. Besides the *Summa Theologica*, tr. by the English Dominicans, 22 vols., 1912–36 (frequently reprinted), there are in English: *Commentary on the Nicomachean Ethics*, tr. by C. I. Litzinger, 2 vols., 1964; *The Virtues in General*, tr. by J. P. Reid, 1951; *On the Truth of the Catholic Faith* (*Summa contra Gentiles*), Bk. III, tr. by V. J. Bourke, 2 vols., 1956. Consult also: V. Bourke, *Ethics*, 1951; A. D. Sertillanges, *La philosophie morale de s. Thomas d'Aquin*, 1946; M. Wittmann, *Die Ethik des hl. Thomas von Aquin*, 1933; *PACPA*, XXXI (1957) containing many papers on ethics, notably those of G. P. Klubertanz and I. T. Eschmann.

VERNON J. BOURKE

Tillich, Paul Johannes

Tillich (1886–1965) rejects theological ethics as a separate theological enterprise. Ethics as such involves an analysis of the moral function and a judgment upon its changing contents in view of this analysis. Theological ethics implies, according to Tillich, a religious determination of moral principles. It issues in the imposition of so-called 'divine commands' on human behaviour. Now the subjection of moral inquiry to external religious authority is a form of heteronomy, and must, therefore, be denied. Ethics, he insists, is a part of philosophy, and should be treated accordingly.

Hence, if a theologian speaks of morality and the moral imperative, he does so as a 'philosophical ethicist'. And the weight of his arguments depends upon their experiential and rational cogency, not upon his theological assertions.

Tillich's philosophical ethics proceed on two assumptions: the ultimate character of the moral form (the sense of 'oughtness'), and the relative character of all moral content. Concrete ethical norms are determined by cultural, social and personal factors, that is, by the contingencies of time and space. But the experience of the moral imperative is absolute. It is, in fact, the distinguishing feature of man as person.

The source of the moral imperative is, in Tillich's view, man's *essential* being – which, from a theological standpoint, may be termed 'the will of God' for man. This accounts for its unconditional seriousness, its intrinsically religious quality. It contrasts man's true nature with his actual being, and commands him to fulfil his created potentiality. The ultimacy of this demand is experienced through the conscience.

It follows that man's knowledge of ethical value derives from his knowledge of his essential or created nature. But how can existential man discover his essential nature? In two complementary ways: the intuitive and the experiential. Intuitively, man sees the contrast between what he is and what he ought to be. But since this intuition is open to error and distortion, he must subject it to the wisdom of experience, both individual and collective. He should be especially attentive to the experiences embodied in the ethical traditions of the past.

What norms or principles of moral action issue from knowledge of man's essential nature? Just one, according to Tillich: love, which includes and transcends both power and justice. Such love is not merely an emotional state, but is 'the moving power of life'. 'Life', in Tillich's terms, 'is being in actuality', and love is its moving force.

Because of its ontological status, love is the ultimate principle of moral action. Love is one, but it manifests itself in a hierarchy of 'qualities': in *epithumia* – the drive towards sensual fulfilment; in *eros* – the desire for reunion with the good, the true, and the beautiful; in *philia* – the person-to-person relationship between equals; and in *agape* – the all-inclusive and self-transcending quality of love.

Love as the ultimate ethical principle relates to both power and justice, also grounded in being as such. Power is the power of being, the dynamic self-affirmation of life in spite of that which resists it. And 'love is the foundation, not the negation, of power'. The dynamics of love and the dynamics of power are the same: reunion overcoming separation, being overcoming non-being.

Further, love relates to justice as its vital principle. Justice, as the form in and through which the power of being actualizes itself, '... must include both the separation without which there is no love, and the reunion in which love is realized.' Thus, love is immanent in justice, as justice is immanent in power.

In God as being-itself, love, power and justice are essentially united, although not identical. There remains a tension between love and power, even in the divine. And this is reflected in physical and moral evil. The tension between love and justice in the divine is ultimately resolved in the atonement: 'the Cross of Christ is the symbol of the divine love, participating in the destruction into which it throws him who acts against love.'

It is noteworthy, in conclusion, that Tillich's ontological analysis follows the same dialectical method developed in Hegel's early writings. Both describe life – human and divine – in terms of the dynamics of separation and reunion. Both interpret human existence as the process whereby love, power and justice become one, as in the divine.

Paul Tillich, *Love, Power and Justice*, 1954; *Morality and Beyond*, 1961; *The Protestant Era*, 1948, Chaps. IX and X.

WILLIAM B. GREEN

Tolerance

Tolerance is not valuable in itself; its value lies in the doctrines of God and man it expresses and the type of community it supports. Tolerance is not the creed of those who hold that it does not matter what a man believes as long as he goes his way without molesting others. In politics tolerance means that the government in power allows minority groups to hold political beliefs contrary to the government's without their being deliberately submitted to open violence or hidden coercion. In religion, tolerance means a refusal to use violence or coercion to banish or convert those of different religion or of no religion at all. *See* **Persecution and Toleration.** In the life of the Church tolerance means accepting that Christian doctrine is descriptive rather than definitive and consequently there is room for differences within limits in doctrinal explanations. Intolerance in politics is a result of the belief in one-party government and leads to the stamping out of all detected opposition. Intolerance in religion is seen in the determined attempt to convert people at any cost and is also seen as a result of believing that doctrines are absolute, definitive statements which must not be questioned.

Tolerance is not the refusal to use power but a resolution to use it in the interests of truth, justice and mercy. Intolerance has no regard for truth, justice and mercy and thus misuses power. No man or institution can be completely and consistently tolerant but the sustained attempts to achieve tolerance enrich the whole human community. In some cases people tolerate anything but intolerance; in other cases men have no concern for either tolerance or intolerance because they do not believe in human freedom.

The Christian is to be tolerant towards the arts and sciences, respecting artists and scientists for their perception and expressions of truth. Therefore he does not deride works of art he cannot appreciate or decry scientific discoveries as dangerous or of no immediate usefulness. Those who are intolerant towards the arts and science usually only want entertainment or propaganda from the arts and amenities from the sciences.

R. E. C. BROWNE

Toleration. *see* Persecution and Toleration.

Total Abstinence. *see* Temperance and Temperance Movements.

Total Depravity

The confidence in reason which was a feature of the Renaissance has been undermined by Freud and Marx as well as by some elements in the teaching of Barth. Reason, so far from being what Platonism took it to be, something uncorrupted by evil, can deteriorate into rationalization. If the doctrine of total depravity simply meant that every part of man is affected by sin, it would be accepted in fairly wide circles today. But the doctrine goes much further and holds that there is no good in man at all, that every part of him is *entirely* corrupted. As the Westminster Confession puts it (Chap. VI), Adam and Eve at the Fall became 'Wholly defiled in all the faculties and parts of soul and body' and from this original corruption we are 'utterly indisposed, disabled and made opposite to all good, and wholly inclined to all evil'.

How did such a doctrine come to be held? One reason is that the Bible says some fairly pungent things about the depravity of the human heart. 'The heart is deceitful above all things and desperately corrupt' (Jer. 17.9). 'Behold I was brought forth in iniquity and in sin did my mother conceive me' (Ps. 51.5). 'For I know that nothing good dwells within me' (Rom. 7.18). But it is one thing to take a realistic and even a dark view of human nature and another to hold the doctrine of *total* depravity. If all men are totally bad then there is no difference between the good and the bad. Jesus, however, draws such a distinction in at least three places, Matt. 5.45; 13.49; 25.37 and 46. St Paul does the same in Rom. 13. It should be noted also that even when Jesus and St Paul are emphasizing the basic evil in life, they do not hold that it excludes manifestations of good (cf. Matt. 7.11 and Rom. 7.18). Another reason for acceptance of the doctrine has been the evangelical emphasis that we are saved by the grace of God and not by our own merits. But to say that our good actions are irrelevant for our salvation is not to say that we do not do any good actions.

IAN HENDERSON

Totalitarian State. *see* Fascism; State.

Transference

Transference is the term employed technically in psychoanalysis (q.v.) for that phase in therapy in which the patient experiences impulses or feelings in relation to the therapist which have their origin in earlier relationships with other significant persons in the patient's life. It is as if the analyst temporarily 'becomes' the father, mother, brother, wife, employer, etc., of the patient and is reacted to accordingly. The analyst permits this transfer in order to assist the patient to explore, understand, and come to terms with, the original impulses and feelings. In successful analysis, these transferences are later withdrawn and relationship to the analyst adjusts on a realistic basis. The name *Counter-transference* is given to the therapist's irrational and unconscious reactions to the patient, arising from the therapist's own personal psychic needs and problems. Transference continues to occupy a central role in psychoanalytic therapy and requires expert handling if it is to prove constructive. Karl Menninger in his *Theory of Psychoanalytic Technique* (1958) sets out contemporary Freudian approaches to transference.

In other forms of psychotherapy the role of transference varies in importance. Carl Jung regards it as an inevitable feature of every thorough analysis but it is peripheral and minimized in the 'client-centred therapy' of Carl Rogers. Some other therapists agree with Freud and Jung on the importance of transference but hold alternative views as to how its analysis results in the 'cure' of the patient.

The main significance of transference for ethics lies in its dramatic demonstration of the fact that people react to other persons and to things on bases which are not necessarily determined by the actual characteristics of those other persons or things. An example of this is the carrying over of hostility or ambivalence originally felt in relation to the father (but never adequately worked through) to other persons encountered later in life who also occupy positions of authority, for example, teachers, police, employers, etc. Attitudes towards God may also be distorted by unrecognized and unresolved conflicts with significant human beings. Many irrational prejudices (e.g., against people of a certain hair colour) may also be traced to this perseverance of feelings and attitudes which have been repressed into the unconscious (q.v.) but which have not thereby been rendered inactive. Dealing with the symptomatic behaviour alone is unlikely to produce any finally effective results.

GRAEME M. GRIFFIN

Troeltsch, Ernst

Ernst Troeltsch (1865–1923), German theologian and philosopher of history and culture, was born near Augsburg and taught successively in the universities of Göttingen, Bonn, Heidelberg and Berlin. His work was dominated by an interest in history, but in a very different way from the interest in history shown by his contemporaries of the Ritschlian school.

Whereas the latter tended to isolate the historical events at the origin of the Christian faith, Troeltsch sought to set them in the whole context of history and to relate them to the needs and situations of the present. His understanding of history was strongly influenced by the ideas of Dilthey, who had sharply distinguished between the human sciences (including history) and the natural sciences, and between the connections of events in the human and natural spheres. Troeltsch himself taught that the 'psychological causality' operative in history is capable of creating novelty in a manner impossible for natural causality. Since he considered Christianity as a phenomenon within the total context of history, Troeltsch tended towards relativism and to the denial of the so-called 'absolute' claim of Christianity, as a uniquely exclusive revelation of God. But, like Weber (q.v.), Troeltsch was determinedly anti-Marxist, and refused to see in Christianity or in religion generally merely a product of cultural and social forces. Religion has its own autonomy, and can contribute to the shaping of a culture. On the other hand, the relation is a reciprocal one, and a religion bears the marks of cultural influences. Troeltsch is perhaps best known for his analysis of the different types of Christian organization, on the basis of their attitudes towards the cultural environment. He distinguished three such types: the church-type, the sect-type and the mystical-type. Because of his awareness of the close ties between religion and secular culture, Troeltsch was strongly critical of the traditional Lutheran insistence on the separation of civil and ecclesiastical spheres, the things of Caesar and the things of God, the law and the gospel. He rightly saw the baneful consequences for Germany of this tradition. Although Troeltsch's theological views became unpopular during the Barthian ascendancy, he continues to have a strong influence on Christian social ethics, especially in the USA, where his views were taken up and developed by H. Richard Niebuhr and others. His numerous writings are collected in the four volumes of the *Gesammelte Schriften* (1912–25). His most important book for social ethics is his *The Social Teaching of the Christian Churches*, originally written in 1912 and translated into English in 1931.

EDITOR

Truth and Truthfulness

The heart of the matter is found in Eph. 4.15 where Christians are told to speak the truth *in love*. Truthfulness is the proper use before God of his gift of speech; but it must be in love. That is to say that we are not called upon to utter the whole truth at all times and to all and sundry without further reflection. There are truths better left unsaid; not to speak is not necessarily to sin against truth. Or on occasion part of the truth may be better withheld. Only those who are devoted to the truth will have the sensitivity to know when and how much of the truth to speak. Otherwise we become sly. In the NT it is the epistle of James which stresses most fully the right use of the tongue and condemns most strongly its misuse (cf. 3.2,6), but in doing so it only echoes Matt. 12.36 f. *See* **Lying.**

The question of professional secrets is involved in that of speaking the truth. Put briefly, what is known solely in such a capacity should not be revealed without the consent of the person concerned. The supreme example of this is the confessional. For a fuller treatment of this point works of pastoral theology should be consulted. The legal position varies in different countries. In some, professional secrecy is explicitly safeguarded, in others it is not. In the latter it may nevertheless in fact be respected. In any event the moral duty of the person concerned is to preserve his professional secrecy.

RONALD PRESTON

Tutiorism

Tutiorism or rigorism is that system in moral theology which holds that in all cases of doubt, the 'safer' course must be followed, or, in other words, that 'when in doubt, obey the law no matter how probable it may be that the law does not apply in this case'. The only exception allowed is where the probability that the law does not apply amounts to a moral certainty. But this only amounts to 'never disobey a law unless you are certain that the law has ceased to exist or does not apply'. The system has always held an appeal for persons of Puritan outlook and of scrupulous conscience. Its main weakness is that it encourages scrupulosity and inhibits action. For if we may not act until we are sure that the act is legitimate, until all our doubts however slender have been removed, often we shall never act at all: and often so not to act will be, in truth, a neglect of duty.

R. C. MORTIMER

Two Realms

Luther's social ethic tries to re-establish the theological co-ordination of civil and religious authority which had been advocated in St Augustine's *City of God* prior to the late mediaeval church's programme of subordinating the civil to the ecclesiastical realm.

The uniqueness of Luther's formulation lies in his rejection of any kind of biblical-philosophical synthesis, as with Plato in Augustine or with Aristotle in Thomas. Instead he interprets the totality of human experience within the strictly biblical categories of God's twofold rule of mankind through his law as Creator and through his gospel as Redeemer. Ultimately, Luther's doctrine of the 'two realms' is grounded firmly in the Pauline eschatology of the 'two ages' (*aeons*) in Adam and in Christ (Rom. 5).

Luther wrote in *Secular Authority: To What Extent It Ought to be Obeyed* (1523, XI, pp. 249 f.):

> We must divide all the children of Adam into two classes; the first belong to the kingdom of God, the second to the kingdom of the world. Those belonging to the kingdom of God are all true believers in Christ and are subject to Christ and the gospel of the kingdom.... All who are not Christians belong to the kingdom of the world and are under the law. Since few believe and still fewer live a Christian life, do not resist evil, and themselves do no evil, God has provided for non-Christians a different government outside the Christian estate and God's kingdom, and has subjected them to the sword.... For this reason the two kingdoms must be sharply distinguished, and both permitted to remain; the one to produce piety, the other to bring about external peace and prevent evil deeds; neither is sufficient in the world without the other.

The key points in Luther's position are these: (1) God is the Lord of both kingdoms, although he rules each by different means (law and gospel) for different ends (peace and piety); (2) every Christian lives in both kingdoms simultaneously – in the kingdom of God insofar as he is righteous, and in the kingdom of the world insofar as he is sinful; (3) the two kingdoms are to be sharply distinguished from one another, which means that the realms of law and gospel are to be neither separated (in secularism) nor equated (in clericalism). Both kingdoms should be permitted to coexist in harmonious interaction and co-ordination as complementary expressions of the triune God's creative and redemptive activity among men.

Through this doctrine of God's 'two realms', or better, 'twofold reign', Luther reaffirmed the 'sacred secularity' of the ordinary tasks of the common life as those which best meet our neighbours' needs in the service of Christ.

WILLIAM H. LAZARETH

Unconscious

Because of the work of Sigmund Freud it is now widely accepted that there are within the person unconscious mental processes which the individual person is not aware of and which he cannot consciously control. These unconscious processes are nevertheless potent factors in determining attitudes, feelings and behaviour. Unconscious wishes and desires may thwart or frustrate conscious actions or intentions, may produce 'irrational' feelings of guilt (q.v.), ambivalence, dissatisfaction, etc., and may precipitate conflicts leading to mental illness. Prior to Freud's time the existence of the unconscious was doubted by most psychologists and philosophers but this is no longer true.

In Freud's view, the contents of the unconscious consist of repressed material (*see* **Repression**) and material relating to the original, instinctual, primitive and infantile elements of psychic life. These contents obey their own laws and adopt their own modes of expression. The unconscious contents cannot voluntarily be brought into consciousness – the acknowledgment of their presence would conflict too painfully with the individual's socially learned ideas of what is good, proper or acceptable. Contents temporarily forgotten, but which can be recalled into consciousness, are termed preconscious. The unconscious repressed contents may only enter, or re-enter, consciousness with the sort of assistance available in psychotherapy, or in disguised or distorted form either in pathological symptoms or in the more normal phenomena of dreams, wit, slips of the tongue, etc. The two basic mechanisms which operate in the unconscious are condensation and displacement. *See* S. Freud, *A General Introduction to Psychoanalysis*, rev. edn., 1920; *The Psychopathology of Everyday Life*, 1904.

Most, but not all, contemporary theories of the unconscious are based on the Freudian model with modifications in detail. One significant addition has been suggested by Carl Jung, who claims that as well as those contents which derive from the personal life-experiences of the individual, there is also a stratum of the unconscious which is held in common by persons of the same tribe, race or culture. This 'collective unconscious' forms part of a living deposit of all human experience right back to the remotest beginnings. The powerful images which arise from the collective unconscious (called archetypal images) recur widely in religions, mythologies, folk-lore and in individual dreams. These images tend to cluster around a limited number of themes concerning the basic power of life, the development of wholeness, salvation, etc. In Jung's view, the unconscious tends to act as a corrective to one-sidedness or imbalance in conscious psychic life. *See* C. G. Jung, *Two Essays on Analytical Psychology*, 1928; *Psychology and Religion*, 1938. *See also* **Defence Mechanism; Dreams; Ego; Id; Inhibition; Instincts; Oedipus Complex; Psychoanalysis; Repression; Superego; Transference.**

GRAEME M. GRIFFIN

Underdeveloped Countries

Countries are considered underdeveloped when they exhibit low standards of living due to lack of modern industrial production. While this cannot strictly be applied to some exceptional cases, a yardstick often used is an annual per capita production of less than £70 or $200. Economic underdevelopment is also reflected in psychological, political and social lags. In a worldwide stirring of expectations, less privileged areas are attempting to complete in decades the industrial, democratic and racial revolutions which required centuries in other lands.

On grounds of self-interest, unless more fortunate nations move with the vanguard of world revolution, they may be trampled under foot by it. On deeper levels, Christian concern should move us to become allies of the worthy aspirations of mankind. Instead of trying to preserve privilege by policies of delay, we ought to champion responsible movements for change and more generously provide technical assistance and economic aid.

The Bible stresses the particular responsibility of the privileged. 'Every one to whom much is given, of him will much be required' (Luke 12.48). The rich and powerful are strictly required to discharge a stewardship unlimited by rationalization.

The underprivileged on the other hand have a particular claim to the response of love. Service is to be directed especially towards those in unusual need. In meeting human want the Christian is called even beyond the standards of mutuality. The needs of the neighbour are to be given priority, when necessary, to the point of sacrifice.

Support for underdeveloped areas is further reinforced by the all-inclusive nature of Christian love which allows no major distinction between the near-neighbour and the far-neighbour. The distinction which both Augustine and Aquinas made has diminishing importance. Modern communication allows transferring funds to other continents with little more loss than if they were used at home. Arguments we commonly use to justify the use of resources in discharging our vocations in family and community, also apply to the right of parents and citizens in poorer lands to the resources necessary to discharge their similar vocations. It is impossible to justify unnecessary luxury in some places while poverty exists in so many places. A certain priority may still be given to genuine needs near at hand, but this becomes less convincing in the face of such impressive needs as exist in underdeveloped areas. *See* **Economic Aid; Imperialism.**

HARVEY SEIFERT

United Nations

The UN represents a major beginning stage in the development of world organization. Comparatively young and disparately supported, it has nevertheless compiled an impressive record.

As a continuing conference and a forum for world opinion it exposes the policies of nations to steady challenge and debate. It makes possible limited but significant collective action against threats to peace. It has contributed to the emancipation of colonial areas and erected international standards for conduct, as the Universal Declaration of Human Rights. The specialized agencies related to the Economic and Social Council co-ordinate and supplement activities of the nations for human welfare. Resources from many lands have been pooled on such varied matters as methods of basic education, research in fish farming, vaccination of children and economic assistance. The UN is the world's best political hope for substituting the conference table for the battlefield, and for mobilizing the earth's resources for the service of humanity.

There are still serious weaknesses in the UN. Important gaps exist in membership and support. The proper weighting of votes and the misuse of the veto constitute problems. Threatening acts by great powers cannot be controlled. International actions are still infected by tensions between existing national power structures. The purposes and programmes of the UN often lack the enthusiastic support of governments and populations.

The prestige and effectiveness of the UN would be considerably improved if nations turned to it more consistently. Many citizens still consider it virtue to stand aside from world community in an egoistic isolationism. Governments often conduct the diplomacy of tomorrow with the methods of yesterday. Comparative neglect of the UN is increasingly perilous. The UN ought to be regarded not only as a symbol of our faith, but also as a pattern for our practice, making full use of its actualities as one way to develop its potentialities. *See* **World Government.**

HARVEY SEIFERT

Urbanization. *see* Contemporary Society.

Usury and Interest

The charging of interest by Jews to their own people was forbidden by the Law (Ex. 22.25; Deut. 23.19–20). In the early Church it gradually came to be regarded as unlawful and was formally condemned by the Third Lateran Council (1179), on the basis of Aristotle's argument about the barren nature of money.

The mediaeval attitude to usury was related to the doctrine of the just price. The essence of this was that in any transaction justice demanded an equivalent return by the buyer to the seller. In the contract of mutuum, or loan, where the money lent became the property of the borrower, subject to the obligation to return an equal amount, it was held that the mere passage of time did not reduce the value of the money and hence gave rise to no claim for more than repayment of the principal. Interest could, however, be justified where there was a cessant gain or an emergent loss to the lender, where he forewent a gain or suffered a loss through the loan, for which compensation should fairly be paid. In practice, as commerce developed in later mediaeval and early modern times, most actual forms of interest payment in business came to be so justified, though the condemnation of usury as such continued to be maintained by writers in the Scholastic tradition.

Modern economic thought sees the reason for interest both in the greater productive power which can be achieved when resources are diverted from consumption and used for investment, and in the need to provide an inducement to income receivers to abstain from consumption and forego control of liquid resources, to make them available to investors. It is also seen as an essential price, allocating a limited supply of capital between alternative uses. An investment can be regarded as worth making if it promises a return that equals the current market rate of interest, and some equivalent to a notional interest rate is used in investment calculations even in Communist economies.

Modern Christian thinking tends to accept these pragmatic justifications for this as for other cases of the working of the market system, though in some circles the influence of the traditional fear of usury can still be seen, for instance, in the attraction of 'social credit' theories for certain schools of Christian thought.

JOHN F. SLEEMAN

Utilitarianism

Utilitarianism is the name given to those moral theories which seek for moral obligations an end and ground outside themselves by which alone they are justified, or which, after the manner of Hume and Shaftesbury, subordinate all virtues (including justice) to that of a disciplined pursuit of the maximum human happiness.

The end or ground of moral obligations sought by utilitarians is very differently conceived by Jeremy Bentham and James Mill on the one side and by G. E. Moore and Goldsworthy Lowes-Dickinson on the other. The latter reject the simpliste Benthamite identification of that which is good with pleasure and the absence of pain, finding moral obligation justified by its promotion of intrinsically excellent states of affairs, namely, personal relations and the appreciation of beautiful objects. The great utilitarians, the so-called 'philosophical radicals', sought to criticize the institutions of their society, political, legal, moral, by the yardstick of their tendency to promote or to impair the greatest happiness of the greatest number of people. Anything which might be called a critique of satisfactions was rejected, and in the field of government the theory which was later invoked to justify a strong element of *dirigisme* in the economy,

was first used to defend thorough-going laissez-faire. As a study of John Stuart Mill (q.v.) brings out clearly, this doctrine was a most effective dissolvent of entrenched moral superstitions and legal and political fictions. *See also* **Pleasure.** We can trace its temper in the work of urgent social reformers today in the sphere of penology, for example, Baroness Wootton.

What men initially receive as liberation they quickly tend to experience as bondage. Here the student may with profit turn to such works as John Stuart Mill's *Autobiography* (1873), Dickens' novel *Hard Times* (1854), and Lord Keynes' essay, *My Early Beliefs* (1949), the last an excellent comment on Moore's moral breach with Benthamism.

There is in thorough-going Utilitarianism of the kind professed by Bentham and James Mill an element of the sheerly Philistine suggested by Bentham's frequently quoted *mot*, 'poetry is misrepresentation' (a thesis, however, which in a different form was certainly held by Plato). Indeed a knowledge of Benthamism is essential for a proper appreciation of the targets of Matthew Arnold's polemic in *Culture and Anarchy* (1869). With Moore and his followers, reaction against this strongly marked element in the Benthamite temper issued in the cultivation for their own sake of the sort of attitudes regarded as characteristic of the 'Bloomsbury Circle' which so provoked the rage of D. H. Lawrence.

What, however, is permanently significant in the utilitarian approach to the problems of ethics is the insistence that moral principles shall be justified by reference to the promotion of human happiness and perhaps more particularly to the diminution of human suffering. Although Utilitarianism does not in any of its forms provide a complete moral theory, the demand that precepts shall be justified by reference to the extent that they further recognizable human ends is a most powerful dissolvent of entrenched moral beliefs based on the *ipse dixit* of traditional authority. The cake of moral custom needs continually to be broken, whether we think of the traditions of sexual behaviour or of the tendency (frequently found among Christians) to commend heroic self-sacrifice as something of value for its own sake. Thus we shall welcome, not least as we recall Martin Heidegger's seemingly spontaneous, if short-lived, espousal of the Nazi cause, a utilitarian critique of the way of life suggested in his writings as 'humanly authentic'. To speak in paradox, one might say that in a way analogous to Kierkegaard's own lonely *marturia* it supplies in its very different way an indispensable 'corrective' to Christian readiness to flirt with the self-consciously heroic as somehow supremely expressive of the claims and presence of the transcendent.

It may be argued against the utilitarians that they identify a kind of prudence, expressed in a disciplined concern for observable human welfare, with the whole of virtue, and not only play down what Hume called the 'monkish virtues' but diminish the tragic heights and depths of human existence. In judging, however, the practical worth of an ethical theory, it is worth asking whether or not it would have justified an unhesitating and uncompromising refusal of service in Hitler's *Wehrmacht* in furtherance of the Führer's monstrous purposes of aggression. There is little doubt that much so-called Christian discussion of the problem of political obligation can be invoked to set a question-mark against the validity of such refusal. Further, it is not a matter on which Dr Rudolf Bultmann, for all his concern with the excision of mythology from the presentation of the gospel, seemingly has much to say. Indeed, his ethics might well be thought to leave the matter an open question. But the utilitarian conception, for all its limitations, none the less in virtue of its unflinching universalism seems to provide strong foundations for such a refusal, unaffected alike by chatter concerning the place of obedience in the Christian life, the role of government in the providence of God, the frontiers of human existence, etc. Thus it would seem that utilitarian insights have an important role to play at a time when, if men and women are indeed 'come of age', they must show their adulthood by a properly 'aseptic' and deeply critical attitude to the claims made for established authorities and the alleged moral and spiritual value of obedience. If there is kinship here with elements discernible in the Marxist temper, this makes appreciation of the points made of even greater contemporary relevance in respect of the need to reopen dialogue not only between Christians and Marxists but between the latter and apologists for so-called 'western values'.

D. M. MACKINNON

Utopianism

Utopianism in ethics means lack of realism in one's aims, or striving for goals that are not attainable in the actual situation.

Values and Value Judgment

'Value' is a modern term used to indicate what traditionally has gone by the name of 'good' or 'the good'. While for some the new term is taken to have a basically subjective connotation because it is believed to imply the identification of what is good with human interest and desire, not all philosophers hold this view. At one end of the spectrum there is the subjectivist view that asserts an essential connection between value and human interest as in Ralph Barton Perry's thesis: 'That which is an object of

interest is *eo ipso* invested with value. Any object, whatever it be, acquires value when any interest, whatever it be, is taken in it. . . .' At the opposite end of the spectrum stands the objectivist view, running through western thought from Socrates and Plato to Nicolai Hartmann, according to which value is an intrinsic part or aspect of whatever has value; since value is taken to be independent of the observer it is his task to develop the necessary sensitivity for perceiving the values presented to him.

Despite a long tradition which identified all questions concerning the good for man as a goal, or individual goods involved in particular situations, as 'ethical' questions, the aim behind the development of a general theory of value is to characterize value in its *generic* sense. This means that moral value represents a special form of value with its own distinctive characteristics and is not co-extensive with value as such. The way is then open for recognizing values in the religious, aesthetic, legal, economic and political domains. In each case a proper understanding of the values involved is to be gained only by combining the generic meaning of value with the special features that define each context in which value figures. In economics, for example, we are interested in the values of commodities in exchange, whereas in ethics we may be concerned instead for the intrinsic worth of persons in a sense that takes us entirely beyond the idea of an exchange value.

One of the central questions about the nature of value has already been indicated – the issue about 'subjectivity' and 'objectivity' – and it concerns the status of value in existence. The topic is endlessly complex involving the subtle distinctions characteristic of contemporary 'meta-ethics'; only the main positions can be marked out. The subjectivist position asserts that 'good' and any synonymous value term means no more than the human response – interest, desire or expression of approval – that is made by a person when confronted with the object or when it is considered by him for the purpose of evaluation or appraisal. On this view the value term is *constituted* by the feelings aroused in the person. It is sometimes said that the one making the judgment is *expressing* his feelings – the most extreme form of the so-called emotive theory of values – but generally it is claimed that the individual is *asserting the existence* of the appropriate feelings in relation to the object when he uses a value term in referring to it. In either case value does not reside in the object as something antecedent to the mind that judges, but depends instead on the subjective response.

The main criticism urged against this view by proponents of one or another of the various objectivist positions is twofold; on the one hand, it is held that while we may discover the value of something by attending to it and responding, the value does not thereby come into existence on this occasion, and on the other hand, it is claimed that many of the things and actions that have attracted human interest or called forth desire are not in fact good but represent instead something bad or evil and hence something to be avoided. Over against the attempts of subjectivists to show that value terms like 'esteemed', 'coveted', 'admirable', etc., are one and all translatable into responses made by judging persons, objectivists are concerned to show that the value terms denote instead characteristics of objects, either simple qualities or complex rational properties, that belong to the objects themselves and are discovered by the mind sensitive to their existence. Frequently the objectivist appeal is to intuition or direct insight as the appropriate means of apprehension, and most intuitionists have laid down the condition that only a trained mind, sensitive and sincerely attending to the relevant features of value situations, will be in a position to grasp the values presented.

The attempt to pass beyond the opposition of subjective and objective in value theory was made by the instrumentalists whose major spokesman was John Dewey. For him value considerations are relevant wherever there are alternative courses of action. Distinguishing between 'prizing' and 'appraising', Dewey held that while the basic materials of value must be acknowledged to be human desires and preferences, we cannot remain content merely with the reports of what people actually prize or find satisfying. Instead we must appraise our immediate desires, which means subjecting them to a test. Instead of taking such desires for final values, we must use them as starting points for ethical inquiry. To know that some object or situation has been deemed satisfying is to have but a subjective report; the next step is to see whether the claim made on behalf of the object can be sustained in a critical test. The aim is to discover whether the objects in question really are satisfactory or have the capacity claimed for them. It is important to notice that whereas the starting point of this approach is in the desires and satisfactions of persons, the outcome of critical inquiry is meant to refer to the capacities of objects. To the thirst-crazed man, the immediate desire is for liquid; drinking sea water, however, though it may be immediately satisfying can never be satisfactory because the constitution of the water itself is inadequate for meeting the demand that is put upon it. Our prizings themselves must be appraised, and we must weed out short-run and immediate satisfactions in favour of values 'approved on reflection' by which Dewey meant longer-range satisfactions arrived at through a knowledge of the natures of things and by considering the means required to obtain them.

Value judgments have to be considered as special cases of the general function of judgment. Judgment of value embraces both the basic assertion of values or goods as values, and the application of the standards implied to individual situations, actions and objects. Judgment presupposes standard or leading principle whether it is made fully explicit or not. Even if we interpret judgment as a record or report of preferences, a standard is still involved. Explicitly expressed judgment belongs to the sphere of reflection; that in actual deliberation or the process of deciding what we are to do, we are not aware of making judgments of the fully explicit sort that are to be found in books on ethics, does not alter the fact that judgment is present. In the sphere of moral judgment, 'conscience' is the name for the judging activity. Quite apart from the questionable metaphors that have been used to describe conscience, it is essentially a process of comparing our conduct or state of mind with a standard expressing what is good or which ought to hold.

In addition to the logical problems that arise in connection with the interpretation of value judgments, there are also moral considerations attached to judging in this sphere. The ancient injunction 'Judge not!' leads to a distinction between judgments passed by a person on his own conduct and judgment passed by another on that same conduct. The moral quality of a person is revealed not only through the conduct dictated by his own judgments, but also through his understanding and forbearance in passing judgment on others.

Brand Blanshard, *Reason and Goodness*, 1961; A. C. Ewing, *The Definition of Good*, 1947; Nicolai Hartmann, *Ethics*, 3 vols., tr. by S. Coit, 1932; Ralph Barton Perry, *General Theory of Value*, 1932.

JOHN E. SMITH

Vice

Vice is the name given to the root sins, or sinful dispositions, which engender and nurture acts of sin. The Middle Ages adopted a catalogue of seven vices: pride, envy, anger, sloth, avarice, gluttony, lust. All men sin, baptized or unbaptized, each in his own fashion. The Christian gospel does not tell men and women to attack their sins but to acknowledge them and to repent. Therefore the life of an individual Christian is not a continual interior warfare between virtues and vices. This would be a way of living which would keep vice in the centre of the Christian's life and make it a constantly determining factor. The Christian life is always to be described as living creatively rather than as avoiding vice. The Scripture says, 'overcome evil with good' (Rom. 12.21), an activity which might be described as behaving creatively in thought, word and deed in the love of God and all his creatures, visible and invisible.

The more fully a man lives the stronger both his virtues and his vices become and the more trouble he has in mastering himself. Virtues and vices make themselves felt on every plane of living; thus a man can be tempted to be proud of his lack of pride; a Christian can be angry with God for not giving him more consolation, more knowledge or more help; a Christian can be angry with himself for his slow growth in holiness.

The Christian Church in the West has tended to concentrate on sin, atonement and moral behaviour in such a way that emphasis has fallen on the sins of the flesh, theft and other offences against property. The life of those called to be the light of the world can neither be adequately described nor lived in such small, negative, moral terms.

The mediaeval tables of virtues and vices, in spite of their emphasis on the individual, have a certain value in describing the Christian life and give some guidance for Christians in this generation who attempt to live the good life in terms of freedom, creativity and personal relations. In all consideration of vices and virtues the words of our Lord are to be remembered – 'I came that they may have life and have it abundantly' (John 10.10). Abundance of life makes both great goodness and great evil possible and shows that there is something more important than the mere avoidance of evil.

R. E. C. BROWNE

Virginity

Virginity, as a physical state, is innocence of physical intercourse, and may be predicated of either sex; hence St John is often referred to by the Fathers as John the Virgin. The Bible assumes virginity as the proper state of one about to be married (cf. Deut. 22.13–21). Hence it may be used as a metaphor for the proper relation of Israel to God, or of the Church to Christ (II Cor. 11.2). Physically a woman is *virgo intacta* when the hymen (or maidenhead) has not been broken, whether by intercourse or accident. But as a moral quality virginity is not lost by involuntary violation – a point developed by St Augustine in connection with the Gothic sack of Rome in 410 (*City of God* 1.15–17).

As a spiritual quality or virtue virginity is no mere negative condition. It is the state of one who has not wasted or misdirected his deepest forces of body and soul, but either reserves them for due fulfilment in marriage or dedicates them in obedience to God according to his call. The virgin state dedicated to God was highly esteemed by the early Church, in accordance with the example of Christ and the counsel of St Paul (I Cor. 7.8 ff.) – although the virgin martyrs who figure prominently in the accounts of the persecutions are often simply young girls, as are also the bridesmaids of Matt.

25.1–13. The dedicated virgin became so by her own vow, as noted by Hippolytus of Rome c. 200 (*Apostolic Tradition*, 13), without separation from society. But since there was little place in the ancient world for the unmarried adult woman – though there was some (for example, the virgin who is said to have concealed St Athanasius in her family vault was obviously an old maid) – the protection of virgins became the responsibility of the Church in default of family, and hence one of the problems faced by the bishop (cf. Chrysostom, *On the Priesthood*, III, 17). A natural solution was to bring them together under the guidance of older women such as the widows whom the Church also supported. Hence monastic or conventual communities of women are somewhat older than those of men (cf. Athanasius, *Life of Antony*, 3).

Tertullian (*On the Veiling of Virgins*) discusses a rather amusing practical problem: Should dedicated virgins assume the matron's veil, as brides of Christ, or in token of innocence continue to go bare-headed, which might imply that they were marriageable? The former custom prevailed, and by the mid-fourth century Rome developed a ceremony of the 'veiling of virgins', along the lines of an ordination – first referred to by St Ambrose with reference to the veiling of his sister by Pope Liberius, c. 360. By the Middle Ages, however, dedicated virgins were normally members of monastic communities, and the liturgical *velatio* became obsolete, being succeeded by the taking of vows and the blessing of Abbesses. In the later Middle Ages the older institution reappears in the form of the recluse, who lived in a cell attached to a church. The most famous is the mystical writer Dame Julian of Norwich, at St Julian's Church in the city c. 1380–1410. *See* Celibacy; Monasticism.

E. R. HARDY

Virtue

In its basic sense, the word means 'power' or 'excellence'. In ethics, virtue is moral excellence, a settled attitude which conduces to habitually good action in some respect. The virtues have been variously classified. The intellectual virtues (e.g., wisdom) are distinguished from the practical virtues (e.g., courage), the former being associated with the life of contemplation, the latter with the life of action; or the cardinal virtues of classical philosophy are distinguished from the so-called 'theological virtues' of the NT; or the natural virtues are distinguished from those that are attained only through God's working in us (*virtus infusa*). *See* articles on the individual virtues, *also* **Cardinal Virtues; Good and Goodness; Habit; Theological Virtues.**

Virtus Infusa. see Virtue.

Vocation

Vocation is used in the AV only at Eph. 4.1; it translates *klēsis*, and in the other nine places where that occurs the AV uses 'calling'. The RV and RSV are consistent in using 'calling' at Eph. 4.1 as well. Closely related is *klētos* (called) which occurs ten times. Both primarily refer to the call of God in Christ to membership in the community of his people, the 'saints', and to the qualities of Christian life which this implies. But in I Cor. 7.20 St Paul also applied the term to the daily work of the Christian. The RV brings out the double sense of the word in this verse, 'Let each man abide in that calling (i.e., job) wherein he was called (i.e., when he became a Christian).' This was to have momentous consequences at the Reformation. In the intervening centuries the doctrine of the 'double standard' had grown up, according to which life in the world is a second best. Some are called beyond the *precepts* (binding on all) to the *counsels of perfection*, to poverty, chastity and obedience. To them the term 'religious' was given, and it remains a technical term for them in the Roman Catholic Church.

Luther rebelled against this and developed on the basis of I Cor. 7.20 a theology of the Christian's calling in the world. (The German word is *Beruf*.) The idea of vocation was brought from the monastery to the market place. The Christian's calling is to carry on the world's work to the best of his ability. The vocation of a cobbler is to cobble shoes properly; he can have no higher calling, for through this he loves God and serves his neighbour (cf. Gustaf Wingren, *The Christian's Calling; Luther on Vocation*, 1957).

St Paul's view is static. He does not envisage the Christian changing his job. 'So, brethren, in whatever state each was called, there let him remain with God' (I Cor. 7.24). The reason is the same as for the grudging permission he gives the unmarried to change their state; at this time of his life he thought that 'the appointed time has grown very short' (v. 29). Luther showed a similar apocalyptic conservatism. Calvin took a more dynamic view, and it is easy to adapt St Paul's teaching in this way. The Catechism in the Prayer Book of the Church of England picked up the more flexible use when it refers to getting one's living 'in that state of life unto which it *shall* please God to call me'. For modern uses of vocation *see* **Work, Doctrine of.**

RONALD PRESTON

Voluntarism

In ethics and in theodicy, voluntarism is a view closely (though not inseparably) associated with the nominalist philosophy. In answer to the question whether a thing is good because God wills it or whether God wills it because it is good, voluntarism chooses the first alternative. Voluntarist ethics is thus based on revelation, an ethic of the divine command rather than of natural law; and, similarly, God's dealings with men are known in the mandates of his inscrutable will (the divine decrees) rather than in the effects of the divine intelligence discerned in the nature and purpose of things. From the first Reformers (and especially Calvin) until today, voluntarism has been a recurrent strain in Protestant thought. In spite of the crudities in which it has sometimes been expressed, the view has sought to safeguard the sovereignty of God, and the personal nature of his dealings and his commands.

JAMES A. WHYTE

Vows

A vow is a definite promise made to God. It differs therefore from an aspiration or an intention, or even a resolution. It is a definite undertaking whereby a man binds himself to do or not to do, or to give something by a promise to God. A vow therefore is not something to be undertaken lightly or carelessly, but only after full deliberation and recognition of all that is involved.

Vows may be private or public. A public vow is one that is accepted in the name of the Church by a legitimate ecclesiastical superior. A private vow is one made without seeking such acceptance. There is a further distinction within public vows, between simple and solemn vows. The distinction is not nowadays of much importance and concerns certain juridical effects attaching to solemn vows. Simple and solemn vows, public and private vows all create the same obligation.

Any person is competent to make a vow, provided that he has the full use of his reason. For the vow to be valid, there must be (1) a clear intention to make a vow, (2) adequate deliberation, that is, a man must understand what burden of obligation it is that he is laying on himself, and (3) free choice, that is, the vow must not be taken as a result of fear. The object of a vow, or what is promised to God, must be (1) something that is possible, (2) pleasing to God – you cannot make a vow to do something which you know to be wrong, nor make a vow about some triviality – and (3) something which effects an improvement in the present moral or spiritual state of him who makes the vow. For example, chastity is an improvement on unchastity. A vow of chastity therefore is a valid vow.

Every valid vow creates a moral and religious obligation. Unless the vow itself specifies a time at which it is to be discharged, it should be discharged as soon as possible. A negative vow, that is a vow *not* to do something, becomes obligatory at once. Because a vow is a restriction on liberty, it is to be interpreted strictly.

A private vow ceases automatically to bind if there is such a radical change in the situation of the man who made it or in the thing vowed that had things been so at the time, the vow would not have been made. For example, a rich man vows to give a large sum annually to charity, but later loses his money and becomes poor. Or a man vows to build a church on a given site, and then finds he cannot get planning permission. Public vows cease by dispensation granted by the appropriate authority. For a valid dispensation a just and sufficient cause is required. Such a cause is either the general good of the Church or the private necessity or advantage of the man under the vow. So that a monk who is dismissed by his Community because of his scandalous conduct, may be dispensed from his vows for the good of the Church. A monk who becomes convinced that he has mistaken his vocation, is finding it increasingly difficult to live in the spirit of his vows and is under constant grave temptation to break them, may rightly be dispensed for the sake of his own good. Indeed, in the case of life-vows, though a dispensation may often be delayed in order to give the man who asks for it time for further reflection, it is seldom, if ever, finally refused.

A vow may be commuted, that is, something else may be substituted in place of the original vow. If the thing substituted is something better than or, at least, not worse than the original vow, no just cause is required and it may be done by the man who made the vow himself. If something less than the original vow is to be substituted, there must be an adequate reason and also recourse to superior authority.

The Reformers frowned on vows, both public and private, and especially on the life-vows of poverty, chastity and obedience taken by the religious. Their main objection was that vows restrict future liberty of action, and changing circumstances may and often do create altered duties. A vow may prevent or seem to excuse a man from discharging these new duties. Yet vows are of value both as affording strength and determination to the will, and as an expression of devotion and obedience to the will of God. The objections are met if care is always taken to prevent rash and ill-considered vows, and if wise and charitable use is made by those in authority of their dispensing and commuting powers.

R. C. MORTIMER

Wages. see Industrial Relations;
Just Wage.

War. see Peace and War.

Wealth

There is a fundamental ambivalence, rooted in the NT, in the Christian attitude to wealth. On the one hand, material goods are God's gifts, the product of the talents which he has given to man, using the natural resources which he has created. They are therefore to be used to his glory. On the other hand, the pursuit of riches is always in danger of becoming an end in itself, blinding men to their need of God and making them careless of the claims of others, so that the love of money becomes a root of all evil.

Traditional thinking has never regarded the possession of wealth as wrong in itself, but has always stressed that it is a privilege and a responsibility, involving obligations to use it to meet the needs of others, and with regard for the effects of its use on their welfare. The doctrine of the just wage (q.v.) was held to imply that remuneration for each occupation should be such as to enable the recipients to keep up the state of life appropriate to their position, though at the same time frugality in personal expenditure and the duty of almsgiving were always emphasized. More recently, the doctrine has been held to imply the right of workers to organize in order to ensure that they get rates of pay equal to the value of their work, and also to imply the provision, by social security or otherwise, for the maintenance of spending power through such vicissitudes as sickness, unemployment, large family or old age. Hence theorists of the just wage would accept differentials according to skill and training and to some extent according to changes in relative supply and demand for different types of labour, as being consistent with the principle of equal and maximum pay for equal ability. See M. P. Fogarty, The Just Wage, 1961.

Other writers would take a more radical attitude. D. L. Munby and D. Jenkins both hold that Christianity implies equality as the only ultimate standard, though they would admit that, for practical reasons, such as differences of skill, training and opportunity, the need for incentives, and relative shortages of various types of labour, there will always be some differences of income. Great inequalities, however, are a barrier to real community and a denial of men's fundamental equality as children of God.

The present situation is in many ways a new one. In the West, although differences of income are still great, the general level of wealth is now such that most of the people can live at a level that looks like affluence to the two-thirds of the world's population who are still in poverty. Traditional thinking on wealth and poverty has been based on a situation with a small minority of rich people in a society in which most were poor. We have not yet worked out the Christian ethics of an affluent society. How far is the stimulation of ever new wants by advertising justified? How can the community use its affluence to help those of its own members who do not fully share it, to improve the quality of life for all, and help the poor majority of the world's people outside North America and Western Europe to break out of their age-old poverty? Christians have to develop a style of life which is appropriate to true stewardship of the opportunities of a rich society.

M. P. Fogarty, *The Just Wage*, 1961; D. Jenkins, *Equality and Excellence*, 1961; D. L. Munby, *Christianity and Economic Problems*, 1956; *God in the Rich Society*, 1961; J. F. Sleeman, *Basic Economic Problems, A Christian Approach*, 1953.

JOHN F. SLEEMAN

Weber, Max

Max Weber (1864–1920) is one of the most seminal and distinguished German social thinkers. A principal founder of modern sociology, his profound influence in contemporary social science is particularly marked in such areas as sociological theory, sociology of religion, political power, economics, urbanization, bureaucracy, class stratification, and the sociology of law.

Born in Erfurt, Thuringia on April 21, 1864, the son of a trained jurist and prosperous politician, Weber grew up in an intellectually stimulating environment. In his father's house young Weber came to know such men as Dilthey, Mommsen, Julian Schmidt, Treitschke, and Friedrich Kapp. Having suffered from an attack of meningitis at the age of four, he grew up as a weakly child who preferred books to sports. Weber developed into a precocious student who wrote historical essays at the age of thirteen.

Weber occupied the chair of political economy at Freiburg, taught at Heidelberg, and later at Munich. Active in the political life of his day as consultant to government agencies and as a consultant to the German Armistice Commission in Versailles, he was also one of the founders of the Deutsche Gesellschaft für Soziologie and editor of *Archiv für Sozialwissenschaft und Sozialpolitik*. His close associates and friends included George Jellinek, Paul Hensel, Karl Neumann and Ernst Troeltsch, who for a time lived in the Weber household.

Viewing sociology primarily as a science of understanding, Weber's massive scholarly erudition is best indicated in his *Wirtschaft und Gesellschaft* (1922), often hailed as the greatest achievement of German sociology. Weber's best-known work, *The Protestant Ethic and the Spirit of Capitalism* (1930), sought to demonstrate that Protestantism, especially the Puritan ethic and Calvinism, laid the foundation for the emergence of modern western capitalism. To establish this thesis Weber argued that religious orientation has a profound influence upon the social structure. These orientations are not mere reflections of differences in the economic

situations of the religious groups, but are partially independent of the group's social situation. Indeed, prime causal significance may be attributed to the factor of 'religious orientation' as an initiating factor in the evolution of human society.

Weber's interpretation was a direct challenge to the economic determinism of the Marxists and has generated much discussion and controversy. His classic study has stimulated dozens of scholarly works and a large body of literature which has sought to sustain, qualify or repudiate his thesis. One should bear in mind that Weber's analysis of the impact of Protestantism on the spirit of capitalism was only the beginning of a series of comparative monographs in the sociology of religion. In studies of Confucianism and Taoism, Hinduism and Buddhism, and ancient Judaism, Weber explored the significance of religion for economic activity. At the time of his death of pneumonia in June, 1920 at the age of fifty-six, he had planned similar studies of Islam, of early Christianity, and of mediaeval Catholicism.

Max Weber, *The Protestant Ethic and the Spirit of Capitalism*, tr. by Talcott Parsons, 1930; *The Sociology of Religion*, tr. by Ephraim Fischoff, 1963; Reinhard Bendix, *Max Weber: An Intellectual Portrait*, 1960; H. H. Gerth and C. Wright Mills, *From Max Weber: Essays in Sociology*, 1958.

ROBERT LEE

Welfare State

This term can best be understood in contrast to the laissez-faire theory of the State (q.v.). When modern capitalism and industrialism developed, the theory of the market economy held that if everyone was left free to pursue his private interests the total effect would be the maximum common good. On this view the role of the State was mainly to provide law and order. Many of those who held this theory thought of it as a powerful weapon against privilege, and also expected it to work out in a somewhat egalitarian way. It was never in fact acted upon in all its rigour, and in the course of the last century all kinds of 'interferences' with it developed, such as trusts, tariffs and cartels, or defensive human associations like trade unions (for the theory dissolved all social and organic ties between men and left only the bleak association of the labour contract). Moreover it did not work in an egalitarian way but had a built-in tendency to inequality, intensified by the rights of inheritance. This led governments to redress through progressive taxation the balance of incomes arrived at by the forces of the market. Little dent so far has been made on the distribution of property (e.g., in Britain 1 % of the population still owns about 47 % of the property). A striking feature of the laissez-faire economy was its tendency to proceed in a cycle of boom and slump roughly every ten years, and this was the cause of much hardship. The casualties of society, as well as its basic services like schools and hospitals, were to begin with provided for by private charity, but it could not cope with the scale required, and so both national and local public provision began to be made. Germany pioneered social legislation under Bismarck. Britain took notable steps forward after the election of the Liberal government in 1905.

It was only after the war of 1939–45, however, that the term welfare state came into general use. It means that the community makes corporate provisions for its citizens and adopts a minimum standard of life which it guarantees them. It is not a matter of effort or desert, but of status as a citizen; it is not a charity but a right. It covers different things in different countries, but it is likely to include positive policies to provide full employment or a guaranteed minimum subsistence in case of unemployment. It may also include compulsory education, a health service, minimum housing standards and a variety of other benefits. It may be financed by weekly contributions from workers, employers and the government, by direct and indirect taxes, by specific charges, or by various combinations of all these. To some extent it is likely to mean a compulsory redistribution of income among the working population.

The welfare state is a recovery of a more positive doctrine of the State which should be welcomed by Christian theology. Much of the Christian tradition, perhaps influenced by apocalyptic pessimism, has had too negative a view of the State, and regarded it as mainly a 'dyke against sin' provided by the preservative mercy of God to prevent human life being 'nasty, brutish and short' (to use Hobbe's phrase). But the State has also a positive function. It cannot itself make the good life, but it can make it easier for its citizens to achieve it, and it can express the corporate nature of human life by its corporate provisions.

The administration of the welfare state requires an efficient and uncorrupt civil service. It also draws in citizens to run aspects of it (e.g., the British Regional Hospital Boards).

Two criticisms are sometimes made of the welfare state. The first is that it is 'totalitarian' and seeks to take the place of God. Whether this is so depends entirely on the nature of the State. If it is totalitarian its welfare activities will be totalitarian. If it is democratic so will its welfare services be. The other criticism is that it kills the spirit of voluntary action. This is only the case if the ordinary citizen allows it to happen. A democratic state needs the fullest participation of citizens at all levels of its life. While many of the social services which in the past were pioneered by voluntary activity have been taken over by the State, this should be

seen as a triumph of voluntary initiative. It has shown something to be universally necessary and beyond the scope of voluntary effort to provide. The call is to pioneer new services, reveal new needs, and to realize that there will always be scope for efficient voluntary work that it is not appropriate for the State to undertake.

The upshot is that modern welfare state capitalism is very different from laissez-faire capitalism. Social injustice remains, but the sting has been taken out of Marxist criticism by the positive government policies which have alleviated the alternation of boom and slump and raised corporate standards of life. However its social philosophy is expressed there is no economically advanced capitalist country which is not in greater or lesser degree a welfare state.

RONALD PRESTON

Widows

Widows are women whose husbands have died and who have not remarried. Among the Hebrews the practice known to anthropologists as the levirate was laid down in Deut. 25.5 ff. wherein a widow had a definite claim to be treated as a wife by her husband's brother. There was, in fact, a reproach attached to permanent widowhood (cf. Isa. 54.4) based on the assumption that the brother would not have her. Nevertheless widows and orphans had a special call on the protection of God (Ex. 22.22). A widow, particularly one with young children, is in a position of great weakness for the breadwinner and traditional protector of the family has gone. In English law this frailty was made more acute by the fact that before the Married Woman's Property Act of 1882 the property of a woman became the property of her husband on marriage and she had no prescribed right to any part of his estate on death, and the husband could, in fact, will the estate away from his relict. This was altered by an act of 1938 which gave a wife certain claims on the estate.

Most husbands left little or no property and widows were cared for either by relatives or by some form of public assistance. In most cases the English Poor Law was more generous to widows than to most other applicants for relief, but at certain times even they were forced to take institutional aid. England introduced a system of widow's pensions in 1925. This lasted for the rest of the widow's days. In the post-war recasting of social insurance the pension was substantially increased but was receivable only while the children were at school and not earning.

Mary Penelope Hall, *The Social Services of Modern England*, 1952; Peter Morris, *Widows and Their Families*, 1958.

BRIAN RODGERS

Will

Will is a word no longer much in fashion among either moral philosophers or psychologists. It savours too much of the old faculty psychology, as if the will were some definite organ or department of the mind or personality. The will is not a thing or anything thinglike, but denotes a kind of behaviour – the kind that we call 'action' (q.v.), that is to say, the kind that is done knowingly and responsibly, when the self consciously seeks to bring about some change in the existing state of affairs, or tries to prevent some change from taking place. This is the kind of behaviour that can have moral quality or be the subject for moral judgment, and so we can speak of a good will or a bad will. This moral sense of will and willing must be distinguished from such usages as 'will to power' and 'will to live', where the will is equated with drives or instincts, especially in German *Lebensphilosophie*. *See also* **Free Will.**

EDITOR

Williams, Roger

Roger Williams (*c.* 1603–1683), apostle of the liberty of conscience, was educated at Cambridge under Puritan auspices. Though he was ordained in the Church of England, by the time he arrived in America in 1631 he had already espoused a separatist position. He refused to serve in the church at Boston because he did not deem it to be clearly separated from the Church of England. He served in the ministry at Plymouth and then at Salem, but continued to be critical of the effort of the leaders of the Massachusetts Bay colony to enforce religious conformity. Civil magistrates, he insisted should rule only in civil and not in religious affairs. Tried and banished, he fled into the wilderness, and founded Providence in 1636 on land bought from the Indians. For a short while he espoused the Baptist position and was a founder of the first Baptist Church in America, but soon he became a Seeker, not knowing where among the warring sects the true Church was. Theologically, he remained a Puritan Calvinist all his life, as may be seen from his contentious and difficult work, *George Fox Digg'd out of his Burrowes* (1676). He engaged in missionary work among the Indians, among whom he became a trusted peacemaker.

Recognizing the need of a charter to protect the young colony of Rhode Island, Williams sailed for England in 1643, and the next year his efforts were rewarded. His first book, *A Key into the Language of America* (1643) won favourable attention. While in England he contributed to the debate concerning Church and State raging in those early years of the Puritan revolution. In *The Bloudy Tenent of Persecution for Cause of Conscience* (1644), he argued on biblical, historical and theological grounds for full religious liberty and the separation of Church and State. In later writings he continued his crusade, never more forcefully than in a little work published during a second trip to England, *The Hireling Ministry None of Christs* (1652).

As a social thinker, Williams shared many of the views popular in his time, but in his advocacy of democracy and liberty of conscience he was a bold pioneer. He believed that families, not individuals, were the foundation of government. He put great emphasis on the necessity for law and order. He believed that the origin of the State lay not in civil agreement but in the community consciousness of a common social purpose and a desire for civil peace and welfare. This consciousness should find expression in an orderly assembly through the will of the majority. Long prominent in the political life of the colony he founded, where the principle of religious liberty was put into practice, he frequently had to employ great skill in dealing with local contentions that threatened the colony from within.

James Ernst, *The Political Thought of Roger Williams*, 1929; Perry Miller, *Roger Williams: His Contribution to the American Tradition*, 1953; Ola E. Winslow, *Master Roger Williams, A Biography*, 1957.

ROBERT T. HANDY

Wisdom

There are two articles on this subject. The first considers wisdom in the Bible; the second considers wisdom as a virtue.

Wisdom · I

With respect to form there are two types of material in Proverbs. Most of the contents of 1–9 together with 22.17–24.22 (an imitation in part of the 'Instruction of Amenemope') and 31.1–9 have a form similar to the Egyptian 'Instruction' (*ANET*, pp. 412–25). The remaining material in the Book is, for the most part, in the form of wisdom sentences in which generalizations of practical wisdom are elegantly expressed. With respect to content there are sentences which illustrate the absence of ethical commitment in old wisdom and those which illustrate the subordination of wisdom to the 'fear of the Lord' and an ethics of piety.

In Job and Ecclesiastes we pass from the *How* of practical, godly, wisdom to a more heart-searching *Why*. Job is tortured by the threat of unbelief, but Ecclesiastes asserts with iconoclastic relish the impossibility of theodicy. Both books make much of the inscrutability of God. In Ecclesiastes this leads to the conclusion that a man must extract as much pleasure as he can from his fleeting life and that all else is nothingness. In Job it constitutes a demand for reverence and submission. Job was wrong in supposing that his faith could be made conditional on the intelligibility of God's dealings with him and on justice being seen to be done.

The 'scribe' or 'sage' in the ancient Near East was near to the centre of government and such a wisdom of statecraft existed in Israel from the time of David onwards. In Isaiah and Jeremiah particularly there is a reaction against the claims of this statecraft. The intellectual grasp in which the sages take pride exists only in God and is evidenced in creation and history. This is further developed in Prov. 8 where the hypostatized wisdom is a master-workman who presided over the creation of the world (v. 30) and is the source of the wisdom of rulers (vv. 14–16). In the NT, especially in I Cor. 1–2, we find the antithesis between worldly wisdom and the wisdom of God. The new element here is the emphasis on the foolishness of preaching and the foolishness of the cross which is yet the wisdom of God. The idea that the wisdom of God is enigmatic, which is characteristic of Jewish apocalyptic, is also seen in St Paul's reference to 'hidden wisdom' (I Cor. 2.7 and perhaps 2.1). This also appears in the representation of the parable as a 'mystery' in St Mark and pre-eminently in the Apocalypse.

W. Baumgartner, 'The Wisdom Literature', in *The Old Testament and Modern Study*, ed. by H. H. Rowley, 1951, pp. 210–37, with accompanying bibliography.

WILLIAM MCKANE

Wisdom · II

Christians are told to be wise. It is not easy to say what wisdom is or how a man becomes wise. A great deal of wisdom is shown in the refusal to look for it in oneself or to search for it too intently in others. Wisdom is the light by which men understand what they see. It is in the ability to make judgments – spiritual, aesthetic, moral, legislative or scientific. It may be seen in the ordering and carrying out of necessary daily routine affairs, domestic or administrative. It may be seen in offices, workshops, airports, laboratories, hospitals, schools, universities. It may be known when a man confides in his friend or addresses a public meeting. Poems, paintings and music manifest qualities that give form to a wisdom that their authors have not made merely by their own efforts. Men of prayer, whoever and wherever they are, live with frequent stillness and silence in which both prayer and wisdom grow and develop through the grace of God.

A description of wisdom is best made by an attempt to note some of the characteristics of a wise man: (1) The wise man knows himself (insofar as this is possible) yet he is not self-centred, (2) he sees life in proportion and therefore does not waste life on trivialities, (3) he recognizes that there are situations in which he cannot help others directly but he is always at the disposal of those who need him,

(4) because he is not self-centred he is more able to discern the trend of events in both Church and State than those who are concerned with their own safety and gain, (5) he knows that the acts men call good are often worse than those they admit to be bad, (6) he finds life more than tolerable because he believes that the might of God is most often expressed in deeds of mercy.

For several centuries decision-making, good works and character have been emphasized at the expense of wisdom. How can there be decision-making of value without wisdom? How can there be good works and character unless these are nurtured by wisdom? The Church has never proclaimed that amiable foolishness is a necessary qualification for the Kingdom of Heaven. On the contrary, Christians are expected to be as 'wise as serpents and innocent as doves' (Matt. 10.16); nevertheless the voice of wisdom is often cried down at all kinds of church assemblies, for the freshness and vigour of wisdom disturbs the best laid plans for the sort of action which the majority understand. Crowds long for action but the wise man knows that the typical human state is not activity or idleness but watchfulness – 'Watch and pray'. The good life does not consist of the quantity or cost of acts but of their appropriateness. Appropriateness depends largely on the timing of the act, and wisdom is a safeguard against hastily conceived actions, presumption and the caution which stifles love.

The Scriptures say: 'The fear of the Lord is the beginning of wisdom' (Prov. 9.10). Fearing the Lord is the experience through which a man recognizes the purity and power of almighty God, the limitations of human knowledge and action, and the traces of sinfulness in the best of human achievements.

R. E. C. BROWNE

Women, Status of

A world-wide study of the place and work of women in the churches was sponsored by the World Council of Churches following the 1948 Assembly meeting. Dr Kathleen Bliss's interpretation of the survey remains the one most complete interpretation of the status of women in the churches. Fundamentally, women's status is a question of the relationship between men and women, a relationship which is never entirely fixed. The churches recognize both an order of creation in which God created male and female, and the order of redemption in which there is neither male nor female. The widest possible divergence of opinions has found expression in the churches from both doctrines. In addition, the Church's concept of women and their relationship with men is affected by society. In the present period of rapid social change the question of the status of women in the churches has become a vital issue in many of the denominations and countries. Persons in modern society face a complex of questions regarding the changing patterns of family life. Changing patterns in family life are interwoven with emerging new attitudes towards sex and sexual morality. The participation of men and women in the economic and political spheres of life raises questions about the roles of men and women in the policy-making and legislative bodies in society and in the churches.

The Bible has no direct answer for the specific questions raised in our period of history. Scripture, however, reveals guide lines for inquiry and reaching new understandings. The task of describing the status of women in modern society and in the churches today is to find the relevant word of God as he speaks to the concrete situations in this period of rapidly changing relationships in all areas of life. In biblical literature the status of woman is deeply rooted in the stories of creation. In the earlier account of creation, God created Adam from dust. Woman is created from the rib of Adam in order that he may not be alone. It is Adam who names the living creatures, and Adam who calls his helper woman. In the chronology of this creation account, man, created first, is seen as superior to woman and all the living creatures. The relationship of the two, however, is a unitive one-flesh relationship. Therefore, a man shall leave his father and his mother and cleave to his wife, and they become one flesh.

The second account of creation reflects a contrasting view and understanding of the creation of man and woman. In this account man and woman are created by God simultaneously, in the image of God, and both are empowered with dominion over the earth and all of life. Being created in the image of God, man and woman are each responsible beings before God. The relationship of man and woman suggested in this account is the complementary one of man to woman, and both under the dominion of the Creator.

In the creation stories there is no sex-conscious distinction in man or woman. In the created order all living creatures live at peace with one another. It is in the story of the Fall that the knowledge of sex consciousness comes to man and woman. The result of the disobedience is that woman is to bear children in pain and to be in subjection to her husband who is to rule over her. In the OT the place of woman is strongly influenced by the prevailing patriarchal form of family life. The place of woman is related to her role as wife and mother and her status in the marriage and family relationships. The subordinate position of woman is evidenced in the development and the history and religious life of Israel. But her place was both influential and revered. The biblical narratives record positions of honour accorded to the wife and mother. Some women reached positions of prominence in the OT society. In the patriarchal society of the Hebrew culture these positions were achieved by women working through men who held the ranking power. Behind the new status given to women in the NT is the attitude of Jesus himself. He deals with women as persons, worthy to be talked to and listened to, in need of salvation equally with men. All four Gospels testify that he made women the first witnesses and heralds of his resurrection. NT overtones of the male dominated culture are particularly reflected in the Epistles of Paul. Paul's attitude towards woman is the subject of much debate. On this subject Suzanne de Dietrich (*The Witnessing Community*, 1958, p. 177) notes:

> Paul is anxious for women to submit themselves to the accepted customs of their time. This is a matter both of dignity and decency. It seems to us that one should retain the spirit, not the letter of such advice. Customs change, but every sensitive women will feel, I believe, that what Paul wants to preserve is something of the essence of womanhood, her dignity and reserve. By stating that in Christ there is neither male nor female, Paul has expressed the fundamental equality of men and women as heirs of the same promise.

The NT affirms a new creation, an *agape* relationship of all persons in Christ. The relationship of men and women is subject to demands and the gifts of grace in Christ's redemptive fellowship. The status of women is articulated in the profound question asked by Visser't Hooft, 'whether the Churches have really faced up to the basic tenets of their own faith concerning the relationship of men and women in the fellowship of the Church of Christ'.

Throughout the history of the Christian churches women have been engaged in two major tasks – nurture and education of the young and the care of the sick, poor and aged. The avenues which have been available to women for carrying out these tasks have varied in the periods of church history, reinforcing the fact that the status of women in the church and the use of women's gifts and talents has never been entirely static or fixed.

Much of the work that is being done by women in the churches today is through the channels of women's organizations. The voluntary organization for women in the churches is a phenomenon of the later part of the nineteenth century. Most of these groups were organized for support of the Church's missionary work. Today, women's organizations are an accepted feature of church life. In the USA these groups tend to organize locally with co-ordination and organizational structures on a regional and national basis with programmes for women including service, study, fellowship and stewardship. Often the only channel for women to participate in the work of the church is through these organizations, and the status of women is defined in terms of women's organizations. Where or when women's groups are isolated from the total life and functioning of the church women do not have respectable status in the church.

The status of women and opportunities to participate in the governing and policy-making bodies differ from denomination to denomination as does their status in the full-time service and ministry in the various churches. There are women who are educated, trained and willing to serve in the church. The way the churches use the services of these women is a question of much concern, often centring around the question of ordination of women. The question of women in the ministry raises questions of interpretation of ministry, laity and priesthood – on which there are divided counsels in most churches. A number of churches have opened the full ministry to women on equal terms with men. Even in churches where ordination of women is possible their status is not readily acknowledged by local congregations. The ministry of women directly affects only a minority of women in the church. The raising of the question has compelled those charged with answering it to re-examine the nature of the ministry, and to look to the broader aspect of the place of all women in the Church.

The status of women is most frequently raised as a problem or a question. It may well be that in our time the discussion will be centred on the potential and opportunities for women, as persons, to contribute to the Church and the work of the Church.

Kathleen Bliss, *The Service and Status of Women in the Churches*, 1952; Beverly Benner Cassara, ed., *American Women: The Changing Image*, 1962; R. W. and Wynn Fairchild, *Families in the Church: a Protestant Survey*, 1961; Superintendent of Documents, Washington, D.C., *American Women: Report of the President's Commission on the Status of Women*, 1963; Gibson Winter, *Love and Conflict*, 1958; Polly Allen Robinson, 'Women in Christ', *USQR*, XIX, 1964, pp. 193–7.

JOHANNA K. MOTT

Work, Doctrine of

Daily work is a central reality of existence. It has a new importance in Christian theology because of the renewed concern for the role of the 'laity' in the total mission of the Church, and because of the rapid technological and social changes which have transformed the conditions of work for most people in developed countries; underdeveloped ones are trying hard to go the same way. Sometimes Christians are sentimental about agriculture, so it is worth noting that in developed lands it is highly mechanized, and that the aim of underdeveloped ones is to get people off the land and to produce

more food with fewer people. Then follows a shift of the working population to manufacture and, at a further stage, to administration and to services. Even in a highly industrialized society only about 3% will be engaged in the 'professions', and of these not more than 0.1% will be professionally religious, that is, earning their living directly as Christians. This should be remembered because there has been a tendency to regard paid religious work, for example, that of the clergy, as in a special sense a Christian vocation. The term is allowed to spill over to other professions with a high personal content (for example, nursing, teaching), but there it stops. This leaves the bulk of the world's work out. It gives a *cachet* to the work of a small elite, often educationally and culturally privileged. A keen Christian entering industry tends to think he should be a personnel manager rather than actually engaged in production. Manual work still tends to be despised; people want white collar jobs in which they don't get dirty. This attitude has spread to underdeveloped countries. A church which has a truncated doctrine of work cannot deal with this.

The Reformation recovery of a doctrine of vocation in everyday life was soon corrupted by Pietism. *See* **Vocation**. Also the culture of the West has its roots in Greek as well as Hebrew thought. The educated Greek thought ordinary work degrading for a free man. He had slaves to do it. It was the creative work of the artist he respected. Greek influence on Christian thought tended in the same direction. This is in striking contrast to the Bible which, while it may not do enough justice to creative art, has a down to earth attitude to daily work and is not at all fastidious. The only exception is Ecclus. 38 (which comes significantly from hellenized Judaism). The double aspect of work, as joy and as drudgery, comes out in the 'parable' of the Fall; it is empirically true that it is both and, like idleness, can be both a blessing and a curse. The NT stresses the need to work and not be idle, and to work well and cheerfully (cf. I and II Thess., *passim*; Col. 3.23).

The Christian doctrine of work sees it as a necessary means of pleasing God by serving human needs. Needs must be interpreted in a broad sense, but not as broad as wants. There are some wants which it is impossible to please God by supplying (e.g., pimps and prostitutes). But in general we should not be too fastidious. If, for example, gambling is regarded to a limited extent as a legitimate activity (though not advocated), then it is legitimate to supply facilities for it. For this reason the Church has never excommunicated bookmakers. When it comes to a choice of jobs, those who have the longest and most specialized training will have the greatest responsibility for the use of it. Those with the least differentiated skills will find it easiest to change. Work is made for man, not man for work, and so it is the legitimate needs of society which matter, not work for work's sake. Otherwise we might as well dig holes and fill them in again. For this reason efficiency is an important virtue, to be balanced against others. The citizen cannot claim the right to a particular job throughout his working life, but he has the right to a job, and it is the function of the State so to arrange economic affairs that there is no long-term unemployment, which is a public impoverishment and a personal disaster. A wise society moves younger rather than older men to new jobs, and provides generous adjustment allowances and new training facilities when a change is necessary. Some have a good deal of choice not only as to what job they will do but where they will do it. Here those with professional and technical skills in developed countries need to remember the great need of them in developing ones. For the problems of organization and management in work *see* **Industrial Relations.**

Alan Richardson, *The Biblical Doctrine of Work*, 1952; J. M. Todd, ed., *Work*, 1958 (a Roman Catholic symposium).

RONALD PRESTON

World Council of Churches. *see* Ecumenical Movement, Ethics in.

World Government

The ecumenical Oxford Conference in 1937 saw the heart of present international difficulties in 'the claim of each national state to be judge in its own cause'. 'The abrogation of absolute national sovereignty' was therefore listed as a duty to be urged by the Church upon the nations. Other church bodies have joined leading political scientists in similar testimony.

The close modern interdependence of nations suggests solutions similar to those congenial with the inclusive nature of Christian love. Brotherhood must now be given social structure among the nations. The largest world community of which man is a part exerts a crucial influence on minute concerns of each individual. The same purposes specified by theologians for the State must be assigned also to an international organization. Such a supplementary world structure is now essential to the preservation of order and freedom, the restraint of national sin, and the provision of full opportunity for individuals.

Goals for an adequate international organization include inclusive membership, democratic procedures, and provision for minimal legislative, executive and judicial functions. Powers of an international body need to be sufficiently limited to safeguard against dictatorial control or threat to legitimate interests. Yet these powers need to be adequate to deal with serious international disputes and to police the world against war.

Beginnings of international action have been accepted in international unions for specific purposes like postal service, in alliances or unified commands in wartime, in regional organization and in the UN. There are still serious obstacles to any structure with more dependable power. One of these is the lack of a comprehensive enough world ethos. When sufficient consensus and trust exist, nations are willing to delegate functions to international groups. A world ethos will not come into being by declaring the need for it. Yet there has been sufficient overlapping of national interest to start the process of international organization. A more powerful motivation may develop as the threat of an unorganized world is becoming increasingly clear. Furthermore, ethos follows as well as precedes organization. Effective education for citizenship in larger units may be found in the experience of living under limited organization. The increasing necessity for world government may yet be matched by the inventiveness and energy which contribute to its possibility. Here also the definition of man's task is always found in the need of the situation as defined by the purposes of God. *See* **Internationalism.**

HARVEY SEIFERT

Worldliness

The ambiguity of the concept of the 'world' in Christian thought is present from the beginning. In the NT the world is the world of men, in opposition to God, but it is also the world which God loves and which he has reconciled to himself in Christ.

The history of Christianity may be seen in terms of the dialectic which arises from this ambiguity. Sometimes the world-denying ascetic element has prevailed, as in the early monastic movement, sometimes the assertion of the world and its claims, as in Luther's words to the German nobility: 'The sphere of faith's work is worldly society and its order.' Yet even in the great periods of world-denial, or the periods of greatest insight into the necessity of world-affirmation, there has never been established a final resting-point for Christian thought: no direct or simple solution, either simply in the world or simply out of it, has been found. The tension which has consequently been maintained has been immensely fruitful for all spheres of Christian thought and enterprise. In the realm of ethics there has thus been a long-drawn-out struggle with classic views, especially with the Stoic view. At this point the recognition of the reality of the intra-mundane ethical demand has worked powerfully to save Christianity from simple denial of the world. Yet even here the issue has not been resolved. For how may the Christian speak of harmony with the rational order, in face of his belief in the revelatory reality both of evil and of suffering as historically focused in Christ? On the other hand, the Christian cannot take refuge in total resignation either. Worldliness, even 'holy worldliness', is often thought of today (the terminology is usually influenced by the later thought of Dietrich Bonhoeffer) as the necessary form of Christian life. But since this conception flows primarily from a specific though not always articulate christology, it is not possible to identify it with any straightforward naturalistic ethic. The Christian, though recognizing that he is entirely within this world, and has his duties and claims alongside all men, is still not simply 'of' this world. His 'worldliness' is thoroughly dialectical. This dialectic arises out of his faith that the absolute demand upon him is simultaneously the demand of a Demander: he acknowledges God as a personal will active in history. This absolute will, acknowledged as concentrated in the historical person of Jesus Christ, asks for the Christian's total commitment in an ultimate relation. At the same time, this absolute claim upon him puts him back into the world, where he must be engaged, in the penultimate sphere, with the same problems and demands as everybody else. The problem of a Christian secularism arises here, and the unfinished discussion on this and related points is an indication of the continuing vitality of Christian faith in relation to the world.

D. Bonhoeffer, *Letters and Papers from Prison*, 3rd edn., revised and enlarged, 1967; W. G. Maclagan, *The Theological Frontier of Ethics*, 1961; H. R. Niebuhr, *Christ and Culture*, 1952; R. Gregor Smith, *Secular Christianity*, 1966; A. R. Vidler, 'Holy Worldliness' in *Essays in Christian Liberality*, 1957.

R. GREGOR SMITH

Wrong. *see* Right and Wrong.

Zeal

The word 'zeal' is not now in common usage; enthusiasm (q.v.) has taken its place.

Enthusiasm, Christians hold, should be creative. It should not be quenched but given approval when those concerned with it have asked some such questions as the following: (1) Is it more than a sudden excited response to an appeal for action? (2) Is it enthusiasm for its own sake because the feeling it generates is more bearable than inactivity, dullness and depression? (3) What line of thought and overt action does it indicate? (4) If this action is both necessary and possible, are the enthusiasts who support it ready for danger, monotony, hardship and misunderstanding? In these questions

there is a concern as to how the immature may be best helped to examine their enthusiasms in the light of Christian doctrine.

In our society which leads its members to be analytical above all else, churchmen are called to be enthusiastic about the unanalysable – the ecstasy of prayer, the sense of completeness that the arts give, the adventure of scientific discoveries and inventions – and at the same time to examine the grounds for these enthusiasms and the expression of them, so as to prevent a tendency to self-deception or despair about the value of human actions.

R. E. C. BROWNE

Zoroastrian Ethics

Schwerer Dienste tägliche Bewahrung,
Sonst bedarf es keiner Offenbarung.

In the years 1814–5, Goethe gave expression to his deep interest in eastern religion, history and literature in a cycle of poems to which he gave the title *West-östlicher Divan*. His study of the religion of Zoroaster (Zarathushtra), the prophet of ancient Iran, and his desire to achieve a synthesis of eastern and western thought and philosophy resulted in a lengthy poem, written in 1815, to which he gave the title 'Vermächtnis' (heritage). In the two pithy lines quoted above, Goethe seems to indicate that the Zoroastrian mind has no need for a revelation other than the daily performance of one's burdensome duties.

In Goethe's days little precise knowledge of Zoroastrianism had reached the western world. In addition, Goethe's summary statement gives as much an insight into his own mind as it reflects Zoroastrian philosophy. Yet, diligence in the performance of one's daily duties is truly one of the essential tenets of the Zoroastrian way of practical behaviour. As it is put by Zarathushtra himself, it is '. . . dawn, noon and evening that remind the "faithful" of his (daily) obligation(s)'.

In the 2,500 years that lie between the first half of the sixth century BC, the most likely period of Zarathushtra's activities, and the present-day Parsees in India, who profess Zoroastrianism as their creed, important changes, if not complete reversals, in ideology, beliefs and practices have taken place. Indeed, as Zaehner has pointedly observed:

The history of [the Zoroastrian] religion, even in its heyday, has been so chequered that a Parsee would have no difficulty in finding scriptural evidence to justify a total monotheism, an uncompromising dualism, or even a barely disguised polytheism.

But, perhaps, the relative validity of statements based on the non-homogeneous materials contained in the Avesta and in the Pahlavi books which date from Sassanian times (250–650 AD) is in no need of further emphasis.

A case in point is the often-mentioned practice of good thought[s] (*humata*), good word[s] (*hūkhta*) and good deed[s] (*hvarshta*) which, according to Parsee and western interpreters alike, is 'the fundamental principle of the Zoroastrian creed' (Masani) and 'the quintessence of the moral and ethical teachings of Zoroaster' (A. V. Williams Jackson). A recommendation of this practice as such, however, is not included in any one passage of the *Gāthā*, those portions of the Avesta that are supposed to be the true reflection of Zarathusthra's own thoughts. On the other hand, the three terms occur frequently in other Zoroastrian texts. They are part, for instance, of a well-known prayer ('We are praisers of good thoughts, good words, good deeds [that are being thought, spoken and] done and [have] been [thought, spoken and] done . . .'), they are used at several important moments in the Zoroastrian liturgy and they symbolize the three steps by which the soul of the true Zoroastrian approaches paradise after death.

Cases like this are not rare; in fact, they are the rule rather than the exception. It is not until later, particularly Sassanian, times that a systematic code of Zoroastrian ethics was developed. This code was in part derived from the original teachings contained in the ancient writings; other parts of it were based on more recent ingredients. The mainspring of this code lies in the Zoroastrian assumption of the original and complete separation of the principles of good and of evil. The triple injunction implied in the (Sassanian) terms *humat*, *hūkht* and *huvarsht* is the practical conclusion drawn from this view. It is also part of the consequence of the well-known Zoroastrian premise that man by his origin belongs to *Ahura Mazdā* ('I belong to *Ohrmazd*') and as such is in a position to choose for the good on his own.

Statements on ethics abound in the Sassanian texts. The old virtues, already recommended or suggested by Zarathushtra, of husbandry and agriculture ('till the earth . . . for all men live and are nourished by the tilling of . . . the land'), of truthful and righteous behaviour in accordance with the nature of *Asha* ('truth') ('speak the truth so that you may be trusted'), and the obligation to keep earth, water and fire free from contact with impure matter, are repeatedly mentioned. Other passages refer to such virtues as generosity ('be as generous with your property as you can'), hospitality ('make the traveller welcome so that your yourself may receive a warmer welcome in this world and the next; for he who gives, receives and [receives] more abundantly'), industry ('rise before dawn so that your work may prosper'), education ('be zealous in the acquisition of education, for education is the seed of knowledge and its fruit is wisdom'), moderation ('show restraint in your eating [and drinking] so that you may live long'), content-

ment with one's lot ('do not be unduly glad when good fortune attends you, do not be unduly sad when misfortune befalls you'), tact ('all actions depend on the proper time and place' – 'speak sharply only after much reflection, for there are times when it is better to speak out and times when it is better to hold your peace' – 'so far as you possibly can, do not bore your fellow men'), or provide bits of 'popular wisdom' ('put out of your mind what is past and do not fret and worry about what has not yet come to pass' – 'do not make a new friend out of an old enemy, for an old enemy is like a black snake which does not forget old injuries for a hundred years'). In short, 'live a good and useful life, be considerate to others, fulfil your religious duties, cultivate the land, rear a family and bring up your children to be literate and educated', while keeping in mind that 'men are like a water skin full of air; when punctured nothing remains; men are like suckling babies, creatures of habit who cling to their habits.'

These quotations show that on the basis of the old ideas of Zarathushtra a set of new values was developed. On the one hand, these values reflect the polished standards of behaviour characteristic for Sassanian civilization; on the other, they are the outcome of the acceptance, for theological as well as secular purposes, of the doctrine of the avoidance of extremes. 'Neither too much, nor too little' has become the favourite theme of both theologians and laymen. In this connection, it is worth noticing that theological speculation developed a list of vices to be avoided as opposites of each virtue to be pursued. This systematization is, in part, the consequence of the basic Zoroastrian distinction between the separation of good and evil as symbolized by *Ahura Mazdā* (*Ohrmazd*) and *Angra Manyu* (*Ahriman*). Falsehood became the standard opposite of truthfulness, stinginess of charity, greed of contentment, sloth of industry, bad manners of education, and so forth.

The controversial matter of the next-to-kin or consanguineous marriage can only be mentioned. Its occurrence is actually attested in Achaemenian and Sassanian times, it is critically mentioned by Syriac authors and not infrequently recommended in Sassanian texts. The evidence has been contested by modern Parsee authorities and western interpreters have looked upon the custom as to be of foreign (Median) origin (Zaehner).

Since its arrival in India about the eighth century, the Parsee community in Bombay and other places in north-western India has strived to live up to the ancient ethical values in its religious and social behaviour. In the words of one of its distinguished members,

Some of the sterling qualities of the Parsi community . . . are its vitality . . ., its adaptability to changing circumstances . . ., its industry and spirit of citizenship; and above all, its philanthropy.

J. Duchesne-Guillemin, *La religion de l'Iran ancien*, 1962; *Symbolik des Parsismus*, 1962; A. V. Williams Jackson, *Zoroastrian Studies*, 1928; R. Masani, *The Religion of the Good Life: Zoroastrianism*, 1938; J. J. Modi, *The Religious Ceremonies and Customs of the Parsees*, 2nd edn., 1937; M. Molé, *Culte, mythe et cosmologie dans l'Iran ancien*, 1963; G. Widengren, *Iranische Geisteswelt*, 1961; *Die Religionen Irans*, 1965; R. C. Zaehner, *The Dawn and Twilight of Zoroastrianism*, 1961; *The Teachings of the Magi*, 1956; J. M. Unvala, 'Die religiosen und sozialen Sitten und Gebrauche der Parsen,' *Worter und Sachen*, XVII (1936), pp. 174–92 and XVIII (1937), pp. 145–63.

M. J. DRESDEN

Zwingli, Huldreich

Zwingli (1484–1531), a Zürich theologian and minister, was partly responsible for the Protestant Reformation in German Switzerland. Like all the Reformers, Zwingli was deeply concerned with the problem of action. During his influential years, he devoted a large measure of time reflecting upon and directing the organization of religious, moral and civic behaviour in Zürich and surrounding areas. Many of his most well-known writings exhibit this involvement in practical moral affairs: *Concerning Choice and Liberty Respecting Food* (1521), *Warning Against Control of Foreign Lords* (1522), *On Divine and Human Righteousness* (1523), *The Pastor* (1524) and *Advice on Excluding Adulterers and Usurers from the Lord's Supper* (1525).

Zwingli's ethical thought, though largely unsystematic, treats problems and moves in categories that are very familiar throughout Reformation literature. For example, his position is decidedly shaped and conditioned by the notion of a fundamental dualism between 'internal' and 'external' morality between 'divine' and 'human' righteousness. Nevertheless, his own particular development and application of this distinction – especially in connection with Church-State relations in Zürich – marks his own rather unique contribution to Reformed ethics.

In his famous sermon, 'On Divine and Human Righteousness', Zwingli draws a bold line between the law of inner man and the law of outer man. The first has to do with faith in and the worship of God, as well as with the love of neighbour. This sort of righteousness is clearly 'higher' in Zwingli's opinion; it embodies the fulfilment of man, for it sets the standard of right relations between God and man. However, the demands of this law are achieved in no wise by human striving, but only through God's grace in Christ. For Zwingli divine righteousness is the exclusive action of God which man can only concede or acknowledge in the inner life of heart and conscience.

Of course, by rights such inward acknowledgment should issue in loving, harmonious action, that is it should affect external behaviour. But as the result of sin, the continuity between God's action and man's is all but broken. Because sinful men are all rebellious 'rogues' (*Schelme*) when judged by divine righteousness, God is moved to provide a special law of human (or external) righteousness that is accommodated to the perversities of fallen men. This second law, the law of outer man, of external action, lays down the minimum conditions that prevent human society from degenerating into animal-like existence; it enables societies to live in relative peace, and permits each man to obtain his earthly due. Zwingli places the jurisdiction regarding this law almost entirely in the hands of the secular, political authorities.

As the result of his views about inner and outer laws, Zwingli comes to conclusions concerning Church-State relations that set him off from such Reformers as Oecolampadius, Bucer and Calvin. The task and authority of the Church is restricted to the supervision of the internal life of man, to preaching the gospel, administering the sacraments, and generally nurturing the renewal of heart and conscience. On the other hand, external behaviour, including matters of ecclesiastical organization and discipline, is properly subject to the civil authorities. Zwingli even went so far as to claim that the civil magistrate 'is necessary to the completeness of the ecclesiastical body' (*Exposition of Faith*, VI).

Alfred Farner, *Die Lehre von Kirche und Staat bei Zwingli*, 1930; Oskar Farner, *Huldrych Zwingli*, 1943–49; S. M. Jackson, *Huldreich Zwingli: The Reformer of German Switzerland*, 1901; Roger Ley, *Kirchenzucht bei Zwingli*, 1948; Heinrich Schmid, *Zwinglis Lehre von der göttlichen und menschlichen Gerechtigkeit*, 1959; Robert C. Walton, 'Zwingli's Theocracy', unpublished doctoral dissertation, Yale University, 1963; Erik Wolf, 'Die Sozialtheorie Zwinglis', *Festschrift Guido Kisch Rechthistorische Forschungen*, 1955.

DAVID LITTLE